BLOOD MOON HAS ESTABLISHED A PRECEDENT OF PUBLISHING GUIDES TO GAY & LESBIAN FILMS. HERE'S WHAT CRITICS HAVE SAID ABOUT THEM:

"Authoritative, exhaustive, and essential, *Blood Moon's Guide to Gay and Lesbian Film* is the queer girl's and queer boy's one-stop resource for what to add to their feature-film queue. The film synopses and the snippets of critic's reviews are reason enough to keep this compendium of cinematic information close to the DVD player."

Books to Watch Out For (www.btwof.com)

"This 400-page first edition of everything fabu in movies for 2005 is an essential guide for both the casual viewer and the hard-core movie watching homo. It's comprehensive and entertaining, with an introduction that announces the **Blood Moon Awards** (they call them the "Bloody Moons"), an amazingly thorough look at their best picture winner, *Brokeback Mountain*, as well as a conclusion packed with sexy pics of three hunks that played gay last year: Colin Farrell, Jake Gyllenhaal and Heath Ledger. While it seems *Brokeback* is all over this book — from the cover to the last pages — there are over 135 feature films and 60 shorts discussed, including big ones like *Transamerica* and *The Family Stone*, as well as lesser-known releases like *D.E.B.S.* and *Hubby/Wifey*. This year's Gay and Lesbian Film festival movies are in it, too. Scattered throughout the listings are "Special Features;" tongue-in-cheek essays about the best and worst mishaps in film last year. Case in point: the essay explaining how Farrell's full frontal was, err, cut from *Home at the End of the World.*"

Bay Windows (Boston)

"Something new that's a lot of fun is *Blood Moon's Guide to Gay and Lesbian Film*. It's like having access to a feverishly compiled queer film fan's private scrapbook. This first edition gives a snapshot of where we are in Hollywood now, which should be updated with each further annual edition. It's valuable and a lot of fun and, like screen representations of us, it verges wildly between tribute and titillation. Now, I'm ready for my closeup…"

Gay Times (London)

"Startling. This exhaustive guide documents everything from the mainstream to the obscure, detailing dozens of queer films from the last few years."

HX (New York)

50 Years of Queer Cinema

OTHER BOOKS BY DARWIN PORTER

Biographies
Steve McQueen, King of Cool, Tales of a Lurid Life
Paul Newman, The Man Behind the Baby Blues
Merv Griffin, A Life in the Closet
Brando Unzipped
The Secret Life of Humphrey Bogart
Katharine the Great: Hepburn, Secrets of a Life Revealed
Howard Hughes: Hell's Angel
Jacko, His Rise and Fall (The Social and Sexual History
of Michael Jackson)

Coming Soon:
Humphrey Bogart, the Making of a Legend
And in collaboration with Roy Moseley
Damn You, Scarlett O'Hara: The Private Lives of Vivien Leigh and Laurence Olivier

Film Criticism
Best Gay and Lesbian Films- The Glitter Awards, 2005
Blood Moon's Guide to Recent Gay & Lesbian Film--Volume One (2006)
Blood Moon's Guide to Recent Gay & Lesbian Film--Volume Two (2007)

Non-Fiction
Hollywood Babylon-It's Back!
And Coming Soon:
Hollywood Babylon Strikes Again!

Novels
Butterflies in Heat
Marika
Venus (a roman à clef based on the life of Anaïs Nin)
Razzle-Dazzle
Midnight in Savannah
Rhinestone Country
Blood Moon
Hollywood's Silent Closet

Travel Guides
Many editions and many variations of *The Frommer Guides*
to Europe, the Caribbean, California, Georgia, and The Carolinas

50 Years
of Queer Cinema

500 of the Best Gay, Lesbian,
Bisexual, Transgendered, and Queer Questioning
Films Ever Made

Another Hot, Startling, and Unauthorized Examination
of America's Entertainment Industry from

Darwin Porter and Danforth Prince

50 Years of Queer Cinema
500 of the Best GLBTQ Films Ever Made

Manufactured in the United States of America

ISBN 978-1-936003-09-9

First Edition, First Printing, April, 2010

Cover designs by Richard Leeds (Bigwigdesign.com)
Videography and publicity trailers by Piotr Kajstura
Distributed in North America and Australia
through The National Book Network (www.NBNbooks.com)
and in the UK through Turnaround (www.turnaround-uk.com)

**Blood Moon acknowledges Marianne Bohr and the NBN
for their support and savvy guidance during the compilation of this book.**

DEDICATION

This guidebook showcases the astonishing breadth of talent, insight, and creativity associated with the legacy of people who have described themselves as GLBT or Queer.

As such, it's dedicated to the filmmakers—producers, directors, scripters, investors, actors, publicists, distributors, and support staff, living or dead—whose work is reviewed within its pages.

GAY AND LESBIAN FILMS

"The sorry state of American Gay Cinema has for too long been a source of frustration for many in our community; Typically horrible production values, poor scripts, inane plots, bad performances, and lousy direction have combined over the years to create very low expectations among LGBT filmgoers. We as a group have been so desperate to see images of our lives portrayed on the silver screen that we have tossed out the high expectations that we as a community have a reputation for in such areas as art, creativity, and style to tolerate and even embrace garbage cinema as long as it was gay themed. So it is refreshing and exciting that American Gay Cinema seems to finally be improving."

Herb Krohn

"I won't be directed by a fairy! I have to work with a real man."
Clark Gable, snarling about his then-director,
George Cukor, on the set of *Gone With the Wind*

"I am prepared to believe that the sense of romance in those of our brothers and sisters who incline towards love of their own sex is heightened to a more blazing pitch than in those who think of themselves as normal."
Lord Laurence Olivier

"Half the people in Hollywood are dying to be discovered. The other half are afraid they will be."
Lionel Barrymore

CONTENTS

BLOOD
MOON
Productions, Ltd.

INTRODUCTION

IN 50 YEARS, QUEERS HAVE COME A LONG WAY, BABY

And Now, Mr. De Mille, We're Ready for Our Close-Up!

JOE GILLIS: Norma Desmond! You used to be *VERY* big.

NORMA DESMOND: I AM big! It's the pictures that got small!

"WE HAD *FACES* THEN"

Despite the many ongoing setbacks that gays and lesbians face in their struggle for equality, the doors of "The Celluloid Closet" were thrown open decades ago, at least since 1960. These locked doors were forced open with crowbars by the most daring and avant-garde directors and scripters on the planet.

Today, gay and lesbian artists have their place in the cinematic sun. They're not only queer and here, but they're likely to stay, gaining even greater prominence than they did during the final decades of the 20th century.

Filmmakers are producing increasing volumes of scenarios about everything queer, including same-sex stories about love and marriage and the continuing struggle for equal rights in America. Collectively, out and proud directors are sending powerful messages, especially to hate groups. But are those messages being registered and received?

Who knows? Thirty years from now, George Bush's daughters may be choreographing same-sex wedding ceremonies on their ranch at Crawford, as was already proposed to nationwide television audiences by out-and-proud Ellen DeGeneres.

In this reference source and gossip guide, we've previewed the staggering diversity of fifty years' production of gay, lesbian, transgendered, and bisexual films. Illuminated in all the colors of the rainbow are archetypes which include gay cowboys, gay Nazis, nude marines, ballsy detectives, hit men, porn stars, women in love, bears, twinks, chicken hawks, bull dykes, lipstick lesbians, muscle fags, hustlers, gay-for-pay guys, johns, chicks with dicks, and most definitely boy-on-boy or girl-on-girl romances.

Whatever your brand of queer, this book contains a description and review of a film someone has made about it.

***

For years Hollywood, on screen, has tried to deny the very existence of homosexuals.

As late as 1958, Paul Newman, cast as a gay Tennessee Williams character in *Cat on a Hot Tin Roof*, was not allowed to play it lavender, the way the role was intended by its playwright.

The liberated 60s brought on a slow revolution, but until relatively late in the history of filmmaking, gays and lesbians were pictured as psychotics, vampires, serial killers, child molesters, or as misfits on the verge of either suicide or emotional breakdowns.

The depiction of gays on screen, at least officially, began with those silly queens in *Boys in the Band* and moved on to *Milk*, the story of a slain gay activist in San Francisco. En route, there was a detour across the ridges of *Brokeback Mountain*.

Since then, however, the so-called *Love That Dare Not Speak Its Name* can't shut up, judging from the profusion of gay and lesbian films today. Almost every subject has been tackled, from pedophilia to bestiality, with lots of good old-fashioned gay comedies and love stories thrown in for seasoning.

This pioneering book contains hundreds of reviews of films ranging from the obscure to mainstream. Many relatively obscure films, some produced outside Europe, Canada, and the US, are previewed for the first time in a major publication.

In selecting films, we paid close attention to the choices that the juries had made at gay and lesbian film festivals around the world. As such, we've documented both major and minor films across the lavender spectrum, many of them small-scale productions from independent, relatively unknown filmmakers whose works have never been configured as major releases.

Some of the films we've reviewed have been amusing but trivial—the gay world's interpretation of what to watch during a snowstorm with popcorn and a lover. We've uncovered and reviewed dozens of documentaries and dramas. We've even added descriptions and the artistic/political context of a half-dozen porno films which, at the time of their release, either made history or broke cinematic records in terms of their box-office success, with anecdotes about some of the *brouhahas* associated with their production. An example is *Boys in the Sand*, the first X-rated film to ever receive full critical reviews and coverage in *The New York Times*.

Fifty Years of Queer Cinema doesn't just document well-known gay movies of yesterday—*Fortune & Men's Eyes*, for example. It uncovers films that were never released to the general public in theaters, but are available on DVD. In these films, no subject is taboo. There's a lot to learn here, including revelations about iconic players in gay and lesbian history.

This anthology is filled with special features too, with information about brouhahas not generally known outside the film community, and commentary on the state of queer entertainment today. One of those features is devoted to the myth that playing gay onscreen is a career breaker for any actor brave enough to accept the role. Today, that simply isn't so.

Making Love (1982), a Golden Oldie for many gay men, was the first gay-friendly romance to ever emerge from a major Hollywood studio. Back in 1982, many movie-goers, not necessarily having understood the content of the film, walked out, especially when Michael Ontkean and Harry Hamlin kissed. *Making Love*'s failure at the box office postponed the production of most other mainstream gay films for years.

Sherry Lansing, president of Fox when *Making Love* was released, still stands by her decision, even though the film made only $12 million at the box office. "I absolutely fell in love with the script, and I thought it was going to be one of the biggest movies in the history of film."

Michael Douglas turned down the role, even gay-friendly Richard Gere transmitted his regrets. Hamlin claimed that *Making Love* paralyzed his movie career, but says that even so, he has no regrets.

Regrettably, both mainstream and independent filmmakers tend to focus more aggressively on gay men than on lesbian women, at least judging from the films reviewed within this guidebook. But all is not lost. *Desert Hearts* from 1986, which has been hailed as the greatest lesbian drama ever made, was recently re-released as a DVD. At the time of its filming, the stars of *Desert Hearts*, Patricia Charbonneau and Helen Shaver, were warned about career suicide if they "played nakedly lesbian."

"We went ahead anyway," Shaver told the press. "And that was long before lesbian chic. Donna Deitch, the director, had guts."

Emerging technologies, coupled with a hunger for gay-themed entertainment and an increased willingness on the part of film studios to invest in restoration and re-digitalization, has catalyzed the re-release of many marvelous classics as DVDs. These have included *The Lost Language of Cranes* (1991) in which both a father and a son come out to each other.

Another film ahead of its time also has been released in DVD. *The Naked Civil Servant* (1975) is based on the witty memoirs of the eccentric Quentin Crisp as he struggles to maintain his artfully personalized brand of flamboyance. Crisp's refusal to compromise, despite "fag-bashing" and mass intolerance during an era when (male) homosexuality was still illegal in Great Britain, led to his elevation to the status of a gay icon and an international celebrity. In a vivid cinematic portrait, John Hurt plays Crisp in a biopic about his life.

"Lost films" of yesterday are also coming back, with restorations. An example includes Gus van Sant's *Mala Noche* (Bad Night) from 1985 with a new 35mm print. Whole new generations of gay men and women have emerged since some of these golden oldies first came onto the market. "And Everything Old Is New Again," as the song blithely recites.

The queer presence in current cinema traverses a wide spectrum of the rainbow flag, including tragic star-crossed lesbian lovers in *Imagine Me & You*; "well-heeled" and deeply politicized cross-dressers in *Kinky Boots*; an effeminate author (Truman Capote) in *Infamous*.

"During the past couple of years," said Lisa Daniel, director of the Melbourne Queer Film Festival, "films have leaned further away from the concept of the *angst*-ridden lives of gays and lesbians, and to an increasing degree, they're avoiding the coming-out sagas. Instead, we're seeing interesting stories about queers. We're growing up. It has been said that a film is a reflection or mirror of society and its social realities. It's a two-way street as well; sometimes society is a reflection of what's in film, but more often film reflects what is going on in society at that time. We're seeing an increased acceptance of queer life in general. That is, as long as it's not too scary or confronting."

Although unheard of only a few years ago, films with gay themes are now global. One film from Israel, for example, deals with an Israeli soldier falling for a (male) Palestinian. Many of the new queer films share common themes about the difficulties that queer people face in homophobic societies. Some even tackle such sensitive subjects as what to do about trannies incarcerated in prison.

There aren't many "happy ever after" stories. Most films show that despite good intentions, things do go wrong for gay men and lesbians. The impact that AIDS has on the worldwide community continues to be a dominant feature.

Hundreds of gay or lesbian films are released every year, but only a fraction of them are shown in movie houses, even in such liberal and liberated cities as Los Angeles, Miami, San Francisco, and New York. Many gay-themed movies are shown at film festivals, events where producers hope they'll be able to find a distributor and consequently get viewed by a wider audience. Regrettably, only a small percentage is ever picked up by a major, or even a medium-sized distributor.

Both gay and lesbian filmmakers continue to be hot for documentaries, as evoked by the 2001 release of *101 Rent Boys*, where you see all these male hustlers in the skin trade with everything showing in most cases. The viewer is entertained with the unveiling of bodies and/or souls. Most of these men are in their early 20s, and some claim they are gay-for-pay, with wives or girlfriends stashed away somewhere. The rent boys range from a Joe College football player to a Japanese slavemaster in full fetish drag. This is a film about love for sale minus the love.

Mireya Navarro, writing in *The New York Times*, noted that never before have gay story lines been so prominent—in recent months there have been at least 83 gay and lesbian, bisexual, or transgendered characters on TV, not counting *Logo* or *Here!*

"Yet for most gay actors, Hollywood is not a warm and fuzzy episode of *Will & Grace*," she

4

noted. "Today, it is certainly more acceptable to be openly gay. But these actors must still answer wrenching questions: Just how candid do you want to be? Would you be happy appearing only in comedies, or being pigeonholed as a character actor? And what does the line, 'You're just not right for the role' really mean?"

Another pressing question asked is this: Why are lesbian flicks in such short supply? Industry insider Ed Gonzalez ventured an opinion. "Perhaps a future symposium will reveal that lesbians are less interested in making movies than gay men or that distribution companies are more willing to bank-roll boy-on-boy stories."

Yet another critic, David Lornelius, issued another challenge to gay filmmakers. "What hurts about the current gay cinema movement is just how reliant filmmakers are on mainstream storytelling. Case in point: *Long-Term Relationship*, a film that opens with a few brazen scenes of homosexuality at its sweatiest yet finishes with such clichéd trappings that you might as well dump Sandra Bullock and Hugh Grant in the damn thing."

"The industry is persuaded that being known as gay will undermine your credibility both as a romantic lead or as an action star," said Larry Gross, author of a book on media portrayals of gays and lesbians. "They don't test it. We're waiting for the Jackie Robinson moment when someone tests that assumption and discovers it's not true."

As cinema moves into the second decade of the 21st century, the explosion of GLBTQ movies continues unabated. Films for the community play an important role in their traditional market, but also are breaking through into mainstream cinema, the most prominent example in recent times being *Brokeback Mountain*, of course.

With all its challenges and all its setbacks, gay and lesbian cinema has come of age. If the world survives as we know it, gays and lesbians might eventually reach the promised land of full equal rights, as forecast to African Americans by Martin Luther King Jr.

On the 50th anniversary of the launch of gay and lesbian cinema, queer filmmakers can truly proclaim, "We've come a long way, baby."

But, of course, there's a long way to go. When some publisher in 2060 surveys the immediately previous 50 years of all things associated with Queer Cinema, the contents of that book will hopefully appear remarkably different from what's previewed by us within the book you're reading now.

That future guidebook will contain less about homophobia and persecution of gays and lesbians, and more about their triumphs.

SIR IAN MCKELLEN:

ENGLAND'S STATELIEST HOMO

In the summer of 2006, at London's Gay Pride Festival, the largest in Europe, McKellen topped the *Pink List* as Britain's most influential homosexual. Pop legend Sir Elton John came in second on an annual list which documents gay men and women who are leaders in fields ranging from the arts and media to politics and business.

McKellen, who played Gandolf in *The Lord of the Rings* film trilogy, was 67 at the time. "There can be few actors who manage to produce such extraordinary variety and quality while connecting with so many people," *The Independent* proclaimed in London. "He is our Number One."

Oscar-winner McKellen not only nabbed a key role in the hugely successful *The Da Vinci Code* in 2006, but reprised his role as Magneto, a villainous mutant who uses his ability to control metals to take on his heroic fellow freaks of nature in *X-Men: The Last Stand*, the third film in that franchise.

Of course, he was never better than when he appeared in the 1998 *Gods and Monsters*, in which he succeeded in getting hunky Brandon Fraser to strip naked for him.

An outspoken gay-rights activist since declaring his homosexuality in the late 1980s, McKellen likens fear of mutants in *X-Men* with societal homophobia.

As regards his role as Magneto, he told The Associated Press, "We've got to peddle the lie that we're all the same so we all buy the same products. That's why they don't like openly gay people on TV. We upset the view that we're all the same. What is Magneto going to say about that? Well, what everybody should say. Not on your life! There are people who think you can cure homosexuality. Scientologists will tell you they can cure you. That they can CURE you! But the truth is, 'We ARE the cure! And when I realized that, Magneto suddenly became an easy part to play."

QUEER AESTHETICS FOR THE NEW AGE: SHOULD WE *SWISH* OR SHOULD WE *SWAGGER*?

In his book, *Becoming the Kind Father*, author Calvin Sandburn wrote, "Society used to assign certain characteristics to men, including power, aggressiveness, professional success, and autonomy. Other, shall we say, swishier traits were expected of women, such as the ability to create and nurture connections, kindness, and communication."

In their race to compete, especially since the 1960s, women have sometimes rejected some of these more "feminine" attributes, in favor of something more macho and "testosterone-pumped."

But perhaps things are changing. Role model Johnny Depp in his third reprise as the sexually ambiguous Captain Jack Sparrow in *Pirates of the Caribbean: At World's End* seemed just as gay as ever. His mascara is thick, his gestures are regal, and as a Beau Brummel clone inspired by the fashions and mannerisms of Regency England, he sports jewelry, an elaborate sense of protocol, and a wisp of white lace tied just above his left hand.

So what's a guy to do? Stay manly or start acting like the straight world's interpretation of what it is to act gay?

Laura Sessions Stepp wrote: "Increasing numbers of young men bend the gender role freely, especially if their buds are doing the same. A preppy guy in high school might pair a lime-green Polo by Ralph Lauren shirt with light yellow J. Crew pants, a Lily Pulitzer belt and Rainbow flip-flops. And whereas men used to greet each other with a handshake, now it's a hug."

Her words are echoed by William Albert, deputy director of a pregnancy prevention group in Washington, D.C. "Guys who are virgins are still more troubled by their virginity than are virgin girls. Not as many teenage males are having intercourse as in the past, but more of them are having oral sex."

"Maybe Depp with his *Pirate* movies is teaching us something," Stepp said. "There's no longer a defined line between *swish* and *swagger*. Maybe it's both!"

Let's face it. When all is said and done, and in spite of the queer content appearing more and more in mainstream cinema, there's nothing quite like watching a gay film with a gay audience.

The Queer Aesthetic goes mainstream: Johnny Depp as a Pirate of the Caribbean

PART ONE

A SLAM-DUNK A-Z ROMP THROUGH THE BEST OF 50 YEARS OF GLBTQ FILM

"Most of our pictures have little, if any, real substance. Our fear of what the censors will do keeps us from portraying life the way it really is. We wind up with a lot of empty fairy tales that do not have much relation to anyone."
Samuel Goldwyn

"Perhaps most actors are latent homosexuals, and we cover it with drink. I was once a homosexual, but it didn't take."
Richard Burton

"All my life, I've spent time with gay men. Montgomery Clift, Jimmy Dean, Rock Hudson. There is no gay agenda. It's a human agenda."
Elizabeth Taylor

*"**The Celluloid Closet** is a profound account of how the movies have consciously and consistently denigrated homosexuals. Written by Vito Russo, it's militant and marvellous, and must be read by anyone who goes to the movies, and that's just about everyone."*
Arthur Bell,
in *The Hollywood Reporter*

WHEN IS A FILM ABOUT HOMOSEXUALITY NOT ABOUT HOMOSEXUALITY? WHEN HOLLYWOOD BECOMES AFRAID OF ITS CONTENT.

Even during the 1960s and 70s, hip and sophisticated people went into public denial about the queer content of their films. Perhaps "loneliness" was just the newest moniker for *the love that dared not speak its name.*

"*The Sergeant* is not about homosexuality. It's about loneliness."

Rod Steiger (1968)

"*Staircase* is not about homosexuality. It's about loneliness."

Rex Harrison (1971)

"*Sunday, Bloody Sunday* is not about the sexuality of these people. It's about loneliness."

John Schlesinger (1972)

"*The Children's Hour* is not about lesbianism. It's about the power of lies to destroy people's lives."

Billy Wilder (1962)

10 Attitudes

(2001)

L.A.'s Gay Dating Scene

In a quick one-line summary, what is this film about? It's the story of a Jewish man who discovers that throughout the previous decade, his boyfriend has been cheating on him. Josh Stevens, as played by Jason Stuart, discovers his boyfriend, Lyle (Rusty Updegraff), getting  head in his red Jaguar convertible from a boy ten years his junior. The tagline for the film is, "Can a regular gay guy find love in L.A.?"

Making his directorial debut with this low-budget quickie is Michael Gallant, who co-wrote the film with his leading man, Jason Stuart, not an unheard of situation. If you don't mind the grainy, poor quality of the film, you might have some fun with this flick.

Actor/comedian Stuart brings a certain pixie-like charm to the role of Josh, playing a "pushing 40" gay male who came to California from conservative Cleveland a decade earlier. With him was his significant other, Lyle, who adapts to the L.A. scenes more quickly than Josh, who isn't able to yank up his Midwestern values by the roots.

Devastated by the news that his lover is a back alley slut, Josh is comforted by his best friend, Brandon, as played by Christopher Cowen. Brandon persuades Josh that all he needs is a series of ten dates—hence, the title, *10 Attitudes*—to find Mr. Right or Prince Charming—take your choice. Consequently, Josh hits the Internet looking for love.

Josh dreads dragging his paunch and his aging face into the shark-infested dating pool of West Hollywood. But he ventures forth. Since the film is set in West Hollywood, the men he meets on his dates tend to be either hustler/actors or actor/hustlers. If not that, then an actor/waiter or a waiter/actor/hustler/druggie. Everybody in town seems to be on the make.

Josh ends up kissing more than his share of frogs in his search for "the man of my dreams."

100% Human

(*100% Menneske;* 2004)

A Male-to-Female Transsexual

100% Menneske (Human) is the helmer achievement of Jan Dalchow and Trond Winterkjaer.

It's a docu where Monica Voilås Mykebust plays herself. When Monica was born, her parents believed she was a boy and named her Morton. In April of 2002, at the age of 22, she had her body surgically altered to correct this mistake. Basically, the docu is a search for one's true identity.

The film is a rare video diary in that Monica confided to the camera her story during the months before and after her operation. To the film, she brings total honesty and a sense of humor. The movie consists not only of a video diary, but musical performances and re-enactments and traditional cinema verité scenes. A musical twist in a docu of this sort is most unusual, but the songs add depth to Monica's story in a poetic and untraditional way.

Monica's mother, Sissel Voilås, stands by her daughter and is astonishingly supportive, realizing that for her offspring the choice for Morton is Monica or suicide.

The most telling line is from Monica's doctor. "A human being is like a closed box. You have to open it up to see what's inside."

The film is in Norwegian with English subtitles.

WHAT THE CRITICS SAID
"Truthfulness, compassion, and dignity lend this film a stand-alone quality. Monica is an inspiration within a social context that juxtaposes gender with humanity, yet, as she so succinctly puts it, 'Those who live a lie live a cold life.'"
Jim Norrena

"Specially written ballads of self-realization also strike an overly earnest chord, played far too straight and screaming for parody. The good news is that Monica can sing, but one number in particular, on the operating table with dancing masked surgeons whirling through dry ice, recalls Rosa von Paunheim at his campiest, minus the self-conscious sense of outrageousness."
Jay Weissberg, *Variety*

101 Rent Boys

(2000)

Why Young Men Peddle Their Meat

The one thing you cannot say about this project from co-helmers Fenton Bailey and Randy Barbato is that it's boring. It definitely is not. The docu-makers rented 101 actual rent boys--and paid them $50 each to spill their guts--or else show the full monty.

The docu was shot on location in various motel rooms situated along the length of Santa Monica Boulevard. The backgrounds of the hustlers in West Hollywood are explored along with details of their private lives and their attitudes toward their work. These same motel rooms were where some of the men screwed (or got screwed by) their johns.

For the most part, the male whores range in age from their early 20s to their late 30s. Many of them had been abused as children, many of them sustained drug habits. Some of the boys are remarkably good looking; others look like they've spent too many nights hustling their meat along the boulevards.

Perhaps the most shocking scene in the docu involves a hustler extinguishing a cigarette on his ass--he's into pain, of course. Many of the "hos" are either married or have a girlfriend, often with children in tow.

WHAT THE CRITICS SAID
"This flashy blitz of sound bites and mild voyeurism does offer some insight into the diverse human reality behind L.A.'s male prostitution trade. Interviewees deliver an interesting, wide range of comments on their physical selling points, attitude toward customers, turn-ons/turn-offs, sexual self-definition (several are only gay for pay), drug use, and periods of homelessness."
Dennis Harvey, *Variety*

15

(2002)

The Seedy Streets of Singapore

Still in his 20s, Royston Tan has been hailed as the most promising young filmmaker in uptight Singapore, where authorities might arrest you and paddle your bare ass for throwing a candy wrapper on the sidewalk. Known for his distinctive knack for cinematic narrative, original directorial style, and an innate ability to connect with his audience, he has collected more than 26 international and local film awards for his work.

Tan's first full-length feature is '15', which he extended from his award-winning short of the same title.

The movie charts the misadventures of teenage boys on the fringe of Singaporean society, a real street kids' drama that exposes the gritty side of modern-day Singapore—the kind of seedy realism that travel brochures never show you.

The scrappy suburban existence of five boys is portrayed in a progression of disturbing sequences that bit by bit reconstruct the psychological and ad-hoc family dynamics of the teen rebels. Tan masterfully explores this counter-culture adolescent world whose inhabitants are addicted to video clip and videogame aesthetics. The fragmented narrative and visual style throttles the viewer's senses.

The boys in the film form a tight but complicated bond among themselves. It's a brotherhood whose code allows the shedding of blood, perhaps, but never tears. Skipping school, taking drugs, rehearsing gang raps, piercing and ritual cuttings of their bodies— this is pure drama.

Tan is very attentive to the underlying intimacy of the boys' shared suffering and the need each one eventually shows to be close to someone, even in a late-night embrace out of sight of the others.

The movie manages to depict some of the best traits of human nature—patience, caring, forgiveness, loyalty, and a willingness to be vulnerable to one another. In the end, '15' emerges as a brave and unique depiction of young lives pitted against a hostile world and often giving back better than the world deserves.

2 x 4

(2002)

The Man in the Tight Leather Pants

This 90-minute drama is the oeuvre of a triple threat, writer/director/star Jimmy Smallhorne, who has cast himself as the foreman of a group of illegal Irish immigrants working construction in the Bronx.

Johnnie Maher (Smallhorne himself) has a girlfriend Maria (Kimberly Topper), who asks him, "Do you like men?" He thinks for a second and then responds, "Try anything once."

When she buys him a pair of tight leather pants, he reluctantly tries them on and rubs his crotch. He fears he'll be mistaken for gay in these pants. In spite of that, he's not afraid to use eyeliner and don a boa to become King of Karaoke at a rowdy bar.

Johnnie is haunted by the demons of his subconscious, as he discovers his repressed homosexuality through a series of fuzzy nightmares from his past.

Sexually confused, he meets an Australian hustler, Christian (Bradley Pitts), who has the face of an angel. He takes Johnny to a nearby crack house for a night of torrid sex. The hustler shows Johnnie some tender, loving care, which the young construction worker desperately needs. Predictably, Maria catches the two men kissing one night.

A subplot revolves around Johnnie's uncle, "Trump" (of all names). He carries a secret that Johnnie will discover.

If the film shines with brilliance, it's in its cinematography, winner of the 1998 Sundance Award. Declan Quinn (Leaving Las Vegas, Monsoon Wedding) evocatively captures the nitty gritty Bronx landscape.

With Johnnie, we visit dark streets, dark bedrooms, and dark gay bars, one of which was seemingly designed by Dante for his deepest Circle of Hell.

Surprisingly the film carries subtitles even though it's in English—heavily accented English, that is.

29th and Gay

(2005)

A Movie for the Gay Everyman

A lot of gay men, mired in everyday lives, will identify with this comedy. It tells the story of James Sanchez (as played by James Vasquez), who is an unemployed actor rapidly approaching thirty. In his Twenties, he dreamed of fame and fortune...and, yes, love.

Trapped in the role of a tour guide for a movie studio/theme park, he's facing up to reality. If he didn't, that twenty-seven dollars he has in his bank account is a reminder. He drives around town in a car that has 227,000 miles on it. As Peggy Lee in her famous song might ask, "Is this all there is?"

There's more. James doesn't have a six-pack. Not only that, he's missing a full head of hair. Mostly, he's minus a boyfriend. He's not ready to give up, however. Secretly he stalks the coffee boy, and discovers the world of on-line dating. And he even earns extra cash dressed as a giant bunny rabbit.

His friends offer some comfort, especially Roxy, an actress turned activist. Actually, her full name is "Roxy Hymen." The role is creditably played by Nicole Marcks. She tries to convince James that there is life "beyond the glitz and glamour of a disco ball."

James also has a male friend, Brandon Bouvier, as played by David McBean. Unlike James, Brandon is comfortable in his own lavender skin. He urges James to "at least talk to a boy."

The film is about James as he moves to find *A Place in the Sun* (to steal the title of an old Elizabeth Taylor movie). He's not comfortable in the gay world of circuit boys. He also has to deal with his Hispanic-American cultural heritage. In Hollywood, he feels he's the boy at the window staring in at others living the life.

The director, Carrie Preston, skillfully guides us through James's dilemma. Incidentally, James Vasquez, the film's star, also wrote it and was the executive producer and helped in the film editing. James's partner, Mark Holmes, did the cinematography, and helped in the editing.

3 Guys, 1 Girl, 2 Weddings

(3 garçons, 1 fille, 2 marriages; 2004)

Boy-Wants-Boy-Who-Wants-Girl

This 90-minute film is light, it's French, it's campy and somewhat stereotypical, and an amusing diversion. First released in France in 2004, and directed by first-time helmer Stéphane Clavier, it gives a slightly new twist to a time-tested theme, all the while inserting supportive comments about gay relationships and gay marriages. It's worth a look, and it's now available on Home Video,

Dan (Olivier Sitruk) and Laurent (Arnaud Giovaninetti) are not only best friends, but roommates. Dan, a professed "commitment-phobe" and a womanizer, hosts a radio show called "Let's Talk Sex." Although Dan has a new girlfriend every week, Laurent is in love with his roomie. The plot thickens when Lothario Dan meets Miss Right, Camille (Julie Gayeet).

Laurent, horrified at the prospect of losing Dan, takes on a lesbian roommate "Sam" (Anne Azoulay). The insensitive Dan asks Laurent to be his best man. Laurent steps up a campaign to scare Dan away from marriage. He sends Dan to meet Camille's parents, and even writes letters to Dan pretending to be an old girlfriend. He wears Camille's wedding dress to a rally for legalizing gay marriages in France. He'll stop at nothing, even trying to convert Dan from the straight-and-narrow path.

Hipper than her prospective groom, Camille is aware that Laurent has the hots for her husband-to-be. She even encourages Dan to try gay sex just to determine if he's making the right choice between a male partner and a female bride.

The results are . . . . We can't really give away the plot, such as it is. The ending includes two weddings, but you'll have to see the film to understand the significance of the title.

Many gay viewers have had to confront that "moment of truth" with a so-called straight roommate. If nothing else, this movie will remind us of that crucial turning point in our lives.

3 Needles

(2005)

Ignorance, Greed, Fear, & Superstition

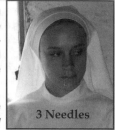

3 Needles

This sometimes frustrating Canadian film examines the AIDS epidemic on three continents. Ironically, the word AIDS is never heard in the film.

Thom Fitzgerald, who gave us the 1997 *The Hanging Garden* and the 1998 *Beefcake*, directed and wrote the film. In spite of all the actors and crew, it remains his personal baby.

The trilogy tells the story of a novice nun in South Africa; a black marketer in China, and an HIV-positive porn star in Canada. This three-in-one film provides very different perspectives on the struggle against AIDS.

A grim prologue launches the film with a tribal initiation rite in which African boys are led into a forest and circumcised to mark their passage into manhood. As a trivia note, many of the Pondo and Xhosi people of Africa cast in 3 Needles had never seen a movie in their lives.

At the beginning of the first section, the porn actor Shawn Ashmore, playing Denys, schemes to pass his mandatory blood test. In the second part, a young nun, Chloë Sevigny as Sister Clara, makes a personal sacrifice for the benefit of a South African village. In rural China in part three a black-market operative, Lucy Liu, cast as Jin Ping, posing as a government-sanctioned blood drawer, jeopardizes an entire village's safety.

The Canadian plot mimics the 1998 scandal that focused on real-life straight porn star, Marc Wallace. Denys' screen escapades end when it's discovered he's been faking negative HIV test results.

Also appearing in the film is one of the greatest broads on the screen today, Stockard Channing, as Olive Cowie, delivering an Oscar-worthy performance as Denys' mother.

One of our favorites, Olympia Dukakis, playing a nun, delivers the film's benediction, a rambling and eccentric message from the Great Beyond.

300

(2006)

A Gory Historical Drama with the World's Best Abs

Although it contains a bit of sexuality and nudity, the reason *300* is on the Gay-Dar is because of the army of bare-chested men on voyeuristic display throughout the film. Talent scouts combed the world to find some of the most buffed actors ever to appear on camera.

The script calls for the male cast to spend much of their screen time showing their tits, as per Frank Miller's original graphic novel. To prepare themselves for the cameras as the deadliest fighting force of the ancient world, the entire principal cast underwent a rigorous training regime for six weeks prior to shooting. The 37-year-old Scottish actor, Gerard Butler, trained for eight months to play buffed King Leonidas.

The Spartans on parade are certainly male beauties cast as holy warriors in their scarlet cloaks, loincloths, and sandals. Whether stuffed or the real thing, most of their leather pouches appear amply endowed.

The film is often a shot-for-shot adaptation of Frank Miller's comic book novel, similar to the film adaptation of *Sin City*, making extensive use of computer-generated imagery.

Miller was inspired by the original 480 B.C. Battle of Thermopylae after viewing the 1962 film, *The 300 Spartans*, as a child. If you remember from college history, the brave Spartans fought to the last man against the pagan Persian King Xerxes and his army.

Violent death in the film is often choreographed as a ballet. Talk about heads rolling. More computer blood was used in this film than any other ever released.

The Persian king is played by Rodrigo Santoro. As Xerxes, he would definitely fit the bill of one of Arnold Schwarzenegger's "girly men." One columnist thought the traveling throne of the god-king evoked "a louche Brazilian gay pride carnival float."

3-Day Weekend

(2008)

There Is Indeed Gay Life After 40

Eight gay men gather for a long weekend of R&R in a California mountain cabin. A committed couple, Jason (Douglas Myers) and Simon (Derek Meeker), to shake things up, have invited two friends to their cabin. Each of the foursome has also invited a single friend to make sparks fly.

Rob Williams both directed and scripted this man-on-man drama, on a micro-budget, using "threes" as a theme—three ways, three takes on sex, three men sunbathing, three men who have bedded the same guy. As one fan said, "it's not *Citizen Kane*, but doesn't try to be."

One of the men, André (Daniel Rhyder), is a hustler who Simon invited because he is a client.

The cast is rounded out by Cooper (Derek Long) and Ace (Stephen Twardokus) a "daddy-boy" leather vibe who are strictly monogamous; Mac (Chris Carlisle), an insecure computer geek; Cameron (Joel Harrison), old college roommate of Ace's who he also used to sleep with, and Kevin (Gaetano Jones), Cooper's New Age "naked yoga" instructor.

The combination of new and old friends creates more tension than either of the hosts realized. Some 72 hours pass, with a complex array of sexual couplings. New liaisons are formed, as others disintegrate.

WHAT THE CRITICS SAID
"Unlike, say, *The Boys in the Band* or *The Broken Hearts Club*, *3-Day Weekend* is populated by uniformly nice guys. There's not a single bitchy queen throwing barbed remarks among them. While the addition of one might have helped add a little zip to the script, it would also have led the film into cliché territory, so Williams chooses instead to make his points in a relatively calm atmosphere, even if André the hustler does shake things up by bouncing from guy to guy when not lounging nude (with one knee strategically bent for modesty) by the hot tub."
Dom Willmott

50 Ways of Saying Fabulous

(2005)

The Lows, the Trivia, & the Joy of Growing Up in Rural New Zealand in the 70s

A well-told story riddled with gentle humor, this 90-minute film premiered at the Toronto International Film Festival in 2005 and won many fans. It plays out against the dramatic landscape of Central Otago in New Zealand in 1975.

This is basically the story of 12-year-old Billy, beautifully acted by Andrew Patterson. A farmer's only son, he soon discovers that growing up is not without its pitfalls. Kiwi helmer Stewart Main adapted Graeme Aitken's novel.

Billy's fame takes note of his fondness for "dressing up" and his love of theatrics. Billy is earmarked as a "poofter" in the making, a local term for "budding queer."

Also a misfit is his best friend, Lou (Harriet Beattie), playing the role of an androgynous tomboy. There is a hilarious scene as Lou is horrified at her mother's attempts to get her to wear a bra. She doesn't welcome the growth occurring on her chest, as she is an ardent rugby player on an otherwise all-boy team.

In their one-room school in the country, Billy is a target of ridicule and abuse by the home-grown tough—that is, when he doesn't have Lou around to fight his battles.

Rejecting the world around him, Billy is a dreamer, imagining a life in outer space. In this make-believe world, a turnip paddock can become a lunar landscape, a cow's tail a head of beautiful blonde hair which can transform Billy into "Lana," the heroine of his favorite TV show.

Billy's world is changed forever with the arrival of Roy (Jay Collins), the class freak, and Jamie (Michael Dorman), a sexy young farm laborer.

WHAT THE CRITICS SAID
"Some viewers may find pic off-key, overfamiliar in gist or in questionable taste. Despite its whimsical tone (and title), '50 Ways' is far from affirming or inspirational. A lukewarm ending seems to shrug off the seriousness of what's passed before."
Dennis Harvey, *Variety*

Abnormal Beauty

(2004)

Sadistic Slasher Film from Hong Kong

If you like your movies R-rated and strong on violent content, with some nudity, grab a copy of this creepy thriller shot in Hong Kong, where it was released under the title of *Sei Mong Se Jun*. It was both directed and written by Oxide Pang Chun, with Danny Pang listed as co-producer. Known to Chinese cinema fans as "The Pang Brothers," this duo is the most famous in the Hong Kong film world.

On a tantalizing note, the two stars of the film, Race Wong as Jiney and Rosanne Wong as Jas, are actually sisters playing lesbian lovers. Both are a well-known music duo, "2R." Although skilled musicians, they are less experienced at acting, especially in stark horror melodrama.

Running for 101 minutes, *Abnormal Beauty* centers around Jiney, a beautiful, rich, and talented student studying photography but finding it unfulfilling—"something missing" from her life.

That begins to change when she witnesses a car wreck and photographs a female pedestrian lying face up on the road. After the crash, her latent schizophrenia begins to take over, and she becomes obsessed with death. Her greatest moment comes when she captures on film a suicidal woman's falling body in mid-flight. She even hires a chicken peddler to decapitate fowl so that she can shoot successive death throes from various angles.

There are scenes of intimacy with Jasmine, but this is hardly a flick devoted to lesbianism.

The plot takes an about-face when Jiney receives a mysterious videotape labeled "Take a Look." In the film, a masked man is bludgeoning a young woman to death with a lead pipe, the horrendous beating deliberately caught on tape.

Is death-obsessed Jiney his next victim? By now we know that it's inevitable that Jiney will come face to face with her potential killer. Long before the movie ends, we are aware of the identity of the S&M killer. It hardly takes Miss Marple to figure that one out.

Adam and Steve

(2005)

Post-Millennium Take on Adam & Eve

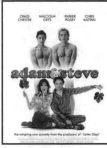

This comedy/romance was both directed and written by Craig Chester, who also stars as Adam. The veteran actor is known to gay audiences for his roles in *Swoon* and *Kiss Me Guido*. We first see him back in 1987 when he's a high school sprig in black goth regalia. His fag hag, played by Parker Posey, steals the show as his gal pal. Posey is so good, in fact, that she steals every scene in which she appears.

Adam is intrigued with a glittery glam dancer, Steve (played by Malcolm Gets of *Caroline in the City*). Steve takes substance-abuse virgin Adam and turns him onto drugs. Back at Adam's apartment where torrid sex is in the offing, the combination of coke cut with baby laxative removes Steve from the game. He's so sexually embarrassed that he's traumatized.

The movie jumps forward seventeen years. The setting is a psycho ward where a hysterical Adam seeks medical help for his accidentally stabbed dog. The psychiatrist-in-residence is none other than Steve, who does not remember his earlier embarrassment with Adam years ago.

In contrast to Steve's successful career, Adam is an underachiever, hired as a birdwatcher tour guide in Central Park. He's also a recovering addict, attending AA meetings presided over by Sally Kirkland as Mary, a manic ex-addict herself.

Romance blooms once again between Steve and Adam until Steve realizes that years previously, Adam witnessed the most humiliating sexual moment of his life.

As Michael, Steve's best friend, actor Chris Kattan delivers a creditable performance, as does Julie Hagerty as Sheila, the fab mom of Adam's cursed family.

The dance numbers are first-rate, one featuring a showdown in the form of a cowboy line dance, with Adam leaping, somersaulting, and whirling; the other a choral offering sung in a bar that will bring one tear to your eye.

Adored:
Diary of a Male Porn Star

(2003)

Not Porn, but the Joy of Sex

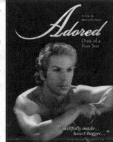

Playfully and even hauntingly erotic at times, this Italian film (*Pocco più di un anno fa*) drips with romance. Written and directed by Marco Filiberti, it stars himself in the lead role of Riki Kandinsky.

After a long separation, Riki and his older brother, Federico (Urbano Barberini), meet again at their father's funeral in France.

They journey to Riki's apartment in Rome where Federico learns that his brother is a male porn star. Shocked at first, he comes to accept his brother's lifestyle, showing up on the set of Riki's porn shoot the next day. Federico also feels the rock-hard bulge in Riki's underwear.

Is Federico also a closeted gay with incest on his mind? Perhaps not, since he eventually falls for Rosalina Celentano, cast as Luna, playing Riki's *agita*-prone fag hag.

Riki isn't bad to look at, evocative of one of those Luchino Visconti blond fantasy figures, especially Helmut Bereger or Bjord Andresen in *Death in Venice*.

The film takes an abrupt turn when Riki witnesses the death of a lesbian mother in a traffic accident, leaving an adorable little tyke, Plapla, played by Edoardo Minciotti. Riki wants to adopt the boy, but to gain custody he has to face off against the boy's grandparents.

Filiberti, in defining Riki, called him "a mixture of harmoniuous contradictions, cheeky and discreet, deep and superficial, elegant and trashy, aristocratic and common, luminous and melancholic, generous and selfish. He's like an angel lighting up the lives of others, but not his own, because he is still a prisoner of his own physique."

Planet Out defined the film as a "throwback to an era when directors like Roger Vadim stylishly mixed sex, sets, risqué humor, and melodrama."

Adventures of Priscilla, Queen of the Desert

(1994)

3-Queen Drag Act Rattling the Outback

In *Priscilla*, a heavily mascaraed Terence Stamp, who once flashed his well-endowed goodies onscreen, is now a magnificent, though sardonic and world weary, transsexual named Bernadette. He travels toward a gig on a bus tour through the wilds of Australia, encountering the bigots and the bumpkins. This unholy trio is shaking the kookaburras out of the trees.

Bernadette is joined by Hugo Weaving (Tick/Mitzi) and Guy Pearce (Adam/Felicia). Together they've made a road movie with a difference: Bitchy, outrageous, and vulgar, yet essentially warmhearted and endearing.

Incidentally, Bernadette is in mourning over her lost young lover, who was accidentally asphyxiated by peroxide fumes.

A highlight for us was when one of the aborigines joins the trio in a spirited rendition of "I Will Survive." Any director—in this case Stephan Elliott—who uses a soundtrack featuring Abba, Patti Paige, Lena Horne, and the Village People has to be doing something right.

For wild, wicked costumes, call on Lizzy Gardiner and Tim Chappel to design your next gown for the drag ball. These two know their way around spangles, sequins, and ostrich feathers.

Hop aboard. Watching this movie is a hell of a ride. So what if it "drags" a bit? (Pun intended.)

Priscilla should be screened for all high school kids as a lesson in tolerance of diversity.

WHAT THE CRITICS SAID
"I guess the scenes of homophobic hostility in the movie are obligatory, but Stephan Elliott doesn't seem to have his heart in them, and I wonder if he would have been happy to make the whole story as lighthearted as his best scene."
Roger Ebert

Affinity

(2008)

The 'Lady Visitor' and the Female Prisoner

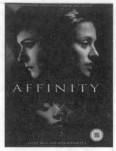

A costume drama set in Victorian England, this latest adaptation of a Sarah Waters' novel evokes *Tipping the Velvet* and *Fingersmith*.

It is a rather bizarre lesbian romance about a grieving upper-class woman who becomes a "Lady Visitor" at London's Millbank prison, where most of the inmates are awaiting mandatory transport to Australia. As part of the "Lady Visitor" program, she is introduced to a strange young woman, Selina Dawes (Zoe Tapper), who pretends to have supernatural powers.

Margaret Prior, played by Anna Madeley, has something to grieve about. Her former lover has married her brother, who is unaware of his sister's love affair.

A figure of mystery, Selina claims she is a spirit medium who can channel the souls of the dead. She was sentenced for murder and assigned to Millbank because she is alleged to have caused the death of a participant at one of her séances. Selina convinces Margaret that she is innocent, claiming that the evil spirits caused the death—not her. The jury didn't buy that.

Margaret is obviously attracted to Selina and falls under her spell. This upper-crust lady is taken in by Selina when mysterious events begin to occur in her life. A vase of flowers shows up in her bedroom, seemingly coming from nowhere. A plait of Selina's hair appears under Margaret's pillow. One of Margaret's most valued lockets mysteriously disappears. Is Selina merely a con artist, seductively using Margaret, hoping she can secure her release?

You get mystery, romance, even the quasi-supernatural, but these moody histrionics may not be enough for the average viewer as *Affinity* is slow moving, even gloomy, and somewhat disjointed. Maybe the Waters novel was too complicated to condense.

Directed by Tim Fywell, the film has authentic period costumes, a noble cast, and there are bits and pieces of brilliance here. If only the whole came together like a jigsaw puzzle.

The Aggressives

(2005)

An Aggressive? Or a Bull-Dyke?

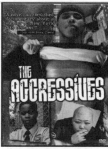

In this Secret Gallery Production, Daniel Peddle was both director and casting director. It took him five years to film *The Aggressives* and to tell the intimate stories of six very different women, each a self-styled "Aggressive."

Of course, Aggressives are women who stress their masculine sides. Traditionally, such women have been called bull-dykes by the general public. But Aggressives don't label themselves as such. Perhaps the subtle difference between a bull-dyke and an Aggressive is a question of attitude and self-description.

The cast of characters is often startling. It includes Tiffany, whose masculine persona is that of a "faggot." She is sleeping with a transvestite undergoing female hormone treatments. Kisha, another subject, works as a freelance femme model but also fulfills her duties as a part-time messenger in masculine attire.

Another performer, Rjai, proclaims, "My sexuality has nothing to do with my gender." At one of the celebratory drag balls, Rjai wins trophies for striding around as a construction worker, accented with a cement block balanced on her shoulder.

Flo, the film's sole Asian interlocutor, defines an Aggressive as "being a special kind of man." She is big, bulky, and with a shaven head. She also seems, as one critic put it, "joyously at home in her chosen milieu."

Marquise, one of the lesbians depicted, does biting exercises to keep her jawline firm and also adopts—rather predictably—baggy clothing and a close cropped "butch" hairstyle. Naturally she flattens her chest, not wishing to call attention to her tits. "That's not the illusion that I want to give you," she says.

One of the characters, Octavia, is tossed into prison for dope-dealing. When she's eventually released, she laments, "I miss the girls."

Agnes and His Brothers

(*Agnes und Seine Brüder;* 2004)

Which Sibling Is the Most Fucked-up?

Oskar Roehler juggles this tale of three brothers—one of them transgendered—who try to escape from both the real and perceived traumas of their childhood. The film moves adeptly along between drama and farce, with the drama winning out.

Sex-starved Hans-Jörg, played by Munich's Moritz Bleibtreu, one of the brothers, is convinced that the neuroses of his family come from repressed memories of their horrible father (Vadim Glowna) molesting Agnes as a child. With his long, shaggy mane, Glowna, an affluent hermit, suggests a "near-catatonic acid casualty of the 1960s," to one reviewer.

Hans-Jörg plays an introverted sex addict, working as a librarian. The therapy-addled Peeping Tom turned porn actor is on intimate terms with his right hand. He keeps a mannequin in his apartment for stimulation at night, but during the day slips into the bathroom, where he jerks off while spying on women through a peephole in the stall.

His older brother, Werner (Herbert Knaup) has his act a little more together, but not by much. A boorish, deluded Green Party politico, he lives in a mansion in the suburbs. Only problem is, his beautiful wife, Signa (Katja Riemann), hates him. She seems more sexually interested in their son, Ralf (Tom Schilling), whom she likes to massage. Ralf sets up surveillance cameras to catch dear old Werner taking a dump on the floor of his office.

Riemann evokes Annette Bening, and is one of the most talented of the cast. Her role in *Rosenstrasse* earned her the Best Actress Award in Venice in 2005. Bleibtreu and Knaup have worked together before in *Run Lola Run.*

Last but not least is Martin Weiss in the title role of Agnes, a gentle fragile dancer, a lonely male-to-female trannie, whose transgendered status is inseparable from her tragic aura. On top of those high heels, she is the most sympathetic of the brothers.

Aimée & Jaguar

(1999)

First Lesbian Romance of WWII

This was Germany's entry in the category of Best Foreign Film in 1999 at the Academy Awards. It's the story of a forbidden love larger than death, set during the time of the Battle of Berlin (1943/1944), with Allied bombs bursting overhead.

The stars are Maria Schrader, playing Felice (nicknamed Jaguar), and Juliane Köhler playing Lilly (nicknamed Aimée). The German director was Max Färberböck, who was also the co-author of the screenplay.

Living in the shadow of death, Felice has five damns: She's a Jew. A Communist. A spy. A lesbian. And she's having an affair with a German officer's wife.

When the two potential lovers meet, they give each other "that look."

Forever smoking like Marlene Dietrich, the "It Girl of Nazi Berlin" (Felice) works in the propaganda ministry by day, then parties at night with Jewish lesbians when not spying for the Communist underground.

Then Felice meets Lilly Wurst, mother of four blonde little Aryans and the wife of a Wehrmacht officer.

The true story of this couple is recounted in a 1994 book by journalist Erica Fischer, which became a bestseller in Germany.

Aimée and Jaguar certainly prove the cliché: opposites attract. Almost from the beginning, though, the audience knows that the love of these women is doomed. But on the way to that tragedy, Färberböck spins a story of love in all its extravagantly emotional moments, evoking Bertolucci or even De Sica at times. Lustrously shot, it is brilliantly acted.

Both Ms. Schrader and Ms. Köhler won the Best Actress honors at the 1999 Berlin International Film Festival, and they richly deserved it.

The film asks you to make a big jump: Did Felice actually trade a few moments of "the perfect love" for the eternity of the grave?

AKA

(2001)

Three Windows Into One Fractured Soul

In many ways, this avant-garde film evokes Patricia Highsmith's *The Talented Mr. Ripley* minus the murders. Director/writer Dundan Roy based the film on his own life story.

He folds the screen into a triptych to trace the saga of a disaffected young man in his search for status, love, and identity, even if that identity is false.

Set in Britain in the 1970s, it is acted by Matthew Leitch who plays the lead, Dean Page. He begins life almost in a Dickensian setting of working-class London. Here he is trapped between an abusive stepfather (incest is clearly suggested). The parent from hell is played by Geoff Bell, the doormat of a mother brilliantly acted by Lindsay Coulson.

Fleeing this horrid landscape, Dean advances himself up the London social ladder, arriving in Paris where he assumes the identity of a young British lord who is Oxford bound and headed for a life of wealth and privilege.

In Paris, Dean becomes involved with a tax exile, David (George Asprey), and his cute American toy boy, Benjamin (Peter Youngblood Hills). David in time kicks out Benjamin and adopts Dean as his new pet.

AKA is an indictment of the horrid aspects of the English aristocracy, portraying its members as decadents from hell, lost in a world of snobbery, cocaine sniffing, homosexuality, and wife-swapping. And, yes, like proper Victorians, they beat their servants.

It is not always an easy ride for Dean, since he has to serve a year in prison for stolen identity and credit card abuses.

The question asked is this: Can Dean find love while living a lie?

The poignant film is both insightful and consistently amusing, and the triptych is a device but never a gimmick to tell the story.

In a word, the movie is a TRI-umph.

All About My Mother
(1999)
Tennessee, Truman, & *All About Eve*

"The Spanish John Waters," Pedro Almodóvar, has done it again with *Todo sobre mi madre* (its Spanish title). The film suggests that part of every man is a woman.

Manuela, wonderfully played by Cecilia Roth, is a nurse employed in a Madrid hospital. Her son, Esteban (Eloy Azorin), doesn't know who his father is. On his 18th birthday, he is taken to see Tennessee Williams' *A Streetcar Named Desire*. After the show, he is killed in an accident trying to get an autograph from legendary actress Huma Rojo (as played by Marisa Paredes).

Overcome with grief, Manuela goes to Barcelona to tell Esteban's father that his son is dead. The father (Toni Canto), as we learn, is now a transvestite prostitute called Lola.

The melodrama unfolding is aptly defined as "Almodrama." Visiting a Barcelona slum, Manuela calls on Agrado, a good-hearted transsexual (Antonia San Juan), who introduces her to a friendly nun, Hermana Rosa (Penélope Cruz). Get this: Rosa is knocked up and HIV-positive. The daddy is none other than Lola.

Manuela becomes the personal assistant of Huma Rojo (evocative of *All About Eve*), whom her son so admired. Cruz fits easily into her role as a nun working in a shelter for battered prostitutes. Huma's lover is drug-addicted Nina (Candela Peña). Agrado soon takes over when Manuela must care for Sister Rosa's risky pregnancy.

Death, pain, and disease parade in front of us, with performances that are first-rate, aided by razor-sharp dialogue and bouts of comic relief.

Almodóvar lives up to his reputation as expressed by critic Vincent Canby who called him "Spain's most reputable disreputable filmmaker."

All About My Mother is an Almodóvar extravaganza that, like Blanche DuBois, depends on the kindness of strangers. The film is woven into a rich tapestry of love that takes many forms.

All the Rage
(1997)
The Call That Never Comes

You've seen them so many times, the buffed clones of New York's Chelsea District, West Hollywood, South Beach, and Key West. *All the Rage* is arguably one of the best films devoted to the cult of gay narcissism. In this overview of the gay clone life, a question emerges. Can a leopard truly change his spots?

Roland Tec both wrote and directed this serio-comedy, casting John-Michael Lander as Christopher Bedford, every gay man's fantasy—gorgeous, young, wealthy, totally buffed.

The audience for this film is the gay male urbanite. The world of the superprivileged gay Bostonian is explored in the 1990s. Christopher, a successful lawyer, is an egomaniac who brushes off his hopeful one-night stands with a promise "I'll call you." He is the perfect 10, but, so far, the only mate worthy of him is the one staring back at him in the mirror.

His colleague, Larry (Jay Corcoran), is also a lawyer and fellow gym bunny. He seems happy to take Christopher's cast-offs.

Along comes Stewart (David Vincent), complete with love handles. He is shy, unjaded, cute but nebbish, and in a lowlife position as a book editor. He's not at all Christopher's type, so why is he interested in this nerd? In contrast, Stewart's roommate, Kenny (Alan Natale), is a chiseled hunk that Christopher has lusted for in the gym for weeks. The plot thickens.

All the Rage is both diverting and delicious, but ultimately damning, emerging as a cautionary tale about both the heart and the eyes having different tastes.

WHAT THE CRITICS SAID
"A-gays look good in the shower, so *All the Rage* opens with close-ups of soaping up and rinsing, with beads of water thrilled to be on such perfect gym-toned skin."
The New York Times

All-Star:
The Films of Todd Verow

(2009)

Iconoclastic Maverick Bares All

You'll either love or hate the controversial Maine-born filmmaker, Todd Verow. Some of his devoted fans adore his work; others, especially those who once voted for George W. Bush, find it utterly repellent. Born on November 11, 1966—"a day that will live in infamy," according to his critics—he's been called the Spielberg of film's new digital age or New York's underground cinema posterboy. He's also been called a lot of other things as well, but we can't print them in case kids have gotten a copy of our reviews.

Verow burst onto the scene when he made his first feature film, a notorious version of Dennis Cooper's novel, *Frisk.* After that he started his own production company, Bangor Films. *Frisk* was about the exploits of a gay serial killer. The movie was set in an erotic world of sado-masochism, exposing the sexual appetites of a young man to whom killing and cannibalizing the victim becomes the ultimate thrill.

After the completion of *Frisk*, Verow established his own production company, Bangor Films, which was the corporate entity which subsequently produced most of his other films.

All-Star is a DVD containing 13 queer short films and videos directed by Verow. They share a common thread of raw sex and shredded emotions, and as a plus for men who love dick, most of them contain a degree of porn, including in some cases at least one cum shot. *Frisk*, incidentally, is not included in the All-Star collection.

WHAT THE CRITICS SAID
"In Todd Verow's horribly, hauntingly candy-colored films and videotapes, beauty like Verow's camerawork exists in a state of divine agitation. The filmmaker's frenetic and corrosively low-rent visions of the American verities, raw sex and shredded emotion, portray glamour as a kind of drug-induced condition. Gender assignments collapse, narrative logic disintegrates and memory dissolves in a frenzied spin-art spew of teased hair and tangled psychodrama, baubles, bangles and bulging briefs."
San Francisco Bay Guardian

And the Band Played On

(1993)

A Fight for Many, Fought by Few

The Black Death of the 1980s caught the world by surprise, especially gay men. The teleplay by Arnold Schulman was based on the 1987 non-fiction book *And the Band Played On: Politics, People, and the AIDS Epidemic* by Randy Shilts.

Director Roger Spottiswoode asked Richard Gere to appear in the film. Gere accepted a small role, breaking a long taboo where major movie stars did not take part in TV productions. In his wake Steve Martin, Alan Alda, Phil Collins, Lily Tomlin, Angelica Huston, and others agreed to appear.

The end result is a powerful human drama, showing a threat that no one in major authority wanted to face. AIDS was a word that no one wanted to speak, especially the presiding ruler of America, Ronald Reagan.

The former president is clearly the villain of the film, and with good reason, as he seemed indifferent to the plight of "the gay disease"—and later hemophiliacs, drug users, and newborn babies who had contracted AIDS.

Gays in the teleplay are real people, not a stereotype, except for one or two characters.

Dr. Bob Gallo (Alda) is an AIDS researcher who tries to hog credit for discovering the virus, although credit more properly should go to a team of doctors in France.

The cameos by such major stars is a bit of a distraction, especially when Collins appears as a cynical bathhouse owner.

The film is most effective in depicting how the gay community in San Francisco was divided about the disease and what to do about it.

WHAT THE CRITICS SAID
"The telefilm takes measures of the battle against red tape, egos, lack of funding, and countless self-interests. The film mirrors the struggles as researchers in France and the U.S. fought to isolate and identify the virus despite public resistance and government neglect."
Tony Scott, *Variety*

Angels in America

(2003)

A Gay Fantasia on National Themes

How can this TV series, running 352 minutes, go wrong? The drama fantasy is by Out playwright Tony Kushner, and it's got everything from full frontal nudity (Justin Kirk of *Weeds* shows the full monty) to Meryl Streep impersonating an old Rabbi. She also plays the doomed Ethel Rosenberg and a Mormon housewife.

It's got gay Mormons, sex, romance, and, just for fun, an oversexed angel (Emma Thompson) who, we're told, has eight vaginas.

Kushner's masterpiece is a political epic of the AIDS crisis that came like the Black Death during the Reagan era of the 1980s. Director Mike Nichols holds the rambling piece together, infusing both grandeur and extravagance into Kushner's two-part epic, divided into "The Millennium Approaches" and "Perestroika."

Al Pacino is brilliant as Roy Cohn, the self-loathing homosexual and anti-Communist zealot. Even when dying of AIDS, he cannot admit it to himself, brow-beating his doctor into asserting that he has liver cancer.

Five younger actors each give outstanding performances. They include Mary-Louise Parker, Jeffrey Wright, Ben Shenkman, Patrick Wilson, and Justin Kirk. Plot twists multiply and characters collide, and there is dialogue, dialogue, and more dialogue, most of it witty, poetic even.

Critic Chris Barsanti assessed the series accurately as a "landmark piece of work that stretches too far and flies too high, but even when plummeting back to earth, makes for a riveting and heady spectacle." Despite the gloom and doom of death, Kushner ends on an optimistic note. Actor Justin Kirk is clearly speaking for the playwright when he said: "This disease (AIDS) will be the end of many of us. And we are not going away. We won't die secret deaths any more. The world only spins forward. We will be citizens when the time has come."

Anonymous

(2004)

Satyriasis Dominating a Human Life

Todd Verow is becoming an increasingly famous name in the world of underground films. Once again, as in so many of his other films, he's the writer, producer, and helmer. He also plays a character named Todd on screen.

This original psychological portrait is provocative in its violent and frequently degrading "anonymous" sexual encounters with nameless strangers. Todd is a Manhattanite involved in a long-term relationship but also fatally attracted to sex in toilets, which he prowls frequently in search of adventure and dick.

Eventually—and inevitably—his boyfriend, John (Dustin Schell), catches him *in flagrante* in the stalls of a theater men's room. He beats him up and leaves him lying half naked in a pool of blood. When Todd gets home, he finds that John has changed the locks on the door. Homeless, Todd moves into his office, where his compulsion for anonymous sex throws his job into jeopardy. Todd is the night manager of a movie theater but his supervisors notice his increasing indiscretions and neglect of the popcorn concession. In one extended sequence Todd strips off his clothing in his office, prancing around in his jockstrap.

In the unlikely event you grow bored with Todd's package, the plot turns a corner. Arriving is an IRS official come to "audit" Todd. An unlikely choice for such a part, Craig Chester is cast as the IRS agent. Todd discovers an unusual method of settling his bill for back taxes.

WHAT THE CRITICS SAID:
"The real love story here may be between Todd the exhibitionist and Mr. Verow the voyeur, peeping in on his character's activities. They look to have a long and happy future together."
Dave Kehr, *The New York Times*

"Sordid beatings, joyless sex, and a sullen synth score create the air of a home-brewed 60s sexploitation-noir flick, or a pre-Stonewall pulp homosexual novel, complete with narrative clichés and the occasional bit of ugly beauty."
Ed Halter, *Village Voice*

Another Country

(1984)

Gay British Spies at Eton

If you like caning, male nudity, boarding school sex, and gay Commies, this drama/romance is for you. A very young Rupert Everett, never looking handsomer, and Colin Firth give outstanding performances as the gay and Communist members of a 1930s British 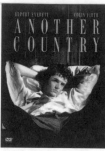 public school such as Eton. (Americans call it a private school).

The movie is based on a play by Julian Mitchell and follows the life of Guy Burgess, who became a Soviet spy and defected to Russia in 1951. He was a member of the notorious Cambridge Spy Ring, an infamous quartet, three members of which were homosexuals working for the KGB-- notably spies Guy Burgess, Kim Philby, and Donald Duart Maclean.

This scandal set gay rights back ten years, as homophobes loudly proclaimed that gays couldn't be trusted in sensitive government positions.

As directed by Marek Kanievska, the movie begins in 1983 in Moscow as an unrepentant Guy, made up to be an old man, is interviewed by a British reporter. The rest of the film is an extended flashback.

The object of Guy's schoolboy attraction is James Harcourt (as played by Cary Elwes). Soon he and gorgeous Cary are in each other's arms. Guy's friend is Tommy Judd (Firth), who is a "pinko" right down to his jockey shorts.

Everett seems to delight in playing a narcissistic mama's boy, who is both obnoxious and "out" (long before the term was invented). A talented cast drew raves from one viewer. "If you're into pretty, clean-cut British men, the film will basically make you cum in your pants," he claimed.

This is the story of what makes a man like Guy Burgess, with his educational pedigree (he even knows the secret handshake of the elite), break with both his class and Mother England.

Unlike Everett, the other cloistered teenage boys frequently pair up for secret trysts in the closet, all the while preserving their straight credentials.

Apartment Zero

(1988)

Psycho Roommate Thriller

Director Martin Donovan provides a lot of close-ups of his co-star Hart Bochner, perhaps thinking he is another James Dean. But the curled lip and arched brow, it was suggested, more often evoked Elvis Presley in *Blue Hawaii*. The helmer teamed  Bochner as Jack Carney, opposite Colin Firth as Adrian LeDuc.

This thriller, set in modern-day Buenos Aires, centers around the relationship of two emotionally crippled roommates.

Adrian is the owner of a movie revival house in the city where the seats are often empty. He is a tenant in a run-down apartment building, and is forced to take in a roommate. The handsome, charming Jack shows up and takes the room. Adrian is clearly attracted to this stranger.

Reports spread through the building that serial murders are occurring, the blame centering on mercenary foreigners who came to Argentina where they were employed by Death Squads. There is a suspicion that Jack may be a member of these Death Squads.

WHAT THE CRITICS SAID

"Edgy and unsettling, with terrific performances from its stars, Colin Firth and ultra-sexy Hart Bochner, this suspenseful tale of violence and madness never connected with audiences. But it has grown in cult stature over the years. *Apartment Zero* should have made Bochner a star if only people had seen it."
Pam Grady, *DVD Review*

"Perhaps derailed by the force of his own originality, or possibly suffering from novice's overdrive, Donovan loosens his grip somewhat during *Zero*'s final act. But the sardonic, gruesome conclusion is nonetheless entertaining; a minor skid for Donovan is sure driving for others by the time you've felt *Zero*'s full impact."
Desson Howe, *Washington Post*

April's Shower

(2003)

How Far Would You Go for True Love?

This feel-good movie, a comedy/romance, was written and directed by Trish Doolan. Doolan also cast herself as Alex, a lesbian chef.

The title comes from the depiction of what appears to be a traditional wedding shower at the beginning of the movie. Before long, the shower turns into a free-for-all, as the inner motives of the leading characters are revealed. The plot becomes zanier and more complex as the party progresses.

As maid of honor, Alex (Doolan) must throw the mandatory bridal shower for her friend and former lover, April (Maria Cina). Even April's own mother doesn't know that she and Alex were former lesbian lovers. But revelations are on the way.

The women are not alone, as the eclectic guests file into Alex's house, filled with their own hilarious insecurities and troubling life situations. One of the guests, for example, is being stalked by a one-night stand that followed her from Scotland.

The sexual tension builds as the guests—fueled by too much red wine—hysterically re-examine their own histories and relationships. This only comes after Alex explodes and reveals the true nature of her clandestine relationship with the supposedly straight bride-to-be. The news comes as great interest, of course, to the groom.

"All you need is wine, sex, and garlic", says Alex.

WHAT THE CRITICS SAID
"The cast of unknowns is commendably game for this typically talky low-budget effort, but it could have used a much stronger script—and we could have done without the onslaught of poignancy in the final act."
Sara Cardace, *New York Magazine*

"The gender twist is a quirky enough take on the genre, but it's the fun cast of characters that makes this movie great."
Lesbiannation.com

Auntie Mame

(1958)

A Queer Icon for the Ages

Let's face it. All of us wanted Auntie Mame for our relative, so we could run away to New York and do gay things with gay people. The memorable line of the movie was "Life is a banquet, and most poor suckers are starving to death." Since 1958, gay men seemed to have adopted "Life is a banquet" as their motto.

Its director was Morton DaCosta, the screenplay by Berry Comden and Adolph Green, but the show belongs to the free-spirited and flamboyant Auntie Mame (Rosalind Russell as Mame Dennis). Tallulah Bankhead turned it down ("too many costume changes, dah-ling").

An orphan goes to live with Mame. The character of Patrick Dennis is played younger by Jan Handzlik, older by Roger Smith. In New York he meets all sorts of zany characters, none better than Peggy Cass as Agnes Gooch or Coral Browne as Vera Charles. Fred Clark (remember him in *Sunset Blvd.*?) was cast as the executor of the estate of Patrick's father who objects to Mame's lifestyle.

It's been suggested that Patrick is secretly gay, but Rosalind Russell certainly isn't. She ends up marrying Forrest Tucker, a rich southern plantation owner, Beauregard Jackson Pickett Burnside. Lucky Mame. Tucker in real life was one of those 12-inch "clubbers."

Along with such films as *All About Eve* and *Sunset Blvd.*, *Auntie Mame* remains one of the great gay movies of all time. Of course, you might ask the question, how could an ostensibly straight film be called gay? It's a question of camp, darlings.

In her timing, delivery, and comedic presentation, Rosalind Russell is perfect for the role, although it would have been fun to watch what Tallulah would have done. "I would have fucked Patrick," she once told a group of gay writers.

In your DVD search, get the Rosalind Russell version, not that hideous remake with Lucille Ball in 1974. "Lucy" played it completely over the top, and her version was an infamous flop.

Backstage

(2005)

Girl's Teenage Crush on a Diva

This French film was directed by Emmanuelle Bercot, who also shared writing credits with Jérôme Tonnerre.

In *Backstage* the groupie girl is effectively played by Isild Le Besco, cast as star-struck Lucie. Her idol is Lauren Waks, a role interpreted by Emmanuelle Seigner, who at times appears to be even more mentally confused than her obsessive fan.

The plot starts to move when Lucie's mother, played by Edith Lemerdy, arranges a surprise but televised visit to the home of the regally remote diva. Once there, Lauren sings a tender love song to her fan, who goes into meltdown. Lauren seems to view the visit as a mere publicity gimmick which she must endure before being driven back to Paris in her limousine. But to Lucie, it's a dream come true, a visit from her idol, whose photographs adorn the walls of Lucie's bedroom.

As part of a plot that's slightly evocative of *All About Eve*, with Anne Baxter and Bette Davis, Lucie flees from her home in the French provinces and heads for Paris. She virtually camps outside Lauren's hotel, hoping for a glimpse of her goddess. Somehow, she's able to bamboozle her way into Lauren's suite. Actress Noémie Lvovsky delivers a superb performance as Juliette, the star's "gate-keeper." Although Juliette initially grants only five minutes to Lucie, the fan ends up staying on to serve her mistress and volunteering to run personal errands.

The diva herself is emotionally distraught, having lost her latest boyfriend, Daniel, as played by Samuel Benchetrit. When Lucie encounters Daniel as part of a chance meeting, she starts plotting to get him to return to Lauren, but not for the reasons you might think. We don't want to give away the plot.

Bercot, as director, is clearly a master of the naturalistic camera style in depicting how Lucie is able to storm the "fortified" walls of Lauren's carefully guarded world.

Bad Education

(2004)

Pedro Almodóvar's Ode to *Film Noir*

Two kids, Enrique and Ignacio, discover love, cinema, and fear in a religious school at the start of the 1960s. Father Manolo, the school principal, is witness to and part of these discoveries. The three characters meet twice again, at the end of the 70s and 80s. Their reunion will mark the life and death of some of them.

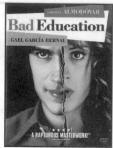

Almodóvar, the writer and director, has done it again, brilliantly, with this Spanish-language film.

Bad Education follows the filmmaker's Oscar-winning *Talk to Her* and *All About My Mother*. But this film is very different, the story of two priest-abused boys who become lost souls in Almodóvar's most personal film to date.

We agree with movie critic Roger Ebert. In a limited amount of space, it's too difficult to summarize the convoluted storyline. Ebert believed, and we concur, that *Bad Education* is a movie that "we are intended to wander around in."

The setting is in the Franco era, when sexual abuse of young boys by priests was generally hushed up. The Catholic Church is indicted in *Bad Education*, not only for abusing its enormous power, but for pedophilia in the priesthood.

Almodóvar brings charm and grace to this *film noir*. Gael García Bernal shines brilliantly as a drag queen, and Fele Martínez as the director-writer is perhaps a quasi-autobiographical symbol for Almodóvar himself. Enrique is played convincingly by Raúl García Forneiro, a young Ignacio by Nacho Per Peréz. Gleaming like a pedophile, Father Manolo is interpreted with razor-sharp finesse by Daniel Jiménez Cacho.

Film-goers are left with a lot of puzzles to solve in *Bad Education*. Of all the actors, Gael García Bernal brings the same kind of dazzling screen presence that's evoked by an earlier Almodóvar discovery, Antonio Banderas.

If your passion is for melodrama and you adore role playing, you've rented the right film. In such a complex web of fantasy, illusion, and reality, you can lose control of what is actually happening.

Big Bang Love, Juvenile A

(46-okunen no koi; 2006)

What's Wrong with Japanese Men?

Enjoying an international cult following, helmer Takashi Miike is both prolific and controversial, having directed some 70 productions since his debut in 1991. A literal translation of this film's Japanese title is *The Love of 4,600 Million Years.*

The director is notorious for depicting horrid scenes of extreme violence and so-called sexual perversions. In one film he depicted the vertical slicing of a man in half from head to groin.

In *Big Bang Love*, Miike used the format of a 1940s style whodunit as a means of exploring his ideas on what's wrong with Japan and also what's wrong with Japanese men. (No, it's not what you think.)

Homoerotic prison life is depicted as a metaphor for what's wrong with Japan. The film is about two male prisoners, each of them jailed for unrelated murders. One Jun (Ryuhel Matsuda) had brutally killed a john who picked him up in a gay bar. The other, Shiri (Masanobu Ando), seemingly has been an outlaw since the day he popped out of the womb.

Don't expect anything to be crystal clear. That is never Miike's intent. The movie has been called "a drippingly hallucinatory confessional." Expect unexplained gaps, unclarified motivations.

The audience is limited for this film. As one viewer put it, "A threadbare homoerotic prison film exposé on masculinity at the pace of a drunken snail isn't exactly going to play in Nebraska."

Ultimately, the film ends as a tribute to homosexual love. There are, however, no overt scenes of sex.

One lesson learned, according to one critic: "Japanese juvenile detention centers are hotbeds of homosexual activity. If only George Michael could travel back in time."

Bar Girls

(1994)

A Romantic Comedy Without Men

Lauran Hoffman concocted this film about the life and loves of a group of gay women who hang out at a local tavern. It might also have been called the "Lavender Circle Mob."

The movie is fun stuff, including the soundtrack that plays "Everybody's Fuckin' My Baby." This lesbian romp has been hailed by many women as one of the first films to accurately portray girl-loving girls on the prowl.

Bar Girls was originally written by Lauran Hoffman as a play, and later as a screenplay. The cast of barflies includes, among others, Chastity Bono, daughter of that gay fave, Cher.

During the course of the movie, most of the barflies get around to sleeping with each other. Of course, it's like a soap opera, but that doesn't mean it can't be entertaining. The women are seen falling in love and having their hearts broken—in other words, getting on with life.

Marita Giovanni with her smooth direction has assembled a savvy cast who parades through a movie which in some respects evokes the stylistically innovative *Go Fish*. Loretta (Nancy Alison Wolfe) is the most fully rounded character, but you also get a congenial assemblage of archetypes: Beautiful "straight" Veronica, tough diesel dyke Tracy, aggressive flat-footer J.R., and virtuous Sandy.

Rachel (Liza D'Agostino) is the second lead. She's involved in a failing marriage, but getting pussy on the side. Surely there has never been such an array of makeups and breakups, with hearts cracking every minute until a new love comes along.

Barbarella

(1968)

Taking Sex into Outer Space

That devastating beauty, John Philip Law, immortalized himself in the Jane Fonda cult classic, *Barbarella*. He is still best known for his role as the blind angel, Pygar, in this psychedelic piece of trash.

Gays were enchanted by Law's six-foot-five presence and his steel blue eyes. Guys who went to bed with this homosexual actor were also enchanted by an 8 1/2-inch penis, rather thick. (Okay, so he was once married.)

In no time at all, gays made Law the male sex symbol of the 1960s, at least in poster art. Nearly all bathrooms of gay males had a poster of the shirtless, blond-haired pin-up whose nipples (according to his bedmates) "were the most sensitive in Hollywood."

Of course, if you like girls you were treated to the "five-star, double-rated astronautical aviatrix," Fonda herself in a minimum of clothing—Nancy Sinatra go-go boots, hard and shiny metallics, and furs. Barbarella, a sex kitten from the 21st century, pursues an evil scientist, Durand Durand, in outer space before he can launch his reign of terror. The 80s group, Duran Duran, took their name from this silly film, using a slightly different spelling.

The picture was directed by the whoremonger, Roger Vadim, who married three of the world's hottest women: Brigitte Bardot, Jane Fonda, and Catherine Deneuve. For greater spice, he preferred beautiful drag queens on the side. Barbarella was originally intended as a role for Bardot.

Anita Pallenberg portrays the lesbian Black Queen who, in her dream chamber, can make fantasies take form.

The highlight of the film for lesbians was when Fonda performs her zero-gravity striptease, which became a movie legend. The major disappointment of the film is when John Philip Law didn't show the full monty . . . hard, that is.

Director Roger Vadim referred to the intergalactic *Barbarella* as "a kind of sexual *Alice in Wonderland* of the future." And so it is.

Basic Instinct

(1992)

A Bisexual Ice Pick Murderess

When this controversial film starring Sharon Stone and Michael Douglas was released, gay and lesbian activists protested having yet another lesbian in movies portrayed as a psychotic murderess. Their protests only seemed to increase box office.

Joe Eszterhas, the screenwriter, hauled in $3 million for the script. The question is, why? Dutch-born director Paul Verhoeven included "the money shot," in this case the vagina of Stone which created shock waves in theaters across the country. Signing on for mega millions, Michael Douglas, in another *Fatal Attraction* turn, plays the police detective setting out to investigate the brutal murder of a rock star.

The corpse of Johnny Boz (Bill Cable) is found tied to a bedpost, with his body pierced with ice pick stabs. The beautiful and bisexual novelist, Stone (Catherine Tramell), is the prime suspect.

Douglas, a fucked-up cop, plays his scenes well in dealing with this twisted and manipulative woman. He's mesmerized by her sex appeal and perhaps attracted to her danger. Never before has Stone exuded such sexual magnetism, certainly not in *Basic Instinct 2: Risk Addiction* (2006), which bombed.

Regardless of the controversies, and regardless of the debate of whether this is a good or bad film, *Basic Instinct* in the last reel emerges as an erotically charged thriller that's Grade A pulp fiction—nothing more, nothing less.

One critic noted that the end result is "a barrage of flesh hacking, shooting, red herrings, and bed-bumping, but in the end a predictable, surprisingly uninvolving affair."

Desson Howe of the *Washington Post* made a wry comment. "If you're unfamiliar with the genitalia of either gender, *Basic Instinct* is the movie that will clear things up."

Nick the detective ends up with the best line. He describes the Sharon Stone character as "the fuck of the century."

Bear Cub

(*Cachorro*; 2004)

Fatherhood Is About to Get Hairier

Calling all bears. Innocent childhood nostalgia is combined with graphic sexuality in this compassionate, life-affirming Spanish comedy/drama. The bears in this movie are bearded, burly, and in some cases, balding. They wouldn't have a  chance getting cast on *Queer as Folk*.

Pedro (José Luis García Pérez) is a sexually free-spirited, HIV-positive dentist. Pulling teeth by day, he hangs out with hairy gay guys at night, the type who like to party.

Then one fine day, his sister Violeta (Elvira Lindo) shows up on his doorstep with his nine-year-old nephew, Bernardo (child actor David Castillo). Violeta is off to India with her hippie boyfriend, but soonafter, she gets arrested for drug trafficking, so she'll have to spend some time in jail.

Pedro finds himself a full-time parent which means he'll have to activate some lifestyle changes. Enter the villain. The kid's grandmother shows up plotting blackmail and legal action. In the role of Doña Teresa, Empar Ferer comes off like a Spanish version of Olympia Dukakis.

By this time the kid, wise beyond his years, has bonded with his uncle as a surrogate dad and wants to stay with him.

José Luis García Pérez is a well-known Spanish stage actor, and David Castillo has been trained in TV drama.

Bernardo is the best advertising for gay parenting that has come along by making it clear to the viewer that he doesn't give a shit about his surrogate father's sexuality as long as his daddy loves him.

There are two cuts of this film in DVD release, the unrated director's cut containing an opening sex scene with two hairy men, plus another gay sex scene in a steam bath. Male frontal nudity is shown in the "uncut" version (and uncut is the right word).

The movie teaches us how fucked up Goldilocks was. It's fun living with bears.

Beau Travail

(1999)

Billy Budd in Boot Camp

The French army didn't want this film by director Claire Denis made, interpreting it as a scandal about the army and homosexuality. The brass preferred that the subject remain taboo. But Denis forged ahead with the script set in a French Foreign Legion outpost in Africa and based on Herman Melville's *Billy Budd*.

Plot aside, the gay male will take delight in viewing the beautiful bodies of the young men in motion. They have sleek, buff bodies as they train to turn themselves into fighting machines.

Lisa Schwarzbaum put it aptly: "[Claire] Denis builds the sinister struggle, with its homoerotic undertones. But mostly she marvels with joy and wonder at the beauty of men—white and black, European and African—engaged as a unit in activities as rote as gun drills, as ecstatic as romping in the ocean; her visual style is hypnotic, rapturous, and she makes barren landscapes look gorgeous, hard men look vulnerable."

The film is narrated by the character of Galoup (Denis Lavant), a former sergeant who has been expelled from the Legion for his brutal treatment of a young recruit, Sentain (Gregorie Colin),

Galoup lusts for Commander Bruno Forestier (Michel Subor) and becomes consumed with jealous rage when Sentain replaces Galoup as the object of his affection.

The hugfests in the film might have been choreographed by Martha Graham. A highlight is when Galoup and Sentain stage a one-on-one bare-chested face-off, circling each other on the African coast.

The film is imbued with eroticism and riddled with repressed homosexual desire. *Beau Travail* is minimalist in characterization and dialogue, but the film has a stunning visual sense, one of the most beautiful gay films made in the 90s.

Beautiful Boxer

(2004)

He Fights Like a Man So He Can Become a Woman

This poignant mix of testosterone and estrogen is based on the real-life story of Parinya Charoenphol, a Muaythai boxer who underwent a sex-change operation to become a woman. Filmed in the Thai language with English subtitles, the movie was directed by Ekachai Uekrongtham, who also co-authored the screenplay.

To find someone to play the role of Parinaya Charoemphol (a.k.a. Nong Toom), the director held nationwide auditions across four regions of Thailand. Winning out over 300 contenders, Asanee Suwan, a 22-year-old professional kickboxer from Chiangmai province, clinched the role.

To prepare for the role, the champion boxer studied acting and went through "personality enhancement" training designed to groom beauty queens.

The film chronicles the life of the boxer from his days as a young boy who likes to wear lipstick to his sensational career as a kickboxer, and, finally, the sex change op itself. One startling moment in the film is when the young boxer un-nerves his opponents by performing a makeup application ritual in full view of the spectators before each fight.

We watch as Nong evolves through stages that include mama's boy, a young monk, a novice boxer, a mega-celebrity, and, finally, a beautiful woman.

In a nutshell, let's call this pic "Rocky in Heels."

WHAT THE CRITICS SAID
"Beautiful Boxer at times feels repetitive and haltingly paced, but its blazing emotional core is the real-life boxer Asanee Suwan's joyously physical performance as Nong Toom. Whether lifting weights with his teeth or engaging in a delicate ritual dance before each match, Mr. Suwan paints the character's simultaneous sweetness and toughness with subtlety."
Dana Stevens, *The New York Times*

Beautiful Darling

(2009)

The Life & Times of a Warhol Superstar

Candy Darling, the transsexual version of Lana Turner, burst on the scene in the 1960s starring in such Andy Warhol films as *Flesh* (1968). She later starred in *Women in Revolt* (1971), playing a Long Island socialite drawn into a women's liberation group called PIGS (Politically Involved Girls). Vincent Canby, in reviewing the film, called Candy "a cross between Kim Novak and Pat Nixon." Candy admitted that indeed she did have Pat Nixon's nose.

In this docu, we learn that Candy appeared in *Klute* with Jane Fonda and in *Lady Liberty* with Sophia Loren. She campaigned for the role of Gore Vidal's *Myra Breckinridge* (1970), but lost. She also appeared in Tennessee Williams' *Small Craft Warnings* at the invitation of the playwright himself. On Off-Broadway in 1973 she starred in *The White Whore* and *The Bit Player*, her character based on Marilyn Monroe.

Darling died of leukemia on March 21, 1974 at the age of 29. The docu uses a series of interviews and archival footage to re-create Candy's life. Members of Warhol's Factory appear along with Tennessee Williams, John Waters, Peter Beard, Holly Woodlawn, Bob Colacello, Geraldine Smith, Pat Hackett, and Ron Delsener.

It's out of print today, but Candy confided her hopes, doubts, dreams, and beauty secrets to a diary which was published as *My Face for the World to See* in 1997. She describes her wild life from the Warhol years. The diary is also the moving story of someone born a boy (James Lawrence Slattery) in Forest Hills, Queens, and it is illustrated with photos and Candy's own sketches.

A slightly jealous drag queen, Holly Woodlawn, once wrote that Candy became "the social sweetheart of the underground, her fame going mainstream. She was fawned over by celebrities, artists, and socialites. And there I stood in her shadow, envious as well."

Candy arguably was the most charismatic of the Warhol superstars. She had looks and talent, evoking Golden Age Hollywood beauties. She also had a sharp wit.

Beautiful Thing

(1996)

Gay London Teenagers Find Love in a Slum

This coming-out fable set in a dreary London housing project features two adorable working-class teens. Jamie (Glen Berry) is an introspective boy avoiding sports. He lives next door to Ste (Scott Neal), a handsome kid and an athlete. Jamie's mother is tough-minded, but generally supportive of her son's gayness. In contrast, Ste's father, a drunken bully, often beats his kid.

This is a tender, sweet story of a budding romance of two sensitive teens living in a hostile world. Sometimes the minor players steal the scene, as in the case of an African-British teenager, Leah (Tameka Empson), who drugs and dreams all day of becoming the next Mama Cass.

This impressive feature debut of director Hettie Macdonald cleverly uses a soundtrack featuring the music of Mama Cass and the Mamas and the Papas.

In one scene, Sandra offers Jamie's bed when Ste flees from his father's violence. At first the mother felt guilty for invading her son's privacy by inviting another boy into his room. When she understood that two young boys were engaged in homosexual love making, she had a different point of view. Sandra tells Jamie: "There's me going to bed at night worried 'cause you had to share a bed with Ste, and all this time you were doing 70 minus one."

Trivia note: One of the cast is named Garry Cooper (with two Rs-no joke).

WHAT THE CRITICS SAID
"Though the movie is gay-themed, its broad range of personalities and light, straight-faced comic style positions it well outside the usual viewing ghetto for such pics. At heart, it's a working-class dramedy with a couple of gay characters, propelled by a sense of humor that comes as much from its non-correct approach to the subject as from one-liners."
Derek Elley, *Variety*

Before I Forget

(*Avant que j'oublie*; 2007)

When A Hustler Stops Selling & Starts Buying

Jacques Nolot directed, wrote, and starred in this portrait of an aging Parisian hustler (he used to refer to himself as a gigolo), who is battling his inner demons on a search for self-discovery at twilight time. He's been HIV positive for 24 years, refusing to take a more advanced medicinal cocktail for fear of losing his hair. "I don't want to have the face of an Auschwitz victim."

Before I Forget is the third cinematic installment of Nolot's memoiristic trilogy. The film is a study of the decay of a man, his insufferable fall from the grace of yesterday, and his abject humiliation. For this 58-year-old Frenchman, he seems to have grown weary of the world, with a string of cigarettes and endless cups of coffee.

He is not afraid to appear nude in front of the camera, exhibiting a sagging chest and a protruding belly. As such, he faces a mercilessly scrutinizing *verité* camera.

Nolot's future has been bleak since the death of his patron—"My father, my mother, my bank." After his lover's death, the patron's family is grabbing up an inheritance intended for Nolot.

No longer the hustler himself, he patronizes Parisian hustlers to fellate them, their bodies reminding him of his own former physicality. He seems to order fellatio as one might call out for a pizza. He has a regular stud Marc (Bastien d'Asnieres), whom he engages for rough sex.

Occasionally he meets with a member of his dwindling group of friends, one of whom is Georges (Jean Pommier), a married, closeted attorney. They compare the price of call boys, discussing young flesh the way you might talk to your butcher about meat prices.

In this self-lacerating portrait, Nolot maintains a haughty independence, and is perfectly aware that the clock is ticking away. One critic defined the director/star as being composed of equal parts Marcel Proust and Joe Dallesandro.

The movie could also be called *Remembrance of Flings Past*.

Before Stonewall

(1984)

Back When Gays Were Called "The Third Sex"

Filmmakers Greta Schiller and Robert Rosenberg took on a big job in this 87-minute docu, narrated by Rita Mae Brown, the writer. The history of the gay and lesbian community is articulated with talking heads and archival footage, everybody from

BEFORE STONEWALL

Beat poet Allen Ginsberg to Harry Hay, founder of the Mattachine Society.

Do you know who Sylvia Rivera is? She was a Puerto Rican drag queen who is sometimes credited with throwing the Molotov cocktail that launched the Stonewall Riots on June 27, 1969, as gays were mourning the death of their icon, Judy Garland. That cocktail, and others on that memorable night, launched the gay revolution.

Gays and lesbians have come a long way from that night (and they have a long way to go), but *Before Stonewall* shows us just how awful it was to be G or L or B or T in the not-so-good-ol' days.

To openly admit to homosexuality meant ruined careers, possible imprisonment, enforced admission to a mental institution, or, in so-called gay novels of the time, suicide.

The docu goes back to the 1920s when there were a few pockets of tolerance for gays in New York's Harlem, New Orleans' French Quarter, and San Francisco's Barbary Coast.

The film travels to World War II which saw a major breakthrough in homosexuality. Thousands of young service men and women went out ostensibly seeking members of the opposite sex and ended up in bed with each other. Archival footage captures many gay icons on camera.

WHAT THE CRITICS SAID
"When you think that only 40 years ago, women, African-Americans, and gays were considered second-class citizens, it's mind boggling. This film makes you feel like you're struggling just to be able to live with all the constraints. Even as late as 1969, police would routinely raid gay bars and haul off every single patron to jail. Imagine: You're having a drink with friends, and the cops come in and take you all away."
DVD Verdict Review

Before the Fall

(*Napola--Elite für den Führer;* 2004)

Hitler's Elite Young Men

It's a bit sad when a film has the potential for greatness and misses the mark. Such is the case with the German film *Napola*, released in the United States as *Before the Fall*, with Dennis Gansel directing. Actually, its complete German title is *Napola—Elite für den Führer*.

Napola was just one of the famous Napolas, brutal training schools for a carefully selected Hitler elite destined one day to preside over such cities as Washington, Moscow, and London, had the tawdry Third Reich survived. Of these schools, Hitler himself said, "Men make history; we make the men."

Potentially, the film could have been one of the great German homoerotic love stories of the post-millennium, but it falls far short in that department, getting lost somewhere along the way in Nazi fetishism. The brutality of the training regime at the school, Napola, is depicted frequently.

Variety was the first publication in America to note how the director, Dennis Gansel, never fully developed the homoerotic undercurrent of the film. There was the perfect setup between the boxer character of Friedrich Weimer, as played by heartthrob Max Riemelt, and the sensitive poet, the role of Albrecht Stein, as interpreted by actor Tom Schilling.

Another potential for a homoerotic relationship was between young Friedrich and the Nazi boxing trainer, a role played by actor David Striesow. In his role, Striesow discovers the well-muscled Friedrich working out at a Berlin boxing club. A more homosexually inclined director would have Striesow, in his role of Heinrich Vogler, follow Friedrich into his dressing room after the boxing bout. There Vogler could have watched Friedrich undress, shower, and dress again in street clothes.

That doesn't happen. Vogler does, however, offer Friedrich a chance to enroll in Napola at a towering castle in Poland along with other budding Nazi generals-to-be.

The Believers

(2006)

Transgendered Persons Singing Gospel

If they ever went to see it, right-wing Christians would surely stage protests over this intriguing docu. The film follows the nation's first all-transgender gospel choir as they overcome obstacles and raise their voices praising God and lifting their own feelings of self-love and dignity.

Filmed over a three-year period in San Francisco, *The Believers* traces the choir's shaky origins as its members learned to sing with transitioning voices and fight over wardrobe. Director Todd Holland focuses on 15 core members of the choir as they learn to sing. Their intimate, personal stories are told in ways that evoke *A Chorus Line* on Broadway.

The Transcendence Gospel Choir homepage summed it up rather nicely. "We endeavor to demonstrate that the preconceived notion of a bipolar, heterosexual, hetero-gendered 'natural order' is not reflected in the nature of God or the ministry of Jesus Christ. In this way we will challenge intolerance and hatred, transcend boundaries and restore hope to our communities."

At docu's end, the film had moved heartwarmingly through its trials and tribulations into a polished, award-winning choir and a close knit family.

The Transcendence Gospel Choir has presented major performances across the country, and in 2004 the choir won an Outmusic Award for its album, *Whosoever Believes*. Although the choir stresses its interdenominational roots, it's loosely affiliated with the United Church of Christ.

WHAT THE CRITICS SAID
"At the heart of the dilemma is a struggle for acceptance within two worlds historically at odds with one another. As one of the film's subjects eloquently says, 'I'm living in a window. I get to see both sides.' *The Believers* is a unique story of determination and perseverance and an important look at the intricacy and diversity of spirituality and the LGBT community."
Justin Kolling

Bent

(1997)

Gay Love in a Time of Genocide

Bent is the first dramatic film to concentrate solely on the Nazi persecution of gays during World War II. Nearly all Holocaust films are about the Jews who went to the death camps. One day some filmmaker may take up the gypsy cause as well.

Based on Martin Sherman's 1979 Broadway play starring Richard Gere, the film version features Clive Owen as Max and Lothaire Bluteau as Horst, both of them prisoners in a Nazi concentration camp. In this bleak, deadly setting, they fall in love as the central dynamic within this intense and essentially romantic drama.

The film opens during The Night of the Long Knives. The transvestite Greta (Mick Jagger) is hosting a gay orgy. Bodies are strewn about in sexual congress, and many participants are Nazis.

Under the weak direction of Sean Mathias, the orgy is disrupted by Nazi thugs intent on killing members of the homosexual ring centered around commander Ernst Rohm.

Max has picked up one of Rohm's men at the Jagger bacchanal and taken him home. Later that night storm troopers break down Max's door and slice the soldier's throat.

Max and his boyfriend, Rudy, try to escape but are captured and put on a train for the death camp at Dachau. Claiming he is Jewish, Max opts to wear the Yellow Star of the Jew instead of the Pink Triangle of a gay man. On the train he is forced to beat Rudy, the poor wretch dying in a crowded cattle car.

In camp, Max befriends Horst (Bluteau), whom he'd first met on the train. Their desire and love for each other grows.

The film's greatest notoriety comes from the scene where Max and Horst, standing shirtless in the hot sun, manage to have sex without touching each other, only using their words and their erotic imaginations. It's called the language of love.

Bernard and Doris

(2007)

Gay Butler Inherits Duke Tobacco Millions

Bernard and Doris

The tobacco heiress, Doris Duke (1912-1993), was the richest woman in the world, with Barbara Hutton (1912-1979) coming in number two. Duke was not only obscenely rich, but idiosyncratic. Upon her death, the world was shocked to learn she'd left control of her empire to her gay Irish butler, Bernard Lafferty.

In this mostly two-character movie, the roles are interpreted by Susan Sarandon and Ralph Fiennes. Bob Balaban, known for acting gigs on *Seinfeld*, directs this unlikely pair as they move into a special relationship (no sex, please).

The sound track of jazzy Peggy Lee-era tunes seems ideally suited for both characters, who find they have a need for human companionship beyond the bed. Of course, Doris has her share of gigolos. (Her favorite form of sex was having her toes sucked, but that's not in the movie). And she never wanted to mess up her mouth with anything less than ten inches, and that's not in the movie either. Obviously that's why she married Porfirio Rubirosa, known as "Peppermill."

Fiennes assures Doris that all he wants is "to take care of you." Athough, understandably, she's suspicious, he finally wins her heart.

The script is a bit undercooked, but Sarandon and Fiennes make up for any inadequacies with their unique personalities. Much of what went on between Bernard and Doris will never be known, so the scriptwriter, Hugo Castello, had to do some guesswork. Despite some serious time in rehab, Fiennes, as Bernard Lafferty, bounces back to be at the side of Doris when she dies.

The movie explores money, class, and the sexuality of these two spectacularly different individuals. An alternative title might have been *The Princess and the Pauper*.

Both characters emerge, as they did in real life, as damaged goods, and both are also in the twilight of their years. Bernard was not a pauper after Doris died and left him in control of 1.3 billion dollars. But the butler didn't live long enough to enjoy it, dying in 1996 at the age of 51.

The Best Man

(1964)

A Gay Presidential Candidate?

In Gore Vidal's play, *The Best Man*, a question is asked: "Does the best man always get to the White House?" Vidal, of course, is one of the most cynical observers of politics in America. The answer is an obvious no. But this film has some political fun in getting to its resolution.

Henry Fonda as William Russell and Cliff Robertson as Joe Cantwell play the two battling presidential candidates. One of the best casts assembled in a 1964 movie provides backup, including Edie Adams (wife of Cantwell) and Margaret Leighton (wife of Russell), along with Shelley Berman playing a sleazeball, as well as Lee Tracy, Ann Sothern, Gene Raymond, Kevin McCarthy, Mahalia Jackson, Howard K. Smith, Richard Arlen, and Penny Singleton.

Leighton is brilliant (as usual) as Russell's long-suffering British wife. Her husband has had multiple affairs. At the end of the movie, they agree to try to salvage what's left of their marriage, although Fonda warns her that the fires of autumn burn on a low flame.

Shelley Berman as Sheldon Bascomb is the rotter who surfaces out of Cantwell's military past, airing charges. Ann Sothern is splendid as a lobbyist, the only known link between the John Birch Society and the Communist Party.

This film gives you a real insider's look at what goes on behind the scenes at a political convention, as Cantwell and Russell are neck and neck for the presidential nomination. At one point, each candidate seems to have a dark secret that will cost them the election. Russell once had a nervous breakdown, and Cantwell is accused of having been a homo during WWII.

Cantwell releases his smear, but Russell does not. He tells his backers, "I don't believe it. No man with that awful wife or those ugly children could be anything but normal." That leaves the implication that if Cantwell might have practiced homosexuality, Russell would smear him.

The Best of "So Graham Norton"

(2004)

Outrageous Host, Outrageous Guests

Graham Norton, the Irish-born actor, comedian, and television presenter, is famous for his outrageous talk show, *The Graham Norton Show*. In this DVD, Graham introduces highlights from the first three seasons of his Channel 4 chat show, including unseen footage.

Openly gay Graham is usually charming and always outrageous, and he likes to stir up controversy, as when in October of 2006 he described cocaine and ecstasy as "fantastic."

Appearing in archival footage are some of his more provocative guests: Beatrice Arthur, Jacqueline Bisset, Dustin Hoffman, Elton John, Ricki Lake, Shirley MacLaine, Lee Majors, Roger Moore, Dolly Parton (at long last), and Ivana Trump. Other guests include La Toya Jackson, who posed topless for *Playboy* back in 1989. She once tried, for a half-million dollars, to sell evidence that the charges that her brother Michael was a pedophile might be true.

Grace Jones, who has a large gay following, is the Jamaican/American singer, model, and actress. She was once called "The Queen of Gay Discos." Her masculine appearance, height (5'10"), and manner influenced the cross-dressing movement of the 1980s. Regrettably, Graham didn't ask her the one question that many gay males wanted to know: What are the exact measurements of Dolph Lundgren's dick?

Not the sharpest knife in the drawer, Bo Derek also appears. She'd met pedophile and former male hustler, John Derek, who was 30 years her senior. To get this babe in the woods, he divorced his wife (Linda Evans) and fled to Germany to avoid being charged with statutory rape. Amazingly, the star of *10* turns out to be a conservative Republican who supported Daddy Bush.

Graham can count on Naomi Campbell to be a provocative guest. The London-born model became famous for assaulting people, but Graham escaped unbruised during their interview, which could have been much deeper.

Better Than Chocolate

(1999)

Lesbian Chocolates in the Box

The confections within this box of lesbian chocolates have soft centers and hard centers. Regardless of which one you bite into, the taste is sweet in this 101-minute, Canadian comedy/drama that is a delicious romp.

Two attractive young lesbians, Maggie (Karyn Dwyer) and Kim (Christina Cox), meet in Vancouver. The attraction is immediate, and they develop a romance. Moving in together, they become lovers.

A lovely nineteen-year-old Maggie abandons college to learn what life is about, and that means outing herself as a lesbian. Kim, an artist, arouses long suppressed feelings in her.

Naturally, complications arrive when Maggie's mother (Wendy Crewson) shows up with Maggie's brother (Kevin Mundy). Crewson plays Lila, who has recently caught her cheating husband in an affair and left him.

Dear Ol' Mom has a lot to learn about her daughter, beginning when she finds a box of "toys" under the bed.

Other discoveries include that Maggie has a lover and that she works in a lesbian bookstore. Mom doesn't even know that her daughter also dances in a lesbian nightclub.

Peggy Thompson's screenplay deftly handles these developments, along with a complicated roster of subplots. One of these involves Judy and/or Jeremy (Peter Outerbridge), Maggie's transsexual friend who's in love with Frances (Ann-Marie MacDonald), the owner of the lesbian bookstore.

There's even trouble with the censors, who harass Frances over her inventories of books and videos, even seizing at one point a copy of *Little Red Riding Hood*.

A bunch of skinheads supply the hate, as pressures surge in from the straight community. Director Anne Wheeler cleverly handles her talented cast, even such scenes as Lila discovering that she can still have a satisfying orgasm.

Big Eden

(2000)

A "Northern Exposure" Look at Gay Romance

If Frank Capra or Preston Sturges made gay movies, *Big Eden* might have been their epic. Set in a tiny fictional town in northwestern Montana, it's a gay love story unfolding in Timber and Cowboy Country.

Our hero Henry Hart (Arye Gross) is a successful New York artist who returns to his childhood hometown to take care of his ailing grandfather (George Coe), who brought him up.

For years, Henry has nursed a crush on the local hunk, Dean Stewart (Tim DeKay). Dean is now divorced, and Henry's hopes rise. Lurking in the background is Pike Dexter (Eric Schweig), who runs the general store and hankers for Henry himself. To add some spice to the plot, Pike is a Native American.

What is unrealistic about this rather charming flick is that everybody seems pro-gay—in red state Montana of all places. Montana lies next door to another red state, Wyoming, where a young gay man, Matthew Shepard, was brutally murdered.

Even those "bewhiskered, pipe-puffing, jeans-wearing, cowboy-hatted old cowpokes" gathered at the general store become cheerleaders for Henry's gay romance.

The thing that keeps you in your seat is the big question in Big Eden: Will Henry find true love, with either Dean or Pike, or will he return to the fleshpots of New York?

Thomas Bezucha, who wrote and directed the film, makes spectacular use of the Glacier National Park, and he cast the supporting players well, especially Louise Fletcher as a kindly schoolmarm.

Some critics called *Big Eden* "stupefyingly benign," but many gay men found it a wish fulfillment of a giddy Utopia that might one day come to America, although obviously not in the lifetime of anybody now alive.

A Bigger Splash

(1974)

The Private Life of David Hockney

At long last in DVD, this formerly banned semi-docu from 1971 is now available for our viewing pleasure, depicting a lot of hot dudes from the 70s. Seemingly anticipating reality TV, it traces the life of the legendary painter David Hockney, presenting a sexy and stirring portrait of the artist.

Real people play themselves in this partly fictionalized tale of Hockney, who was noted for his color and specialization in "California subjects," centering around gay life. In his paintings, Hockey was fascinated by the swimming pools of Los Angeles—hence, the name of the film. Of course, within the film, those swimming pools are filled with handsome young men in the buff.

For three-and-a-half years (1970-1973), Hockney allowed filmmakers Jack Hazan and David Mingay to follow him around with a camera as he interacted with friends, lovers, and business associates. Reportedly, Hockney, with his white blond hair (*à la* Warhol) and thick black-rimmed glasses, was shocked at the final result because it penetrated his personal life as deeply as it did.

The action, such as it is, takes place during a period in which Hockney and his lover, the model, Peter Schlesinger, are breaking up. The beautiful and androgynous Schlesinger served as both Hockney's lover and muse. In the docu, Hockney is attempting to finish his last painting of Schlesinger after destroying and repainting it several times.

Most daring of all is a scene in which Schlesinger and another young man make love.

With all its flaws, this is nonetheless a very important addition to gay cinema.

WHAT THE CRITICS SAID
"However, accurate (or not) the film may be depicting Hockney's daily life, it's undeniably a powerful time capsule—a vivid, intense depiction of the swinging London of the 60s during its last dying gasps. In a lot of ways, *A Bigger Splash* plays like *Blowup* with a lot of gay sex. The film has abundant full frontal male nudity."
Jesse Ataide

Bijou

(1972)

The Size of It!!!

In the early 1970s, the director Wakefield Poole needed a follow-up to his *Boys in the Sand,* which, thanks to its star, Casey Donovan (a.k.a., Cal Culver), had been the most successful gay porn movie in the history of cinema. *Bijou* needed a star  that was equally as well-hung and equally charismatic.

In a real-life scene that evoked something from *The Boys in the Band,* a San Francisco-based friend of Poole's had been sent a hustler as a birthday present. The stud bore a striking resemblance to Robert Redford. Later, Poole's friend showed a grainy snapshot of the guy to Poole. Based on the photo and his friend's recommendation, Poole arranged for the handsome six-footer to come to New York. Porno history was made.

Remembering the first time Poole saw his star, Bill Harrison, naked, he said, "When he took his dick out for the first time, everyone on the set gasped." So did gay audiences throughout America. His thick, foot-long dick was right up there in the John C. Holmes category.

The rest of the cast was comprised mostly of New York men, one of the actors, Bill Cable, resembling a muscular Warren Beatty. A self-proclaimed heterosexual, he was surrounded in the film by gay men.

Many of this film's scenes transpire in a club named Bijou, a self-defined "place of sexual freedom with a mystical, almost religious atmosphere." A key moment occurs when Harrison encounters a naked body lying on its stomach. Poole had not allowed his actor, Bob Stubbs, to meet or even see Bill prior to the filming.

"I just wanted him to lie there, get fucked, and not move a muscle," Poole said. Stubbs was completely unaware that he was about to be penetrated "by a cock that never seemed to come to an end."

Later Stubbs told Poole that the invasion of his body by Harrison "was the most erotic sex I'd ever experienced."

The Birdcage

(1996)

The Queers vs. The Squares

Shaking a layer of dust off the sequins and ostrich plumes, the director of *La Cage aux Folles*, Michael Nichols, returns the romance/comedy to the screen as *The Birdcage*, an American remake of that 1978 French movie.

Birdcage was written by Elaine May and starred Robin Williams, Nathan Lane, and Gene Hackman.

If you don't already know it, here's the plot:

Armand (Williams), the owner of a flamboyant drag club called The Birdcage, is planning a big party for his life companion, Albert (Lane), a flamboyant drag queen and temperamental diva on stage and off. Armand's 20-year-old son, Val, is coming home. Val is getting married to his fiancée, Barbara, the daughter of Senator Keeley (Hackman), the most Right Wing politician in Washington.

The character is obviously modeled on the notorious Jesse Helms, senator from North Carolina, who built a career on tormenting gays. Thankfully, Helms has now gone to Hatemongers' Heaven.

This new version is set in South Beach in Miami instead of St. Tropez. The film whirls around the meeting of these colossally incompatible future-in-laws.

Lane, incidentally, has nice gams and looks good in pearls.

Much of the gay press condemned the film upon its release for its campy portrayals of homosexuals. A typical comment by critic Michael Bronski claimed that the movie "trivializes and diminishes gay lives by refusing to take them—or homophobia—seriously."

In spite of its trappings, *Birdcage* is actually a love story between two men (Williams and Lane), even though Lane is often in drag (even when he's not), displaying effeminate mannerisms. It's all in good fun, and Nichols operates in an AIDS-free universe where homosexuality is equated with a wacky fashion sense.

Black Is...Black Ain't

(1994)

A Stewpot of Blackness

Few names have been as controversial in public television as Marlon T. Riggs, who died of AIDS in 1994. He stirred up the Right Wing with his controversial 1990 film *Tongues United*, a study of the black homosexual experience and an exposé of racist and anti-gay attitudes.

Conservatives bitched that the movie docu was partially funded with government money and wanted him cut off. Many public TV stations refused to air the docu because of the backlash.

Riggs' last docu, *Black Is . . . Black Ain't* was not completed by the time of his death and had to be finished by his collaborators, working from his notes. His last oeuvre dealt with definitions of blackness and the self-conception of blacks in America. Self-hating racism, sexism, and homophobia are explored.

Many figures in the film, including Angela Davis, appear as themselves. What has emerged is a simmering stewpot of thought and emotion, and a call for pride in diversity. A genuine cry from the heart, it is both poetic and intelligent.

The film shows Riggs traveling through America, showing black diversity in such places as South Carolina where Afrocentric blacks have constructed a traditional African village, and Los Angeles where gays and lesbians have created their own church.

The ostracizing of gays from black society is a sad comment on the homophobia that runs through the black community. Rapper Ice Cube said it, cruelly but succinctly: "True niggers ain't faggots."

Riggs "final solution" to the problems exposed by the docu involves "talking to each other about the ways in which we hurt each other."

Black White + Gray:

(2007)

A Portrait of Sam Wagstaff & Robert Mapplethorpe

James Crump made his debut as a director with this docu on the relationship between curator Sam Wagstaff, the notorious photographer Robert Mapplethorpe, and musician-poet Patti Smith. The film is a biography of a diabolical art world power couple, who both died of AIDS in the late 1980s.

Born into wealth and privilege, Wagstaff was called "the debs' darling" until one night he met working class *provocateur* Mapplethorpe. Their explosive bonding transformed the art of photography and helped define the burgeoning gay liberation movement.

Mapplethorpe was 25 years younger than Wagstaff. The elder would introduce the younger to "the darker pockets of the gay demimonde." His great fans called Wagstaff "the last great aesthetic champion of the late 20th century." The relationship between this infamous pair was defined as "the most prophetic of Faustian bargains."

The film's title refers to Wagstaff's obsession for collecting photographs after he inherited his mother's millions in 1973. That led him to Mapplethorpe, and the rich dilettante became the photographer's most ardent champion, or even "inventor" if you will. Wagstaff single-handedly drove up the market for vintage photographs.

WHAT THE CRITICS SAID
"Mapplethorpe's posthumous renown has completely eclipsed Wagstaff's. Crumb evidently wants to redress that imbalance, and his witness list includes several voices that denounce Mapplethorpe as a gold digger. The photographer inducted Wagstaff into Manhattan's gay S&M subculture, and he took to it with the same ardor he brought to the roles of curator and collector."
Kenneth Baker

"Wagstaff and Mapplethorpe exude the glamorous mystique of insolent movie and rock stars: think of James Dean and Jim Morrison but with a kinky gay twist. Talent, beauty, sex, death, and finally pots of money; their storm is a perfect storm around which to spin a profitable legend."
Stephen Holden, *The New York Times*

Blackmail Boy

(2003)

Greek Soap Opera with a Handsome Young Stud

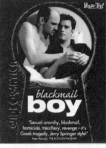

This soapy Greek drama with English subtitles combines early Almodóvar with *Dynasty*. For gay men, its main audience in America, the interest focuses on the very handsome young Christos, who is twenty but looks much younger parading around in his white jockey shorts. The plot revolves around his clandestine homosexual affair with an older married man.

Directed by Michalis Reppas and Thanassis Papathanasiou, *Blackmail Boy* is set in a small provincial town in Greece. The plot is a bit convoluted and hard to follow, mainly because the English titles in white letters appear on a pale background many times and are hard to read. The exploitation of a plot of land triggers a chain of blackmail that draws the main characters in a cynical game of mutual extermination.

Magda is the mother of Christos, and she dotes on her son. She has a much more troubled relationship with her daughter, Giota, who lives upstairs along with her husband Stelios. He's an evil bastard, but he manages to seduce Magda into giving him a blow job. The menacing Stelios' discovery of a gay affair between Christos and the older man puts the young man at the epicenter of the blackmail plot. But Christos is not without plans of his own.

In spite of its faults, the movie is well cast. The star, the handsome but arrogant young man, Yannis Tsimitsells, evokes a young Elvis. His older lover, a doctor, is played by Akyllas Karazisis. The young man is also having an affair with an older woman, Tzia (Joyce Evidi). The older doctor has a sweet, unsuspecting wife (Maria Kavoylanni), and yet another character, Nena Mendi, playing the mother of Yannis, is saddled with the care of her paralyzed husband, trying to keep tabs on her son, and having sex with her son-in-law.

WHAT THE CRITICS SAID
"Sexual anarchy, blackmail, homicide, treachery, revenge-it's Greek tragedy, Jerry Springer style."
Peter Keough, *The Boston Phoenix*

The Blossoming of Maximo Oliveros

(*Ang Pagdadalaga ni Maximo Oliveros;* 2004)

Remember the First Time You Fell in Love?

A buoyant and endearing film, this Filipino movie is groundbreaking in that it presents a 12-year-old queer boy without trepidation or compromise. Nathan Lopez plays a girly little boy, Maxi, a kid growing up on the seedy side of Manila.

He dotes on his father and two brothers but falls for a handsome and older police officer, Victor (JR Valentin). The film is directed with charm, clarity, and insight by Auraeus Solito working from a perceptive script by Michiko Yamamoto. A colorful, exotic portrait of sexual awakening is presented. The young teenage boy has a desire for cross-dressing, and his family earns their living with petty thefts.

The scenes are erotic between the rookie cop who takes Maxi under his wing, and there are near romantic encounters at times, although the helmer keeps it platonic.

Maxi's family consists of Paca (Soliman Cruz), who loves Maxi, as do his older brothers, Boy (Neil Ryan Sese) and Bogs (Ping Medina). Maxi cooks for "the men in his life," and also mends their clothes. He is in fact the wife of the family, since the mother is dead.

Maxi, wearing lipstick, walks the shantytown back alleys of Manila with a kind of hip-swiveling fabulousness, as if these dark alleys were pageant catwalks.

Stick around for the final scene, a heartfelt tribute to Carol Reed's 1949 masterpiece, *The Third Man*.

This film comes as a wake-up call—dare we suggest mini-Renaissance?—in the country's long dormant cinema.

WHAT THE CRITICS SAID
"Maxi is such an intriguing mix of the streetwise and the innocent, self-aware yet emotionally vulnerable. Solito's ability to inspire such a daring, unself-conscious portrayal from Lopez is no less than astonishing."
Kevin Thomas, *Los Angeles Times*

Borat:

(2006)

Cultural Learnings of America for Make Benefit Glorious Nation of Kazakhstan

Before the release of *Borat,* directed by Larry Charles, Sacha Baron Cohen, its star, was famous for his HBO series *Da Ali G Show.* In it, the comedian's alter-egos interviewed ignorant people and humiliated them for our pleasure. He continues that theme in *Borat,* but with a cultural vengeance against redneck America.

In the scenario, Borat plays a clueless Kazakhstan TV reporter coming to America to find the bosom of Pamela Anderson, even if those tits aren't completely real. Anderson gamely plays herself.

The release of the film created a boom in little-known Kazakhstan, where tourists wanted to see if you could really purchase a local bride for 15 gallons of pesticide. Americans, often baby boomers, flocked to the country, anticipating views of locals drinking horse urine. Potential travelers got an early taste of the culture of Kazakhstan when they learned that booking hotels online did not necessarily mean that the hotel actually existed.

Borat flies to New York with his obese producer, Azamat Bagatov (Ken Davitian), on a vaguely defined trip to interview locals about American customs.

For gay audiences, Borat is a riot, especially when he joins a gay parade and goes back to the hotel room not knowing that he's being entertained by queers. Later Borat asks a stranger, "Are you telling me that the man who tried to put a rubber fist into my anus was a homosexual?"

Borat kisses men on the lips, and even shares sexually provocative photographs of an underage male relative. At one point he meets up with a Bible Belt redneck, telling him that gays are hanged in his country. The homophobic moron responds, "We're trying to do the same here."

But nothing is more provocative than Borat's nude brawl with the rotund monster, Azamat. They end up in positions that even the Kama Sutra hadn't envisioned.

Both

(2005)

Twilight World of Intersexuals

As the politically correct now know, hermaphrodites are no longer called that. Once consigned to the world of freak show porno, genital ambiguity is now better understood, as it occurs in one out of every 2,000 births. Parents must make painful decisions, and doctors often "choose" a sex for the child, using hormones to "normalize" the baby's body.

Both is based on the experiences of the filmmaker as well as those of many other intersex adults. Lisset Barcellos directed it based on a script by Rafael Dumett. San Francisco stuntwoman Rebecca (Jackie Parker) discovers that she was born a hermaphrodite in Peru and reared as a boy. At the time of her discovery she is engaged in affairs with both an actress (Nicole Wilder) and a male mechanic (J.D. Brumback).

An aunt in Peru sends an old photo album which includes a shot of Rebecca's brother, who purportedly died as a kid. Rebecca's mother (Yvonne Frayssinet) refuses to talk about the tragedy with her. The "boy" was, in fact, Rebecca *née* Pedro. At an early age he was given a clitorectomy to correct nature's mistake. Sent to the U.S., Rebecca was given a new identity.

WHAT THE CRITICS SAID
"Raw, nervy and groundbreaking—for the first time ever, a narrative film looks at what it's like to have been born a hermaphrodite—and, worse still, to have had doctors perform post-natal surgery to assign the 'proper' gender. Acting that sometimes misses the mark and low production values only mildly hamper the effect of Lisset Barcellos' moving story."
Kathleen Wilkinson

"Graphic sex (hetero as well as homo), believable characters, and a genuine feel for its East Bay and city locations mark this impressive debut by SF State grad Lissett Barcellos, which benefits from natural multicultural ambience, something that cannot be faked."
Kelly Vance, *New York Times*

Bound

(1996)

Lesbians vs. the Mob

Bound is a gangster movie, a sex film, a caper flick, and a slapstick comedy. It's the creation of two first-time film-makers, Larry and Andy Wachowski, self-described college dropouts when they made this movie in Chicago while still in their 20s.

Corky (Gina Gershon), a lesbian ex-con hired to work in an apartment as a plumber, meets her new neighbors Caesar (Joe Pantoliano), who launders money for the Mafia, and his girlfriend Violet (Jennifer Tilly). Violet falls for Corky, al-though she's afraid to tell her Mafioso shack-up that she's a lesbian.

The sex scenes between these two hot women are not gynecological drudgery, but hot and steamy the way we like it. The low-budget film is more than an erotic excuse to sell popcorn, but has an ever-thickening plot as we descend into a fandango of blood, sex, murder, and big bucks.

When the women learn that a bag man named Shelley (Barry Kivel) will arrive at Caesar's apart-ment with $2 million in cash, the two women plot to steal the loot, leaving Caesar to take the blame, which will almost mean certain death from the gang.

Bound drew a widely diverse critical reception, though found honor at various film festivals.

WHAT THE CRITICS SAID
"Joe Pantoliano has some of the trickiest scenes in the movie, bouncing from paranoia to greed to lust to abject fear like a pinball in the wrong ma-chine."
Roger Ebert

"Novelty of having two sultry babes hook up with each other while pulling a fast one on some mob-sters wears thin before becoming ludicrously con-trived. Debuting writer-directors Larry and Andy Wachowski come off like Coen brothers wannabees with no sense of humor. Sapphic angle will arouse some curiosity and want-see in certain circles, but this is otherwise a low-end gangster melodrama."
Todd McCarthy, *Variety*

The Boys in the Band

(1970)

A Coming Out Party for Inner Demons

Arguably, this was the "Stonewall film" that brought gays to the screen as they'd never been seen before. Re-grettably, it wasn't a pretty picture, but at least homo-sexuality was no longer the love that dared not speak its name.

The play with self-loathing homosexuals was based on an off-Broadway presentation in 1968 written by Mart Crowley. Amazingly the play proved a trendsetter, forcing many gays out of the closet. It did all this in spite of such dialogue as "You show me a happy homosexual and I'll show you a gay corpse."

The dialogue, for its time, was shocking and provocative, especially to homophobes, many of whom walked out of the theater during the movie's general release.

The Boys in the Band opens as Michael (Kenneth Nelson), a recovering alcoholic, is preparing to host a birthday party for his friend Harold (Leonard Frey), "a 32-year-old, ugly, pockmarked Jew fairy."

Cast members are stereotypes, the supporting actors including self-medicating Donald (Freder-ick Combs), fiercely swishy Emory (Cliff Gorman), a studly cowboy (Robert La Tourneaux), and is-he-or-isn't-he? Alan (Peter White) as the token married man in this gay bunch. Bernard (Reuben Greene) adds a minority viewpoint to this all-white cast. As a sad reflection of its time, half the cast of *Boys in the Band* later fell to AIDS.

The film is climaxed by a cruel telephone game, in which each of the party-goers must call some-one and tell him (or her?) of his love for them.

WHAT THE CRITICS SAID
"Mart Crowley's work was celebrated as bold and compassionate—a breakthrough play on a taboo subject. But when the Stonewall riots of 1969 trig-gered the movement toward gay self-esteem, it rapidly became dated. With gays redefining them-selves as strong and proud, a play about acid-tongued, self-pitying fairies was bound to resemble the gay equivalent of a minstrel show."
Edward Guthmann, *San Francisco Chronicle*

Boys in the Sand

(1971)

The Landmark Gay Porno Film

On a budget of $8,000, *Boys in the Sand* was shot over three successive weekends in August of 1971 in the gay resort of Fire Island, New York. It made film history.

Variety claimed, "There are no more closets!" *The Advocate* predicted, "Everyone will fall in love with this philandering fellator."

Wakefield Poole, its director and writer, clearly turned out a gay porno classic, making an underground star out of a blond Greek god, Calvin Culver (8½"), also known as Casey Donovan. The movie also starred Peter Fisk, the lover of Poole; Danny Di Cioccio, and Tommy Moore.

Boys became the first porn film to include on-screen credits for its cast and crew, although many were assumed names.

The plot, if you'd call it that, revolves around hunky Culver in various sexual escapades, all of which are set against the most beautiful cinematography in any gay porn. The sexual scenes are both passionate and erotic. Culver knew how to perform on camera. Off screen he became a male hustler, star fucker, and failed actor. If you had the price, Culver would make love to you. Sadly, he died of AIDS in 1987.

Boys consists of three segments, including "Bayside," in which Culver appears naked out of the ocean. Arguably, this appearance is the most famous scene in gay porno. Both anal and oral sex is performed with Fisk.

In "Poolside" Culver penetrates Di Cioccio in a variety of positions, and in the third segment, "Inside," Culver performs sex with an African American phone repairman, Moore. The most shocking scene is when Culver penetrates himself with a large black dildo.

By the time *Deep Throat* was released the following year, "the egg had cracked," Poole claimed. "The 70s porno chic era had begun."

In 1984 Poole made a sequel, *Boys in the Sand II*, with Culver again as the star.

The Boys of St. Vincent

(1992)

Painful Look at Pedophilia

Although accused in some circles of being anti-Catholic and homophobic, this controversial film was originally made for Canadian national television and broadcast as a two-part miniseries in 1992. The first part delves into the abuse of young, orphaned boys in St. John's, the capital of Newfoundland.

The second details court proceedings many years later in which shattered lives were revealed under official gaze.

The star of the film is an abusive brother, Peter Lavin, brought to forceful life on screen by Henry Czerny, with his piercing, almost diabolical eyes. He has won awards for his performance in Canada, and has even been compared to the horrifying Anthony Hopkins as Hannibal Lecter in *The Silence of the Lambs*.

Lavin's lust focuses on a button-eyed, 10-year-old named Kevin Reevey (Johnny Morina). When not trying to make love to the boy, Lavin beats him viciously.

A kindly janitor (Phillip Dinn) discovers the battered Kevin and rushes him to the local hospital. Here the film becomes almost Dickensian. Although the crime of child molestation is brought to light, it is covered up with a far-reaching conspiracy.

Taking place 15 years later, Part II shows ex-priest Lavin being arrested in Montréal to face charges of sexual assault and gross indecency and misconduct. The boys from the orphanage, now in their mid-20s, are called upon to reopen childhood scars to nail their former tormentors.

WHAT THE CRITICS SAID
"The story plays out as a coolly detailed fictional drama that wisely stays away from being overly graphic yet is still unflinching. It is a bleak picture of evil portrayed in entirely convincing human terms. Too tough for some, an outrage to others."
Peter Stack, *San Francisco Chronicle*

Breakfast on Pluto

(2005)

Candide Meets Tom Jones in Drag Heaven

This is a comedy (of sorts). It's about a young man's travails with clothes, gender, absent fathers and mothers, religion, and terrorism in Ireland and London in the 1970s. "I decided to make the film an object lesson in survival, about how a beautiful heart can triumph over  every disaster life throws at it, how a good attitude and great clothes can mean more than all the rancid little ideologies that battle for our souls," said writer/director Neil Jordan. "Kitten (the heroine of the film) wins in the end because he has more grace, more humor, and in the end, more charity than all the grotesques that confront him. And he has much better clothes. He takes his happy endings where he finds them."

Neil Jordan revisits the central concerns of *The Crying Game*—sexual identity and Irish/English political strife—in *Breakfast on Pluto*. Helmer's second adaptation, after *The Butcher Boy*, of a novel by Patrick McCabe relates the Candide-like odyssey of a flighty, gorgeously feminine young man through the 60s-70s British Isles as he searches for the mother he's never known. Young Patrick is played by Conor McEvoy who grows into the Kitten character as interpreted by Cillian Murphy. Both actors playing the same character at different ages flaunt gender proclivities in their church-dominated small town. Patrick is reared by a tough, homophobic foster mother who is horrified when he begins to don dresses and put on lipstick at an early age. Patrick inevitably meets a hostile reaction from his Catholic school superiors.

Abandoned as a baby in his small Irish hometown, Patrick (Kitten) Braden, as brilliantly played by Cillian Murphy, is aware from a very early age that he is different. Kitten is an endearing, deceptively tough young man. When he travels to the swinging London of the 1970s and takes to the stage as a transvestite cabaret singer, he uses his wit and charm—and sometimes his fists—to make sure nothing gets him down and nobody tries to change him.

Romance is on the way.

Breakfast with Scot

(2007)

Gay Hunks Adopt a Girly-Boy

Based on a novel by Michael Downing, this is the story of a fairly closeted gay couple who become guardians to a flamboyant 11-year-old, who loves boas, beads, and Broadway musicals, and isn't adverse to kissing boys at school.

Breakfast with Scott

After his mother dies of a drug overdose, Scot is taken in by Eric (Tom Cavanagh) and Sam (Ben Shenkman). Eric is a Toronto Maple Leafs hockey player, turned sportscaster, and his partner, Sam, is a sports lawyer.

In an amazing first, the national Hockey League allowed a gay film to use real team logos and likenesses. "The people there thought it was a family comedy, and they wanted to support it," said Laurie Lynd, the director.

The 'tween queen Scot (Noah Bernett) steals the show. He's so effeminate he embarrasses Eric, who is afraid the dippy little kid will call attention to his own gayness. In this refreshingly snarky and quick-witted movie, the action is aimed for mainstream audiences—no gay sex please, although we missed seeing these two handsome, hunky guys get it on. After all, they are a committed couple of many years.

Eric, no great lover of kids, especially one with a flouncing gait and a fondness for Christmas carols, only begins to bond with Scot when he discovers he can skate. He tries to channel the boy's twirling and dipping figure skating talent toward hockey.

As the movie progresses, we learn that the two hunks are not only going to have breakfast with Scott, but that he's sticking around for dinner, too.

WHAT THE CRITICS SAID
"Mr. Cavanagh gives a convincing performance. The bulk of the movie's heavy lifting falls to Mr. Bernett, an endearing young actor who imbues Scot with a cheeky I-am-what-I-am attitude toward his temporary surrogate parents and his persecuting peers."
Stephen Holden, *The New York Times*

Brother to Brother

(2004)

The Harlem Renaissance of the 1920s

This heartfelt, fascinating, and absorbing film is a sensitive and entertaining journey into the sexual politics of the glory days now known as the "Harlem Renaissance" of the 1920s. This captivating drama that seesaws between modern times and the Roaring Twenties was both written and directed by Rodney Evans.

The cast of skilled actors brings to life such legends as Langston Hughes, Zora Neale Hurston, James Baldwin, and Eldridge Cleaver in their youth. Some of these were the creators of the seminal literary journal, *Fire!*, that even angered the NAACP.

In the many "Cotton Club film depictions" of this stormy time in Harlem, *Brother to Brother* is the pioneering movie to deal with that era's vibrant gay and lesbian subculture.

Thrown out of his Brooklyn home by his homophobic father, Perry heads to Manhattan where he becomes a student at Columbia, working part-time at a homeless shelter. Along the way he looks for love in the form of a good-looking white male student, "Jim," as played by actor Alex Burns.

Described accurately as "young, gay, black, and beautiful" in the film, Perry goes to the homeless shelter after his classes. In both venues, he aspires to be something that he can't articulate. In the shelter he encounters an elderly Bruce Nugent, as brilliantly portrayed by Roger Robinson.

Nugent is a black gay poet who lived from 1906 to 1987. Through the eyes of this old man, the Harlem Renaissance lives anew. Nugent becomes Perry's guide not only back to the days of the Renaissance but as a role model on the virtues of an uncompromised life. It's a voyage of self-discovery for Perry.

Rounding out the cast, and doing so admirably, is Daniel Sunjata as Langston Hughes and Aunjanue Ellis as Zora Neale Hurston.

The Bubble

(*Ha-buah;* 2006)

Forbidden Love

Helmer Eytan Fox won a lot of gay fans in America with his love story between two Israeli soldiers, *Yossi & Jagger*. With *The Bubble* he set off a firestorm in Israel and elsewhere when he made one of the lovers, Ohad Kroller, playing an Israeli man, fall in love with Yousef ("Joe") Sweid, a Palestinian. The film sparked controversy not only in Fox's native Israel but in other parts of the homophobic Middle East.

First, there was resistance at many European film festivals, which refused to screen any film from Israel because of its war with Lebanon. In Tel Aviv, movie goers charged that the film was "pro-Palestinian," which it really isn't, of course. As for Arab countries, exhibitors would not screen any movie from Israel anyway, especially a gay one.

The most irreverent moment of the film is when the subject of gay suicide bombers is brought up. Do they receive virgin women or virgin men when they get to heaven?

The movie is well crafted and deserves to be seen in spite of efforts to suppress it. Other films have been made about lovers who cross dangerous lines, both political or social. Take *Romeo and Juliet*, for instance.

Love scenes in the film are exquisite, especially the tender relationship between the two men. The acting is excellent, dialogue often witty, and Eytan Fox does it once again. We applaud him for daring to take on such a provocative subject matter.

WHAT THE CRITICS SAID
"As with prior films, Fox's greatest strength lies in conveying genuine affection between youthful lovers and friends, which in turn lends eventual cruel twists of fate greater poignancy. Climatic events that push the central gay Israeli-Palestinian pairing toward predictable tragedy feel over-contrived and psychologically less than credible."
Dennis Harvey, *Variety*

Buddies

(1985)

A Moving, Realistic Look at AIDS

Director J. Bressan Jr. in this 81-minute film presents his drama somewhat like a home movie. That's not a criticism. If anything, this technique brings Buddies closer to the actors and the story of a man dying of AIDS. The helmer cast two unknowns—Geoff Edholm as Robert Willow and David Bennett as David Schachter.

David is writing a book about the AIDS crisis. As for himself, he still lives in the closet, but he decides to lend his hand in working with AIDS patients. His assignment is Robert, a gay political activist, who is dying of the disease.

Robert is candid about his sexual preference and his sense of gay pride. Through his dialogues, David begins to emerge from the closet himself. In the wake of Robert's death, he flies to Washington where he joins in the march to fight against AIDS.

WHAT THE CRITICS SAID
"The characters say exactly what might be expected, and say it more often than would be necessary to get the point across. The performances are unrelievedly sincere."
Vincent Canby, *The New York Times*

"Nothing is glossed over, and the touching aspects of both their disease and personal commitments are presented truthfully."
Archer Winstein, *New York Post*

"*Buddies* rushes in where no other dramatic work about AIDS has dared to tread. It shows us sex; not the memory of sex or its disparagement, not the platonic embrace that will have to suffice for homosexual passion on prime time. I can't remember a more riveting moment in any film than the image in *Buddies* of a dying man masturbating while being held by his friend."
Richard Goldstein, *Village Voice*

Bulgarian Lovers

(2003)

Immigrant Hunk Peddles Flesh to Older Man

In this sex comedy and drama, Eloy de la Iglesia returns to the screen. He first won international acclaim with his *El Diputado* released in 1978.

It's a love story . . . sort of, although the love is rather one sided. It's no secret that hundreds of refugees—both men and women—have fled from the former Eastern Bloc countries to the West in hopes of a better life. For gay men, especially older and affluent homosexuals, this has been like winning lotto.

The pampered middle-aged narrator, and star, Daniel, as played convincingly by Fernando Guillén Cuervo, isn't adverse to preying on young and impoverished new arrivals in Madrid, especially if they are hot, handsome and hung. He picks up Kyril (as played by Dritan Biba), a 23-year-old Bulgarian hottie. After checking out Daniel's apartment, Kyril proves to be a crude but effective lover, so much so that Daniel falls and falls hard. In Cuervo's performance, we have a virtual Spanish version of Kevin Spacey.

Daniel is backed up by his screaming queen best friend, Peón Nieto as Gildo. Perhaps the funniest exchange in the film is when Daniel virtually falls before Kyril and claims, "I'd give my life for you." In response, Kyril informs him, "I'd also give your life for me."

Those who like their gay movies with graphic nudity, strong sexual content, racy language, and some drug use will find comfort here. As the plot deepens, Daniel learns that his hunk isn't adverse to stealing and smuggling—maybe and rather improbably a radioactive bag that Kyril stashes at Daniel's house. Daniel, blind with love, gets involved in Kyril's shady business affairs—yes, gangsters, drugs, even possibly radioactive materials.

Into this love nest emerges Kyril's girlfriend, arriving to come between the two male lovers. Anita Sinkovic is cast in the thankless role of Kyril's girlfriend, Kalina. Still in love, Daniel even pays for Kyril's wedding to his girlfriend in Bulgaria.

Burnt Money

(*Plata Quemada*; 2001)

Gay Bank Robbers in Edgy Heist Film

Called it a South-of-the-Border gay version of *Bonnie and Clyde*. This Argentine film is about bank robbers—two men who also happen to be lovers. El Nene (Leonardo Sbaraglia) and Ángel (Eduardo Noriega) and their accomplice, El Cuervo (Pablo Echarri), stage a botched bank robbery in 1965 in Buenos Aires, then hide out from the police in Uruguay while the gang falls apart.

The film is based on two ultimately ruthless bank robbers, a 1965 page in Argentinian crime history. Ángel and Nene are known as "the twins," because they look so much alike. But they are, in fact, not brothers but hottie lovers involved in a passionate gay affair.

Enter a woman into their lives, Giselle (Leticia Brédice). She is a prostitute and she allows Ángel and Nene to move in with her when they are forced to abandon their nest. When Nene gets hostile and breaks with Giselle, she goes to the police to turn in the gay lovers.

What happens next became the stuff of legend in Argentina.

WHAT THE CRITICS SAID
"Director Marcelo Piñeyro interweaves the Ángel and Nene story lines with finesse, underscoring the symbiotic obsessive nature of their bond. At one point, when Nene is having sex with a stranger in a public lavatory, the film cuts to Ángel going to church and lighting candles. Ángel, beautiful and mentally unbalanced, is played by Noriega, the actor who had the Tom Cruise role in *Abre los Ojos*, the Spanish film that inspired *Vanilla Sky*."
Edward Guthmann, *San Francisco Chronicle*

The Butch Factor

(2009)

The Testosterone Quotient of Gay Men Today

This film by Christopher Hines asks the provocative question, "What kind of man are you?" There is no straight answer for sure.

In *The Butch Factor,* you get all kinds, as the helmer surveys everything from the Castro clone culture of the 70s to today's Bears and gym rats. The film is an intriguing study of gay men, their stereotypes, and masculinity.

Intertwined are muscle men, rodeo riders, rugby players, and cops. Yes, gay men aren't all drag queens. From homophobia to metrosexuality, the men interviewed speak openly about their feelings, even about the subject of effeminacy.

Entertaining and informative, the film also is eye candy for many who like looking at extremely masculine gay men, some in skimpy apparel.

WHAT THE CRITICS SAID
"The strength here is the breadth of likable men interviewed and the moments when old but persisting stereotypes are confronted."
EDGE San Francisco

"Definitely a must-see. Blows the lid off some strongly entrenched stereotypes in the gay community."
Reel Affirmations

"Clever and fast-paced!"
Frameline

"Stereotyping seems to be a way of life in America. Gay men seem to be the prime victims of stereotyping. *The Butch Factor* looks at these stereotypes and blows them away. Hines takes a comprehensive look at the subject of masculinity, and he has done his research well. It is not often that you can be entertained and learn something at the same time. But that is what *The Butch Factor* does."
Amos Lassen

Butch Jamie

(2007)

The Lesbian Version of Tootsie

Michelle Ehlen, a woman of talent, directed, wrote and starred in this comedy/romance, appearing in the lead role of Jamie Klein, an out-of-work butch lesbian actor willing to try almost anything for a role. Butch Jamie is a gender-bending comedy about struggling for success in Hollywood.

As a femme, Jamie gets turned down on all casting calls. But when she goes as "herself," she finds work in a man's part.

There are complications along the way. Tiffany Anne Carrin, cast as Jill, gets the hots for Jamie, thinking she's all man. Rounding out the cast is Olivia Nix who performs well as Nola, Jamie's roommate. Nola's aim in life is to make a star of her cat, Howard.

In general, Ehlen's performance as Jamie won her acclaim and some prizes. But there is always dissent, especially from male critics such as Rich Danko. "This is the worst movie I have ever seen. Ehlen is a horrible actress. The writing is not funny at all. I understand it's a budget film, but good writing and acting don't cost money if you've got talent. What is the point of reviewing things if you think every piece of crap media involving lesbians is great?"

WHAT THE CRITICS SAID

"Many familiar topics come up, including a few tried-and-true bisexual jokes, but the tone is conversational and nonconfrontational at all times. The script is smart to acknowledge its roots in Dustin Hoffman's comic masterpiece, *Tootsie*. A lesser cast would likely mangle the delicate balance between 'cute and smart' and 'completely clichéd,' but the talented performers do wonders."
Danielle Riendeau

"*Butch Jamie* is entertaining as a comedy, but also gives insight into societal gender roles and how often they blur with one another. Ehlen's role as Jamie has been described as a modern-day *Tootsie* for a whole new generation."
Lisa Cohen

Butley

(1974)

Wife and Boy Friend Leave Him for Other Men

In the 1970s and 80s, the talented, ruggedly handsome Alan Bates became a cinematic sex symbol, never afraid to take on a gay or bisexual role.

Simon Gray wrote the screenplay, *Butley*, based on his original play, and Harold Pinter shows a certain precise brilliance as the director.

But it is clearly Alan Bates's moment to shine, even though the cast also contains Jessica Tandy. She plays a middle-age teacher and his female associate whose lifelong book project has been accepted while his tome on T.S. Eliot lies unfinished.

Bates, playing Ben Butley, an English professor, does so with astonishing virtuosity. And does he have humiliation to face. His wife, Anne Butley (Susan Engel), tells him she intends to marry another man.

His lover, Joey Keyston (Richard O'Callaghan), also informs him that he is saying good-bye, heading off with a man closer to his own age. A snob, Butley ridicules Joey's choice of Reg Nuttall (Michael Byrne) as a Northern working-class bloke, the son of a butcher and a female traffic warden.

In the film, we watch as Butley slowly disintegrates before our eyes. Even though he's bitchy, he emerges as suavely likable.

WHAT THE CRITICS SAID

"The play hasn't been opened up so much as opened in. The camera gets closer to the characters and sees more. What it sees in *Butley* is a man with a desperate problem. He needs other people, and his only strategy for attracting them is to drive them away."
Roger Ebert

"A *tour de force* for Bates as the appalling yet touching Ben Butley. The trenchant dialogue illuminates the academic scraping bottom; however, the film never lapses into self-pity."
London Movie Express

Butterfly

(2004)

Sexy Hong Kong Made Lesbian Drama

With empathy to spare, this well-made drama, shot in Hong Kong (but also issued in English), tells the story of Flavia, played by Josie Ho, who is more than 30 years old and a married teacher. Somehow she has suppressed the memory of her adolescent lesbian fling with Jin, as played by Stephanie Che. Young Flavia, as seen in flashback, is acted by Yat Ning Chan. The older Flavia is stuck in a stifling marriage to Ming (Eric Kot).

A chance encounter in a supermarket with a playful and seductive singer, "Yip," re-awakens dormant lesbian feelings within Flavia. Yip (Tian Yuan) says to Flavia: "Cry to me whenever you want. Just buy me a beer."

Yan Yan Mak both directed the film and wrote its screenplay. She succeeds rather admirably except for her attempt to link her drama with the Tiananmen Square demonstrations. Somewhere along the way, her parallel story plot lines become knotted.

WHAT THE CRITICS SAID
"The lengthy Hong Kong lesbian drama has hot women, sensual love scenes, and episodes of tender and erotic sex, without any explicit nudity. The movie will also seduce lesbians hoping to see positive images of gay women."
Dinah Shore

"Butterfly finds that little empty space that you keep to yourself, grabs its hand and takes it away for a serious talk."
Imogen Neale

"In a nutshell, Butterfly delivers a potent message about the need to be brave and stand up for ourselves in pursuit of happiness."
Adrian Sim

By Hook or By Crook

(2001)

A Raw Work of Lesbian Outlaw Expression

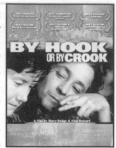

A child asks Shy (Silas Howard), "Are you a man or a woman?" A valid question. Her poetically evasive reply is "both." With her close-cropped hair, mannish attire, and tattoos, she is a small-town butch with a nagging messiah complex. She heads to San Francisco to immerse herself in a life of crime.

Once there, she bonds with Valentine as "Harry Dodge" (Harriet Dodge), a wise-acre adoptee who is searching for her birth-mother. The two stars of this innovative butch buddy movie also wrote and directed the picture.

The film accurately proclaims itself as a "movie about butches by butches." When Shy encounters Valentine or Harry Dodge, she meets another gender bender, plus a refugee from a psychiatric institution. As for her sexuality, she claims, "I'm a special—two for one."

WHAT THE CRITICS SAID
"By Hook or By Crook is really a corny old romance at heart, with almost all the attendant clichés intact. Pic's obvious derivations include the Jean Genet tradition of gay criminal as society's ultimate outsider, Kerouac road stories, Boys Don't Cry, and in several unfortunate instances, John Cassavetes' improvised noodlings."
Robert Koehler, Variety

"By Hook or By Crook isn't a love story, exactly: Dodge and Howard have earthy sex scenes, but not with each other. The movie instead explores the electric connection that occurs when a person with a unique sensibility meets a kindred spirit. The premise alone—the friendship of two dogged eccentrics—sets By Hook or By Crook apart from the 'we're just like everybody else' romantic comedies and cautionary tales that dominate queer cinema. The thrill is that Dodge and Howard plainly aren't like everybody else."
Noel Murray

Cabaret

(1972)

A Musical for the Age of Aquarius

Bob Fosse directed this award-winning smash hit musical that remains as Liza Minnelli's most memorable performance. "Come to the Cabaret" became part of the international language. The basic material came from gay author Christopher Isherwood's *Berlin Stories* and a 1951 dramatic play by John Van Druten, filmed in 1955 as *I Am a Camera*. The film version came from the 1966 John Kander-Fred Ebb Broadway musical.

Judy's daughter heads a superb cast, with Michael York playing Brian Roberts and delectable Helmut Griem cast as Maximilian von Heune. Who can forget Joel Grey's bizarre, devastating portrayal of the Master of Ceremonies at the Kit Kat Club?

Minnelli put her unique stamp on the role of a young American, Sally Bowles, who becomes involved with an aimlessly bisexual Britisher, Brian Roberts. Both of them get involved with Baron Von Heune. When the baron leaves Berlin, Sally tells Brian she's pregnant. He offers to marry her, but she refuses, preferring an abortion instead.

Julie Harris was miscast in *I Am a Camera*. In the same role, Minnelli, on the other hand, inhabits her part as the heartless, ingenuous vamp, especially when she dons garter belts and a bowler hat, singing "Bye Bye Mein Herr." Think Marlene Dietrich in *The Blue Angel*.

The most disturbing part of the film is not any sex scenes, but when a young S.A. man sings a song called "Tomorrow Belongs to Me." It begins on a nostalgic level but turns into a Nazi call for world domination.

WHAT THE CRITICS SAID
"Minnelli is overwhelming. York is a somewhat ineffectual leading man, overshadowed by tiny Joel Grey as the drag-Danteian guide to the rotting city's netherworld. The film's bisexuality is bold but not belabored, and its German Jews are anything but caricatures."
ABC Movie Express

Caligula

(1979)

Rape, Fisting, Beheadings—Roman Politics as Usual

This 156-minute film is debauched, depraved, disgusting, campy, a costumed classic for the ages in a remastered, uncut version on DVD, Arguably, it is the most controversial film of all time.

Penthouse's Bob Guccione, one of the co-directors, had scouts search Italy for cocks big enough to appear in this graphic, shocking, and tragic story. It was based on an earlier screenplay by Gore Vidal, but when Guccione went to work to sex up his script, the gay author withdrew his name.

This is the saga of Caligula, Rome's most infamous Caesar, to whom power was the ultimate aphrodisiac. So what does this randy Roman, magnificently played by a young Malcolm McDowell, do? He declares himself a god, opens a state-sponsored brothel, and lets the good times roll.

He's supported by an all-star cast, including Helen Mirren, Peter O'Toole, and John Gielgud, who referred to *Caligula* as "my first pornographic movie."

Caligola (its Italian name) is our kind of guy. He sleeps with his sister and organizes elaborate Roman orgies. He gives his horse political office and humiliates and executes anyone who even slightly displeases him. He also marries Rome's most infamous whore.

In the hardcore version, nothing is left for the imagination. The XXX-rated scenes were inserted after the big name actors had departed Rome. This full version is as gratifying as a day of debauchery.

WHAT THE CRITICS SAID
"Rather than rethink the process of photographing sex, the makers of *Caligula* use *Penthouse* as their only artistic reference. *Caligula*'s gratuitous decapitations and disembowelments—presumably far less common in everyday life—are now accepted in everyday cinema, and even then went largely unremarked upon."
Daniel Kraus

Callas Forever

(2002)

It's Easier to Be Worshipped Than Loved

Callas Forever is arch, stylish, and stylized, and about a minute into its run, if you're gay and of a certain age, you'll realize that this is an "impressionistic sketch," or an aria, to remembered beauty. There's a demurely worded caveat at the end, acknowledging that the script portrays Maria Callas as remembered by director Franco Zeffirelli—not necessarily as the historical figure she was. And from here, the film plays with your emotions, your sense of whimsy, your heartstrings, and your memory of what you thought you already knew about Callas.

The story line is a fictionalized account, a nostalgic "what if" tale, of what might have happened if circumstances had been different during the final year (1977) of Callas's life.

Fanny Ardant as Callas delivers a divine performance. She recaptures the spirit of Callas, and also looks stunning in all that Chanel. The plot requires the proposal and development, as part of the film, of a hypothetical arts venture which—because of Callas's extravagant (and perhaps overblown) sense of artistic integrity—eventually fails. And it fails despite the basic soundness of the reasoning behind the venture. Jeremy Irons plays gay musical entrepreneur Larry, perhaps as an autobiographical allegory for Zeffirelli himself.

After picking up a new and handsome gay lover at the Paris airport, he bashes down the fortress doors of Callas's self-imposed isolation within her Paris apartment. He wants her to go back to work.

Once inside, he finds a feisty diva in a state of hugh dudgeon. She's drinking, popping pills, weeping uncontrollably and being an insomniac. She also lovingly picks up portraits of Aristotle Onassis, her only true love, and rages against Jacqueline Kennedy for stealing her man from her.

What's the venture? To lip-synch the words to recordings that she made of the Bizet opera back 20 years ago when her voice was in its prime.

Camp

(2003)

A *De Facto* Remake of *Fame*

Back in their hometown schools, this cast of young people would be called "a misfit," "a dyke," or "a faggot." But at a musical theater summer camp, they are on fire and filled with life.

Todd Graff wrote and directed this comedy/musical/drama and selected a young, inexperienced, but talented cast to pull it off as a show-stopper.

The cast includes supposedly straight Vlad Baumann (Daniel Letterle); a queeny cross-dresser Michael Flores (Robin de Jesus), Ellen Lucas (Joanna Chicoat), a bit of a nerd; and Jenna Malloran (Tiffany Taylor), whose parents had her jaw wired shut so she won't gain weight. Other cast members include Fritzi Wagner (Anna Kendrick) who becomes a strange personal slave to Jill Simmons (Alana Allen). Kendrick was singled out for the most acting awards in the supporting category.

After a series of flops on Broadway, washed up songwriter Bert Harley (Don Dixon) is the instructor of these young performers. Ultimately he achieves success by staging a dramatic altogether-new production, introducing the number "Here's Where I Stand." Many critics felt this song should have gotten an Oscar nomination. The great Stephen Sondheim makes a cameo appearance as himself.

WHAT THE CRITICS SAID
"*Camp* is another of those summer movies that want to pluck at your heartstrings. If it would just stop plucking for a second, it might be enjoyable. Ok, so we've established that this is a unique subculture among the high school population. But that's not all. If you're a guy at Camp Ovation, you're almost certainly gay. In fact, when Vlad shows up with a football, a guitar, and an interest in girls, everyone is positively stunned. 'A boy,' marvels one of the counselors. 'An honest-to-God straight boy."
C.W. Nevius

Camp Out

(2006)

Gay, Young & Christian

The film traces the odyssey of 10 teenagers to the country's "first gay Christian Bible camp." Unlike other films of this nature, this camp doesn't try to turn its interns straight, but hopes instead to help them reconcile their sexual orientation to a faith that so often condemns them.

The skilled helmers are Larry Grimaldi and Kirk Marcolina, who so amused us with their TV series on Bravo, *Boy Meets Boy*.

For these six Midwestern boys and four girls, it's just as hard to come out as a Christian as it is to come out as gay. They're caught in the battle between religion, politics, and sexuality.

These kids are outsiders--their straight classmates ostracize them and their churches reject them. But like all teens, they yearn to feel at home, somewhere. Struggling to find a way to be true both to their spirituality and their sexual identity, these teens come to camp hoping to finally find a place of acceptance.

WHAT THE CRITICS SAID
"From pre-interviews with select participants in bunkhouse confessionals where campers can gossip about each other, the soundbite-driven docu gives these ostracized teens, many of them virgins seeking same-sex life partners, a platform that will likely cause some Christians to reconsider their biases against homosexuals--and vice versa."
Peter Debruge, *Variety*

"The directors get some profoundly personal and even deeply philosophical portraits of the teens. They range from chubby, depressive Tim, who's fresh out of drug rehab, to Stancy, a gregarious, fuchsia-haired dyke who's loud and proud. These kids offer up rich, funny, and poignant pictures of gay youth."
Marc Thomson, *The Bottom Line* (Palm Springs)

Carandiru

(2003)

Who You're Likely to Meet in a Brazilian Jail

Set within the sweaty, high-pressure environment of Latin America's biggest prison, this is an epic, sprawling, and ambitious film that shows North American viewers a side to life in the Third World that they might never have otherwise imagined. It was adapted from a Brazilian work of bestselling non-fiction (*Carandiru Station*).

The book's author, Brazilian oncologist Drauzio Varella, came late in his life to the world of book authorship. He was already in his late 50s when his experiences as a volunteer in one of South America's biggest and roughest prisons (São Paulo's *Casa de Detenção*, also known as *Carandiru*) prompted him to record his experiences. It was his friendship, and his role as physician to noted Brazilian director Hector Babenco, that led to a commitment on the part of the director to make the film even before the book had been published. The filmmaking process brought together some of South America's finest actors and technicians, eventually attracting huge media attention.

Gathering together the doctor's stories about life in Carandiru Prison, Babenco composed a sweeping tapestry that's loaded with pathos.

The doctor, winningly played by a good-looking Danish-trained Brazilian actor named Louis Carlos Vasconcelos, is faced with horrendous problems inside this, Latin America's largest jail: decaying facilities, diseases such as TB, leptospirosis, cachexia, and the beginning of a full-blown AIDS epidemic. With more than 7,000 inmates and only rudimentary medical equipment, Carandiru is a huge challenge for the newly arrived doctor. But his work begins to bear fruit, and the doctor eventually earns the respect of the inmates. And with respect comes secrets, and his ability to deal with issues beyond disease. The doctor's meetings with patients become "windows" into both the world of crime and into the sociology that's peculiar to the lives of the inmates, many of whom are engaged in active homosexual lifestyles.

<table>
<tr>
<td>

Caravaggio

(1986)

He Paints. He Loves. He Fights. He Murders.

</td>
<td>

Casablanca

(1942)

We'll Always Have Each Other

</td>
</tr>
</table>

Derek Jarman, its director and co-writer, has created a stylishly bold and homoerotic tribute to the volatile, darkly handsome Renaissance artist. Jarman depicts the controversial painter torn between his hunky, rough trade lover and his mistress. This biopic comes from the UK.

Not that much is really known about Michelangelo Merisi da Caravaggio (1571-1610), so Jarman had to take great liberties in fashioning a narrative. The cinematography is superb, and Caravaggio's artwork brilliantly incorporated into the movie. Some scenes, for example, bathe the shot in *chiaroscuro* lighting, which was a signature of the artist's work.

Caravaggio, as played by Nigel Terry, is a thrill-seeker and bisexual voluptuary. One night at a bare knuckles boxing match, he discovers the object of his desire, Ranuccio Thomasoni (Sean Bean), a street thug he makes his model. The relationship develops into a *ménage à trois* with Ranuccio's mistress, Lena (Tilda Swinton).

Jarman, known for such films as *Last of England* and *Edward II*, was a tireless advocate of gay rights. He died of AIDS in 1994 at the age of 52.

WHAT THE CRITICS SAID
"Derek Jarman's *Caravaggio* triumphantly rises above its financial restrictions and proves, once again, that less can be a lot more. Jarman's film, in classical tradition, is told in flashback as the artist lies dying in poverty. Story takes a back seat, however, since much of the joy of the film is to be found in the way Jarman and his team recreate the look and color of the original paintings. But film lacks a certain warmth and emotional depth."
Variety

"*Caravaggio* dramatizes the painter's need for patronage, his religious beliefs, and his sexuality. Curiously, Jarman undercuts narrative conventions through his use of obvious anachronisms, including typewriters and motorbikes."
TV Guide

Why does one of the most famous of all straight love stories, the celluloid romance of Humphrey Bogart and Ingrid Bergman, always end up on a list of most favorite gay films?

That's because gays claim that the real love story is not between Rick and Ilsa, but between Rick and Captain Louis Renault, as played by Claude Rains.

Set in unoccupied Africa during the early days of World War II, an American expatriate meets a former lover, with unforeseen complications.

The film is filled with memorable lines. "Of all the gin joints in all the towns in all the world, she walks into mine." "Here's looking at you, kid." "Round up the usual suspects." "We'll always have Paris."

One viewer claimed that for him the most interesting relationship in the movie is between Rick and Louis. "Theirs is a relationship of almost perfect cynicism, one-liners, and professions of neutrality that provide much humor, as well as gives a necessary display of Rick's darker side before and after Ilsa's arrival."

Many famous movie reviewers, including Roger Ebert, knew that Rains was playing a "subtly homosexual police chief."

Rains as Louis is obviously besotted with the super-butch Rick. In Rick's presence, Rains becomes almost like a school girl. Gays picked up on such lines as when Louis says to Rick: "You were never interested in any woman."

Louis also tells Rick: "She [Ilsa] was asking questions about you earlier, Rick, in a way that made me *extremely jealous*." Rains said "extremely jealous" in such a way that only a redneck homophobe could not have picked up on what he meant.

After Ilsa's airborne, the captain walks away with his man. Bogie famously drawls, "I think this is the beginning of a beautiful friendship." World War II audiences didn't get this homoerotic overtone.

Cat on a Hot Tin Roof

(1958)

Castrated Williams Still Exudes Testosterone

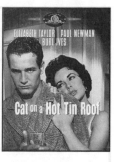

Playwright Tennessee Williams hated the film adaptation of his hit Broadway play, *Cat on a Hot Tin Roof*, but audiences in 1958 flocked to see gay-friendly Elizabeth Taylor as Maggie the Cat and blue-eyed Paul Newman play a repressed homosexual.

Brick, an alcoholic ex-football player, drinks his days away mourning the loss of Skipper, the only person he ever loved (a suicide victim) while spurning the advances of his wife, Maggie.

In the meantime, a brilliant Burl Ives as Big Daddy is dying of cancer. A soap opera Southern potboiler but what fun. It's also great drama, although, because of the censorship of the 1950s, the film could not deal openly with the homosexuality of Newman's character. But your gay grandfather, watching the movie, understood Brick's dilemma.

A dysfunctional Southern family gathers to await the death of "Big Daddy" (Burl Ives). He is disturbed by the childless marriage of his favorite but alcoholic son Brick. His other son, Gooper (Jack Carson), is filling the house with little "no-neck monsters" born to Mae (Madeleine Sherwood). Judith Anderson delivers her usually superb performance as the long-suffering "Big Momma."

Grace Kelly was originally slated to star as Maggie the Cat, but went off to Monaco with her prince. Elizabeth Taylor was second choice. Richard Brooks was the director, having helmed the studio's *Tea and Sympathy* in 1956.

Williams deplored the ending when Britt throws his pillow besides Maggie's on the bed. It is suggested that they are about to make love and bring Big Daddy's long-hoped-for child into the world. Memories of past wrongs and misunderstandings are laid to rest, so to speak. After all, Maggie, in the movie, hinted—however obliquely—at Brick's satisfying sexual technique and, presumably, his fabulous endowment.

Dipsomania, sexual frustration—in this case gay angst—and family dysfunction never got so sweaty, or so humid, deep in the heart of Dixie.

The Celluloid Closet

(1995)

Butch & Sundance Should Have Kissed at the End

Too bad Vito Russo died of AIDS in 1990 and didn't live to see Rob Epstein and Jeffrey Friedman bring his 1981 book to the screen. His highly acclaimed *The Celluloid Closet* was a landmark that dealt with the portrayal of homosexuals in film through Charlie Chaplin in drag to the 1980s.

In film clips, some of them obscure, we see two men dancing together in Thomas Edison's *Gay Brothers* in 1895; Marlene Dietrich cross-dressing in *Morocco*, and Peter Lorre toying with a walking stick in *The Maltese Falcon*.

The love that dare not speak its name on the screen had to be suggested in veiled exchanges, such as that between John (Big Dick) Ireland and Montgomery (Little Dick) Clift in *Red River*. John says to Monty, "There are two things more beautiful than a good gun—a Swiss watch or a woman from anywhere. You ever had a Swiss watch?"

The film is narrated by Lily Tomlin, who notes that, "The sissy in film made everyone feel more manly or more womanly by filling the space in between." Interviewees include Gore Vidal who created a gay relationship between Stephen Boyd and Charlton Heston in *Ben Hur*, or Matt Crowley who wrote the watershed *Boys in the Band*. Shirley MacLaine, Tony Curtis, and Tom Hanks are also interviewed.

Of course, when gays were first depicted on the screen, they had to end their lives in madness or suicide. Sandy Dennis, for example, playing a lesbian in *The Fox*, was crushed by a falling tree. Yes, we got the Freudian symbolism.

Trivia note: The filmmakers planned a sequel, showing how gay figures were portrayed as heterosexual in films. However, Charlton Heston declined use of *The Agony and the Ecstasy* (1965), falsely claiming that Michelangelo was straight. Richard Burton's estate denied the rights to *Alexander the Great* (1956), and MGM denied use of *Hans Christian Andersen* (1952), fearing that Epstein and Friedman were going to "out" gay comedian Danny Kaye.

Chasing Amy

(1997)

Redefining the Boy-Meets-Girl Formula

It's a hell of a lot better than *Gigli*, where lesbian mobster Jennifer Lopez falls for Ben Affleck. In this time around, comic book artist Holden McNeil (Affleck) falls for a cartoonist Alyssa Jones (Joey Lauren Adams), only to discover that she too is a lesbian. Basically, it's a movie about how straight people relate to gay people.

Before the entrance of Alyssa, Holden has been hanging with Banky Edwards (Jason Lee). He too is a comic book artist, and he and Holden have been best friends for years. Their buddy relationship is threatened by the appearance of this beautiful young lesbian.

Kevin Smith, who directed and wrote the movie, avoids the pitfalls of another empty-headed sex-com, developing the film into insights in the way of love. His dialogue is sharp, ironic, and alive.

Scene-stealer Hooper (Dwight Ewell) plays a gay African American who assumes a black militant pose to be taken seriously by the readers of his comic books.

WHAT THE CRITICS SAID
"Still showing his touch for garrulous, hair-splitting conversation, Smith engages his characters in a bright, spirited demonstration of just how difficult modern love can be. Total candor, shifting sexual orientations, and an atmosphere of teasing, free-wheeling argument make *Chasing Amy* a spiky comedy with engaging honesty at its core."
Janet Maslin, *The New York Times*

"Smith pivots his yarn on two central intimate questions: The possibility of a confirmed lesbian's crossing over to begin a serious affair with a man, and the ability of that man to deal with the woman's extensive sexual past. The hyper-sensitive climate makes these matters, delicate ones for a straight filmmaker."
Todd McCarthy, *Variety*

The Children's Hour

(1961)

Shirley MacLaine Goes Dyke

Lillian Hellman's celebrated stage play, *The Children's Hour*, opened on Broadway in 1934 and ran for 691 performances. The play was a strong psychological drama that dealt with lesbianism. Director William Wyler brought it to the screen two times, failing both times.

To Wyler's credit, he wanted to present the drama as Hellman wrote it. But Samuel Goldwyn even insisted on a title change, calling the film *These Three* (1936). Lesbianism was changed to a charge of adultery. That film starred Joel McCrea trapped between Miriam Hopkins and Merle Oberon.

In 1961 Wyler remade the film with Shirley MacLaine and Audrey Hepburn, with James Garner in the male lead. In the new version, lesbianism raised its head but was treated like leprosy.

Audrey played Karen Wright, with Garner her love interest, Dr. Joe Cardin. Shirley was cast as the lesbian, Martha.

Interviewed for the film, *The Celluloid Closet*, Shirley said, "We were in the mindset of not understanding what we were basically doing. These days, there would be a tremendous outcry, as well there should be. Why would Martha break down and say to Karen: 'Oh my god, what's wrong with me? I'm so polluted. I've ruined you.'"

In the film Mary Tilford (Karen Balkin) spread a malicious lie about Karen and Martha, who are teachers in a school for girls. This lie travels, destroying not only enrollment in their school but their private lives as well. As in most films of that time, the gay man or lesbian has to die. In this case, Shirley cannot bear the guilt she feels and hangs herself.

WHAT THE CRITICS SAID
"*The Children's Hour* in its reincarnation is somewhat dated, but bold, brisk and a faithful remake. Wyler's direction is arresting, penetrating, and sensitive."
Variety

<table>
<tr><td>

A Chorus Line

(1985)

Hit Stage Show Trashed in Film

</td><td>

Chris & Don: A Love Story

(2007)

No One Believed They Could Last So Long

</td></tr>
</table>

We loved it on Broadway but the show did not translate well onto film. In fact, Universal Pictures held an option on the movie rights for five long years before finally coming up with a workable idea on how to adapt it for the screen.

The plot is simple enough, depicting a director casting dancers for a Broadway show. The numbers are narrowed down, as more and more hopefuls are eliminated. The road for those remaining, in Judy's words, "gets lonelier and tougher."

A Chorus Line, called the quintessential backstage musical, celebrates both the lives and hard times of the gypsy dancers, who turn up for auditions for the handful of jobs left on Broadway. The film celebrates the masochism of being a Broadway gypsy in song and dance. Most dancers use rejection as their middle name.

Richard Attenborough, of all people, was called upon to direct, filling in for the stage's Michael Bennett. Attenborough made a big mistake in casting Michael Douglas as Zach.

But the Britisher himself, Attenborough, was the wrong choice for the director.

For us, the most fascinating part of the movie, and also the play, is when the platoons of dancers have been winnowed down to a chosen few, and they are asked to share details of their personal lives. The most melodramatic point is when Sheila (Vicki Frederick), Zach's former girlfriend, shows up for an audition. Once she was a star, but now she needs a job in the chorus line.

WHAT THE CRITICS SAID
"The result may not please purists who want a film record of what they saw on stage, but this is one of the most intelligent and compelling movie musicals in a long time-and the most grown up, since it isn't limited, as so many contemporary musicals are, to the celebration of the survival qualities of geriatric actresses."
Roger Ebert

This is the true story of a love between the British writer, Christopher Isherwood (whose *Berlin Stories* inspired the musical *Cabaret*), and Don Bachardy, the American portrait artist. Directors Tina Mascara and Guido Santi Wisely allowed Bachardy himself to be the narrator.

Chris & Don tells the story of a gay English blueblood who in the 1950s picked up a working-class stud muffin 30 years his junior on a Santa Monica beach and became obsessed with him.

At first Bachardy may have been Eliza Doolittle to Isherwood's Henry Higgins. The younger man even learned to talk like Isherwood after a year of living together. One critic noted that Bachardy today sounds like Katharine Hepburn in *Suddenly, Last Summer*.

But in time Bachardy became an exceptionally gifted portrait painter in his own right.

The docu draws on a rich treasure trove of archival and home-movie material. W.H. Auden, viewed in rare film glimpses, was just one of the cultural elite that Isherwood introduced his young protégé to. Others include Igor Stravinsky, Aldous Huxley, and Tennessee Williams.

WHAT THE CRITICS SAID
"After Bachardy became successful in his own right, he and Isherwood had periods of estrangement, took lovers, and pushed the limits of domesticity. But he was there at Isherwood's deathbed, drawing him compulsively, then drawing his body for hours after his passing. The sequence, like the movie, is stunningly open and heartfelt. We look at those final drawings of Isherwood and sense what Bachardy is doing: capturing the surface details in a feverish attempt to go beyond them to get to the core of his lover's being. *Chris & Don* is the rarest of documentaries: a realistic portrait of the human spirit."
New York Magazine

Circuit

(2001)

Life-Endangering Drugs & Anonymous Sex

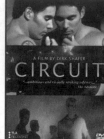

Unrequited love, homoeroticism, steroid abuse, gay bashing—it's all here. Let's party. Director Dirk Shafer, who also co-wrote the script, has created the best circuit party film around.

John Webster (Jonathan Wade-Drahos) lives and works as a police officer in a small town in Illinois. Tiring of the homophobic life there, he heads west for Los Angeles, where his muscular, athletic, and beautiful body is likely to be devoured.

Under colored lights, he enters a world of glitter on the circuit party. He's sucked into drugs and unsafe sex, all played out against the sound of techno-pop disco music.

The gay cult of youth worship and "body fascism" are explored, perhaps as never before.

John's guide into Dante's Inferno is a cool hustler (Andre Khabazzi). Together they experience disco-soaked bacchanals. For John, shooting steroids and snorting Special K are just a breath away. The hustler and the former cop spiral into a world of self-medication and self-improvement.

To enliven the scene, the director brings in celebrities, including Bruce Vilanch, Nancy Allen, William Katt, and Jim J. Bullock.

WHAT THE CRITICS SAID
"*Circuit* is as slick and attractive as its cast. But the movie gets away from Shafer, as did his previous film, *Man of the Year*, which drew from his real-life experiences as a *Playgirl* centerfold."
Noel Murray

"The artistic-design is amazing; the camera-work and cinematography incredible—especially remembering that the filming was completed with a digital camcorder. But the heart of this movie is the story. The main characters John and Hector have a dangerous love for one another, and both yearn to experience the true intimacy between them. But the shallow and tumultuous world of the *Circuit* keeps them tragically separated."
Christopher W. Blackwell

Clapham Junction

(2007)

Discrimination, Prejudice, & Violence

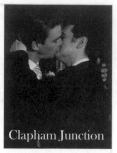

Clapham Junction

This British film was attacked in some quarters for presenting too negative a view of homosexuality. It follows 36 hours in the lives of a number of gay men in Clapham in South London. *Clapham Junction* was originally made for TV in the UK when Channel 4 ran a series of specials, commemorating four decades since the decriminalization of homosexuality in Britain.

Aided by scripter Kevin Elyot, director Adrian Shergold follows the trails of a number of homosexuals where all their stories come together.

Gays looking for role models won't find them here. Gavin (Stuart Bunce) and Will (Richard Lintern) are a middle-class gay couple celebrating their civil union with a big bash commitment ceremony. But, wait, all is not what it seems. One of the happily married couple is a slut. When his chance comes, Will flirts with a handsome waiter Alfie (David Leon).

Alfie has problems of his own. After work he goes to a gay bar to unwind. There he encounters a bloke named Terry (Paul Nicholls). He has a nasty hobby of picking up gay men, taking them to some secluded place to have sex with them, then violently beating them up. Terry is that sad gay cliché: a homosexual man who hates himself because of his gayness.

Julian (James Wilby) is a sad closet case who likes to go "cottaging" (a British term for men who go to public toilets seeking other men for sex). The United States Senate has men like that. Robin (Rupert Graves) unexpectedly encounters Julian at a dinner party just after having discovered him looking for sex in the "loo." His overbearing wife Marion is played by Samantha Bond.

Enter Tim (Joseph Mawle), a fourteen-year-old who takes advantage of his parents' absence to sow some gay seeds. He makes himself available to a 29-year-old neighbor, Theo (Luke Treadway). They end up having a hot time, but the prospects for a future relationship between them are dim, not to mention illegal.

The film shows that cruising is still alive.

Close to Léo

(Tout contre Léo; 2002)

A Strong Family Growing Stronger

This is a well acted and scripted film directed by Christophe Honoré, who was one of the script writers.

Léo (Pierre Mignard) is 21 years old, the oldest of four brothers. One night he announced to his rural French family that he's HIV+. Up to now this loving family has supported Léo's homosexuality. The disease will test their family bonds.

The father and mother (Dominic Gould and Marie Bunel) are also the parents of two teenage brothers, Tristan (Rodolphe Pauley) and Pierrot (Jeremie Lippman), as well as an 11-year-old Marcel (Yannis Lespert). The family agrees that Marcel is too young to handle the news of Léo's affliction.

Unknown to them, Marcel has eavesdropped on the family table, and is aware that his near-perfect world is about to come tumbling down.

Mom and Dad and the younger brothers are supportive of Léo, who is plunged into a morbid depression, resisting all the daily medications available to patients with HIV+.

Finally, Léo decides to go to Paris to seek treatment. He gets the family's permission to take Marcel along on a road trip, since both of them have been acting strangely lately.

In Paris, Léo confronts former lovers and old friends. The reunions aren't happy for him. Tensions arise between Marcel and Léo, leading to Marcel's return to rural France on the train alone. He doesn't know if he'll ever see Léo again.

WHAT THE CRITICS SAID

"Director Christophe Honoré dares to make Marcel the emotional center of this deeply felt film, and luckily, Lespert rises to the challenge, turning in one of the best juvenile performances of recent years. Marcel goes through a lot and hangs tough throughout."
Dom Willmott

Cold Showers

(Douches froides; 2005)

An Emotionally Awkward *Ménage à Trois*

This French film marks the debut of filmmaker Antony Cordier, better known for his documentaries. It is an erotic coming-of-age story that spins around two good-looking young men and a beautiful girl whose lives become entangled.

Brunette newcomer Salomé Stevenin as Vanessa gets naked and shows off every crevice of her body. Full frontal male nudity will also give gays in the audience a treat.

The plot spins around Mickael (played by Johan Libéreau), a judo enthusiast who lives in poverty with his parents. Mickael is Vanessa's boyfriend. The storyline picks up speed with the entrance of Clément (Pierre Perrier), the new kid on the block. He's also a judo freak and comes from *nouveau riche* parents. Clément quickly bonds with Mickael. The three teenagers propel themselves into sex. Although this encounter passes breezily at first, it later leads to jealousy on Mickael's part. Call this one a tragic comedy. The director is in love with his stars on a sensual level.

WHAT THE CRITICS SAID:
"Tech package is adequate but uninteresting, with the general look and sound on par with similar low-budget French pics. Full frontal male and female nudity, as well as the sex scenes, will probably stop film being seen by the teen demographic depicted in most territories."
Leslie Felperin, *Variety*

"When the pair bond over an upcoming tournament, and Clément helps Mickael to lose some weight for the meet, Vanessa is hesitant to accept the outspoken newcomer. As the bond between Mickael and Clément strengthens, Vanessa's increasingly complex role in the pair's friendship leads the trio through a series of sacrifices and emotional revelations that will result in a profoundly affecting sexual encounter for all three conflicted teens."
Jason Buchanan

Color Me Kubrick

(2005)

A "True-ish" Account of a Flamboyant Con Man

John Malkovich delivers a hilarious performance as a flamboyantly gay fruitcake con-man who successfully impersonates director Stanley Kubrick despite scant knowledge of the helmer's work. The British film is actually based on a true event that occurred during the production of Kubrick's last film (a disaster), *Eyes Wide Shut*. If you were unfortunate enough to have seen that one, it starred the very heterosexual Tom Cruise, walking around on platform shoes, and Nicole Kidman. (That's the picture where they sued one journalist who claimed that Kubrick had to bring in a sex therapist to teach them how to play straight love.)

In full camp mode, Malkovich romps through the film as con-man Alan Conway, who as Kubrick's impersonator leads the good life at other people's expense and cons hopeful young men into taking off their pants to satisfy his libido. Most of the action takes place in London during the 90s.

Malkovich is awash in accents, mannerisms, and constant narcissistic invention—and in some ways he's never been better. It was the role he was destined to play, insulting living actors by referring to them as "Little Tommy Cruise" or "Miss Kirk Douglas."

From the inception of the project, both the screenwriter and director were deeply familiar with the material. Helmer Brian Cook, who made his feature debut with this film, worked with the real Kubrick for some 30 years, and was assistant director on such films as *The Shining, Barry Lyndon,* and *Eyes Wide Shut.* The scripter, Anthony Frewin, first worked with Kubrick on *2001: A Space Odyssey.*

In a rather brilliant scene, the Kubrick posturing comes to an end when Conway meets New York Times theater critic Frank Rich (William Hootkins) and his wife Alex (Marisa Berenson) in a London restaurant. Rich becomes suspicious and eventually exposes Conway.

The aptly named con artist, Conway, died in 1998, three months before Kubrick himself.

Come Undone

(*Presque rien;* 2002)

First Love and the Havoc It Can Wreak

This is a sensual French film, the work of director Sébastien Lifshitz, who also was the co-author of the script. It stars two handsome young teenagers cavorting in the summer surf on the north coast of France and falling in love. A shower jerk-off and a naked beach sex scene add welcome touches of eroticism.

Mathieu (Jérémie Elkaïm) spends the summer in his mother's summer house in Brittany. There, one day on the beach, he meets ex-hustler Cédric (Stéphane Rideau), and a love affair blossoms between the two boys. Rideau, incidentally, is one of France's biggest indie stars (his t*our de force* was *Wild Reeds*).

The story line is a bit difficult to follow, consisting of long flashbacks and bits and pieces of the present, even time forward movements into the future. Nonetheless, it's engrossing, ranking up there with *Beautiful Thing*.

It wouldn't be a film without its complications. Mathieu's mother (Dominique Reymond) is very ill and confined to her bed, where she's taken care of by the boy's aunt, Annick (Marie Matheron). Mathieu's sour younger sister Sarah (Laetitia Legrix) is thoroughly bitchy.

The story of 18-year-old Mathieu's initiation into homosexuality and first love, his subsequent suicide attempt and recovery, leaves a lot unexplained for viewers. But, even so, it captures that emotional turbulence of late adolescence when many teenagers are trying to figure out who they are and come to terms in this case with their sexual preference.

WHAT THE CRITICS SAID
"The depiction of Mathieu and Cédric's intense affair, whose ecstatic interludes are interrupted by angry spats, feels utterly real. While the movie has abundant male nudity and one hot sex scene, the camera never seems voyeuristic because everything is seen from Mathieu's essentially innocent perspective."
The New York Times

Compulsion

(1959)

The Love That Dare Not Speak Its Name

This movie was released just before the ban on mentioning homosexuality on the screen was lifted. Under such restrictions, director Richard Fleischer and screenwriter Richard Murphy had to tiptoe through the tulips to re-create the drama of the famous Leopold and Loeb case.

Two brilliant law students, nineteen-year-old Nathan Leopold and eighteen-year-old Richard Loeb at the University of Chicago, murdered fourteen-year-old Bobby Franks on May 21, 1924. Their desire was to commit the "perfect crime."

Variety claimed "That the boys have a homosexual relationship is quite clear, though the subject is not overstressed." *The New York Times* also noted the screenplay's "showy inference of homosexuality."

Giving two of the best performances of their careers, Bradford Dillman was cast as Artie Straus and Dean Stockwell, former child star, as Judd Steiner. Judd's eyeglasses are found near the scene of the crime, which is the artifact that leads to the capture of the killers.

Many critics noted that Stockwell and Dillman, as the two leads, were "snobbish, self-satisfied, young, homosexual college men who are unbelievable in their utter smugness and of their almighty attitude." The conceit of their intellect was so profound that neither one had any remorse whatsoever for the cold-blooded murder that they so heartlessly committed. In real life, little Bobby Franks put up a fight for his life—blood, not his own, was found underneath his fingernails—but the men overpowered him and strangled the kid to death.

Orson Welles is the defense lawyer. He is called Jonathan Wilk in the script but he is clearly based on the famous lawyer Clarence Darrow.

The performance of Welles is short, but is one of the finest of his career. One reviewer noted he appears as "heavy set, beetle-browed, gray hair descending in a drooping cowlick, the personification of a wise humanitarian."

The Conrad Boys

(2006)

How Far Would You Go for Love?

Captivating newcomer Justin Lo makes his film debut as Charlie Conrad, a 19-year-old history buff with the weight of the world on his shoulders. In descending order, Lo is also the producer, director, editor, and writer. One reviewer suggested that he should have hired a better actor for the lead "but then this low-budget indie would lack its vanity project *raison d'être*."

Just when Lo, playing Charlie, a high school senior, is accepted at Columbia University, his mother suddenly dies. He is forced to postpone college to work at a local joint to support his 9-year-old sibling, Ben, whose real name is "Boo Boo" Stewart.

Strapped with new parental responsibility, Charlie yearns for freedom and romance. He gets part of his dream when he meets Jordan Rivers (Nick Bartzen), a charismatic drifter. They embark on a torrid romance. We admire Lo for treating Charlie's gayness as a non-issue; his Eurasian genes are also handled matter-of-factly.

And then the villain of the piece arrives in the form of Doug (Barry Shay), Charlie's long-lost father. He returns to town and wants to take care of Ben himself, claiming he has reformed. Caught in a struggle to keep Ben and eager to hold onto Jordan, Charlie must do some soul-searching to make the most momentous decision of his life. *LA Weekly Film + TV Reviews* suggested that "the script's insights are drawn straight from freshman-dorm late-night rap sessions."

WHAT THE CRITICS SAID
"Charlie gets involved with sexy but irresponsible drifter Jordan (Nick Bartzen, persuasive in a sketchy part), whose troubled past instigates eventual silly melodramatics that nonetheless enliven tepid screenplay. While Lo's multi-hyphenate moxie is admirable, his bad bowl haircut, scant screen charisma and pedestrian dialogue suggest future projects should be more collaborative."
Dennis Harvey, *Variety*

Consenting Adult

(1985)

"Mother, I Am a Homosexual"

Novelist Laura Z. Hobson became famous for her book about anti-Semitism, which was made into a widely acclaimed movie, *Gentleman's Agreement*, released in 1947 and starring Gregory Peck.

Director Gilbert Cates brings to the screen another novel of hers, *Consenting Adult*, in which a teenager confesses to his family, "I am a homosexual." Barry Tubb (Jeff Lynd) plays the son of Tess (Marlo Thomas) and Ken Lynd (Martin Sheen) who are devastated by the news of their only son's homosexuality.

Gay son tells mother: "I know you don't want to believe it. I don't want to believe it either. I've been fighting against it for years. But it's true and it just gets truer."

It took a decade for Hollywood to finally green light this film. The "gay 70s" had come and gone before ABC-TV finally broadcast the 100-minute feature. By then the AIDS hysteria was in full bloom.

Marlo Thomas was cast in an unattractive role of a mother having to deal with her son's "sickness." Eventually she tries to understand and come to terms with her son. But Sheen, as the humorless father, would rather die, and in the end he does just that, never having reached a reconciliation with his offspring.

Previously, Sheen had been cast as a gay man having an affair with Hal Holbrook's character in *That Certain Summer* (1972).

The young boy's sister, Margie (Talia Balsam), unlike her parents, is able to accept her brother's homosexuality with grace.

In the end, as can be predicted, dear ol' Mum comes around. At college, she calls her son and invites him for Christmas. And, yes, his lover, Stu (Joseph Adams), is also invited to join in the Yuletide cheer.

Contadora Is for Lovers

(2006)

An Engaging Bisexual Romp Through Paradise

This film was written, produced, developed, and directed by Hollywood iconoclast, Brazilian/Panamanian Jorge Ameer, producer of several other GLBTQ films.

Contadora Is for Lovers represents the fruition of a complicated series of negotiations whereby Ameer persuaded the tourist authorities of an unspoiled tropical paradise, the Panamanian Island of Contadora, to turn their beaches and jungles over for a film production which, presumably, brought the island's many charms to the attention of North American holiday-makers. (By anyone's standards, Ameer's persuasiveness quotient is high—the fact that local authorities agreed to the use of their island for the production of a bisexual-themed film is remarkable.)

This sun-drenched paradise provides a sensual and sybaritic setting for Ameer's study in the expression of and acceptance of bisexuality. Newlyweds Mike (as played by Vincent De Paul) and Helen (Renée Pietrangelo) arrive on-island to celebrate their recent marriage. Into the equation steps Gabriel (Tony Sago), the ingratiating and very humpy guest services director of the resort they've selected. Gabriel, we learn, is not above preying upon the occasional (willing) male guest for whom palm trees, piña coladas, and feminine charms simply aren't enough.

During an all-male circumnavigation of Contadora, Mike and Gabriel do, indeed, become physically entangled, and eventually swap fluids between bouts of nude sunbathing and swatting at fire ants and mosquitoes.

As might be expected in these brouhahas, their growing sense of commitment to each other eventually forces a confrontation with Helen, who by now has spent a lot of time dining alone and staring at the sea. The holiday isn't completely ruined, however, and before long, everyone manages to pile into the same hammock, ensuring that a good time is had by all. By the end of the film, it's virtually guaranteed that this new gringo marriage can't continue as a closed or self-contained system ever again.

Côte d'Azur

(Crustaces & coquillages; 2004)

The Family That Lays Together, Stays Together

Real-life partners Olivier Ducastel and Jacques Martineau both wrote and directed this French farce set on the *Côte d'Azur* (French Riviera). Its genre is a comedy/musical/romance. It's all here: Masturbation, adultery, homosexuality.

For a summer vacation, Marc (Gilbert Melki) and his sexy wife, Béatrix (Valeria Bruni Tedeschi) take their kids to the seaside house of Marc's youth. Almost immediately their daughter, Laura (Sabrina Seyvecou) takes up with a biker and heads west for Portugal.

Romain Torres plays Charly, the curly-haired son whose purported homosexuality has the *paterfamilias* in a tizzy. "Being Dutch," Mom is more tolerant as she pursues her own adulterous lifestyle.

Charly invites Martin (Édouard Collin), a former schoolmate, to enjoy the holiday with his family. Martin is in love with Charly. Martin's sexual frustration propels the plot in unexpected directions. There is one scene in which daddy watches Martin masturbate in the shower.

While mama is engaged in her affair with her ardent lover, Mathieu (Jacques Bonnaffé), the plot takes a detour. An old flame of Marc's appears, the hunky local plumber (Jean-Marc Barr) who really knows how to fix pipes.

The original title of *Crustaces et Coquillages* (Crabs and Oysters) is, of course, a reference to the infamous speech that Lord Laurence Olivier delivered to a half-clothed Tony Curtis in the film, *Spartacus.*

We get all this and singing and dancing too, French style.

WHAT THE CRITICS SAID
"Watching the featherweight French farce *Cote d'Azur* provides the oxymoronic sensation of looking at a pornographic movie with no real sex or even a credible approximation of erotic heat. The stream of gay and straight couplings in this dizzy pansexual comedy is contrived and ludicrous."
Stephen Holden, *The New York Times*

The Country Teacher

(Venkovský ucitel; 2008)

A Gay vs. Straight Variation of Maugham's *Rain*

It is rare when a Czech gay-themed film arouses world interest, but such is the case with this film. Director Bohdan Sláma both directed and wrote the screenplay for this excellent movie which won 5 international awards.

Tired of the gay life in Prague, Petr (Pavel Liska), a young teacher of natural sciences, leaves the big city for a rural setting where some of the houses don't even have indoor plumbing. In doing so, he breaks up with his boorish lover (Marek Daniel).

In a small village, Petr establishes a bond with a farm woman, Maria (Zuzana Bydzovská), who becomes a sort of soulmate. When she makes a move toward him, he does not respond. Unaware that he is a homosexual, she feels he's rejecting her because of her age.

Maria keeps Petr in her life, but makes a mistake when she asks him to tutor her rebellious seventeen-year-old son, Lada (Ladislav Sedivý) who seems to have a perpetual hard-on. But for girls, alas. The boy would rather be fucking some girl in a barn loft.

WHAT THE CRITICS SAID
"The sad, serious joke of *The Country Teacher* is that the tender love and care Petr lavishes can't begin to kindle desire in a young, straight teenager who is entirely unaware of Petr's true feelings. Eventually, against his better judgment, Petr makes his move. His nature has its way. The flesh is weak, and lust is lust, no matter how lofty, well-meaning gestures are thrown in as camouflage."
Stephen Holden, *The New York Times*

"Sláma explores a basic situation with such insight into the human heart that it becomes an instance of a small, intimate film that quietly develops an emotional impact of unexpected power."
Kevin Thomas, *Los Angeles Times*

Cowboys and Angels

(2005)

Coming of Age in Modern Ireland

Shane Butler is a handsome but geeky 20 years old who feels that life is passing him by. A talented artist who longs to go to Art School, he spends his days stuck in a horrible job behind a desk in the civil service. When he moves into an apartment in Ireland's Limerick City with Vincent Cusack, a gay fashion student, things begin to look up. Despite being poles apart on almost every level, Shane and Vincent soon become close friends.

Vincent's artistry, evident in everything he puts his hand to, inspires Shane to greatness. When he meets and falls head over heels in love with Gemma, an ex-art student and best friend of Vincent's who now works in a fast food joint, he feels compelled to make some radical changes to his life.

Fate steps in to lend a hand in the form of Keith, a drug dealer who lives downstairs. Keith offers Shane the opportunity to make a lot of money by going on a drug run to Dublin. At first Shane refuses. But he desperately needs the cash.

He goes on the drug run and lives to regret it. With the money he has made Vincent transforms himself—"Pretty Woman" style—into one of the hippest cats in town. Unknown to Shane, though, some shady figures have tailed him back from Dublin and are now watching his apartment.

When Vincent finds out the source of Shane's cash they have a terrible confrontation which spells the end of their friendship. With the death of Shane's closest friend at work, Shane goes off the rails and plunges into an emotional abyss, culminating in an unforgettable night at the "Mud Club" after which Shane re-examines his whole life.

Shane renews his friendship with Vincent and helps him complete the collection for his graduate fashion show. At home, celebrating their success, the police burst in and arrest both of them.

Convinced that this is the end of the road, Shane and Vincent are unaware that redemption is near.

Cruel and Unusual

(2006)

Transgendered Women in Men's Prisons

This unusual 66-minute docu takes an unflinching look at the lives of transgendered women in men's prisons. Shot over a period of three years, the film challenges the viewer's basic ideas about gender and justice with graphic stories, vibrant landscape portraits, and stark prison footage.

The film's creation was a labor of love by directors Reid Williams, Janet Baus, and Dan Hunt, who told the story of such transgendered women as Ashley, Linda, Anna, Yolanda, and Ophelia, each of whom was incarcerated in a men's prison anywhere between Wyoming and Florida. Denied medical and psychological treatment, and ongoing victims of rape and violence, the docu asks if the punishment for their crimes is indeed cruel and unusual.

Prison officials determine where to place inmates based on their genitalia, not their gender identity. Ophelia, for example, has lived in a man's body for all of her 46 years. She now is jailed in Virginia, having been sentenced for 67 years for bank robbery with an unloaded gun. Denied female hormone treatments, Ophelia felt she had no choice but to mutilate her genitals to force the system "to finish what I started."

Anna Connelly had been living successfully as a woman, raising her son, and working toward sexual reassignment surgery. She was on hormone therapy as prescribed by a doctor for five years before she was incarcerated. Thereafter, she was refused additional hormone treatments and placed into solitary confinement, which contributed to her later attempts at suicide.

Ashley, an inmate in Arkansas, said, "A lot of times I wake up, and I look around at my surroundings—and I see all these men. And I think, what am I doing here?"

Once a person begins estrogen treatment, their body stops producing hormones, which is akin to denying a woman hormones after a hysterectomy. Coupled with the psychological effects of returning facial hair and losing breasts, transsexuality in prison becomes an untenable situation.

Crutch

(2004)

A Student & His Teacher in Love

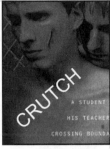

Crutch is a dark and intensely personalized family drama that's based on a historical and autobiographical recitation of catastrophes from the filmmaker's childhood in suburban New Jersey. It transmits a belief in the premise that the exorcism of psychological demons can occur in the aftermath of a public disclosure of pain.

It's doubtful that anyone will see this without disturbing memories of his or her own Gothic childhood. More than anything else, good writing and a red-hot performance from lead actor Eben Gordon keep viewers tuned to the nuances of this personalized exorcism of family-derived anguish.

Eben Gordon plays David, the cutest, brightest, and most talented 16-year-old in the history of the Garden State. Members of the audience are not the only ones who want to adopt him: The character of Kenny, skillfully portrayed by the film's writer, co producer, and director, Rob Moretti, succeeds in actually maneuvering his way into legal custody of this brilliant but isolated teenager when his mother, foggy and in the throes of detox, signs over his care and custody.

Thirty-something Kenny, toxic and bitter, and unimpressed with his present gig as a method acting teacher in a public high school, has already "made it" in Hollywood, impressing his young pupils with his acting resumé, but never answering their query about why he has descended from Olympus for residency in the suburban hinterlands.

Emphasizing the fact that he's underaged, David is adorable as a teenager barely old enough to have a learner's permit. Their first kiss occurs after Kenny successfully navigates David through a driving lesson. Considering the 16-year-old's raw and surging talent, and the shit that seems to tumble down upon him from all sides, what red-blooded older gay male wouldn't develop a Lolito-obsession, reinforced by pride at having rescued the lad from his existential hell?

The Crying Game

(1992)

The Famous Movie with "The Twist"

Irish director Neil Jordan's seventh film was his best. This movie was one of the most daring and controversial in 1992. It begins when a blue-collar English soldier named Jody (Forest Whitaker), is seduced by a foxy member of an IRA group (Miranda Richardson), and then kidnapped by her cronies and held as hostage to be exchanged with the British for one of their own men. The film unfolds as both a thriller and an unconventional romance, exploring themes of race and gender, certainly sexuality.

Jody is black, noting that Northern Ireland is "the one place in the world where they'll call you a nigger to your face." In captivity, an unlikely friendship develops between Jody and Fergus (Stephen Rea), an IRA volunteer who has been assigned to guard Jody. The relationship becomes rather intimate when Jody asks Fergus to take out his penis so he can urinate. "It's only a piece of meat."

In an attempt to escape, Jody gets hit by a British army tank before squadrons of soldiers shoot up the secret IRA hideout. Fleeing to England, Fergus keeps a promise he made to Jody while he held him as a prisoner.

He looks up his "special friend" Dil (brilliantly played by Jaye Davidson). Calling himself "Jimmy," Fergus is hired as a day laborer. He starts dating Dil, who is unaware of his IRA connections. But there's a lot about this hairdresser that Fergus doesn't know. He's about to find out.

As one critic noted, Dil is a "fascinating creature with myriad contradictory traits . . . hot and cold, petulant and seductive, needy and fiercely independent." She lures Fergus into a relationship that will test how far he's willing to go in the name of love.

When Fergus finally gets around to exploring below the belt, he discovers that Dil has a penis—not a vagina. Initially, at least, he appears revolted.

The Damned

(1969)

A Nazi Movie of Great Perversity

The Damned (La caduta degli dei in Italian) is a movie of great perversity. If only Eric von Stroheim were alive, he might have directed it. Instead we get Luchino Visconti, who shows us he can be as perverse as the master himself. In Europe, the film was generally released under the title of *Gotterdammerung*. How apt.

In a nutshell, this war drama is about the collapse of a rich industrialist family during the early reign (1933-34) of the Third Reich .

What's not to like about this movie? Incest, rape, gay orgies, suicide, murder, drug abuse, jet-black Nazi uniforms, transvestite SA gatherings, a son stripping and bedding his own mother, the divinely beautiful Helmut Berger in a brilliant drag impersonation of Marlene Dietrich. Film and theater critic John Simon claimed that Berger didn't do his own Dietrich vocals. Actually he did, and did so perfectly.

Most critics, except for Pauline Kael and Rex Reed, claimed that Berger played it gay. It would appear so on first viewing, but actually he was playing a "prissy heterosexual." Such creatures do exist, as you know.

If you can't always follow the plot, welcome to the club. The film seems to have been based loosely on the fortunes of the Krupp dynasty. An SA man Konstantin (Rene Kolldehoff) moves toward Nazifying the family's vast assets. Frederick Bruckman (Dirk Bogarde), as the lover of Baroness Sophie von Essenbeck (Ingrid Thulin), hopes to prevent that from happening, with the aid of his cousin, an SS member named Aschenbach (Helmut Griem).

Griem, a stunningly handsome man, is better known for his appearance as the bisexual baron who seduces both Liza Minnelli and Michael York in *Cabaret*.

Frederick's dreams are usurped by Sophie's *über*-Nazi son Martin (Berger), whose pastimes include child molestation and incestuous longings.

Daphne

(2007)

Daphne du Maurier's Lesbian Romps

"Last night I dreamt I went to Manderley again." Who can forget Daphne du Maurier's immortal line from *Rebecca*?

Would that there could have been more of them in Clare Beavan's helmed script by Amy Jenkins based on the Margaret Forster bio.

Actress Geraldine Somerville attempts to bring the bisexual British writer to the screen. The author referred to herself as a boy and was smitten by both sexes. The story unfolds between her post-war plagiarism trial and the writing of *My Cousin Rachel*, which was made into a movie starring Olivia de Havilland.

The movie primarily focuses on Du Maurier's unrequited love for Ellen Doubleday (Elizabeth McGovern), who is married to the author's publisher. Christopher Malcolm (*Absolutely Fabulous*) camps it up as Nelson Doubleday.

At a party, Noël Coward (Malcolm Sinclair) introduces Du Maurier to the actress Gertrude Lawrence (Janet McTeer). "She's one of us," Coward tells Du Maurier.

Du Maurier's lusting for an unattainable woman (Ellen Doubleday) grows a bit tedious, but Gertrude is more receptive to a relationship.

In one sense, *Daphne* is the story of a woman's struggle with her own sexuality. It highlights excerpts from her letters of the time. "I was a boy of 18 all over again, nervous hands and a beating heart, incurably romantic and wanting to throw a cloak before his lady's feet. I wanted to ride out and fight dragons for you." Sounds like love to us.

The BBC first introduced this film to mark the centenary of Du Maurier's birth. It followed in the wake of the groundbreaking BBC miniseries about Vita Sackville-West's turbulent affair with Violete Trefusis. Later *Daphne* was released on DVD in the United States by BBC Warner.

Dare

(2010)

Do Something You're Afraid Of

The cast of queer star icons—Sandra Bernhard, Katy Huffman, and Alan Cumming—might be enough to get you to rent this DVD. Originally a short on the *Boys Life 5 Collection*, this gorgeously crafted film is directed by Adam Salky based on a script by David Brind.

Presented in a clean, crisp style, *Dare* gives a fresh new spin on the much-clichéd tale of coming out. The action, such as it is, takes place in a tony suburb along Philadelphia's Main Line.

A mysterious and very hot bad boy, Johnny Drake (Zach Gilford) becomes the object of lust from both Alexa (Emmy Rossum) and her so-called boyfriend Ben Berger (Ashley Springer).

Before coming to the party at Johnny's home, Alexa has performed a scene for Grant Matson (Cumming), a successful actor. She wants his opinion of her talent, or lack thereof.

He tells her that her acting shows that she's a virgin and lacks life experiences. His advice is for her to pursue lust and desire, which will favorably affect her performances on stage. As a remedy for her "ignorance," she plots to seduce Johnny.

Ben has the same idea. The hottest scene is out by Johnny's pool where Ben confesses that he's never been kissed before. Johnny decides to remedy that situation. Once Johnny's lips descend on Ben, his pent-up lust is unleashed.

Is a *ménage a trois* in the works?

Although Ben's homosexuality is obvious, Johnny's true sexual preference remains blurred. At any rate, that scene by the pool made the waters bubble.

WHAT THE CRITICS SAID
"Smart and edgy"
San Francisco Chronicle

"Surprising and dangerous"
New York Magazine

Death in Venice

(*Morte a Venezia;* 1970)

Lusting for the Beautiful Boy Tadzio

Luchino Visconti directed and scripted this screenplay based partly on the concept of passion as a metaphor for confusion and degradation. It was based on the novella by Thomas Mann, first published in German in 1912 as *Der Tod in Venedig.* The rigorously disciplined Gustav von Aschenbach (as played by the late gay actor Dirk Bogarde) was to some extent based on the avant garde composer Gustav Mahler.

Von Aschenbach arrives at the Lido near Venice where he checks into the Grand Hotel des Bains. Suffering from mental exhaustion, he discovers a city ripe with Freudian insights and orgiastic Dionysian imagery.

His monastic aesceticism is interrupted when he spots the stunningly beautiful Tadzio (Björn Andrésen), a fourteen-year-old in a sailor suit who evokes "Narcissus smiling at his own reflection." Tadzio's aristocratic and ferociously protective mother, a Polish aristocrat, is played by the famous Italian actress Silvana Mangano.

Like Marlon Brando in the film he shot with Elizabeth Taylor, *Reflections in a Golden Eye*, Von Aschenbach dyes his hair and pathetically paints his face. He is getting ready for "the hunt," a hopeless undertaking, as if the young boy could possibly be sexually attracted to him.

The setting is before the Great War when Venice is under siege from a cholera epidemic, the existence of which is denied by city officials, not wanting to lose the tourist lire.

After weeks of agony, wherein the older man admiring the youth from afar, they encounter one another briefly. Rising from the ruins of his own dignity, the older, impotent man whispers, "You must never smile like that to anyone. I love you."

This is a platonic love story involving dreams one almost dares not dream. Von Aschenbach's last memory is seeing Tadzio in the ocean lifting his arm. Is he beckoning to Von Aschenbach? It's too late. As the older man lifts his arm in response, he struggles to rise from his beach chair. But at this crucial moment, his heart fails him.

Deathtrap

(1982)

Murder, Mayhem, & Betrayal

When the first reviews of *Deathtrap* came out, there was hardly a mention that the two leading male characters, Michael Caine (Sidney Bruhl) and Christopher Reeve (Clifford Anderson) were homosexual lovers. Of course, Sidney has a wife, Myra, as played by Dyan Cannon.

To write too much about this "play within a play" would give away the surprises and gimmicks that inhabit this movie, which was based on a play by Ira Levin (*Rosemary's Baby*) and adapted for the screen by Sidney Lumet as director. Twist upon twist makes an absorbing mystery, even though it's a bit overdone.

Sidney, a once-celebrated playwright, is slipping. As one member of his audience put it, "It's the worst play I've ever seen." Another said, "I can't believe Sidney Bruhl wrote it."

Sidney receives a script from Clifford, and is insanely jealous as he reads it. He tells his wife, "The play is so good a gifted director couldn't even hurt it."

Sidney concocts a scene whereby he will kill Clifford and claim the play as his own, thinking it would run for years and make millions.

Shortly after Clifford's arrival, however, things aren't what they're supposed to be. Viewers must speculate where the line between truth and deception begins.

Both Caine and Reeve play off each other brilliantly, each actor at peak performance. As the wife, Cannon provides set decoration.

WHAT THE CRITICS SAID
"Deathtrap still contains its fair share of claptrap, but it's become a dandy little movie, faithful to Levin's flamboyant theatricality yet artfully transcribed by a cinematic style that gives the illusion of reality."
David Ansen, *Newsweek*

The Deep End

(2001)

What to Do with the Dead Lover of Your Gay Son

This thriller is based on a 1947 crime novel named *The Blank Wall* by Elizabeth Sanxay Holding. Originally, Max Ophuls brought it to the screen in 1949 as *The Reckless Moment* with James Mason and Joan Bennett.

In this updated version, directors Scott McGehee and David Siegel changed the gender of the child in the movie, making him a homosexual.

The movie pivots around the mother, Tilda Swinton, playing Margaret Hall, a woman who spirals out of control trying to keep her son from being found culpable in a murder investigation.

This mother of three lives in a home on the shores of Lake Tahoe in Nevada. Her husband, an admiral, is away at sea, and she struggles to bring up her three kids.

The one that causes her the most trouble is the oldest, 17-year-old Beau (Jonathan Tucker). From the beginning, we know he's gay when he visits a club in Reno where he's involved with Darby (Josh Lucas), who is 13 years older than him.

Although Margaret does not make her son's homosexuality an issue, she feels that Darby is bad news for her boy. One night when Darby visits Beau at their lakeside boathouse, they have a fight. Later the drunken Darby stumbles, falls, and (accidentally) kills himself.

When Margaret finds the body the next morning, she assumes that Beau killed the older man. From that point on, Margaret begins a cover-up to protect her son.

Blackmail is just one of her problems. A critic claimed that *The Deep End* "creates that kind of suspense Hitchcock liked, in which an innocent person is wrongly accused, looks guilty, and tries to cope and lacks essential information."

In its focus on a mother/son relationship, the film becomes more than a thriller, examining what people will do, however unreasonable, when faced with extreme circumstances.

Deliverance

(1972)

A Machismo Nightmare in Troubled Waters

John Boorman helmed this screen adaptation of the James Dickey novel. Dickey also wrote the screenplay about four Atlanta urbanites who set out to see the Cahulawassee River before it's turned into a huge lake. Their river-rafting trip, filmed in northeast Georgia, turns into a nightmare as they explore one of America's most dangerous back countries.

The film put Burt Reynolds, with his Mephistophelean swagger and chewy, good ol' boy drawl, on the Hollywood map.

In a very different role from that of Joe Buck in the Oscar-winning *Midnight Cowboy,* Jon Voight delivers an equally stunning performance.

The supporting cast includes Ronny Cox as Drew and Ned Beatty as Bobby. Poor Bobby (Beatty). For the rest of his life, he has had to endure "squeal like a pig" heckling in the wake of *Deliverance's* notorious hillbilly rape scene.

The creepy rednecks, many of whom still live in the State of Georgia, turn the lives of this adventuresome quartet into hell. These city slickers should have stayed on the golf course. They discover a forgotten wilderness where the scenery is beautiful, the toothless, grinning tobacco spitters demons from hell.

Before this trip is over, one of the canoe party will be dead; another will be raped by a demented hillbilly, and the other two men have each killed a redneck psycho with a bow and arrow.

WHAT THE CRITICS SAID
"Dickey lards this plot with a lot of significance—universal, local, whatever happens to be on the market. He is clearly under the impression that he is telling us something about the nature of man, and particularly civilized man's ability to survive primitive challenges. Survival is the name of the game, the macho Burt Reynolds assures us. The scenes of violence and rape work, although in a disgusting way."
Roger Ebert

De-Lovely

(2004)

Cole Porter in Pursuit of Beautiful Young Men

This latest biography of composer Cole Porter takes great liberties with the facts. Porter was a ravenous homosexual, not a discerning bisexual as the film portrays. But, even so, it's a far greater improvement over the 1946 biopic, *Night and Day,* where the gay actor, Cary Grant, played Porter as rigorously hetero.

Although he fooled his fans and the censors at the time, many of Porter's lyrics were actually written about men instead of women. Take this line for instance: "They're not her lips, but they're such tempting lips that, if some night, you're free, then it's all right, yes, it's all right with me."

Director Irwin Winkler miscast Kevin Kline as Porter. The actor was 57 at the time, and he's unconvincing as the late composer who was in his late 20s in some scenes of the movie. At least Winkler directed Kline to play it gay, even though the script sanitized much of his life.

Ashley Judd as Porter's loving wife, Linda, in many respects was no more than a "beard." Judd appears rather stiff in her vital role, though looking "De-Lovely" in all that period dress.

The film follows Porter from New York to Hollywood, and on to Paris. Focusing on Porter's love for Linda, and presenting his homosexuality as an occasional flirtation, it departs from reality.

Big stars such as Sheryl Crow, Natalie Cole, and Elvis Costello were brought in to sing Porter's usually radiant songs. Regrettably, the songs come off as rather joyless, not the show stoppers they were when first heard by audiences. Our favorite moment is when Kline and an actor, John Barrowman, sing "Night and Day" and then go off together to make love.

Because of an accident, Porter was wheelchair bound for his last 27 years and endured great pain. When he died, hits which reflected the popular taste of the day, such as "Gay Divorcee," "Anything Goes," "Kiss Me, Kate," and "Can-Can" survived, but without their original gusto, of course.

Desert Hearts

(1985)

Called the Best Lezzie Film Ever Made

Wolfe has released a new two-disc Collector's Edition of the lesbian classic *Desert Hearts*, originally filmed in 1985. Packed with bonus features, the new DVD feature includes never-before-seen bonus footage from that now-famous woman/woman love scene.

This release heralds the launch of the new Wolfe vintage collection, whose aim involves the reintroduction of classic queer imagery to new generatins of today's audiences.

Based on a novel by Jane Rule, and directed by Donna Deitch, *Desert Hearts* is set in 1950s Nevada. Professor Vivian Bell (Helen Shaver) arrives to get a divorce. At the time of casting, Shaver was an underrated Canadian actress of cool elegance. Arriving in Reno by train, she meets Cay Rivvers (Patricia Charbonneau), an unabashed lesbian who falls in love with Vivian at first sight.

The third star of the film is Frances Parker (Audra Lindley), a no-nonsense older woman who runs the guest ranch where divorcees-in-the-making wait out their Nevada residency requirements.

Eventually Vivian and Cay perform what became a notorious sex scene, although this is not a soft porn movie. Back in the Reagan era, it caused a lot of steam and a lot of comments. The emotions released by the developing intimacy of the relationship of the two women, and Vivian's insecurities about her feelings toward Cay, are played out against a backdrop of rocky landscapes and country and western songs, including those of Patsy Cline.

This was one of the first films to portray lesbians in a normal, positive manner.

WHAT THE CRITICS SAID
"The chemistry between these two women is amazing and it shows on film. Their intense stares, awkward fumblings, and deep passion make even the worst of dialogues shine."
www.opinions.com

The Devil Wears Prada

(2006)

The Gayest Mainstream Movie Ever Made

As the Queen of all she surveys, and the fearsome editrix of *Runway* magazine, Meryl Streep proves once again that she's incomparable. Within this fashion world fantasy, she plays the terrifying editor, Miranda Priestly, who bears a strong resemblance to Anna Wintour.

With a crested gray mane and laser glare, Streep as Miranda wears the world's chicest wardrobe, one dazzling outfit after another. With her modulated stealth missile sarcasm, she is a monster…but what a glorious monster.

The movie is based on a best-selling *roman à clef* drivel that was inspired by Lauren Weisberger's stint as assistant to the editor-in-chief of *Vogue*, Anna Wintour. Within Weisberger's book, the fictional Elias-Clark publishing company is said to be modeled after Condé Nast.

Wintour—pardon, Miranda—runs the magazine like Stalin presiding over the Kremlin. Andy Sachs, as played by *Brokeback Mountain*'s Anne Hathaway, is a recent university grad with journalistic ambitions. She gets hired as Miranda's flunky. She is told repeatedly that a million girls "would kill for this job."

Andy settles uneasily into her new job and her 15-minute lunches, performing tasks that rival the Twelve Labors of Hercules, obtaining a pre-pub copy of the newest Harry Potter novel, and getting her boss a flight out of Miami in the middle of a hurricane.

Prada exerted an enormous appeal on gay men. It was estimated that some 20% of the opening audiences in Los Angeles and New York were gay. "And for gay male filmgoers, there's the Meryl factor," said Michael Jensen, editor of afterElton.com. "She's been an icon forever, because gay men admire strong actresses."

There's also the potent appeal of *Devil*'s gay character, Stanley Tucci, who plays a witty, deeply embittered art director. He's not a stereotype, and in fact represents a nice trend toward meaningful gay roles.

The DL Chronicles

(2005)

Men on the Down Low

Focusing on men who lead double lives, this is a sexy, independent anthology of short films by indie directors Quincy LeNear and Deondray Gossett. It tells the story of sexually duplicitous men of color with secret lifestyles. This provocative and intriguing world of sexual discovery, denial, betrayal, love, and loss is called "The Down Low."

"Down Low" African-American men, for appearance's sake, are outwardly straight but secretly engage in sex with men. They date women, have children, and often marry in an effort to appear heterosexual to the public. Deeply closeted, they do not identify as either gay or bisexual. They refuse to hang out in a gay community.

Our favorite episode within this anthology is the story of Wes Thomas (brilliantly performed by Darren Schnase). Its protagonist is a successful real estate broker married to the beautiful Sarah (Jessica Beshir). But he's unhappy because of his closeted attraction to men. When Wes' sexy brother-in-law comes to stay with the couple for a while, the inevitable happens.

Wes is only human and falls for the forbidden fruit in a sexy scene. When Wes wakes up alone the next morning, we are treated to a glorious shot of his naked ass as he lies in the bed.

Jessica Beshir comes on as a sultry blend of Salma Hayek and Dorothy Dandridge. She was born in Mexico City to a Mexican mother and an Ethiopian father. Darren Schnase hails from Down Under. He relocated in the U.S. in 2004 and has appeared in a number of independent film projects.

Another episode, *Robert*, is a romantic dramedy that introduces us to the character of Robert Hall as portrayed by TV star, Terrell Tilford of *Guiding Light*. He plays a closeted talent agent who falls for a hot health food store manager 20 years his junior. What Robert fails to share is that there is a special woman in his life. When his new lover grows suspicious about his many secrets, a game of cat and mouse ensues.

Do I Love You?

(2003)

A Lesbian Woody Allen Roundelay in London

As writer, star and director, Lisa Gornick attracted acclaim as a possible rising talent on this scene in this lesbian comedy/drama/romance. Hers is a romantic philosophical comedy about life and the questions it throws at you.

One viewer suggested that, "If Annie Hall had been made by a bike-riding lesbian Londoner, it might well have turned out something like this."

Viewers noted the "Sapphic navel-gazing and frank sex talk," and many were won over by the film's "honesty, intelligence, and offbeat humor."

At the beginning, Marina (Gornick herself) tells her mother she's breaking up with her girlfriend Romy (Raquel Cassidy). A series of flashbacks follow—at one point Marina considers sleeping with men again. A sub-plot involves Louise (Sarah Patterson) who is investigating and writing about the Sapphic impulse. Will her report lead to any new breakthroughs in the lesbian sexual impulse?

Marina is forever biking around the city, airing her neurotic musings in voiceover. In the meantime, other lesbians couples in her orbit are questioning their own lives, even experimenting with infidelity. The pic lacks a firm backbone and depth of character, but at times conveys real feeling in the lesbian community. Scenes are fragmented and sub-plots not well sewn together, but it does try to answer the question of why Marina "prefers a taco to salami."

WHAT THE CRITICS SAID
"Not so much a conventional narrative as a patchwork of fragmented scenes and barely related sub-plots. *Do I Love You?* is clearly a labor of love for its first-time writer-director-star. So it's a pity it's poorly lit, haphazardly assembled, indifferently acted except for Raquel Cassidy. It's also a shame that Gornick feels the need to demonize men as 'violent creeps' with a penchant for road rage and inappropriate sexual advances."
Neil Smith

Dog Day Afternoon

(1975)

What I Did for Love

Sidney Lumet's famous film, starring Al Pacino, was based on the true events that took place on August 22, 1972 at a Brooklyn bank. Pacino, cast as Sonny Wortzik, attempts to rob a bank so that his male lover can have a sex change operation.

At one point Pacino quit the film, and the role was offered to Dustin Hoffman, but Pacino was persuaded to come back. And well that he did. *Dog Day Afternoon* is now added to some of his most memorable films, side by side with *Serpico* and the three *Godfather* movies.

John Cazale is excellent in the less flashy role of Sonny's partner in crime, Sal. Charles Durning is his usually brilliant self as police lieutenant Moretti.

Almost from the beginning, the bank robbery runs afoul. One of the problems is that the bank is almost out of cash. Outside, as the hours drag on with hostages taken, a circus of rubber-neckers, including aggressive news people, form to watch a reality show.

Two "wives" appear—first Sonny's legal wife, Angie (Susan Peretz), to whom Sonny vows his love as he does for his three children. The second appearance is a surprise. His second wife is Leon Schermer (Chris Saradon), a transwoman whom Sonny "married" in a drag wedding some months earlier with his mother as a witness.

Saradon plays the role with just the right mixture of "fear, dignity, and silliness," in the words of one reviewer. Saradon surprises the police when it's revealed that his would-be patron has tried to kill him on several occasions.

When Sonny realizes he can't make a simple getaway, he demands to be put on a jet to fly out of the United States. Of course, as the viewer already knows, that plan for escape will not work out.

The real-life bank robber, John Wojtowicz, was arrested and convicted in court, and sentenced to 20 years in prison, of which he served 14.

Dog Tags

(2008)

What's Sexier Than a Man in Uniform?

This film stars hunky Paul Preiss (Nate Merritt), playing a young Marine exploring his sexuality with Andy (Bart Fletcher), a queer Goth.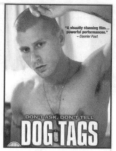

Damion Dietz's drama was said to have been based on his own experiences, from which he fashioned the script and later became its director. Dietz said that part of his inspiration also came from *Midnight Cowboy*, with Dustin Hoffman and Jon Voight, which was voted Best Picture of the Year in 1969.

Fresh from a leave at boot camp, Nate arrives home to surprise his fiancée, finding her with another man. In an unlikely plot twist, Nate sets out AWOL cross country with Andy who has his baby son Travis in tow.

We learn that Andy is longing to relive a romance he had with another Marine. There seems to be several movies rolled into one here, with plots and motivations heading in various directions. There are even issues of overbearing mothers.

Nate became a Marine for all the wrong reasons. He was hoping to impress his mother (Candy Clark) and his trashy fiancée (Amy Lindsay), maybe even the father he's never met. Eventually, he goes on a search for his father, but doesn't seem to impress the indifferent parent.

Highlight of the film is when Nate and Andy end up in a motel room for a tentative sex scene, which is not played out very well. In a review by Don Willmott, he noted several inconsistencies. "Andy's thick eyeliner comes and goes, and Nate's shaved head grows hair and then loses it. Even his dog tags change, appearing both with and without black edges. What's going on?"

The viewer might suspect that a gay romance is about to develop, but it never gets airborne. Nate is nothing if not non-commital.

Even with all its flaws, Blockbuster check-out counters across the country reported a heavy demand for this film. Maybe they were hoping that macho Paul Preiss would show it hard.

The Dresser

(1983)

Part Bossy Nanny, Part Abject Slave

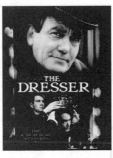

Peter Yates directed Albert Finney as "Sir" and his dresser Norman (Tom Courtenay) in this first-rate theater drama scripted by Ronald Harwood. He was said to have based his script on his experiences working as a dresser for the noted Shakespearean actor Donald Wolfit (1902-68).

The play revolves around a reclusive and deteriorating old actor—barely able to make it on stage—and his "mother-hen" valet. Both Finney and Courtney are brilliant in every scene. Finney certainly looks the part, though he was only 47 when the movie was shot. Gone was his male beauty and the charismatic charm he showcased in *Tom Jones*.

In a touring Shakespearean theater group, the dresser is slavishly devoted to "Sir," as they struggle to carry on during the London Blitz of 1942. The pathos backstage mirrors the theme of *King Lear* that is being presented on the boards.

Courtenay in his self-sacrificing part is every bit as good as he was in *Billy Liar* or *The Loneliness of the Long Distance Runner*. As Sir, veteran actor Finney challenges the great Olivier.

In bondage to the egomaniacal actor, Norman is a morale booster, bather, masseur, doctor, nurse, and, yes, a dresser. Sir takes his gay dresser for granted. Incidentally, homosexuality doesn't come up, although the dresser may well be in love with his master.

In a reference to the so-called pansy fraternity, Sir himself claims, "I don't hold a brief for buggerers."

Vanity Fair dismissed the role of Norman as "all lavender-tinted prissiness—*The Boys in the Band* style gay-face." Quentin Crisp, that stately British homo, was offended by the play, especially the role of Norman. "He speaks through his teeth, arches his back, walks with tiny, hurried steps, and holds his hands before him like a begging Pekinese dog."

The two stars are ably backed up by a strong cast, including Edward Fox playing a homophobic actor, Oxenby.

Drift

(2001)

Three Different Ways to Seek Love

The protagonist Ryan (Reggie Lee) is an Asian-Canadian in his late 20s. He has dreams of becoming a screenwriter (who doesn't?) but serves coffee at a café to make a living. His domestic partner Joel (Greyson Dayne), with whom he is not completely satisfied, is about to be left behind.

At a party, Ryan meets Leo (Jonathan Roessler), an aspiring novelist and college student. They have a mutual interest in such dark obsessions as serial killer lore and horror movies.

Ryan laments that Joel "just doesn't understand what I'm passionate about." But Leo seems to. Could Leo be Mr. Right?

Ryan moves in with gal pal Carrie (Desi del Valle) to begin his pursuit of Leo. Joel, meanwhile, is on tenderhooks.

Three different possibilities for love face Ryan and each is explored in the film. First, there's Leo. A possibility of a reconciliation with Joel is another way to go. Finally, there is yet a third ambiguous denouement.

Audiences liked *Drift* because it was not cast with perfect 10s. Give the boys a 6, perhaps a 7 on a good hair night. The cast looks naturalistic, and not overly macho. One even has a slight case of acne, and the men are a little bit fem.

WHAT THE CRITICS SAID
"Ryan wants someone who can make him whole, who will know and understand him. He is full of romantic notions based the readings of Plato and Wordsworth. He feels that something is wrong with his relationship with Joel."
Alan Jacobs

"A gay breakup tale that springs its structural-gimmick surprise midway—but remains just moderately interesting nonetheless—*Drift* reps a respectable soph feature effort for writer-helmer Quentin Lee."
Dennis Harvey, *Variety*

Drifting Flowers

(2008)

Three Poetic Tales of Lesbian Love

Fresh from her success with *Spider Lilies*, award-winning lesbian director Zero Chou doesn't quite hit a home run the second time at bat, but the film has an undeniable, dreamlike charm. It's in Mandarin and Taiwanese with English subtitles.

The film is a trio of parts centering around the cliché of a group of women struggling to find their identity—read that lesbian identity. Obviously, this time around, Chou is taking a trip down memory lane.

The movie starts with its most fully developed segment, running 40 minutes out of the 90. It tells the story of an eight-year-old May (Chih-Ying Pai) who develops a friendship with Diego (Chao Yi-lan), a woman accordionist who accompanies May's blind sister Jing (Serena Fang) in a lounge bar act.

May becomes very jealous when she sees Diego, acting very butch, and Jing, acting very fem, canoodling one night.

Diego also appears in another segment, where we see her as a teenage rebel, binding her breasts and filled with sexual confusion. When she gives in to the advances of a showgirl, she discovers her true desires.

The third segment Lily, an elderly lesbian and Yen, her gay friend, create an unexpected bond and support each other in a time of crisis. Playing the Alzheimer's victim of Lily is Lu Yi-cheng. Her childhood friend (Sam Wang) is now HIV-positive and a cross dresser. This 30-minute part has a mellow appeal but plays like an interruption between the first and second segments.

WHAT THE CRITICS SAID
"Newcomer Chao is the most striking presence, and makes Diego a believable character. However, the young thesp gets little original to work with beyond lesbian wish-fulfillment clichés. A whole movie could be made about Diego."
Derek Elley, *Variety*

The Dying Gaul

(2005)

A Tragic End to Lurid Love

The film is directed by Craig Lucas and based on his 1998 play. Jeffrey (as played by Campbell Scott) is a beady-eyed Hollywood studio executive. In a remark that is so painfully true, he claims that "Most Americans hate gay people." That is also his reason for wanting writer Robert (Peter Sarsgaard) to rewrite his screenplay about a male lover who died of AIDS and turn it into a heterosexual tear-jerker. If Robert will do that, Jeffrey will offer him one-million dollars. To define the arrangement even more clearly as a bargain with the Hollywood devil, Jeffrey also wants Robert to sodomize him. You see, Jeffrey is a closeted bisexual with a wife and two adorable children.

As we move forward into this melodrama, only the script lets us down. The three actors, including actress Patricia Clarkson as Elaine, Jeffrey's wife, each emote brilliantly.

The title is a bit far-fetched. Of course, it's taken from one of the most famous statues in the world resting in Rome today. It depicts an injured soldier dying from battle wounds. Robert became intrigued with the statue when he and his lover, Malcolm (played by Bill Camp), discovered it on a sightseeing tour. Malcolm's death of AIDS—told in flashback—is one of the more gruesome aspects of the film. He underwent a hideous experimental treatment for tuberculosis that involved injections directly into his brain.

Jeffrey and all that money are very persuasive, and soon Robert is having his computer replace the screenplay's 1,172 references to Malcolm with the name of Maggie. As a subplot, Robert is paying child support to a former wife, who, coincidentally, happened to be Malcolm's sister.

Making his debut as a director, the name Craig Lucas is familiar to gay males. He wrote the screenplay for the still-remembered *Longtime Companion* about the coming of the great plague.

Film noir certainly meets Greek tragedy in this flicker. To really appreciate it, you must abandon reason and go along with its improbable plot twists.

An Early Frost

(1985)

The First Human Face on AIDS

In the White House, President Ronald Reagan wouldn't touch the subject of AIDS. Hollywood wouldn't go there until *Philadelphia* (1993) with Tom Hanks and Antonio Banderas playing lovers.

But in the autumn of 1985, NBC-TV bravely presented *An Early Frost*, the first movie to deal with the subject. Wolfe Video has now produced a DVD edition for those who weren't around to see it in its initial release.

Director John Erman assembled a top-rate cast who included Gena Rowlands, brilliant as the mother; and Katherine Pierson, playing opposite her bigoted husband, Nick (Ben Gazzara). Old-time actress Sylvia Sidney is a lovable grandmother. The star is definitely Aidan Quinn, who wasn't afraid to play gay in an era when accepting such a role was known as a career breaker.

Aidan, a young, successful gay man, is struck down with AIDS in the prime of his life as a Chicago lawyer. His longtime lover, Peter (D.W. Moffett), lends love and support.

The story is set in an era when little is known about AIDS and how it was transmitted. Aidan's sister (Sydney Walsh) reacts with panic, fearing he might contaminate her children. Caregivers even refuse to attend to him.

During the making of the movie, heartthrob Rock Hudson came out with his diagnosis and died just one month before the TV film was broadcast.

Of course, the film, seen through the knowledge of today, is very retro, but remains exceedingly ballsy.

The greatest line is delivered by Michael to his father: "I'm not going to apologize for what I am, because it has taken me too long to accept it." The most touching moment in the film is when Michael attempts suicide, and Nick (Gazzara) comes to realize that his love of his son is far more overriding than his own phobia about homosexuality. The talented Quinn delivers his most moving performance.

East Side Story

(2006)

A Heartfelt Gay Love Triangle With a Twist

Most films about Los Angeles are set in the relatively prosperous western sector of the city, not the east. Carlos Portugal, the director and co-author of the script, takes us into the wilds of East Los Angeles in his comedy of interracial romance.

This debut film from Portugal is the fiery tale of a young hottie, Diego (René Alvado), who works in his family's restaurant. Diego is involved in a stifling relationship with Pablo (David Berón), a local real estate bigwig. Pablo is deeply closeted, and the relationship seems to be going nowhere.

When Diego's man-eater of a sister Blanca (Gladys Jiménez) returns, she steals Pablo from her brother. Pablo seems to brush Diego aside, telling him their gay love affair was "just a phase I was going through."

Diego's life grows more complicated when new neighbors Wesley (Steve Callhan) and Jonathan (Cory Schneider) move in.

They are the new gay couple on the block, and they invite Diego to a party. Wesley and Diego bond, and he is in danger of breaking up a gay marriage. We can't give the plot away from this point on. But the ending is unexpected.

The story also tackles some problems of gentrification, especially when *gabachos* (a pejorative term for English-speaking, non-Hispanic people—and gay ones at that) start moving into the neighborhood that had been typically *mexicano*.

As these new gringos start renovating houses and adopting children from abroad, the Mexicans in the neighborhood feel challenged. Even the restaurant where Diego works might be threatened with closure.

East Side Story was shot in Spanish with English subtitles.

Eban and Charley

(2000)

A 15-Year-Old Boy and a 29-Year-Old Man

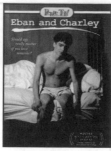

James Bolton, who helmed and scripted this February/April romance, faced a predictable mixed reaction when the controversial movie was released. One viewer said, "I'm torn. Half of the time I hated this movie, and half the time I loved it."

At its best, it's a voyeuristic look at a boy, just turning 15, engaged in a sexual relationship with a 29-year-old that raises legal complications.

Whether right or wrong, nobody, not even fear of the law, can stop love from blossoming. Charley (Gio Black Peter) since his mother's death has lived in Seaside, Oregon (the scenery is beautiful), with his stern, unloving father (Nolan Chard).

During Christmas week, Charley meets Eban (Brent Fellows), a coach who may be pushing thirty but doesn't look it. Eban is home for the holidays for a Yuletide visit with his parents.

The boy and man bond, exploring their shared love of poetry and singing. During walks along the beach, they fall in love. When knowledge of this becomes evident to the 15-year-old's parents, anger (of course) ensues.

As the plot unfolds, viewers learn that the soccer coach, Eban, had to flee Seattle to escape prosecution after an (unrelated and earlier) affair with a younger student. When the authorities learn about what's going on, the man and boy must end their relationship, or escape as fugitives.

WHAT THE CRITICS SAID
"Lead thesps do well making these recessive characters intriguingly ambiguous, just as script's plain, everyday dialogue avoids psychological/social problem literalism. Still, at times this deliberate reserve seems clunky or just undernourished, with pacing occasionally lax. Charley's friends, two heterosexual teens, also on the verge of running away, provide sole subplot; parents' roles are sketchy."
Dennis Harvey, *Variety*

Eden's Curve

(2003)

A 70s Coming-of-Age Romantic Drama

Based on a true story, this is about Peter, an 18-year-old who enrolls in a conservative Southern all-male university "in order to discover myself." Peter is convincingly played by the star of the film, Samuel A. Levine, a beefcake who evokes Ryan Philippe, as noted by several viewers. The film is directed by Anne Misawa.

Peter takes up with his roommate Joe (Trevor Lissauer) and his girlfriend Bess (Amber Taylor). They are an aggressively predatory hetero twosome, and soon Peter is lured into an orgiastic three-way. Soon after they're floating, *à trois,* in a blurry haze of drugs and sensuality,

It doesn't take Joe long to realize that Peter is more sexually thrilled by him than by Bess. The situation gets messy. Peter escapes to the home of a sympathetic teacher (Julio Perillán).

Peter is at a crossroads in his life, and the decisions he makes will affect his life forever.

WHAT THE CRITICS SAID
"Set in the swinging 70s, this intense gay soap opera follows a clean-cut All-American boy through his first year at college. Along with long hair, tasteful retro outfits and a total absence of AIDS, Misawa relies on a quasi-impressionistic palette to paint the period. Against all odds, Misawa makes amateurish acting read as unformed adolescence, and occasional excursions into the ludicrous (our hero taking woodsy refuge with his poetry teacher in Thoreau-esque skinny-dipping idylls) feel like sexual awkwardness."
Ronnie Scheib, *Variety*

"The subject matter is strong, especially in the period when the hippy-ethnic freedom hid an undercurrent of homophobia. Strangely, Misawa makes very little use of the time period—we have to keep reminding ourselves this is 1972 because she rarely does. And the gravity of the story is further undermined by amateurish film techniques."
Rich Cline

Edmond

(2005)

American Psycho or *Dr. Jekyll & Mr. Hyde?*

This dour movie is for fans of the controversial playwright David Mamet, who enjoys a cult following. He wrote the screenplay for *Edmond* based on his off-Broadway play which was inaugurated during the "Morning in America" Reagan era.

In one of his most difficult roles ever, William Macy plays Edmond, an angry white man, and does so brilliantly.

Helmer Stuart Gordon brings this drama/thriller to the screen with a knife-like plunge into the gut. The story is far too bleak for those faint of heart.

The foul language and raging machismo long associated with Mamet are here, but also some insight as to how a decent white man can be plunged into a horrifying urban hell, which is what makes this film so compelling.

In the early 1980s, Mamet, ignoring political correctness, attacked women, gays, and especially blacks. He was called a "spit-in-your-face playwright," and his incendiary language still exists in this sleazy film.

Edmond's descent into hell begins along New York's 8th Avenue, a world of hookers, pimps, and peep shows. That scene is largely gone post-millennium, and *Edmond* has somewhat the allure of a period piece.

"You are not where you belong," says a fortune teller to Edmond in one of the opening scenes. Beset with inner demons, Edmond is about to plummet into a free fall.

Edmond plunges into the world of the homicidally berserk, taking on a leering, gold-toothed pimp who lied to him and even a young waitress and aspiring actress (Julia Stiles).

It isn't long before Edmond is thrown into prison where he becomes a sex slave to his hulking black cellmate (Bokeem Woodbine). Through degradation and disgrace, Edmond reaches a personal transcendence.

Mamet is stalking big game in *Edmond*—God, fate, man, sex, and death.

The Education of Shelby Knox

(2005)

Sex Education & Gay Rights

This is a film about Red State reaction vs. Blue State enlightenment. The 76-minute film is basically a coming-of-age tale about a teenage girl from Lubbock, Texas, who joins a campaign for comprehensive sex education in her district. It's about the "salvation" of a Red State soul.

Shelby Knox is a Christian high school student coming of age in a George Bush value system. Unlike the American president, she is intelligent and capable of changing her point of view.

An avowed "virgin-to-marriage," she does not transform herself into a dope-addicted slut. Unlike the former U.S. *el presidente,* she becomes an activist for sex education and the separation of church and school. Her civil disobedience takes a mild form of protest but puts her at odds with her parents, the pastor of her Southern Baptist church, and the local, very uptight and right-wing school board.

Horrors of horrors, she even takes up the controversial banner of gay rights. In the end, Shelby with her brightness and her charm emerges as a feminist (albeit not a radical one) and a liberal Christian.

This documentary, directed by Marion Lipschutz and Rose Rosenblatt, is a film that teens and their families could watch together, if only they would. To the film's credit, Shelby is not always presented as Joan of Arc. There are those who question her motives, suggesting she's "just a spotlight-grabber."

Some members of the far right claimed that the film was "anti-Christian" and that some of the more extreme characters, such as the abstinence-preaching pastor, border on caricature. The pastor, Ed Ainsworth, does make such comments as, "Sex is what two dogs do on the street corner."

Moronic Lubbock was the ideal setting for such a film.

Edward II

(1991)

The King Who Was a Queen

Derek Jarman's erotic, brutal reworking of Christopher Marlowe's 16th century play about Britain's only openly gay monarch is intriguing and wildly homoerotic. Jarman also co-scripted this classic tale of sex, revenge, and love.

Marlowe's Elizabethan drama, surprisingly, even shockingly, is played out amid a mixture of Plantagenet presuppositions and modern costumes and settings. Shakespeare it isn't.

There was a reason for Jarman to set the film in modern dress. In the end, the film emerges as a radical assault on homophobia in contemporary British society.

Steven Waddington as Edward II, it becomes clear, is "mad about the boy," in this case Andrew Tiernan cast as the king's lover, Piers Gaveston. "My father is deceased. Come Gaveston, and share the kingdom with thy dearest friend."

Tilda Swinton plays Edward's queen with an imperially icy hauteur. Her clothing and jewels become more opulent as her fury turns her into a murderous Tory monster.

Of course, being so obvious in his choice of a lover, and an ambitious one at that, the stage is set for the gay twosome to be removed from the throne into a torture dungeon.

Historically Edward II's love for Gaveston sparked a conflict with his barons, providing an excuse for their eventual incitement of a civil war.

WHAT THE CRITICS SAID
"As King Edward and his lower-class favorite Piers Gaveston, Steve Waddington and Andrew Tiernan radiate heat and joy, and while Jarman emphasizes their love story and means for us to see their plight as tragic, he doesn't canonize them."
Joe Brown, *Washington Post*

An Englishman in New York

(2009)

The Big Apple's Adopted Version of Oscar Wilde

Quentin Crisp

John Hurt once again portrays pithy gay icon Quentin Crisp in this poignant sequel to *The Naked Civil Servant* (see review). Expect gay zingers and witticisms rivaling those of Oscar Wilde. Hurt is backed up by a talented supporting cast that includes Swoosie Kurtz (our favorite), Denis O'Hare, and Cynthia Nixon.

The film depicts Crisp in his testy later years, enjoying celebrity in New York City. In London as a young man, he was often beaten up in the streets, but in gay New York of the 1970s he becomes a role model and icon. His barbs and eccentric behavior make him the toast of New York during the era just prior to AIDS.

Director Richard Laxton takes us on a gay merry-go-round, aided by scripter Brian Fillis.

In "the city that never sleeps," Crisp makes friends with Philip Steele (Denis O'Hare), a gay magazine editor, and Patrick Angus (Jonathan Tucker), a lonely young artist.

The major attraction is the chance to hear Crisp's acerbic philosophies. "Never keep up with the Joneses: Drag them down to your level—it's cheaper."

But in the AIDS-ravaged decade to come, Crisp made several comments that sounded insensitive at best, or homophobic at their worst. This angered many members of the gay community who confronted him. In the past it was menacing straights that Crisp had to fear.

With the help of performance artist Penny Arcade (Nixon), Crisp finds his way back into the limelight and a peace truce with the gay community.

Crisp, with his hats and ascots, was the role Hurt was destined to play. With zest and a certain outrageousness, this remarkably talented actor takes us for a final glib romp through the streets of NYC.

Entertaining Mr. Sloane

(1970)

Handsome, Sexy, & Completely Amoral

This film was considered quite daring when it was first released. Remember the 70s had just begun. Directed by Douglas Hickox, *Entertaining Mr. Sloane* was based on a play by the British playwright, Joe Orton.

At the age of thirty-four, Orton was murdered by his lover, who then killed himself. When the play opened in London, it caused an outrage, sending fans flocking to the theater. It remains Orton's most popular play and is still revived today in both the U.S. and Britain. The movie isn't as cutting edge as the play.

The stars of the play are involved in a three-way affair. Beryl Reid plays Kath, Harry Andrews her brother Ed, and Peter McEnery the notorious and apparently bisexual Mr. Sloane. Alan Webb was cast as Kemp or "Dadda."

The strikingly handsome hunk, McEnery, was the blackmailer in *Victim*, but in *Entertaining Mr. Sloane* it is he who is blackmailed.

The very sexy Sloane joins Kath's household as a lodger. But he is recognized by Dadda as the murderer of Kemp's former employer, a photographer who had asked Sloane to pose nude.

Sloane murders the old man Dadda. But the killer gets his "just desserts," in more ways than one.

The middle-aged nymphomaniac (Reid) and her misogynist brother Harry learn that Sloane has killed their aging Dadda. Instead of reporting him to the police, they hold him in bondage to become a love slave to both of them.

Reid, the star of the lesbian-themed *Killing of Sister George*, camps it up as the aging nympho, and seems to have a hell of a good time doing so. As her closeted gay brother, Andrews was perfectly cast. He seems to express his sexual preference primarily through his hatred of women.

When brother Ed meets Sloane, he is infatuated and hires him as his chauffeur, dressing him in leather from head to toe.

Erotikus:
A History of the Gay Movie

(2004)

A Definitive Take on Gay Porn

Many young readers are searching for this 1973 movie that in 90 minutes surveys the history of gay porn from the nudie/not-quite-nudies of early filmdom to the "money shot"-filled feature-length releases that introduced such "stars" as Casey Donovan (Cal Culver) with his 8½ inch dick. We even get to see clips of Monte Hansen whose nude pictures used to adorn the bathroom walls of many a gay man. He was one of the first and most successful nude models of the 1970s, and he never had a problem being photographed with a hard-on (or never had any trouble raising one). His thick sausage is shown in archival footage.

Fred Halsted (1941-89) is the narrator. What gay man coming of age in the 70s doesn't remember the films of Halsted, including *LA Plays Itself/Sex Garage* (1972). A scene in *Sex Garage* got a New York City movie theater raided. Halsted himself appeared in this one.

He also brought us *A Night at Halsted's* (1980), often considered a classic, especially its Plexiglas glory-hole scene. Halsted in *Erotikus* not only narrates but jerks off in one scene. The movie also highlights the first cum shot shown (no pun intended) in public release (i.e., not as a scene within a secret "blue movie"). The porn helmer hired blond and skinny models of the California surfer type. "My type," he said.

Halsted's lover was Joey Yale, who appeared in some of his films. Halsted recalled that he first met Yale in front of a Hollywood leather bar in 1969. The kid was too young to go inside. "He was the cutest blond I'd ever seen, and I decided I had to get into his pants. There was no sense in going into the bar and getting drunk. So I took him home and fucked him, and we've been doin' it ever since."

Halsted committed suicide at Dana Point, California, on May 9, 1989, overdosing on sleeping pills after the death of Joey Yale.

The director of *Erotikus*, Tom DeSimone, is credited with having produced the first so-called "homosexual feature film," *The Collection,*

Everything Relative

(1996)

A Sapphic Big Chill

What's the best thing about this lesbian flick? Harvey Fierstein appears in a cameo as the moyle presiding over the baby's ritual circumcision.

A group of women—six lesbians and one straight—unite in this provocative and sexy ensemble comedy.

The old college friends with their memories come together for a reunion in Massachusetts to celebrate the birth of one of the member's babies. The women dip into nostalgia and also speak of their struggle in their lesbian political feminist movement.

The occasion for the get-together is Daniel, a newborn baby of a Jewish mother, Katie (Stacey Nelkin) and her WASP lover and "co-mother" Victoria (Monica Bell). Victoria's brother fathered the child.

Other cast members include a Mexican, Maria (Olivia Negron), who lost her kids in a custody battle to her homophobic husband; Josie (Ellen McLaughlin), a recovering alcoholic; Luce (Andrea Weber), a daredevil stunt woman; a former hooker/singer Gina (Gabriella Messina); and Sarah (Carol Schneider) an activist for the Planned Parenthood Association.

WHAT THE CRITICS SAID
"Writer-director Sharon Pollack's strategy is shamelessly forthright and boring, alternating collective sessions of singing, dancing, and swimming with more intimate interactions whose sole purpose seems to be reconciliation of old conflicts and tensions."
Emanuel Levy, *Variety*

"Back in the late 70s, the pals were part of a political street-theater troupe. Today they're approaching 40, drinking less, eating low-fat, enjoying the benefits of lesbian mainstreaming, and wondering where the time went and what they've learned."
Edward Guthmann, *San Francisco Chronicle*

Excavating Taylor Mead

(2005)

Warhol's Superstar as a Lonesome (Old) Cowboy

"All art is a scandal," said Tennessee Williams. "Life tries to be. Taylor Mead succeeds. I come close." The playwright was talking about the first Andy Warhol superstar, Taylor Mead, in this clip-rich docu. When people meet to talk about Warhol  and the history of underground film, the name of Taylor Mead surfaces. Whether cavorting through Ron Rice's Beat touchstone, *The Flower Thief*, to pitching camp in Warhol's *Lonesome Cowboys*, Mead defined a small sliver of the 1960s.

Today he lives in a cluttered hell-hole of an East Village apartment, from which he might be evicted. He admits to living on a "fixed income and the kindness of bartenders."

The docu shows the fading old star of yesterday walking lonely New York streets or feeding stray cats for company. The scenes are almost unbearably poignant.

Mead was more than a mere Warhol superstar. He did "only 10 films with Andy," but, as he recalls, he appeared in some 100 movies, many of which were seminal moments in the American indie movement.

The narration is by Steve Buscemi, who also resembles Mead physically. The film does not totally succeed in presenting us with a clear portrait of what Mead's contribution to our culture was. Those who "grew up on Mead" will understand, of course, but those who weren't even born when *Lonesome Cowboys* was released may be a bit baffled by this star's peculiar allure.

Mead was born in 1924 to a rich but unstable Detroit family. His father was a Democratic political boss, and his mother wanted to abort him.

If you ever see Mead in a seedy East Village bar, buy him a drink (as we recently did) and toast the underground films of yesterday.

During your time together, Mead will likely tell you: "I'm the biggest star in the world, but I'm buried in museum *cinemathèques* and foundations."

eXposed: The Making of a Legend

(2004)

A Look at the Making of the Porn Film *BuckleRoos!*

Nudity and graphic sexual context? Right on! It's not often that adult entertainment guys allow documentary filmmakers onto their closed sets, let alone a blonde, pig-tailed, free-spirited woman named Pam. But producers John Rutherford and Tom Settle agreed to do just that. Pam (aka Pam Dore) was the videographer and talented if zany director. Pam has edited films for such gay porn legends as Chi Chi LaRue.

Running for 1 hour and 35 minutes, *eXposed* takes you on a day-by-day journey through the lives of some of the biggest names in the all-male Industry. You meet the directors, the tireless crew members, and, of course, the big-dicked studs themselves. In all, you'll get to know 39 men, both reel and real. Each of them is intent on building all-male fantasies, often for jerk-off purposes.

The film explores how the porno flick, *BuckleRoos!* was made. You'll see such scenes as Marcus Iron holding a camera with one hand while he strokes his hard cock with the other. Or Marcus and Dean Phoenix in the middle of their climactic, romantic scene in the barn being interrupted when a cow breaks the mood with a loud groan.

WHAT THE CRITICS SAID

"*eXposed* is a making-of docu that's entertaining if not necessarily no-holds-barred. Chronicling the three-week shoot of a gay porno extravaganza *BuckleRoos*, pic benefits from female helmer Mr. Pam's light touch."
Dennis Harvey, *Variety*

"Dean Phoenix is so cute and charismatic, he could easily be doing mainstream films. Zak Spears is a deep-voiced combination of Bruce Willis and The Rock, a perfection action star. There is actor Ricky Martinez, so proud of his manhood that it is jutting out of his shorts at full attention during the entire interview. The film is full of nude men sporting and rubbing their erections. It is a gay porno shoot, after all."
Charles Tatum

Eye on the Guy

(2006)

Alan B. Stone and the Age of Beefcake

Alan B. Stone was a businessman who lived life in Montréal as a quiet suburbanite back in the 50s and early 60s. But his hobby was the homoerotic pin-up of scantily clad, beefy men, many wearing only underwear covering their crotches.

Alan B. Stone produced thousands of images of men, ranging from Montréal bodybuilders to Pacific fishermen, from rodeo cowboys to the workers who built Expo '67. He inhabited a distinct gay subculture back in the days when homosexuality was illegal. This docu explores the little-known world of "physique photography," as it was called, a scene that paved the way for gay liberation. From his Montréal basement, he ran an international mail order business in male pin-ups, catering to the inner desires of closeted gays throughout North America.

Most of Stone's beefcake pin-ups models, or so it is believed, were straight, which seemed to add to their allure among purchasers of the erotica, in other words, a peek at forbidden territory.

In the film, former models recall the heyday of Stone's studio. Stone traveled far and wide, and his photographic legacy provides a rich document of the Canadian West in the 1960s. Wherever he traveled, his eye was always on the guy.

For 48 minutes, Philip Lewis and Jean-François Monette re-create this long-gone world through vintage footage, old pictures, and interviews. Stone's pictures were published in muscle magazines which in time gave way to the openly gay porn magazines that began to circulate in the late 60s and early 70s.

Stone's work came to light in the mid-1980s when Thomas Waugh, a film studies professor at Concordia University in Montréal discovered them. "I was struck by how ingenious much of Stone's photography was," recalled Waugh. "It created this sanitized yet prurient image of the male body. The pouches the men were wearing, the coy nods to homosexuality—it was all very clever, and was a product of the repression of the time."

In a word, this docu is archival eye candy.

<table>
<tr>
<td>

Eyes Wide Open

(2009)

Married Butcher, Seductive Young Man

</td>
<td>

Fabulous!

(2006)

The Story of Queer Cinema

</td>
</tr>
</table>

This was a very controversial film in Israel, emerging from director Haim Tabakman from a script by Merav Doster. It tells the story of a repressed, married orthodox Jewish father of four, who falls in love with a handsome male student, only 22 years old.

Giving credible performances is Zohar Shtrauss in his breakthrough role as the kosher butcher, Aaron. The reigning Israeli heartthrob, Ran Danker, plays the seductive young man, Ezri. The thankless role of the wife goes to Ravit Rozen as Rivka.

Conforming to a rigid lifestyle of home and hearth is one of the tenets of this orthodox community which will go to great extremes to ensure obedience.

Ezri's mere presence incites passion in Aaron, who has long lived in the closet, repressing his desires. Aaron offers Ezri a job and shelter, but he cannot—at least for long—conceal his passion for the young male beauty.

Their love grows as they are depicted singing in their Torah study group, with their arms around each other's shoulders. Is this spiritual joy or sexual passion?

In a subplot and in performing his duties to his church, Aaron has to join his rabbi in paying a threatening call on a man who is involved with a woman shopkeeper. She has already been promised by her father to another man. In spite of his own "deviant" behavior, Aaron warns the man of what a visit by the "purity police" would involve.

WHAT THE CRITICS SAID
"Gritty, realist art direction reinforces the sense of the characters' enclosed world. Taboo-breaking *Eyes Wide Open* is an intense, restrained drama sensitively helmed, boasting a tightly structured, multi-layered script."
Alissa Simon, *Variety*

Helmers Lisa Ades and Lesli Klainberg painted in broad brush strokes when they surveyed the history of gay and lesbian cinema, the love that dared not speak its name in early films. But any docu that attempts to do that in 82 minutes is destined to be broad. Even so, we were rather startled not to see the seminal film, *The Boys in the Band*, surveyed. Also missing from the lineup are such classics as *Philadelphia*. What about *Jeffrey*? Left out was *TransAmerica, Midnight in the Garden of Good and Evil, In and Out, Compulsion, Party Monster,* and even *My Own Private Idaho*. We also didn't see mention of the classic, *The Children's Hour,* by bisexual playwright Lillian Hellman.

Much of the cast is predictable. We just knew John Waters would turn up, and we got our wish that Ang Lee, the director of *Brokeback Mountain,* would make some comments. Gossip maven Michael Musto can always get a laugh just by showing up. John Cameron Mitchell, the creator and star of *Hedwig and the Angry Inch,* appears, as does *Queer as Folk*'s Peter Paige as well as Don Roos who directed *The Opposite of Sex.*

For those coming to the subject for the first time, this is an entertaining lesson in gay history. For the old sailors on the deck of gay cinema, it's everything we've mopped up before. Where the docu succeeds is in showing how G&L cinema came into its own after long struggles, with men playing sissies on screen and lesbians playing serial killers or vampires.

The film clips alone are worth the price of admission, and the gay glitterati "talking heads" give valuable opinions. It's entirely appropriate that the filmmakers in such a short time start with Kenneth Anger's *Fireworks*.

The directors trace gay cinema up to *Brokeback Mountain*. The boy-meets-boy stories are better represented than fine lesbian cinema, although we do get a preview of *Personal Best, Go Fish, Desert Hearts,* and even *DEBS*. Transsexuals get short-changed in this breezy, fast-moving docu.

Fag Hags:
Women Who Love Gay Men

(2005)

They Include the Queen Mother and Liz Taylor

The term "fag hag," presumably dates from the infamous Studio 54 era in New York. Could Judy Garland, daughter Minnelli, and certainly Liz Taylor be called fag hags? In its original usage, the term was used as a putdown for desperate and dateless women. After all those episodes of *Will and Grace*, the term increasingly has become a cheeky comment, at least after the introduction of Charlotte in *Sex and the City*. *Fag Hag* has also become a cliché of popular culture, and a descriptive term for Jennifer Aniston in *The Object of My Affection*.

The 20th century's most famous fag hag was the Queen Mum, who surrounded herself with gay male courtiers. At her gin-and-tonic hour, she once said, "I don't know what you old queens are doing, but this old queen needs a drink."

This 52-minute Canadian flicker, directed by Justine Pimlott and written by Maya Gallus, explores a group of women and their best friends, all gay males. It's the tale of a trio of Canadian couples, and in its limited time slot delves seriously into the psychology of gay man/straight woman relationships. The film reminds us that platonic love has a life-altering power.

WHAT THE CRITICS SAID
"Formerly the object of suspicion and scorn, fag hags grew from kitsch-value to mainstream novelty, *à la Will & Grace*. Now we also have this homegrown hour on the rise and relations of gay-men-trapped-in-chicks'-bodies. *Fag Hags* follows three memorable pairs of life-long pals, splicing their stories with celluloid moments in film and TV, including clips of Margaret Cho. It manages an admirable and wide swipe at complex issues surrounding intimacy, companionship and sex, but doesn't go quite far enough to reach any fresh insight or discernable conclusion. Worse yet, not one drop-dead hot, skinny hag featured dispels the most nagging stereotype of all: that we're all fat and dateless."
www.eye.net

The Fall of '55

(2006)

Boise Witch Hunt and Gay Paranoia

In the fall of 1955, now notorious in the history of Idaho, the citizens of Boise were overcome with mass hysteria aimed at gay people. As Halloween approached, they were told that there was a giant sex ring preying on their local teenage boys—perhaps their own son.

No such ring existed, but a witch hunt was launched. Before it was over, 16 men had been convicted and dozens more intimidated. The men were charged with sex crimes, including accusations of having relations with other consenting adults. One family fled to Mexico; others left town never to return.

With *Time* magazine and other media fanning the flames, the fire spread by "The Boys of Boise" swept across the nation. There were calls for a "morals drive" to rid the country of "undesirables."

Even with homophobes still sitting in the Senate, this 81-minute docu from journalist Seth Randal shows how far we've come since the Eisenhower era.

Scars of that post-McCarthy witch hunt remain unhealed in the Boise of today, as descendants express their bitterness over what happened.

The docu was five years in the making, and the production team visited actual locations for their shoot. Excerpted letters to the prison warden by traumatized relatives evoke "the almost unbearable pain" of that time. Regrettably, so many of the principals are long gone, and for interviews Randal had to rely on second-hand sources in many cases.

As an example of its media coverage, one headline from a 1955 issue of Holiday read: MALE PERVERT RING SEDUCES 1,000 BOYS.

In reviewing the case in 1967, *CBS News* broadcast a saner sentiment. "The people of Boise tried to 'stamp out' homosexuality. They discovered it couldn't be done. In the learning process, everybody suffered."

Far From Heaven

(2002)

What Imprisons Desires of the Heart?

In his fourth feature film, *Far From Heaven*, director/scripter Todd Haynes drew heavily on those 1950 Douglas Sirk melodramas, such as *All That Heaven Allows* (1955) that starred Jane Wyman and Rock Hudson.

From all outward appearances, Cathy Whitaker (Julianne Moore) and Frank Whitaker (Dennis Quaid, never looking handsomer), are the all-American couple. They live a seemingly near perfect life in an affluent northeastern suburb of Hartford, Connecticut in 1957. They have a station wagon, kids, a beautiful home.

One night, Cathy, the perfect wife, decides to bring dinner to Frank at his office. There she catches him, clothing in disarray, kissing another man. Trying to be understanding, she insists that Frank get psychiatric help. After all, homosexuality was considered a sickness.

While all this is going on, she befriends her black gardener Raymond Deagan (Dennis Haysbert). If she thinks her husband is breaking the taboos of 1957, what about herself?

The friendship between Cathy and Raymond is at first tentative, blossoming into an affecting tenderness. Cathy's social circle is shocked.

Obviously, as the plot spins, Frank and Cathy are about to cross a bridge over troubled waters, and her life will change forever.

WHAT THE CRITICS SAID
"As an exercise, *Far From Heaven* is never less than fascinating, but two-thirds in it becomes clear that the experiment is failing. Haynes' attempt to make a move with the cathartic effect of a good 50s weepie falls into an emotional dead zone between melodrama and camp comedy. An audience that cackles knowingly one minute can't be expected to get all choked up the next."
Mic LaSalle

Far Side of the Moon

(*La face cachée de la lune*; 2004)

Rewarding But Frustrating Drama

In French with English subtitles, this film is a showcase for the internationally acclaimed filmmaker from Québec, Robert Lepage (*Le Polygraphe, No*). For *Far Side of the Moon*, he has adapted one of his theatrical works for the screen in a whimsical and gently humorous adventure.

In the 1960s, a Soviet lunar probe exposed the far side of the moon (which can never be seen from Earth) as scored and disfigured by storms of celestial debris. From this discovery, Lepage crafts an engaging metaphor of mysterious dualities, juxtaposing sibling rivalry with the U.S.-Soviet space race.

Lepage masterfully tackles his dual role, delivering a bravura performance as each of the brothers (one of them is gay). The two brothers are Philippe and André. In the film, the estranged brothers cope with their mother's death. She's played by Anne-Marie Cadieux.

Philippe is cynical, going for a Ph.D. in space exploration. André is a famous and fatuous weatherman. "The idea is that the far side of the moon is a metaphor—there's two sides to it," said Lepage. "They're the same person. So playing both brothers was a metaphorical choice."

Throughout the movie, Philippe makes piquant social observations such as this comment about his brother. "I don't care if he's gay, but like most gays I know he's carefree, rich, and lucky."

La face cachée de la lune is a captivating but quirky cinematic journey, probing issues of competition and reconciliation.

WHAT THE CRITICS SAID
"Both brothers are obstinate in equal measure—Philippe, though, is a cancer survivor, and hence more bitter—and Lepage patiently brings the two mirror-image narcissists in line, like planets on parallel orbits. Reworking his own raw material, Lepage spins a rich, moving film that acknowledges humanity's power to break out of Earth's daily gravity; in the process, he leaves audiences floating."
Mark Peranson, *The Village Voice*

Farm Family

(2004)

In Search of Gay Life in Rural America

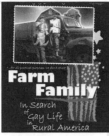

This 73-minute film, directed by T. Joe Murray, looks at gay men living in redneck hostile rural American terrain. The men depicted in the film are not the common stereotypes. We see them rearing children, milking cows, or even living as hermits. There's even a radical fairy or two.

These are not the buff boys of Chelsea. No lingering nights at Splash, no long drawn out sessions with their hairdressers.

Murray, an Out gay man and a product of rural America himself, got the idea for the docu on a trip back to his childhood farm home.

Most of the gay men in the film are part of a couple. They include a male/male duo on a working dairy farm in Wisconsin. One member of the couple notes that, "I have 11 gay relatives in my family. At my sister's wedding, you had the Bob Joneser section—you know, the Bob Jones University section—you had the alcoholic section, and you had the gay and lesbian section."

One segment of the film features gay rodeo. Many of the neighbors are accepting of the same-sex couples, although homophobes are also depicted. In one scene, a gay man is sitting on his front porch. Someone drives by, screaming at him, "Go home, faggot." The geeky driver of that car didn't seem to realize the man was at home.

To tell his story, Murray traveled across the country, filming gay couples as they told their stories. One couple he met had five adopted kids. Wyoming's gay pride celebration evoked sad memories of the slaying of Matthew Shepard by two deranged country morons.

We also visit a gay Moravian "hermitage" in Pennsylvania where a couple live without electricity or running water, facing ugly local prejudice.

Murray gives vent to voices from gay rural America which are rarely heard. The stories are poignant and funny, but sometimes frightening.

Loneliness emerges as the biggest drawback to being queer in the heartland.

Fat Girls

(2006)

"We're All Fat Girls"

Homophile viewers of both *Napoleon Dynamite* and *American Pie* might enjoy this original offbeat comedy feature, even though it hardly strives for nuance. The jokes are hit-and-miss, with enough hits to make it worth viewing.

In the movie's opening voiceover, budding writer/director/actor Ash Christian stakes out his premise: "You don't have to be fat to be a fat girl. You don't even have to be a girl. It's a state of mind. And whenever you're in a fellow fat girl's presence, you know it right away. It's almost like an unspoken club no one really talks about."

In a nutshell, this is another coming-of-age drama set in a dipstick Texas town. It zeroes in on a coterie of Texas teens (both gay and straight) who, for different reasons, are condemned as "outcasts" by their redneck peers.

Christian is skilled as an actor and promising as a director. Wisely he cast two great supporting roles—his best friend, fat girl, 300-pound Sabrina (played by newcomer Ashley Fink), and Sabrina's BF, Rudy (Robin de Jesus of the recent indie hit film, *Camp*).

Like members of the Three Musketeers, the outcast trio of misfits band together to overcome their mistreatment. To make for more character development, each of the three carries baggage. Rodney (Christian) is the gay son of fundamentalist Christians; Rudy, a Cuban refugee adopted by black parents, and Sabrina, the overweight daughter of two lesbian moms.

Gay actor Christian actually grew up in Texas where he claims that "someone is being harassed or beaten up every day because they're gay," in an interview with *The Advocate*. "I've always sort of felt like a fat girl on the inside, someone who didn't really fit in." After settling into California, Christian landed roles on TV shows, including *Boston Public* and *Cold Case Files* while pursuing his dream of filming *Fat Girls*.

The film is about the triumph of the nerds, as Rodney learns to accept the "fat girl" within himself.

Fathers & Sons

(2005)

Dysfunctional Triptych

This 101-minute drama revolves around the intertwined tales of three families who grow up on the same street. The movie was made for Showtime, but didn't really have that made-for-television aura about it. The triptych was written and directed by a trio of men: Rob Spera, Rodrigo Garcia, and Jared Rappaport.

In the first segment, directed by Serpa, Bradley Whitford plays Anthony with Samantha Mathis cast as Jenny. It focuses on the father-son bond that develops between Anthony and his newborn boy over a period of three decades. Nick is played by different actors as an infant, a toddler, at 5, at 10 to 12, and older.

In the second segment by Garcia, the plot centers on an adulterous airline pilot, Gene (played by John Mahoney). He shares a house but not a life with his wife, Nora (Kathy Baker). In the film he spends an extraordinary night with his son, Tom (Ron Eldard).

This second segment will have the most interest to gay viewers. The pilot tries to understand his gay son's lifestyle. The most poignant moment is when Mahoney interacts with his son when his boy's first love succumbs to AIDS.

Rappaport was charged with the final chapter, which depicts Elliot (Gale Harold) in a homecoming with his estranged family as played by Barbara Barrie, Lisa Edelstein, and Joe Bologna. Even though his father is dying, Elliot meets and falls in love with Nell (Vanessa Shaw).

WHAT THE CRITICS SAID
"The families are loosely connected and the name of the street on which they all live serves as the name of each of the three segments. A good idea, a bit of varying showmanship of concept, and in the end it all works fairly well. The actors are consistently fine with some cameos by older actors we haven't seen in a while. There are no solutions to father/son roles here, only a gentle exploration of how important the impact of that relationship is on forming future lives."
Grady Harp

Fellini Satyricon

(1969)

Petronius' Study of Roman Decadence

Director Federico Fellini turned to the nearly 2,000-year-old unfinished work of the Roman writer Petronius for his film about a surreal Roman world in a state of moral flux. It is inferior to his *La Dolce Vita*, but a film of power and majesty nonetheless.

We follow the picaresque adventures of two lusty Romans, the beautiful Encolpio (blond-haired Martin Potter, an Adonis) and the darker, crueler, and priapic Ascilto (Hiram Keller). Their lover is Giton (Max born), an epicene Ganymede.

Fellini called his film "a pre-Christian film for a post-Christian age." His young men move through various picaresque adventures in Nero's Rome. *Satyricon* sparked world interest, the most notorious Roman-made spectacular since Elizabeth Taylor's *Cleopatra*.

Fellini, in an interview, also announced, "I am examining ancient Rome as if this were a documentary about the customs and habits of Martians."

The movie is fragmented, following no particular storyline, as we're taken into a "universe of grotesques and dwarfs, and cripples, lesbians and homosexuals and hermaphrodites, gluttons and murderers and the robbers of graves." Oh, yes, there are beheadings, disembowelments, suicides, and death by fire and lance—even cannibalism.

WHAT THE CRITICS SAID
"His film is a fantastical journey to a pre-Christian Rome that resembles no civilization that ever was, in Heaven or on Earth. And it is a masterpiece. Some will say it is a bloody, depraved, disgusting film; indeed, people by the dozens were escaping from the first sneak preview I attended, but *Fellini's Satyricon* is a masterpiece all the same, and films that dare everything cannot please everybody."
Roger Ebert

Female Trouble

(1974)

Nice Girls Don't Wear Cha-Cha Heels

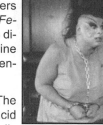

Only a warped mind like director/scripter John Waters could have conceived *Female Trouble*, starring the divine drag queen, Divine herself as "Dawn Davenport."

And what a fun script. The bitch gets raped, has acid thrown in her face, brutally murders her daughter Taffy (Mink Stole), and opens fire on a crowd. Talk about female trouble. The movie is an outrageous send-up of "bad girl" films.

The bitchy dialogue is some of the best released since those 50s movies, *Sunset Blvd.*, with Gloria Swanson, and *All About Eve*, with Bette Davis.

We won't go into the various plot twists that will lead Dawn to the electric chair. She's even thrilled at that prospect, considering all the publicity she'll get by being killed by the state.

Her final words, "Tell everyone they have my permission to sell their memories of me to the media."

At least Ida Nelson (Edith Massey) gets in a plug for gaydom when she urges Gator (Michael Potter) to turn queer. "Queers are just better. I'd be so proud if you was a fag and had a nice beautician boyfriend. I'd never have to worry. The world of heterosexuals is a sick and disgusting life!"

Female Trouble is for you if you like a thoroughly deranged comedy in bad taste, one filled with psycho social misfits and dysfunctional lunatics. If you like sluts, the film is also for you. It's definitely a date movie if you want to dump your nerdy boyfriend for one more adventurous fling.

WHAT THE CRITICS SAID
"Repeating from *Pink Flamingos* in the stellar role of Divine is a mammoth 300-pound transvestite with a tinsel soul. Though Divine doesn't stoop to devouring dog excrement as at the *Flamingos* fade-out, he does everything else, from cavorting on a trampoline, to playing a rape scene opposite himself, and 'giving birth' on camera. Camp is too elegant a word to describe it all. A true original."
Variety

Fifth of July

(1983)

Richard Thomas Makes Love to Jeff Daniels

Gay playwright Lanford Wilson's acclaimed play, which originally starred *Superman's* Christopher Reeve as a gay lover, was turned into a film with a punch.

Actors Richard Thomas and Jeff Daniels (repeating his stage role) play lovers in Missouri in the post-Vietnam era.

Born in Missouri himself, Wilson has long been one of the leading American dramatists, a fixture on Off-Broadway. He received the Pulitzer Prize for Drama in 1980 for *Talley's Folly*.

The original Broadway production of *Fifth of July* opened at the New Apollo Theater on November 8, 1980, running for 511 performances. It was nominated for the 1981 Tony Award for Best Play. It didn't win, although the brilliant Swoosie Kurtz won for Best Featured Actress in a Play.

Fortunately the producers retained her for the movie version, along with Daniels, Jonathan Hogan, Danton Stone, and Joyce Reehling, who also reprised their roles in the film.

The movie version is "opened up" by director Kirk Browning, who depicts outdoor exteriors of the two male lovers in Lebanon, Missouri, in the summer of 1977. It is here that Kenneth (Richard Thomas), a paraplegic Vietnam vet, is reunited with several friends from his days as a student activist.

As critic Jeff Shannon put it, the characters "reflect on their past, present, and future with varying degrees of trepidation, hope, and wisdom."

Daniels is superb as Kenneth's supportive lover. What we especially like is that both men are openly gay, but no one is making a big fuss about that. The film owes much, it would seem, to *The Big Chill*.

These college friends seem to be searching for a way to revive youthful dreams.

Fighting Tommy Riley

(2005)

A Fierce Left Hook of Hidden Desire

Stunningly photographed and impeccably acted, this is the tale of a trainer who fights his homosexual orientation and the gorgeous boxer he loves.

Following the trail of Sylvester Stallone and his *Rocky* script, the strikingly handsome J.P. Davis, an unknown actor and script writer, refused to sell his scenario unless he would play the title role. Director Eddie O'Flaherty took the challenge and it paid off.

Davis has been compared to Jean-Claude Van Damme—"a glowering charismatic Abercrombie with total K.O. cheekbones," in the words of one fan. He plays Tommy, a stud with a short fuse and a tendency for self-destruction. After blowing it at the 1999 Olympic trials, his dream of going for the big time seems over. He might as well quote Marlon Brando's famous line, "I could have been a contender."

To his rescue comes veteran actor Eddie Jones, playing the Melville-quoting, gone-to-seed trainer. He immediately spots Tommy's raw talent—might we add raw beauty as well?

Jones gets the role of a lifetime as the trainer who has lost the battle of the bulge, playing the portly, white-haired trainer. Once Tommy comes to trust Marty, he comes alive outside the ring as well as inside it. Marty is overjoyed to be spending a month at his mountain cabin with the hunk.

Once there, the drama suddenly shifts.

WHAT THE CRITICS SAID
"A retreat to the woods for training before a title bout raises the stakes, even as Tommy gets pressure from the powerful, smooth-tongued fight promoter Bob Silver (Paul Raci) to sign with him and leave Marty. The old trainer has his own secrets and desires, which Jones manages to keep so well hidden that when they burst forth, it has the shock of a jolting scene in an Arthur Miller play. The film doesn't end in Milleresque tragedy."
Robert Koehler, *Variety*

The Fine Art of Love: Mine Ha-Ha

(2005)

Homoerotic Overtones in a Girls' Orphanage

Here is this film's plot reduced to a sound bite: Set in an oppressive boarding school for girls, sexually inquisitive young women are kept in line by stern supervisors and the always beautiful Jacqueline Bisset, who pays the headmistress suppressing her own desires and secrets.

John Irvin directed this film based on the novel *Mine-Haha or Physical Education of Young Girls* by German author Frank Wedekind. This co-production was made with forces in England, Italy, and the Czech Republic. It was shot in the Czech Republic in a bucolic setting.

Under the Bisset's unrelenting baton, the girls are being groomed for the ballet. Supporting cast members include an adventurous girl Vera (Natalia Tena), who, with her friends Hidalla (Mary Nighy) and Irene (Hannah Taylor-Gordon), enter a locked library where they discover a hidden chamber with the details of their pedigrees. Vera gets locked in, and Bisset's cruel punishment leads to tragedy.

WHAT THE CRITICS SAID
"Subtlety is not Irvin's strong suit, but neither is an understanding of how to use the text's rich symbolism to further a commentary on sexual desire and suppressed freedom. In a scene that could have been reminiscent of *Salò*, an elderly female aristocrat touches two of the undressed girls, but the montage fails to make any extra-textual comment. Add to that such Gothic elements as a couple of lascivious lesbian servants, and the poignancy of *Maedchen in Uniform* appears increasingly affecting."
Jay Weissberg, *Variety*

"When two of the girls disappear mysteriously, the initial fairytale atmosphere grows more and more eerie. Will the inspector from the nearby city discover the real purpose of the college? Will Hidalla be successful in her revolt against the destiny assigned to her by the Headmistress?"
Federico Del Monte

Fingersmith

(2005)

Lesbian Erotica with Dickensian Intrigue

Divided into three parts and adapted from the Sarah Waters novel, this 181-minute drama, available on DVD, was aired on the BBC in England in 2005. The TV version of the series was split across three one-hour episodes but on DVD it is divided into two 1½ hour segments. Director Aisling Walsh brought the drama to the screen, with a screenplay by Peter Ransley.

Waters gained a large lesbian following, particularly after the publication of her novel, *Tipping the Velvet*. In 2003, she published her novel, *Fingersmith*, just as the BBC TV production of *Tipping the Velvet* was appearing on the screens. Thanks to the success of *Tipping the Velvet*, it was almost inevitable that *Fingersmith* would also be filmed.

Set in London in 1862, it is the story of a young orphan, Susan Trinder, who grows up among petty thieves—they were called "Fingersmiths" back then. Sue is played by Sally Hawkins, who is brought up by Mrs. Sucksby (Imelda Staunton). The woman looks after orphans and unwanted babies, finding work for them in her gang of thieves and pickpockets. Shades of *Oliver Twist*.

Like that of most Victorian dramas, the plot is intricate. A member of the gang, Richard "Gentleman" Rivers (as played by Rupert Evans) schemes to marry a rich heiress, Maud Lilly (Elaine Cassidy). Gentleman (who isn't) plans to send her off to a madhouse and steal her fortune. He arranges to have Sue employed as Maud's maid and he promises her a vast fortune at the time, 3,000 British pounds.

When Sue meets Maud, she discovers a frail, sensitive girl to whom she feels sympathy. Her mistress suffers from nightmares, and Sue soon joins her in bed to offer comfort . . . and more. Sue even teaches Maud some lessons in lovemaking as a relationship between mistress and maid develops.

We won't give away the rest of the plot, but expect the unexpected in twists and turns.

Floored by Love

(2005)

Love, As Interpreted by Two Diverse Families

Director and co-author Desirée Lim is the creator of this 60-minute Canadian drama in which a lesbian couple contemplates marriage, and a family with a gay teen son takes in an unexpected visitor from the past. Did we forget to mention that the lesbian couple is Chinese/Japanese and that the family is African-American/Jewish?

Cara (Natalie Sky) thinks she's happily attached in a perfect relationship with her beautiful, loving partner, Janet (Shirley Ng). Along comes a same-sex marriage bill approved in British Columbia, and Janet wants to get married. All hell breaks loose for Cara who is pressured by her lesbian lover to say "I do." In the meantime, Cara's parents want her to marry a man.

The other family in Vancouver centers around a gay son, Jesse (Trenton Millar). His straight stepdad, a mild-mannered accountant named Norman (Michael Robinson), must compete for Jesse's affection with Daniel (Andrew McIlady), the boy's biological father. A trendy, hip, and now openly gay actor, Daniel breezes back into the family after a long absence.

The foundation of the family threatens to crack when the gay teenage son decides to follow his dad back to New York. His liberal, New Age mother reluctantly agrees, even though the idea of her son moving across the continent is breaking her heart.

In this flick of two multicultural families, the characters navigate through different layers of universal love for their life partners, children, and parents, each on his/her own, finally to discover their lives aren't so far apart.

WHAT THE CRITICS SAID

"*Floored by Love* has flashes of wit, but mostly it's merely amusing. The weak pun of the title (revealed in the film's final scenes, so I won't ruin it for you) is emblematic of a script that could have used a lot more punching up in the early draft stages."
Nancy Legato, *MetroWeekly*

The Fluffer

(2001)

Johnny Rebel, Heartthrob and Sexual Fantasy

If there's any gay man who doesn't already know what a fluffer is, it's a person who sexually stimulates a porno star to make him camera ready. Fluffers get their man hard by playing with his penis and/or performing fellatio.

Becoming a fluffer was not what the film's protagonist Sean (Michael Cunio) had in mind when he arrived in Hollywood hoping, like thousands of others, to break into the movies. One day he rents a film that he thinks is *Citizen Kane.* As it turns out, it's a gay porno film starring a streak of sex with a ten-inch dick, Johnny Rebel.

Sean becomes transfixed by the star and seeks employment at Men of Janus pictures. Hired as a cameraman, he finds out that his duties will involve "work" as a fluffer.

By coincidence, he's assigned to fluff the beautiful but self-destructive star Johnny Rebel himself. Scott Gurney, who plays the stud, is a talented actor in his own right. In the film, he plays it as a straight man who's "gay for pay" because gay porn pays more than straight porn.

Obviously Johnny will not fall in love with his puppy but inevitably will use and abuse him. On the side, Johnny has a girlfriend named Julie (Roxanne Day), who works as a stripper under the pseudonym of Babylon.

Directors Richard Glatzer and Wash Westmoreland (who wrote the script) conceived *The Fluffer* as an inside look at the gay porn scene, and they succeeded in making a movie of substance. They even managed a cameo spot for Deborah Harry who plays the manager of the club where Day performs.

WHAT THE CRITICS SAID
"*The Fluffer* begins as the light satire on the gay porno industry its title suggests, but then develops parallel stories of thwarted love and ultimately emerges as a coming-of-age odyssey of notable substance and honesty. Writer and co-director Wash West researched the world of gay porn so thoroughly that he ended up making some adult videos himself."
Kevin Thomas, *Los Angeles Times*

Fögi Is a Bastard

(*F. est un salaud;* 1998)

A 15-Year-Old Boy in a Dysfunctional Gay Affair

Bastard might not be the right translation—perhaps "rotter." This French film helmed by Marcel Gisler (also the co-scripter) traces the love story of a 15-year-old boy Beni (Vincent Branchet) who falls in love with Fögi (Frederic Andrau), the gay singer in a rock band.

Fögi sings in English although the band is French, dreaming dreams of becoming the next French Velvet Underground. Beni has developed a crush on Fögi and sends him a note, making himself available. Fögi takes the bait. Even though he has no previous sexual experience, Beni seems all too willing to take off his clothes and hop in bed with his idol. Both leads show the full monty.

The rock singer at first merely uses the young boy for sexual relief, later turning him into a "slave dog" in S&M submission rituals. Fögi's punk band is called "The Minks," but they quickly fade from favor. Fögi returns to his former occupation of dealing drugs, even heroin. He turns young Beni onto acid.

Both men, the younger and older versions, are well cast. When cash runs short, Fögi hires Beni out as a call boy. Still strung out on his fixation on Fögi, Beni is only too willing to follow his hero along any downward path.

WHAT THE CRITICS SAID
"Beni is Fögi's dog. Too bad *My Life as a Dog* was already taken. It sounds unpromising, yet the film is such an unsparingly realistic portrayal, and it is beautifully shot in a gritty style with a very mobile camera."
Ken Rudolph

"Beni's hustling (and some modeling) brings in enough money to support them both, and Fögi does not even have to deal drugs any more. He has a horror of growing old and refuses to do so. The movie shows how self-destructive love can be."
Stephen O. Murray

Food of Love

(2002)

A Film Adaptation of Leavitt's *The Page Turner*

Helmer Ventura Pons adapted this script from David Leavitt's novella *The Page Turner*. It is more than a routine coming-of-age story, although it has a strong element of that too.

A handsome and talented music student, Paul Porterfield (Kevin Bishop), is employed as a page-turner at the San Francisco concert of a world-famous pianist, Richard Kennington (Paul Rhys).

Looking into the void of middle age, Kennington, a former boy wonder, is now aging. His looks as well as his zest for life are fading. He needs a transfusion of vitality the way a vampire needs blood. Along comes the little cutie.

Paul's mother, Pamela, is portrayed by Juliete Stevenson, who plays it scatty and jittery. One day she discovers that her husband is having an affair. Taking Paul with her, she flies to Barcelona to escape her trouble.

Just by chance, Paul discovers that Kennington is performing in Barcelona. He looks up his idol, and the two men have an affair, perhaps even falling in love. There's a problem. Paul's mother also fancies Kennington. When she goes to his hotel room to seduce him, she discovers a pair of her son's shorts.

Back in the states, Paul faces the reality that he's not the great musician his mother wants him to be. In another coincidence, he runs into Joseph Mansourian (Allan Corduner), Kennington's agent. The manager also seduces the young boy.

WHAT THE CRITICS SAID
"One-movie-a-year cult Catalàn helmer Ventura Pons makes his fifth consecutive appearance with *Food of Love*. Attempts by Iberian helmers at Anglophone fare have generally been misfires, but Pons has aimed for a performance-drive drama whose virtues are of the small-scale, low-key variety, with the director working within narrow dramatic limits as always but here doing so brilliantly."
Jonathan Holland, *Variety*

For the Bible Tells Me So

(2007)

Tossing a Grenade at Religious Zealots

Daniel G. Karslake both co-authored and directed this 95-minute docu exploring the "intersection" between religion and homosexuality in the U.S. and how the religious right has used its interpretation of the Bible to stigmatize the gay community.

Regrettably, it's preaching to the choir (the G&L people likely to take in this movie). Such noted homophobes as orange juicy Anita Bryant, the "sinning" Rev. Jimmy Swaggart, and that ferocious crocodile of the right, James Dobson of the *Focus on the Family* group, aren't likely to show up to see it.

The film deals with a hot-button issue, and Karslake isn't afraid to press that button. It's ambitious and daring, attacking the traditional Christian stance against homosexuality, offering other interpretations of the very few verses in the Bible that specifically deal with the subject.

Providing reintorprotations are such heavy-weights as Archbishop Desmond Tutu among other illustrious defenders, notably Gene Robinson, the first openly gay bishop to be consecrated by the Episcopals. That set off a firestorm which is still threatening to split that church.

Robinson provides his own story about coming out to his parents. Other heavyweights weighing in are former Rep. Dick Gephardt, wife Jane, and daughter Chrissy. Presented also is Mary Lou Wallner, who became a cultural warrior against homophobia following the suicide of her lesbian daughter. Missing is Dick Cheney's daughter.

WHAT THE CRITICS SAID
"With great conviction, Tutu and others repeatedly point to Jesus' teachings of love and inclusion as the standard by which the church must regard the gay community—a standard certainly not upheld by the legacy of hate crimes, fire-and-brimstone sermons and condemnations perpetrated in the name of God, as recapped in extensive archival footage."
Justin Chang, *Variety*

Forgive and Forget

(2000)

Unrequited Love & Obsession

This bittersweet drama was originally produced for Scottish television and aimed primarily at a straight audience. It arrived in the United States and Canada at various gay and lesbian film festivals before making its way to video.

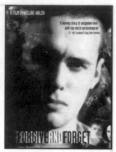

For 14 years, a working class plasterer David O'Neil (Steve John Sheperd) and a perpetual student Theo (John Simm) have been best mates. As the more macho member of the pair, David is a kind of protector and defender of Theo. They seem so devoted to each other that they would appear to be lovers.

Then one fine day Hannah (Laura Fraser), a photographer, enters the picture. She meets Theo on the rebound as she is recovering from a broken relationship with a male lover who was unfaithful. As Theo moves deeper and deeper into his new relationship, David is neglected. The bond that held them together so tightly is loosening.

Life is made more difficult for David because he lives with virulently homophobic parents. A closeted gay man, he is deeply in love with Theo but has never made his desire known to "my best mate."

At first Theo tries to bring David into his new life but he balks, having meaningless sexual pickups in London's Soho district all the while plotting how to break up Theo and Hannah. Theo becomes suspicious and confronts David to talk about his motives in trying to break him up with Hannah.

Unable to tell Theo that he is in love with him, David, in a surprise move, goes on a popular UK confessional show, *Forgive and Forget*, that evokes memories of episodes of Ricki Lake's former show or *Jerry Springer*.

On the show in front of the UK, David admits that he's gay and declares his love for Theo. Not only do David's parents reject him, but Theo beats him into a bloody mess until David is rescued by the intervention of Hannah.

The only good that seems to come out of this is that David is freed at last of having to lead a lie.

Fortune and Men's Eyes

(1971)

The Boys in the Band Go to Jail

When that handsome hunk, Sal Mineo, directed the prison drama, *Fortune and Men's Eyes* in Los Angeles, the lead actor dropped out at the last minute. Mineo took over the role, appearing frontally nude in front of an all-gay audiences, revealing for the first time that his leg-

endary nine inches were not just legend. Regrettably, Sal Mineo did not appear as the star in the film version, and consequently did not reveal for all the world to see what a magnificent man this Bronx-born Italian was.

This brutal drama, released by Metro-Goldwyn-Mayer and directed by Harvey Hart, based on John Herbert's play (he also scripted the film), is not for the squeamish.

Caught with pot, Smitty (Wendell Burton), still a teenager, is sentenced to six months in jail in a Québec prison. Here he meets his cellmates: Queenie (Michael Greer), a flamboyant drag queen; Rocky (Zooey Hall), the strong silent type but a cocky con; and Mona (Danny Freedman), an effeminate Shakespeare-quoting prisoner.

Rocky spells it out to Smitty. Unless he places himself under the protection of one of the more powerful prisoners—Rocky himself, for example—he'll become the victim of gang rape by virtually anybody in the cell block who wants his beautiful young ass.

Rocky's words hold true when Smitty is almost gang raped by brutish prisoners but rescued by Rocky. This leads to Rocky becoming Smitty's "old man," which means he has to surrender his ass for a pounding anytime Rocky chooses.

The tide turns when Smitty, taunted by Queenie, fights Rocky, emerging the victor. Humiliated, Rocky commits suicide. Smitty is now the stud on the block. He demands that Mona become his love slave.

One of the highlights of the film is a bump-and-grind strip that Queenie performs at a Christmas variety show in front of the warden and his wife. The climax of the act is when Queenie shows the full monty.

A Four Letter Word

(2007)

A Latter Day Queer Wonderland

Reviewer Richard Hellstern made this startling statement: "This movie is either total crap or the best gay movie ever made. Maybe both." The opening certainly attracted our attention, taking place in a naked yoga class. Expect breezy shots of male genitalia and characters named "Long John."

Exploring gay relationships, this romantic comedy was directed by Swedish-born Casper Andreas, known for his *Slutty Summer* film. He's at it again in this pacey, raunchy, well-crafted, sleek, and hilarious *tour de force*.

The film's star and slut-on-the-prowl is Luke (Jesse Archer), who lives like AIDS never happened. Entering a gay bar, he shouts, "Let the manhunt begin."

Then he meets Stephen (Charlie David), a world-class beauty and a hunka man who puts stars in Luke's eyes and a hard-on in his jeans. Luke falls for Stephen, thinking he's the heir to a fortune. Actually, he turns out to be a hustler. The film might have been called *The Playboy and the Prostitute*.

This "total top" (Stephen) declares serial "hoe" (Luke) to be a "gay cliché." One of Luke's typical *bon mots* is, "There's a party in my pants and everybody's coming."

By day, Luke works in a lube-and-dildo store in New York's Chelsea district. Here his friend Zeke (played by Cory Grant—is that name for real?) is involved in social activism and provides commentary on Luke's lack of morals.

The cast is talented, including Mace, as played by Jeremy Gender, a self-styled "penile anthropologist." The fag hag role is performed especially with conviction by Virginia Bryan, a recovering alcoholic. She's a masochistic, frazzled mess, who can't stop obsessing about her upcoming wedding, even when receiving cunnilingus. A subplot involves an interracial couple.

The film is not just about love and sex, but about living life on your own terms.

Fox and His Friends

(1975)

Or, Fassbinder's Fox Has No Friends

As Hollywood producers tentatively took on gay subjects in the 1970s, Rainer Werner Fassbinder had more co-jones than any of them. A queer script didn't frighten him at all.

Before his death at the age of 33 from a drug-related suicide, he'd turned out 36 feature films, including *Ali: Fear Eats the Soul* in 1974 and fascinating *The Marriage of Maria Braun* in 1979. The director dealt with gay characters with an amazing frankness, portraying them just as selfish, brutal, or grasping as straight people. Evil, he suggested, does not depend on your sexual preference.

Fassbinder cast himself in the lead role of Franz Bieberkopf ("the Fox"). Since the film required him to appear in a full-frontal nude scene, the normally portly director dieted strenuously to lose weight in order to play Fox. Fassbinder not only directed and starred in this controversial movie, he co-scripted it with Christian Hohoff.

Fox is a poor circus worker who is at loose ends when his lover (and barker) Klaus (Karl Scheydt) is arrested for tax fraud. Fox must turn tricks to buy a lottery ticket, which he hopes will bring him vast riches.

Indeed Fox wins the lottery but falls in with a group of queer snobs, including Eugen (Peter Chatel), who hooks onto him for his money. Eugen is the son of an industrialist who is on the verge of bankruptcy. Eugen's family successfully sets out to milk Fox of his 500,000 German marks. In that they succeed, humiliating the now-broke Fox by forcing him to work at their factory as slave labor.

At the end of the film, Fox lies dying on a subway station floor, as greedy kids pick his pockets and his so-called "friends" step over his body.

WHAT THE CRITICS SAID
"At the delicate art of combining the bizarre and the mundane, nobody is more skillful than Fassbinder."
Roger Ebert

The Fox

(1968)

D.H. Lawrence's Spin on Lesbian Love

This was one of the most controversial lesbian movies of the 1960s, and was banned in certain movie houses. True, it makes explicit use of lesbian scenes that might have been merely hinted at in the Lawrence novella. *The Fox* was hardly as graphic as his infamous *Lady Chatterley's Lover*.

Shot during a cold Canadian winter, mostly around Toronto, *The Fox* had an all-star cast, with Sandy Dennis playing Jill Banford, Anne Heywood, cast as Ellen March, and Keir Dullea (then at his most beautiful) cast as the male intruder Paul Renfield.

Director Mark Rydell makes the most of the Canadian winter, its early sunsets, its cold, and its snow. He does it so effectively that the viewer wonders if there will ever be a spring.

A sickly, chattering Jill and a quieter, stronger Ellen are hopelessly trying to run a chicken farm in Canada. They are hampered by a rapacious fox that keeps eating up their profits.

The crisis arrives in the hunky form of Paul (Dullea) whose grandfather once owned the farm. During his shore leave, this merchant seaman offers to help the women get the farm up and running so they can make a living from it.

Love blooms between Ellen and Paul (who symbolically, of course, is the fox). They become lovers in front of the jealous eyes of Jill.

Jill makes her intentions known, and there is an explicit scene where the two women make out in their bedroom, with Jill kissing Ellen's neck, shoulders, and chest.

Paul has left the farm briefly but returns to find the women chopping down a tall tree. As the macho of the trio, he takes charge of the axe, but warns Jill to move from the tree's path. When she refuses she is killed by the falling tree (we get the symbolism).

At the end Ellen sells the farm and goes away with Paul.

Fried Green Tomatoes

(1991)

Lesbians in the Gothic Deep South

This is a stellar adaptation of Fannie Flagg's novel *Fried Green Tomatoes at the Whistle Stop Café*. Flagg herself appears in an amusing cameo.

It's a story-within-a-story, with an all-star cast. Told in flashbacks, a repressed Southern wife, Evelyn Couch (Kathy Bates), meets Ninny Threadgoode (Jessica Tandy) at a nursing home. Evelyn becomes fascinated by Ninny's tales of two feisty female friends and their escapades back in the 1920s and 30s.

In Flagg's novel, Idgie Threadgoode (Mary Stuart Masterson) and Ruth Jamison (Mary Louise Parker) are lesbian lovers, but in director Jon Avnet's film, they are just best friends. Forget that Idgie wears brogans and has an obvious crush on Ruth. Idgie is definitely the tomboy next door, a distaff Huck Finn.

She rescues the pregnant Ruth from her abusive husband, redneck Frank Bennett (Nick Searcy), aided by black Big George (Stan Shaw).

Idgie takes Ruth back to Whistle Stop. Here they are helped by Sipsey (Cicely Tyson).

Later Idgie and her loyal manservant, Big George, stand trial on a charge of murdering her brute of a husband.

John Avnet (*Risky Business*), when asked about the film's lesbian sub-theme, said, "I had no interest in going into the bedroom."

WHAT THE CRITICS SAID
"A drama about strong, giving, funny women, *Fried Green Tomatoes* seems plucked from the same patch as the play-turned movie *Steel Magnolias*. It's not exactly a successful hybrid, but you could get a craving for it anyway. Celebrating the crucial, sustaining friendships between two sets of modern-day and 1930s Southern femmes, pic emerges as absorbing and life-affirming quality fare, but for a story celebrating fearlessness, it's remarkably cautious."
Variety

Friends and Family

(2001)

Gay Couple Are Hit Men for the Mafia

Talk about a reverse of stereotypes. In this film the gay guys are the machos, the straight fellows prefer cooking and sewing. In the mob world depicted in *Friends and Family,* it's okay for a gay guy to make out with another, providing they can each shoot straight. In the case of two enforcer lovers, Danny (Christopher Gartin) and Stephen (Greg Lauren), they can indeed. Nobody who owes the Mafia money seems beyond their reach.

Directed by Kristen Coury, with a script from Joseph Triebwasser, *Friends and Family* depicts two handsome mob lieutenants armed to the teeth and sworn to protect their *padrone.*

When the hit men's families come to visit, they put their guns, knives, and brass knuckles away. It even seems cool that they are gay to their Midwest parents (a bit of a stretch).

The cover used by these guys is that they're employed as caterers, which explains why they work nights and wear tuxedos. But it's also a bit of a stretch when the audience has to swallow the fact that two gay men, in their 30s and living together in a Manhattan apartment, wouldn't know how to boil an egg when our heroes must demonstrate their skill as caterers.

WHAT THE CRITICS SAID
"Stephen and Danny essentially play the straight men to hysterically mincing gunslingers. As Stephen, Greg Lauren is a poor man's George Hamilton, all crisp tux, inky hair, and charm. As Danny, Christopher Gartin is fine as the adorable, loving boyfriend who likes to strap a pistol to his ankle, just in case."
Francesca Chapman

"First-timer Coury's fast pace can't outrun Joseph Triebwasser's predictable script, saddled with mobster clichés and queer stereotypes. A Judy-quoting queen helps mob thugs pass as gay by showing them Liberace videos."
Jorge Morales

Friends of God
A Road Trip With Alexandra Pelosi

(2007)

Human Crocodiles in Red-State America

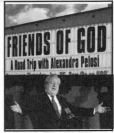

Alexandra Pelosi's mother, Nancy, is the most powerful woman in U.S. history—yes, even more so than Hillary Clinton. Daughter Alexandra Pelosi decided to go on a road trip to film some of America's gay-bashing religious nuts, including the disgraced pastor, Ted Haggard, "victim" of that embarrasing hustler problem.

Her film highlights "The Big Three" flashpoint points of controversy in contemporary American politics: Evolution, Abortion, and Homosexuality. But it does so much more, hitting the Holy Land Experience Theme Park in Orlando, a drive-through church, a visit with "Cruisers (of cars) for Christ," and even a stopover with the Christian Wrestling Federation (we're not making that up).

The God-fearing wrestlers pummel each other in a ring surrounded by cheering crowds of young children, including prepubescent girls screaming for God to "invade" their bodies. They appear to be sexually turned on by the wrestlers, which seems to suggest they are eager to lose their cherries. Please, say this impression isn't true.

For *Friends of God*, Alexandra rambled through 16 states in a rental car. She meets these "Christlers," who place scripture in truck-stop menus and put huge crosses alongside state highways.

The film has a voyeur factor—maybe better called "The Mom Factor." Here is the daughter of a woman who is more hated by the Christian Right than Hillary herself. Nancy Pelosi was vilified by conservative Christians during the midterm elections as the leader of the supposed ultra-liberal San Francisco gay rights agenda.

A former producer for NBC News, Alexandra, in her docu, is not an attack dog, and she's learned to distinguish those old dragons of hate—the lardy Jerry Falwell, the increasingly wacko Pat Robertson, and that vicious scorpion, the very, very anti-gay James Dobson—from some younger evangelicals.

"Young evangelicals tell you that these men don't speak for them," Alexandra noted.

Frisk

(1996)

He Picks Up Guys & Kills Them

Director Todd Verow's first feature film remains his most notorious. It also made Verow infamous in gay circles.

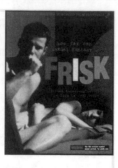

When first shown in San Francisco at a film festival, it caused what one reviewer called "a pink riot—queen threats and hissy fits."

Set in an erotic world of sado-masochism, the film portrays the sexual appetites of a young man for whom killing and eating the victim is the ultimate thrill.

Dennis, the main character, is played by Michael Gunther, who also does nude scenes. He is quite handsome, a veteran of adult cinema. Cast also includes Craig Chester and Parker Posey in supporting roles and a cameo from Alexis Arquette as a punk for hire.

The story unfolds in a series of letters Dennis writes to his sometimes lover and best friend Julian (Jaie Laplante), and the object of his desire, Julian's younger brother, Kevin (Raoul O'Connell).

The film is not for everyone, except for devotees of bondage, S&M, leather, fetish culture, homicide, suicide, and snuff. Call it art-house erotica.

Dennis meets up with Henry in the movie. Played by Craig Chester, this character likes to be bloodied while having sex. "Doesn't everyone?" asked one queen out loud at the San Francisco showing.

No moral judgment is imposed in the film, and no punishment is dished out.

WHAT THE CRITICS SAID
"Sensual and suggestive, it is a serious and discreet work of considerable dark impact and no little humor."
Kevin Thomas, *Los Angeles Times*

"Awkwardly, distressingly real."
Dennis Harvey, *Variety*

Führer Ex

(2002)

Neo-Nazi and Queer

Winfried Bonengel, who both directed and co-scripted this film, presents a cinematic study of the effects of changing political ideologies on two friends.

Führer Ex

Fair-haired and virginal Heiko (Christian Blümel) becomes friends with Tommy (Aaron Hildebrand), who is a juvenile delinquent. Arrested on a minor flag-burning crime, he is sent to jail where he emerges tattooed.

Both young men dream of escaping East Germany to the West. If only they had waited for The Wall to fall.

One night they try to break through the barbed wire but are caught and arrested. Both are sentenced to a cruel Communist prison. To survive, Tommy joins a neo-Nazi group, whereas Heiko allows himself to fall under the protection of an older prisoner who inevitably rapes him.

The two continue to plan to escape the prison and flee to the West. In that, Tommy makes it but Heiko does not. He remains in the harsh prison.

Years later when the Berlin Wall has come down, Tommy is seen living a settled life in West Berlin. Freed from prison, Heiko is now a Neo-Nazi himself. The roles have shifted: Heiko is the bad guy, Tommy the good guy.

WHAT THE CRITICS SAID
"What makes the film so sad is that Tommy is absolutely right about the dying East German government, and the freedom he wants is just around the corner, but he has no way of knowing it. Both he and Heiko waste time and energy on an impossible revolution that turns out to be totally unnecessary. How ironic, and how tragic."
Don Willmott

Funny Kinda Guy

(2004)

Simon de Voil from Female to Male

This 83-minute docu from the UK traces the saga of singer and songwriter Simon de Voil who changed his gender from female to male. Although he finally achieved his long-sought masculinity, he sacrificed the elegantly trained quality of his singing voice, the result of extended hormone treatment.

Directed by Travis Reeves, *Funny Kinda Guy* is very slow moving, although de Voil himself is charming.

All his life, de Voil apparently knew he was in the wrong skin, preferring to be a "transman" to a butch lesbian. The docu is very realistic, even depicting de Voil giving himself his first shot of testosterone.

The happy ending shows the blue-haired lead in a Tranniboy T-shirt becoming all man and dancing in the rain with his bride-to-be.

WHAT THE CRITICS SAID
"*Funny Kinda Guy* is not a likely title for a documentary about a transgendered singer-songwriter who, while gaining his true identity as a man, must sacrifice his voice to hormone treatment. Yet Scotland's Simon de Voil is so charismatic and good-natured, the title quickly grabs and never lets go."
Jim Norrena, *San Francisco LGBT Film Festival*

"A strong sense of compassion towards a clever guy struggling to come to terms with his own masculinity . . . *Funny Kinda Guy* scores by simply telling it straight."
Isla Leaver-Yap, *The List*

"A standout at the Melbourne Queer Film Festival is *Funny Kinda Guy*, a painful journey taken by transgendered singer-songwriter Simon de Voil's transition from male to female."
Lesa Beel

"*Funny Kinda Guy* travels from Scotland to Australia through transgender protagonist Simon. The main character, Simon, actually falls in love with an Australian girl from Brisbane."
Megan Carrigy

Garçon stupide

(*Stupid Boy;* 2004)

Existential Heartache and Sex

Shot in French with English subtitles, this is a comedy/drama that spins around Loïc, a young, handsome gay man in Switzerland who works in a chocolate factory by day and seeks anonymous sex at night. It's an existential coming-of-age story—call it a gay version of *Alfie*.

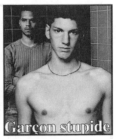

Director Lionel Baier, who also co-wrote the screenplay with Laurent Guido, is audacious and voyeuristic. Yes, he even moves in for a close-up of Pierre Chatagny's dick. It looks meaty and uncut in repose. The young, inexperienced actor plays Loïc. His part calls for hardcore sex, which he manages to convey rather convincingly. Amazingly, in spite of all the sex and the nudity, the film is strangely un-erotic.

In a surprise turn, Baier appears as himself, one of Loïc's tricks, although we never see his face, only hearing his voice. Baier puzzles Loïc. The man wants to get to know the impatient young kid before enjoying his sizable endowment.

Loïc's sole friend is Marie, who delivers the best performance in the movie. She is the low-key but very experienced Natacha Koutchoumov, playing a student who works in a natural history museum where illicit lovers sometimes go to fuck.

She listens to Loïc's erotic tales but is clearly too advanced in her soul to be a mere fag hag with voyeuristic interests. She is clearly losing patience with Loïc, with whom she might be in love.

A poignant moment in the film occurs when Loïc becomes infatuated with a local black soccer star, Rui Pedro Alves. He stalks him and eventually meets him. But the unlikely pairing hardly develops into the romance that was at first suggested. Alves is just too much of a family man for that. He's also boringly straight.

The sex scenes are stark and clinical, and apparently Loïc would even go to bed with a troll.

The young man's existential ache is believably but often boringly portrayed. But, of course, that is the nature of the ache itself.

The Gay Deceivers

(1969)

Two "Normal" Guys Posing as Faggots

This low-budget comedy, a rarity in the 1960s, fails in many respects, but is an amusing diversion seen on DVD. Director Bruce Kessler summed up the plot this way: "They had to keep their hands off girls in order to keep the Army's hands off them."

Made in the era of the Vietnam War, when men (that is non-gay men) were being drafted, the film delivers a message, but it's not a preachy one. It does show how gays are discriminated against, all the while being a send-up of gay stereotypes as well.

The *British Monthly Film Bulletin* summed up the case for the opposition: "A sick joke at the expense of homosexuals, whose presumed mannerism of speech and behavior are grotesquely parodied to occasionally amusing but more often tasteless effect."

Good buddies (non-sexual) Danny Devlin (Kevin Coughlin) and Alliot Crane (Larry Casey) plot to avoid the Army draft where they would be shipped to the rice paddies of Vietnam.

In spite of their being a "couple," Lt. Col. Dixon (Jack Starrett) isn't convinced. He intends to sniff around to find out if they are really gay.

To convince the Army, the young men move into a gay complex inhabited by the most outrageous gay stereotypes this side of Fairyland. The "Queen Bee" and landlord Malcolm (Michael Greer) is his most flamboyant self. He also created a sensation in *Fortune and Men's Eyes.*

He also personally designed the garish décor of the bungalows, including the one in which the "new couple" lives. When word reaches girlfriends, family, and employers, the consequences are dire for the couple who find that they have been relegated by society to second-class status merely because of their sexual orientation. Elliott, for example, is fired as a lifeguard from a private athletic club.

Gay Republicans

(2004)

What's Wrong With These People?

In the view of some gay men, for a homo to be a Republican in the era of that horror, ex-President George W. Bush, is like a Jew praising Hitler on his way to the gas chamber. A bit harsh, but Bush was the most fiercely polarizing figure in the U.S. presidency. Not since Lincoln has a nation been so divided about this moron who rode to Washington from Texas on Daddy Bush's coattails.

President Clinton disappointed gays by not living up to his early promise. But Bush took a decided anti-gay stance, virtually unknown in the history of U.S. presidents, many of who were anti-gay but hardly took to the air waves to vent their prejudice.

In lieu of all that, the question remains, why would an active gay man with reasonable intelligence want to join the Log Cabin Republicans? Of course, that just proves that there is nothing homogeneous about the gay community.

Wash Westmoreland, the film's director and writer, takes a compassionate look at this group of conservative homos. He makes it clear that the year 2004 was rough on the Log Cabin boys as they were put to a test when the Bush creature in the White House declared his unequivocal opposition to gay marriage.

That presented queer GOP guys with a stark choice: whether to be a good Republican and support this ill-chosen idiot or to stand up for their civil rights as gay Americans. The decisions afforded them a historic chance to affect the election but it also opened schisms that threatened the unity of the Log Cabin itself. In this docu, politics gets personal as the Republican gays wrestle with an issue that goes to the core of their identity.

The most penetrating attempt to explain the political oxymoron comes from the "poster boy" of the Log Cabin, Steve May. "Our party [meaning the GOP] is supposed to be one of freedom and liberty, and that's what we were. Unfortunately, our party has been hijacked by people who don't really believe in freedom and democracy."

Gay Sex in the 70s

(2005)

From Gay Libertarian to Gay Plague

"It was wilder than you thought."
— *Entertainment Weekly*

Ed Gonzalez in *Slant Magazine* stated the case very well: "If Jake Gyllenhall's character from Sam Mendes's Gulf War drama *Jarhead* were queer and had lived in New York City during the 70s, he might have had an easier time getting off."

In this 72-minute documentary, middle-aged men wax nostalgically about a long-gone era when New York was turned into a great bacchanalia which began with the Stonewall riots in 1969 and lasted until the coming of the black death in 1981.

Distributed by Wolfe Releasing, the documentary is obviously a labor of love for its director and co-producer, Joseph F. Lovett. A highly skilled professional, Lovett was one of the producers/directors for ABC News "*20/20*" for ten years, breaking off in 1989 to found Lovett Productions.

The era lives again. Through the depictions of the notorious Christopher Street piers; the dark, dank backrooms of sleazy bars; the Rambles in Central Park, the dangerous truck orgies at night in the Meat Packing district; orgies among the sanddunes of Fire Island, and, of course, the Continental Baths where fag hag Bette Midler was "strewing poppers like flower petals in her wake."

Gay men in New York and San Francisco flocking to this movie hoping to see pre-condom porn will be disappointed. They'd be better off spending the night at home watching the best of Jeff Stryker on DVD.

Gay Sex in the 70s takes nostalgia buffs back to those fondly remembered times when a young, suited Wall Street junior executive, with a wife and two kids at home in the suburbs, could duck into an anonymous doorway for a quick blowjob on the way to work.

For younger viewers, who grew up after the party was over, the film's own synopsis makes a telling point: "For those who became sexually active after the age of AIDS, this film may be a startling revelation of what everyday life was like when American youth were cutting loose from Puritanical values and ascribing to the watchword of the time, 'If it feels good, do it!'"

George Michael, A Different Story

(2004)

Candid, Self-Deprecating, & Altogether Winning

Londoner George Michael has certainly had his triumphs and tragedies. As a one-time member of one of the most successful bands of the 80s, *Wham!*, he's a most worthy subject for this docubio that runs for 93 minutes.

In it, in addition to George himself, we get appearances from Sting, Mariah Carey, Elton John, and Boy George. Each of these artists, including George Michael, plays himself/herself.

After Michael split with *Wham!*, he launched a massively successful solo career, beginning with the album, "Faith," in 1987. The album featured a series of chart-topping hit singles and sold more than 7 million copies.

In the most regrettable and saddest episode in Michael's career, he was arrested on a charge of lewd conduct in a men's public restroom at a park near his Beverly Hills home. Following the incident, the singer appeared on CNN to publicly reveal his homosexuality. The artist later made a music video mocking the whole incident. The undercover police officer who arrested Michael later filed a civil suit against him for defamation as Michael in the song portrayed himself as a victim of entrapment. The case was dismissed.

Michael's autobiographical film premiered in Berlin, during which time he made public appearances. "I think my own genre is dead," he said. "I don't really think that there is anyone in the modern pop business who I feel I want to spar with."

In the film, directed by Southan Morris, Michael takes viewers through the highs and lows of his career. He reveals stories of his childhood growing up in Hertfordshire, and he gets together with Andrew Ridgeley to discuss the *Wham!* Years. He also talks about his later career, including his battles with record label Sony, as well as his more recent protest songs, speaking out against George Bush and the Iraq war.

The singer also offers some candid insights into his private life, discussing the pain of losing his Brazilian boyfriend, Anselmo Feleppa, to AIDS, as well as his notorious 1998 arrest.

Gia Carangi (1960-1986) was an American fashion model who became almost legendary in the late 70s and early 80s. The beauty was featured on the covers of both *Vogue* and *Cosmopolitan*. Regrettably she became addicted to heroin, and her modeling career declined. At 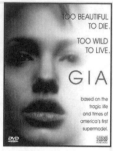 the age of 26, she was one of the first famous women to die of AIDS.

In 1998, Angelina Jolie, as Gia, starred in a biographical film, dramatizing the tempestuous life of the superstar from Philadelphia.

She was bisexual, leaning more toward the lesbian side. In the film Jolie portrays Gia as being sexually intimate with both women and men. In the wake of the model's death, she is said to have epitomized "lesbian chic".

WHAT THE CRITICS SAID

"Angelina Jolie shows her tits. It's a shame that's all this film is known for, for two reasons. Firstly, it's a good movie in its own right, with more interesting directorial flourishes than most made-for-cable films, and strong performances from Jolie and Mercedes Ruehl, as Gia's mother. And secondly, because seeing Jolie's tits are not a good thing. While most people seem to find her irresistibly attractive, that is because most people are stupid. To me, she looks like she's eaten improperly canned tomatoes, and her face is puffing up like a sprained knee from botulism. And her lips? Those bee-stung, cocksucking lips? I wouldn't let those anywhere near my cock. They look fucking contagious. I know I'm poorly hung, but I'd rather not have my genitals get whatever gargantuan elephantitis is disfiguring her face."
Karr Karreau

"Since Gia was a real person, even the facts may hook you in, because it captures a time and a scene and a person you may be interested in. The story does have the ring of truth to it, the script presents Gia 'scars and all,' and Ms. Jolie is a charismatic (and daring) performer."
Scoopy Web

Based on a true story, *A Girl Like Me* relates the tragedy of Gwen Araujo, born Eddie Araujo. It documents his self-discovery that he was born into the wrong sex. As he grew older, he changed his name from Eddie to Gwen, naming himself after his favorite singer, Gwen Stefano.

The murder of this teenage trans girl occurred in Newark, California in October of 2002. Gwen had sex with her killers, performing fellatio and passive sodomy. She told the men that she was menstruating and pushed their hands away from her genitalia.

At a party, a girlfriend of one of the men conducted a forced inspection on Gwen, discovering that she had male genitalia. When she reported it to the men at the party, they went ballistic, brutally attacking her. The torture and beating went on and off for five hours, leading to her death. An autopsy later revealed that she died from strangulation and blunt force trauma to the head.

After she died, she was hog-tied, wrapped in a blanket, and placed in the bed of a pick-up truck. The men drove four hours away and buried her near the Sierra Nevada Mountains. Her murder went unreported for days.

One of the assailants finally broke down and led authorities to the gravesite, providing he would exchange a guilty plea to voluntary manslaughter. The Alameda County assistant district attorney, Chris Lamiero, representing the prosecution, said, "Gwen being transgendered was not a provocative act. She's who she was. But I don't think most jurors are going to think it's OK to engage someone in sexual activity knowing they assume you have one sexual anatomy when you don't."

Two of the defendants were convicted of second degree murder, but not convicted on the charge of a hate crime. The other two men pleaded guilty to voluntary manslaughter. Two of the men offered a plea of "gay panic" self-defense. The crime attracted nationwide attention and was compared to the Matthew Shepard case.

Girl Play

(2004)

A Narcissistic Love Song

A hot lesbian drama that brings together such stars as Dom DeLuise and Mink Stole can't be all bad. Lee Friedlander both directed and co-authored this comedy/drama of two women in love. Gabriel (Dom DeLuise) casts Robin (Robin Greenspan) and Lacie (Lacie Harmon) to play lesbian lovers in his latest production. Unwittingly, he sets into motion a true-life lesbian drama.

Based on the original play, *Real Girls*, this drama is the personal story of its writers/actors, Greenspan and Harmon. They actually met and fell in love while rehearsing a play in which they were cast as lovers.

Girl Play remains rather stage-bound, but does offer insights into love and sex. Obviously lesbians will appreciate it far more than straight or gay male audiences.

As an actor DeLuise camps it up (doesn't he always?) pushing the women to greater intimacy. Too much so. Greenspan's jealous girlfriend (Katherine Randolph) delivers a mandate (or is it womandate?): "No tongues, no noises."

We're always a sucker for John Waters vet, Mink Stole. She plays Greenspan's melodrama queen and Jewish mother who must adapt to her daughter's coming out.

As the movie's dilemma, the girls must ask themselves if their affair involves true love?

WHAT THE CRITICS SAID
"Tedious narcissists Robin Greenspan and Lacie Harmon star as themselves in this adaptation of their play, *Real Girls*. The she-said, she-said, punctuated by artless flashback, essays lesbian bed death, coming out to Mom, and schoolgirl crushes. Greenspan and Harmon's paltry song of themselves concludes with five minutes of outtakes, capping the self-love."
Melissa Anderson

"Any Pirandellian motions are far from this work's extremely unsophisticated exploration of love. Even fans of Stole may tire of seeing her in her now-familiar slot as the homophobic mom."
Robert Koehler, *Variety*

Girlfriend

(2004)

Hindus Riot Over Its Depiction of Lesbians

It's a rare day when a film—a mere movie—touches off rioting, even the burning of a theater. Such was the impact of this Indian lesbian film directed and written by Karan Razdan about a man who comes between two female lovers, forming a triangle with bleak consequences. This film is a black-hearted Bollywood spectacle in which a female relationship threatens straight romance.

It was the girl-on-girl action that led to violent protests from the right-leaning lunatics of the Shiv Sena party. But—get this—even gay activists joined in the protests but for different reasons, of course. The Organized Lesbian Alliance for Visibility and Action charged that the film damages the image of lesbians in India. The exact charge is that *Girlfriend* is "a cheap and titillation-oriented film masquerading as one that's liberal."

The film explores the brutal, violent childhood of Tanya (played by Isha Koppikar), who flees home at the age of eighteen. A "man-hater," because of her father's brutality, she becomes a street fighter and is an expert in kick-boxing.

When she meets Sapna (Amrita Arora), the Sapphic love story begins. The two women settle into a relationship that goes more or less well for five years.

But without conflict there would be no picture. So we face the arrival of Rahul Choudhary (played by an actor called Aashish Choudhary—same last name). He's a London-based owner of a shipping company. He meets Sapna and love blooms. At least we realize now that she is bisexual. The couple plan to get married.

Still deeply in love with Sapna, Tanya experiences a collapsing world at the loss of her girlfriend. Tanya won't let go but plans to hold onto Sapna by hook or crook, conceiving a devious scheme to break up Sapna's relationship with Rahul.

Tejal Shah of the Forum Against Oppression of Women claimed that the film was made to give pleasure to straight males. "All the negative popular myths about lesbians are here."

Girls Will Be Girls

(2003)

Three Men Portray Three Aspiring Actresses

This is a tongue-in-cheek, drag comedy depicting three actresses who are not exactly at the top of the Hollywood food chain. All three parts are played by men in this picture written and directed by Richard Day.

Living in the Hollywood Hills in a split-level that was dated even back in the 1970s, Evie Harris (Jack Plotnick) is what one critic called "a hobbling nightmare of egomania, nymphomania, and dipsomania." A true bitch diva, she's on the comeback trail which is climaxed by her appearance in a one-woman variety special for cable called *All About Evie*. For his portrayal, Plotnick must have been inspired by all those 1940s movies that starred Joan Crawford and Susan Hayward.

Evie's maid, companion, and doormat is the long-suffering Coco (Clinton Leupp), who dreams of Mr. Right who got away. When not catering to Evie, Coco longs for romance and a child.

Enter Vera (Jeffrey Roberson)--plump, dark, and headed for a life of prostitution. Ironically, Vera just happens to be the daughter of a tragically deceased starlet originally cast in *Asteroid*, a role that Evie stole, the one that made her famous.

WHAT THE CRITICS SAID
"Each taking an archetype to its logical extreme, three cross-dressing leads know how to strike a pose and deliver an off-color line. Their sharply defined perfs ballast uneven material whose episodic nature is underlined by the blackouts and coy 'chapter' titles that lazily separate scenes."
Dennis Harvey, *Variety*

"The movie follows each of the women, but Evie—sexually ravenous and repellent, cruelly ambitious but completely past having any kind of career is Day's best creation. In her, we have a character completely without conscience, so that almost everything she says is appalling."
Mick LaSalle

A Glimpse of Hell

(2001)

The Navy Blames an Explosion on Gay Sailors

This is the story of a tragedy, an explosion that killed 47 Navy men aboard the *USS Iowa* and the subsequent cover-up by the Navy, who ridiculously blamed a homosexual affair between two sailors as the reason for the blast.

Mikael Salomon helms this 1989 story based on a book by Charles Thompson. The movie of this real-life disaster probes into deep issues such as honor and justice.

The story of the battleship *USS Iowa* is told through the eyes of Lieutenant Meyer (Robert Sean Leonard). The real reason that *Iowa* blew up was because it was an aging ship with faulty equipment. Obviously, the Navy didn't want to admit that and blamed an onboard homosexual relationship that had gone awry.

The ship's commander, Captain Fred Moosally (James Caan), at first goes along with this decision, but the young gunnery officer, Lt. Meyer, is not so sure. He risks his own career in the Navy by seeking the truth.

The innocent men, accused of being homosexual lovers, are Kendall Truitt (Jamie Harrold) and Dashiell Eaves (Clay Hartwig). Meyer was considered disloyal until a Congressional hearing forced the Navy to revise its findings.

WHAT THE CRITICS SAID
"The most confusing element of the film has us guessing what the truth really is. Depicting Truitt and Hartwigg as close friends with underlying issues is no accident, but leaves us wondering if there was any truth to the original claim. *A Glimpse of Hell* is a convincing adaptation of an unfortunate, yet important event in U.S. military history. It's a story worth telling, and one about which the Navy is long since due to come clean."
Janet Branagan

Go Fish

(1994)

A Lesbian Version of *The Matchmaker*

This black-and-white film from helmer Rose Troche is virtually a legend in the lesbian world. It's discovered every year by gay women just emerging from their closet. It stars Guinevere Turner as Camille (Max) West, who also co-scripted the film.

Max is a trendy, pretty, young lesbian looking for love and not finding it. She's been celibate for "ages." Her roomie, a professor named Kia (T. Wendy McMillan), sets her up with Ely (V.S. Brodie), who already has a lover but one who has moved to another town.

Ely is not Brigitte Bardot in St. Tropez in 1959. In fact, she's rather plain. Ely appears charmingly awkward in her blushing pursuit of the highly adorable Max. The relationship advances as they play the card game "Go Fish" (hence the title).

The awkward sponteneity of their first kiss reflects the way romance often blossoms in real life, not in the movies.

WHAT THE CRITICS SAID
"The film begins with an amusing opening segment in which friends speculate on which women in history were closet lesbians. The list includes Eve, Peppermint Patty, and Marilyn Quayle. Its high spirits, candor, wit, and heart prevail over its outward cheesiness. That's not to say that everyone will be comfortable with a film in which naked babes nibble one another nilly-willy."
Rita Kempley

"The movie's strength is also a weakness: Its matter-of-factness. It records everyday life in an everyday way, and introduces us to some people we are happy to know. But not a whole lot happens, and there are times when a scene continues simply to show the unplanned passage of time. Troche and her collaborators have the right note here. The film is honest, forthright and affectionate, and it portrays the everyday worlds of these ordinary gay women with what I sense is accuracy."
Roger Ebert

Gods and Monsters

(1998)

The Final Days of the Director of *Frankenstein*

This is the semi-fictionalized story of gay director James Whale's last days. Director Bill Condon, who also co-wrote the screenplay, obviously had seen *Sunset Blvd.*

Ian McKellen as James Whale and Brendan Fraser as Clayton Boone have some of their best roles, with Lynn Redgrave cast as the housekeeper Hanna.

Whale, of course, gave the world such films as *Frankenstein* (1931) and *The Bride of Frankenstein* (1935). In *Gods and Monsters*, he develops a friendship with his gardener, a handsome hunk of an ex-Marine, who takes such gestures as a sexual advance.

His mind fading, Whale relives moments of his life to his muscle-bound gardener, including details of his life in the trenches during The Great War.

As his time is passing away, he indulges his fantasies by having the gardener pose for him. He also invites him to use his pool. "We're quite informal here—no need to use a bathing suit."

One of Britain's stateliest homos, McKellen, gives a riveting performance as Whale, who is still living comfortably, although he hasn't made a movie in 16 years. He dabbles a little at painting, lusts a bit, and remembers.

Near the end of the movie, Clayton (Fraser) strips for Whale. But, regrettably, the actor's backers decided it would be wrong for his career to show the full monty, so we are merely tantalized. Actually, the full monty might have made his career skyrocket.

WHAT THE CRITICS SAID
"*Gods and Monsters* is not a deep or powerful film, but it is a good-hearted one, in which we sense the depth of early loss that helped to shape Whale's protective style, and the California openness that allows Clayton Boone to care for a man he has nothing in common with."
Roger Ebert

Goldfish Memory

(2004)

A Thin But Likable Irish Version of *La Ronde*

Written and directed by Elizabeth Gill, this 85-minute comedy/drama is a light-hearted look at the dangers and delights of dating in contemporary Dublin. It's filled with as many romantic entanglements as *La Ronde*.

The film centers around Tom, as played by actor Sean Campion, a literature professor in his forties. He likes to seduce gullible female students—or, as one reviewer put it, he uses "Irish whimsy to get into these girls' knickers."

The teacher's current pet is flighty Clara (as played by Fiona O'Shaughnessy). She spots Tom flirting with another attractive student, Isolde (played by another Fiona, Glascott in this case). Clara's refusal to sit back and sulk sets off a veritable chain reaction of Dublin metrosexuality.

Fickle Tom drives Clara into the arms of a love-struck lesbian TV star, Angie (Flora Montgomery). With Annie, Clara decides to experiment in "alternative love."

The best pal of Annie is a gay bike courier, Red (Keith McErlean), who has taken a shine to a shy young waiter David (Peter Gaynor). David is straight but is having trouble with his long-time girlfriend, and suspects that Red might offer him a way out.

As the film proceeds, expect every coupling combo on the books. This is a tale about *Sex in the City,* Dublin to be precise.

WHAT THE CRITICS SAID
"An ensemble of metrosexual Dubliners populates this vapid relationship comedy, reminiscent of the sponsorship ads that wrap around the commercials during TV's *Friends*. Everyone chatters in a perky romcom language not used by ordinary carbon-based lifeforms. An aging Lothario lecturer serially seduces and discards cute young students who start hooking up with each other in a merry-go-round of decaffeinated love and bowdlerized sex. Like goldfish, they forget the heartbreak and swim on to the next romantic adventure. The movie's forgettable, too."
Peter Bradshaw, *The Guardian*

Gone, But Not Forgotten

(2003)

Amnesia Victim Discovers Who He Really Is

This romantic and erotic film tells the story of Mark Reeves (Matthew Montgomery), who cannot remember who he is. He's been rescued during a flash flood by a hunk of a forest ranger Drew Parker (Aaron Orr). Michael Akers helms this low-budget flick dealing with repressed desire.

After his recovery, Mark is released from the hospital into the care of his rescuer, who takes him to an A-frame house in the hills. Beginning in front of a crackling fire, Drew's hospitality extends to a seduction that Mark enjoys. Mark's brother, Paul, and his wife take a dim view of this emerging relationship.

Flashes of memory begin to come back to Mark. Was there a woman in his life? A fancy car? A job where he's required to wear a business suit?

Of course, Mark's identity will inevitably be revealed, which sets the next stage in this melodrama. Will Mark remain with his handsome forest ranger or will he go back to the life from which he fled?

WHAT THE CRITICS SAID
"Tainted with connotations of soapy melodrama, amnesia is a plot device screenwriters should approach with great caution. Luckily, Akers has a deft touch, and his *Gone, But Not Forgotten* gets beyond the traditional 'Who am I? Where am I?' moments quickly to take on deeper issues of identity and relationships."
Dom Willmott

"There are random sequences that feel like irrelevant padding, such as a hospital corridor wheelchair race, a lame dress-up montage, and a soft-core porn scene that's somewhat sexy but doesn't actually feature any sex. On the other hand, the dialogue is bracingly natural, and there are some very strong scenes in which the actors get to really flesh out their characters (no pun intended)."
Rich Cline

Good Boys

(Yeladim Tovin; 2005)

Rent Boys in Israel

Israel is not a place you'd associate with an indie film about two rent boys. But Yair Hochner, who served for three years in the Israeli Defense Force, both wrote and directed the film.

As a film critic for *Seret*, the leading website in Israel about cinema, he grew up loving movies. He admits that *Good Boys* was inspired by some of his favorite films, including Jean-Luc Godard's cinematic masterpiece, *Vivre sa vie* (My Life to Live) and even Gus Van Sant's *My Private Idaho*. He also owes a debt to Brian De Palma and his erotic thrillers. His intention for the future is to make "a pure camp John Waters style movie."

His film, with English subtitles, tells the story of two male hustlers. They are hired by a trick to perform together. In so doing, they develop a personal relationship.

The star of the film is Daniel Efrat, playing Menni, a 17-year-old Armani-dressed rent boy who when not selling it by the inch listens to music and goes to the cinema. Even at such an early age, he's already a father, having had a baby with Mika (played by Nili Tzerruya), a young drug-addicted prostitute.

Gila Goldstein is already a gay icon in Israel. This transgendered performer was a former football player and ballet dancer (obviously a most unusual combination of professions). In the film, she has one of the most attention-getting roles. Cast as Grace, she plays Menni's adoptive mother who is also a prostitute on the side.

Another young hustler, Tal, is the co-star of the film. The role is played by Yuval Raz, an actor in Habima, the Israel National Theater. Both Raz and Efrat perform their difficult parts with sensitivity.

We won't give away the ending but both characters face an obvious dilemma. Can Menni and Tal forge a new life together after such tawdry beginnings?

Call this film about two young male whores *My Own Private Idaho* set in Tel Aviv.

Grande école

(2003)

French Students Play Sexual Power Games

Robert Salis, director and co-scripter, has created a passable drama about French students experimenting with power and sexuality. And, yes, there is lots of full frontal male nudity for devotees of French dick.

Before the titles fade, a young man and a young woman are going at it. But this is no ordinary French romance. Our chief character Paul (Gregori Baquet) is beset with internal struggles. He's been going with Agnès (Alice Taglioni) for some time, but would rather live with his roommates than her.

Without really knowing what is happening to him, Paul develops a powerful attraction for one of those roomies, Louis-Arnault (Jocelyn Quivrin).

Agnès becomes jealous, realizing that Paul is bewitched by the charismatic Parisian, Louis-Arnault. She challenges Paul to act on the homosexual desire he is blocking from his consciousness.

If Paul seduces Louis-Arnault first, she'll walk away. If she seduces him first, Paul will belong to her.

But Paul has a mind of his own. While all this betting is going on, he meets Mécir (Salim Kechiouche), a young Arab worker born in France. Mécir is subjected to racist tirades, and Paul comes to his rescue. Paul is attracted sexually to Mécir, and they make love. The director allows us to see their post-orgasmic full-frontal nudity.

Many hormones are stirring in this French potboiler: Sexual politics, racial tension, working class vs. upper class, new vs. old money, gay sex as opposed to straight sex.

There are also a lot of literary references and serious student-like pronouncements on the meaning of life.

If you hook up with this DVD, play the bonus feature, which also includes young men showing the full monty.

Gray Matters

(2006)

Lost Lezzie Struggles with Desire

This is a romantic comedy/coming-out flick from debut director Sue Kramer. Heather Graham stars as the film's namesake, Gray, playing a winsome New Yorker living with her brother, Sam (Tom Cavanagh).

The action gets moving when Sam, after a whirlwind romance, falls for Charlie, as played by Bridget Moynahan, a sexy zoologist.

Gray's got a problem. She's not only losing her brother, to whom she's devoted her life, but she realizes she's in love with his bride-to-be, Charlie. Talk about sexual confusion.

The most memorable scene is a now infamous kiss shared between Graham and Moynahan. Graham told the press she was "really looking forward to it," although Moynahan remained "a little creeped out."

Regrettably for their lesbian fans, there was also an X-rated love scene, but the foolish director cut that out.

Naturally, all these young New Yorkers have a profession. Sam is an up-and-coming heart surgeon, Gray an advertising copywriter. But Charlie is a candidate for that old TV series *What's My Line?* She studies the homosexual behavior of fish at an aquarium.

The supporting players and veteran actors steal scenes from the stars.

The question we found most puzzling was this: Why is such a talented actress as Sissy Spacek, playing a flaky therapist in a downright embarrassing performance, drawn to such a silly script? The obvious answer is that roles are hard to come by once you're no longer twelve. Spacek, as the wacky shrink, conducts sessions while bowling and rock climbing.

In his role as a taxi driver, Alan Cumming is such a good sport that even after he's rejected by Gray, he dresses in drag before accompanying her on her first excursion to a lesbian bar.

The Great Pink Scare

(2006)

Witch Hunt Destroys Smith College's Literary Elite

On Labor Day weekend in 1960, as part of a McCarthy-style witch-hunt against gay men, state troopers launched a raid in the little New England town of Northampton, Massachussetts. At the end of their rampage, they had hauled 15 men off to jail, three of whom were professors at the elite Smith College. The next day, newspaper headlines screamed—POLICE BREAK UP HOMOSEXUAL SMUT RING!

Considered utterly harmless by today's standards, the so-called smut was actually a stash of physique pictorials that wouldn't raise an eyebrow today—or raise anything else either.

Through vintage footage and interviews, directors Dan Miller and Tuggelin Yourgrau recreate that horrible era in a docu originally entitled *Independent Lens*. One of the faculty members arrested was Joel Dorius, who later said: "I thought sharing photos was unwise, considering the laws. But it never occurred to me that it could be fatal."

Among those arrested were Ned Spofford, another Smith College faculty member, and Newton Arvin. Arvin was labeled by the authorities as the so-called ring leader of the group. One of America's leading literary critics and a great love of Truman Capote, Arvin personally betrayed his friends in an act of cowardice. All three professors lost their positions.

The Northampton witch-hunt is re-created through archival and film commentary.

After all this scandal, Arvin became suicidal and was subsequently incarcerated in a mental hospital. He did not try to appeal his conviction, but Dorius and Spofford struggled to get the case overturned. In time their criminal records were erased but the stigma remained. All three men migrated in and out of mental hospitals for years, their once-promising academic careers destroyed. In declining health exacerbated by these issues, Arvin eventually died three years after the incident, in 1963.

If the film does nothing else, it reminds us that government does not belong in the bedrooms.

The Gymnast

(2006)

A Vertiginous, Voluptuous & Aerial Lesbian

Jane Hawkins (played by Dreya Weber) was one of America's leading gymnasts, at the top of her game until a devastating injury ended her career. The accident prevented her from fulfilling her Olympic destiny.

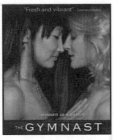

In the film, almost 20 years have gone by while Jane has languished in obscurity, working hand-to-mouth as a massage therapist while slowly disappearing into a passionless marriage with David (David De Simone).

Secretly, she has been trying to get pregnant, although David doesn't want a child. Jane's doctor tells her that she may have waited too long to have a kid. Without her husband's financial support, she can't afford the fertility drugs that might make her pregnant.

A chance meeting with Denise (Allison Mackie), a former gymnastic teammate, provokes Jane to re-examine her life and past—to "spread my wings." On a visit to a gym, Jane is recognized by a coach and is recruited for a different kind of venture—becoming part of a Cirque Du Soleil type of aerial act.

When the ex-gymnast meets an enigmatic Korean dancer named Serena (Addie Yungmee), a sexual tension arises. Their aerial performances together become mesmerizing and beautiful—and something else as well.

The developing relationship is not without its complications. But, of course, Jane is distressed by her lack of children, and Serena is a closeted lesbian with "coming out" problems as the adopted daughter of Jewish parents. As the stunning pair prepares to audition for their act in Vegas, the gravitational pull between the two of them becomes increasingly unavoidable.

After Denise convinces Jane that the affair with Serena is a form of denial, Jane must choose between having a child with her suddenly willing husband—or creating a completely new life for herself. This is a story of midlife liberation, a debut feature from helmer Ned Farr, who also authored the screenplay.

Hannah Free

(2009)

A Lifelong Affair Between Two Women

This is the story of a love affair spanning decades between an Out lesbian and an unassuming housewife. Directed by Wendy Jo Carlton from a script by Claudia Allen, it focuses on the life of Hannah (Sharon Gless) and Rachel (Maureen Gallagher), who grew up as little girls together in the same small Midwest town.

Traditional gender expectations—that is, marriage to a man—challenge their deep love for each other. In contrast to Rachel, Hannah becomes an adventurous, unapologetic lesbian, Rachel preferring the life of a strong but quiet homemaker.

The helmer weaves back and forth with the story, from the past to the present. The movie reveals how the two women maintained their love affair despite a marriage, a world war, infidelities, and family denial.

Sharon Gless (*Queer as Folk*) stars in this passionate lesbian drama, and does so admirably.

WHAT THE CRITICS SAID
"Hannah played by Gless is a free spirit who refuses to abide by the rules and has constant wanderlust even though she is incredibly in love with and happy with Rachel. It takes Rachel a lot longer to fully be with Hannah even though she does love her. Their struggle to love each other and be accepted is symbolic of the evolution of the struggle for gay civil rights. Sharon Gless is a forceful presence as Hannah."
Melissa Silverstein

"Touching and haunting, this love story as told through the ages is both sad and encouraging, a must-see for anyone who has loved and lost—or still has hope for the future."
Fresno Reel Pride

"Ms. Gless delivers a stellar performance that is gritty, poignant, and real."
Huffington Post

Happy Endings

(2005)

Sex, Secrets, Babies, and Deception

There was great hope for writer-director Don Roos, whose debut feature *The Opposite of Sex*, was a razor-funny human-need farce. In this film from the semi-indie school, Roos flirts with a by-now-familiar edge of complexity but doesn't quite live up to the promise of his launch feature. That said, *Happy Endings* is still worth watching.

The film's three tales involve women who exploit gay men for sex or pregnancy. The first consummation is seen in a prologue, as Mamie, age 17 (played by Lisa Kudrow, who sheds all traces of her ditzy *Friends* persona), beds her British stepbrother Charley (Steve Coogan). The encounter results in conception. "I only did it to get out of this house!" she proclaims.

The second subplot of *Happy Endings* involves Charley, who it turns out is gay and in love with Gil (David Sutcliffe) who has inherited his father's restaurant. They've befriended a lesbian couple (as portrayed by Laura Dern and Sarah Clarke) who have asked Gil to provide a sperm sample as a means of impregnating one of them. Later they claim that the sperm donation didn't work and that the ensuing birth was not associated in any way with Gil. Charley, growing obsessed over the paternity of the child as it applies to his lover, Gil, resorts to drastic measures to learn if the baby is or isn't really Gil's.

Finally, as the third element to this film's triptych of subplots, there's Otis, a closeted 24-year-old with musical ambitions who works as a staff member in Charley's restaurant. When the lead singer in Otis' band has to go into rehab, Otis asks Jude (as portrayed by Maggie Gyllenhaal) to fill in. Otis quickly becomes part of an elaborate sub-plot to extort money from Otis' rich and recently widowed father (as portrayed by Tom Arnold, who is well cast and loveable in his post-Rosanne incarnation). Jude, as a 24-karat gold-digger, manages to sleep with both Otis, despite his being gay, and his father Frank, thereby leaving both men in confusion and disarray. Gyllenhaal's offbeat presence and pixie-like smile evoke a young Shirley MacLaine.

Harry + Max

(2004)

When Two Brothers Do It, Is It Incest?

In this drama, directed and written by Christopher Münch, two brothers, 23 and 16, who are both teen idols from the music world, come to terms with their dysfunctional family past and deep affection for each other. The casting is perfect, with Bryce Johnson playing Harry and Cole Williams cast as Max.

The two brothers embark on a camping trip, wherein Max makes it clear that he's got the hots for his older brother. We soon learn that the two hot young men have a sexual history with each other. Remember that time in Bermuda? This edgy feature indie is not for the faint-of-heart troubled by incest issues.

The supporting cast was well chosen by Münch, particularly in the casting of Michelle Phillips (of the Mamas and the Papas) playing the mother, and Rain Phoenix as the girlfriend, Nikki. Phoenix was seen in *Even Cowgirls Get the Blues.*

In the film, Harry is in a boy band. He faces a crisis of career, with his band's fortunes hinged on the success of a new album. Is his band's allotted 15 minutes of fame up? Max is following in his brother's musical footsteps but with more success. Max is the rising star, Harry the fading glimmer. When a girl hiker asks for Max's autograph—but not Harry's—it's all too apparent who has become the star of the family. Harry's alcoholic and temperamental insecurities are laid bare.

As the dramas within the film unfold, the two brothers each spend separate afternoons methodically seducing each other's former lovers: Max gets cozy with Nikki, Harry's former girlfriend, while Harry gets down and dirty with Max's yoga teacher and former (male) lover, as played by Tom Gilmore, known for appearances, among others, on *Sex and the City* and *Law and Order*. (What's not addressed in this film, by the way, is the subject of pedophilia, despite the fact that Max is very obviously underaged.)

The question advanced here is simply this: Will the emotional dependency of the two brothers keep them from moving into adulthood?

Hate Crime

(2005)

Homophobes in Church

The director of *Hate Crime*, Tommy Stovall, who is also the author of its screenplay, is a former wedding videographer. He'd never been on a movie set before filming *Hate Crime*. What he concocted is a serious drama/ thriller about two men, Robbie Levinson (Seth Peterson) and Trey McCoy (Brian J. Smith), who suddenly encounter intolerance and hostility at the hands of their new neighbor.

This pair makes the perfect gay couple—in fact, they could be the poster boys for gay marriage. By profession, Robbie is a C.P.A. and Trey works in his recovering alcoholic father's (Sean Henningan) veterinary practice. After six years of living together, Trey wants a commitment ceremony with Robbie, and he also would like to expand their family by more than just their beloved dog.

The villain of the piece is the new neighbor, Chris Boyd, as played by Chad Donella, the son of Pastor Boyd (Bruce Davison), a fire-and brimstone fundamentalist preacher.

One night as Trey goes for a walk with the family dog, he is savagely murdered. Both Chris Boyd and, ironically, Robbie become the prime suspects.

Shot on location in Dallas, Texas—Bush country—*Hate Crime* deals with Robbie's attempt to discover who killed his lover. He will go to great ends, even turn lives upside down, to bring justice to the case regardless of consequences.

A friendly police detective, Elizabeth Fisher (Farah White), heads the investigation into the assault. The case is eventually transferred to Sgt. Esposito (Giancarlo Esposaito), not a well-developed character.

The picture emerges as a testament to the power of love and the destructive qualities of radical religion-based prejudice.

WHAT THE CRITICS SAID
"Stovall's freshman outing is a surprisingly emotional and often suspenseful film that captures both the good and the bad that might be found lurking in a neighborhood near you."
Greg Archer, *PlanetOut*

Head On

(1998)

A Greek Boy Struggles with Sexual Identity

Alex Dimitriades is an Australian TV star and teen heartthrob, who plays Ali with robust impetuosity. He even does an erect jerk-off scene in this vivid, sexually intense portrait of a closeted Greek-Australian hunk whose life changes dramatically when he meets sexy blond Shawn (Julian Garner).

Ana Kokkinos, who also co-scripted the film, cast her feature debut well. It is the story of a Greek family who must adapt to a foreign culture (Australia) and a gay son's coming out. The helmer is particularly good in showing a happy Greek family dining, dancing, making music, and partying. But trouble looms on the horizon with a father who abhors homosexuality.

Ari has a lot of homosex, including a scene where he is forced to give head to a man his father's age. Up to now, he's been a top. Later Ari forces the man to jerk him off. In another scene Ari and a drag queen are arrested and brutally harassed at police headquarters.

Along comes Sean (Julian Garner), a white Aussie. Sean sees more in Ari than he sees in himself, and in their interactions lies the nucleus of Ari's transformation into something better than he is.

WHAT THE CRITICS SAID
"Its missteps and excesses aside, *Head On* is a promising feature film debut for Kokkinos. The director puts Ari through no end of macho paces, but doesn't revel in his bravado. She's clearly fond of the character, even moved by his predicament."
Daniel Mangin

"*Head On* seems hopelessly divided against itself. On one hand it glamorizes Ari as a heroic sexual rebel. On the other it portrays him as a lazy, violent, self-hating bigot headed for imminent self-destruction. The images don't jibe."
Stephen Holden, *The New York Times*

The Heart is Deceitful Above All Things

(2004)

Why Couldn't Mom Have Been Courtney Love?

This gritty, slice-of-life drama was based on what was later revealed as a literary fraud, the so-called "autobiography" of "JT LeRoy," a character and author who never really existed. LeRoy, the male teenage hustler who supposedly endured Satanic levels of emotional, physical, and sexual abuse, is, in fact, merely the fictitious creation of a woman named Laura Albert. Ms. Albert obviously believes in Oscar Wilde's statement that "Lying, the telling of beautiful, untrue things, is the proper aim of art." Except that in Albert's case, she had nothing beautiful to say in her fraudulent kid-in-peril narrative.

During TV promotional appearances, JT LeRoy was impersonated by 25-year-old Savannah Knoop, half-sister of Albert's long-time partner, Geoffrey Knoop. For these TV appearances, Savannah adopted a persona that included a Hitchcockian getup of big shades, floppy hat, and long blonde hair. You can't make this up—that's why reality always gives novelists a hard time.

After the literary fraud was exposed, one critic said, "If you think the heart is deceitful, you should meet the author." Albert quickly became labeled as the James Frey for the hipster set. Early boosters of LeRoy included both Dennis Cooper and Dave Eggers, who predicted that LeRoy's autobiographical works would "prove to be among the most influential American books of the last 10 years." To that comment, Manohla Dargis, writing in *The New York Times,* responded, "Somewhere, probably in hell, William S. Burroughs laughed."

Before the hoax of the book was exposed, stars were lured into the web of deceit. In the film, Winona Ryder appears as a social worker, Jeremy Sisto, a meth-head, Michael Pitt as "Buddy," and Marilyn Manson as a skuzzy boyfriend—yes, male.

Asia Argento, the Italian actress and filmmaker, directed, wrote, and starred in this episodic slice-of-low-life reality flick that strings together lurid but unfounded tales of addict behavior.

Hedwig & the Angry Inch

(2001)

An Anatomically Incorrect Rock Odyssey

This is John Cameron Mitchell's botched transsexual odyssey. Hedwig, played by Mitchell himself, is a transsexual punk rock girl from East Berlin. As a boy named Hansel, she grew up and fell in love with an American officer. To marry her and take her back to America, he tells her that she has to have a sex-change operation. But the surgery didn't come out right, leaving her with neither penis nor a vagina—just an "angry inch." Since he (she) is of no more use to her would-be Army husband, he deserts her.

Heartbroken, she falls in love with a dorky teenager Tommy (Michael Pitt), whom she instructs in Rock 'n' Roll 101. As Tommy Gnosis, he steals her songs and, with them, becomes a huge success as a rock star.

In the film, Hedwig is leading her rock band on a tour of America, telling her story through a series of concerts at Bilgewater Inn seafood restaurants. Her tour dates coincide with those of Tommy.

WHAT THE CRITICS SAID
"*Hedwig and the Angry Inch* occupies an almost extinct movie category. It's an original rock musical—indeed, according to its maker, a 'post-punk neo-glam rock musical,' a category almost as specialized as the not dissimilar *Beyond the Valley of the Dolls*, which was a camp rock horror musical. Filmed with ferocious energy and with enough sexual variety to match the late Fellini, it may be passing through standard bookings on its way to a long run as the midnight successor to *The Rocky Horror Picture Show.*"
Roger Ebert

"Mr. Mitchell sings in a voice whose lofty elocution and frosty, slightly inhuman tone echo David Bowie's as spiked with a tiny whiff of helium. Fleshing out the story is a meaty rock score by Stephen Trask whose reaching-for-the-heavens anthems brilliantly parody Mr. Bowie's songwriting in the *Ziggy Stardust* era without lapsing into caricature."
Stephen Holden, *The New York Times*

Henry & June

(1990)

An Erotic Masterpiece

This controversial film was based on the first diary of Anaïs Nin, which covered the most significant year of her life. In 1931 Nin (played by look-alike Maria de Medeiros) lived in Paris with her stuffy banker spouse, Hugo Guiler (Richard E. Grant). While he was away during the day, she was researching material for her slim volume on D.H. Lawrence.

Nin is lured into the sensual bohemian world of Henry Miller (Fred Ward), who had not yet published his notorious *Tropic of Cancer*. She also had an emotional and sexual relationship with his wife June (Uma Thurman).

The diarist's relationship with June and Henry is dark, sensual, and at times very graphic. The music of Stravinsky, "Le Sacre du Printemps," sets the mood. The film also captures decadent Paris "between the wars," with its smoked-filled jazz clubs and whorehouses.

Anaïs and her husband help finance Henry's *Tropic of Cancer,* a pseudo-biography of June.

When not in bed together, Henry and Anaïs have many arguments about their different styles of writing. The film might have been called *Henry and Anaïs* since June is off camera for a lot of the time, as she migrates between Paris and New York trying to find acting jobs.

WHAT THE CRITICS SAID
"In its depiction of Depression Paris and sexual candor, *Henry & June* succeeds. The central performances of Fred Ward, as the cynical, life-loving Miller, and Maria de Medeiros, as the beautiful, insatiable Anaïs, splendidly fulfill director Philip Kaufman's vision."
Variety

"You'll be watching this for the fantasy ride it is, a sort of *Life* magazine spread on Literary Paris! Anaïs is the experience-hungry, sex-fascinated diarist and erotica writer."
Desson Howe, *Washington Post*

Here's Looking At You Boy

(*Schau mir in die augen, Kleine;* 2007)

Hit-and-Miss Docu on Gay & Lesbian Movies

The bad news first: this German film is not a worthy successor to *The Celluloid Closet*. But for lovers of gay and lesbian cinema, it's worth a look. André Schafer, who directed and wrote it, subtitled it "A Coming Out of Queer Cinema."

The docu is a short trip down memory lane as it begins in the early 70s with "the first films to mention gays positively." Instead of a world overview, the docu concentrates mainly on the U.S. and Europe where—let's face it—most queer cinema is shot.

The usual talking heads are invoked, along with clips from highly selective films. Naturally, John Waters makes an appearance. He's practically become the granddaddy of gay cinema, a honor bestowed if for no other reason than his direction of *Pink Flamingos* in 1972. In light of subsequent developments in the field, that's almost prehistoric.

In this documentary, we get insights from other talking heads as well, including Gus Van Sant, who at one point emerged as the candidate most likely to direct *Brokeback Mountain* with a cast that at the time looked as if it would focus on Brad Pitt and Matt Damon. He tells of his fight to preserve the shower scene between the two boys in *Elephant*.

Other big names seen in clips include Rainer Werner Fassbiner, and a "big fish" such as Tilda Swinton, who played the gender-shifting title character in *Orlando*, alongside Quentin Crisp as Queen Elizabeth.

Clips also include Stephen Frears' *My Beautiful Laundrette* as well as Bill Sherwood's *Parting Glances*.

WHAT THE CRITICS SAID
"This roundup is best viewed as a quite watchable filmmaker's notebook of familiar gay titles and cheery interviews that should fulfill the goals of its consortium of small screen producers."
Deborah Young, *Variety*

The Hidden Führer
Debating the Enigma of Hitler's Sexuality
(2004)
Adolf is Pulled Screaming from the Closet

Homosexuals have enough problems without German historian Lothar Machtan trying to drag the closeted Führer into the bright light of gaydom. Gay men are proud to claim Michelangelo or Leonardo da Vinci as one of their own, but what about the dreaded World War II dictator who sent millions of Jews, homosexuals, and gypsies to the gas chamber?

The creators of *Party Monster* and *The Eyes of Tammy Faye*—award-winning filmmakers Fenton Bailey, Randy Barbato, and Gabriel Rotello—explore hidden areas of the Führer's private life. Their film was derived from Lothan Machtan, who in September of 2001 tossed a bombshell into the world of Hitlerian studies with the publication of his explosive book *The Hidden Hitler*.

As could be predicted, it ignited a storm of worldwide controversy. After dedicating a good hunk of his life to the study of Hitler the private man, the historian (who is not gay) concluded that Hitler was a homosexual. Many Hitler-era survivors were interviewed in this film, and their testimony is alternated with some extraordinary and rarely viewed vintage images.

Before the camera, arguments pro and con about Hitler's sexuality are presented. Although Machtan makes a compelling case, there are arguments on the other side to suggest that Hitler was not a homo. The opinions expressed are often passionate.

Hitler himself said, "I cannot love any woman until I have completed my task." He also once claimed that he was "married" to Germany.

Especially effective are the encounters with Rudiger Lautman, himself a homosexual. This sociology professor once taught author Machtan himself. They engage in some challenging banter, mainly from Lautman who demands to see proof of Hitler's homosexuality, more than the author offered in his book.

After seeing the pros and cons of Hitler's sexuality, as presented in this film, what's a girl to think? *Sieg heil* or *sieg homo*?

High Art
(1998)
Jaded Artist & Ingenue in a Spider Web

The break-out hit from lesbian helmer/scripter Lisa Cholodenki (*Laurel Canyon*) stars Ally Sheedy (*The Breakfast Club*) as a junkie and washed-up photographer who embarks on a messed-up romance with a young bisexual photo-editor (Syd), as played by the super-hot Radha Mitchell. Syd lives with her unsupportive cad of a boyfriend James (Gabriel Mann). She goes to complain to her neighbor about a leak in the ceiling, and encounters photographer Lucy (Sheedy). Love blossoms in this story of ambition, sacrifice, and seduction.

Lucy is talented yet mysterious. In time Syd is shown her past work which brought her a certain acclaim. The young woman also meets Syd's junkie friends. Syd encourages Lucy to shoot new pictures for the magazine, *Frame*, which employs her.

Greta (Patricia Clarkson) portrays a complex character without overplaying her stoned behavior. Lucy's mother, Tammy Grimes, was once a leading Broadway star when she was younger.

WHAT THE CRITICS SAID
"The film sacrifices any hope of raw edges and real emotion to its own chic sensibility, which is so studiously alluring that it overwhelms the story. In its own fashionably nonchalant way, *High Art* proves every bit as sleek as *Frame*, the film's emblem of poisonous commerce corrupting creative purity."
Janet Maslin, *The New York Times*

"Finally, at what seems like the emotionally inevitable moment, Syd and Lucy sleep together. This is one of the most observant sex scenes I have seen, involving a lot of worried, insecure dialogue. Syd feels awkward and inadequate, and wants reassurance. Lucy provides it from long experience, mixed with a sudden rediscovery of the new. They talk a lot. Lucy is like ground control, taking a new pilot through her first landing."
Roger Ebert

Hilde's Reise

(*Hilde's Journey*; 2004)

Love, Friendship, Hope

In this Swiss film, directed by Christof Vorster, who co-wrote the script with Gabriele Strohm, Carpenter Steff (played by Oliver Stokowski) inherits the estate of his ex-lover, Martin Hilder, who is the scion of a wealthy family. The ex, known as Hilde (hence the title), has died of AIDS, and Steff finds himself the sole heir to his fortune.

At long last, Steff can fulfill his dream of starting his own business. But there's trouble in paradise. He must confront Hilde's controlling, homophobic mother.

There are more clouds on the horizon. Hilde's most recent boyfriend, Rex (Mitchell Finger of *Utopia Blues*), appears on the scene. A handsome young man, Rex is headstrong and unpredictable. He is sexy but HIV-positive. He's also determined to honor his lover's last wish to have his ashes scattered at sea. The mother from hell is adamantly opposed to that wish.

Steff makes a deal with Hilde's family to receive a fraction of the inheritance in exchange for the ashes and no contest of the will. But Rex takes matters into his own hands. He refuses to let Steff betray the will and "kidnaps" the urn.

This action on Rex's part sets off a chain of events that forces Steff to re-examine both his life and his priorities.

WHAT THE CRITICS SAID
"*Hilde's Journey* holds interest despite an undeveloped script that relies too heavily on cut-out characters and the fact it mostly covers paths visited in earlier pics. Helmer Christof Vorster doesn't inject anything new into this story of how a gay man's death wishes affect those he loved, but the excursion occasionally reveals insights, if in an overly earnest way."
Jay Weissberg, *Variety*

"*Hilde's Journey* is a story of honor and betrayal that reminds us that love, friendship, and hope hold us all together even when we're faced with life's most heartbreaking choices."
www.newfestival.org

His Secret Life

(*Le fate ignoranti*; 2001)

A "Straight" Italian Man's Gay Lover

"This film appealed to gay men because it broke a barrier—many married Italian men have secret lives with gay men," said the film's screenwriter and director Ferzan Ozpetek. In *Le fate ignoranti*, I gave a face and a body to all those secret love affairs."

One of Italy's leading men, Stefano Accorsi, signed on for the gay lead of Michele. The director claimed that even though Accorsi is straight, he did not have any problems playing a gay character, including when he kissed two guys or appeared totally nude in a *ménage à trois*.

From all outward appearances, AIDS doctor Antonia (Margherita Buy) has a happy marriage to her husband until he is killed in a car accident. She belatedly learns that he has been cheating on her. When she goes to confront "the other woman," she discovers to her surprise that "she" is a he—in this case Michele. In some respects, he turns out to be a mirrored image of herself.

She enters Michele's life, finding him living in a large apartment shared with gay and transgendered friends, including a Turkish immigrant and a prostitute. In this melodrama, a relationship slowly develops between the pair who is in mourning for their lost lover.

Antonia in time is charmed by the extended family she discovers in that apartment. She revives the spirits of an AIDS patient and even attracts a younger Turkish stud who wants to bed her.

Ozpetek, who is Turkish by birth, also directed *Steam: The Turkish Bath*.

The film deserves a look and is diverting and has a certain charm, although some reviewers found it "innocuous and unremarkable."

WHAT THE CRITICS SAID
"Mr. Ozpetek's curiosity also feels somewhat limited; the film is lovely and touching, but also tactful to a fault, declining to pluck at the deeper knots of emotion that might complicate the characters' careful, defensive maneuverings."
A.O. Scott, *The New York Times*

The History Boys

(2006)

Cute Teenage Boys Pursue Sex & Higher Education

We loved Alan Bennett's play, and we also adore the way he adapted it for the screen under the direction of Nicholas Hytner. This is a warm, wonderful, beautiful film.

As *The Christian Science Monitor's* Peter Rainier put it, "If the literacy of *The History Boys* is deemed uncinematic, then give me uncinema anytime."

Vibrating with exuberance and erudition, the film is set in Yorkshire in 1983, the era of Iron Lady Margaret Thatcher. It's a comedy/drama that has been called "A spirited elegy for a way of educating that is passing away."

The plot, such as it is, spins around eight boys who have been chosen for special tutoring in history to help them pass their difficult entrance exams for Oxford and Cambridge. The officious headmaster of the school (played by Clive Merrison) channels the *Zeitgeist* by hiring a young Oxford history graduate, Irwin (Stephen Campbell Moore), to teach the boys new techniques that will grab the examiners' attention. As a goal-rather than a truth-oriented teacher, his methods put him in competition with general studies teacher, Hector, as played by the Falstaffian Richard Griffiths.

Both teachers are gay, Hector remaining in the closet but Irwin being more forthright about his preferences. Both teachers also use all the weapons in their arsenal—wit, charisma, and, yes, even logic—to win the boys over to their way of thinking. The students are left confused as to which teacher to follow.

Hector is married but has the hots for his students—and his proclivities get him in serious trouble. He likes to take his male students for rides on his motorbike and he enjoys copping feels as he does so. The very tolerant students are well aware of his proclivities, as he's already grabbed most of their dicks.

The History Boys sympathizes with Hector, whom Griffiths plays not as a predator but as a lonely dreamer whose ineffectual gropes are not much different from pats on the back.

Hollywood, je t'aime

(2009)

Another Tinseltown Dream Is Shattered

This is writer-director Jason Bushman's pedestrian debut feature.

The City of Lights grows dim for gay Parisian Jérôme Beaunez (Eric Debets) after he's deserted by his boyfriend Gilles (Jonathan Blanc), "the love of my life."

Impulsively he heads for Los Angeles, with dreams of making it big in Tinseltown.

Once in Hollywood, he meets a limited circle of lovable eccentrics, notably an energetic pot dealer, Ross (Chad Allen). Allen's fans will delight in his portrayal, the finest in this film. His performance is both quirky and magnetic. Allen stands in contrast to the star of the picture, the thuddingly inexpressive Debets.

Among the other eccentrics encountered is a trannie prostitute (Kaleesha Diarra Kilpatrick), plus a world-weary drag queen Norma Desire (Michael Airington).

Finding a rent-free room in the drag queen's house, Jérôme sets out to pursue an acting career. In her scenes with Jérôme, Norma Desire "gets to spout out all manner of aphorisms about Hollywood, broken dreams, lost youth, and loves—pretty much everything you'd expect to hear from a slightly paunchy guy in a sparkly gown and a Dolly Parton wig," said one viewer.

For devotees of free-swinging genitalia, there are a few nude scenes. There is also some guy-on-guy sex action.

WHAT THE CRITICS SAID
"The story of a naïf seeking fame and fortune in Hollywood is about as old as Hollywood itself. You'd think it would have been exhausted by now, but here and there, filmmakers continue to dip into this well of clichés. In the lead role, non-actor Eric Debets has the most unengaging screen presence this side of plankton. All the other characters fall in love with him, he charms strangers, he impresses casting directors, but the guy has the personality of last week's oatmeal."
Tom Becker

A Home at the End of the World

(2004)

Sexy Colin Farrell Plays It Gay

Adapted by Michael Cunningham (*The Hours*) from his 1990 novel, this film was directed by one of the year's most promising newcomers, stage director Michael Mayer. It was the romantic *ménage à trois* of 2004, but with a definite gay twist, carrying an R rating for its  strong drug content, sexuality, nudity, language, and a disturbing accident. But what generated headlines around the world was a frontal nude shot of Colin that was removed from the final release, although seen by preview audiences.

In the film, the real-life, headline-making wild Irish boy, Colin, plays an orphan, Bobby Morrow, in a story that moves from 1967 to the 1980s era of "the plague." Orphaned as a teenager, Bobby comes to live with his friend Jonathan, as played by Dallas Roberts. When the two boys are caught smoking pot by Mom, as interpreted by the always brilliant Sissy Spacek, she joins them to enjoy a little weed herself. Growing up with Jonathan, Bobby is the sweetest boy who ever lived. Gay Jonathan falls for his bedmate, and sexual experimentation follows.

As the years go by, Jonathan has left for New York City, where he leads an openly gay life. Eventually Bobby follows him there from Cleveland, finding Jonathan living with an eccentric hatmaker roommate, Clare, as played luminously by Robin Wright Penn. In no time at all, the trio has created a makeshift family.

Clare is really a fag hag and falls for Jonathan's boyhood friend. Eventually they move to Woodstock, New York, presumably the end of the world, at least in the view of Cunningham. Clare manages to seduce Bobby after he confesses that he's a virgin. A daughter is the result of their liaison.

The nontraditional family as depicted in the film was attacked by the religious right but was all about love. We won't spoil the ending by telling you which character, Jonathan or Clare, the placid Bobby chooses at the end of the film.

Hope Along the Wind: The Story of Harry Hay

(2002)

The Founder of the Gay Rights Movement

A visionary with a courageous spirit, Harry Hay in 1950 founded the Mattachine Society, giving rise to the modern-day gay rights movement. This documentary is about that pioneer of gay activism (1912-2002) who, along with his partner of 40 years, John Burnside, appear as themselves in this docu directed by Eric Slade.

Harry Hay

Brave Harry, born in England, launched the Mattachines at a time when two notoriously closeted homosexuals, Joseph McCarthy, and his pit viper, Roy Cohn, were interrogating suspected Communists and "deviants" in government. Slade follows Harry from his roots in the Communist Party and the Labor movement to his championship of "America's most hated minority."

Slade was racing against the clock to film this docu. Harry, in fact, died at the time of its release. Many subjects interviewed were already in their 80s.

In spite of his longtime love affair with Burnside, the aging radical still proclaimed the joys of sexual promiscuity. There's no doubt about it. Harry was a radical, and many modern-day queers may not agree with some of his positions.

His support of NAMBLA (the North American Man/Boy Love Association, formed in 1978), got him kicked out of the Mattachine Society. Harry was also a co-founder of Radical Faeries, a counter-culture group which explores a spiritual dimension of their gay sexuality. Or, as another critic defined them, they are "a cross between Born Again queers and in-your-face frontline shock troops practicing gender-fuck drag."

The Advocate praised the docu for its "incredibly penetrating interviews and archival footage."

We suggest that the epitaph on Harry's tombstone should have read: HE TRIED TO MAKE THE WORLD A BETTER PLACE FOR EVERYONE.

Horror in the Wind

(2008)

A Ban on Sex Breeds Queer Results

Would you call this a sci-fi movie? Directed and written by Max Mitchell, it was one of the most bizarre movies made in 2008.

The year is 2017. That dreaded homophobe, the creepy Pat Robertson, has become President of the United States. His vice president is his fellow homo-hating James Dobson. They declare a war on sex. The President pays Richard and Ed, two best friends and bio-engineers, to alter their research and create an abstinence drug, with an antidote that will be given only to "Christian Married Couples."

The President steals their formula before testing is complete and inundates the world with it. Formula 4708 doesn't suppress your sex drive. It reverses it. If you were straight, you become gay and vice versa.

After that, the world goes topsy turvy. Suddenly, two straight buddies find themselves looking lustfully at each other's asses. Birth control companies file for Chapter 11, and and the *King James Bible* is replaced with the *Princess Diana Bible.*

When an antidote is finally found and offered to the world, not everyone who has been re-oriented from straight to gay is eager to take it.

WHAT THE CRITICS SAID
"Mitchell has a wonderful gift for turning the absurd into hard-hitting social commentary and genuine comedy."
James Wegg

"Hilariously subversive. A for ingenuity. The two leads are great."
Robert Nott, *Santa Fe New Mexican*

"For the most part, the newly homosexual characters weren't depicted as whoring freaks or leather-clad queens (save for those in the Oval Office). They were depicted as monogamous."
Jonny Metro

Hotel Gondolin

(2005)

Argentinian Sex Industry Workers Bond Together

Transvestism, prostitution, and the homosexual lifestyle as lived in Argentina come together in this Spanish-language film with English subtitles. The 52-minute docu was both written and directed by Fernando López Escriva, and the drag queen "stars" use what they call

Hotel Gondolin

their "pussy names" such as Monica or Wanda even though their real names might be Juan or Fernando. Incidentally, they prefer to be known professionally as sex workers, and not called by the Don Imus name of "ho."

The she-men have taken over a dilapidated hotel on the "wrong side" of Buenos Aires and painted it the world's most garish shade of purple. They live in an association where each roommate pays a monthly rental.

The motto of the girls is, "We're poor but we don't have to be homeless." Each girl has a different story to tell. One inmate, for example, says, "I don't want to be a woman, I want to be a transvestite." Others aim to go all the way surgically, whereas one girl says, "I want to get hips and a butt—the breasts can come later." Another crossdresser claims, "Right now I want to keep my penis." One of the reasons for that is that many clients desire getting fucked by a she-male.

For most transvestites in Argentina, the only professional option for them is prostitution. The film ends with the trannies fighting politically for their civil rights and confronting difficulties with the local police.

WHAT THE CRITICS SAID
"A portrait of a unique building that is collaboratively run by MTF sex workers as a haven from the dangerous life of the streets, *Hotel Gondolin* shows the power of grassroots activism to enact real change against discrimination and violence against transgendered people."
Fernando Lopez Escriva

The Houseboy

(2007)

Wanting a New Toy for Christmas

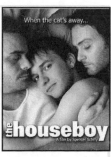

In his early 20s, Ricky (Nick May) is involved in a three-some with his older employ-ers, Simon (Tom Merlino) and DJ (Brian Patacca). Be-fore they go away for Christ-mas, he overhears DJ suggesting that he and Simon should find a new toy-boy.

Left alone in his despair, Ricky has to care for the apartment, the goldfish, the cats, and the gerbils. In an unlikely scenario, he contemplates suicide.

To escape his depression, he pursues men and drugs . . . and, oh yes, self-pity.

This is one of the few gay films to tackle the sub-ject of polyamorous relationships, and, as such, it's rather compelling. The helmer and scripter, Spencer Schilly, has cast some handsome eye candy in this film, but doesn't seem to spend much time exploring character.

Instead, we get an orgy of bodies and random hookups (who's complaining about that?). Except for a fleeting dick and some bare-ass shots, we don't get many full frontals in this flick.

Along comes Blake (Blake Young-Fountain) who turns Ricky on. Blake has two mothers, inciden-tally. At first the African-American turns down Ricky's advances, but a relationship appears pos-sible, although there's not enough time left in the film to fully explore the connection.

At least the movie resolves the question: "Has Ricky reached the end of the rope, or could sal-vation await in the form of a friendly neighbor?"

WHAT THE CRITICS SAID
"The director can't seem to get underneath Ricky's skin in any meaningful way. We under-stand the young man has problems. The more compelling story is Ricky's inner turmoil. He tells several visitors he plans on killing himself. We're never sure if it's a bluff to get attention or the truth."
Jason P. Vargo

How Do I Look?

(2006)

The Harlem "Ball" Community

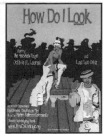

A follow-up to the successful *Paris Is Burning,* this docu takes the voguing and fashion battle zone to the runway where various competitions showcase talents. You may re-member this group from Madonna's *Vogue* video and her *Truth or Dare* docu. Wolf-gang Busch is the helmer behind this ambitious project.

For those unfamiliar with the genre, the "illusion of a runway" is created at ball events that let gay, lesbian, bisexual, and transgendered people live out their fantasies and express themselves artis-tically. As expressed by their drag, they certainly do that—and do so exceedingly well. They are or-ganized into "houses" with an elected "mother" or "father." These houses organize balls to raise money for HIV/AIDS, or whatever.

Some of the stars of the show, including Tracy Africa, Willi Ninja, or Jose Extravaganza, went from these runway walks into a profession. *How Do I Look?* traces 10 years of Harlem "Ball" his-tory and features special appearances by the out-rageously brave Kevin Aviance, out costumer Patricia Field (*The Devil Wears Prada*), and the always-unique Michael Musto. "Starring roles" in-clude cameos by Harmonica Sunbeam (don't you love that name?). How about CoolAid Mizrahi or Anthony Revlon?

Award-winning director Busch was born in Ger-many, but has been part of the "Ball" community since the mid-1980s. Since 1997 he has been a dominant presence at the ball, capturing the drama queens through the eye of a camera.

"*How Do I Look?* is a tool to showcase talent, bringing the ballroom community together, gain-ing artistic and human respect, and providing hands-on video. We aim to improve the quality of life and send HIV/AIDS awareness messages through the many we lost to AIDS and the ones living with HIV now." So commented Wolfgang Busch himself.

Howl

(2010)

The Eisenhower Era's Literary H-Bomb

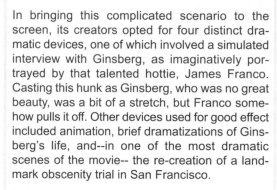

Allen Ginsberg's in-your-face *Howl,* a 1956 literary work, practically paved the way for the sexual revolution of the 1960s. Or so some people said.

Longtime docu helmers Rob Epstein and Jeffrey Friedman have made an amazing film of this work, and its premiere at the Sundance Festival created a buzz.

In bringing this complicated scenario to the screen, its creators opted for four distinct dramatic devices, one of which involved a simulated interview with Ginsberg, as imaginatively portrayed by that talented hottie, James Franco. Casting this hunk as Ginsberg, who was no great beauty, was a bit of a stretch, but Franco somehow pulls it off. Other devices used for good effect included animation, brief dramatizations of Ginsberg's life, and--in one of the most dramatic scenes of the movie-- the re-creation of a landmark obscenity trial in San Francisco.

In it, the publisher of *Howl,* Lawrence Ferlinghetti (Andrew Rogers), is on trial before a somewhat baffled judge, as played by Bob Balaban. David Straithairn is a morally indignant prosecutor dueling with a defense attorney, as played by the always-appealing Jon (*Mad Men*) Hamm.

At one point in the film Franco's Ginsberg reads *Howl* in a Beat Generation coffee house. The crowd seems to respond to this foray into homoerotic love, with its nihilistic endorsement of drugtaking.

The film is not perfect, but we can only applaud its daring in trying to deconstruct such a literary masterpiece and put it on the screen.

WHAT THE CRITICS SAID
"Every piece of film involving Franco is terrific. But the problem is that there isn't enough. The film never takes the leap into treating Ginsberg as a flesh-and-blood character but rather shoves him up on a stage or in front of a tape recorder as a cultural icon. Franco certainly delivers the performance, but the filmmakers haven't given it shape."
Kirk Honeycutt

Hubby/Wifey

(2005)

At Home with Gertrude and Alice

In Paris from 1911 to 1946, Gertrude Stein, "mother of the Lost Generation," and Alice B. Toklas lived together in Montparnasse as husband and wife. Although they were not "out" in today's terms, they ultimately became the most out lesbian couple of the 20th century, the poster duo for an enduring same-sex union.

This short film is based on a love letter Stein wrote late one night in the early 1920s for her beloved to find on the morning of her birthday. In this new film, a modern lesbian couple shares a fever dream of their foremothers, Gertrude and Alice, of the joys and trials of gay marriage. Dominique Dibbell is cast as Gertrude Stein, Jamie Tolbert as Alice B. Toklas.

Appealing to all those with literati taste, the film is the creation of the husband-and-husband team of director Todd Hughes (*The New Women, Ding Dong*) and producer P. David Ebersole (*Stranger Inside, Death in Venice CA*).

Their movie also pays homage to Stein's legendary salon of Parisian visionaries, including Man Ray, Dalí, Buñuel, and Picasso, who painted Stein's infamous portrait.

WHAT THE CRITICS SAID
"Todd Hughes' take on Gertrude Stein and Alice B. Toklas is exquisitely original."
Kevin Thomas, *Los Angeles Times*

"I show this film in a course on American families in order to illustrate the rich variety of family forms today. The film encourages students to consider how families have changed over time—and how they have remained the same."
Diana Selig, Assistant Professor of History, Claremont McKenna College

I Love You Phillip Morris

(2009)

Jim Carrey Loving Ewan McGregor

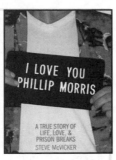

At Sundance when Jim Carrey was asked what it was like to kiss Ewan McGregor, Carrey responded: "A dream come true. I mean, look at the guy!" These two unlikely stars appear together in a deranged gay love story, an epic romance taking place in prison.

Steven Russell (played by Carrey) is a "happily" married police officer who on Sunday plays the organ at church. He prays nightly with his wife (Leslie Mann). Somewhere along the way he decides he's gay and leaves home and hearth to pursue his new flamboyant lifestyle. He moves to Miami and snares himself a boyfriend (Rodrigo Santoro).

The high life is expensive, and the former cop turns conman. When the law catches up with him, he is arrested, tried, and sent to prison. There he meets and falls in love with Phillip Morris (McGregor).

To be with the love of his life, Carrey will go to any end, including fraud, embezzlement, impersonations of attorneys, prison escapes, and even efforts to fake his own death.

Glenn Ficarra and John Requa both wrote and directed this farce.

WHAT THE CRITICS SAID
"Throughout the movie, Steven continually slips away from prison to reunite with his partner, pulling a number of amusing tricks that suggest Chaplin by way of James Bond. But Carrey's performance runs from wild slapstick to puppy-eyed sentimentalism, often making it tough to discern the tone of any given scene. However, because of the perpetual inconsistency, *Phillip Morris* remains a unique oddity, fascinating to watch."
Eric Kohn

"The cutting, juxtaposition of scenes, and reaction shots hit their targets precisely, with Steven's occasional suicidal plunge turned into a laugh."
John Anderson, *Variety*

Imagine Me and You

(2005)

At Her Wedding, a Bride Falls for a Woman

Writer/director Ol Parker's comedy/romance, *Imagine Me & You*, was shot in London. It's about a bride-to-be who steals away from her wedding after spotting an unexpected guest who turns out to be a woman. In other words, it's the story of a girl who falls in love on her wedding day. . . and not with the groom. The title might also have been, *Two Gorgeous Girls, a Wedding & No Funeral*.

The movie is well cast. Piper Perabo appears as Rachel, the prospective bride. She's slated to marry Heck (Matthew Goode), who appears as a terrifically likable guy. Rachel locks eyes with a florist at the wedding, a gay woman named Luce (Lena Headey), who easily steals the movie from all the competition. She'll win the hearts of lesbians everywhere. Heck is slow to catch on to his bride's new crush. After all, he thought she was straight. So did Luce. . . at first.

Lena Headey plays her role as "warm, funny, thoughtful, sensitive, charming, sassy and ridiculously gorgeous," or so was the spin at the film-festivals.

Born in Yorkshire in 1976, Headey is a straight woman who can engagingly play a lesbian. Beginning in the early 90s, she has piled up a respectable list of film credits. She won a Silver Iris Award at the Brussels Film Festival for her role in *Aberdeen* opposite Charlotte Rampling. She also filmed *Possession* opposite Gwyneth Paltrow and *The Brothers Grimm* with Matt Damon and Heath Ledger.

Piper Perabo shot to fame in the 2000 *Coyote Ugly*, and has appeared in *Cheaper by the Dozen* as the older daughter of Steve Martin. Perabo is not from England in spite of her accent. She's from Toms River, New Jersey. Her mother is Norwegian, her father Portuguese. She takes her name from the 1950s actress Piper Laurie, rumored lover of Ronald Reagan.

"A slick but slight Brit pic, chockfull with tart one-liners and pretty posh people, with one major twist: The romantic leads are both women."
Leslie Felperin, *Variety*

The Incredibly True Adventure of Two Girls in Love

(1995)

Prejudice Against Lesbians

"God, Evie, if you were going to turn gay, you could have at least chosen someone pretty."

This is the sentiment expressed when a rich black belle, Evie Roy (Nicole Ari Parker), falls for a butch dyke named Randy (Laurel Holloman). Not much is made of the interracial bonding, but prejudice against lesbians is on parade.

The two young students couldn't be more opposite of each other. Holloman from *The L Word* brings reality to the part of a girl who lives on the wrong side of the tracks, and isn't particularly pretty. She's not one to take to the queen's garden party, as she smokes weed, is a poor student, and likes loud rock music.

In contrast, Evie takes trips to Paris with her mother, listens to opera, reads books, dresses impeccably, and lives on the right side of the tracks.

Randy lives with other lesbians, including her gay aunt. Evie has a boyfriend and seemingly has never thought much about lesbianism before. However, when she meets Randy at a gas station, sparks ignite.

Neophyte helmer/writer Maria Maggenti shows a strong sense of narrative in revealing the characters of the women, but perhaps bogs down with the ending.

WHAT THE CRITICS SAID
"Because the movie is about lesbianism, of course, it has an R rating and a strong MPAA warning about a sex scene involving teenage girls. A scene of similar frankness between a boy and a girl wouldn't have qualified for the word 'strong.' The MPAA is shocked by the homosexuality. The R rating is ironic when you reflect how much healthier and more thoughtful this film is than so much mindless, action-oriented 'family entertainment,' and how likely it is to inspire conversation about its values."
Roger Ebert

Indie Sex: Censored

(2007)

Seduction, Sex & Sleaze

Sex and controversy are examined in this IFC miniseries released on DVD. It commemorates all of the sex scenes that took us to the theater and pushed us to our limits.

The movie follows the history of sex and censorship in the movies from silent flickers and college stag movies to the biggest of blockbusters today.

Indie Sex shows how cinema moved us into new realms on the screen: kink, bondage, homosexuality, domination, "perversion," and just about everything else imaginable. Breaking new ground were *Lolita, Midnight Cowboy, Myra Breckenridge, Last Tango in Paris, The Night Porter, Caligula, 9 ½ Weeks*, and onward and upward (?) to depictions of full on-screen penetration between actors in *Shortbus*, including one scene that depicted auto-fellatio. Some cool commentary is provided by such sexperts as John Waters or burlesque performer Dita Von Teese.

The modern world didn't discover screen sex. Director Lesli Kainberg digs up some amazing examples of early silent stag films and porno that are shocking to some in their explicitness, even by today's raunchy standards.

For some viewers, *Indie Sex* will feature more on-screen penetration and sex acts than they've seen before. *Indie Sex* is unabashedly pro-sex in cinema.

WHAT THE CRITICS SAID
"The series showcases the groundbreaking films that pushed the envelope in terms of what could be expressed on the screen throughout the decades. There are the big ones; the films that really got critics' panties in a bunch, and started up a discourse that lasted years, even decades. During the 1960s, North America lagged something terrible behind the rest of the cinematic world in terms of what could be shown, and much of the early influential films came from France, Italy, Japan, and so on. America soon caught up, pushing the *oeuvre* right in the pants, and once we got going, there was no slowing down."
Adam Arseneau

Inlaws and Outlaws

(2005)

The Gay Marriage Debate

Whether you're gay or straight, this film directed by Drew Emery is timely and goes beyond the usual rhetoric about gay and lesbian bonding to explore what it means to be married. What is rendered here is a look at the basic human connection between couples, regardless of sexual orientation or social attitudes pro or against gay marriage. *Variety* even went so far as to say that the film will be "a fine educational tool in fundamentalist school districts."

Inlaws and Outlaws gets going with snippets of children commenting about what they anticipate the future will hold for them in terms of relationships. From there the shift goes to adult perceptions, as couples recall how they met and in some cases married.

Made in Seattle, the film is a documentary, and it was worthy to note that Emery tied for third place for Best Director in the 2005 Seattle International Film Festival Golden Space Needle Awards.

To explore marriages—its joys, failures, frustrations--Emery has brought together a widely diverse cross-section of the population, including both gay, straight, and lesbian couples. We see, for example, a male couple who've lived together for half a century, their entire lives spent in the closet.

Another highlight is an older woman who married a man as her female lover looked on as a bridesmaid. In yet another story we hear the tale of a former marine who only "found himself" after leaving Vietnam.

In another revelation, we hear from a Mormon lesbian (the cult denies the existence of such a person) who was in love with another woman but married a man in the Mormon Temple in Salt Lake City even though she didn't love him. In another case, we learn that one man became suicidal when his male partner died. He was saved by the welcoming congregation at the Everett Church in Seattle.

Even a male/female couple who opposes same-sex marriage is brought on in all their horrible bigotry. That couple wants marriage rights "limited."

Innocent

(2005)

Vulnerable Asian Teen at Crossroads

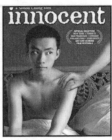

A vulnerable young teen, Eric Tang (played by Timothy Lee) follows his parents during their immigration to Canada, thereby abandoning his boyfriend in Hong Kong. Here in this new land he is forced to confront different emotional and cultural problems as he comes to terms with his gayness.

On the brink of adulthood, he struggles with his sexual identity while his nuclear family begins to experience meltdown. His father (Wilson Kam Wing Wong) lies about getting blow-jobs from young girls in the park. His mother (Jovita Adrineda) launches a restaurant business with another immigrant, an actor billed only as "Mr. Huang" in the role of "Mr. Chia."

Before long, Eric establishes sexual links in Canada, including an ongoing affair with a middle-aged Canadian "rice queen" (Larry Peloso), who functions as a sometimes protector. Despite this involvement, Eric falls for a number of other candidates, often straight guys, including his hunky cousin (Justin Penaloza). Eric also has his eye on Jim (David Yee), a rebellious classmate whose sexuality is ambiguous. His putting the move on Jim leads to Eric's banishment from the friendship.

Eric even attempts to befriend a worker (David Lieu Song Wei) in his mother's restaurant, resulting in a disillusionment so great that he runs away.

In the words of one festival critic, "Although helmer Simon Chung has an appealing quiet sensibility, he never develops dramatic momentum and the film's obtuse personalities never quite gain our sympathies."

WHAT THE CRITICS SAID
"Remarkably free of adolescent angst, Eric's gentle alienation tends to leave him open to a procession of new sensations and exotic experiences, whether wandering through the wheat fields or dancing with older men in a discothéque. Thesping is fine overall."
Ronnie Scheib, *Variety*

It's in the Water

(1997)

Raging Homophobia in a Texas Town

Gays and lesbians who migrated to civilization from redneck towns such as those in Georgia and Texas will appreciate this flick. Helmer/scripter Kelli Herd set the drama in the fictional town of Azalea Springs, Texas. This is a romantic comedy by first-time director Kelli Herd, who knows, like Sacha Baron Cohen, how to send up homophobes.

Alex Stratton (Keeri Jo Chapman) is unfulfilled in a sexless marriage with Robert (Matthew Tompkins). She horrifies the ladies with the big hair and her witchy mom by taking a job at an AIDS hospice. There she bonds with an old friend Grace (Teresa Garrett). This divorced nurse has two children and is already out as a lesbian. As the film moves along, the two women are caught kissing.

Spencer (John Hallum) has a bit of tongue-in-cheek fun spreading the word that the local water supply releases latent homo potentials. Paranoia spreads across the town. Mothers hide their children, as panic rules.

Mark Anderson (Derrick Sanders) works at a local newspaper his father owns. He regularly attends the "Homo-No-Mo" meetings of Brother Daniel. To his own surprise, Mark finds himself becoming involved with Tomas (Timothy Vahle), a Latino house painter. Tomas mistakes the down-with-gays meeting for an A.A. gathering.

In spite of all the homo hysteria sweeping the town, two gay/lesbian love affairs bloom in the midst.

WHAT THE CRITICS SAID
"As in many gay-themed comedies, the straight opposition is virtually all hysterical, hateful buffoons with none of the conflicted feelings which make life with hets so problematic for real-world gays and lesbians. But, again, subtlety was clearly not in Herd's game plan. What she attempted, with considerable success, was to create a good-natured tribute to people who've suffered the trauma of coming out in a less than supportive environment and lived to laugh about it."
Russell Smith

It's My Party

(2002)

"And I'll Die If I Want To"

This is a morbid rendition of the old Lesley Gore hit, "It's My Party." Handsome but AIDS-afflicted Nick Stark (Eric Roberts) is about to die. But before he does, he decides to throw himself a pre-suicide party while he's still coherent enough to recognize everybody.

Imagine attending a party where your host is about to commit suicide. Randal Kleiser's script make it all sound plausible.

It's My Party was shot on a meager budget, the movie based on real characters and inspired by a real party that was thrown in December of 1992.

When he learns of his disease, Nick asks his lover Brandon (Gregory Harrison), "You won't leave me, will you?" But Brandon does just that, other friends like Charlene Lee (Margaret Cho) remaining loyal.

Even though he faces resentment from Nick's loyals, Brandon shows up for a final farewell. Friends feel that Brandon abandoned Nick in the time of his greatest need. As family and friends gather, Nick tries to comfort them, especially his mother (Lee Grant), a Greek woman. Even George Segal, his Jewish father, shows up, although it appears he still is not very accepting of Nick's homosexuality.

Roddy McDowall appears as a devout Catholic, who argues that only God should decide when a man should die.

WHAT THE CRITICS SAID
"Pic feels like a highly personal work but is severely flawed because its narrative consists entirely of background detail, with no dramatic core to contain its multiple subplots and characters. With its loose-knit screenplay, dozens of characters, overlapping dialogue, and other devices, *It's My Party* boasts an Altmanesque structure, but without Altman's savvy or wit—it's more *Ready to Wear* than *Nashville* or *Short Cuts*."
Emanuel Levy, *Variety*

Itty Bitty Titty Committee

(2007)

Clits in Action

Director Jamie Babbit (*But I'm a Cheerleader*) is even more outrageous with this revolutionary romantic comedy about the CIA (Clits in Action), queer feminist radicals reclaiming the streets for girls everywhere. The tagline is "Every generation needs a new revolution."

Fresh out of high school Anna (Melonie Diaz) seems just waiting to be "deflowered." On an impulse, she joins a posse of feminist pranksters. During the day, Anna works as a receptionist in a plastic surgeon's office, moping about after having split up with her most recent girlfriend. Her mother (Ana Mercedes) wants her to be more girly—for example, putting on make-up for her sister's upcoming wedding.

In the feminist coven, Anna meets Sadie (Nicole Vicius), one of the founding members of the guerilla group. She also meets a frustrated artist (Deak Evgenikos); a woman-to-man wannabe transsexual Aggie (Lauren Mollica), and a self proclaimed intellectual Shulamith (Carly Pope).

WHAT THE CRITICS SAID
"The film is a gentle send-up of young activists' excesses, but it's hard not to get swept up in the fun and mayhem as the group, Clits in Action, wreaks havoc on sexist window displays and anti-marriage equality protestors. And through it all is a Le Tigre and Bikini soundtrack that makes you want to run out and fight 'the Man.'"
Jessica Stites

"Great title, shame about the movie. That's likely to be the most common reaction to indie comedy *Itty Bitty Titty Committee*, about a young lesbian who joins a posse of feminist pranksters. With its particular brand of radical politics and 'Riot Grrrl' soundtrack, third feature by helmer Jamie Babbit feels quaintly retro, but that's not enough to redeem pic's hardly witty script."
Leslie Felperin

Jailbait

(2004)

Fragile Young Convict as Potential "Bitch"

Randy (Michael Pitt) commits a victimless crime that would normally get him probation and a hefty fine. But in the "three strikes" world of California justice, he ends up in prison. He finds himself locked up for 25 years.

His cellmate is the brutal Jake (Stephen Adly Guirgis), who casually informs Randy that he slit his wife's throat because she slept with another man just three months after they exchanged vows. Jake takes Randy under his wing, and he has a lot more in mind than offering help to a younger man filled with fear. The domineering cellmate is determined to make Randy his "bitch," in this film by Brett C. Leonard (director and scripter).

WHAT THE CRITICS SAID
"*Jailbait* chronicles the mind game that Jake plays en route to subverting Randy's will and dignity, and it's a hideous process of dehumanization."
Jack Mathews, *New York Daily News*

"For most of its 90 minutes, *Jailbait* rarely strays from the claustrophobic confines of their cell; whether or not that feels like a harsh sentence will depend upon your tolerance for intense, two-handed psychodrama."
Tom Beers, *Time Out New York*

"In the final analysis it all feels very much like a successful acting exercise that while psychologically acute, doesn't really bring much more to the table than we've already gleaned from a few episodes of *Oz*"
TV Guide

"Claustrophobic and overwrought, *Jailbait* is an unpleasant excursions into gay panic mitigated somewhat by performances that are hard to shake."
Philadelphia Inquirer

"Becomes the umpteenth prison drama to focus on the lurid threat of forced submission."
Village Voice

Jeffrey

(1995)

Giving Up on Love in the Age of AIDS

Paul Rudnick's acclaimed off-Broadway hit stars Steven Weber as Jeffrey, a highly sexed gay man who decides to give up on love out of fear he might have sex with a man who is at least HIV-positive.

Then Jeffrey meets the man of his dreams, Steve (Michael T. Weiss). Working out at Jeffrey's gym, Steve makes a pass. In spite of his powerful attraction to the hunk, Jeffrey tries to suppress his feelings.

The subtitle for this comedy/drama might be, "Love is an adventure when one of you is sure and the other positive."

Jeffrey has to decide whether or not love is worth the danger of experiencing a boyfriend dying.

As Sterling, (Patrick Stewart) is a deliciously bitchy decorator, the devil's advocate to Jeffrey. Sometimes the butt of his wit is his boyfriend, Darius (Bryan Batt), a chorus boy in *Cats.*

The supporting cast is first rate, with lively cameos provided by Nathan Lane as a horny Catholic priest; Christine Baranski as a giddy, do-gooder socialite; Sigourney Weaver as a hypocritical New Age evangelist; Olympia Dukakis as the proud mom of a pre-operative lesbian transsexual, and Kathy Najimuy as Weaver's gushing, badly permed acolyte.

WHAT THE CRITICS SAID
"Jeffrey is not without its moments, but the movie never really convinced me it knew what it was doing. It's more a series of sketches and momentary inspirations than a story that grows interesting. Although 'death' has long been a code word in poetry for the moment of climax, the linking of sex and death by AIDS has made it difficult to tell gay male lover stories that don't have at least the possibility of a macabre subtext."
Roger Ebert

A Jihad for Love

(2007)

Go West, Young Men

This docu, which is painful to watch, is about gay life in Muslim countries. Of course, the president of Iran (let's not even mention the creep's name) at Columbia University (of all places) claimed that his country doesn't have homosexuals.

Previous documentaries have explored homophobia in the Orthodox Jewish world (Trembling Before God) and in the evangelical Christian world (*For the Bible Tells Me So*). Now director and scripter Parvez Sharma focuses on gays, lesbians, and transgendered people in the Muslim world, where in some countries young men have been stoned to death for committing "that unpardonable sin."

Filmed in 12 countries and in 9 languages, *A Jihad for Love* is the first-ever feature film to explore the complex global intersections of Islam and homosexuality. Of course, many gay and lesbian Muslims end up renouncing their religion. But other characters in the film aren't willing to abandon a faith they cherish in spite of its flaws.

In the opinion of many Islamic scholars, a short passage cited in the Qur'an was attributed to the prophet Mohammed. It suggests that male-male sexual contact is a crime punishable by death. Other scholars claim that this text was a reference to rape as practiced by the denizens of ancient Sodom to humiliate visiting foreign men.

WHAT THE CRITICS SAID
"Imprisonments, beatings, and personal shame haunt the doc's brave testifiers, who revel in their sexual identity while still hoping to retain a devout sense of faith. The toughest scenes are their confrontations with clergymen who, despite gentleness, point to textual passages that strictly forbid. Ultimately an unanswered question haunts *A Jihad for Love* (and proves its undoing). Why would gay Muslims stay true to a religion that hurts them?"
Joshua Rothkopf, *Time Out New York*

Johan

(1976)

Shortbus, Eat Your Heart Out!

Très risqué! Ooh la la! Back in the 1970s, this was one of the first gay-oriented films released that featured extreme sex scenes pulling no punches. You get plenty of nudity, both male and female, and even incestuous love. As one viewer put it,  "Any film that has two naked men riding a horse into the sunset has our vote."

In its day, this was a chic French retro porn hit. A novice filmmaker searches for an actor to portray his seductive and enigmatic jailed lover in this surreal and sexually explicit film.

Scandalously graphic in 1976, the rediscovered footage of Johan can still shock the faint-of-heart in the 21st century. After the film received an X rating at the Cannes Film Festival in 1976, many scenes were removed, including erect dicks.

The negatives of the cut scenes were destroyed but later a print of them was discovered, and their restored versions were added to the American DVD release. Director Philippe Vallois (also the co-scripter) was very much in your face in his day, or even today as far as that goes.

Out director Vallois wanted to make a movie about his love affair with a young man named Johan, who was in the French Foreign Legion. Before he could, Johan was arrested and sent to jail. Vallois conceived the film as a valentine to his incarcerated lover. But he had to search for another actor to appear as Johan in his film, finding him in Éric Guadagnan.

WHAT THE CRITICS SAID
"There are a number of graphic male-male sex scenes plus some less graphic ones, dance sequences, one with a nude male dancer, one with a nude female dancer, and a drag ballerina. The passage of time and resolute civic attacks on public gay cruising spots (in Paris as in New York) has made the scenes of cruising historical documents. The movie as a whole documents the gay liberation era, which came later to Paris than to American metropolises."
Stephen Murray

Julie Johnson

(2001)

Courtney Love in Love With a Chick

This is a movie about taking charge of your life and realizing your dreams, even exposing one's hidden desires. Lili Taylor plays the title role, with her best friend Claire (Courtney Love) adding good back-up support.

Julie Johnson

A working-class New Jersey housewife, Julie is saddled with a cop husband and two kids. One day she decides she'd going to end this existence and make something of her wasted life. She enrolls in a computer class at an adult school and sets out to enter the professional world in spite of the objections of her domineering husband.

Directed by Bob Goose, *Julie Johnson* depicts its heroine kicking out her husband and finding a job to support herself and her children.

Claire (Love) is also married to a cop. She deserts him and moves in with Julie, her best friend. Somewhere along the way, Julie confesses that she's in love with Claire. It seems that the two women hadn't considered that they might be in love with each other in all their 15 years of friendship. Each of them must cope with the implications of a lesbian affair.

The dialogue is not stellar, and there are flaws in the storyline, but *Julie Johnson* emerges as worthy of a look.

WHAT THE CRITICS SAID
"Taylor practically carries the film with her characteristic flair. Her performances are typically so nuanced, she could make nearly any character believable. She makes an unlikely story seem plausible. Love is surprisingly subtle and not annoying in her role as Claire, and she turns in an equally impressive performance. She's believable and even likable as a bleach blonde with feathered hair, a gum-cracking, tightly clothed Jersey girl."
Shauna Swartz

Junked

(1999)

Bisexual Hustler Tries to Go Straight

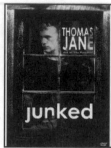

Inspired by actual events, *Junked* is a real-life story written and directed by Lance Lane. It's not everyone's cuppa, but it has its devotees. The film vividly tells the story of a former criminal and bisexual hustler, as played effectively by Thomas Jane.

Switch wants to turn his life around not only for himself but for his best friend, Jimmy (Channing Rowe).

Switch's kid sister, Nikki, is brought to the screen by Jordan Ladd in a completely convincing performance as a junkie and prostitute. Given this premise, the film sets out to explore how difficult it is for Switch to go straight. Vengeance is waiting to ungulf him. The score by Kurt Weill helps a lot. The depiction of criminal low-lifes who inhabit the streets is stark and realistic, so much so that one reviewer called the film "almost unwatchable."

The picture clearly belongs to Thomas Jane, a promising actor best known for his starring roles in *The Punisher* and *Dreamcatcher*.

Junked first saw the light as a play but it has been successfully adapted to the screen. The movie was a long time in being filmed. Budget considerations were no doubt responsible. Filming began in 1998 with the completion date not coming until 2004.

Naturally, you expect drug abuse and strong language. "Of course," we heard one movie-goer comment, "Why else would we be here?"

WHAT THE CRITICS SAID
"Unfortunately Switch's past doesn't want to be forgotten, and when vengeance comes knocking at his door, he must revert to his old ways if he wants to get out alive."
Jason Buchanan, *All Movie Guide*

Keep Not Silent

(*Et sheave nafshi;* 2004)

The Ortho-Dykes of Jerusalem

This is a poignant, even haunting, docu about lesbians living in the ultra-Orthodox communities of Jerusalem. Directed, written, and produced by Ilil Alexander as her film debut, the movie was the winner of an Israeli Academy Award for best documentary.

It's a bold statement about women torn between faith, their families, and their love for each other. In other words, two worlds on a collision course. Their stated goal: To be themselves and live with the women they love.

We meet Ruth, who is married. Her life comes as a surprise in that her husband amazingly allows her to bed her girlfriend twice a week. The daughter of a rabbi, Yehudit, is "out" about her lesbianism and tries to reconcile the two disparate parts of her life. Yet another, Miriam-Esther, has led a closeted life for 20 years, staying married to her husband for the sake of their ten children.

Moving and very personal, the docu is about these various courageous fights for self-realization and acceptance.

All three women join an underground support group to help them cope with their conflicts. As a filmmaker, Alexander knows how to treat her subject with sensitivity and compassion.

The funds to make her film came from the National Foundation for Jewish Culture. The film met with a lot of hostility in Israel, although it certainly had its supporters there, as it did when premiered in San Francisco.

Alexander perceived the idea for her film back in 1996. A woman's body, killed in a suicide bombing on a bus, went unclaimed. The director later found out that the dead women came from an Orthodox family who had excommunicated the victim after discovering that she was a lesbian.

The Kids Are All Right

(2010)

My Two Moms

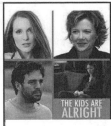

Any film by director Lisa Cholodenko (*Laurel Canyon* and *High Art*) is eagerly awaited, and this *bon bon* to lesbian parenting was warmly received at Sundance.

Jules (Julianne Moore) and Nic (Annette Bening) have been engaged in a lesbian relationship for 20 or so years. Given the red hot debates over gay marriage, particularly from the moronic right, this film is timely.

Nic is a doctor who likes to control; she's also slipping into alcoholism and on the slope of middle-aged danger zones. Jules has tried several professions, and is now being bankrolled into an eco-conscious landscape design business. They are slowly drifting apart.

The pair also has two kids by artificial insemination. Laser (Josh Hutcherson), a typical teenager, is interested in sports and girls. Joni (Mia Wasikowska), sweet 18, is planning to head off for the university. Laser and Joni plot to meet up with their biological father Paul (Mark Ruffalo).

The kids take to their father, and eventually the moms find out. Jules is cool about it, Nic not so much. Paul invites Jules to redesign his over-grown backyard, which leads to an attraction developing between them. Soon they are screwing like honeymooners, despite their shared guilt. Nic inevitably discovers this "adultery," sending the family into a tailspin.

WHAT THE CRITICS SAID
"*The Kids Are All Right* ranks with the most compelling portraits of an American marriage, regardless of sexuality, in film history. Even more remarkably, it's an overwhelmingly affirmative warts-and-all portrait, not a Bergman-style descent, into the pit of marital darkness. Watching two of our finest actresses play unglamorous, flawed, and complicated women is a rare privilege."
Andrew O'Hehir

"Its power lies in how consistently funny and deceptively lighthearted it feels. But there is much more at play here than simply a sharp romantic comedy."
Peter Knegt, *Indie Wire*

Kiki and Herb on the Rocks

(2005)

Boarding a Boat With a Hilarious Duo

First, let's get one point clear: we love Kiki and Herb and would follow this deranged, demented, and devilish cabaret duo at least to hell. That said, it is disappointing to note that this 65-minute documentary made in the UK is a poor vehicle for the gin-soaked Kiki and Herb, both of whom deserve greater immortality on the screen. Nonetheless their talent is such that even a bad film can't completely obliterate them.

Kiki DuRane is actually Justin Bond, and her ever-loyal sidekick, Herb, is Kenny Mellman. Even if *On the Rocks* isn't a great showcase, it includes hilarious bits of comic genius.

Critic Dennis Harvey best stated the case: "Bond's Kiki DuRane is a gravel-voice chanteuse of indeterminate age whose Phyllis Diller laugh and fuchsia pantsuit suggest time froze circa 1973 in a Holiday Inn lounge. Twitchy Herb looks in need of medication whenever he's not furiously pounding the ivories."

Along the way, Kiki, as always, tells of her coke-fueled, battle-scarred life in and out of men.

Until the duo is better showcased, you might prefer to see Kiki and Herb live.

WHAT THE CRITICS SAID
"A drag-camp cabaret duo that started in San Francisco and went on to conquer New York City (even playing Carnegie Hall), *Kiki & Herb* constitutes a great act that doesn't quite get the film the showcasing it deserves in *On the Rocks*. Barely feature-length quasi-docu follows Justin Bond and Kenny Mellman alter egos on a booze-soaked disaster-strewn trip to London, focusing on so-so 'behind-the-scenes' mock-doc footage rather than on-stage sequences."
Variety

"Like Elaine Stritch on nerve powder, Kiki DuRane (Bond) is a cabaret phenomenon still hanging in there (just) after about 70 years in the business. With her faithful keyboardist Herb (Mellman), she arrives in London with delusions of grandeur."
Rich Cline

The Killing
of Sister George

(1968)

America's First A-List, X-Rated Film

Amazingly, this film's leading role, that of lesbian actress, "George" Buckridge, was first offered to Doris Day. She turned it down, as she'd rejected the role of Mrs. Robinson in *The Graduate*. Bette Davis also turned it down, although she would have been most suitable. Eventually, the part went to Beryl Reid, who turned in a larger-than-life performance worthy of an Oscar. The film was directed by Robert Aldrich.

Julie Christie was considered for the role of Alice (aka "Childie"), George's lesbian girlfriend, the part ultimately going to Susannah York.

If you saw the original release of this film, you may want to catch the DVD version. In the original all the sex scenes were cut completely but they've been restored in the latest version.

George is an actress whose current gig involves portraying a cheerful district nurse in a BBC soap opera. She worries, with good reason, that she may be written out of the show. When that actually happens, she laments that the only other job she's been offered is the voice of a cow in a children's program.

A conflict arises when a hard-nosed BBC program director (Mercy Croft, as played by Coral Browne) steals George's lover, Childie. Browne is fabulous as the pernicious older dyke.

Some of the scenes were shot at Gateways, a notorious lesbian bar in London. Reid's performance is a *tour de force*, especially in a scene where George and Alice dress up as Laurel and Hardy for a party.

WHAT THE CRITICS SAID
"*The Killing of Sister George* contains the most erotic sequence ever seen in an otherwise artistically respectable, responsible production. The baring of Susannah York's breast is less a demystification of lesbian tactics than a celebration of all sexual mysteries."
Andrew Sarris, *The Village Voice*

The King and the Clown

(*Wang-ui-namja*, 2005)

Korean Film Tugs at Closet Door

This became the highest-grossing Korean film of all time, eventually earning some $70 million U.S. dollars. The movie centers on a homosexual love triangle in the royal court of Korea during the 1700s.

A young male clown is torn between his love for a fellow clown and a king on the make. The men's display of affection is tame by American standards but taboo-shattering in Seoul.

Homosexuality wasn't removed from the list of "socially unacceptable acts" until 2004. As a depiction of the "love that dare not speak its name," this film was viewed as a breakthrough when it opened. Some 12 million filmgoers, or 25% of South Korea's population, bought a ticket. A local movie distributor said, "It was the equivalent of your *Brokeback Mountain*."

One of the clowns (Jang Sang) is relatively masculine-acting; the other, Gorig-gil, more femme. When the two men begin entertaining the court as jesters, the king becomes enamored of Gil. Naturally, Sang becomes pissed off.

The film is a groundbreaker in more ways than one. As late as 1990, or so a survey revealed, many people living in South Korea were unfamiliar with the existence of gays. One woman thought it was physically "impossible" for two men to mate. She suggested that to fornicate one of the partners "would have to have a hole to penetrate, and only women have holes!" Another viewer said that in the future, "Because of this movie, I will now equate all pretty males as being gay. Before I did not know that a pretty boy was gay." Those viewers have a lot to learn.

Its director, Jun-ik Lee, told *The New York Times*: "This is not homosexuality as defined by the West. It's very different from *Brokeback Mountain*. In that movie, homosexuality is a fate, not a preference. Here, it's a practice."

Kinky Boots

(2005)

Drag Queens Bond with Blue-Collar Blokes

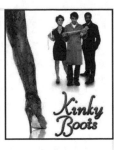

This Britcom was inspired by the true story of a traditional English footwear factory in Northamptonshire which turned to the production of kinky boots for transvestites as a means of saving the ailing family business and safeguarding jobs in the local community.

The Aussie thesp, Joel Edgerton, plays the rather lackluster lead, Charlie Price. In his effort to save his old man's shoe factory, he finds an unlikely ally in "Lola," a black drag queen from London whose real name is Simon. The role is played by the charismatic black actor, Chiwetel Ejiofor, called "Chewey" by his friends and TV announcers who are afraid of mispronouncing his name.

Kinky Boots became the feel-good movie of the year by depicting how a London drag queen finds common ground with a bunch of working stiffs in the Midlands. The parade of erotic women's boots for cross-dressers competes with the actors themselves. By the way, whoever designed those kinky boots, including the size-18 stilettos, should go into business.

In any film, someone has to be annoying, and the thankless role falls to Charlie's whiney fiancée, Nicola (Jemima Rooper). When Charlie is forced to pink slip more than a dozen of the firm's faithful employees, one of them, Lauren (Sarah-Jane Potts), suggests that instead of just firing people, he start a new product line. That leads Charlie south to London's Soho district to check out the footwear on a group of transvestites.

After Charlie helps the hulking drag queen, Lola, fend off attackers in a London back alley, the two form an unlikely alliance. In no time at all, Lola is showing up in Northampton where she encounters one homophobic bruiser who mistakes her for a genetic woman.

Ejiofar, who can also be viewed in Denzel Washington's *Inside Man*, clearly steals the show. He lends his husky voice to musical numbers.

Straight audiences attended this movie and didn't have to worry that there would be any gay sex to offend grandpa.

Kinsey

(2005)

The Mystery of Human Sexual Behavior

Academy Award winner Bill Condon (*Gods and Monsters*) turns the microscope on Alfred Kinsey in a portrait of a man driven to uncover the most private sexual secrets of a nation. What begins for Kinsey as a scientific endeavor soon takes on an intensely personal relevance.

Professor Kinsey is a remarkable man in this film. He's smart enough to launch a sexual revolution, smart enough to get it funded by nothing less than the (very uptight at the time) Rockefeller Foundation, and smart enough to avoid unpleasant accusations of Communist leanings from the (then dauntingly powerful) McCarthyites. He's even smart enough to take things gracefully in stride when the sexual energies of his good-looking male research assistant are unleashed first upon Kinsey himself (we learn as the film unfolds that Kinsey is part of the 48% of the American population that his famous study defines as bisexual), and then upon his wife, a role that's played with aplomb by Laura Linney.

Mrs. Kinsey, it's revealed, had a thick-walled and particularly robust hymen that made penetration from donkey-dong Kinsey (we learn that he has a prodigious willie during a scene at her gynecologist's office) virtually impossible. Early in the film, thanks to an enlightened surgeon, Venus's barrier is surgically and painlessly cut asunder, and coitus is fulfilled.

Kinsey, as eloquently and alluringly played by Liam Neeson (was the real Kinsey as good-looking as that?) rocks and rolls confidently through the evolution of his sexual hypotheses. With an endearing kind of open-handedness, he bumbles and blunders his way through the compilation of statistical information that will, eventually, rock the foundations of America's self-image. "Do you masturbate?" even when queried within the cocoon of a movie set and replayed on DVD, still elicits some of the same red-faced "aw shucks" apologies that we might have experienced in sex-ed classes back in junior high school.

Kiss Kiss, Bang Bang

(2005)

SeX, MuRdEr, MyStErY

Robert Downey Jr., playing Harry Lockhart (a thief masquerading as an actor), and Val Kilmer as "Gay Perry" (a homosexual private eye) might become the next romantic duo in buddy movies. If William Powell and Myrna Loy in *The Thin Man* series  enthralled movie audiences of the 1930s, so can Downey and Kilmer, as a handsome same-sex couple, bring a new twist to the mystery genre in *Kiss Kiss, Bang Bang*, a Warner Brothers release.

This is a comedy crime thriller, bigger on humor than suspense. Making his directorial debut, former Hollywood *wünderkind*, Shane Black, seems to lose control of the screenplay. It was based in part on the 1941 novel by Brett Halliday.

The title of Halliday's detective novel was *Bodies Are Where You Find Them*. But Black felt that *Kiss Kiss, Bang Bang* was the catchier title. Actually, it wasn't his original. He wanted to call it *You'll Never Die in This Town Again*.

The movie is divided into five "chapters," each named for a Raymond Chandler title. The film begins with *Trouble Is My Business*, ending with *Farewell My Lovely*.

Let's take a hopeless stab at plot summary for this smarty-pants mystery thriller. From the first shot, Black is back with his wise-ass insider tone, as he sends up Los Angeles with cleverness that Harrison Ford and humpy Josh Hartnett failed to do in *Hollywood Homicide*. Ford and Hartnett never survived their lame script. Black gives Kilmer and Downey more of a fighting chance.

Our advice would be to sit back and enjoy the movie and not even attempt to follow the convoluted plot. One reviewer found that the logic of this movie is as hard to find as the Lost City of Atlantis. Bodies appear and reappear so fast in this picture of mayhem madness that it's hard to keep tabs. All you know for sure is that Downey's character seems to have booked a one-way ticket to the Los Angeles morgue.

Sexy and macho, private eye Kilmer advertises himself as a faggot dick.

Kiss Me, Guido

(1997)

Exactly What Does GWM Mean?

This is a silly little film, an amusing trifle scripted and directed by Tony Vitale. Warren (Anthony Barrile) has an extra room in his apartment for rent, and he's five months behind on the rent after his lover moved out. He advertises in the *Village Voice*, a  GWM (gay white male) seeking a roommate.

Frankie (Nick Scotti) unwittingly thinks GWM stands for "guy with money." In spite of complications, he becomes the roommate of gay, gay Warren.

As is inevitable, Frankie and Warren, after a lot of false starts, develop some sort of friendship without any major conversions to homosexuality. The relationship never crosses into the sexual realm.

One critic defined the film as "*La Cage aux Folles* in reverse—that is, a pair of gay men coaching a strictly hetero Italian American stud in the fine points of swishing." That's so he can play a gay male on stage in a play.

Everybody's a stereotype in this movie, even the parents and best friends.

A pizza baker, Frankie has aspirations to become an actor. He's wanted to leave the Bronx behind ever since he came home one night and walked in on his brother making love to his girlfriend.

The question is asked: "Can a gay man and a *guido* (Italian American) live together in platonic harmony when both harbor prejudices against each other?"

The supporting cast includes a horny landlady (Molly Price), who jumps at men "like a Rottweiler on a soup bone." Warren's ex-lover is played by Christopher Lawford, son of Peter Lawford and Patricia Kennedy.

Kiss of the Spider Woman

(1985)

A Gay Fantasy About Seducing a Straight Man

The Brazilian director, Hector Babenco, directed his two American stars in this steamy drama set entirely in a jail cell in an unnamed Latin country, presumably Argentina.

Raul Julia stars as Valentín, a macho political prisoner who shares his cramped cell with a hopelessly romantic gay man, Molina (William Hurt). Molina has been jailed for molesting a young boy.

The two men, to pass the time, enter Molina's fantasy world of romantic films in this legendary adaptation of Manuel Puig's classic novel.

Hurt, then at his hottest (*Altered States, Body Heat, The Big Chill*) originally wanted to play the role of Valentín himself. We can be grateful that he went back to the Molina part, with his henna hair. One critic, for reasons not altogether explained, called *Spider Woman* "a gay Casablanca."

Brazilian star Sonia Braga plays three roles, two of them as the star of the old movies Molina recalls, and the third a surprise.

WHAT THE CRITICS SAID
"What *Kiss of the Spider Woman* at first seems to be about is the changing nature of the relationship between two very different men who have been locked together in the same cell. They are opposites in every way. But they share the same experiences, day after day, and that gives them a common bond. Gradually, an affection grows between them, and we assume that the movie will be about the ways in which they learn to accept each other. Only gradually, mysteriously, do we realize that the movie is about a good deal more."
Roger Ebert

"Don't be too quick to jump on Hurt with complaints of old-fashioned gay stereotyping. Only with a development well into the movie will the audience realize the layers he brought to Molina's role-playing."
Bob Graham, *San Francisco Chronicle*

Kiss the Bride

(2007)

Guess Who's Coming to the Wedding?

In high school Matt (Philipp Karner) and Ryan (James O'Shea) were best friends. More than friends, actually. Time has separated them. But when Matt learns that Ryan is getting married—to a woman, no less—he heads for his old hometown determined to put a stop to it.

Tori Spelling is cast as the third wheel (Alex Golski). This bride-to-be is about to discover that her fiancé may be gay.

Director C. Jay Cox showed poor "grooming" in casting Tori Spelling as a visibly pregnant Alex, who is supposed to be an innocent bride waiting at the altar.

One scene was called "squirm-inducing," and that was when Matt and Alex meet. She's blindfolded at her bachelorette party, and he's mistaken for the stripper.

WHAT THE CRITICS SAID
"At first, the supremely silly vibe offers a fair amount of fun. But then Cox switches gears and gets serious, which is a huge mistake. A movie this preposterous should never have been played straight."
Elizabeth Weitzman, *New York Daily News*

"Matt is relieved to discover that he and Ryan still have chemistry, though flashbacks to their 'innocent' high school strip-poker games seem unintentionally laughable, since neither actor passes as an awkward teen. What Matt doesn't expect is just how much he likes Alex, which leads to an awkwardly contrived moment when they kiss—for no reason except that the screenplay requires it. Naturally, Ryan walks in on them, sending everyone's sexual-identity issues into a tailspin."
Peter Debruge, *Variety*

"Will Matt divulge Ryan's sordid past and put a stop to the wedding? A pressing question to be sure, but here's one to trump it: Can you believe a camp icon like Tori Spelling playing a character with no gaydar?"
Kyle Buchanan, *The Advocate*

Kissing Jessica Stein

(2001)

A Lesbian Comedy of Ideas

All the straight world is busy around Jessica Stein (Jennifer Westfeldt). Her brother's getting married, her best friend Joan (Jackie Hoffman) is pregnant, and her mother (Tovah Feldshuh) is urging her to find a single Jewish male, aged 20 to 45.

Kissing Jessica Stein

Disillusioned with her hopeless dates with heteros, Jessica answers an ad placed by Helen (Heather Juergensen), who quotes the poet Rilke in her personals. Helen is aggressively bisexual, sneaking away for a quickie with her toy boy during an art gallery opening.

After Jessica answers her ad, Helen learns that Jessica has never had a lesbian experience. If Jessica is fluttery, Helen is grounded.

Jessica is reluctant to invite Helen to her brother's wedding, lest the family find out who she's been dating. As Jessica starts to fall for Helen, she has to deal with her own securities.

Director Charles Herman-Wurmfeld has taken a script by Heather Juergensen and Jennifer Westfeldt (also the star) and turned it into a fresh take on the subject of sex.

Helen and Jessica muddle through their hilarious courtship with a certain sincerity. They make up the rules as they go along. Many critics noted how Jessica blurred the lines between friendship and romantic love.

WHAT THE CRITICS SAID

"*Kissing Jessica Stein* is pure pleasure. A fresh take on sex and the single girl, this buoyant, well-crafted romantic comedy blends pitch perfect performances with deliciously smart writing.
Lael Lowenstein, *Variety*

"Same-sex romance, a controversial topic in movies millions now alive can still remember, is a lifestyle choice in *Kissing Jessica Stein*. Yes, a 'choice'—although that word is non-PC in gay circles—because one of the two women in the movie is nominally straight, and the other is bisexual."
Roger Ebert

A Knock Out

(2004)

Who Is S/He?

Dealing with social issues, this docu is the story of an undefeated world champion boxer whose career comes to a sudden end. She did not actually retire, but ran out of fighters who were willing to face her. Her title was eventually "vacated" for non-defense.

Should Aboro decide to remain inactive and, ultimately, to retire from boxing, she would join Rocky Marciano and a handful of others in boxing's history to retire as an undefeated world champion.

Michele Aboro, born in London in 1969, is a world-champion pro-boxing two-time K1 winner and three time *Pound for Pound* Best Woman Fighter of the world. As the documentary depicts, she wins all 21 fights and ends 18 of them with a knock-out. This is, of course, an exceptional achievement in women's boxing.

Aboro was of Nigerian descent. Growing up was hard for this mixed-race lesbian. But her tenacious spirit and uncanny talent for combat sports sustained her.

She refused to "vamp up" her image and pose naked in magazines. Faced with little choice, she had to more or less abandon the sport of boxing, finding it was more interesting in selling sex than sport.

A Knock Out interweaves her personal story with interviews from boxers whose wild success strikes a painful contrast to Aboro's own struggles.

In search of reason behind this case, the docu, as viewed by *Vrij Nederland* magazine, leads us into the world of international women's boxing and its marketing. It also explores social issues that go way beyond the world of boxing: the meaning of gender, sexuality, and identity. The film lifts this individual story to a universal one of fighting for one's identity and how far one is willing to go to win.

The film was directed by Tessa Boerman and Samüel Reiziger.

L.I.E.

(2001)

**A 15-Year-Old Boy Sexually Involved
With an Ex-Marine**

L.I.E. are the initials for the Long Island Expressway. As the movie opens, Howie Blitzer (Paul Dano) is hazardously balanced on one foot, standing on a guard rail above the speeding traffic. He has lost his mother in a car accident. His voice-over intones that, "There are the lanes going east, there are lanes going west, and there are lanes going straight to hell."

His father is hardly a responsible parent. He's embroiled in a legal case against his budding contracting company and absorbed with his new bimbo girlfriend. No emotional support there.

Howie spends his time robbing neighborhood houses with his hustler friend Gary (Billy Kay), to whom he is sexually attracted. When Howie leaves behind some evidence in the house of ex-Marine Big John (Brian Cox), the Vietnam veteran tracks him down. It seems that Big John likes the company of young boys.

In soulless American suburbia, where helmer/scripter Michael Cuesta has set this drama, he screens an ambiguous relationship that develops between the 15-year-old boy and the middle-aged pederast.

WHAT THE CRITICS SAID
"Make no mistake. L.I.E. is not an apologia for pederasty. It does not argue in defense of Big John. But Cuesta has the stubborn curiosity of an artist who won't settle for formulas but is intrigued by the secrets and mysteries of his characters. Many men can remember that when they were boys there were sometimes older men around who used friendship or mentoring as a metaphor for a vague unexpressed yearning. The movie is balanced along that murky divide just as Howie is balanced above the expressway."
Roger Ebert

"Skillfully negotiating a thin line between the abhorrent and the sympathetic, this superbly acted film is likely to provoke discussion through its courageous depiction of an unapologetic pedophile as an oddly honorable man."
David Rooney, *Variety*

La Cage aux Folles

(1978)

The Cult Classic Deserves Its Reputation

Birds of a Feather (its English name) tells the story of nightclub owner Ugo Tognazzi (Renato Baldi) and his transvestite lover Michel Serrault (Albin Mougeotte).

Michel as "Zaza Napoli" is the star drag queen at the couple's notorious St.-Tropez club. Renato's son is bringing home his fiancée's ultra-conservative parents to meet Michel and Ugo. The gay couple work frantically to conceal their lifestyle before the arrival of their son's fiancée.

With its gags, uproarious complications, and a tender, touching ending, *La Cage* won over an international audience. Even some homophobes liked it.

The film inspired two sequels and an American remake entitled *The Bird Cage* that was directed by Mike Nichols and starring Robin Williams and Nathan Lane.

The most wickedly funny moments in the film occur when "Auntie" Serrault, the live-in maid and a black transvestite, appears.

The father of the intended bride just happens to be the "Minister of Moral Standards" in France. *Guess Who's Coming to Dinner?*

WHAT THE CRITICS SAID
"The dilemma of dinner guests inspires the film's hilarious middle section, in which Tognazzi's garishly bizarre apartment is severely redecorated in crucifixes and antiques. Tognazzi goes to visit the woman who bore his son two decades ago to ask her to portray the mother for one night. She agrees. Too bad, because in the course of the uproariously funny dinner party, at least two reputed mothers are produced, one of them suspiciously hairy around the chest."
Roger Ebert

"Yes, *La Cage aux Folles* is funny and poignant and charming and even a touch satirical, but I think what makes it all work so well is that its characters are both engaging and endearing."
John J. Puccio

La Vie en Rose

(La Môme; 2007)

France's Iconic Songbird Gets a Biopic

Marion Cotillard plays "the Little Sparrow," Edith Piaf, the waiflike French songbird whose personal traumas fueled her art. Burned out at the age of 47, Piaf died in 1963, but her memory lingers on.

A bisexual, she loved men but also had affairs with women, including Marlene Dietrich, her great friend.

The helmer, Oliver Dahan, also co-wrote the script. He draws moments—the good, the bad, and the ugly—from Piaf's failures and triumphs—and weaves them into a celluloid mosaic.

If there are any souls on the planet who are not familiar with the career of Edith Piaf, she was a Gallic fusion of Judy Garland and Billie Holiday, only more so. Cotillard's portrait of the French singer is brilliant, going from famished alley cat to stooped, feeble wreck prematurely aged.

The first half hour or so focuses on Piaf's traumatic childhood when she was abandoned by her mother and lived in a bordello. She went temporarily blind and began to sing for her supper on the streets of Paris. Her adult life had all the makings for French drama: she was accused of murder, endured the death of her only child, married twice (unsuccessfully), and became involved with the French Resistance.

The biopic also stars Gérard Depardieu as Louis Leplée, the cabaret owner who discovers Piaf.

Watch for brief appearances of Caroline Sihol as Marlene Dietrich and Alban Casterman as Charles Aznavour.

Millions of people around the world were touched by the music of Piaf. Thousands will be touched by scenes in this somewhat successful film.

WHAT THE CRITICS SAID
"Marion Cotillard's feral portrait of the French singer Edith Piaf as a captive wild animal hurling herself at the bars of her cage is the most astonishing immersion of one performer into the body and soul of another I've ever encountered."
Stephen Holden, *The New York Times*

The Lady in Question Is Charles Busch

(2004)

She-Bitches and Vampire Lesbians

"The Lady" in question is known to all the gay world. Directors John Catania and Charles D. Ignacio in this fascinating "doc" bio will make their writer/actor subject known to even more fans. Those of us in New York already know Busch from his appearances in cabaret and theaters. Others know the performer through his (we almost said her) film work. The one with the most memorable title was *Vampire Lesbians of Sodom*. More recently Bush was seen in the film, *Die, Mommie Die*.

His play, *The Tale of the Allergist's Wife*, ran for 777 performances on Broadway and won Busch the Outer Circle Critics John Gassner Award. He also received a Tony nomination for Best Play.

A poignant moment in this documentary comes when we learn that some of Busch's early collaborators died in that great plague that swept across New York's artistic community in the late 80s, when President Reagan was still refusing to mention the A word.

Told in what one reviewer claimed was a "talking head-meets-flashback-style," the film includes appearances by longtime partner Eric Myers to sing Busch's praise. Other observers of the New York theater and cultural scene include Julie Halston. Yes, that's Boy George caught in the act, and even an appearance by Michael Musto playing himself, of course (what else?). Rosie O'Donnell also appears as herself as do Kathleen Turner and Paul Rudnick.

"Theodora, She-Bitch of Byzantium" (we mean Charles Busch, of course) comes alive in rich archival footage that recreates an era in all its cross-dressing madness. Remember *Red Scare on Sunset* or *Psycho Beach Party*? Mae West used to call herself an institution. But in New York, Charles Busch, "The Lady in Question," is also an institution and a forever entertaining personality but only after dark.

WHAT THE CRITICS SAID
"A cleverly constructed movie."
Time Out New York

The Laramie Project

(2002)

Bigotry That's Hard to Watch

Director/scripter Moisés Kaufman (Gross Indecency) and the Tectonic Theater of New York explore University of Wyoming student Matthew Shepard's brutal gay-bashing murder in 1998. His death attracted nation-wide attention, even sup-  portive comments from President Clinton.

It can be said that this western town lost its inno-cence the night young Shepard was murdered. Laramie itself has become a name that will live in infamy. The man who discovered Shepard's body recalls, "He was the first gay person I ever saw." Depicted is policewoman (Amy Madigan) who cut the cord that bound Shepard's wrists. She later experienced her own scare when it was revealed that the student was HIV-positive.

Hundreds of hours were spent interviewing local residents, although many turned down the op-portunity to appear on camera. The docu pres-ents a mixture of direct reportage, re-enactment, and dramatization. Actors play certain roles, none more famous than Peter Fonda cast as the chief physician at the hospital.

Two local morons, Aaron McKinney and Russell Henderson, rednecks from hell, were charged with driving Shepard from a local bar to a remote point on the outskirts of town. They later claimed that he came on to them seductively.

He was savagely pistol whipped and beaten and then tied up, shoeless and bleeding, to a cattle fence in the mid-October cold. He was discov-ered by a passing bicyclist and rushed to the hos-pital, where he never regained consciousness.

Candlelight vigils and protests made the case a cause célèbre.

WHAT THE CRITICS SAID
"The artifice inherent in recasting this story via so many familiar professional faces does lend this Laramie Project a hybrid, pseudo-real quality that's often distracting. That said, the heart-wrenching nature of the material does eventually come through."
Dennis Harvey, Variety

Latter Days

(2004)

Slutty Party Boy Meets Uptight Mormon

Expect fireworks when a wild, gay "party animal" falls for a handsome young Mor-mon missionary. Needless to say, the Mormons are not known for promoting gay lib-eration.

Christian, as charmingly played by Wes Ramsey, is a hunky, 20-something, West Hollywood slut. He gets more than he bargains for when he tries to seduce 19-year-old Elder Aaron Davis, as delightfully acted by Steve Sand-voss, so boyishly handsome you'll want to abduct him.

Davis is a sexually confused Mormon missionary who moves into an apartment complex in gay West Hollywood.

When Christian exposes Davis's secret sexual desires, Davis rejects Christian for being shallow and empty. The encounter shatters each boy's re-ality, drawing the two into a passionate romance that risks destroying their lives.

Latter Days is charming, sexy, and moving, a tale that will leave you believing in the transforma-tional power of love.

Jacqueline Bisset comes as a total and rather de-lightful surprise in this film. She is the tolerant owner of a restaurant where Christian works as a waiter.

This is the directorial debut of C. Jay Cox, a long way from home and his screenplay for the ro-mantic comedy, Sweet Home Alabama.

The film ran into trouble in Salt Lake City where it provoked outrage among some members of the Mormon community. We weren't there, but would love to have stood in the lobby to see if any gay-bashing Mormons showed up.

For the most part, the characters, except for the gay-haters, are well conceived and sympathetic.

Leaving Metropolis

(2002)

Gay Man and Married Couple in Love Triangle

The out, outspoken, and gay Canadian playwright Brad Fraser is one of the writers for the hit television series, *Queer as Folk*. In *Leaving Metropolis*, he has filmed a movie based on a stage script *Poor Super Man*.

This is a tale of a gay Winnipeg artist who has an affair with a married man. A painter, David (Troy Ruptash) has writer's block. He decides to take a job as a waiter.

The glorified diner is owned by yuppie marrieds Violet (Cherilee Taylor) and Matt (Vincent Corazza). The puppyish Matt certainly inspires him all right. David finds himself falling for his guileless, hunky Matt, who may be a repressed homosexual.

Violet grows suspicious about her hubby's late nights out. Eventually Matt is forced to confess all to Violet when the nude portraits David has painted of him are unveiled at a public exhibit.

Will David break up Matt's marriage? What will Violet do when she learns the truth? Will David and Matt learn the true meaning of love?

The major supporting roles include a transsexual Shannon (Thom Allison), living in David's loft. He has long wished for a sex change operation (male-to-female) but is on hold because of his HIV-positive status.

The part of an aging, bitter, fag-hag journalist Kyrla (Lynda Boyd) barges into the diner one day to taunt her incognito pal. Up to now, David has tried to keep his two lives separate—that of a painter and that of a waiter. But Kyrla is about to change all that.

WHAT THE CRITICS SAID
"Well-played characters are drawn in decisive strokes, even if pic's headlong progress allows little room for psychological back stories or breathing space. Individual scenes occasionally retain a too theatrical air."
Dennis Harvey, *Variety*

Lesbianas de Buenos Aires

(2004)

Dreams, Hopes, & Desires of 3 Women

This courageous docu is, in essence, a celebration of a despised minority: lesbians living in the macho man's world of Buenos Aires, Argentina. It tells the story of three women: a lesbian activist, a soccer coach, and a mother. They share stories about their first fantasies, the consequences of coming out, the desire to have children, and of love between women in a repressive society.

In Spanish with English subtitles, the docu is the creation of helmer/scripter Santiago Garcia.

Argentina, of course, is not as repressive against gays and lesbians as—say, Iran, which has put to death 4,000 men and women since 1979 because they were homosexual.

Nonetheless, lesbians have limited freedom of expression, sexual or otherwise, in this male-dominated Latino culture. Many homosexuals in Argentina are harassed and even arrested just for being gay, without committing any civil or criminal trespass.

The docu features a lesbian parade, evocative of one in New York but much smaller, of course. One woman criticizes the event, noting, "There's nothing to celebrate here."

One vivid portrait narrates the life of a soccer coach, who encourages young women to take up this sport, heretofore almost the sole privilege of men.

There is the inevitable coming out story. In one case a lesbian outed herself to her parents, and she was outed from her home as a result.

The derogatory word for lesbian in Argentina is "tortilla." Since that also means an omelette, confusion sometimes reigns.

WHAT THE CRITICS SAID
"The film becomes one-sided and small in scope so that the richness of a specific reality in Latin America is not fully investigated. But all in all, the film has no grand ambitions, and though it feels incomplete, the women's specific experiences are well told."
Roxana M. Ramirez

The Life and Times of Allen Ginsberg

(1994)

Beating the Drum for a Poet-Visionary

Allen Ginsberg

Helmer Jerry Aronson in this bio-docu augmented his 1993 cinematic portrait of the beat poet Allen Ginsberg with 6 hours of extra material for a double-disc release in 2005.

The life and work of Ginsberg, the greatest of the Beat Generation poets, is put into focus in this film. Famous people in archival footage appear as themselves, including Joan Baez, William F. Buckley, William S. Burroughs, Abbie Hoffman, Jack Kerouac, Ken Kesey, Timothy Leary, Norman Mailer, and Ginsberg himself.

The film follows the young poet from his middle-class upbringing in New Jersey, through the media outpost of the Beat Generation, his role in the flowering hippie movement of the 60s, and his final years as a devout Buddhist and political activist.

Aronson spent 12 years filming Gainsburg, as he read poetry, answered questions, or cavorted with his famous pals

Tantalizing snippets include Ginsberg and Bob Dylan visiting Jack Kerouac's grave in Lowell. Even Andy Warhol appears, but Johnny Depp comes as a surprise.

This is a rich slice of cultural history, lovingly presented.

WHAT THE CRITICS SAID

"Strictly routine as filmmaking, adhering fairly consistently to the sound-bite approach. But given the subject, there's still a great deal of interest here about the life, art, milieu, and political activity of Ginsberg."
Jonathan Rosenbaum, *Chicago Reader*

"It is scintillating, nutty, madly inspired, or ecstatically preposterous. Ginsberg himself is all these things, but the movie is not."
Hal Hinson, *Washington Post*

The Life of Reilly

(2006)

More Than Just Kitsch Celebrity

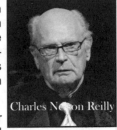

Charles Nelson Reilly

Fans of the *Match Game* on TV still recall Charles Nelson Reilly, a Bronx-born native with a reedy voice. He became the small screen's swishiest stealth weapon, an out gay man pre-Stonewall.

He also became a familiar face to millions who watched his 90-plus appearances on *Johnny Carson's Tonight Show.* These appearances were only the fluff. Behind that wicked *repartée* beat the serious heart of an artist.

Directors Frank Anderson and Barry Poltermann reveal Reilly as more than a kitsch celebrity. The video is built around *Save It for the Stage*, a one-man show by Reilly, who was an actor, Tony Award-winning theater director, and general showbiz gadfly. The docu is filed with bittersweet anecdotes, interspersed with archival images.

Revealed is his impression of his acting coach Uta Hagen, his friendship with Hal Holbrook, and the influence of his bigoted, fiercely protective mother.

One viewer asked the question, "What if it was 1940 and you had a lobotomized aunt, an institutionalized father, a racist mother, and you were the only gay kid on the block? What do you think the odds would be that you'd become a generational icon?"

WHAT THE CRITICS SAID

"With equal measures of wit, gleeful pride, and bemused gratitude, Charles Nelson Reilly looks back at his life, and invites his audience to share the view, in this thoroughly engaging filmization of his one-man stage show. Except for some fleetingly serious scenes—recollection of a troubled childhood, a miraculous escape from a 1944 circus fire—the tone is light, bright, and shamelessly dishy. There's a suggestion of still-simmering anger when he recalls a brutal brush-off by an NBC talent scout in the early 1950s. 'They don't let queers on television.' Ultimately, however, *Life of Reilly* is vivid proof that living well, and laughing heartily, can be the best revenge."
Joe Leydon, *Variety*

Like a Virgin

(Cheonhajangsa Madonna; 2006)

"Be What You Want to Be"

This South Korean film follows the travails of a boy who wants to be a woman. Within its country of origin, it's viewed as something of an oddball, since a few years ago gay-themed movies virtually didn't exist.

The film was both directed and scripted by Hae-jun Lee and Hae-yeong Lee, and stars Ryu Deok-hwan as Dong-gu, a tubby South Korean high school boy whose grand ambition involves having a sex-change operation.
To fund the operation, he enters a *Ssireum* (also spelled *sirum*) or traditional Korean wrestling championship. Even though he is much smaller than the other sumo wrestlers, he seems to have superhuman strength.

Dong-gu is not only a great wrestler but a dancer as well. He learned his formidable dancing skills by mimicking Madonna—that's how the name of the pop star ended up in the Korean-language title of this film. Until he slowly earns their respect, his fellow wrestlers resent this girlish boy in their midst.

The boy soon develops an adolescent crush on his Japanese teacher (Tsuyoshi Kusanagi). Dong-gu believes that his teacher will love him if he becomes a woman. The Japanese teacher is so effeminate, we suspect he'd love Dong-gu more as a boy than a woman.

Oh, yes, the wrestler waiting to become a woman has a miserable home life, centering around his alcoholic father who was a former boxing champ.

WHAT THE CRITICS SAID
"Ryu is a versatile, charming delight in the lead role, and manages to charm as he walks a tightrope in depicting one of South Korean cinema's trickiest characterizations in recent memory. Despite the nation's rep as a homophobic environment, Dong-gu is incredibly at ease with himself. That said, the character isn't allowed to show much interest in physical sex for a teenage boy of any persuasion. Film themes in South Korea are changing fast . . . but not that fast, it seems."
Russell Edwards, *Variety*

The Line of Beauty

(2006)

Love, Class, and Tragedy in Thatcherite London

Helmer Saul Dibb strikes again. This time he no longer explores the gritty lower rungs of the economic ladder as he did in his sleeper debut, *Bullet Boy*. Within a mini-series originally broadcast on the BBC in three one-hour parts, he's moved up to where the rich folks—all Torys—live.

Andrew Davies adapted the plot from Alan Hollinghurst's Prize-winning novel about a young gay man, Nick Guest (played by the divinely handsome Dan Stevens), who, during the 1980s, moves into the innermost circles of power.

At Oxford, Nick becomes "best mates" with Toby (Oliver Coleman), the son of a rising member of Parliament, Gerald Fedden (Tim McInnerny). Is the relationship platonic? We don't know for sure. There was that certain gleam in Nick's eyes.

After graduation, Nick moves into the Fedden family's London mansion and becomes a member of their glittering world of lavish parties and summer homes on the Continent. If he has a job in this household at all, it's to befriend Toby's troubled sister, Catherine (Hayley Atwell).

But instead of maneuvering his way into Toby's pants, Nick turns to Leo (Don Gilet), a bicycle-riding socialist immigrant from Jamaica.

The film fast forwards to 1986 when Nick is still living within the Fedden family's orbit, but carrying on with a sometimes lover, Wani Ouradi (Alex Wyndham), the closeted son of a Lebanese tycoon.

As the series nears its end, scandal looms. Trouble lies ahead as an ongoing series of financial and political embarrassments burst out.

WHAT THE CRITICS SAID
"As Gerald's career skyrockets toward a possible cabinet position, private matters become increasingly at risk of becoming public. While the clan privately tolerates Nick's sexuality, different standards apply to the 'gay issue' in Tory political terms."
Dennis Harvey, *Variety*

Little Ashes

(2008)

When Salvador Dalí Loved Federico García Lorca

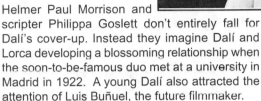

The surrealist artist, Salvador Dalí, always denied that he and the Spanish poet Frederico García Lorca had a torrid romance. "We were just friends."

Yeah, right.

Helmer Paul Morrison and scripter Philippa Goslett don't entirely fall for Dalí's cover-up. Instead they imagine Dalí and Lorca developing a blossoming relationship when the soon-to-be-famous duo met at a university in Madrid in 1922. A young Dalí also attracted the attention of Luis Buñuel, the future filmmaker.

Cast as Dalí, with his famous roller-coaster mustache, Robert Pattinson will horrify his 13-year-old fans playing it gay. But no tweens were in sight at screenings for the star of *Twilight* and *Harry Potter* in this 2008 venture. Playing Lorca with a certain passion is Javier Beltran.

The relationship between Lorca and Dalí was "passionate but platonic," in *Little Ashes*. In real life, there's a good chance they balled each other.

WHAT THE CRITICS SAID
"By 1936 García Lorca was dead, murdered by Spanish fascists. Buñuel fled Spain to Mexico, then later returned as one of the world's greatest filmmakers. Dalí betrayed his early talent, embraced fascism, Nazism, and communism, returned repentant to the church, and became an odious caricature of an artist, obsessed by cash. 'Each morning when I awake,' he said, 'I experience again a supreme pleasure—that of being Salvador Dalí.' Yes, but for a time, he was a superb painter."
Roger Ebert

"*Little Ashes* is a trifling historical fantasy, gossip wrapped in gossamer, beautiful to watch but it takes only a light wind to leave the story in tatters."
Betsy Sharkey, *Los Angeles Times*

Little Miss Sunshine

(2006)

Dysfunctional Family Road Trip Comedy

Of course, an offbeat indie film with a flawless cast would have a gay character in it. In this case, it's the suicidal brother Frank (Steve Carell). Known in scholarly circles for his infinite knowledge of Marcel Proust, Frank has just lost to a rival academic both the young grad student who was his male love, plus a MacArthur Foundation grant. Movie viewers know Carell for his appearances in *The 40-Year-Old Virgin* and *The Office*. In *Sunshine*, he delivers a morosely deadpan characterization, and does so brilliantly.

It was the film's "winning" look at "losers" that drove audiences to buy tickets. The youngest player in this megahit, Olive, "Little Miss Sunshine" herself, a 9-year-old New Yorker, Abigail Breslin, may be diminutive (4-feet-1), but she towers tall as an actress.

Greg Kinnear as Richard plays her dad, with Alan Arkin cast as her raunchy grandfather.

A broken-down VW transports the dysfunctional Hoovers from their home in Albuquerque on a foolhardy trip to Redondo Beach so Olive can compete in a beauty pageant. The mother, Sheryl, is winningly played by Toni Collette. Their teenage son, Dwayne (Paul Dano), is a silent Nietzsche devotee. This comedy/drama was directed by husband-and-wife team, Jonathan Dayont and Valerie Faris, from a script by Michael Arndt.

WHAT THE CRITICS SAID
"As a chaotic, cathartic bonding experience, the film works, in part because the family members are so caught up in their individual frustrations and insecurities."
David Rooney, *Variety*

"Carell follows Richard Dreyfuss in *Poseidon* in what appears to be a new stock role: the post-suicidal gay man recently dropped by a younger lover whose sexuality has little to do with the rest of the movie."
Bruce C. Steele, *The Advocate*

The Living End

(1992)

On the Lam With 2 Hunks with AIDS

Helmer/scripter Gregg Araki made one of the great breakthrough movies about the early years of the AIDS pandemic in 1992. It's been remixed and re-mastered and is now available on DVD.

The director told *The Advocate*, "Young people today can't even imagine what it was like to be gay in the late 80s and early 90s when people were dying every day all around you and it felt like a war zone."

In the film Luke (Mike Dytri) is a gay hustler. His friend Jon (Craig Gilmore) is a movie critic. Both are HIV-positive. Together they go on a hedonistic, dangerous journey. You might call this the first movie about an AIDS-affected road trip. Chronicled in this movie are the exploits—"mostly erotic and excretory," in the words of one viewer, of an HIV-positive couple on the lam, as they explore (Araki's words) "the desolate, quasi-surrealist American wasteland."

HIV+ or not, both of the film's stars appear as hunky homosexuals. When they shot the movie, it was under the working title of *Fuck the World*.

Gay men come out better in this flick than lesbians, who are depicted as "foul-mouthed, green-eyed man killers," as evoked by Mary Woronoz and Johanna Went.

In an episode that might have been inspired by *Bonnie and Clyde*, Luke runs into gay bashers and shoots them dead.

Perhaps the most touching moment in the film is when Jon rescues blood-splattered Luke and takes him home. Right before they make love, Jon confides that he has learned he's carrying the AIDS virus. "Welcome to the club," Luke whispers in his ear.

WHAT THE CRITICS SAID
"Jon, a conventional sort, is infatuated by the rebellious Luke, a Valley Guy who says 'dude' a lot and drinks bourbon from a Ninja Turtles water bottle. When Luke kills a cop off-screen, he persuades Jon to run away with him."
Rita Kempley, *The Washington Post*

Liza With a Z

(1972)

Resurrection of a Broadway Baby

When diva Liza Minnelli and Broadway legend Bob Fosse created the spectacular musical special *Liza with a Z* in 1972, they made TV history and carted home four Emmys. Since around the mid-80s, it was widely believed that the film had been

lost. Now it's back in a digitally restored version that returns that old glamour of our favorite Broadway baby when she was just 26.

Today in her 60s, Liza is hardly a has-been. We prefer to call her an "always was." Okay, so she's not as great as Judy Garland. But who in the hell ever was?

Liza gave this one-woman concert at the Lyceum Theater in New York in 1972. For audiences not around in those days, the remastered 16-millimeter film reveals Liza at the very apex of her career. At least a newer generation will understand why she looms so large in both pop culture and gay iconography.

Luckily for us, Liza sings a medley from her hit *Cabaret*, the film musical that brought her an Oscar and her greatest and only plausible movie role as a romantic lead.

In the DVD, we love Liza when she does her own rendition of such standards as "Bye Bye Blackbird" and "Son of a Preacher Man." Not only that, but we get music by Kander & Ebb.

Many critics viewed this new release as required viewing for the classroom of Gay 101. If you have not already become enraptured by the spell cast by Liza, this DVD might turn you into an Ohmigodit'sLiza! Homo.

We're still listening and watching . . . still in Liza's camp. But some post-millennium critics are a bit harsh, including *The New York Times* which suggested, "Of late, she has become a Michael Jackson-ish figure, too preposterous to function even as a nostalgia act."

That's pretty harsh. Wherever Liza appears today, we'll be there . . . with all that pizzazz.

Loggerheads

(2005)

One Son, Two Mothers, Three Endangered Lives

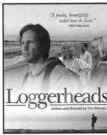

Winner of the Grand Jury Prize at the Sundance Film Festival in 2005, *Loggerheads* is three different but intertwined stories set in three different years: 1999, 2000, and 2001 at various places in rural North Carolina: Kure Beach, Eden, and Asheville.

We first meet Mark (Kip Pardue), a young gay man without a home, passing through the sea-bordering town of Kure Beach and occasionally sleeping on the beach himself.

Born in Atlanta, Pardue is a talented and handsome young actor who grew up playing football and baseball, graduating from Yale in 1998. *Variety* has proclaimed him one of the "10 actors to watch." He starred in *The Rules of Attraction* (2002) based on the Bret Easton Ellis novel.

The title of the film, *Loggerheads*, comes from Mark's attempt to save turtles near Kure Beach. An endangered species, the loggerhead turtle returns to its birthplace to lay eggs that it then abandons. Mark was put up for adoption as a baby. Get the symbolism? His self-imposed mission is to save the loggerhead from extinction.

George (Michael Kelly), a local man with a boring job at a motel, takes a liking to Mark. George is mourning the loss of a male partner who drowned mysteriously. He offers free lodging to Mark, who confesses that he is HIV positive. The two men develop a sad, tentative romantic bond.

As the story unfolds, the film moves to Eden where a minister's wife, Elizabeth (Tess Harper), is wracked with guilt. Her adopted son left home years earlier because of the disapproval of her husband, Robert (Chris Sarandon), a preacher, when the teenage boy came out as gay. Mention of their runaway gay son is taboo.

In Asheville, we encounter Mark's birth mother, Grace (Bonnie Hunt), who has returned from Atlanta to her childhood home after a breakdown and a suicide attempt. She hires Rachael (Robin Weigert) to track down the son she gave up for adoption two decades previously.

Lonesome Cowboys

(1968)

Hot, Hunky Gay Caballeros

Gay men in 1968 wanted to be the Andy Warhol superstar Viva (playing Ramona Alvarez) in this film which Warhol directed, with a lot of help from its scriptwriter, Paul Morrissey.

Viva is raped by five cowboy hunks and also has sex with Little Joe (Joe Dallesandro), who is not always that little. After Ramona seduces Little Joe, she claims that they should commit suicide together after experiencing such a glorious union. He turns down the bitch's request, riding off into the wilds of California with one of the cowboys. (Good thinking, Joe).

The crude film was shot in 16mm in Tucson, Arizona, featuring the inestimable Taylor Mead, one of the wonders discovered by the Warhol Factory.

The transvestite sheriff was played by Francis Francine, the cowboys by Julian Burroughs, Alan Midgette, Eric Emerson, and Louis Waldon. They like to dance a ballet or work on their coiffures.

Congratulations to Warhol for having the *cojones* to release such a picture back when Hollywood was presenting gay characters as either sociopathic killers or suicide prone.

WHAT THE CRITICS SAID
"*Lonesome Cowboys* is simply an unedited but in-focus home movie for homosexuals and a 'drag' in every play on the word."
Variety

"Part of the problem is that Warhol's cowboys, unzipping their flies with the same reflex alacrity that their conservative prototypes display in reaching for the holster, become at least as predictable as any old B-feature heroes. The improvised satire is more than blunted by the self-admiring, stoned haziness of the non-performances."
British Monthly Film Bulletin

Long-Term Relationship

(2006)

The Hard Things in Life

This is the first feature from writer/director Rob Williams, who set out to make movies that he himself would like to see. He's teamed with his partner and co-producer, Rodney Johnson.

Cast in the film are Matthew Montgomery as Glenn—a Richard Gere type—and Windham Beacham as Adam—a Brendan Fraser type. One reviewer said that you should see the film "if you've ever wanted to see Gere make love to Fraser."

Out of all the gay men in Los Angeles (and sadly, he's tested out more than a few), Glenn has finally found his soul mate—a cute Southern boy named Adam. Their relationship started, as so many great relationships have, with the personal ads ("GWM seeks LTR"). From the moment they met, it was instant attraction. Now Glenn's in love for the first time, and it feels great.

There's only one problem. Well, actually a few problems. For starters, Adam is a Republican—not the biggest turn-on for a dedicated Democrat like Glenn. But more importantly, when they finally decide to have sex, it's bad. Really bad. And they can't figure out why their everyday chemistry and compatibility don't extend to the bedroom. Are these problems big enough to be deal-breakers, or can Glenn and Adam work through their differences?

Glenn's straight friends (including married couple Mary Margaret and Andrew) encourage him to stick it out and make it work—after all, everyone's happier as part of a couple, right? Meanwhile, his gay friends (including best friend Eli and roommate Vincent) tell him to move on if he's not happy, especially where sex is concerned. Of course, Vincent has his own agenda in wanting to keep Glenn and Adam apart.

Ultimately, only Glenn and Adam can decide what it takes to sustain a long-term relationship in this classic romantic comedy that appeals to both gay and straight audiences alike.

Longtime Companion

(1990)

Putting a Human Face on AIDS

Predating even the big-budget *Philadelphia*, the little independent film, *Longtime Companion* was the pioneering drama that put a human face on the AIDS epidemic. The movie was not only a landmark in the history of cinema in that it dealt with the "gay cancer" crisis, but it was one of the very first to portray gay men as actual human beings. They were not murderous faggots, queenie caricatures or closeted effeminate cases thrown on the screen for derisive laughter. The characters shown in *Longtime Companion* are real people, loving and dying on the screen.

The title, incidentally, referred to the way that *The New York Times* at the time allowed a gay man's lover to be listed in an obituary.

Norman René's film begins the day when a small story in *The New York Times* mentions a disease that seems to be striking gay men. The drama ends after AIDS has profoundly affected all of the lives of the men in the film, mostly for the worse, including killing them.

The cast was well chosen, beginning on pre-AIDS Fire Island where Willy (Campbell Scott) and Fuzzy (Stephen Caffrey) meet and begin a relationship. The most touching scenes involve a TV script writer Sean (Mark Lamos) who is dying but cared for in a very tender way by his lover David (Bruce Davison).

The film began as a play by Craig Lucas, who also scripted the screen drama, which became a milestone of gay cinema. The movie has arguably the greatest final scene in gay cinema.

WHAT THE CRITICS SAID
"The sad effect is that the filmmakers have inadvertently turned their characters into victims. In being so delicate, René and Lucas have cut into their subject's power. Still, there are moments in *Longtime Companion* that make you feel as if bits of your heart are being scissored away. After a time, the film becomes less about AIDS and more about death. The chord it strikes, finally, is universal.
Hal Hinson, *Washington Post*

Looking for Cheyenne

(2006)

Politics, Philosophy, Sex, & Love

This is a sure-handed debut feature by helmer/scripter Valérie Minetto, who has made a movie about love and longing in many of its permutations, and done so admirably.

Lesbian love comes unglued in this French tale of a journalist abandoning her modern Paris life for a simpler existence. Parisian journalist Cheyenne (Mila Dekker) loses her job and is unable to find another one. This loss triggers a fury in her against the establishment and the ways it exploits her and other common people.

She decides to live in the wild, without running water or electricity. She uses candles for light and bikes to get around.

The isolation means leaving her blonde girlfriend Sonia (Aurelia Petit), a high school science teacher who likes her job and doesn't want to go with Cheyenne.

WHAT THE CRITICS SAID
"An utterly refreshing look at work, love, and politics centered on two attractive young women who are nuts about each other, *Looking for Cheyenne* is suspenseful, funny, touching, sexy, and painlessly pertinent. Rich distillation of romances both sour and sweet manages to breathe new life into the question of whether one should play along with 'the system' or drop out of consumer society for a life of self-reliance. A date movie for auds of every persuasion."
Lisa Nesselson

"At heart, the film is about the ways in which money-driven politics and big business wreak havoc on everyday lives, with its great strength being its casual positioning of a lesbian relationship as the nexus for those conversations. And without a bit of saccharine, it makes the case that human connection is the one true glitch in the matrix."
Ernest Hardy

Looking for Langston

(1998)

Gay Men in the Harlem Renaissance

The freedom of gay black men in 1920s Harlem is both suggested and celebrated visually. Award-winning British filmmaker Isaac Julien recaptures the life of the poet Langston Hughes both lyrically and poetically. The black gay cultural icon lives again in this celebratory meditation.

This original work of cinematic art incorporates poetry with archival footage of the Harlem Renaissance, including romantic shots of two intertwined lovers and Robert Mapplethorpe's photographs of beautiful black men—all set to a disco soundtrack.

Cinematographer Nina Kellgren shot the film in black and white, including fantasy sequences and an imagined love story. The nature of black gay desire is presented most evocatively in this stylish avant-garde film. Especially intriguing is the presentation of original footage of Harlem's Cotton Club back in the 1920s.

The Harlem nightclub morphs into a London dance club from the late 80s. The dream sequences pay homage to both Jean Cocteau and Jean Genet. The soundtrack consists of the words of Hughes himself, along with novelist James Baldwin and a contemporary poet Essex Hemphill. "Freakish Man," an early gay blues recording, is compelling.

WHAT THE CRITICS SAID
"First and foremost Julien's film is not a mainstream one. It exists within a number of cinematic ghettos which will no doubt deter the casual viewer. Moreover, its 'narrative' focus is never clean cut: The film is both a documentary and fantasy, a paean to gay sexual desire and gay filmmakers. Despite having never been behind the camera on such an ambitious project, Julien manages to pull off the challenge with a remarkable deftness."
Anthony Nield

Lost and Delirious

(2001)

Teenage Idealism & Teenage Hormones

Early reviews portrayed this movie as a picture of steamy lesbian sex in a girls' boarding school. But, as one critic put it, that's like "reviewing Secretariat on the basis of what he does in the stable."

The helmer, Lea Pool, has created a lush, carefully thought-out movie that is well framed and composed. The story is told through the eyes of a young and innocent new girl called Mouse (Mischa Barton). She's a bit slow to catch on that her new roomies are lesbians. The first time she sees them lip-locked, she says, "I thought they were just practicing for boys."

Piper Perabo's character, Paulie, is engaged in a lesbian relationship with her best friend, Tori (Jessica Paré). Tori doesn't have the courage to out herself to her parents and decides to end the love affair. This causes Paulie to freak out. She becomes desperate in her attempts to win Tori back.

WHAT THE CRITICS SAID

"Yes, there is nudity in *Lost and Delirious*, and some intimate moments in the dorm room when the movie recalls the freedoms of the 1970s, before soft-core sex had been replaced by hardcore violence. The movie would be dishonest if it didn't provide us with visuals to match the libidos of its two young lovers—Paulie and Tori represent two types familiar from everyone's high school—the type who acts out and the type who wants to get all the right entries under her photo in the yearbook. Footnote: the movie is being released 'unrated,' which means it is too poetic, idealistic, and healthfully erotic to fit into the sick categories of the flywheels at the MPAA. Mature teens are likely to find it inspirational and moving."
Roger Ebert

"Lea Pool's *Lost and Delirious* represents a solid, if somewhat cloying romantic, over-earnest English language bow for the Swiss-born Québec-based director. Overwrought story of growth, discovery, adolescent love, and passion in the halls of an exclusive girls' boarding school is bolstered by a gutsy lead performance from Piper Perabo."
David Rooney, *Variety*

The Lost Language of Cranes

(1991)

A Father & Son Emerge from Their Closets

This is classic GLBTQ cinema. It began life as a novel by David Leavitt which used New York as its setting. The title refers to a mysterious incident involving construction cranes hanging over the cityscape. When the BBC optioned the film for production, director Nigel Finch changed the location to London.

When Philip (Angus Macfadyen) comes out to his parents, he triggers hidden emotions and startling actions. His father, Owen (Brian Cox), decides that he, too, can no longer live a lie and embraces his own homosexuality.

The long-suffering mother, Rose (Dame Eileen Atkins of *Cold Mountain* and *Vanity Fair*), believes that "keeping certain secrets secret is essential to the balance of life."

The love scenes in the movie make you think that the BBC certainly has one up on American TV, including cable. The characters may not be fully developed, but that is only a minor flaw.

Philip's journey will not be an easy one, and he longs for a permanent relationship. But the young man he's dating is an American, rather cruel and self-centered. His mother takes news of her family's outing themselves rather hard.

When broadcast in England on public TV, *The Lost Language of Cranes* created quite a stir because of its frank treatment of homosexuality.

WHAT THE CRITICS SAID

"Like the novel, the film is concerned with mapping out the emotional and mental grief the drama provides. The plot didn't have much to do with AIDS other than the perfunctory mention of the disease, and instead offered a very real, poignant look at the struggle gay men go through when coming out. More than that, it also showed a nice counterpoint between marriage and relationships for men with other men. The film was ahead of its time, and set the stage for a rash of films that gave 'the gay 90s' its cinematic identity."
Brett Collum

Love Forbidden

(Défense d'aimer; 2002)

Love Triangle Tests the Limits of Desire

In this French drama, Rodolphe Marconi helmed it, wrote it, and starred in it as a character called Bruce. Arriving in the French Cultural Institute in Rome, he is housed in the luxurious Villa Medici. He had fled Paris, hoping to escape from the pain of his brother's recent death and his abandonment by his girlfriend.

Once in Rome he is drawn into the orbit of Matteo (Andrea Neccik), who is an assistant in the library of the institute. Matteo comes on strong, showing Bruce the Eternal City and showing up at night in his room unannounced.

The inevitable happens. The two men sleep together, and Bruce begins to realize he is gay. What for Matteo might be a mere fling becomes an obsession for Bruce.

Matteo does not share Bruce's love desire. His interest turns to Aston (Echo Danon), a punk American woman who's writing novels about serial killers.

Still filled with love and passion, Bruce stalks the couple, eavesdropping outside their window as they make love.

Love Forbidden enters into dangerous territory. The French call it *l'amour fou*, meaning "the more unaccountable the passion, the more extravagant its expression."

WHAT THE CRITICS SAID
"Unlike so many American independent films on gay themes, *Love Forbidden* is unconcerned with presenting positive images. Bruce's infatuation with Matteo is a malignant force, growing out of his fear of abandonment more than a healthy, affective drive. Beginning as a youthful romance not unlike Cédric Klapisch's recent *Auberge Espagnole, Love Forbidden* gradually and gracefully develops into a gothic tale."
David Kehr, *The New York Times*

Love in Thoughts

(Was Nutzt Die Liebe in Gedanken; 2004)

Two Young Men Lost in Love and Life

Two handsome young men, with their shirts unbuttoned, standing in a field of golden grain, was the picture that lured gay men into seeing this German release with English subtitles. The director, Achim von Borries, based it on a true story, an incident that occurred in 1927, during the heyday of the Weimar Republic—the Steglitz Student Tragedy. In Germany, the case was the equivalent of the tragedy instigated by two gay psychos, Leopold and Loeb, in the United States.

Paul (Daniel Brühl) and Günther (August Dieh) are two school buddies who visit Günther's country manor for the weekend. The jaunt will turn into a four-day binge of alcohol, drugs, and sex.

Paul is actually in love with Günther's sister, Hilde (Anna Maria Mühe). She's got the hots for Hans (Thure Lindhardt), who is also the object of Günther's affections. In a bizarre twist, Günther and Paul promise to kill themselves when they no longer love. And they might take Hilde and Hans with them.

From the beginning of the film, we know black deeds are afoot, as Paul is being interrogated by the police.

Expect joyriding, nude swims, fortune telling, plenty of heavy drinking, gunplay, brawls, and, of course, sex. Even though the film ultimately falls, it contains scenes of raw emotion.

WHAT THE CRITICS SAID
"*Love in Thoughts* is moody and well made and even though we know Günther will end up dead, we're not sure until the end who pulled the trigger and why. Directed by Achim von Borries (*Good bye, Lenin!*), the film is the work of a craftsman who obviously cares about the topic and his subjects, even if their pseudo-philosophies are juvenile and untenable. More to the point, we keep wanting Paul—the only character here with a shred of sense—to break away from the clan of phonies and the shallow Hilde, but he just never wises up. That, ladies and gentlemen, is how you make a tragedy."
Christopher Null

Love Is the Devil

(1998)

Full Frontal Nude by Daniel Craig

Let's face it: a lot of gay men watched this film about the homosexual British painter, Francis Bacon, to catch a glimpse of the dick of "James Bond." Craig, of course, played 007 in *Casino Royale*. Before that, he was cast as Bacon's rough trade lover in *Love Is the Devil*, where he had to do a lot more than show the full monty.

As George Dyer, a former small-time crook, Craig supplies stud service to Bacon (Derek Jacobi).

In a film helmed and scripted by John Maybury, this bio of the British painter is loosely based on David Farson's *The Gilded Gutter Life of Francis Bacon*.

Roger Ebert in his critique of the film accurately captured Bacon's style of Abstract Expressionism. "He defiantly painted the figure, because he wanted there to be no mistake: His subject was the human body seen in anguish and ugliness. Flesh clung to the bones of his models like dough slapped on by a careless god. His faces were often distorted into grimaces of pain or despair. His subjects looked like mutations, their flesh melting from radiation or self-loathing. His color sense was uncanny, his draftsmanship was powerful and unmistakable, his art gave an overwhelming sense of the artist."

In their sex life, as depicted on film, Dyer dominates, with Bacon playing the masochist. But as the relationship deepens, Dyer's bouts of depression, drinking, pill popping, and satanic nightmares puts a strain on the affair. Dyer had to put up with Bacon's casual infidelities.

WHAT THE CRITICS SAID
"Unconventional, audacious and uncompromising in every sense, John Maybury's *Love Is the Devil* is a very personal interpretation of the destructive relationship between British painter Bacon and his lover and muse, George Dyer. This provocative film's unflinchingly unsympathetic portrayal of the artist—ferociously played by Jacobi—and its often experimental style, make it clearly an item for niche audiences."
David Rooney, *Variety*

A Love to Hide

(*Un amour à taire*; 2005)

The Persecution of Gays During World War II

Christian Faure, the director, gives the TV-movie treatment to this French-language film in France during World War II.

A Love to Hide, with English subtitles, stars Jérémie Renier as Jean. The actor created a stir in François Ozon's Criminal Lovers. Playing his lover Philippe is Bruno Todeschini.

The plot unfolds in 1942 when much of France is under German occupation. Two young gay lovers, Jean and Philippe, must keep their "third sex" relationship secret under peril of their lives.

Into the scenario falls Sara (Louise Monot), a young Jewish woman who's a former girlfriend of Jean's. While Jean and Philippe harbor Sara from the Nazis, Jean's brother, Jacques (Nicolas Gob), a black marketer, returns from prison. As everyone tries clandestinely to keep their respective secrets, Jacques' jealousy and his potential for betrayal threatens all of them.

WHAT THE CRITICS SAID
"Intense, riveting, and earnest, *A Love to Hide* is a beacon of wit and sophistication in an age of too many vapid gay DVDs. The story of a Jewish girl who loses her family to the Nazis and finds sanctuary with a gay companion, the film weaves haunting authenticity with beautiful, unwavering human hope."
Randall Shulman, *Instinct*

"Extremely well acted, *A Love to Hide* is a worthwhile and deeply affecting film that sheds light on how various people coped during this horrible period of history."
Gary Kramer, *San Francisco Bay Times*

"Bad, stupid decisions made by bad-seed—if later semi-redeemed—brother Jacques gets Jean sent to a labor camp. Subsequent horrors are piled on a tad melodramatically, but polished perfs and package keep the twisty, eventually decades-spanning tale engrossing."
Dennis Harvey, *Variety*

Love! Valour! Compassion!

(1997)

Terrence McNally's Depiction of a Gay House Party

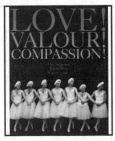

Terence McNally's play opened at the Walter Kerr theater on February 14, 1995 and ran for 248 performances, winning the 1995 Tony Award for Best Play.

Director Joe Mantello has fashioned it into an absorbing drama about eight men spending Memorial Day, Fourth of July, and Labor Day in a remote house in New York State. In scene by scene, the film shows how these gay men deal with sex, love, and ultimately, AIDS. The host is Gregory (Stephen Bogardus), a handsome, stuttering, and aging dancer and choreographer. His lover is Bobby (Justin Kirk) who is blind.

In the most difficult role, John Glover plays identical twins, John and James Jeckyll—"good twin, bad twin."

Some reviewers compared this filmed play to the viperish *The Boys in the Band*, but the comparison isn't apt. Only Buzz (Jason Alexander) belongs in *The Boys in the Band*. He plays a musical comedy fanatic living with AIDS, and utters one witty epigram after another. He claims that his nightmare would be a revival of *West Side Story* featuring Cher and Robert Goulet.

His weekend date is Ramon (Randy Becker), a handsome, on-the-make Latino hunk who's a Puerto Rican dancer. Buzz calls him "Chiquita."

Perry (Stephen Spinella) is the effeminate one—there's got to be one in the crowd. He's celebrating the 14th year of his affair with Arthur (John Benjamin Hickey), who spews racist and misogynist epithets.

WHAT THE CRITICS SAID
"There is still ground to be broken and depths to be discovered in drama about homosexuals. There will eventually be a play like this in which one of the characters need not be an expert on the works of Ethel Merman and Gertrude Lawrence and none performs in a tutu. But *Love! Valour! Compassion!* is a touching and perceptive film about themes anyone can identify with: loneliness, jealousy, need, generosity."
Roger Ebert

The Loved One

(1965)

A British Satire on the American Way of Death

It is said that after World War II, the great English author, Evelyn Waugh, came to Hollywood to work on a movie adaptation of his novel *Brideshead Revisited*. While there, he attended a funeral at Forest Lawn Memorial Park and was outraged by the pretense of the American funeral industry. He decided to satirize it in a novel, *The Loved One*. After its release, it became a cult favorite. In its day, it was seen by thousands upon thousands of gay men and women.

Helmer Tony Richardson must have had his tongue in his cheek—or somewhere—when he cast the most famous satire on the funeral business ever made. Although he had a few straight actors in the cast, including Robert Morse as Dennis Barlow, the director decided that gay's the word.

He cast John Gielgud, one of England's most stately homos, as Sir Francis Hinsley; gay blade Tab Hunter (who outed himself in his autobiography), bisexual actor Dana Andrews as Gen. Buck Brinkman, Roddy McDowall (Dame Elizabeth's gay pal), and even Liberace in this film. We could name several others among the cast and crew but they have never officially outed themselves so we'll be discreet.

Margaret Leighton, also cast in the film, was not a lesbian, but she was married to Laurence Harvey, who once told Frank Sinatra, "I have this thing for black men."

Warner Home Video has re-released this 1965 film on DVD, allowing a whole new generation of young men and women to see it in all its campy glory.

Hunter was at his most fuckable when he appeared as a Whispering Glades Tour Guide, and Roddy McDowall comes off queenly as "D.J. Jr."

Liberace was at his most repulsive as an unctuous coffin salesman.

Jonathan Winters appears in a dual role, both as the owner of Whispering Glades and as his twin brother, who operates the graveyard for pets.

Luster

(2002)

A Sexy Look at Unrequited Love

There are a lot of crushes and crises to sort out during this film's depiction of a complicated weekend, set in Los Angeles, during the mid-90s.

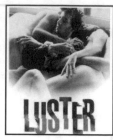

Director and co-scripter Everett Lewis centers his story around a punk, party-going, sometimes poet named Jackson (Justin Herwick). Jackson is cute, lanky, and blue haired, standing at the core of this twisted black comedy.

The other night he developed a crush on Billy (Jonan Blechman), a guy he met at an orgy. There's a complication: Billy isn't into Jackson.

But two other men are attracted to Jackson, including Derek (Sean Thibodeau) and Sam (Shane Powers), the so-called straight owner of the record store. Into this melting pot is thrown Jed (B. Wyatt), Jackson's hunky corn-fed cousin. Just as Jackson is considering the possibilities of incest, Jed is seduced by Jackson's lesbian artist friend Alyssa (Pamela Gidley). She lures the stud into the desert for a nude photo shoot, much to the distress of her lover Sandra (Susanna Melvoin).

Jackson is hired to pen lyrics for the closeted rock star Sonny Spike (Willie Garson), only to discover that Billy and Sonny have a thing.

WHAT THE CRITICS SAID
"*Luster* has a charming, skittish quality, and Lewis finds pathos and humor in his characters' often painful search for love. There are moments in which the actors seem a bit self-conscious, yet this low-budget picture is a calling card for pretty much everyone in front of the camera. *Luster*'s finale comes out of left field, although it becomes more credible as it sinks in."
Kevin Thomas, *Los Angeles Times*

"A less snarky trip through the L.A. gay/punk terrain hitherto identified with Gregg Araki, Everett Lewis' micro-budgeted indie *Luster* is an ensemble seriocomedy that's initially loose to a fault, but gradually wins one over with its shaggy charm—and by the close has grown more ambitious and poignant, than initial reels lead you to expect."
Dennis Harvey, *Variety*

Ma Mère

(*My Mother;* 2004)

An Incestuous Version of *Mommie Dearest*

In this sordid French mother-and-son drama, Isabella Huppert continues to reign as "the Queen of Edge." She's up to her old tricks, as perfected in *The Piano Teacher*, where she played a compulsive voyeur who prowled porn shops and performed genital self-mutilation. One critic called Huppert "Garbo for an age of postmodern kink."

In *My Mother*, under the baton of Christophe Honore, Huppert stars as a mom from hell. She guides her teenage son through various orgies and bondage sessions, predictably ending in an Oedipal clinch that transcends mere incest between mother and son.

The film was based on a 1960s novel by the late philosopher, Georges Bataille, called "the metaphysician of evil."

Louis Garrel is well cast as Pierre, Huppert's son. Pierre is only 17, dark, leonine, and freshly returned from Catholic school when he comes to live with his mother in the Canary Islands. "The pleasure only begins once the worm is in the fruit," Hélène tells her son. In one scene she urges her son to have public sex with Réa (Joana Preiss) in a late-night subway station while Ma Mère watches.

As the perversely tormented teenager, Garrel appears quite at home masturbating on screen and then urinating on the floor.

WHAT THE CRITICS SAID
"All manner of deviant sex in all manner of pairings (some involving mother and son) follow, to an especially shocking finale."
V.A. Musetto, *New York Post*

"*Ma Mère* drops the awful hint that we may never connect with another human being besides the one in whose womb we started out."
Ty Burr, *Boston Globe*

"Yet another stylish exercise in depravity in which Huppert floats through the sordid proceedings in a calm haze. If only the film she inhabits was as sexy as it aspires to be."
Frank Scheck, *The Hollywood Reporter*

Madame Satã

(2002)

Marlon Brando and Vivien Leigh in the Same Body

This is a loose cinematic portrait of João Francisco dos Santos (1900-1976), known also as Madama Satã, a chef, transvestite, lover, hustler, father, hero, and convict from Rio de Janeiro.

Actor Lázaro Ramos was cast by director Karim Ainouz in the dual role. The director told his star, "I want you to be Brando and Vivien Leigh in one body," referring to their performances as Stanley Kowalski and Blanche DuBois in *A Streetcar Named Desire*.

Resident of a Brazilian slum during the 1930s, João became a celebrated female cabaret entertainer with a passion for gay sex and violence. Thanks to a hair-trigger temper, he killed a man and was sentenced to a combined total of 30 years in prison. Lean and muscular, he was described as an "aggressive strut with an attitude to burn," becoming a gay outlaw folk hero to Brazil's homosexual community.

Even though his contract called for no love scenes, at the last moment Ramos agreed to be filmed having hot sex with a man, in this case Marqés Fellipe, playing Renatinho.

WHAT THE CRITICS SAID
"Homosexuality is an invitation to violence in the milieu of the film, but João is more than able to defend himself, and indeed makes a point of telling one of his attackers that being a queen makes him no less of a man. His domestic life is a parody of the nuclear family; he lives with a female prostitute named Laurita (Marcelia Cartaxo) and her child, not by him. At home João rules with a short temper and an iron hand of the stereotypical dominant male, and is in many ways the most masculine character I've seen in any recent movie.
Roger Ebert

"First feature director Karim Ainouz's vivid 1930s set biopic recreates the key period in the life of the legendary gay streetfighter, criminal, and killer, an uneducated black Brazilian descended from slaves who doubled as a cabaret singer and drag *artiste*."
David Rooney, *Variety*

Maggie and Annie

(2002)

It's a Whole New Ballgame

Annie (Amy Thiel) is a happily married woman with a loving husband and daughter. She decides to join her company's softball team where she befriends her fellow player, the out Maggie (Joy Yandell). Much to Annie's own surprise, her friendship with Maggie gradually develops into a strong attraction.

Filmed on an $80,000 budget, the movie is devoid of special effects, with fairly simple camera work. The actors play their roles well. Kimberly Wilson wore three hats: writer, director, and producer.

Although Maggie does not move in on Annie like a vampire, a night of celebration, with lots of drinking, alters that plan.

The film did not meet with favor in the lesbian community because of its unanticipated ending that didn't end up happy for the lesbians involved.

WHAT THE CRITICS SAID
"I respect this film because Wilson made challenging choices that ring of tremendous authenticity. She broke clichés, broke stereotypes, and instead focused on the humanity of these relationships. None of these people were really shown in a negative light. They were shown as human beings trying to make human choices based on human feelings. When Maggie and Annie finally get together, the scenes of intimacy are among the most honest, tender scenes I have witnessed on screen. I forgot that I was watching two lesbians. I was watching two women who so completely loved each other. Quite simply, it was beautiful."
Richard Propes, *The Independent Critic*

Making Love

(1982)

A Groundbreaking, Much-Maligned Film

Harrison Ford, Michael Douglas, and Richard Gere turned down this film by scripter Barry Sandler, who based it on a story by biographer A. Scott Berg. The homosexual movie didn't do well at the box office, which set gay films back, or so it was said, for at least a decade.

This was an attempt to make an honest film about homosexual love. It didn't succeed, but it gets our vote for sheer entertainment. Many gays were delighted just to see themselves presented on the screen as human beings.

Director Arthur Hiller wisely chose handsome hunks as his male leads: Michael Ontkean as Zach, a doctor working with cancer patients, and sexy Harry Hamlin, a novelist with a commitment-phobia. They actually kiss on screen, something Tom Hanks and Antonio Banderas failed to do in *Philadelphia.*

The plot has Zach "happily married" to Claire (Kate Jackson), a fast-rising network executive. If Zach is so happy, why does he hang out in gay bars populated by extras who look as if they were posing for "*Ah! Men!* catalogues? At one point Zach drives down an alley lined with shoulder-to-shoulder hustlers.

When Hamlin comes into Zach's office for a physical exam, both hotties are immediately attracted to each other.

As is inevitable, Jackson finds out, and throws her husband's clothes out of the closet (get the symbolism?). She perceives that their entire life together has been a sham. Perhaps it was. Both Zach and Claire will go on to find other men, Zach in the final scene ending up with a stud that looks like "Hunk of the Year."

WHAT THE CRITICS SAID
"Gay liberation has turned into gay romanticization. Evidently the film industry now feels free to have homosexuals in love as foolish as their heterosexual counterparts."
Robert Asahina, *New Leader*

Mala Noche

(*Bad Night*; 1985)

Veal Cake *Mexicano*

The director, Gus Van Sant, first made a name for himself with this 1985 release which has been restored. Set in some of the real dreary streets of Portland, Oregon, it tells the sad story of a liquor store clerk (Tim Streeter), who lusts for a Mexican street kid, Johnny (Doug Cooeyate), although the viewer may wonder why. You can find hotter *mexicano* street kids on the corner of any big city in America.

What makes this movie almost unbearable is that the street hustler is straight—not even gay for pay. Of course, he'd be gay for pay if Streeter, playing Walt Curtis, offered him $25 instead of the $15 which is all he's got on him.

In the 78 minutes he allows to tell his tale, Van Sant manages in this film noir to capture Twilight Zone Portland with B&W photography that is both stunning and seductive. The helmer effectively uses *chiaroscuro* to tell his tawdry tale of unrequited love. Streeter is the only brilliant performer here. Johnny is weak in his role.

Based on the Walt Curtis autobiographical novel of the same name, *Mala Noche* is the tale of an *amour fou*. In the movie, Walt in his mad love/lust, says, "I wanna show this Mexican kid that I'm gay for him." But the object of his unrequited affection speaks no English and finds Walt "strange and undesirable." In other words, he wants *gringa* pussy as he makes it clear several times in the film.

Johnny's friend in the movie is Roberto Pepper (Ray Monge) who, unlike Johnny, doesn't mind crashing in Walt's pad and fucking him.

Ultimately what we liked about *Mala Noche* then and now is that Van Sant refuses to treat homosexuality as something deserving of judgment. Openly gay, the helmer has dealt unflinchingly with homosexuality and other marginalized subcultures without being particularly concerned about providing positive role models.

At the screening we attended, several senior citizens, presumably straight couples, got up and walked out after the first 20 minutes.

Mambo Italiano

(2003)

"My Big Fat Gay Wedding"

Minus the male nudity and the sex scenes that were shown on stage when this script was a play, *Mambo Italiano* was also scripted for the screen by Steve Galluccio, with Émile Gaudrealt as director.

The son of Italian immigrants living in Montréal, Angelo Barberini (Luke Kirby) struggles to find the best way to reveal to his parents that he's gay. When he moves out, he shocks both of his parents, Gino (Paul Sorvino) and Maria (Ginette Reno).

In a chance encounter, Angelo meets once again with his school buddy, policeman Nino Paventi (Peter Miller), who prefers to live deep in the closet. Even so, he and Angelo become lovers and move in together. Except for a kiss, don't expect much man-to-man action in this film. It's a send-up to Italian prejudices more than it's a gay fuck film.

Angelo shocks his parents even more when he comes out, although his sister, Anna (Claudia Ferri), is more accepting. The revelation from Angelo causes chaos in his neurotic family.

Nino is a man's man, a macho police officer. Like Angelo, Nino comes from a traditional Italian family. When Nino's controlling Sicilian mother Lina (Mary Walsh) hears of the scandal, there is a funny altercation with Gino over which of their sons is the "top" in the love affair.

WHAT THE CRITICS SAID
"In *Mambo Italiano*, the hero's Italian-Canadian parents grade sex for their son as follows: (1) No sex at all is best—just stay here at home with us; (2) If you must have sex, have it with a nice Italian girl; (3) If you get engaged to a non-Italian we'll kill you; but (4) If you become a homosexual, we will first die of mortification and then kill you, and (5) No points for having gay sex with an Italian boy, because no Italian boy has ever been gay, except for you, and you're not gay anyway, you just haven't met the right girl, and look, here she is."
Roger Ebert

The Man of My Life

(*L'homme de sa vie*; 2006)

A Married Man & His Gay Neighbor

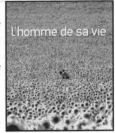

A happily married man and his new gay neighbor hit it off a bit too well in this French film that tries to evoke the sublime moral comedies of Eric Rohmer.

Under the direction of Zabou Breitman, from a script he wrote with Agnès de Sacy, this is a lyrical exploration of male bonding as examined from a feminine perspective.

Frédéric (Bernard Campan), a chemist in his late 40s, seemed locked into wedding bliss with his beautiful young wife Frédérique (Léa Drucker). His life begins to change when he invites his next door neighbor Hugo (Charles Belrin) over for a cookout. This lean graphic designer with his cold, penetrating eyes has them set on Frédéric. After the party is over, Frédéric and his new friend stay up until dawn, talking about love and life. After that, Frédéric loses sexual interest in his wife. She sinks into despair.

In one scene the two men almost kiss, but the camera backs away. In addition to talking, the two men, who are about the same age, like to go running together. Perhaps that releases their sexual tensions. Hugo works to convince Frédéric that his role as a dutiful husband and father has robbed him of his earlier lust for life.

WHAT THE CRITICS SAID
"Exploring the man-crush between a happily married heterosexual and a gay devotee of emotionless physical gratification, the movie is a big tease. Even auds inclined to indulge its pretentiousness will start tuning out as its endings drag on, none of them satisfying or revelatory."
David Rooney, *Variety*

"As it ponders father-son relationships and the quasi-erotic attraction between two middle-aged men, one straight, the other gay, this soft-hearted movie portrays both men and women as coming from Venus; forget about Mars. The men talk about relationships, not sports, and when they go jogging, they don't compete. When one man twists his ankle, the other tenderly carries him home on his back."
Stephen Holden, *The New York Times*

Mango Kiss

(2004)

A Humorous Celebration of Lesbian Sexuality

It drew very mixed reviews, but director Sascha Rice's *Mango Kiss* earned a devoted lesbian following. Rice and her writer, Sarah Brown, set the film in 1993 in San Francisco, including scenes both authentic and poignant. Watching the scenes made

us nostalgic for the pre-George W. Bush era. We wished we could go back and relive our times in San Francisco—enjoying a hot cup of mocha at Red Dora's Truckstop Café, a spicy enchilada in Dolores Park.

The movie is a sometimes funny and sometimes amusing look at the struggle to maintain a relationship while being liberated enough to explore new frontiers. *Mango* can be both campy and romantic at the same time.

Many indie films take themselves too seriously, and are filled with social commentary on the struggle of lesbians in modern society—or whatever. This one does not.

The basic plotline has a "lipstick lesbian," Sass (Danièle Ferraro), moving to San Francisco with her butch buddy, Lou (Michelle Wolff) where they become roommates and more. Wolff, incidentally, looks a lot like Sarah Jessica Parker, with perhaps a gene or two contributed by Winona Ryder. As the two baby dykes move deeper into their relationship, a little role-playing is in order, with Sass—actually "Sassafras"—pretending to become "Princess Sass," whereas Lou transforms herself into "Captain Daddy."

Other characters emerge to challenge the relationship. Captain Daddy allows Sass to have a son. He's Mickey (Shannon Rossiter), a punk bassist. Meanwhile, Daddy herself fantasizes about Chelsea Chuwawa (Tina Marie Murray), the neighborhood dominatrix, a sexy black bitch mommy. There's also an all-too-brief cameo by Dru Mouser from MTV's *Undressed.* Mouser comes on as a character named Leslie.

The best acting in the film comes from the always marvelous Sally Kirkland. Playing the mother of Sass, Kirkland is a liberated artist from the era of "free love."

Mango Soufflé

(2002)

India's First Real Gay Male Movie

Indian audiences were delighted (or revolted) by a real man-to-man kiss in *Mango Soufflé*, which may not seem groundbreaking to Western viewers but is big news in Bollywood. As it opens, the film recycles serio-comic conventions dating back to

The Boys in the Band. Mahesh Dattani, the director, adapted the script from his stage play, *On a Muggy Night in Mumbai.*

Clothing designer Kamlesh (Ankur Vikal) invites friends to his huge estate in the country for a mysterious announcement. The big news is that he is moving to Canada, in the wake of a recently ended love affair.

His guests are fairly stock characters, including women such as Deepali (Sheeba Shah), a disillusioned woman who wants her straight love affairs as harmonious as her platonic relationships with gay men.

Sharad (Faredoon Dodo-Bhujwala) is revealed as a catty queen concealing his hurt feelings behind a viper-like wit. Naturally, television star Bunny (Sanjit Bedi) wants to stay in the closet to protect his career. And there are others.

WHAT THE CRITICS SAID
"Mango Soufflé predictably turns into a case-pleading melodrama in which social stigma and conformist pressure are decried, and honesty lauded as difficult but the best policy. It is duly noted that the straight world's disdain does no less damage to self-loathing gays than 'the harm we do ourselves.' Apart from a glimpse of underwater nudity in a swimming sequence, talky pic isn't exactly a hot hotbed of sensuality."
Dennis Harvey, *Variety*

"Sharad has concocted a ceremony to help Kamlesh recover from being dumped by the man he fell in love with. Before the ceremony is finished (with Kamlesh tearing up a picture of him and his beloved in a naked embrace), Kamlesh's sister Kiran (Rinkie Rhanna) shows up with her fiancé in tow. He is (of course!) the very man who broke Kamlesh's heart."
Stephen Murray

Markova: Comfort Gay

(2000)

Japanese Soldiers Raped Boys, Too

World War II violence included not just rape of young women, but of boys, too, especially if they were cross-dressers.

Veteran comedy star "Dolphy," cast as Markova, watches a television documentary about an ex-comfort girl and her latter-day quest for justice. These so-called comfort girls in the Philippines were used by Japanese soldiers for sex, enduring one brutal rape after another. Markova wants to spill his story to reporter Loren Legarda, playing herself.

In flashback, the movie tells Markova's early story of growing up as Walter Dempster. A young Markova is played by Jeffrey Quizon, an older Markova is played by Eric Quizon.

Young Markova is tormented by his macho older brother. As a young adult, Markova plays regal den mother to a group of glamorous cross-dressers who spend the Japanese occupation in forced sex work. The invading Nipponese were said to have more brutally raped the cross dressers, using more force, humiliation, and violence in their sex acts with them than they did with the girl slaves.

The film is directed by Gil M. Portes, who presents an unflattering and stereotypical portrait of swishy gays. In the words of one viewer, this distracted "from the human rights theme that the film otherwise presents too starkly."

WHAT THE CRITICS SAID
"Gay themes and exploitative melodrama have often been queasy bedfellows in Filipino cinema, but *Markova: Comfort Gay* may rep a new conceptual low. Spurious spin on the real-light of native females drafted as 'comfort women' by WWII Japanese invaders in fact comprises just one overflow episode in otherwise banal cocktail of drag queen's life and times. Results play like *La Cage aux Folles* with mawkish delusions of pulp-novel grandeur."
Dennis Harvey, *Variety*

The Masseur

(*Masahista*; 2005)

A Dutiful Son Who's Also a Sex Worker

A john enters the massage parlor to take his pick among the young men—often shirtless—on parade. He deals with the queenish male "madam" of the parlor, who assures him that all his boys are good looking—one "can even suck your scrotum dry."

Directed by Brillante Mendoza, the action takes place in Manila. The star is 20-year-old Iliac, who works in the club giving in-depth massages . . . and a whole lot more.

The film depicts the night of December 14 when Iliac's first customer for the day is a homo romance novel writer. Outside the parlor, Iliac's current girl, a bar floozy who works in Japan, asserts her sexual dominion over him.

There is family drama back home. His estranged father dies. As he makes the trip back to his home province, he is faced with the reality of decay, love, life, and survival. He must reconcile his career as a sex worker with his role as son and brother to his grieving mother and siblings.

Coco Martin as Iliac made his debut performance in *The Masseur*. The model has appeared in various TV commercials and print ads in the Phillipines. Helmer Mendoza singled him out from a "cattle call" to work in the film. Among the young male hopefuls wanting the role, Martin was viewed as a potential actor of "intensity, drive, and raw talent."

You can decide if you agree with the director.

WHAT THE CRITICS SAID
"Brillante Mendoza's perfect combination of technique and subject reveals a sense of humanity. The story is told with honesty and integrity giving us a chance to empathize with the central character. *The Masseur* is without contrivance or conceit."
Signis Interfaith Jury, Brisbane International Film Festival

The Matador

(2005)

The Tastiest Cock in Town

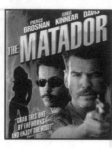

Pierce Brosnan is cast as an anti-hero James Bond type in this hitman-buddy movie that was one of the surprise sleepers of 2006. He plays Julian Noble, a globetrotting hit man on the verge of a nervous breakdown, who does not have a license to kill.

He heads for a bar in Mexico City which has "the tastiest margaritas and the tastiest cock in town." There he meets Greg Kinnear, typecast as the nerdy businessman, Danny Wright, trying to score a big deal after a financial slump from his Denver base.

A new Jack Lemmon in the making, Kinnear is drowning in the shallows of midlife crisis. The actor is perfectly cast as the grown-up Boy Scout who married his high school sweetheart. He was supposed to live happily ever after—except it didn't work out that way.

At first Kinnear wants to flee the scene when he initially suspects that Brosnan is queer and wants to make it with him. But they eventually settle into one of the strangest friendships ever recorded on film.

Written and directed by Richard Shepard, *The Matador* is full of surprises. Brosnan seems to have a ball playing a bisexual, who likes to go to Manila on assignment because the pretty boys there look like chicks.

He's unshaven, a heavy drinker, as vulgar as they come, and completely friendless . . . that is, until he hooks up with this down-on-his-luck businessman.

Incidentally, the film is not about bullfighting as its title suggests. The name comes from a scene in the film in which Brosnan escorts Kinnear to a bullfight in Mexico City.

It is clearly Brosnan's film, with Kinnear playing the straight man for his antics. But Hope Davis, cast as Bean (Danny's wife), has never been more brilliant. She illuminates every scene she's in. Brosnan's chemistry was at work in all his scenes with both Kinnear and Davis.

Maurice

(1987)

Two Men in Love at Cambridge

This James Ivory film was based on the posthumously published E.M. Forster novel. It's a story about coming to terms with sexuality during the Edwardian age.

While enrolled at Cambridge, Maurice Hall (James Wilby) falls in love with another British blueblood, Clive Durham (Hugh Grant at his most beautiful).

Maurice is one of the best filmed gay romances of all time. Forster wrote this novel in 1914 from his own personal pain, and it is no doubt autobiographical in part. It wasn't published until 1971.

When Maurice's doctor advises him to emigrate to a country such as France, where homosexuality is no longer criminal, he answers: "England has always been disinclined to accept human nature."

Clive declares his love for Maurice. At first he is shocked by the come-on, but later gives Clive a passionate kiss and a whispered, "I love you."

Clive prefers an idealistic love, whereas Maurice seems like he'd rather get plowed. In time, Clive, the pursuer, becomes the pursued.

Fearing exposure and disgrace, Clive breaks off from Maurice. Clive will settle down with a wife and enter politics.

One night a rough-hewn gamekeeper on Clive's estate, Scudder (Rupert Graves), crawls through Maurice's window and makes love to him. The sexual mating is what Maurice has been looking for, and he decides to fuck reputation and live together with this hot low-class boy.

WHAT THE CRITICS SAID
"Subtle, sensitive, and every bit as swoony as a Barbara Cartland bodice-ripper, James Ivory's superb screen translation of Forster's *Maurice* is a weezy, unadulterated romance, an intoxicating tuxedo-ripper set against the elegant priggishness of England's post-Edwardian gentry."
Rita Kempley, *The Washington Post*

Memoirs of My Nervous Illness

(2006)

Key Moments in the History of Psychoanalysis

In 2004, Jefferson Mays gave a Tony-winning performance in *I Am My Own Wife*, which replicated the tribulations of Charlotte von Mahlsdorf, a German transvestite caught up in the great European dramas of the 20th century.

Now, directed by Julian Hobbs, he returns again in all his glory to re-create the experiences of Daniel Paul Schreber, an esteemed German judge who, at the turn of the 20th century, composed a highly articulate written account of his own mental illness. Later, Sigmund Freud interpreted his account as a case history of homosexual paranoia and repression.

Schreber was incarcerated in a Leipzig asylum after he started to suffer various delusions, including one in which he imagines having been chosen by God to procreate a new race of men. These mental disorders were carefully charted in his journal, upon which Dominic Taylor and others fashioned this screenplay—a fictionalization of a pivotal moment in the history of psychoanalysis. The judge's lucid and intricately detailed 1903 account of his own insanity inspired both Freud and Jung.

In the asylum, Schreber is given dubious care by Dr. Email Flechsig (Bob Cucuzza), who prescribes opium and tepid baths, and who seems deeply threatened by the possibility that his patient might be sane. The patient's pattern of rapid shifts between lucidity, violent fits, and manifestations of seductive femininity is deeply upsetting to some viewers.

Back in rouge and petticoats, Mays can even turn a straitjacket into a makeshift corset, a bed sheet into a strapless gown.

WHAT THE CRITICS SAID
"Julian P. Hobbs directs by getting out of the way of his star's soulful eyes and considerable talent, allowing Mr. Mays to feed on the tension between the rationality of his character's grand delusion." Jeannette Catsoulis, *The New York Times*

The Men Who Danced:
The Story of Ted Shawn's Male Dancers, 1933-1940

(1990)

Ted Shawn (1891-1972), of course, was the father of American dance, teaching such greats as Martha Graham. He was a partner with his wife, Ruth St. Denis, in the famed Denishawn Company, founder of the world-famous Jacob's Pillow annual dance festival.

Shawn brought the concept of virility to male dancing, especially through his all-male dance groups. Even though married, Shawn himself was gay, and so were many of his dancers, but they were nonetheless macho.

Helmer Ron Honsa has brought this docu to life, beginning in 1933 with the origins of the first all-male dance troupe in America.

The docu traces Shawn and his group right up to 1940, the year before the United States entered World War II. In archival footage, we get to see Shawn himself along with a notable cast of male dancers. Barton Mumaw, for example, is sexily pictured as the first soloist of the men's group. One of his most tremendously popular solos was *The French Sailor.*

Mumaw was lithe, slender, and darkly exotic, showing an impressive package in many of his tight-fitting outfits. As the stabbing warrior in *The Dyak Spear Dance*, Mumaw danced nearly nude.

By 1940, Shawn's approach to dance, even that of Mumaw, seemed dated.

Before the camera, the male dancers discuss their lives not only as dancers but as members of this daring new venture. "What's a dance troupe without a woman?" one critic of the time asked.

Most of the docu was written by Richard Philip, *Dance Magazine's* editor-in-chief.

Shawn died at the age of 80 and was proud that he'd carved a way for American men to be accepted and respected as dancers—"not viewed as silly faggots mincing around in a ballet costume."

"The seeds sown from 1933 to 1940 are bearing fruit," he told *Dance Magazine* in 1966.

Men, Heroes, & Gay Nazis

(Männer, Helden, Schwule Nazis; 2005)

Uniform Fetishes, Sexual Kink, Skinheads

Yes, Virginia, there are such things as gay Republicans in America. There is also that phenomenon of the gay Nazi, whose political views are to the right of Attila the Hun. Until he was murdered, SA commander Ernst Rohm liked to get plugged by his "golden god" storm-troopers. One book recently published even makes a case for Hitler being a homosexual, although the gay liberation movement should probably stick to the adoption of more benign posterboys such as Leonardo da Vinci and Michelangelo.

The film focuses on the "new Führer," Michael Kuhnen, a closeted neo-Nazi leader who died of AIDS. He once claimed that gay men make better fighters since they have no sentimental family attachments and therefore could take greater and more daring risks in battle.

Shocking but true, German journalist Rainer Fromm estimates that some 10% to 15% of today's neo-Nazi party leadership is gay. Amazingly, in spite of their notorious past for sending homosexuals as well as Jews to the gas chambers, the fact of this gayness is both known and tolerated within today's Nazi party in Germany.

Of course, Hitler had the same so-called "toleration" in the early days of the Nazi party until he decided to have his elite troopers shot.

The documentary is the creation of the controversial Rosa von Praunheim, who both directed and wrote it. In German with English subtitles, it runs for 90 minutes.

Von Praunheim is a household name in Germany and a very visible public personality. Over a period of some four decades, he has created a library of sociopolitical-docu oeuvres. He's up to his old tricks in *Men, Heroes, and Gay Nazis*, using archival footage when needed and spewing few anti-immigrant sentiments and (as always) über-masculinity fixations.

Portrayed are such characters as a skinhead, André, who hangs out with other bald-headed right-wingers, who, surprisingly, tolerate his gayness.

Merci, Docteur Rey

(2002)

An Opera Diva, Her Gay Son, and a Murder

This farce was helmed and scripted by Andrew Litvack, a protégé of Ismail Merchant and James Ivory.

It's a madcap romp about a young phone sex addict and his narcissistic opera diva mom. Set in Paris, it includes pot brownies, puke jokes, a gay dad, a flying lesbian, and cameo appearances by Jerry Hall and Vanessa Redgrave.

Dianne Wiest stars as Elisabeth Beaumont, a diva preparing for her performance of *Turandot*. While there she dabbles at some belated mothering of her 23-year-old son Thomas (Stanislas Merhar), not realizing he is a hot, young, and gay phone sex addict.

He likes to answer anonymous personal ads, although most of these blind dates end in dismal failure. One ad intrigues him: It's from an older man who offers cash for him to sneak into his apartment and hide in the bedroom closet.

Thomas watches middle-aged Bob (Simon Callow) have sex with a hunky hustler (Karim Saleh). The episode ends with Bob being murdered. Thomas flees, not wanting to call the police.

Going to a shrink, Thomas reveals the details of the episode to a "Dr. Rey." The good shrink has just expired from a heart attack. His paranoid client Penelope (Jane Birkin), who has developed the odd but fascinating delusion that she is Vanessa Redgrave, presents herself as the psychiatrist.

And the plot goes on from here, on and on. "It's all just theater, darlings!" and so it is.

WHAT THE CRITICS SAID
"No thanks are in order for *Merci Docteur Rey*, a disastrous stab at contemporary farce. Featuring career-worst performances from normally fine multinational thesps, this boondoggle set amidst the City of Light's operatic, cinematic, and criminal spheres will cough up barely a chortle for all but the least discriminating auds. Production shingle's arthouse muscle might garner theatrical distrib in some territories. Getting patrons to show up will be another matter."
Dennis Harvey, *Variety*

Metrosexual

(*Gang chanee kap ee-aep*; 2008)

"Sex and the City" on Amphetimines

Shot in Thailand, this comedy has a Thai name which roughly translates as *A Gang of Chicks and a Closeted Gay Man*, and perhaps that is more apt than the one that was officially chosen.

Directed by Youngyooth Thongkonthun, this gay-themed movie was scripted and filmed to appeal to straight audiences. Four "gal pals" set out to investigate a friend's suspiciously sensitive fiancé.

Kong (Thienchai Jayasvasti) is the stylishly coiffed man suspected of being a closeted gay. Is he too perfect? The guy's knowledge of cosmetics, clothing, and cooking make him appear, if not gay, then perhaps a metrosexual. The determined women want to get to the truth of the matter. The fifth member of the gang is sweet Pang (Meesuke Jangmeesuke), who may be about to marry a gay man.

The girls enlist Brother Bee (Michael Shaowanasai) as a "gay-dar" consultant to begin snooping.

For those who aren't familiar with the term "metrosexual" (are there any out there still in the dark?), that term, paraphrasing author Mark Simpson in a 2002 Salon.com article, refers to a single young man with a high disposable income, living or working in the city where all the best shops are. He might be officially gay, straight or bisexual, but this is immaterial because he has clearly taken himself as his own love object and pleasure as his sexual preference. In the 80s he was only to be found inside fashion magazines such as *GQ,* in television advertisements for Levi's jeans, or in gay bars. In the 90s, he was visible everywhere and he did a lot of shopping. A Metrosexual, in other words, is an advertiser's wet dream.

WHAT THE CRITICS SAID
"While happy to have Brother Bee buzzing on the sidelines with gags and campy posturings that have done the rounds for decades, scripters keep the main comic focus on how contempo sexual identity issues suggested by the buzzword title affect women's perception of men."
Richard Kuipers, *Variety*

Midnight Cowboy

(1969)

It Would Have Been a Great Vehicle for Elvis

One studio executive sent director John Schlesinger a memo stating, "If we could clean this up and add a few songs, it could be a great vehicle for Elvis Presley." And as it was being cast, "The King" actually wanted the role of Joe Buck in all his rawness.

The film's two protagonists, Ratso (Dustin Hoffman) and the hustler, Joe Buck (Jon Voigt), are never presented in this film as gay. So even though the picture became the first and only X-rated movie to win an Academy Award as Best Picture of the Year, several million viewers didn't recognize the story for what it was: A love story between two men, even if that love was nonsexual and unconventional, playing itself out in seedy dwellings in a rampantly depraved New York City.

But gay men knew what they were watching, even though thousands of them felt Schlesinger's film was homophobic because of its sordid depiction of homosexual life in a script by Waldo Salt.

Leaving his job as a dishwasher in Texas, Joe heads for New York where he plans to lead the life of a kept man. He tells people, "I ain't a for-real cowboy, but I am one hell of a stud!" Once in the big city, Joe strikes up an unlikely friendship with the crippled Ratso, a third-rate con artist.

In an interview with *The New York Times*, Voigt said, "In a way, I feel I have no right to be in the picture at all. I don't know anything about homosexuality or transferring the feelings I've had for girls to what I might feel for a boy."

The movie reinforced stereotypes that homosexual men are predatory losers. Gay men in the movie, one of them a religious fanatic, were as bizarre as those created in James Leo Herlihy's novel *Midnight Cowboy*. The author himself was gay. Many viewers claim that *Midnight Cowboy* was the first of the "buddy films," idealizing a nonsexual friendship between two men.

The film drew a widely mixed reaction from critics, Vincent Canby of *The New York Times* interpreting it as "so rough and vivid that it's almost unbearable." *Variety* labeled it a "sordid saga."

Midnight Express

(1978)

Gay Rape in a Turkish Hellhole

Critic Pauline Kael called this film "a porno fantasy about the sacrifice of a virgin." It was one of the most controversial movies of all time, and many viewers canceled their plans to visit Turkey forever.

Oliver Stone is credited for adapting the biographical book by Billy Hayes, who was discovered wearing hash strapped to his body and thrown into a Turkish prison where he received a term of 30 years.

Hunky Brad Davis is the star of this hellish drama. In prison he enters a virtual male bordello and is the prime Grade A meat as he moves through a motley crew of homosexual or bisexual inmates.

Brad knows what he's in for when the chief guard (Paul Smith) sodomizes him. In his role, Smith is cruel, vicious, unjust, and verbally abusive.

Helmer Alan Parker outraged the Turkish government with his depiction of Turks as brutal and uncivilized. The director walks a fine line between portraying Billy either as a victim or a criminal.

Fellow convicts include Randy Quaid as Jimmy Booth, a psycho character; John Hurt as Max, a hard-line doper, and Norbert Weisser as Erich, an articulate gay inmate.

WHAT THE CRITICS SAID
"Cast, direction, and production are all very good, but it's difficult to sort out the proper empathies from the muddled and moralizing screenplay which, in true Anglo-American fashion, wrings hands over alien cultures as though our civilization is absolutely perfect."
Variety

"I have no idea if the people who made the film, most of whom are English, have altered Billy Hayes's story thus out of simple stupidity or because of some unexplained grudge against the Turkish people."
Christopher Lehmann-Haupt, *The New York Times*

Milk

(2008)

Gay Rights in Mythic Grandeur

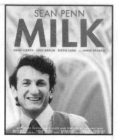

Director Gus Van Sant tackles the story of San Francisco's Harvey Milk, the struggling gay activist who fought for homosexual rights and became California's first openly gay elected official. Of course, California has had at least one gay governor, but closeted.

Van Sant wisely hired gay scripter Dustin Lance Black to chronicle this amazing life, and straight actor Sean Penn to become Milk's screen image. Both did so admirably.

Penn plays a gay so convincingly you'll think he's spent his life plowing boys. He perfectly captures the persona of Milk, who became the heart of the gay rights movement. As an actor, he virtually disappears into the role in an eerily dead-on performance that brought him critical acclaim.

Milk's life story is both jubilant and tragic, ending in his murder by discontent Dan White (Josh Brolin). Milk was assassinated along with Mayor George Moscone (Victor Garber).

Using flashbacks and archival footage, Milk's career is traced from his 40th birthday until his death. He runs for office with his lover Scott Smith (James Franco) as his campaign manager.

On Oscar night, when Penn won for Best Actor, he brought down the house when he said, "You commie, homo-loving sons of guns!"

Penn also noted that, "For those who saw the signs of hatred as our cars drove in tonight, I think it is a good time for those who voted for the ban against gay marriage to sit and reflect and anticipate their great shame." He was referring to anti-gay protesters outside the auditorium.

Black, in accepting for Best Original Screenplay, predicted that "God does love you and that very soon, I promise you, you will have equal rights, federally, across this great nation of ours."

Mishima:
A Life In Four Chapters

(1985)

The De-Gaying of the Japanese Hemingway

This is a fictionalized account of the life of Japan's celebrated 20th century author, Yukio Mishima, as interpreted by Ken Ogata. It was a daunting role for any actor, as the flamboyant homosexual, Mishima, played himself like no other.

Mishima wrote some of the most popular and critically acclaimed novels of post-war Japan.

When not doing that, he lifted weights and posed for body-building photographs, some of them nude. He also created his own private army with uniforms he designed himself, and starred in a series of action films. He was the leading spokesman for the return of the samurai traditions of Imperial Japan.

Director Paul Schrader, who also helmed *American Gigolo* with Richard Gere, fails to capture on screen the real Mishima. Yet his film bears watching as one of the strangest biographies of a homosexual character.

Mishima's widow, Yoko, prohibited depiction of her mate's homosexuality or even his violent death when he disemboweled himself. The author died in 1970 in a *shinji* or double-death pact, with his lover Morita (Mashayuki Shionoya).

Warners released the movie but downplayed the gay angle, referring in a press kit to Morita simply as Mishima's "close friend."

Mishima's family originally cooperated in the project but requested that a scene in a gay bar be removed. When their wishes were denied, they withdrew their cooperation.

WHAT THE CRITICS SAID
"Ours is no longer a world, Mr. Schrader suggests, that tolerates saintly ambitions; psychological wounds and physical circumstance drag such men down, turning would-be heroes into monsters, and messiahs into figures of ridicule. His triumph in *Mishima*, his most completely satisfying film, lies in creating a seeker who is aware of his own absurdity, and who is willing to embrace the ridiculous on his way to the sublime."
Dave Kehr, *The New York Times*

Mom

(2006)

Big Dreams in Little Hope, USA

This is a female buddy movie, running for only 70 minutes, and the creation of Erin Greenwell, who both helmed and scripted it. It stars Julie Goldman as Linda, Emma Bowers as Natalie, and Emily A. Burton as Kelly.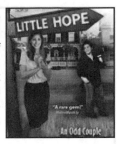

As a duo, Linda and Kelly could remake that hit TV series, *The Odd Couple.*

Market researchers Kelly and Linda are in New Hope for an annual Chili Cook-Off. When not holed up at the hostel, they make the rounds in this light, affable comedy, asking overly specific questions in customer preference surveys.

Kelly is dreaming of a coveted job as a field reporter, and laid-back Linda dreams of tattooing women in her parlor.

One of the interview subjects turns out to be an old girlfriend of Linda's. Her old flame, Natalie, is now settled down and married, but she and Linda rekindle the flame.

WHAT THE CRITICS SAID
"Erin Greenwell's shoestring debut tells the story of odd couple, Kelly, an uptight market researcher, and Linda, a goofy butch cameraperson who dreams of opening a tattoo parlor. Stranded in a New Hope hostel, Kelly struggles with her identity, and Linda confronts an old fling. There are Universal lessons on friendship, love, and happiness to follow. *Mom* takes a while to get going, but the adventures of this offbeat duo—played with heartfelt sincerity by Emily Burton and Julie Goldman—prove that a decent script with a lotta heart can go a long way."
Termeh Mazhari

"Greenwell, in her sophomore outing, relies on little comic touches and bits of business instead of big laughs or elaborate pay-offs. Every encounter adds a touch of sociological satire or oddball color to the comfortable canvas, which is never mean-spirited or judgmental. Burton and Goldman amble along nicely in soft-shoe counterpoint, their routine nonchalantly synchronized to improve rhythms."
Ronnie Scheib, *Variety*

The Monkey's Mask

(2000)

The Gumshoe Is a Dyke

Director Samantha Lang based this crime mystery/thriller on Dorothy Porter's novel. Porter's book, a sensation in literary circles, was a Chandleresque thriller penned in non-rhyming verse, and became the best-selling volume of poetry in Australia since World War II.

The Monkey's Mask revolves around a relationship between an older and a younger woman. Jill Fitzpatrick (Susie Porter) is a 28-year-old street-smart and out-of-work private dick wishing she wasn't celibate. A job comes knocking on her door, just like one did in those Bogie movies of the 40s. Her assignment is to investigate the disappearance of Mickey (Abbie Cornish), a young female student.

During the course of Jill's investigation, she encounters Mickey's poetry lecturer, the seductive Diana as played by Kelly McGillis. Sparks fly. Married to a good-looking young Aussie, Nick (Marton Csokas), Diana does little to discourage Jill's obvious passion. The two women begin a torrid affair that sets the sheets on fire.

Jill seems to be getting nowhere on her case. Mickey was known to sleep around, including having affairs with two older male mentors. Diana remarks to Jill at one point: "You're a great fuck, but you're a very ordinary detective."

WHAT THE CRITICS SAID
"As Lang picks away at the power of danger of infatuation and the link between sex and death, she also turns our perceived notions about poetry (and those who read and write it) on their head, allowing Jill to lift the lid on a rather seamy, literary-academic underworld."
Michael Thomson

"McGillis (remembered from *Top Gun*) brings a combination of fire and ice to this murder mystery from Australia. Poetry, lesbian sex, and murder might be a killer combination if a deadly pace weren't included in the mix."
Bob Graham

Mother Nature

(*Mater Natura*; 2004)

Triangular Love & a Transgendered Romp

This 94-minute Italian film is mildly amusing in parts. Call it a triangular love story and a serio-comic look at a transsexual hooker and her flamboyant friends.

Making a debut as a helmer, Massimo Andrei also co-scripted the project. Cast in the leading role as Desiderio, Maria Pia Calzone is a post-op hooker. But she's willing to confine her blow-jobs to just one man when she bags studmuffin Andrew (Valerio Poglia Manzillo).

Some reviewers called this piece of bronze eye-candy "Ulysses on horseback." His idea of acting is to remove his shirt which is good enough for many gay men. He's got a secret, though. In addition to Desiderio, he's got a fiancée lusting for him as well.

Andrea can't make up his mind as to which gal he wants. Maybe he wants both of them in bed together.

To help Desiderio get over her shock, a group of her adrenalin-filled cross-dressers and transsexuals establish a community of support for her in the shadow of Mt. Vesuvius. There they set up an organic farm, *Mater Natura*. The farm serves many purposes, one of which is to grow luscious produce like eggplant and zucchini with no apparent effort. Another is to serve as a center for transgender counseling. It's even a place where a macho man can find "the faggot that dwells within himself."

The film is not all life on the farm, however. There are some well-delivered songs, even an appearance by Luxuria, Italy's best-known drag performer, whose talents are squandered in a trousers role.

You also get to witness far-out fashion—no *Devil Wears Prada* stuff—and plenty of queer histrionics in this trannie pageantry.

Incidentally, Sharon Stone said she always wanted to play Lana Turner on the screen, but in this romp the honor goes to Fabio Brescia.

Mr. Right

(2010)

The Gay Date Movie of 2010

Set in London, this romantic comedy directed by brothers David Morris and Jacqui Morris, playfully bounces around its romances, dramas, and lusts. Taking place in Soho, Mr. Right moves at a fast pace, introducing a coven of charmers who each discover an inner truth.

Louise (Georgia Zaris) might uncharitably be called a fag hag. She has a history of dating gay men, but she wants to find out if her new beau Paul (Jeremy Edwards) also leans in that direction. As a means of getting an accurate reading on him, she brings him to a dinner party composed of a gaggle of gay men.

Among the couples attending are Harry (James Lance), a reality TV producer who is ashamed of "the crap" he foists on the viewers. His BF is Alex (Luke de Woolfson), a waiter whose acting career is about to take off.

A successful artist, Tom (David Morris), brings his rent boy Lars (Benjamin Hart) to the party. He seems on the make for anyone.

William (Rocky Marshall) is a rugby player who has a problem. It's his 11-year-old daughter, who seems determined to drive her dad's boyfriend away. William is in love with Lars (Leon Ockenden), a TV soap opera star.

The question asked is this: Just how straight is Louise's new boyfriend Paul?

WHAT THE CRITICS SAID
"This is ensemble drama about friends—how they try and fail to make love work with their boyfriends. It's not about Louise, but about how gays search for Mr. Right. Because the film is British, it embodies sophisticated humor and the characters are quite complicated, sometimes a bit too complicated. There are several storylines, but once you understand who the characters are and where they are going, you will find a movie that looks like a fluffy comedy but is in reality a look at the way we live."
Amos Lassen

The Mudge Boy

(2003)

A Boy, A Chicken, & a Burning Gay Crush

First things first: Emile Hirsch, who plays the lead character Duncan Mudge, resembles a softer version of Joaquin Phoenix, or even Leonardo DiCaprio circa *What's Eating Gilbert Grape*. Elegantly shot and intelligently written (both tasks performed by Michael Burke), this is a story of a 14-year-old misfit farm boy, Duncan Mudge, who tries to cope with his mother's death. To do so, he mimics her behavior, even speaking in her voice at table and wearing her fur coat to bed.

His father, Edgar (Richard Jenkins), doesn't quite know what to make of this odd behavior. Set in rural Vermont, the drama deals with love, grief, and coming-out gay sexuality. Burke expanded on his 1998 *Fishbelly White* to make this drama.

Duncan seeks comfort with his pet chicken, not the most cuddly of animals. He develops an oral/poultry fixation, registering as a kind of fellatio. Chicken is called "she," but looks like a rooster. Duncan has a habit of slipping the chicken's head inside his mouth to calm the bird. His mother taught him the skill.

An outsider, "the Mudge Boy" befriends Perry (Tom Guiry), who, one day at the swimming hole, recoils when Duncan reaches out to feel the muscles in his arm. But, in spite of his initial reaction, is this macho tough kid secretly gay?

WHAT THE CRITICS SAID
"When Perry's sexual desire overcomes him, Duncan is pushed into dangerous territory, his responses confused by emotional hunger. But when the older boy betrays his friendship to guard his own secret, Duncan reacts with a dramatic, violent gesture, the shocked aftermath of which draws him closer to his father in grief."
David Rooney, *Variety*

Mulholland Drive

(2001)

A Love Story in the City of Dreams

A car wreck on the winding Mulholland Drive renders a woman amnesiac. She and a perky Hollywood hopeful search for clues and answers across Los Angeles in a twisting venture beyond dreams and reality. It's a crime story, fantasy, mystery, romance and thriller, both directed and written by David Lynch.

Naomi Watts as Betty Elms Diane Selwyn plays a starry-eyed Canadian who wants to make it big in Hollywood. She discovers a very beautiful woman with amnesia, Laura Harring, who gives a sizzling performance as Rita.

Nominated for dozens of awards, *Mulholland Drive* just may be the best movie about movies ever made, although many gay fans would dispute that, citing *Sunset Blvd.* instead.

What is not disputed is that *Mulholland* features the most unabashedly erotic connection between two women ever committed to film. The love scenes between Watts and Harring melt the screen.

The sunny blonde falls hard for the raven-haired amnesiac from the first moment she sees her in the shower and naked. The film is hard to understand—that is, if Lynch himself fully knows. Both women are pulled into a psychotic illusion involving a dangerous blue box, a mysterious night club, *Silencio*, and a director named Adam Hesher (Justin Theroux).

The movie unfolds like a surrealist dreamscape in a form of a Hollywood *film noir*. We're treated to the appearance of Ann Miller, of tap-dancing fame in the 40s. She plays a landlady.

WHAT THE CRITICS SAID
"The movie is hypnotic; we're drawn along as if one thing leads to another—but nothing leads anywhere, and that's even before the characters start to fracture and recombine like flesh caught in a kaleidoscope. *Mulholland Dr.* isn't like *Memento*, where if you watch it closely enough, you can hope to explain the mystery. There is no explanation. There may not even be a mystery."
Roger Ebert

Mulligans

(2008)

Shagging Your Kid's Best Friend

Chip Hale directed this overly melodramatic film that still caught our fancy. Tyler (Derek Baynham) brings his best friend Chase (Charlie David) home to bunk with his family at their Vancouver lakeside cabin for the summer.

Chase is introduced to Tyler's dad, Nathan (Dan Payne) and his wife Stacey (Thea Gill). She is remembered as one half of the token lesbian couple in *Queer as Folk*. The summer appears to be idyllic. But there's a catch, a storm cloud on the horizon. Swimming, golf, and barbecues give way to lust.

Tyler hauls Chase to some Animal House type parties, but the slutty girls don't interest Chase. Finally, he admits the truth to Tyler, telling his best friend that he's gay. Tyler seems cool with that, claiming "I love you, man" but realizes that's not the right thing to say.

Tyler's family also seems cool about the announcement, although Birdie (Grace Vukovic), the eight-year-old daughter, wonders if she's gay, claiming she loves her female tennis teacher.

Nathan finally comes on to Chase after living for 25 years in the closet. A skinny dip later and the torrid affair has begun. Stacey discovers it, and chaos reigns.

In an amazing turnaround, the clan rebounds with a certain equanimity.

WHAT THE CRITICS SAID
"Here's the weird part. All hell breaks loose for only ten minutes. Even Tyler, who has just found out that his father is gay and has bedded his best friend, gets over it shockingly easily. Your reaction may be more that of a family friend who jokes, 'Has anyone called Jerry Springer yet?'"
Dom Willmott

"Just because you're a gay man, it doesn't mean you suddenly can't help yourself and have to act out on every desire you have, but Mulligans seems to disagree, and also seems to think everyone else should just forgive you for it."
Ted Isaac

Murder by Numbers

(2002)

Recycling the Leopold and Loeb Case

This crime drama, directed by Barbet Schroeder and scripted by Tony Gayton, has been told before, but never with Sandra Bullock in the lead role of the detective.

Those who have seen *Compulsion, Swoon*, or Hitchcock's *Rope* are already familiar with the infamous murder pact between two brainy and amoral young men, played by Michael Pitt as Justin Pendleton and Ryan Gosling as Richard Haywood.

In this version, these two brainy high school students plot the "perfect" murder, which engages them in an intellectual contest with a seasoned homicide detective (Bullock in the old James Stewart role).

In real life, Leopold and Loeb were Chicago-based homosexual lovers in 1924. In *Murder by Numbers* the boys are on the brink of becoming lovers but decide to sublimate their passion into this arrogant crime. They pick a victim at random, so there will be no link between corpse and killers. A middle-aged female is murdered in a secluded wooded area.

Perhaps not wanting to "offend" mainstream audiences, Schroeder virtually ignored the latent homoerotic relationship between the two boys. Their link is only superficially presented, and not in any intriguing way at that. By not portraying them as lovers, the script comes unglued a bit. To enter into such a deadly intellectual pursuit—murder, that is—the bond between them needs to be stronger.

The plot thickens when we learn that Bullock as the detective Cassie has some deep, painful secrets in her own past. They are gradually revealed. Her partner is Ben Chaplin, cast as Sam Kennedy, who clearly is not able to stand up to her.

WHAT THE CRITICS SAID
"As Bullock draws the net closer, she runs into more danger and more official opposition. At least the climax shows us that Bullock can stay in character no matter what."
Roger Ebert

Murder in Fashion

AKA *Fashion Victim*; AKA *Target Versace*

(2010)

Celebrity Worship & Narcissistic Self-Loathing

In Memoriam

Andrew Cunanan launched his murderous killing spree in Minnesota, continued through Chicago, and, despite being the object of an intense manhunt, was able to fatally shoot fashion designer Gianni Versace in Miami Beach before committing suicide. What a story. Director Ben Waller brings it to life, casting Jonathan Trent as Cunanan and Robert Miano as Versace.

Cunanan is an over-the-hill rent boy, turning 27 and fretting over his fast-fading looks and a six-pack rapidly becoming an eight-pack. He licks vodka off a magazine cover shot of Versace while delivering a line, "You play for me, you play for keeps—I'm pretty, but I'm deadly."

Critic Nick Pinkerton noted that while shooting this scene "hack Ben Waller worked the jerky-zoom PsychoCam effect liberally. *Fashion* contains the worst FBI procedural scenes in collective memory—possibly good for a laugh in the right frame of mind."

Early on we get the point that this hustler isn't going to take aging gracefully. FBI agent Harry Spalding (James C. Burns) is close on the killer's trail, but he doesn't move fast enough to prevent Versace's death.

Cunanan conducted his hysterical, three-month, four-state, five-victim killing jag in 1997 before he did himself in on a houseboat in Florida.

One reviewer noted that "the real culprit of the movie is the aesthetic tyranny of gay culture."

WHAT THE CRITICS SAID
"Filmed in *Miami Vice* colors and with a *Desperate Housewives* level of credibility, the movie has a touching earnestness that blocks our impulse to laugh. We can almost believe that if only a Miami shop assistant had not urged Cunanan toward liposuction, Versace might still be alive."
Jeannette Catsoulis, *The New York Times*

My Beautiful Laundrette

(1986)

A Fab Gay Romance in Thatcherite London

The film takes place during the reign of the Iron Lady over Britain. Young Omar, a Pakistani, is given the chance to run his uncle's launderette. He enlists the aid of his ex-lover Johnny to get the business back on its feet. Johnny and Omar have gone through their ups and downs in the past, and Johnny is now hanging with a lot of neo-Nazi white punks.

Omar and Johnny, in spite of opposition and prejudice, convert the launderette into a place where you'd like to hang out. Their relationship creates a volatile racial situation, which director Stephen Frears does a superb job of revealing. He also cast the minor roles well.

Daniel Day-Lewis as Johnny stars as a gay punk who transforms a dingy London launderette into a glitzy new emporium with his Pakistani lover Omar (Gordon Warnecke). Together they transcend the neighborhood racists in this landmark film.

This movie along with *A Room With a View* opened on the same day, March 7, 1986. Both films starred Daniel Day-Lewis in very different roles, lower class in *Laundrette* and a snobbish Edwardian upperclassman in *A Room with a View*. When critics saw him in these very different parts, each showing great talent, his career was made.

WHAT THE CRITICS SAID
"The chemistry between Omar and Johnny is palpable and their relationship handled totally matter-of-factly. It's actually about the only part of the film not trying to score any political points and the whole matter is handled without the need for labels and self-defining—which is a breath of fresh air compared to most films where any gay romance appears in the plot. An unexpected kiss in a dark alley is easily the most erotic single shot I have seen in a film."
Nicola Osborne

My Brother's War

(2005)

Rebel Soldier Is Really a Woman

This is a labor of love for Whitney Hamilton, who was the director and writer and also starred in the dual role of Grace (aka Henry) Kieler. Why the dual male/female names? Grace was part of the 400 women who fought disguised as men during the Civil War. *My Brother's War* is her story.

On the day of her engagement, Grace finds her family and fiancé divided on political grounds. Her future husband plans to enlist in the Union Army, but her brother vows to fight for the Confederacy. She is torn between these two conflicting loyalties.

She promises her father she will look after her brother. When her father dies, she cuts her hair and dons her brother's clothing. Taking his name, she joins the Rebel army fighting in the South.

On the way to find her brother, Grace meets Virginia Klaising (played by Dana Bennison). She is both a widow and a mother grieving the death of her only son.

Virginia and Grace team up to travel the back woods, and Virginia finds herself falling for Grace, thinking she is Henry. Henry's secret (really Grace's secret) is revealed when she is shot and brought back from certain death. Even so, the bond between the two women grows stronger.

We won't reveal how the plot unfolds. But the film very dramatically and realistically shows how each woman is able to comfort the other. Predictably, though, each woman must reach her respective destination without the other.

The story is loosely based on the novel, *Firefly*. Rounding out the cast is a team of well-chosen and talented supporting players: Rebecca Damon as Georgianna Walker; Patrick Melville as Lucius Walker; Ed Moran as Zeb Riley, and Thom Milano as Colonel Wright.

My Mother Likes Women

(2002)

An Erotic Almovódarian Romp

Written and directed by Daniela Fejerman and Inés París, this is a 93-minute Spanish comedy with English subtitles.

Within the first few minutes of this film, we're introduced to Sofia (Mamma as played by one of the most famous sitcom actresses in Spain, the intensely likable Rosa María Sardà), who happens to be a celebrated concert pianist and about as hip as they come. Gathering her clan together, she breathlessly announces that she's in love. Before her three daughters can even ask whether the newcomer is good in the sack, or worthy of her, the doorbell rings. The newest usurper to home and hearth is a statuesque (female) brunette.

The rest of the film involves how the clan copes, as they each hammer their way throughout their primal fear of confronting the sexuality of a parent. Each of the three considers herself as too liberal, and too well-educated, to outwardly reject their mother's proclivities. Reasonably, one of the sisters says to the others, "No one ever died of having a lesbian mother." But, then, like the three implacable witches of *Hamlet*, they collectively wave their arms, grieve, rage, and scheme, each with differing degrees of ruthlessness. Adding to their conviction to end the relationship is the news that Mamma has spent all her savings on paying off some of her new lover's debts.

The youngest, and perhaps the least neurotic of the three sisters, is Sol (Silvia Abascal), a blissfully self-involved, pink-haired and exhibitionistic groupie who struts her stuff on stage every weekend with a punk-rock band.

The oldest sister Jimena (María Pujalte) is a hard-edged, unhappily married suburbanite with a young son and an uptight and judgmental hubby whom she later divorces. It is she who urges her siblings to entrap her mother's new lover (Eliska) into a sexually compromising situation that will so enrage their mother as to precipitate the end of the affair. ("If I can get into Eliska's panties, then Mom will come to her senses and dump her.") Sol, the most sexually toughened of the lot, agrees to do the dirty deed.

My One and Only

(2009)

Renée Zellweger & 2 Sons (1 Gay)

This movie re-creates the 1950s on a road trip through America. Ostensibly, it's a rather fictionalized account of suntanned actor George Hamilton, who has also penned a tell-little memoir.

The picture clearly belongs to Zellweger playing Anne Deveraux. She catches her husband Dan (Kevin Bacon) with another woman and decides to leave him. Piling clothes in a suitcase, she cleans out a safety deposit box and pulls her two sons out of prep school. They head off for a grand adventure.

Zellweger wants to find a new breadwinner, perhaps forgetting that she's in middle age and has to compete with younger women for husbands. She tears up the American landscape as she heads out to round up old beaus or find a new one.

Behind the wheel of the car, 15-year-old George (Logan Lerman) steers his mother and his effeminate stepbrother Robbie (Mark Rendall) on their cross-country adventure.

Robbie is obviously gay but that's not a subject that comes up, except for a certain mocking from strangers they encounter along the way. He bides his spare time embroidering a map of the family travels onto the back of a shirt.

In contrast, George is more serious, a bit bookish. He keeps a copy of J.D. Salinger's *The Catcher in the Rye* by his side, and fancies that one day he too will write. Steering Zellweger on her husband hunt is Richard Loncraine, who guides a series of mainly TV actors in and out of their roles as potential mates.

WHAT THE CRITICS SAID
"Rendall does limp-wrist well; Lerman serves as an adequate vessel for Hamilton exorcising adolescent struggles with Mom. Occasionally diverting but ultimately forgettable, *My One and Only* will become unforgivable if it inspires other former competitors from *Dancing With the Stars* to go in search of lost time."
Melissa Anderson

My Own Private Idaho

(1991)

Friendship Between Two Male Hustlers

Under Gus Van Sant's brilliant direction, this story of a friendship between two male hustlers made the late River Phoenix a legend. Mike Waters (Phoenix) and Scott Favor (Keanu Reeves) live on the street, do drugs, and sell themselves to both women and men.

Abandoned as a child, Mike is obsessed with finding his long-lost mother. The twist in the plot is that he suffers from narcolepsy, which means that he goes to sleep a lot, as clients take advantage of him. In fact, he sleeps through some of the more crucial moments in his own life.

Scott is the rebellious son of an upper-class family, and he seems to live his life mainly to embarrass his father. Mike is in love with Scott, who insists that he is straight. Together they go on a search for Mike's mother, which leads them into adventure. The two young men become outlaws on the road, sharing the bedrooms of strangers.

WHAT THE CRITICS SAID
"Although the central characters are prostitutes, the movie is not really about sex, which does not interest either Mike or Scott very much. What Mike wants is love, and by love what he really means is someone to hold him and care for him. He was deeply damaged as a child, and now he seeks shelter. It is a matter of indifference whether he finds it with a man of a woman. The achievement of this film is that it wants to evoke the state of drifting need, and it does. There is no mechanical plot that has to grind to a Hollywood conclusion, and no contrived test for the heroes to pass. This is a movie about two particular young men, and how they pass their lives."
Roger Ebert

"Rather less than the sum of its often striking parts, Gus Van Sant's appealingly idiosyncratic look at a pair of very different young street hustlers is one of those ambitious, over-reaching disappointments that is more interesting than some more conservative successes."
Variety

My Summer of Love

(2004)

Lesbian Love Among Teenagers

No, this is not a remake of *A Summer Place*, that 1959 flick of summer love that starred heartthrob Troy Donahue and Sandra Dee. The title does make it sound like a Sandra Dee teenspoitation movie. But it's far from that.

Natalie Press plays Mona as sprightly, freckly, and yearning for life—"think Sissy Spacek's Carrie meets Peppermint Patty." She's a local Yorkshire girl with a thick accent and red hair.

In contrast to Mona, Tamsin is dark, pampered, exotic, and also a beauty, with a far greater sense of worldliness. We seem to know right from the beginning that the more sophisticated Tamsin will seduce the virgin and later abandon her as she returns to her own class. The movie is rated R for sexuality, nudity, and drug use.

Today's post-millennium lovers are teenage girls in this ContentFilm Release of BBC Films. Directed by Polish-born Pawel Pawlikowski and running for 86 minutes, the story is a drama of the meeting of two girls in a field on a sweltering day in Yorkshire. One is on horseback, the other pushing a scooter. One comes from a rich family, the other from the working class.

Cast opposite Mona is the haughty Tamsin (Emily Blunt), spending the summer in her family's Tudor manor nearby. These two self-searching girls soon lose themselves in a love affair that, in the words of one critic, "has more to do with faith and yearning than reality."

One of the most brilliant performances is by Paddy Considine, playing Mona's brother, Phil. He's lost his heart to Jesus, and is seen pouring brew down the drain of his pub. He's preparing for a new role in life—that of an evangelical minister and "bride of Christ."

The director with his hard-to-pronounce name (Pawlikowski) is not entirely unknown, having given us *Last Resort,* a Kafkaesque tale of a Russian mother and son trapped in immigration limbo. He is said to shoot without a script, relying on improvisation.

The Mysteries of Pittsburgh

(2008)

That Final Summer Before Life Begins

There's one scene in *The Mysteries of Pittsburgh* where Peter Sarsgaard, Sienna Miller, and Jon Foster are depicted at a bar drinking. In this production they share more than drinks in this *menage-à-trois* wiseguy tale.

The film chronicles the defining summer of a recent college graduate who crosses his gangster father and explores love, sexuality, and the enigmas surrounding his life and city.

Director Marshall Thuber also wrote the screenplay. The movie was based on the best-selling novel by Michael Chabon, a debut effort in 1988. The novel's plot and characters are familiar to those who have read the novel, but the film adaptation has many variances. As *The San Francisco Chronicle* accurately pointed out, "The edge, the charm, and dryly pointed cultural observations that made the Chabon novel so auspicious are largely missing in action throughout the earnest but unconvincing film."

In a summer that will change his life, Art Bechstein (Jon Foster), the son of mobster (Nick Nolte), goes to work in a bookstore. He's in search of who he is. He doesn't really find out between the stacks of books when he has sex with his boss (Mena Suvari).

He finds a role more suited to him—that of a third wheel—with the unpredictable, volatile Cleveland Arning (Peter Sarsgaard) and his girlfriend Jane (Sienna Miller). Critics pointed out that Sarsgaard gets to burn on all cylinders in this film. Nick Nolte mixes paternal tough love with genuine threat. In this film, which contains nudity, sexual situations, and coarse language, Art becomes attracted first to Jane, and later to Cleveland.

Art is soon caught up in the couple's manic and thrill-seeking lifestyle. He finds Cleveland mercurial, mysterious, and charismatic. The book's bisexual/homosexual episodes are somewhat downplayed in the film—for homophobic viewers, no doubt—but Art and Cleveland do end up in bed together for some serious fucking.

Mysterious Skin

(2004)

The Aftereffects of Sexual Abuse During Childhood

This poetic fable is based on Gregg Araki's screenplay which in itself was based on the Scott Heim novel of the same name. Araki also directed this drama about a teenage hustler and a young man obsessed with alien abductions.

The film begins when the two stars are only eight years old and Little League teammates. The boys are Neil and Brian. Neil is more hardened to life, Brian the sensitive one. The coach, Bill Sage, has the hots for Neil in particular but takes both boys home one rainy night where he seduces each of them. The event is deeply traumatic to Brian, but not to Neil.

The film moves forward in years to when the two boys are young teens. At this point in their lives, Brian (played by Brady Corbet) has become asexual and is convinced he was abducted by aliens. Neil is turning tricks in the park. Former child TV star, Joseph Gordon-Levitt (*3rd Rock from the Sun*) delivers a haunting, uncompromising performance as Neil, who embraces nihilism not as a fashion statement but as a survival mechanism.

The film is not visually graphic, although there are some tense sexual situations with the coach and the young boys. Both the long-term effects of child sexual abuse and sexual addiction are dealt with in *Mysterious Skin*.

The movie is bold in that it explores both prepubescent and teen sexuality with such honesty it might make some viewers squirm in their seats.

WHAT THE CRITICS SAID
"All the elements ultimately coalesce to create an indirect but stunningly effective approach toward revealing how pedophilia can devastate and scar its victim. *Mysterious Skin* is candid without being graphic but leaves little to the imagination, and its language at times is blunt. But it's hard to imagine a more serious or persuasive indictment of the horrors inflicted on children by sexual abuse than *Mysterious Skin*."
Kevin Thomas, *Los Angeles Times*

The Naked Civil Servant

(1975)

England's Most Stately Homo

Quentin Crisp, John Hurt

John Hurt (*The Elephant Man*) stars as Quentin Crisp, England's most stately homo, who lived his life as an openly gay man in London during the 1930s. It was based on Crisp's remarkable, "warts and all" autobiography which made him internationally famous. He was an ordinary British man who became extraordinary.

Helmer Jack Gold, working with a screenplay by Philip Mackie, brought the life and times of Quentin Crisp to the screen. Hurt is quite brilliant playing an outrageous and flamboyant homosexual, coming of age and growing into old age in conservative England, which was very homophobic territory at the time, and most often hostile to an out queen (and we're not talking about the one who inhabits Buckingham Palace).

Before the film was first aired on TV, the Independent Broadcasting Authority censored a line from Crisp: "Sexual intercourse is a poor substitute for masturbation." During the actual film it was discovered that Hurt had painted Crisp when he was a life studies model at an art school the actor had attended.

This is a film that at the time of its release was way ahead of its time. But it was about a man even more ahead of his time.

Crisp was witty and eccentric. Once author Darwin Porter took him to lunch at a trendy restaurant in Greenwich Village. He ordered his favorite dish, mashed potatoes, but discovered that the chef had left the peel on. "This is the most outrageous thing I've experienced since I was spread-eagled and raped by five men in Her Majesty's Navy."

Crisp, as the film shows, was subject to harassment and humiliation. His life was often in danger. But in spite of homophobic attacks and mass intolerance, he refused to be anything but himself. The movie doesn't hold back its punches. Crisp is not sugarcoated, and at times comes across as vain and pompous. The triumph of the movie is in its depiction of how our hero lived life on his own terms.

Ned Rorem: Words and Music

(2005)

The Leading American Composer of Art Songs

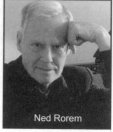

Ned Rorem

James Dowell and John Kolomvakis were co-directors and producers of this remarkable documentary where they were granted almost unlimited access to Ned Rorem, the composer. He is almost as famous for his scandalous diaries as he is for his compositions such as his 1965 opera, "Miss Julie."

His first diary about his life in Paris became almost mandatory reading for gay men in 1965. Rorem became the *protégé* of the Viscountess Marie-Laure de Noailles, a celebrated and wealthy art patron of her day.

The documentary on Rorem was filmed over the course of a decade, and is filled with his pithy observations on art, love, and death. "In the act of stealing, the artist is so guilty that he tries to cover his tracks. The act of covering his tracks is the act of creation."

The docu features interviews with playwright Edward Albee and composer Paul Bowles, along with such other celebrities as Edmund White and John Corligliano. The author's life partner of 32 years, James Holmes, is also featured. He died in 1999, although Rorem lives on into his 80s.

The film skips over the most gossipy aspects of his privileged life, although he was never closeted and apparently enjoyed a full sex life along with struggles with alcoholism.

He was raised a Quaker in a pacifist family. Early in life he showed a love and a talent for music, later studying with Bernstein and Copland. In his lifetime he met virtually everybody who was everybody from Anaïs Nin to Tennessee Williams.

WHAT THE CRITICS SAID
"Performances include a dance interpretation of three 'micro-operas;' Claire Bloom reading poetry to a Rorem score, and Manhattan School of Music's staging of his only full-length opera, *Miss Julie*. Alternately testy and philosophical, the master of art song exudes the complexity of a man secure in his achievements, but perhaps no longer infatuated with self-analysis."
Dennis Harvey, *Variety*

The New Twenty

(2009)

Gay Is the New Straight, Friends Are the New Family

Five best friends in their late 20s discover new truths about themselves and the friendships they thought would last forever.

Julie (Nicole Bilderback) and Andrew (Ryan Locke) are pre-collapse Wall Street yuppies engaged to be married. She is a beautiful Asian woman who is Andrew's match in the world of business. He is a lean, mean, blond alpha-dog.

Once very competitive, Andrew is an investment banker who doesn't have the fire in his belly that he used to. Julie, the only woman in this group, frets over her soon-to-be-husband's disillusionment. Their official coupling is the signal for the beginning of the end, as their utopian bubble of group love must burst.

The court jester is Ben (Colin Fickes). He's gay, overweight, and addicted to online sex sites. When one trick he's summoned from the web appears at his doorstep, the two men reject each other on sight.

Rounding out the group is Felix (Thomas Sadoski), who is drug addicted, and Tony (Andrew Wei Lin) who has a commitment phobia.

"A touch of existential malaise due to late capitalism," is how Felix sums up his "friends since college," who now must grapple with an assortment of social, romantic, and professional anxieties.

Tony is also gay and uneasily conducts his affair with a healthy, HIV positive lover (Bill Sage).

Joining the group is Louie (Terry Serpico), who is called "streetwise, sexy, and Machiavellian." He has his eye on Julie, Andrew's fiancée.

Helmer Chris Mason Johnson, who also co-wrote the script, successfully guides these yuppies on their way to a finale. On the way there, they betray themselves and each other in their abuse of sex, money, and drugs.

The Night Larry Kramer Kissed Me

(2000)

A Filmed Landmark Theatrical Event

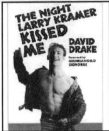

One can imagine a day when closets are a thing of the past. Director Tim Kirkland filmed actor David Drake's solo performance in the off-Broadway hit of the early 90s, *The Night Larry Kramer Kissed Me*. Essentially this filmed version of the play sticks to the theatrical values of the stage production.

The movie begins as an odyssey of a gay child celebrating his sixth birthday on June 28, 1969, the date of the Stonewall riots, as he is thrilled by the sounds of *West Side Story*.

We see him on his 16th birthday, catching *A Chorus Line* with his first boyfriend. We move forward into the satiric finale in 2018 when Drake is a happily married man with two adopted boys in America, a land free of homophobes, such as Rush Limbaugh, who has been assassinated.

WHAT THE CRITICS SAID
"The original finale for David Drake's 1992 *The Night Larry Kramer Kissed Me*, the longest-running one-man stage production in New York theater history, was set in 1999 and celebrated a cure for AIDS (the eponymous smooch refers to Kramer's 1985 watershed play *The Normal Heart*). The film adaptation bumps it up to 2018 and adds to its prognostications a Damon-Affleck remake of *The Way We Were*. If a few pockets of Drake's seven-part, semi-autobiographical narrative of growing up, coming out, acting up, and sleeping around—and of constant, terrible loss— seem a bit dated, his writing is so cogently personal and his performance so versatile that Larry Kramer could have debuted yesterday."
Jessica Winter

"Like the play, film version assumes aud awareness of, first, Larry Kramer's seminal AIDS drama, *The Normal Heart*, and its notorious accusation that *The New York Times* deliberately buried coverage of the rising disease in the early and mid-80s, and, second, the concurrent activist movement led by ACT-UP. Those clueless to these factors will be utterly lost, but Drake's mercurial perf may win them over."
Robert Koehler, *Variety*

The Night Listener

(2006)

Maupin Confronts Another Literary Hoax

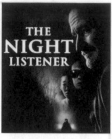

In 2001, before the bogus memoirs of JT LeRoy and James Frey, Armistead Maupin gave us the novel, *The Night Listener*. It was created at the time he was breaking up with his partner, Terry Anderson, and it was written after he was duped into a phone friendship with someone posing as an abused teenage boy.

Helmer Patrick Stettner brings this story within a story to the screen. He cast Robin Williams as Gabriel Noone, the fictional name used for Maupin. In the film, Gabriel is a radio yarn-spinner in the midst of a crumbling relationship with his male lover. This was true to life as Anderson and Maupin called it quits.

In 1992, the real Maupin received a manuscript allegedly written by a 14-year-old boy, detailing the sexual abuse, including rape, he'd suffered as a child. However, he claimed that his nightmare was over as he was spirited away by a social worker.

In the film this social worker is called Donna Logland, as played by Toni Collette. We know it's getting confusing at this point. Over a period of time, the real Maupin developed an intense phone conversation with this "boy."

In 1993 a shocking memoir was published by a so-called Tony Johnson called *A Rock and a Hard Place*. Maupin wrote a blurb for it.

In 2001 "Tony Johnson" was exposed as an invention of his supposed adoptive mother, Vicki Johnson, in a *New Yorker* article by Tad Friend.

So, *The Night Listener* becomes a movie adapted from a novel that was inspired by the "memoirs" of a boy who probably never existed.

Even when Maupin published his novel, he apparently felt that there might be some small chance that Tony actually existed. There was even fear of a lawsuit, though he chose to call his story fiction.

Nighthawks

(1978)

He Leads a Secret Life by Night

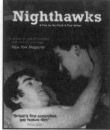

When it was released in 1978, *Nighthawks* was hailed as the first British film to deal with gay life in a positive light. Its backers spent five years planning and raising funds for the movie. Even mainstream film critics at the time hailed *Nighthawks* for its sensitivity and intelligence.

Helmer Ron Peck, who co-wrote the script with Paul Hallam, said, "Almost any film starts off with the burden of trying to redress an imbalance. To make homosexuality visible in the cinema, we need hundreds of gay films, not half a dozen."

Nighthawks is the story of a young man forced to hide his sexuality by day while living a secret life. The depiction of the gay lifestyle is so realistic, the picture could almost be a docu. It was obviously made right before the advent of AIDS.

A closeted gay man, Jim (Ken Robertson) is a schoolteacher in London. At night he frequents gay bars and discos. The director brilliantly depicts gay cruising, his actors expressing the desire in their eyes.

WHAT THE CRITICS SAID
"The camera roams the expanses of a disco in extended takes, forcing—allowing—the viewer to choose what or whom to watch, just as Jim does. The repetition of scenes becomes hypnotic, and without ever growing didactic, the camera's gaze compellingly dramatizes the simple act of sight, of looking as a routine of consumption. Do we consume those around us in the manner that we consume images? It is a question with graver implications than when *Nighthawks* was first released."
Ray Pride

"Since bars and discos, by nature, encourage one-night stands over long-term relationships, Robertson's frequent sexual encounters become routine and dissatisfying. With intimacy and compassion, Peck and Hallam explore the romantic dilemmas of marginalization, using a miniscule budget and few locations to show the suffocating limits of homosexual life."
Scott Tobias

Nijinsky

(1980)

A Comet That Blazes, But Only Briefly

In an era of passionate artistic experimentation, ballet dancer Vaslav Nijinsky burst onto the scene (1906-1917) before disappearing into madness.

George de la Peña, a brilliant dancer from the American Ballet Theatre, recreates the aura of the great Nijinsky in such intricately performed numbers as *Afternoon of a Faun* or *Petrouchka*.

Sergei Diaghilev (Alan Bates) enters his life to become his mentor and possessive lover. It was this Russian impresario who brought Nijinsky world acclaim. But there was a downside when Romola de Plusky (Leslie Browne) enters the dancer's life. The ballerina attempts to draw the increasingly mentally unstable Nijinsky away from Diaghilev. This triangular love turmoil eventually leads to Nijinsky's plunge into schizophrenia. After 30 years of seclusion, he welcomed death in 1950.

A professional ballet director and choreographer, Herbert Ross was a terrific choice as the helmer.

In a supporting role, Jeremy Irons plays Diaghilev's ex-lover, Fokine, who refers to Nijinsky as "a little pederast."

WHAT THE CRITICS SAID
"Is marriage to blame for Nijinsky's balletic fall and decline into madness? Or is the culprit homosexuality? Is Diaghilev trying to convert the boychick to manlove, or is he Nijinsky's only true love? When the men 'kiss,' it's over with quickly, just to indicate their relationship. Ostensibly the story of two extraordinary men, *Nijinsky* should have been much, much more."
Out

"The relationships are vague, although Bates is an admirably imperious Diaghilev, founder of the *Ballets Russes de Monte Carlo* and an aging lover afraid to risk his heart. De la Peña makes the seventeen-years-younger Nijinsky too contemporary, and the famous relationship is nonsexual."
Samedi et Dimanche

No Regret

(*Huhoehaji Anha;* 2006)

Divided by Class, United by Passion

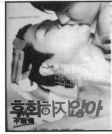

This film, called the first true gay film in the history of Korean cinema, is the story of a have and a have-not falling in love. It's also a story of forbidden love. In one gay parade in Seoul, many young men wore paper bags over their heads to conceal their identity. In spite of this film, and a few others, homosexuality remains a taboo in Korean society.

Director Leesong Hee-Il has helmed the story of the two lovers—Sumin (Lee Young-Hoon) and Jaemin (Lee Han). Sumin is an orphan from the countryside who has come into the city to seek his fame and fortune. He meets Jaemin when he is hired to drive him home after a night of drinking.

In time, Sumin loses his job at a factory, which, incidentally, is owned by the father of Jaemin.

To support himself, he takes a job as a male hustler at X Large, a "host bar," where young Korean boys strip during karaoke, then go off with the customers.

Still infatuated with Sumin, Jaemin tracks him down at the bar and hires him as a prostitute for the night. This leads to Sumin falling in love with his john. Complications ensue as Jaemin's homophobic family has big plans for their handsome son, including his wedding to a girl.

Trapped in their passions, the two men have strong choices to make.

WHAT THE CRITICS SAID
"On the surface, the plot seems like a same-sex treatment from some silent-era weeper. The film is anchored by superb performances by the two young men. Young-Hoon develops his character as much through body language and facial expressions as with dialogue, yet we completely understand the young man's inner turmoil and his need to free himself from a lingering sense of shame in order to achieve adulthood. In contrast, Jaemin is given a number of lines that the Gish sisters could have handled nicely about 90 years ago, if, of course, they weren't making silent films."
David Wiegand

Noah's Arc

(2005)

A Black and Gay Version of *Sex & the City*

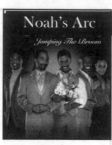

Now on DVD, and running for 200 minutes, the complete first season of this glossy gay TV series was advertised as "the answer to your *Queer as Folk* withdrawal symptoms." The DVD is filled with extra features, including the original pilot, deleted scenes, extended episodes, and cast comments.

The series followed the daily lives of Noah (Darryl Stephens), Alex (Rodney Chester), Ricky (Christian Vincent), and Chance (Douglas Spearman). These were four African-American gay men living and loving in Los Angeles.

The show, acquired by Logo, was wonderfully sexy with hot men. Jensen Atwood, who played Wade in a dozen episodes, was singled out by one reviewer as "the sexiest man on TV apart from Rockmond Dunbar."

Light-hearted moments were mingled with more serious drama. Reportedly, some networks are considering picking up the show and refilming it for a wider audience. But one gay viewer lamented that if that happened, CBS or NBC might give it the *Will & Grace* treatment.

Noah believes that he has finally found true love in the shape of his new boyfriend, Wade. But soon he realizes that he, along with his best friends, must endure the everyday drama and hardships of life in the Big Orange. From new BFs to strained relationships to career misadventures, these men persevere and live their lives with a certain grace and wit, even if they have to sell a beloved car to pay the rent.

What are some of the soap opera problems? Noah wants to meet some of Wade's straight friends. But he feels uncomfortable when he learns that Wade hasn't come out to them yet. When Wade's career takes a downward turn, Noah suggests they collaborate on a project. But the results are disastrous.

In *Noah's Arc*, black queer visibility on TV reached new heights.

The original title was called *Hot Chocolate*.

Notes on a Scandal

(2006)

An Evil Lesbian Juices Up a Thriller

Judi Dench walks away with the picture in this story of two misguided schoolteachers. It's soapy melodrama, of course, a tale of sex, betrayal, and loneliness.

An embittered old lesbian, Barbara Covett (Dench) has the hots for her target, a young new art teacher, beautiful Sheba Hart (played by Cate Blanchett). Sheba mistakes Barbara's affections for friendship because she is distracted by her smoldering affair with a 15-year-old hottie, one of her students. The student is a working-class Irish youth, Steven Connolly (Andrew Simpson), who blurs the line between schoolboy innocence and sexual predator.

When Barbara learns of Sheba's indiscretion, after having caught her in a compromising position with Steven, Barbara confronts Sheba rather ferociously.

Barbara is invited to Sheba's home where she meets her husband, Richard (Bill Nighy), who delivers his usually brilliant performance.

As the film progresses, Dame Dench is delicious at her delusional best, as she begins her manipulation of Sheba.

In the final scenes, Barbara sets into motion the scandal that will rock both their lives in ways they never imagined.

Richard Eyre directed this drama, illustrating that one woman's mistake is another woman's opportunity. It was scripted by Patrick Marber, who based it on a novel by Zoë Heller.

WHAT THE CRITICS SAID
"Though every line spoken by both women is a master class in acting, the resulting film is like a plate of Chinese food: wonderfully good, yet soon after, unsatisfying."
Instinct

"Barbara may be a fright, but, as Judi Dench plays her, she's hardly a stereotype. Abrupt and formidable, she can silence a class of noisy teens with a stare."
David Denby, *The New Yorker*

Nureyev: The Russian Years

(2007)

The Most Iconic Dancer of the 20th Century

Rudolf Nureyev had it all: beauty, charm, genius, passion, and a sex appeal that attracted some of the most beautiful men in the world, many wanting to sample his ample charms.

His defection to the West in 1961 made him an instant celebrity, and his brilliant performances on the stage made him a superstar before he succumbed to AIDS in 1993.

But what is not as well known about him is the Russian years, which are recaptured in this docu in home movies by Teja Kremke. We're treated to rare archival clips and interviews with close friends and colleagues.

Of course, those wishing to learn of his homosexual love life will have to look elsewhere. He bedded almost everybody from Tab Hunter to Cecil Beaton, from Leonard Bernstein to Erik Bruhn, from Mick Jagger to Freddie Mercury, even Anthony Perkins.

Nureyev: The Russian Years traces his meteoric career with new insights. A Tartar from Ufa in the Ural Mountains, the charismatic dancer got a late start in ballet. He was already 11 years old when he took his first ballet lessons. He was 17 when he was admitted to Leningrad's Kirov School.

The docu makes clear that Nureyev wanted to escape to the West to explore his artistic freedom. Had he remained a "prisoner" in Russia, he would have performed in a narrow and conventional ballet repertoire instead of pursuing a diversity of challenges eventually encompassing choreography from George Balanchine to Martha Graham.

It may never be made, but what is called for is a complete biopic of the dancer's life, including his whirlwind social life and his notorious sexual history. He was diagnosed with HIV in 1984, but defied the disease for nearly a decade as he directed the Paris Opera Ballet among other achievements.

At least the docu sheds new light on the unknown years of this towering figure whose fame reached far beyond the ballet stage.

Open Cam

(2005)

Serial Killer Roams Gay Sex Website

The tagline of this film was, "the Internet's not just for sex anymore." Directed and written by Robert Gaston, *Open Cam* is a comedy/drama/mystery/thriller wherein a DC-based gay sex website becomes home for a serial killer with a flair for exhibitionism.

Manny Yates (Andreau Thomas) is a rising young artist whose secret obsession involves cruising the web for possible sexual liaisons. He soon finds himself out of his clothes and into deep trouble when he witnesses a murder online. Think a 21st-century version of Alfred Hitchcock's *Rear Window*.

Hamilton (Amir Darvish), a studly detective, shows up to solve the case and, while he's at it, to top Manny. The original film featured some male nudity, including bubble butts. But the DVD bonus features have more steamy scenes, including shots of guys jerking off and erect dicks on screen. Yes, our hunky hero, Manny Yates, shows it hard.

One fan, who found Andreau Thomas the hottest man on the planet, claimed that *Open Cam* "successfully puts the Cock into Hitchcock."

WHAT THE CRITICS SAID
"*Open Cam* sports some surprisingly high production values, giving all the scenes a slick and polished look that goes far in suspending disbelief. And believe me, that suspension requires some heavy lifting. Just don't spend too much time wondering why a sex hook-up site that broadcast multiple live castration murders of users would ever have traffic again. . . . A couple plot holes aside, *Open Cam* is worth the ride. . . . Oh, and there's a lot of sex, if you're into that."
Sean Bugg, *Washington Metro Weekly*

Other Voices, Other Rooms

(1995)

A Boy's Turbulent Odyssey in the Deep South

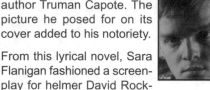

Published in 1948, the novel, *Other Voices, Other Rooms,* brought instant fame to gay author Truman Capote. The picture he posed for on its cover added to his notoriety.

From this lyrical novel, Sara Flanigan fashioned a screenplay for helmer David Rocksavage. Together they have captured the Deep South of live oaks and Spanish moss from which Capote emerged. In a nutshell, *Other Voices* is the story of a gay teen and the summer he spent with a gay relative, but it is so much more than that.

The actual homosexual references in the book seemed to be skirted around in the film adaptation. Capote could be no more thrilled with this adaptation than he was of the movie *Breakfast at Tiffany's.* For the role of Holly Golightly, instead of Audrey Hepburn, he wanted Marilyn Monroe.

Joel Sansom (David Speck) arrives at a decaying plantation to meet his father who he hasn't encountered in nearly a decade. There's a puzzle surrounding his father's ailment. He meets Randolph (Lothaire Bluteau in a command performance), who discloses hidden secrets about his mysterious relationship with Joel's father. As Amy Skully, Anna Thompson plays the bitter mistress of the seedy mansion.

Seen in flashback, we learn of Randolph's unrequited obsession for a prizefighter in Havana, which led to a tragic accident involving Joel's father.

The role of Joel is masterfully acted, depicting an early teen tossed into a decadent world. He must escape to remain sane.

WHAT THE CRITICS SAID
"In evoking Randolph's homosexuality and Joel's possible identification with it, the Capote novel is muted and evasive, suffused with a sad romantic music. The movie scrupulously avoids psychological modernization, leaving Randolph's confessions of his tormented triangle with a woman and a fiery Cuban boxer (managed by Joel's father) as inexplicit as they are in the novel."
Stephen Holden, *The New York Times*

Our House

(2000)

Reinventing the Family

This is one of the best looks at the changing face of the American family. Director Meema Spadola brings to life the inner workings of five gay families of varying backgrounds. The locales range from Arizona and Arkansas to New Jersey and New York.

Depicted are the sons and daughters of five families in rainbow-hued colors—Latin and white; Mormon, Christian, Jewish, and African-American. If anything, the scope of America's gay and lesbian families will come as a surprise to some, who think the American family is still *Ozzie and Harriet* from the 1950s TV sitcom.

Originally broadcast as a TV docu, the film was made by the daughter of a lesbian mom. First seen on public television in June 2000, it was later rebroadcast on the Sundance channel and has been shown at various gay and lesbian film festivals across the country.

In DVD, it also comes with special extras, such as updates on the families, a conversation with filmmaker Meema Spadola and participant Ry Russo-Young, plus other depictions.

WHAT THE CRITICS SAID
"The children's voices are loud, clear, revelatory. Raw, poignant, and humorous, this film will amaze, teach, and inspire."
Barbara Seyda

"Clearly a labor of love."
Rolling Stone

"An uplifting portrait of a situation clearly more common than some might think."
Entertainment Weekly

Our Lady of the Assassins

(*La virgin de los sicarios;* 2000)

You Can't Go Home Again

This is about the tempestuous love between Fernando (Germán Jaramillo), a 60-year-old man, and a 16-year-old boy, Alexis (Anderson Ballesteros). The older man has returned to his hometown, Medellín (Colombia) to die. He finds that it is now the crime-ridden drug capital of the world, through which billions of dollars in illegal money is regularly funneled.

This subtitled Spanish-language film was based on a semi-autobiographical novel by Fernando Vallejo, who also wrote the script for helmer Barbet Schroeder. The director also helmed *Reversal of Fortune,* the story of Claus von Bulow, and *General Idi Amin Dada,* a docu about the fanatical neuroses of Uganda's dictator-killer.

Back in his hometown, Fernando, a homosexual, learns that everybody he knows from 30 years ago is dead. He also discovers that teenage boys are systematically being dragged into a life of crime, becoming assassins.

Fernando meets the teenage Alexis and falls in love with him, dismayed that the boy kills far too easily, often on a whim. When Alexis himself is fatally shot, the grief-stricken Fernando hunts for his young lover's killer in the Medellin slums.

Here he encounters Wilmar (Juan David Restrepo) who bears an uncanny resemblance to the slain Alexis.

Fernando takes Wilmar as a lover, only to discover that Wilmar killed Alexis. But it was Alexis that killed Wilmar's brother. The plot deadens with this shocking news.

WHAT THE CRITICS SAID
"Can a man of 60 have a romantic relationship with a boy of 16? In a sane world, no. They would drive each other crazy. In a world where both expect to die in the immediate future, where plans are meaningless, where poverty of body and soul has left them starving in different ways, there is something to be said for sex, wine, music, and killing time in safety. Fernando and his boys share the same cool disinterest in tomorrow."
Roger Ebert

Our Sons

(1991)

Coming to Terms with Her Son's Gay Life

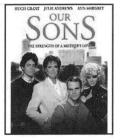

This made-for-TV drama needs to be better known, if for no other reason than its cast. Hugh Grant plays gay son James, and the mothers include Ann-Margret (in a blonde wig) and Julie Andrews.

A young man, Donald (Zeljko Ivanek), is dying of AIDS. His lover James asks his own mother Audrey (Andrews), a supercharged San Diego business person, to fly to Arkansas to persuade Luanne (a tell-it-like-it-is country girl, as played by Ann-Margret) if she'll reconcile, face to face, with her son before it's too late. Luanne, a divorced, working-class mother with an Arkansas twang, has not been on speaking terms with her grown-up son.

The rich, successful Audrey agrees to visit the Arkansas home (a trailer park) of her son's lover. Ever the elitist, Audrey arrives by limousine and convinces Luanne to fly with her to California for a final farewell to her dying son. On their way to his deathbed, the two women discover that they have more in common than they realized.

Donald was thrown out of his home at the age of sixteen when his parents found out he was gay. Luanne's love for her dying son eventually wins out over her prejudice. Donald dies peacefully in California, with Luanne, Audrey, and James in attendance, and Luanne commits herself to hauling his body back to Arkansas for burial.

The film resolves the dilemma: Before you can accept a son's death, you must accept his life.

WHAT THE CRITICS SAID
"The telefilm works through chunks of two-role scenes to build its case against homophobia and against the ignorance of AIDS. All is correctly written, but an emotional wallop is lacking. Grant acts movingly in his scenes with Ivanek, whose makeup is crushingly realistic."
Variety

"Of the two actresses, only Ann-Margret is able to free herself from the movie manacles and perform in a way that touches you. Andrews sort of goes along for the elegant limo ride."
Howard Rosenberg, *Los Angeles Times*

Out of Hand

(2005)

Tragedy in a Teen Wasteland in Germany

This 92-minute German film tells the story of two 16-year-old boys, Sebastian and Paul. Bored with school and homelife, they set out on self-created adventures, stealing liquor, drinking, and bonding. A wolf-like nature deep inside each boy attracts them to each other. Gradually Sebastian falls in love with Paul, but he can't admit that to himself.

They discover a disused factory owned by Sebastian's father and turn it into a lair away from the eyes of the world. On a dare, they abduct Sonja, a woman in her early 30s, and tie her up in the factory. Fear and lust rule the day. They don't really know what to do with their prisoner. They try out a number of ideas.

The deserted factory is discovered by Chris, Sonja's boyfriend. But rescue is not immediate. Chris blames her for creating this mess. He soon ends up just as helpless as Sonja.

Tensions mount as Sebastian clutches his father's gun. He loses all vestiges of self-control. A shot rings out.

The fun and games are over.

WHAT THE CRITICS SAID
"Here's a nasty little German story of teens gone bad. This little triangle could get messy because the last thing you want to do to the unstable Sebastian is get his jealousy fired up. It's interesting how the movie pulls itself into a long holding pattern, leaving you wondering how it will resolve. Eventually it will take a misguided trip back to town by Paul to force an exciting and ugly climax. Given that in Hollywood it's usually male writers and directors who like to see women tied up, it's interesting to note that *Out of Hand* is helmed by Eva Urthaler. While it's not exactly a story of a brave woman conquering her two assailants, the victim does exhibit some smarts and 'girl power' in trying to stay alive, no small trick given Sebastian's rapidly crumbling sanity."
Dom Willmott

Out of the Closet, Off the Screen:
The Life of William Haines

(2001)

William Haines

In 1930 William Haines was America's Number One Box Office Star. But by 1935 his film career was only a memory.

This 45-minute docu of Hollywood's first openly gay star originally premiered on *American Movie Classics.*
Haines was definitely on the A-list of stars, and a frequent guest of William Randolph Hearst and Marion Davies at their castle in San Simeon.

His best female friend was Joan Crawford, whom he called "Cranberry." But when studio chief Louis B. Mayer learned that he had a male lover and liked to suck dick and fuck sailors, plus other rough trade on the side, he was ordered to dump his lover, Jimmie Shields. Haines refused to do that, and Mayer sent him into what he thought would be oblivion.

But Haines was very resourceful and launched himself into a second career as an interior decorator. As such, he decorated the homes of some of the biggest stars in Hollywood, including Carole Lombard in her pre-Clark Gable days. (Incidentally, in a bit of Hollywood lore on the side, Haines in the late 20s once fucked the bisexual Gable.)

"Billy Haines is one of the forgotten giants of the silent era," said Marc Juris, executive vice president of AMC. "Even though he was the number one male box office star, he did something that a lot of people wouldn't have had the courage to do."

"This is a man who sacrificed his career for the man he loved," said the executive producer of the film, Fenton Bailey. "It also will take a rare look at Hollywood's ongoing struggle with how to deal with homosexuality."

Haines, who once "roomed" in Greenwich Village with Cary Grant, often played callow, cock-sure collegians in comedy/dramas. He first came to major American attention in *Brown of Harvard* in 1926.

Amazingly, Haines became as desired as a decorator as he was as a star during his heyday.

Outrage

(2009)

Outing Homophobic Gay Politicians

That hypocritic Idaho senator Larry Craig became a household name for allegedly soliciting sex from an undercover detective in the toilet of a men's room. It's called playing footsies. Craig later claimed, "I'm not gay. I have never been gay." Yeah, right.

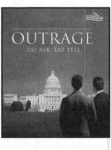

Before getting caught with his pants down, Craig in the Senate had voted adamantly against issues important to the rights of gays.

In this docu, he emerges as a key member of a D.C-based group of "hypocritical" male politicians, each of whom support anti-gay legislation but who are believed to privately have sex with men.

Appearing as themselves is an array of famous names, including Tony Kushner, Barney Frank, Larry Kramer, and James McGreevey, the former governor of New Jersey. The docu also features interviews with journalists, activists, and media personalities. Frank, a formerly closeted politician himself, claims, "There's a right to privacy, not to hypocrisy."

Former NYC mayor Ed Koch is the only prominent Democrat outed in the film. Gay activist David Rothenberg accuses him of having dumped his longtime boyfriend for the more powerful aphrodisiac of political power.

WHAT THE CRITICS SAID
"The director, Kirby Dick, does back up his allegations with firsthand accounts, and he makes an excellent case for outing those actively trying to deny other Americans their civil rights. But without a deeper exploration of the issues he raises, some of the accusations feel more sordid than satisfying."
Elizabeth Weitzman, *New York Daily News*

"It is beyond the resources of any film to prove conclusively the sexual orientation of people such as Sen. Craig, California Rep. David Dreier, and Florida Gov. Charlie Crist. Still, Dick is awfully persuasive."
Kenneth Turan, *Los Angeles Times*

Outrageous

(1977)

The World's Greatest Female Impersonator

A Canadian entertainer, Craig Russell (1948-1990) may have been the greatest female impersonator of all time. Before he contracted AIDS and drank and drugged himself to an early death, he did uncanny impersonations of his favorite ladies, includ-

ing Carol Channing, Bette Davis, Peggy Lee, Mae West, Barbra Streisand, Tallulah Bankhead, Marlene Dietrich, Bette Midler, Judy Garland, and a devastating take on the homophobic OJ queen, Anita Bryant.

Toronto's most flamboyant hairdresser was also a personal secretary for a while to the incomparable Mae West, where he learned all her secrets, or so he claimed. By the way, she was a real woman, not a transvestite as rumored.

Based on *Making It*, a book by Margaret Gibson, *Outrageous* is the story of a female impersonator, Craig himself, who rooms with a pregnant schizophrenic.

Actress Hollis McLaren as Craig's friend Liza urges him to give up hairdressing, move to New York, and make it as a female impersonator. He was on his way. The world could have been his, but he blew it by appearing drunk and/or drugged at just too many performances, including a mega-gig at Carnegie Hall where the audience walked out on him.

WHAT THE CRITICS SAID
"Almost any description of *Outrageous* makes it sound like a sensational exploitation film but that's exactly what it isn't. It's a bittersweet, endearing, sometimes funny little slice of life, and when you describe it as the story of a friendship between a transvestite and a schizophrenic, you have to add that they're loyal and human and deserve one another."
Roger Ebert

"It's the best film made up to now on drag shows, the gay world, and the trials and tribulations of the homosexual. But it's a human story of a relationship. The dialogue between these misfits carries the pic with refreshing ease from start to finish."
Variety

P.S. Your Cat is Dead

(2002)

Life, Love, and Payback

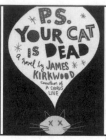

The late writer James Kirkwood (co-author of *A Chorus Line* for which he won the Pulitzer Prize) was to the theater born. His father, James Kirkwood Sr., directed (and had an affair with) Mary Pickford. His mother, the silent screen actress, Lila Lee, co-starred with Valentino in *Blood and Sand*.

Along comes his play *P.S. Your Cat Is Dead*, which had a brief run on Broadway before hitting the road. Sal Mineo in Los Angeles was in rehearsals for it when he was fatally stabbed.

As a labor of love, Steve Guttenberg directed the movie based on his own script. Back when he was making *Three Men and a Baby*, his career was more first rate.

In this movie, he stars as Jimmy Zoole, a failed actor and novelist on his worst day. His girlfriend has dumped him, his most recent show has bombed, and his cat has just died.

Entering his apartment, he discovers a burglary in progress. The crafty burglar (Lombardo Boyar) just happens to be gay in his role of Eddie Tesoro. Jimmy's apartment has been burgled twice in recent months.

Jimmy overpowers Eddie and ties him to the kitchen sink. Once secured, he has to decide what to do with him. At one point he brandishes a butcher knife; at another, the two men are having heart-to-heart talks, getting to know each other's *angst*.

Jimmy now has another problem to face: Is he a closeted homosexual?

WHAT THE CRITICS SAID
"It's tough to generate sympathy for Guttenberg's character and his juvenile case of homosexual panic. He whines, he throws garbage at his girl-friend, and when she returns to the apartment and finds a bare-bottomed burglar tied to the sink—thereby assuming that her ex has suddenly turned queer—Guttenberg cackles madly, as if 'turning gay' were a spurned lover's best revenge."
Edward Guthman

Pageant

(2008)

There She Is, Miss Gay America

Ron Davis and Stewart Halpern-Fingerhut, helmers and writers, went behind the scenes in this docu to prove that on occasion boys will be girls. With all its sequins, glitter, and fab falsies, the film highlights an annual *Miss Gay America* pageant, this one taking place in Memphis (what would Elvis think?).

By the time Victor/Victoria appears shaking her booty in a short baby-blue dress, you're really into faux women. Off the stage, she's known as Victor Bowley. This plus-size diva says, "Call me Pork Chop—everybody does!"

Leopard-print stilettos have hardly been filled so astonishingly, as you get old-fashioned Hollywood glamour and plenty of lip-synching: Liza with a Z, and Judy, Judy, Judy, Fosse, Fosse, Fosse, even Reba McEntire, and, of course, staged numbers from *Chicago* and *Dreamgirls*.

One viewer gave this opinion: "Drag queens are essentially grown men who haven't outgrown playing dress-up." In many cases, these glamorous gals are part of an ugly-duckling-turned-swan narrative. As men, they are less enticing, and no doubt encountered many a school bully in their younger days.

In many ways, these "gals" take the pageant as seriously as their scepter-wielding sisters. Friends and often family members are here to cheer their sons on to victory, which means a tiara, a scepter, and $7,000 in cash prizes.

The drag queens aren't enhanced trannies who pitch their wares on Craigslist. The officials at the pageant forbid hormones and surgical body enhancement. This is not a *Miss California* contest.

Of all the 50 contestants, only two make a living in night clubs as female impersonators. Others have ordinary jobs where they wear pants. One works at Disney World, for example, as a guide. What would Walt say?

One hopeful revealed that she used to be a backup singer at Jimmy Swaggart's ministries.

Pansy Division

(2008)

A Gay Rock Band-Queercore and Punk

Undeniably one of the most important and influential gay music acts in the past 20 years, *Pansy Division* provides an essential history of a genre of alternative music that is only now beginning to be appreciated.

Pansy Division was founded in 1991 in San Francisco (where else?) by Chris Freeman and Jon Ginoli. As the men told the press, "We wanted to be what we didn't see when we were growing up." As was known at the time, most gays were into retro-disco and show tunes. Gay Rock heroes such as Melissa Etheridge were still in the closet.

Their song titles seemed to draw inspiration from *Queer Nation*, and lyrics were raunchy—"Rachbottomoff," "Touch My Joe Camel," "Crabby Day," "Fem in a Black Leather Jacket," "James Bondage," and "Bill & Ted's Homosexual Adventure."

The indie rock club circuit, often liberal straight punks, look to them like female impersonators to cock-sucking. At Madison Square garden they were the opening act for rising pop punk stars Green Day.

But one segment of the audience—you know the type, frat boys with big egos and small dicks—threw bottles at the gay band and heckled them as "faggots."

In both original and archival footage, helmer Michael Carmona employed Chris Freeman, Jon Ginoli, and Larry Livermore as themselves.

In spite of their notoriety and growing fan base among gays, Pansy Division did not sign up with a major label, the uptight music executives rejecting their act as "too gay."

WHAT THE CRITICS SAID
"Members' often jokily racy songs are perhaps ideally experienced in excerpt—complete with subtitled lyrics—making this a docu whose prankish DIY charms reflect the spirit of its subject."
Dennis Harvey, *Variety*

Paper Dolls

(2006)

Transsexuals in Israel

Paper Dolls, written and directed by award-winning filmmaker Tomer Heymann, is a docu about a group of pre-op transsexual Filipino immigrants in Israel. By day they take jobs as home attendants for elderly Israelis, but by night they perform as drag entertainers in Tel Aviv nightclubs.

In this low-budget film, interviews with the ladies are mingled with their observations of daily life in a strange new country that doesn't always tolerate them with ease.

WHAT THE CRITICS SAID
"They [the Paper Dolls] fit in as best they can, speaking pretty good Hebrew and ignoring the occasional stares that come their way, especially in the Orthodox neighborhoods where they work. Most have mixed feelings about their temporary home, which is a more open, less sexually repressive society than the one they left, but also one they find to be cold, materialistic, and bureaucratic. The documentary seeks to illuminate a subculture without allowing its curiosity to become exploitative or prurient."
A.O. Scott, *The New York Times*

"The director, a gay man himself, does not conceal his bias and prejudice when he introduces and interviews the main characters of his film. It is interesting and sweet witnessing how he sheds his own homophobia (tranniephobia, should we say?) and develops respect and affection."
Rafael Solis

"When Israel closed its borders to Palestinian labor in 2000, an influx of 300,000 foreign guest workers flooded into the country to fill the shortage. Among them were a quintet of Filipino caregivers docu-helmer Tomer Heymann found while attending a gay nightclub. The five (Sally, Cheska, Chiqui, Giorgio, and Jan) all perform as a lip-synch collectively known as 'The Paper Dolls.' The filmmaker arranges an audition for 'The Paper Dolls' with the owner of a prominent night club. For a while, it seems as if the group's shared dream to succeed as professional performers may be fulfilled."
Russell Edwards

Paragraph 175

(2000)

Queer Resistance Fighters Opposing the Nazis

"An unnatural sex act committed between persons of the male sex or by humans with animals is punishable by imprisonment; the loss of civil rights may also be imposed."

That is Paragraph 175 of the German Penal Code, passed into law in 1871. During the Weimar Republic, this law was largely ignored. Berlin, in fact, evolved during the 1920s and early 30s into what was called "a homosexual Eden." The Nazis, however, twisted this law to their own cruel purposes. Between 1933 and 1945, 100,000 men were arrested for homosexuality—either imprisoned or sent to death camps.

With Rupert Everett as narrator, historian Klaus Müller interviews survivors of the Nazi persecution of homosexuals. Only a handful of frail survivors remain to recount the traumas they suffered under Hitler's brutal regime.

East Germany reverted to the old version of the law in 1950, limiting its scope to sex with youths 18 and under in 1968, and abolished it completely in 1988. Shockingly West Germany retained the Nazi-era statute until 1969, though limited to "qualified cases," whatever the hell that meant. The law was modified again in 1973 and finally revoked entirely in 1994 after German reunification. Shockingly, some of the men interviewed as witnesses were re-arrested under this draconian law after the defeat of the Nazis in 1945.

This film emerges as a compelling depiction of human resilience in the face of unspeakable cruelty. "I am ashamed for humanity," relates one of the survivors.

WHAT THE CRITICS SAID
"*Paragraph 175* touches on gay resistance fighters and victims, but also gay Nazis and sympathizers. The tales told are bitter, horrific in detail—yet often leavened with irony and humor. Rupert Everett's low-key narration serves the film well."
Elliott Stein, *Village Voice*

Paris Is Burning

(1990)

The Fine Art of "Vogueing"

No, this is not a film about Hitler ordering the burning of Paris before the inevitable Nazi retreat in the wake of an Allied advance, although the title suggests that.

Director Jennie Livingston takes us on a tour of *fashionistas* who created "voguing" and drag balls, turning these raucous celebrations into a powerful expression of personal pride.

Voguing, of course, is a dance invented by black and Latino gay men on the streets of Manhattan long before Madonna made it famous on MTV. In the words of Joe Brown, it's about "combining the stiff, haughty poses struck by high-fashion models with acrobatic spins and dips, evolving as a competition from the black gay traditions of 'reading' (razor-sharp, fast-slashing, finger-snapping verbal abuse) and 'shade' (attitude, the body language version of reading)." You got all that?

WHAT THE CRITICS SAID
"*Paris Is Burning* is a poignant and profound unsentimental and unexploitative examination of a subculture that until now has been invisible to most Americans. Built around elaborately staged mock fashion balls, this alternative world of black and Latin gay men and lesbians has its own elaborate jargon and its own intricate social structure, the self-protective hierarchy of 'houses.' These substitute extended families (or 'gay street gangs,' as one voguer puts it) knock themselves out to imitate society that, ironically, will not have them."
The Washington Post

"*Paris Is Burning* combines footage shot at several balls and interviews with some of the participants. From the competitions, we see the bizarre mated with the mundane, as when there are dress categories such as 'the gay basher who beats you up on the way here tonight.' The competitors are scored by a panel of judges who hold up cardboards with point scores on them—just like in the Olympic diving competitions. The interviews make it clear that some of the competitors—who can look so affluent and 'real' in their expensive costumes—lead marginal lives as hustlers and thieves."
Roger Ebert

Paris Was a Woman

(1995)

Lesbian Legends Between the Wars

Paris in the 20s and 30s wasn't all Ernest Hemingway, Pablo Picasso, F. Scott Fitzgerald, Ezra Pound, and James Joyce. Women (many of them lesbians) who were artists, writers, photographers, designers, and just plain adventurers also settled into the City of Light at that time, and had a profound influence on the culture of Paris. Home movies, rare archival footage, photographs, and interviews bring this fermenting period to life again.

None of the American ex-pats were as famous and celebrated as Gertrude Stein and Alice B. Toklas, the ruling duennas of the day, especially Miss Stein, who once told Hemingway that he had never faced up to his homosexuality.

But there were so many others on parade as well. Acerbic writer Djuana Barnes and the love of her life, Thelma Woods, are introduced, as is painter Romaine Brooks. Heiress Natalie Barney was known for her literary salons, and Janet Flanner went to Paris with a girlfriend in 1923 and stayed for 40 years to write columns for *The New Yorker*.

Other subjects include Sylvia Beach, Gisele Freund, Adrienne Monnier, Berenice Abbot, largely forgotten figures today, but cultural icons of the 20s and 30s.

WHAT THE CRITICS SAID
"Though ultimately flying under false colors, *Paris Is a Woman* still emerges as a very watchable docu on Left Bank artsy expatriates between the wars, and it was painstakingly researched. Main problem is that the film is simply not about its professed subject. Pic purports to be a gender-balancing look at the femme side of the coin, showing there was more to the city's international artistic community than guys like Joyce and Hemingway. More by design than accident, however, the docu focuses solely on lesbian participants and, given their uneven accomplishments, ends up more as an intriguing footnote on a community of sexual self-exiles than a convincing argument that artistic history should be rewritten in any major way."
Derek Elley, *Variety*

Parting Glances

(1986)

A Milestone in the Depiction of Gays

This film by Bill Sherwood, both the helmer and scripter, is a landmark in gay cinema. Its most ardent fans call it "the best gay film ever made." We wouldn't go that far, however.

Although perhaps dated in today's context, *Parting Glances* does not treat gays as sexual stereotypes, but as sensitive human beings, consenting adults going about their lives with its love and tragedies, even death from AIDS. Incidentally, Sherwood would not make another movie. He died of complications from AIDS in 1990.

Basically, it's the story of Michael (Richard Ganoung) and Robert (John Bolger), a gay couple in New York. Robert is preparing to depart for a two-year assignment in Kenya, which may end their six-year relationship. Robert must face his lover's true motives for leaving while dealing with their circle of eccentric friends, including Nick (Steve Buscemi) who is living with AIDS.

This film shouldn't really be called a gay movie. It's a story of gay characters dealing with life.

Parting Glances was ahead of its time. It beat *And the Band Played On, Longtime Companion,* and *Philadelphia* to the screen in its depiction of AIDS.

It was also ahead of its time in its depiction of a same-sex relationship. Most films settle for implied sex or one hot sex scene. In *Parting Glances*, the two young men pepper each other with kisses and embraces, like lovers should.

WHAT THE CRITICS SAID
"*Parting Glances* was filmed at a time when the shadow of AIDS was shorter but the fear was greater than 15 years later. It showed the impact of the disease while portraying the reality of gay life in Manhattan.
Cheryl DeWolfe

"It's definitely very 80s, including music from *Bronski Beat*, and enough wing-backed hair to make a flock of seagulls jealous. Yet it's still a powerful and moving portrait.
Brett Cullum

The Path to Love
(AKA *The Road to Love*)

(Le chemin d'amour; 2001)

Going Gay Among the Arabs

This French-Algerian film is a quasi-docu that interweaves a student's fictive making of a docu with his meditation on the role of homosexuality in various Arab cultures.

The student in Paris is Karim (Karim Tarek). His willowy frame and large, expressive eyes are likened by his girlfriend Sihem to the yearning orbs of Vermeer's *Girl With a Pearl Earring.* That doting girlfriend is played by Sihem Benamoune. Obviously the two leads chose to use their first names.

Eventually, Karim has to ask the question. Did he choose homosexuality as the subject of his docu project because unconsciously it revealed his preference for men?

First he has to track down gay Muslims to interview. He hangs out in front of a gay tea shop in Paris and even places an ad in a newspaper. Naturally, all of his respondents come on strong to this cute boy.

Along comes a potential Mr. Right in the shape of Farid (Riyard Echali), a young flight attendant who knows a lot of gay Muslims in Paris and elsewhere. Soon Farid begins to fall in love with Karim.

Produced and directed by Rémi Lange, *The Path to Love* follows a well-worn trail as Karim flies off to Marrakesh in Morroco for a romantic weekend with Farid.

WHAT THE CRITICS SAID
"Homosexual relationships are tolerated in many Muslim cultures as an outlet for pent-up desires that must otherwise wait until marriage. There was even one relatively modern culture, centered in the Siwa oasis in Egypt, where marriage ceremonies between men were performed, though those marriages dissolved when the time for grown-up reproductive coupling arrived. Only passive homosexuality, Farid explains to Karim, is considered truly shameful. Sex, in other words, is power, in which a sense of domination counts for everything—not, alas, a notion exclusive to the Arab world."
Dave Kehr, *The New York Times*

Patrik 1.5

(Patrik Age 1.5; 2008)

A Gay Adoption That Begins in Hell

This comedy/drama from Sweden, directed and scripted by Ella Lemhagen, tells of a gay couple who adopt what they think is a 15-month-old orphan only to meet their new son, a 15-year-old homophobic juvenile delinquent.

Blame it on a typo. The gay couple had requested a boy age 1.5, not 15 years old.

Even if you can figure out the ending by the time the son arrives on the doorsteps of his new home, the film is amusing—never maudlin or syrupy—though devoid of surprises.

Gustaf Skarsgård as Göran and Torkel Peterson as Sven were well chosen for their roles as a loving gay couple, with Thomas Ljungman playing the son, Patrick, a problem child with a criminal past.

In spite of his new marriage to a man, Sven still maintains a friendly relationship with ex-spouse Eva (Annika Hallin), who often drops in for a meal with her teenage daughter Isabell (Amanda Davin), a sulky Goth Lolita. Eva is a vocal supporter of the couple's right to adopt.

All the actors, even the kid, give nuanced and believable performances. The gay relationship is handled rather straightforwardly with no leering, no condemnation. There is a brief scene of homophobia in this very straight neighborhood in which the two men reside.

As one viewer put it, "*Patrik 1.5* is predictable in terms of where it is going, but it is one of those films in which the journey—not the destination—is what matters."

WHAT THE CRITICS SAID
"*Patrik 1.5* tells us an old story, but one that's still the best: that even though life is messy and complicated and imperfect, it's still possible to be happy. It's been a long time since a movie has so perfectly achieved this uplifting affect. And if you'd told me a gay Swedish adoption comedy with a country-music soundtrack would have achieved this I would have laughed in disbelief."
Sarah Manvel

<table>
<tr><td>

Pedro

(2008)

Young Gay Latino Fighting AIDS

</td><td>

Personal Best

(1982)

When a Lesbian Film Is Not a Lesbian Film

</td></tr>
</table>

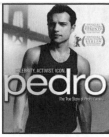

If you don't know who Pedro is, much of the drama of this film by director Nick Oceano will be lost on you. Pedro Zamora was an AIDS activist who appeared on *The Real World: San Francisco* and put a face on the disease for the American public in the early 90s. Sadly, he died just after this film was shown on TV.

He generated a public debate among those who had never known anyone who was HIV positive. He even caught the attention of President Bill Clinton, who provides an introduction for the DVD version of this film.

Alex Loynaz tries nobly to bring Pedro to the screen, not always succeeding. The screen version was scripted by Dustin Lance Black, who was an Oscar winner for his *Milk* screenplay. Depicted is Pedro's life, including his childhood in Havana where he was the youngest of eight children. His emigration to the United States is shown, as well as his hard work as an AIDS activist who even testified before Congress.

Pedro learned he had AIDS when he was 17, and he lived until he was 22, his death generated front-page news across the country, his too early departure provoking a nationwide outpouring of grief.

Helmer Nick Oceano re-creates the most dramatic moments in Pedro's life.

WHAT THE CRITICS SAID
"A more moving tribute to Pedro Zamora was created by MTV in 1994 when they did a special honoring his memory. Also, if you can track down the graphic novel, Judd Winnick's *Pedro and Me,* it is a moving remembrance of Zamora. Asking people to play reality stars poses a unique acting challenge, and perhaps we should not ask thespians to do that. What's the true point, when we have actual film of these people to look back on and honor their legacy?"
Brett Cullum

As an actor, Mariel Hemingway had the defining moment of her career playing the athlete Chris Cahill in this story of intertwined lives and loves of two highly ranked athletes striving for the national team. For her, the role was her *Personal Best.*

The film came as a surprise from Robert Towne, its helmer and scripter. He had given the world screenplays like *Chinatown, Shampoo,* and *Bonnie and Clyde. Personal Best* emerged as his directing debut.

Two female athletes, Chris (Mariel Hemingway) and Tory Tingloff (Patrice Donnelly), meet at the 1976 Olympic trials and become lovers. Their relationship becomes strained as they compete.

Much of the film is devoted to running, pole-vaulting, and hurdling, as well as swimming. What shocked viewers back in 1982 was the movie's lesbianism.

Both the film's director and its star seemed in denial of its subject matter.

On the *Today* Show, she claimed, "For me the love scenes never seemed homosexual. The scene is not explicit. You don't see anything!"

The Advocate challenged her. What you see are two women naked in bed, caressing each other, legs wrapped around each other.

But Ms. Hemingway didn't find that explicit because the viewer didn't see "them going down on each other."

Even though the film dwells on the two women being together for three years, Ms. Hemingway felt, "It's not a statement about lesbians at all!" What would Papa Hemingway have called it then?

As could be predicted in a film that was not about lesbianism, Chris trades in Tory for a male athlete, Kenny Moore (Denny Stites). The three starring parts were rounded out by Scott Glenn playing Terry Tingloff, coach to Chris.

Philadelphia

(1993)

HIV/AIDS and Homophobia

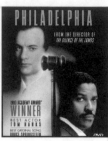

Forrest Gump as a gay man? Hard to believe. But Tom Hanks, cast as Andrew Beckett, a senior associate in a Philadelphia law firm, pulls it off. The story was based on the case of Geoffrey Bowers, an attorney who in 1987 sued the law firm of Baker & McKenzie for unfair dismissal in one of the first AIDS discrimination cases.

With Denzel Washington as Hanks' lawyer and Antonio Banderas as Hanks' lover, and also starring Jason Robards and Joanne Woodward, *Philadelphia* is perhaps the best film ever shot about gays and homophobia.

Hanks won an Oscar as Best Actor that year. *Philadelphia* was the second big budget movie to tackle the issue of AIDS, following in the wake of the TV movie, *And the Band Played On*. The Hanks' movie marked the most realistic depiction of gays on the screen at that time. Even so, director Jonathan Demme, fearing a backlash from the straight public, removed a scene with Hanks and Banderas in bed together.

During the trial, Beckett collapses on the stand. While he is hospitalized for treatment of his disease, the jury votes in his favor, awarding him back pay, damages for pain and suffering, and punitive damages.

WHAT THE CRITICS SAID
"Set in the City of Brotherly Love for ironic reasons, *Philadelphia,* like so many classics of this lofty genre (*To Kill a Mockingbird*), tries the beliefs of the American people. Are they as noble as they imagine? Is not this a land where all men are created equal—or must they be straight men?"
Rita Kempley, *Washington Post*

"For a filmmaker who thrives on taking chances, *Philadelphia* sounds like the biggest gamble of all. Jonathan Demme's film has stubborn preconceptions to overcome as well as enormous potential to make waves. Yet it does not have is much evidence of Demme's acual daring. Maybe that's not surprising: It isn't easy to leave fingerprints when you're wearing kid gloves."
Janet Maslin, *The New York Times*

Pick up the Mic

(2006)

Queer Hip-Hop

File this under the category of what will filmmakers think of next. Imagine a controversial documentary dealing with the world of queer hip-hop, and we thought all hip-hop music makers were homophobic. Alex Hinton filmed searing public performances from such artists as QBoy, J.B. Rap, Marcus Rene Van, and Tim'm T. West.

Running for 95 minutes, it makes a full-feature film, but for what circuit? One viewer who caught the flick at the Sarasota Film Festival accurately summed up the plight of many of the artists featured. "After sitting through the stories of the artists involved, you learn that all they really want is to be taken seriously as musicians. They aren't just trying to push the envelope with being gay/lesbian/transgendered rappers; they are trying to make music that people can relate to."

This is a film about a gay culture within the unforgiving hip-hop industry. It brings its own sensitivity to this form of often cruel music. We were left wondering what that little snot, Eminem, with his gay-bashing lyrics, would think of *Pick Up the Mic*.

WHAT THE CRITICS SAID
"You know this isn't an ordinary hip-hop doc the minute a bouncy rapper drops a shout-out to 'all the TGs in the heezee.' Tracing the history of LGBT rap from the late '80s, Alex Hinton's boisterous doc skimps a bit on the backstory, tossing off references to the heyday of pioneers Rainbow Flava as if they're a household name, but its copious performance footage makes an instant case that queer hip-hop deserves a much larger place in the pop-cult sphere. A few rappers, like the rhythm-impaired Johnny Dangerous, come off as little more than novelty acts, but the varispeed rhymes of San Francisco's Deepdickcollective are enough to send any hip-hop fan searching for MP3s. Mic's focus on performance footage documents the music's audience as well as its artists, although it's too bad we have to wait till the end credits to see if the music's production is as radical as its lyrics."
Philadelphia City Paper

The Picture of Dorian Gray

(2006)

A Modern Adaptation of the Wilde Classic

Duncan Roy has updated and adapted the Oscar Wilde classic tale of vanity and brought it to the screen once again. He cast David Gallagher as Dorian. The handsome young Gallagher, of course, made his film debut with the lead role in *Who's Talking Now* (1993) alongside John Travolta. In 1996 he landed the role of Simon Camden in the TV series, *7th Heaven*.

This latest version of Dorian is more homoerotic than earlier screen versions. It is sexually graphic, including one very hot same-sex scene. As the director was quoted, "We just put the 'gay' back in *Dorian Gray*—I can't help but think that Oscar Wilde would be proud."

Artist Basil Hallward (Noah Segan) has become obsessed with Dorian Gray whose beauty is the focus of a new portrait installation. When the young Dorian sees the installation for the first time, he resents the portrait, wishing it would grow old and ugly instead of him.

Henry Wotton (Christian Camargo) is the cynical, intellectual friend and agent of Basil Hallward. It is Henry who is responsible for Dorian's transformation from angel to devil.

Wilde's novel was first published in 1890. In his reference to it, the only novel he ever wrote, Wilde said: "There is no such thing as a moral or an immoral book. Books are well written or badly written. That is all."

WHAT THE CRITICS SAID
"Duncan Roy's Gotham-set-update of Oscar Wilde's novel flaunts a cavalier disregard for narrative logic, character development, and Wildean wit. Instead, he favors an inchoherent walkabout through New York's decadent 90s art scene, trailing a faint whiff of sour grapes and a rancid trace of homophobia. When it was shown in New York, the film dramatically polarized auds."
Ronnie Schieb

Pills Profits Protest
A Chronicle of the Global AIDS Movement

(2006)

Grass-Roots Activism Against Apathy

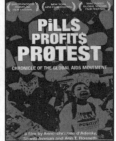

This up-to-the-minute docu about global AIDS treatment is powerful. Sometimes the world seems to ignore AIDS, although some 40 million are now at risk, with hundreds becoming affected every day.

This is a passionate and timely docu about AIDS treatment activism. The movement for access to AIDS treatment is, at heart, a highly personal battle being led by individuals who are motivated by a desire to stay alive and save their communities and, in the process, change the world. Weaving together the perspectives and experiences of activists from Durban to Delhi, from Botswana to Bahia, from Philadelphia to Port-au-Prince, a collective voice, rooted in local struggles, emerges.

This docu examines critical junctures in the battle for access to HIV treatment as the poorest and most marginalized individuals confront larger powers, including government, corporate bodies, and a multi-national drug industry that is motivated by profit.

Pills Profits and Protest are the three thematic touchstones of the film, each reflecting an important aspect of the current battle.

WHAT THE CRITICS SAID

"*Pills Profits Protest* delivers a visually stunning message."
Richard Stern

"The creator's fine filmmaking leaves you charged, energized, ready, and willing to join the fight."
Amanda Lugg

"*Pills Profits Protest* is one of the best films about AIDS I've ever seen. It's a moving portrait of the global struggle to expand treatment access for millions of poor people with HIV/AIDS, and underscores the critical role that grassroots activists are playing in forcing 'Big Pharma' and other powerful interests to adopt responsible AIDS policies."
Paul Zeitz

Pink Flamingos

(1972)

"The Filthiest Person Alive"

In spite of its repugnant nature, *Pink Flamingos* is now a camp classic. It made a star out of rotund Divine, a 300-pound actor-in-drag, and launched director John Waters on a trail of notoriety. Now restored and in re-release, the film contains profanity, nudity, graphic sex, violence, and some things not fit to be printed in a family paper.

The filthiest person alive, Divine, is using a fake name, Babs Johnson, and living in a trailer in the woods with her dysfunctional family in this outrageously sick, perverted, and disgusting movie. Waters' intention was to shock, and he did just that. *Pink Flamingos* is not for the faint of heart, which means we loved it.

Sleaze queen Divine lives with her mad hippie son, the aptly named "Crackers" (Danny Mills), who knows how to sing with his anus. Cracker also likes to involve chickens in his sex life with strange women. Playing Divine's mate is Cotton (Mary Vivian Pearce), who likes to watch her son with these strange women and chickens. Also in residence is Divine's retarded mother Eddie (Edith Massey), who sits in a crib eating eggs. A huge mountain of adipose tissue, Mama performs coprophagy on the fresh product of a miniature poodle while "How Much Is that Doggie in the Window" toodles on the soundtrack.

Divine, who in the words of one viewer dresses like a combination of showgirl, dominatrix, and Bozo, faces competition for her title. Connie (Mink Stole) and Raymond Marble (David Lochary) want to dethrone the bitch and become the filthiest couple alive. Mr. and Mrs. Marble kidnap girl hippies, chain them in a dungeon and force their butler to impregnate them. After these young girls die in childbirth, the Marbles sell their babies to lesbian couples to finance an inner-city heroin ring catering to high school students.

One scene at the end really carved a place for this film in screen history. In one of the most notorious scenes ever filmed, Divine actually ingests (no joke) "the least appetizing residue of the canine," as one critic put it. Put more simply, she ate real dog shit.

Pissoir (Urinal)

(1988)

The Dilemma of Sex in Public Latrines

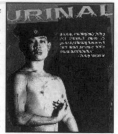

The helmer and scripter of this film, John Greyson, has many awards on his mantelpiece. He is a filmmaker, video artist, writer, activist, and educator.

In 1998 *Pissoir* (a film also known as *Urinal*) won Best Feature Teddy at the Berlin Film Festival. Greyson has also won acclaim for *Zero Patience, Lilies,* and *Made in Canada*. Born in British Columbia, he moved to Toronto in 1980, where he became a professor in the film department at York University.

In many ways, *Pissoir* is his most unusual film to date. The central character is an unnamed man who conjures up a circle of dead gay literary icons as a vehicle for examining some inevitable truths about life and gay life in particular.

The film's cast includes Paul Bettis as Sergei Eisenstein; Pauline Carey as Frances Loring; Keltie Creed as Florence Wyle; Lance Eng as Dorian Gray; David Gonzales as Yukio Mishima; Olivia Rojas as Frida Kahlo; and George Spelvin as Langston Hughes.

These members of the literati investigate a police response to the dilemma of toilet sex in Toronto.

The gay artists of yesterday are given a week to report on the ethics of police tactics such as entrapment. The literary figures infiltrate the police network to learn that they themselves are under surveillance as a politically subversive group.

Greyson's film shocked many viewers, assuming that they were not familiar with toilet sex or the police crackdowns on gays who meet at the urinals. Some relatively innocent viewers went away having learned about a previously unfamiliar lifestyle, including that the word "tearoom" is often used to describe a toilet.

The artists in question explore and report on the "evolution" of toilets and behavior in such places.

Ironically and regrettably, in many parts of the world, toilets are about the only place for gay men to meet other gay men.

Postcards from America

(1994)

The Turbulent Life of David Wojnarowicz

This film directed by Steve McLean traces the life (in three parts) of the controversial gay artist David Wojnarowicz (1954-1992), who died of AIDS. The stories in the movie were based on two of his angry autobiographical books, *Close to the Knives* and *Memories That Smell Like Gasoline.*

The film sketches the horrors of his growing up as an abused child, his sexual experiences on the road as a prostitute, and his battle with AIDS.

Young David is played by Olo Tighe who as a fat, gay child is traumatized by his parents' violent fights. The teenage David is brought to the screen by Michael Tighe, a runaway punk and Times Square hustler. Finally James Lyons is the adult David, a lonely drifter who finds release (or rape) in quick sex, fast cars, and the open road.

As critic Edward Guthmann noted, "The three tales don't play out chronologically but interweave—rotating, encircling, informing one another in a system that feels like three-way eavesdropping."

The artist Wojnarowicz became notorious largely because of that headline-grabbing homophobe, Jesse Helms, the dinosaur ex-Senator from North Carolina and the equally homophobic Rev. Donald Widemon. These two beasts succeeded in getting the National Endowment for the Arts to withdraw funding from an exhibition of Wojnarowicz's work. The artist later sued the fire-breathing reverend for "copyright infringement and misrepresentation."

Singer Connie Francis subsequently sued Universal Music for releasing rights to her music to be used in the movie. Widely recognized as a gay rights advocate, she found the film "overly pornographic and morbid," and didn't want to be associated with it.

Voyeurs will find the postcards rife with male-on-male sex scenes, including casual encounters in latrines or truck stops. There is one particularly vicious rape when Wojnarowicz accepts a ride in a van from a mysterious stranger.

Poster Boy

(2004)

What Would You Do If You Were Jesse Helms' Son?

In this film, Henry Kray (as interpreted by Matt Newton) is the gay son of a North Carolina senator. (That senator's character might have been inspired by that dreaded homophobe, ex-Senator Jesse Helms, who, mercifully, retired in 2003 because of senility and is now dead.)

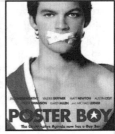

Young Henry has a few problems: Young Republicans across the state have threatened to Out him, and other gays are keeping files on his sexual escapades. His daddy has scheduled a highly visible political rally at his college campus. Playing the role of Henry's father, the arch-conservative senator, Jack Kray, is actor Michael Lerner. The character he plays makes Joe McCarthy look like a den mother.

The senator has problems of his own. In addition to having a gay son, his fur-collared wife, played by Karen Allen, has a drinking problem. Of course, married to him she has plenty of reason to hit the sauce. Allen is quite effective as the salty, wise, and boozy Southern belle.

Just prior to daddy's arrival, his son has had hot gay sex with a jaded AIDS activist (Jack Noseworthy), who also wants to Out Henry. Or has the rabble-rouser fallen in love with our hero?

WHAT THE CRITICS SAID
"The setup is contrived, and the hunky leads ordered directly from the A&F catalog, but *Poster Boy* does manage to touch the eternally raw nerves of gays and American politics."
Tom Beer, *Time Out New York*

"Directed by Zak Tucker, *Poster Boy* is a muddled coming-out movie that for no good reason unfolds flashback style as Henry tells his story to a sleazy newspaper reporter. The device slows the little momentum the narrative builds. Still, Tucker's message is sometimes on target, even if his film isn't."
V.A. Musetto, *New York Post*

"Directed with more sincerity than skill, *Poster Boy* is a plodding indictment of extreme conservative intolerance."
Jeannette Catsoulis, *The New York Times*

Pretty Boy

(*Smukke Dreng*; 1993)

Young Danish Runaway Peddles His Meat

Pretty Boy, a Danish film, another coming-of-age story, is a poignant tale of a young runaway who turns to whoring to survive. Danish director Carsten Sønder's first feature is a compelling, in-your-face exploration of innocence plundered and lost.

Feuding with his mother, Nick (Christian Tafdrup) flees from his dysfunctional home. Fatherless, he actively seeks out the companionship of older men, finding himself in a relationship with Ralph (Stig Hoffmeyer), a closeted, middle-age professor of astronomy. Ralph gives Nick a place of temporary refuge, and the two share an interest in the stars as well as romance.

However, when Ralph's girlfriend returns from vacation, he chooses her over Nick. The boy hits the streets, where he joins up with a gang of violent hustlers who victimize the men who buy their services. Adopted into their ranks, Nick finds refuge again—an unexpected first love—with the gang's only female member, Renée (Benedicte Madsen), an androgynous girl who masquerades as a boy.

Things get complicated once Ralph decides he wants Nick back. Renée, of course, gets jealous. The plot thickens.

The film never rises above the mediocre. In the hands of the brilliant Gus Van Sant in *My Own Private Idaho*, this formula worked much, much better.

The film features an unaffected performance by Christian Tapdrup, who certainly lives up to the billing of pretty boy.

WHAT THE CRITICS SAID
"This sad little film, obviously produced on a modest budget, is likely to be of interest only to a minority audience. It's technically good, with sensitive direction by Carsten Sønder, and is well acted and commendably concise."
David Stratton, *Variety*

Prick Up Your Ears

(1987)

The Life and Tragic Demise of Playwright Joe Orton

Gary Oldman and Alfred Molina star as Joe Orton and his lover Kenneth Halliwell, two young men whose lives ended in bloody tragedy in this mesmerizing film directed by Stephen Frears. It was based on Orton's biography by John Lahr.

In addition to the male actors, Vanessa Redgrave takes top honors as Joe's compassionate and benign literary agent, Peggy Ramsay.

Before the film begins, we already know the ending. Halliwell's 16-year relationship with Orton ended in tragedy on August 9, 1967 when he beat the playwright to death and subsequently killed himself with an overdose of pills.

Frears, who shot *My Beautiful Laundrette*, concentrates on the rocky road of that affair beginning when Orton, 17, met Halliwell, 25. Both of them wanted to be writers, and they began an affair, although sex was not the tie that bound. Never satisfied with what he had at home, Orton cruised at night, seeking rough trade, often in public toilets.

Orton shot to success, Halliwell did not. Drawing upon their life together, Orton scored theatrical hits which included *What the Butler Saw, Loot,* and *Entertaining Mr. Sloane.* Halliwell became almost psychotically jealous of his friend's success.

Frears does not make homosexuality the point of this movie. He's not so much interested in showing them in bed together, but in exposing the deep-rooted neuroses of their respective personalities.

WHAT THE CRITICS SAID
"The movie is not about homosexuality, which it treats in a matter-of-fact manner. It really is about a marriage between unequal partners. Halliwell was, in a way, like the loyal wife who slaves at ill-paid jobs to put her husband through medical school, only to have the man divorce her after he's successful because they have so little in common—he with his degree, her with dishwasher hands."
Roger Ebert

<table>
<tr><td>

Priest

(1994)

Should a Priest Be Forced to Be Celibate?

</td><td>

Producing Adults

(Lapsia ja aikuisia-Kuinka niitä tehdään; 2004)

Just When You Think You've Grown Up....

</td></tr>
</table>

Among the many dilemmas tackled in this film by director Antonia Bird, Father Greg Pilkington (Linus Roache) is torn between his calling as a conservative Catholic priest and his secret life as a homosexual. This film enraged the Catholic Church. In Ireland, the church tried to have its distribution banned.

Father Greg is young, dedicated, and idealistic. He moves into the house of Father Matthew Thomas (Tom Wilkinson), only to discover that the senior priest is having a torrid affair with his maid, played by Cathy Tyson. She steps forward to confirm that celibacy is no longer part of Father Matthew's calling.

Father Greg's dilemma grows even more frightening when he discovers in confession that a young girl is being sexually abused by her father. He fears he can't break the seal of the confessional to have the abuser apprehended, yet he wants to save the girl from her ordeal. Of course, filmmakers have dealt with this old chestnut before, the inviolable secrecy of the confessional.

The plot thickens when Father Greg takes off his collar and goes cruising in a gay bar. Here he meets Graham (Robert Carlyle), and has anonymous sex as part of a one-night stand. Later Graham recognizes him on the street, and their affair continues.

WHAT THE CRITICS SAID

"*Priest*, one critic has written, 'vigorously attacks the view of the Roman Catholic Church on homosexuality.' Actually the film is an attack on the vow of celibacy, preferring sexuality of any sort to the notion that men should, could, or would live chastely."
Roger Ebert

"A far cry from the parishes of Bing Crosby's heyday, St. Mary's is subject to the troubles of inner cities everywhere. Father Greg's conflict lies in his passion for both God and man; for him, religion is both a calling and a defense against his homosexuality."
Rita Kempley, *Washington Post*

Let's don't even try to pronounce the umlaut-laden Finnish name of this film: *Lapsia ja aikuisia-Kuinka niitä tehdään*? Suffice it to say, it was the Finnish entry in the Foreign Film category at the Oscars.

Promoted abroad as a lesbian drama, it is actually more than that. A newcomer helmer, Finnish director, Aleksi Salmenperä, claims his film is about "the success of a marriage is not in producing children, but in children producing adults."

The main character, Venla (played by Minna Haapkyla), is a counselor in a fertility clinic. As such, she grows enchanted with the idea of having a baby of her own. She's been locked into a relationship with Antero (Karl-Pekka Toivonen) for 15 years. He agrees to marry her, but he doesn't want to have kids.

He begins by tricking her into drinking a glass of champagne containing a morning-after pill, the first in a series of secret attempts to prevent her from conceiving. Ultimately he will secretly have a vasectomy.

The plot thickens. Determined to become pregnant, Venla seeks help from a female fertility doctor, a decision that breeds new possibilities for the prospective mother when she falls in love with the doctor. Satu, the woman doctor, is excellently played by Minttu Mustakallio.

At the clinic, Satu hopes to solve Venla's dilemma by artificial insemination. But her boss, Claes (Dick Idman), wants to impregnate Venla in nature's more traditional way. She rejects his pathetic advances.

WHAT THE CRITICS SAID

"Letting go of much of its comedy to illustrate how these kind of dramatic situations are now seriously confronting those in the contemporary scene, the film in a quiet way gives the subject of exploring same-sex romances the dignity and respect it deserves."
Dennis Schwartz

187

Proteus

(2003)

Inter-Racial Lovers in 18th Century South Africa

This joint Canadian and South African film originated with the fascination of its directors, John Greyson and Jack Lewis, for the story of two Dutch-speaking prisoners during the early 18th century in what is today known as South Africa. It's a tale about forbidden love during an era when sodomy was judged as worse than murder, and it's a story that illuminates the institutionalized extermination of men engaged in homosexual acts by a moralistic penal code. Complicating the story was the fact that within European society at the time, interracial love was virtually unthinkable, and that the protagonists in this drama included a white and a black man.

The screenplay was based on South African court records that were meticulously compiled during the trial of Rijkhaart Jacobsz (a white Dutch sailor imprisoned in the 1720s for sodomy) and Claas Blank (a Hottentot tribesman accused but never convicted of cattle theft). Each of them was incarcerated within South Africa's most notorious penal colony, Robben Island. (Ironically, Robben Island, was the much later site of Nelson Mandela's life sentence.)

After lengthy trials, the details of which were meticulously recorded in archaic Dutch script that linguists, including the modern-day Dutch themselves, have difficulty interpreting, they were jointly sentenced to death for their "crimes" by being bound together with chains and pushed off the edge of a ship.

As the film depicts, the men's incarceration occurred during an era when Calvinists and/or vengefully hysterical moralists controlled most of northern European society. Adding to the self-righteous indignation of the South African court was a repressive policy in Amsterdam at the time. Documents uncovered by the filmmakers revealed the trials of tens of thousands of mainly black men in colonial South Africa, many of them for sodomy, and many of them leading to executions as late as the 1870s.

The movie is a bitter and alarming reminder that gay people have paid a high price for their sexual orientation.

Psychopathia Sexualis

(2006)

Case Studies in "Forbidden Desire"

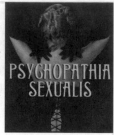

Young gay men in the early part of the 20th century often secured a copy of the 19th-century medical research of the Austrian psychiatrist Richard von Krafft-Ebing (1840-1902) to read "tales of deviance and forbidden desire."

In 1886 Krafft-Ebing published his famous study of sexual perversity called *Psychopathia Sexualis*. It remains well known for its coinage of the term sadism after the Marquis de Sade. He also coined the term masochism, using the name of a contemporary writer, Leopold von Sacher-Masoch, whose partially autobiographical novel, *Venus in Furs*, tells of a protagonist's desire to be whipped and enslaved by a beautiful woman.

Krafft-Ebing often called homosexuality "contrary sexual desire." He felt that the purpose of sexual desire was procreation. In his view, any form of desire that didn't have as its ultimate goal pregnancy was a "perversion." Therefore, rape, although an aberrant act, was not a perversion in his distorted view since pregnancy could result.

This docu is a multi-narrative adaptation of his notorious medico-forensic study of so-called sexual perversity. Before its release, and to get an NC-17 rating, helmer Brett Wood had to remove a shot of urination in someone's mouth. The 2-minute sequence, which included a depiction of male frontal nudity. hit the cutting room floor.

Nonetheless, there remains some strong sexual content, including not only graphic nudity but some violent and disturbing images.

Wood employs an eclectic array of devices to tell his story, even puppet theater and true-crime reality TV. Case histories were selected at random from Krafft-Ebing's files. Flashing on the screen before us are the misadventures, maladjustments, and obsessions of the "sexually inverted" of Victorian England.

The film uses such thesps as Daniel May who has a resemblance to the infamous somnambulist of *The Cabinet of Dr. Caligari*. Lisa Paulsen and Veronika Duerr grapple with the love that dare not speak its name.

<table>
<tr><td>

Puccini For Beginners

(2006)

A Screwball Comedy and Bisexual Roundelay

</td><td>

Queens

(*Reinas*; 2005)

Not Penis Envy, Almodóvar Envy

</td></tr>
</table>

Writer-director Maria Maggenti won many lesbian fans with her coming-of-age drama, *The Incredibly True Adventure of Two Girls in Love*. But that was some time ago.

She's back with this romantic comedy about a separated couple whose members each have affairs with the same woman.

The references to Woody Allen were rife in the reviews. Lou Lumenick in *The New York Post* suggested, "Imagine for a second if *Manhattan* centered not on Woody Allen's teenage-girl-loving character but on Meryl Streep—his lesbian ex-wife. Allen certainly hasn't managed anything remotely this funny lately." Even *The New York Times* wrote of "the crackle of vintage Woody Allen, as any number of stilted duds can attest, applying a Philip Barry or Woody Allen sensibility to 21st century New Yorkers in their 30s is as delicate a craft as diamond cutting."

Davy Ray claimed that *Puccini for Beginners* was "better than Woody Allen's last five movies combined."

Maggenti's movie was summed up in this tagline: Girl Leaves Girl, Meets Boy and Then Meets Boy's Girl.

The plot? Reaser plays Allegra, who is on the rebound from her love affair with Samantha (Julianne Nicholson). Samantha has fled the nest to take up with Jeff (Brian Letscher).

Allegra then takes up with Philip (Justin Kirk), an assistant professor of philosophy at Columbia. This Woody Allen scenario turns into Noël Coward when Allegra meets Grace (Gretchen Mol). What Allegra doesn't know is that Grace is Philip's soon-to-be ex. Are you still with us?

The chemistry heats up between Grace and Allegra. Allegra is now "torn between two lovers," as the song goes. Reaser pulls it off beautifully and steals the picture, just as she did when she played a Norwegian mail order bride who comes to 1920s Minnesota in *Sweet Land*. She is a modern lesbian feminist writer with "commitment issues."

This film is not so much about gay sons getting married but about five mothers (three of them longstanding Pedro Almodóvar muses). Now that Spain has officially sanctioned same-sex marriages, it was inevitable that some filmmaker would come out with a picture about gay marriage.

Too bad it wasn't Almodóvar himself. Instead we get helmer Manuel Gómez Pereira, who failed to pull it off in spite of a cast of some of the most talented actors in Spain.

The movie is about three gay couples and their pending nuptials. The mamas take over as their sons bicker over furnishings. The women's discomfort at the upcoming communal wedding is played out by their seducing the wrong men.

Nuria (Verónica Forqué), for example, seduces her drunken future son-in-law. A successful hotelier, Magda (Carmen Maura), runs to the arms of her head chef while dealing with a strike of her employees. Reyes (Marisa Paredes), a rich actress, lusts after her gardener. She seems to ignore the fact that he (Lluís Homar) will become her new in-law after the knot is tied. Pressed into duty is yet another mother, a judge (Mercedes Sampietro), who will preside over the ceremonies.

For those who don't get off on gay weddings, there's even a dog-poop joke. Not only that, but we're treated to everything from "aggressive" bosoms to a single intimidated penis.

WHAT THE CRITICS SAID
"Despite the rich potential of the movie's basic premise, *Queens* is frantic, shrill, and dreadfully disappointing. (And I'm a gay son of two Spaniards, mind you—good luck finding a film critic more inclined to have liked this movie.) Director Manuel Gómez Pereira and his co-writers fail to create a single character for the audience to relate to or even like. Everyone on screen is so shrill and selfish and irritating that it's impossible to give a tinker's damn about any of them."
Alonso Duralde, *The Advocate*

Queer Duck, The Movie

(2006)

A Fruity Fowl & Cult Hero

What's not to like in this raunch-loaded animated feature? The title alone won us over. We first met Queer Duck, an odd bird if there ever was one, when he appeared on the Internet as part of the Icebox website. The cartoon character was created by Xeth Feinberg who wrote for *The Simpsons* and now is director of the movie. *Queer Duck* shorts went "mainstream" after being scheduled on *Showtime* for Sunday nights, right after *Queer as Folk*.

Jim J. Bullock was hired as the voice of our favorite duck. The other voices are equally wonderful, including Jackie Hoffman as Lola Buzzard; Maurice LaMarche as Oscar Wildcat; and Tress MacNeille as Dr. Laura Schlessinger, a monster who's easy to hate. Kevin Michael Richardson is the voice of Openly Gator, with Bill West doing the soundtrack for Bi-Polar Bear. He sounded like Paul Lynne.

Celebrity voices, all great sports, include cameos by Tim Curry, Mark Hamill, Bruce Villanch, Andy Dick, Conan O'Brien, and David Duchovny as the voice of "Tiny Jesus."

There are parody impersonations of such gay-friendly divas as Rosie O'Donnell, Liza Minnelli, Elizabeth Taylor, and Barbra Streisand, but a rather unflattering portrait of the late Michael Jackson. Most of the humor seems targeted to gay males rather than a lesbian audience.

Seymour Duckstein (Queer Duck) leaves his lover, Openly Gator, when he, the duck, becomes enamored of and marries the Norma Desmondesque-Ms. Buzzard.

As with South Park, you're treated to musical numbers, including such tuneful interludes as "Jimmy Couldn't Master Masturbation" or "Have Sex With Animals." You even get a pastiche from the Village People's YMCA. The black-and-white penciled "What Ever Happened to Baby Jane" remains one of our favorites.

As its writer, Mike Reiss crafted some hilarious lyrics, including a spoof of Gilbert & Sullivan's *Pinafore*.

Querelle

(1982)

Fassbinder Turns to Genet for His Swan Song

The final movie of gay filmmaker Rainer Werner Fassbinder was disappointing, yet intriguing. The controversial movie followed the descent into Hell of a young sailor Querelle, who was called by French writer Jean Genet "the Angel of the Apocalypse." Fassbinder based his "final statement" on Genet's novel *Querelle de Brest*, published in 1953.

Brad Davis in skin-tight sailor pants, showing off his uncut cock, took the starring role of a French sailor who arrives in Brest and starts frequenting a strange whorehouse. The way Brad Davis plays it, the only time he's out of his sailor whites is when he's on his back.

Fassbinder managed to complete the film in ten days before his fatal drug overdose at the age of 36. Salvador Dalí, upon viewing *Querelle*, called it "an authentic surrealist sex farce."

Querelle wants to smuggle a cask of opium into Brest and seeks help at a bordello owned by Mme. Lysiane (Jeanne Moreau), who is wed to Nono (Gunther Kaufmann), a light-skinned black. At the Hotel Feria, horny sailors shake Nono's dice. Winners get to have sex with Lysiane, who is in her mid-50s. If they lose, they get screwed by Nono. Playing the dice, Querelle deliberately loses.

At the whorehouse, Querelle learns that his brother Robert (Hanno Pöschi) is the lover of Lysiane, the "lady" owner of the bordello. Querelle has a love-hate relationship with Robert.

Watching all this is a Peeping Tom, Lt. Seblon (Franco Nero), a naval officer on Querelle's ship. Dressed in a uniform out of *The Student Prince*, Seblon worships Querelle from afar. By fadeout, Querelle will belong to his longtime admirer.

Querelle enlists the help of Vic (Dieter Schidor) as his smuggling accomplice. Vic obviously wants to get plowed by the sailor. But when Vic strips down for Querelle, he gets his throat cut instead. At one point in the film, Querelle also sleeps with Mme. Lysiane. Moreau shocked faint-of-heart audiences when she filmed a scene comparing the cocks of the two brothers.

Quinceañera

(2006)

Ostracism & Liberation

A real couple in private life, helmers and scripters Wash Westmoreland and Richard Glatzer brought us that gay fave, *The Fluffer*, one of the hottest indies we've seen in a long time. Their switch to more mainstream cinema came as a surprise to us when we attended a showing of *Quinceañera*.

In Mexico, a *quinceañera* is a "coming out" party announcing a girl's 15th birthday. Magdalena (Emily Rios) is looking forward to the big day. There's a problem. She's pregnant, although technically a virgin. She became pregnant by her boyfriend in a rare instance of nonpenetrative sex. She is kicked out of the house by her devoutly Catholic papa.

One outcast seeks two other outcasts—in this case her cousin, Carlos (Jesse Garcia), a gay *cholo* who has also been evicted by his family for being gay. He lives with her gentle great-uncle, Tomas (Chalo Gonzáles), a life-loving 80-plus character who hawks *champurrado* (a popular Mexican hot drink) on the street.

The setting is Echo Park in Los Angeles, a neighborhood inhabited in large part by Mexican immigrants though it's going through a gentrification.

The producers were very impressed with their hot new star, Garcia, who hails from Wyoming. "Jesse, as an actor, has so many emotional layers, and he's so ready to go places and try things," says Glatzer. "He's almost a return to that kind of 50s innocence, like Brando and Dean, where you don't need to think of what you are sexually, you just go with it."

We'd endorse that remark, although "innocence" in the case of Brando and Dean might be the wrong word.

WHAT THE CRITICS SAID
"*Quinceañera* exhibits such stalwart faith that its troubled characters will prevail that its underlying bleakness is largely camouflaged. The filmmakers have described *Quinceañera* as kitchen-sink realism in the tradition of British working-class dramas of the late 1950s and 60s. "
Stephen Holden, *The New York Times*

Race You to the Bottom

(2005)

Metrosexual Fluidity

Russell Brown both wrote and directed this 75-minute romance drama about bisexual travel writer, Nathan (Cole Williams). He's assigned to research California's Napa Valley with his girlfriend Maggie (Amber Benson). Each member of this loving couple actually has a boyfriend waiting back home.

There is some chemistry between Williams and Benson, although most of the time we feel we're on a trip with a gay man and his fag hag. Call this a road pic. Actually, if we can believe the plot, Maggie and Nathan have been engaged in an affair for months.

Maggie's boyfriend, Milo (Justin Zachary), could have quickly determined what was going on when he told Maggie good-bye with Nathan in the car.

"Take care of my girl this weekend," Milo says to Nathan. "Don't worry," Nathan responds. "I always take care of our girl. Nice ass!"

What's the hardest line to deliver in the movie? Surely it is when Nathan tells Magie, "The taste of another man on you makes me hot." At the end of the film, you'll still be uncertain who the bottom was.

WHAT THE CRITICS SAID
"Brown's screenplay and direction, both economical and unshowy, sketch character dynamics in crisp terms that resist the temptation to explain all, beg sympathy or heighten drama for purely histrionic purposes."
Denis Harvey, *Variety*

"Where old world queers were traumatized by the thought of an either/or coming out, young queers with fluid sexual boundaries are up against a whole new set of dilemmas."
Anne Stockwell, *The Advocate*

"*Race You to the Bottom* is a sublimely funny take on a new generation some have labeled 'the undefined,' an under twenty-five set for whom the old labels—gay, fag hag, bisexual—are supposedly obsolete."
David Lamble, *Bay Area Reporter*

Radical Harmonies

(2002)

Alternative to 'Cock Rock Culture'

The roots of women's music, often lesbian oriented, is traced from the so-called early days until the 21st century. The well-made docu is a tribute to lesbian music in particular and the history of the genre. For Dee Mosbacher, this represents a masterpiece. Interviews and performances are used to provide an overview of the women's music scene.

The women's music scene eventually blossomed to take in labels owned entirely by women, including the Olivia Collective and Holly Near's Redwood Records. Women not only made the sounds and provided the music, but filled the role of tech crew as well. Festivals were used to showcase this music, which often focused on traditional folk sounds.

From what was mainly white folk-rockers, the movement was widened to take in soul, multicultural jazz, and punk rock groups such as the Indigo Girls.

A lot of time in this docu is spent in the 1970s, and perhaps that is as it should be.

WHAT THE CRITICS SAID
"Put on your Birkenstocks, strum your guitar, and sit back and love the energy of this documentary. It's wonderful, regardless of your age, gender, sex, or sexuality. You will laugh, you will learn, you will sing along, and you may even get a little moisture in your eyes—and you will definitely come out empowered."
"Queer Movie Lover"

"A whirlwind tour through three decades of mostly lesbian-targeted, folk-rocking 'womyn's music' in the U.S. Dee Mosbacher's *Radical Harmonies* is entertainment on its own terms, but offers little for those not already well acquainted with this musical scene."
Dennis Harvey, *Variety*

Rag Tag

(2006)

Love Isn't Just Black or White

The action in this 98-minute English-language Nigerian film by Adaora Nwandu takes place in both Nigeria and the UK. Raymond or "Rag" (Daniel Parsons) and Tagbo or "Tag" (Adedamola Adelaja) met when they were both eight years old.

Rag is from a single-parent West Indian home, while Tag is the only son of middle-class Nigerian parents. They remain inseparable until late in their teens, when Rag goes to London.

A decade passes before Rag attempts to find Tag. The two men still want to be together. Their needs are those of mature men—read that sexual.

Finishing law school, Tag has a white girlfriend and is searching for a job. His lack of credentials doesn't impress his girlfriend's papa.

Rag feels he doesn't have much of a chance with Tag, and he sees even less room in his life when Tag's friend, Olisa (Ayo Fawole) flies into London.

Rag and Tag are invited to return to Nigeria for Olisa's chieftain ceremony. Rag is determined to "save" Tag in this tale of family, friendship, and love.

The director and writer (Nwandu) said, "I wanted to tell a story that demonstrated that we might all seem very different on the surface, but deep down very few real divisions exists. Be you from a Western or African mentality, many underlying values are the same. In the end, people are just people and love is just love."

WHAT THE CRITICS SAID
"Andrea Nwandu's first feature *Rag Tag* is a rough-hewn but likeable seriocomedy very much in the *My Beautiful Laundrette* mode, weaving together albeit less skillfully various business and personal intrigues including a gay male romance in multicultural London. Emphasis on the Nigerian expat community there provides a fresh angle, and character dynamics are entertaining. Erratic writing, directing, and production values."
Dennis Harvey, *Variety*

Rainbow's End

(2006)

Gay Liberation Has a Long Way to Go

Directors and script writers Jochen Hick and Christian Jentzsch suggest that the end of the rainbow with its pot of gold is a long way off for most gays and lesbians living in the advanced countries of Western Europe. Judged on a superficial level, gay liberation has manifested itself in many ways, including the legalization of same-sex marriage in Spain. But the picture's not all rosy.

This docu takes us on a multinational journey to the borders of Europe, from street activism to personal stories (often sad). Peter Tachell of OutRage!, a gay and lesbian activist group, is quoted as saying, "History does not progress in a linear fashion from oppression to liberation. If it did, the extraordinary freedom enjoyed by gay people in 1920s Germany should have been followed by the legalization of homosexuality. Instead, we got the Nazis and their concentration camps."

At a gay pride parade in Warsaw, one homophobic moron shouted, "Hitler should be here." Another scumbag shouted, "Send them to the damn ovens."

One deeply disturbing aspect of the film is the clash between liberal Western Europe values in cities such as Amsterdam and ignorant homophobic opinions held by the majority of émigrés from countries such as Nigeria. Settling into the suburbs, these unenlightened émigrés often harass, threaten, or even attack gay people. Many British teenagers in London have had to leave their birth communities to flee from these new arrivals who carry the prejudices taught in their home countries with them.

Sadly, any attempt by the United Nations to get that body to pass a resolution prohibiting discrimination against homosexuals is defeated by the combined forces of both the Vatican and Muslim countries. At least these two opposite forces agree on something, and that is their mutual loathing of gays.

Ready? OK!

(2008)

Don't Break the Rules. Change Them

This poignant comedy, scripted and helmed by James Vasquez, is the story of a single Mom who struggles to understand her young son's obsession with dresses, dolls, and girls' cheerleading.

Starring as the overcaffeinated single mother, Andy Dowd (Carrie Preston) plays a character who has a late-life epiphany. Lurie Poston is cast as her cheerleading son, Josh Dowd. In addition to cheerleading, he relishes the art of French braid and calls Maria von Trapp his role model. He successfully conveys a boy who knows what he wants and has the guts to follow his dreams.

Michael Emerson plays the gay neighbor Charlie New. He's a kind of next-door fairy godmother.

Tara Karsian is cast as Sister Vivian, the repressive nun who wants to keep Josh on the "straight" and narrow path, as if such a thing were possible.

A wayward brother returns home, compelling the characters to face themselves and what it means to be a family. Alex Dowd plays John Preston with a certain verve.

WHAT THE CRITICS SAID
"What a sweet film this is. The movie is a terrific gem."
Greg Hernandez, *Los Angeles Daily News*

"Hollywood hasn't come up with a sweeter and funnier comedy than this all year. Ready? OK! Is a touching and terrific comedy that you will two . . . four . . . six . . . eight . . . . totally appreciate."
WWW SFist.Com

"This is a finely written and acted movie. The situation of the young protagonist, a boy who longs to be a cheerleader, is a direct and compelling challenge to myriad adults."
Terence Flynn

Red Without Blue

(2007)

Transgender Identity & Family Dynamics

This docu by Brooke Sebold, Todd Sills, and Benita Sills (helmers and scripters) is at times painful to watch. It tells of one man's struggle with his own identity as he tries to accept his twin brother's decision to undergo gender reassignment—all of this in homophobic rural Montana.

Interviews with the subjects get at the heart of their family conflicts. The film also suggests the unswerving bond of twins despite the transformation of one of them (male to female). Clair Farley as (he/she) wants to be known, is the trannie in transition. The twin brother is Mark Oliver Farley.

Even as young boys, Mark and Alex (he had a male name back then) realized they were different from other boys. By the time they were in their early teens, each of the twins knew he was gay. When word got out in Missoula, Montana, that meant harassment from the school bullies.

Mark, an art student, develops his first serious romance, as Alex/Clair debates sexual reassignment surgery.

At one point the lives of the twins became so traumatic they considered drawing up a suicide pact. Mark's initial reaction to Clair's planned sex change was, "He doesn't want to be like me."

Jenny, the mother of these siblings, remains a bit of an enigma. She seems to be "very close" to a platonic female friend. At least we are told it's platonic, but the two women share the same bed. Nonetheless, Jenny claims, "We're not gay!"

WHAT THE CRITICS SAID
"*Red Without Blue* is an understated but compassionate account of twin brothers who struggle to define themselves in terms of individuality and sexual identity. Along the way, the brothers describe childhood traumas great and small, and they must acknowledge the frays in their fraternal bonds. For all its candor and blunt speaking, *Red Without Blue* leaves the audience with a sense that some elements of this family saga are being withheld from closer scrutiny."
Joe Leydon, *Variety*

Redwoods

(2010)

Torn Between Two Lovers

Time was when filmmakers depicted stories like this between a girl and a boy. In this heyday of New Queer Cinema, directors such as helmer/scriptwriter David Lewis can create romantic boy/boy films too.

Shot in the gay resort town of Guerneville, California, along the Russian River, the film, in essence, is the poignant and tragic tale of a young man caught in a stagnant relationship with another man his own age. Everett (Brendan Bradley) and Miles (Tad Coughenour) live and sleep together but the viewer suspects they no longer are making love.

Their non-passionate relationship is held together by the love and attention they devote to Billy, their learning-disabled boy.

Miles decides to take Billy on a visit to the grandparents, leaving Everett at home. Everett doesn't even get a kiss at the door but is told to take care of the mold in the bathroom.

Along comes Chase (Matthew Montgomery), who stops his car in front of Everett's house to ask for directions. Everett conveniently happens to be sitting on his front porch. The attraction between the two hotties is immediate. The flirtations continue later that day when Everett visits Chase's B&B. Foreplay picks up yet again during an antique hunting session with dear old Mom.

Everett is not a slut, but Chase is persistent and he's hard to resist.

In the magnificent redwood forests of Northern California, their passions flare. The story gets a little mushy here. Perhaps you'll know the ending before it's revealed.

Will Everett remain with his dull and chilly BF and his loving child, or run off with the dashing and romantic Chase who's working on a novel that Everett can help him with?

The combination of a Carson McCullers novel with a charismatic box office pair like Marlon Brando and Elizabeth Taylor should have led to a screen explosion, especially when John Huston was hired as director.

But somehow this adaptation of McCullers' 1941 novel didn't work on the screen. The way scripter Gladys Hill conceived it, *Reflections* became a bizarre tale of sex, betrayal, and perversion at a military outpost.

The film was made just at the time the Production Code was being lifted, particularly as regards depiction of homosexuality on the screen. Originally Montgomery Clift was scheduled to play the repressed homosexual, but he died before shooting could begin. Huston then wanted Richard Burton for the role, but Taylor rejected that suggestion, preferring Brando.

He stepped into the role of the closeted homosexual, Major Weldon Penderton, locked into an unhappy marriage to the sexually active Taylor. Finding no sexual satisfaction at home, she turns to Brian Keith, playing Lt. Col. Morris Langdon. All understatement and quiet sympathy, he gives the most nuanced performance in *Reflections*.

He's married to Julie Harris, who, we learn, cut off the nipples of her breasts with scissors after she gave birth to a deformed child.

Brando becomes mesmerized and sexually attracted to Private Williams (Robert Forster), who tends to the Penderton's stables, especially Taylor's horse "Firebird." One day the Major observes the private riding naked in the forest. Brando's lust for the young man is unleashed. Tragic consequences follow.

WHAT THE CRITICS SAID
"*Reflections in a Golden Eye* has one possible virtue: It will send you right back to Carson McCuller's book (hopefully to read it), because one can't imagine that her perceptive novel had nothing more to offer than nutty people and pseudo pornography."
Judith Crist

We really didn't like the stage version of the Pulitzer and Tony Award winning musical about "Bohemians" in the East Village of New York City, who nobly struggled with life, love, and AIDS.

As directed by Chris Columbus (no, not that one!), we didn't like the first 30 minutes of the screen version either. But ever so slowly it won our hearts in places, for the simple reason that it is perhaps the most gay-accepting film ever made for general release.

By now, most movie-goers know that Columbus's résumé includes such un-*Rent*-like blockbusters as *Home Alone* and the first two *Harry Potter* films. Incidentally, the two Potters he directed are now considered the worst of the bunch so far.

In spite of a few cuts or reshuffled songs, it arrives more or less intact from the stage in New York. As noted in several reviews, the original stage actors, now in their 30s, are a little long in the tooth for the young screen roles they are playing.

Jonathan Larson based *Rent* on Puccini's *La Bohème*, telling the story of one year in the life of friends living in a depressingly ugly section of New York's East Village, beginning in 1989 before this district became the chic enclave it is today.

We meet Mark (Anthony Rapp) a cameraman whose former lover, the vibrant, over-the-top Maureen (Indina Menzel) has deserted him. The new object of her affection is a black woman, Joanne (Tracie Thoms), who is well dressed and Harvard educated, a public interest lawyer no less.

Mark's roommate is an HIV+ former junkie, Roger (Adam Pascal). The object of his affection is the HIV+ drug-addicted S&M dancer, Mimi (Rosario Dawson). There's more. In a charming take on his role, the black actor, Tom Collins (Jesse L. Martin), falls for the drag queen and street musician, the charming Angel (Wilson Jermaine Heredia).

Return to Innocence

(2001)

False Accusations of Child Molestation

Tommy Jackson (Andrew Martin) was an abused child. When he was seven years old, his mother shot porno videos of her son and sold them on the Internet. This led to her arrest by the FBI. Tommy was placed in the custody of the Department of Social Services.

At New Horizons, Tommy begins a new life which is complicated when he falls in love with one of his counselors. Glen Erskine (Richard Meese), the chief of staff at the treatment center for abused boys, discovers the affair. When he is about to report it, the counselor dies in an accident. To save the counselor's wife from shame, Erskine does not report the case.

Tommy's love for the older man is so strong that he blames Erskine for breaking up their relationship. To get revenge, he trumps up charges of child molestation against Erskine.

With that accusation, the stage is set for a dark, disturbing, and poignant tale of a decent man trying to clear his name. The agenda of the prosecution of a child sex abuse case is clearly defined in this film directed by Rocky Costanzo and written by Gary M. Frazier.

WHAT THE CRITICS SAID
"The melodrama is ineptly handled. To call Frazier's dialogue wooden is an insult to wood everywhere. That his script is based on his own novel conjures an image of prose stylings that steal my sleep. And Costanzo is a shatteringly unimaginative director, letting actors ramble on in tight close-up and rarely utilizing montage. At least the lighting is inoffensive, an achievement the rest of the production is unable to match."
Travis MacKenzie Hoover

Rice Rhapsody

(*Hainan Ji Fan;* 2004)

Two of Her Three Sons Are Gay

Singapore is a conservative government notorious for its lingering taboo about homosexuality. Yet this gay-themed film is the first joint venture between Singapore's budding film industry and a Hong Kong company backed by Jackie Chan.

In the lead as Mommie Dearest, Sylvia Chang, cast as Jen, walks away with the picture. With a mom like Chang, what son wouldn't turn out gay? Two of her three sons are already queer, and Chang's not certain about the youngest. "The jury's still out on him."

The two confirmed gay sons are Harry (Craig Toh) and Daniel (Alvin Chiang). The third brother, Leo (LePham Tan), is the unknown factor.

The central setting for the film is Jen's dinner table, where the boys gather each night to indulge in her Hainanese chicken rice. In fact, the original title of the film was *Hainan Chicken Rice.*

The film gets humming when dear old mum takes in a French foreign exchange student (Mélanie Laurent). In her breezy role as Sabine, she's wondrous, ending up teaching the family a lot about life, acceptance, and love.

Kenneth Bi both wrote and guided the actors through this soapy comedy/drama which is harmless fun.

We like the way the movie explores the clash taking place in Singapore between traditional Asian culture and oncoming influences from the West. "As the city has prospered, many young Singaporeans are abandoning their parents' Confucian appreciation for social order and harmony, and adopting more Western individualism," said Bi. "Singapore is the only place in Southeast Asia that is a true halfway point between Western and traditional Asian culture."

Singaporean gay activist, Alex Au, claimed that the film's portrayal of gay life in Singapore rings true. "There is quite a bit of shoulder shrugging and 'so what' about homosexuality these days," he said.

Ring of Fire

(2005)

The Emile Griffith Story

Violence, love, sex, politics, and the media are highlighted in this documentary about the boxer, Emile Griffith, a six-time world welterweight champion, born in the Virgin Islands in 1938. Directors Ron Berger and Dan Klores received a Grand Jury Prize when the film was screened at the 2005 Sundance Film Festival.

When a promoter in New York discovered him, he didn't want to box at all. He had a job where he'd proved a hit designing hats for women. As a boxer, he turned pro in 1958.

His most famous fight was in New York on March 24, 1962, when Emile reclaimed the world's welterweight title from Benny "The Kid" Paret. In round 12, Emile charged Paret as he lay defenseless against the ropes. Amazingly, the referee did not bring a halt to the fight.

According to his instructions, Emile pounded Paret a total of 23 times before the fight was stopped. The hopeless Paret had long ago lost consciousness and was never to regain it, dying in a hospital bed nine days later.

This tragedy was played out before millions on nationwide TV, becoming one of the most scandalous events in the history of boxing. Although technically not to blame, Emile never fully recovered his reputation. He finally retired at the age of 39 with a record of 85 wins, 24 losses and 2 draws, with 25 wins by knockout.

What is a film about a boxer doing in an anthology of gay movies of the year? Paret, an illiterate Cuban who spoke only Spanish, had called Emile a *maricon* (faggot) at their weigh-in. Emile had to be restrained from hitting Paret in the locker room.

Emile is still alive today, living modestly, as he didn't save money earned in the ring. Regrettably, his brain is impaired from a vicious attack he suffered outside a gay bar in Manhattan in 1992. He was leaving the bar intoxicated, and therefore could not defend himself, when the attack from a gang of thugs occurred. In this hate crime, he was called a "faggot" as he was severely beaten, coming close to losing his life.

Rise Above:
The Tribe 8 Documentary

(2003)

Topless Lesbian Punkers Waving Giant Dildos

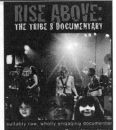

Tribe 8, a leading lesbian punk band founded in San Francisco in 1992, made itself famous with such songs as "Femme Bitch Top," "Castration Song #22," and "Lezbophobia."

What can you say about these semi-naked female punks pushing 40 and performing topless, showing off their not altogether fallen breasts? Or what about the stage business of strapping on giant dildos and inviting some of their straight male fans to come up and perform fellatio?

After watching the group, one viewer compared the experience to being "plunged into a beer scum-covered mosh pit."

Lead singer Lynnee Breedlove is no Cher and certainly no Judy Garland. Her range is below those working-class punk icons "Sham 69." But she's got so much shock in her act that you might not notice how untalented she actually is, with her "ramalama melodies" and her vocal screeches.

Archival segments from the band's concerts are interwoven with portraits of the band members as individuals. It comes as no surprise that most of the group members are from broken homes.

Director Tracy Flannigan manages to blend the lesbian preferences of the band members with their punk lifestyles.

WHAT THE CRITICS SAID
"A suitably raw, wholly engaging documentary, *Rise Above* pays tribute to San Francisco-based Tribe 8. With footage spanning band's history, feature offers a unique perspective on the lesbian community's own shift from 70s feminism-based political correctitude to a more encompassing embrace of rebellious fringe elements. It's also a joyful punk lifestyle manifesto akin to *Another State of Mind* and the original *Decline of Western Civilization*."
Dennis Harvey, *Variety*

Rock Bottom: Gay Men and Meth

(2006)

"Fuck Me Bareback...NOW!"

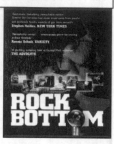

This is a chilling portrait of a community—in this case, New York's Chelsea District—in crisis. With an unflinching eye, this 61-minute docu by Jay Corcoran follows the journeys of seven gay men struggling with meth addiction and recovery.

It is set against a horrific backdrop of an emerging second wave of HIV infection, caused in large part by barebacking among crystal meth users. The docu captures the saga of these young men over a two-year period as they go from sex clubs to hospitals, and in some cases attend family gatherings.

The film delivers a powerful punch and doesn't hold back in its frank and honest portrait of crystal use, going from exciting, even glamorous highs, to devastating lows.

Meth addiction, according to the docu, can be blamed on many reasons—poor self-esteem, HIV burnout, internalized homophobia, and even intensely conflicted feelings about sex.

In one segment, a user is shown dying from drug use and diabetes. What is startling is the appearance of the subjects under the influence of crystal meth and the same men a few months later after freeing their systems of the substance.

The low point of the film is when one user describes in ghoulish detail the blatant signs of gonorrhea.

Perhaps the largest question confronted here is the price some of us pay for the pursuit of sensation.

WHAT THE CRITICS SAID
"The bravado that a jolt of speed gives to men with shaky self-esteem in a still-homophobic culture is an element of its appeal. But as men describe the intensified and prolonged pleasure of sex with meth, you realize that it belongs to the same category of sensation-seeking as race-car driving, skydiving and gambling. A craving for delirious excitement may be hard-wired into the male psyche."
Stephen Holden, *The New York Times*

Rock Haven

(2007)

Homosexuality vs. Christian Dogma

We've seen similar stories like this before—call it scenario 101. Still, in lieu of many boy-on-boy romances, we think it's worth viewing for 78 minutes on a rainy night. It's a good date movie with your prospect for Mr. Right sitting on a sofa in your living room.

A devout Christian, Brady (Sean Hoagland) moves with his mother to the seaside town of Rock Haven. The mother, Marty (Laura Jane Coles), plans to set up a Bible School nearby.

One day Brady spots worldly, seductive Clifford (Owen Alabado). The handsome hunk is shirtless on the beach. For Clifford, it's love at first sight, although he has deep and troubling fears about his gayness.

Clifford brings him out. At one point the two young men are fully nude.

The mother is a problem. Most viewers saw her as a homophobe, although others did not. One film-goer—perhaps misguided—disagreed, claiming, "It's quite possible to be tolerant of homosexuals without changing your religious beliefs regarding their behavior."

Obviously, Clifford has to embark on a personal journey of discovery in the hopes he might reconcile his spiritual beliefs with his sexual conflict. Can he come into his own as an active gay man?

That, dear reader, is the question.

WHAT THE CRITICS SAID
"While we appreciate the skin, the frequently shirtless or even nude boys were not enough to distract us from the bad acting and lack of a unique plot."
Christopher Jones, *Instinct*

"Provocative and romantic, an affecting story about two souls, each looking for an experience of grace."
Frameline

Rome

(2005)

Love, Ambition, Debauchery, Betrayal

This excellent TV miniseries, a BBC-derived costume drama, drew a lot of gay viewers because of its sweeping sense of epic grandeur, cruelty, ambition, passion, an obsessive concern for the aesthetics of ancient Rome, and an unabashed showcasing of frequent male nudity. It includes graphic depictions of masters and slaves giving birth to a Roman Empire that would in time become a symbol for debauchery.

Nominated for two Golden Globes, and created through the united efforts of the teams that created both *Six Feet Under* and *The Sopranos*, it was crafted within the largest standing film set in the world, one that filled up five acres of a backlot at Cinecittà Studios. It is an action/drama centered around the final years of the reign of Julius Caesar and the events that immediately followed.

Ray Stevenson (Titus Pullo) and Kevin McKidd (Lucius Vorenus) star as two soldiers in the army of Caesar, as artfully depicted by Ciarán Hinds.

There are no rules about right or wrong, and soldiers develop their own personal code of morality as circumstances and their individual temperaments dictate. There is no disapproval of ladies who smoke hemp from Persia or men who fuck boy-ass either.

Of course, in terms of sheer flesh-peddling, nothing equaled Bob Guccione's quasi-porno, *Caligula* in 1979, where an actor didn't get cast unless he was well endowed. But *Rome* as a series is a hell of a lot better than the movie *Troy* with small-dicked Brad Pitt or *Alexander* with big-dicked Colin Farrell.

As a historic vehicle drenched with sweat, blood, and verisimilitude, we'd rate *Rome* up there with *Centennial* and *Roots*. Rome contains more than the typical Hollywood glitter that envelops most epics of the ancient world, and it's a long way more artful than any of Steve Reeves' gladiator films.

Round Trip

(2003)

Two Women, One from Israel, One from Africa

Shahar Rozen directed this 95-minute drama from Israel from a script by Noa Greenberg. It's the story of a divorced Israeli woman, Nurit (Anat Waxman), who hires a single African woman as a nanny. The latter role of Nigerian-born Mushidi is played by Nthati Moshesh. The two women, as predictable, form a passionate friendship that leads to a romantic relationship.

Surprisingly for a film set in Israel, there are no references to that country's volatile politics.

A bus driver, Nurit has found herself in Tel Aviv, with her two kids after she leaves her jobless spouse. Rozen carefully establishes the developing relationship, almost as if he were making a documentary.

As Nurit's friendship with Mushidi blossoms, Nurit is forced to make a tough decision.

WHAT THE CRITICS SAID

"The naturalistic acting among all the primary performers nicely compliments the gritty, realistic style employed by Rozen—though his tendency to resort to contrived coincidences (particularly in the film's final act) eventually diminishes the story's impact. In the end, *Round Trip* is a fine effort—the movie deftly manages to overcome its obviously miniscule budget—though Nurit never quite becomes a character we're completely rooting for."
InsideOut

"During most of the film, the main character, Nurit, doesn't smile—she hardly seems to have any personality at all. Then she meets Mushidi, who moves in with Nurit and her two children as a nanny. Nurit and Mushidi become lovers and, finally, Nurit smiles. She is obviously happy with Mushidi. But then her estranged husband finds out about the two women and threatens to take the children from Nurit. She can't give up her children so she gives up Mushidi, who in turn turns herself into immigration and is deported."
P. Bigelow

Running With Scissors

(2006)

A Bipolar Auntie Mame

This is the most frightening depiction of motherhood since Faye Dunaway picked up that wire hanger.

Annette Bening, who has a large gay following, stars in this hilarious and poignant feature based on the memoirs of Augsten Burroughs.

In the film she plays Deirdre, the mother who sends her son (Joseph Cross) to live with her oddball shrink, Dr. Finch (Brian Cox).

As always, Bening is brilliant as the deliciously mad bisexual mom. In the film, Deirdre has two female lovers, both played by amazing young actresses, Kristin Chenoweth and Gabrielle Union.

Nip/Tuck creator Ryan Murphy adapted and directed this tragic-comic memoir in which the young Burroughs lived with his closeted lesbian mother and an alcoholic father, played by Alex Baldwin. How could any helmer cast a gentle, loving man like Baldwin as an alcoholic father?

The movie is so realistic that Burroughs was sued for defamation of character by the family featured in his memoir. One reviewer wrote, "After seeing the movie, you may side with the plaintiffs." Burroughs more or less depicted his adopted family like the Addams family on LSD, including Finch's profoundly depressed wife, Agnes (Jill Clayburgh) who snacks on dog kibble.

Neil (played by Joseph Fiennes) is a 33-year-old patient and adopted son of the family. He is a gay paranoid schizophrenic who immediately takes the virginity of young Augsten.

Playing the disturbed sisters are sex-mad Evan Rachel Wood as Natalie Finch and Gwyneth Paltrow as Hope Finch.

Paltrow acts the unsmiling sister as if she were still appearing in *The Royal Tenenbaums*. The adopted teenage daughter, Natalie, is recovering from an affair with a middle-aged married man. You can tell that Hope is a little off. She buries her cat, then later digs it up for stew meat. When hearing that the stew is feline, Joe's ad lib was "I don't eat pussy." Helmer Murphy kept the line in the final cut.

Saint of 9/11

(2006)

"We All Have Closets"

Narrated by Sir Ian McKellen, this 90-minute docu by helmer Glenn Holstein "stars," among other appearances, Bill and Hillary Rodham Clinton. In archival footage, *Saint* depicts the life of Father Mychal Judge, Chaplain, FDNY. In an inspiring portrait, the film traces the life of this celibate homosexual, a turbulent, restless, spiritual, and remarkable journey.

Everything this ecclesiastic did stemmed from his love for his fellow man. He was ministering to people with AIDS during a time when such victims were treated like lepers in the Middle Ages. His acts were often simple, including giving a warm coat to a homeless person on the streets of New York in winter.

After the 9/11 attack on the World Trade Center, he became famous. "He touched people in an ordinary, consistent way," said Brendan Fay, the co-producer of the film and a long-time friend of Judge's.

Gene Robinson, the first openly gay bishop in the Episcopal Church, claimed he identified with Judge.

The Irish-American priest, a recovering alcoholic and a confidant of tough, gritty firefighters, was a Franciscan friar. He chose to join his men within the North Tower rather than remaining on the sidelines. He died at the age of 68 after giving last rites to a fallen firefighter.

"He became celebrated for how he died," said critic Andrew Sullivan. "But there's so much more to him than that."

WHAT THE CRITICS SAID
"An unabashed tribute to Judge's life, struggles, and Christian mission, does a good job of communicating what made Judge an inspiring figure to many, while making his life's work accessible and understandable."
John Anderson, *Variety*

Salò or The 120 Days of Sodom

(1975)

"The Most Disgusting Film Ever Made"

The gay Italian filmmaker, Pier Paolo Pasolini, shocked the world with the release of this controversial movie. When he was later murdered by a male hustler; some people claimed it was a deliberate killing orchestrated by shadowy Right Wing figures because Pasolini dared make such a film.

In essence, the filmmaker has transferred the Marquis de Sade's 18th-century writings to 1944 Fascist Italy. It is filled with scenes of teen rape, torture, coprophagy, and murder. The severing of a human tongue is one of the most brutal things to watch.

Even filmmaker John Waters lists this movie as sicker than his worst offenders.

Finding his inspiration in de Sade's *The 120 Days of Sodom*, Pasolini delivers a blistering cinematic critique of fascism and idealism that suggests moral redemption may be nothing but a myth. He "chapters" each section within some of the framework of Dante's *Inferno*. Ultimately, the film is about human cruelty.

The plot depicts four fascist libertines who round up 9 beautiful teenage boys and girls and take them to a villa in Northern Italy where they will be physically, mentally, and sexually tortured—gay rape and everything else. Each of the victims is a well-chosen perfect specimen. As a backdrop to all this, there are four older women, three of whom recount arousing stories while a fourth plays the piano.

One of the most controversial elements of the film occurs when the teens are forced to eat excrement. Pasolini's stated reason for that was his belief that modern culture and society were shit, and, thus, it is fed to us by the powers that be.

For gays, the hardest to take was that Pasolini, a gay man himself, linked homosexuality with death and fascism. In earlier works, he had portrayed homosexuality with far more sensitivity. His apologists claimed that he was "out of his mind" when shooting *The 120 Days of Sodom*.

At the end of this marathon of depravity, the young boys and girls are executed while each libertine takes his turn as a voyeur.

Saturn in Opposition

(*Saturno Contro;* aka *Bir ömür yetmez;* 2007)

Lorenzo's Gone. What Now?

A Turk working out of Italy, director Ferzan Ozpetek gave us *Steam: The Turkish Bath*. Here he comes up with a film less exciting but worth viewing. Filmed in Rome, it is a poignant story of loss, despair, and eventual recovery.

Successful author Davide (Pierfrancesco Favino) is happily same-sex partnered to the gorgeous and charismatic Lorenzo (Luca Argentero) who is 30 years old. They spend their time off with a cluster of devoted, mostly heterosexual friends, with the extroverted and diplomatic Lorenzo being the focus of the most attention.

These friends include Antonio (Stefano Accorsi) and Angeli (Marghesrita Buy), an unhappily married couple with children; Davide's acerbic ex, Sergio (Ennio Fantastichini), and a sunny cokehead Roberta (Ambra Angiolini). Other friends are a rather biting Neval (Serra Yilmaz) and her policeman husband Roberto (Filippo Timi).

One night Lorenzo collapses and is rushed to the hospital, where doctors find that he has suffered a cerebral hemorrhage, from which he will not recover.

Upon his death, the core of friends is thrown into chaos, as Lorenzo seemed to be the glue that held these widely divergent people together.

Suddenly, Lorenzo's estranged father (Luigi Diberti) appears, still grappling with his dead son's homosexuality. Our advice to him at this point: get over it.

WHAT THE CRITICS SAID
"Now deprived of the center of their social gravity, the friends bounce off each other recklessly until they get the chance for one big final reconciliation at the lovely vacation home where Davide and Lorenzo first met. It's all quite elegant, chatty, and Italian."
Dom Willmott

Savage Grace

(2007)

Oedipal Docudrama

This mother-son drama could have been fictionally created by Tennessee Williams. Actually, it's based on a true story, that of the murder of a charismatic narcissist Barbara Daly Baekeland (Julianne Moore) by her 25-year-old only child Tony  (Eddie Redmayne), whose alabaster skin was a lure to both women and men.

Tony was the great-grandson of plastics titan Leo Baekeland, and his mother's occasional partner in sexual congress. Moore plays her character of a borderline personality with great intensity, as when she straddles her son and offers to suck him off when he can't come.

The Barbara Baekeland murder case occurred in a posh London flat on November 17, 1972. The bloody crime became tabloid fodder, causing a stir on both sides of the Atlantic. It remains one of the most memorable of American tragedies.

A failure in his dad's eyes, Tony, as he matures, becomes increasingly close to his incestuous, lonely mother. The seeds for tragedy are sown.

Tony is of indeterminate sexuality, although definitely leaning to his gay side. Their "friends" include a hanger-on Sam (Hugh Dancy), a gay "walker" who accompanies Barbara after her husband has left. Mother, son, and "walker" all end up in bed together.

"I was the steam when hot meets cold," comments Tony, the narrator/killer.

Once again Tom Kalin, who made *Swoon* way back in 1992, shows a masterful touch as the helmer. *Swoon* was about another famous scandal, the murder of little Bobby Franks by Richard Loeb and Nathan Leopold.

WHAT THE CRITICS SAID
"That eternally fascinating duo, Decadence and Dysfunction, rear their pretty heads in *Savage Grace*, a crushingly unsuccessful glimpse into the lives of the rich, peripathetic heirs of the Bakelite plastics fortune. Scripter Howard A. Rodman struggles with characterization."
Jay Weissberg, *Variety*

Save Me

(2007)

Fixing "Sexual Broken-ness"

It's hardly news that there's a divide as wide as the Atlantic Ocean separating gays in America from the fanatical religious right. But this film directed by Robert Cary attempts to build a bridge over The Great Pond.

Starring gay favorite Chad Allen as Mark, it dramatizes the story of a sex- and drug-addicted young man forced into a Christian-run ministry in an attempt to cure his "gay affliction."

This is the first feature film from the new gay-focused production company, Mythgarden.

Genius House, a facility "specializing in sexual broken-ness," is run by a married couple, Ted and Gayle (Stephen Lang and Judith Light).

Just at about the time that Mark begins to think he can free himself from his former lifestyle, along comes fellow resident, Scott (played by Robert Gant of *Queer As Folk*). The two men form a fast friendship with an undercurrent of sexual attraction.

At this point most gay viewers can predict the inevitable.

WHAT THE CRITICS SAID
"Helmer Robert Cary and the solid cast of *Save Me* go past potential cliché—or preachiness—by resisting an easy melodrama in favor of stylistic restraint and nonjudgmental empathy. Indeed, the pic loses credibility only in departments where it might be a little too evenhandedly nice."
Robert Koehler, *Variety*

"*Save Me* establishes a clumsy dialectical agenda straight (so to speak) out of the gate, cross-cutting between a day in the life of Mark (Chad Allen), a cocaine-addled young man with a taste for messy sex in cheap motels, and a group of hymn-singing churchgoers with affiliations to the Genesis House, a retreat devoted to converting gay men to heterosexuality. And yet, as the unreconstructed gay might say, look out, girl! Here comes Ted (Stephen Lang), a hunky fellow resident."
Jeannette Catsoulis, *The New York Times*

Saving Face

(2004)

The Wedding Banquet, But With Chicks, Not Dudes

This romantic comedy, written and scripted by Alice Wu, is about a Chinese-American lesbian and her traditional mother, who are reluctant to go public with secret loves that clash against cultural expectations. Wu is especially effective when she focuses on the values of first-generation and second-generation Chinese-Americans.

In Manhattan, Wil (Michelle Krusiec) is shocked when her single mother (Joan Chen) arrives on her doorstep pregnant. Her old-fashioned father has banished her from their apartment in Flushing, Queens, when he discovered that she is pregnant. He will accept her back if she will return with a husband or else prove that it was an immaculate conception.

Wil sets about to find a bachelor Chinese man to marry Ma. Her attempts at dating turn out to be some of the funniest moments in this lighthearted, feel-good film.

There are complications. Wil, a brilliant surgeon, is also a lesbian. She has the hots for a beautiful dancer named Vivian (Lynn Chen), whom she met at one of those socials her mother is forever dragging her to, trying to fix her up with Mr. Right. Chinese herself, Vivian is much more of a free spirit. To thicken the plot, her father is also Wil's boss.

A lot of the humor has a sitcom ring, and the upbeat ending seems a bit forced, but there is amusing material here. Watching it is almost a must for Chinese-American lesbians.

WHAT THE CRITICS SAID
"*Saving Face* deals with familiar subject matter that has been pretty well and tritely trammeled already. But Alice Wu's debut film is so deft, natural, and exquisitely specific, it feels fresh. A former computer programmer, Wu writes like she's been doing it for years, and *Saving Face* avoids the pitfalls of many of the coming-out, coming-of-age, and coming-to-terms-with-your-family movies popular with first-timers. The film is sweet without being saccharine, wry without being cynical, and unabashedly romantic without being cloying or disingenuous."
Carina Chocano, *Los Angeles Times*

Sebastiane

(1976)

Homoerotic Vision of a Martyred Saint

This was Derek Jarman's first effort as a director, getting an assist from his partner Paul Humfress. When asked why there were so many nude bodies in the film—often full frontal—Jarman told the press, "We couldn't afford costumes."

The first film in Latin with English subtitles, *Sebastiane* is a sensuous, lushly photographed, homoerotic vision of the tragedy of St. Sebastiane. It is filled with scintillating images of male bodies and graphic sex scenes.

In 300 A.D., the Roman Sebastianus is exiled to a remote outpost populated exclusively by men, who turn to each other to satisfy their sexual desires. The role of Sebastiane is played by Leonardo Treviglio. The film was aired on TV in Britain and shocked thousands. Gay men, however, not being faint of heart, loved it. This is stating the obvious, of course, but this film is not for homophobes.

In the plot, such as it is, Sebastiano becomes the target of lust from a homosexual Roman centurion, but he rejects the man's advances.

Most film devotees are divided into two warring camps—pro-Jarman and anti-Jarman. We're pro-Jarman. The director has *cojones*. He showed great courage and resourcefulness in bringing this "saintly" film to the screen.

He got us all hot and bothered from the first scene, depicting a feast-orgy at the Court of the Emperor Diocletian.

Made less than a decade after male homosexuality became legal in Britain, *Sebastiane* traveled a more graphic road than any other gay film at that time. It certainly explored the erotic allure of the male body.

English subtitles are often amusingly translated. For example, the word "motherfucker" comes out as Oedipus.

Actor Ken Hicks played Adrian in the film. At one point he presents a full erection. In some versions released of the film, the erection is not visible.

The Secrets

(*Ha-Sodot;* 2007)

Repressed Women Discover Their Voices

One of the best Israeli films in years, *The Secrets* explores an exotic Jewish subculture, focuses on a lesbian love affair, and has a great French star (Fanny Ardant) in its cast. It follows in the wake of several movies that treat Israel's ultra-Orthodox religious communities with a critical eye, the sympathy going to a liberal-feminist point of view which is often suppressed in such male-dominated societies.

Naomi (Ania Bukstein) doesn't relish entering into an arranged marriage with Michael (Guri Alfi), an arrogant rabbinical student. She's a disappointment to her father, Rabbi Hess (Sfi Rivlin). A gifted student of the Torah, she persuades her elders to let her attend the Daat Emet Seminary for women in Safed, an ancient site of reclusion for followers of mystical Judaism.

Here she develops an intense friendship with Michelle (Michal Shtamler). Naomi and Michelle are assigned by the headmistress to help Anouk (French actress Fanny Ardant), who has spent 15 years in prison for killing her lover and is suffering from terminal cancer. Anouk asks for the Kabalistic ritual of purification, and the girls put her through a series of cleansing ceremonies.

This process opens the door to new horizons for the two young women and a fresh desire to be true to themselves, no matter what the cost.

WHAT THE CRITICS SAID
"An intriguing and sensitive exploration of the lives of young Orthodox women. It's a real pleasure to watch the story unfold and enjoy the work of three wonderful actresses: the French superstar Fanny Ardant, and the up-and-coming Israeli Ania Bukstein and Michal Shtamler. Ardant, who was once the muse of François Truffaut, has a riveting screen presence and is still a haunting beauty. Bukstein is in nearly every frame and gives a wonderful, nuanced performance. Shtamler is also appealing and highlights her character's contradictory impulses."
The Jerusalem Post

The Sergeant

(1968)

Suppressed Homosexuality = Homicidal Rage

From the beginning, director John Flynn presents the sergeant (Rod Steiger) as a war hero, depicting a black-and-white scene in 1944 France. His "heroic" deed included the strangling of a helpless, disarmed German soldier, the sergeant's death grip on the younger man betraying a latent homosexuality.

The film was scripted by Dennis Murphy who based it on his 1958 novel of repressed homosexuality back in those "good ol' days" when a gay man had to commit suicide at the end, as indeed Steiger does in this film version made a decade later.

It is now 1952. Steiger arrives at a camp as a first sergeant reporting for duty at a U.S. base in rural France. He finds the unit slovenly and imposes a rigid regime of discipline.

He is strangely attracted to a very handsome young enlisted man, Pfc. Tom Swanson, who is straight and has a French girlfriend. He makes the young man his personal assistant. The sergeant struggles with his latent homosexuality and continuously tries to repress it.

He refuses Law a pass to see his girlfriend—the sergeant is obviously jealous—and tension mounts between the two men. At one point, viewed as shocking upon the film's release, he boldly kisses the object of his affection.

In the aftermath, he wallows in some booze-induced sexual suffering before putting a gun to his head as a means of ending his miserable existence.

WHAT THE CRITICS SAID
"Although Steiger is too good an actor to camp it up, he comes off with all the subtlety of a drag queen—unctuous, mean, commanding, pathetic—in his courtship of the private. As played by John Philip Law, the private also is remarkably dense—he is so hostile that it would seem the sergeant would have to be psychotic to run after him with such boozy abandon."
Vincent Canby, *The New York Times*

Sévigné

(2004)

Torn Between Three Lovers

The name of Sévigné, of course, comes from the famous Madame de Sévigné (1626-96), of letter-writing fame in France. The Parisian marchioness is still celebrated for the collection of 1,700 letters to her daughter. Collectively, they evoke the gossip and values of France's *ancien régime* at the height of its confidence and power.

The writer, director, and star of the film is Marta Balletbò-Coll, often called the "Woody Allen of Catalonia." It's been a decade since she thrilled audiences with her film, *Costa Brava*. Here she's back in all her majesty in this 82-minute drama made in Spain with English subtitles.

The plot revolves around the life of Júlia Berkowitz (Anna Azcona), who decides to direct a play in Barcelona based on the life of *Madame de Sévigné*. The director finds herself identifying with Madama de Sévigné's long ago words: "Sometimes I feel as if I embarked on a life without my own consent."

As we spin merrily along, Júlia has to face a decision: her husband, her young male lover, or the unpredictable female writer of the play.

Tough choice, girl.

WHAT THE CRITICS SAID
"Stunning locations and strong performances keep this witty story bubbling along as it opens up conversations about the role of art in the theater and about following one's heart."
www.outfest.org

"Director Marta Balletbò-Coll, whose feature film, *Costa Brava,* won the Audience Award at Frameline 19, returns with a new comedy which is sure to delight her fans."
Darlene Weide

"A potentially unappealing premise—neurotic crises among middle-aged members of Catalonia's chattering classes—is made quirkily attractive in the bubbly low-renter, *Sévigné*."
Jonathan Holland, *Variety*

Sex Positive

(2008)

Three Men Who "Invented" Safe Sex

In a day when barebacking has returned, and H.I.V. infection rates among gay young men has risen, this docu is something to watch. Those who fail to learn from history . . . you know the rest.

The docu by Daryl Wein asks the question: "What if you knew a deadly epidemic was coming, and no one would believe you?"

Richard Berkowitz, who once made his living as a $100-an-hour dominant S&M hustler, became an AIDS activist. As a student at Rutgers in the 70s, he led one of the first gay protest marches in New Jersey against a homophobic fraternity prank.

In 1995 Berkowitz himself received a diagnosis of AIDS. In the film he appears as himself, and is extremely candid about his life. There are other appearances by notables, none more so than Larry Kramer, today a gay icon.

The revolutionary Berkowitz made an incomparable contribution to the "invention" of safe sex for gay men, and, until this docu came around, he had never been aptly credited.

He was assisted in his fight by virologist Dr. Joseph Sonnabend and performer Michael Callan. All three argued that the more sex partners one had, the greater the risk of contracting HIV, although that should have been obvious even to the most thickheaded.

Footage of gay life in New York in the early 80s seems almost quaint. At the time, little was known about the spread of AIDS. Some gay men (not to mention the straight world) thought you could contract it from a toilet seat. Many dumb straights thought it was the "gay cancer," and somehow their blood streams were immune.

With the deaths of some 40 million people worldwide from AIDS, that appears unbelievably stupid. As amazing as it is, a survey of some men in Harlem in 2009 revealed that many people post-millennium still think you have to be gay to get AIDS. This film addresses some of that ignorance.

Shelter

(2007)

Brokeback Mountain with a Happy Ending

Jonah Markowitz, the director and scripter, said he wanted to make "the anti-*Brokeback Mountain*"—that is, a film where the gay lovers don't end up tragically, either murdered or facing a lonely old age alone in a trailer.

Shelter is a genuine, heartfelt tale about homosexual love between two young men, minus all the shattered lives and tragic fates. Call it queer movie comfort food.

"Avowed heterosexuals," as they were called, were cast in the gay roles of Zach (Trevor Wright) and Shaun (Brad Rowe). Zach has a going nowhere kind of job as a line cook, although he dreams of enrolling in a top art school. In his spare time, he helps his needy but selfish sister Jeanne (Tina Holmes) take care of his 5-year-old nephew Cody (Jackson Wurth).

The rest of his free time is spent surfing with his best friend, Gabe (Ross Thomas), who comes from a wealthy family. Zach's dreary life changes when Gabe's older brother, Shaun, arrives on the scene.

These two California surfer dudes fall in love and, as can be predicted, are headed for a "happy-ever-after" ending. But, of course, there will be problems along the way.

Zach's sister becomes a problem when she tries to sabotage his artistic ambitions. This dysfunctional mother, no doubt a homophobe, at one point asks Zach, "Are you a fag?"

WHAT THE CRITICS SAID
"As the two young men hit the surf and Shaun's mattress with equal enthusiasm, the movie's abundance of tanned bodies, rolling waves, and golden sunsets create an aesthetic of inoffensive hedonism that perfectly matches the subject matter."
Jeannette Catsoulis, *The New York Times*

"Doing a respectable but uninspired multitasking job overall, helmer Markowitz fares best with the scenes between Zach and Shaun, which support a real chemistry that emphasizes affection over eroticism."
Dennis Harvey, *Variety*

Shelter Me

(*Riparo;* 2007)

Will Love Overcome Class Differences?

Helmer Marco S. Puccioni also co-scripted this Italian film with English subtitles. It's the story of a lesbian couple—arguably the most beautiful on screen—and a young Moroccan immigrant stowaway. The star is Maria De Madeiros, who scored so well in *Henry & June* and *Pulp Fiction*. De Medeiros plays Anna, who is both smart and seemingly fragile. She and her lover Mara (Antonia Liskova) are returning from a holiday in Morocco when they discover a stowaway Anis (Mounir Ouadi). The trio embarks on an unusual, emotional relationship. The young man from the Maghreb suddenly storms into their relationship, upsetting its balance.

Mara is employed at a shoe factory which is owned by Anna's family. She begins to resent her lack of power in her lesbian relationship, and considers that Anis might be the right person to help her drown her sorrows.

When Anis discovers that the two women are lovers, this doesn't sit well with him. In his country, women do not love other women openly. When Anna lets Anis move in, they become an uneasy trio.

Anis doesn't understand how two women can find happiness together without a male figure. He thinks all women should have a husband and also children. As one viewer put it, "this red-blooded teenager can't rectify his feelings of disgust and sexual fantasy" by living with two beautiful lesbians.

WHAT THE CRITICS SAID
"Other dramas crop up, like business cutbacks, deaths in the family, stolen shoes, and broken down motorcycles, and frankly, it's all a bit much. The relationship between the two women is so rich by itself (and their performances so vivid) that the film almost doesn't need these other, relatively cheap dramatic devices to move the story forward."
Jeffrey M. Anderson

Shem

(2004)

Dallying With Men, Women, & Drag Queens

This is a muddled stewpot with some sex (not hot) and kinkiness. Ash Newman, playing a teenage boy, Daniel, in Caroline Roboh's *Shem*, is very good looking—and at least that's something. One bright day in London, this bratty 19-year-old decides to abandon his two lovers—a mother-and-son combo. Incidentally, Mrs. Roboh, the scripter and producer, plays the older woman that Newman ditches.

Quitting his job in advertising, he stops in to see his grandmother. This eccentric matriarch (Hadassah Hungar Diamant) sends Daniel on a wild goose chase to locate her father's grave. The search takes him through Paris, Berlin, Prague, Budapest, Belgrade, and Sofia.

The old lady's papa died in 1939, and she is eager to learn the whereabouts of his grave. In looking for it, our handsome but arrogant prick dallies with both sexes and some drag queens of unknown gender. One man blindfolds him and ties him up. "I'm not gay," he says to Daniel, "I like to play." Daniel seems ready to have sex with anybody, but turns down a trio of underage girls he's presented with in a brothel in Sofia.

WHAT THE CRITICS SAID
"As a travelogue, *Shem* (which means 'name' in Hebrew) is pleasant. It just might send you packing for Eastern Europe. As a narrative, *Shem*, directed by Caroline Roboh, is a pointless hodge-podge with a finale that will leave viewers scratching their heads."
—V.A. Musetto, *New York Post*

"Daniel's looks may charm everyone who crosses his path, but he is like the movie: Most of the depth that does exist remains buried beneath the surface."
Laura Kern, *The New York Times*

"A bizarre hybrid between Euro erotic thriller and a parable of Jewish awakening."
Ken Fox, *TV Guide*

Shock to the System

(2006)

Film Noir Private Dick Goes Gay with Vanilla BF

In the wake of the release of *Brokeback Mountain*, Chad Allen, who plays Donald Strachey in this crime drama, told the press: "Until *Brokeback*, there was a huge fear or belief that you couldn't tell a story with a gay hero and have it make money. But a well-made movie with a good story trumps everything. It's not just a victory for gay rights. It's a victory for humanity."

Though not totally satisfying as a thriller, *Shock to the System* is refreshing entertainment for gays. Writing under the pseudonym of Richard Stevenson, Richard Lipez launched the series with his 1981 novel, *Death Trick*. The mystery introduced Donald Strachey, a gay private investigator who evokes Bogie in the 40s. He walks the mean streets of Albany, not New York.

Shock to the System is the second Donald Strachey mystery to be adapted for film. The first of the series was *Third Man Out*.

Cast as Strachey's loving vanilla boyfriend (or husband) is Sebastian Spence, with Nelson Wong playing an enthusiastic assistant. Incidentally, our gay private eye makes his first appearance bobbing up from his husband's lap.

The plot gets rolling when Strachey is hired by a nervous young man who promptly turns up dead.

Morgan Fairchild appears in a freakish cameo. Canuck helmer Ron Oliver (*Queer as Folk*) in this *film noir* cast Dr. Cornell (Michael Woods) as a shady type who runs a gay "reparative therapy" center.

A detour involves Stachey's first love, an Army buddy during the Gulf War. It seems designed to poke fun at the stupid "don't-ask-don't-tell" policy.

We don't know what Dashiell Hammett or Raymond Chandler would have to say about bringing a gay twist to their old *film noir* genre.

Of course, some viewers wanted more sex in *Shock*, though there is some gay hanky panky and a steamy shower scene.

Shortbus

(2006)

Fetishists Perform With Their Genitals

In Cannes at the annual film festival, *Hedwig* creator John Cameron Mitchell insisted that all the orgasms in *Shortbus* be real—not faked.

We believe him too. In one of the opening scenes, a dude sucks himself off. We get to see that and even the jizz. It sure didn't look faked.

His *Shortbus*, perhaps the most provocative and controversial A-list film released in 2006, is a sexually explicit portrait of New York artists and flotsam/jetsam bohemians on a comic and cosmic quest for "connections."

In the film, there is a free-loving Manhattan salon where a hip crowd gathers to converse and share body fluids.

Justin Bond of the fabled *Kiki & Herb* cabaret act is the only big name star in this farce, and he delivers the real standout performance. He is the club's gay host who describes the venue as "just like the 1960s, except with less hope."

Among the chief characters in this candid sex tale is Sofia (Sook-Yin Lee), a sex therapist. Her big problem involves telling her husband Rob (Raphael Barker) that she's never had an orgasm.

Two lovers, James (Paul Dawson) and Jamie (P.J. DeBoy), bring in a third dude, Ceth (Jay Brannan), to spice up their relationship of five years. All this is being video-recorded by the voyeur, Caleb (Peter Stickles), from an apartment across the street.

Lindsay Beamish makes an appearance as Severin, a dominatrix, an artsy Midwesterner who disguises her insecurities and loneliness behind the whip of her adopted trade.

The tagline for this shocker might be, "You're either on the bus, or you're off the bus," that rallying cry of 60s counterculture.

Silkwood

(1983)

Cher Plays It Dyke in a Nuclear Protest

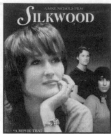

Cher may not be a lesbian—after all, she fucked the very heterosexual Tom Cruise—but her daughter used to be before she became a man. But at least Cher got to play a lesbian on screen when she starred with Meryl Streep as Karen Silkwood and Kurt Russell as Drew Stephens. The film was directed by Mike Nichols and co-scripted by Nora Ephron and Alice Arlen.

It tells the story of Karen Silkwood, a metallurgy worker at an Oklahoma plutonium processing plant, who was purposefully contaminated, psychologically tortured, and probably murdered to prevent her from exposing blatant worker safety violations at the plant.

On November 13, 1974, Silkwood died in a suspicious-looking car accident on her way to a meeting with a reporter from *The New York Times*. Her mysterious death became a *cause célèbre* and still is the subject of lurid speculation.

Silkwood shares her home life in a rundown abode with two of her co-workers, her boyfriend, Kurt Russell, and her lesbian friend Dolly Pelliker, as played by Cher.

The plot heats up at home—not just at the Oklahoma nuclear plant—when a blonde cowgirl, beautician Diana Scarwid, moves in with Cher. In 1983 both Streep (Best Actress) and Cher (Best Supporting Actress) were nominated for Oscars.

WHAT THE CRITICS SAID
"Cher has some wonderful moments, none better than in an intense argument scene with Streep, which turns into a lovely reconciliation. Diana Scarwid is low-keyed but still outrageous as Cher's lover, and the quartet's domestic trials provide some welcome comic relief to the otherwise heavy drama."
David Denby, New York Magazine

"As a nuclear-age horror story, *Silkwood* is both haunting and deeply disturbing."
Sheila Benson, *Los Angeles Times*

The Silver Screen: Color Me Lavender

(1997)

Spot the Closet Cases Within Golden Age Films

Filmmaker Mark Rappaport brought us *Rock Hudson's Home Movies* in 1992. He did it again with this 100-minute docu that unearths gay moments in the often-forgotten past of films from the so-called Golden Age of Hollywood when a certain love dared not speak its name.

The film examines the various subterfuges that screenwriters and actors used to slyly depict "perverted" love. Between 1930 up to the end of the 60s, this was done through the use of oblique references and *double entendres* which usually fooled the "uninitiated," but which were very clear to hipsters. By the end of the 60s, however, many members of the movie-going public had become a lot better educated about what was coming Out of the Hollywood factory.

Rappaport himself wrote, directed, and edited this docu, using a narration by Dan Butler, described in the film's publicity material as "an outspoken gay actor." Butler, of course, is known for playing the skirt-chasing womanizer on the hit sitcom, *Frasier*.

Rappaport sees gay where only gays might see it, not the general public. Were there really homosexual undercurrents between Bob Hope and Bing Crosby in all those Road pictures? Of course, they did kiss a few times, but presumably, it was a mistake. Most of the usual prissy suspects of the 30s are rounded up, including Franklin Pangborn, Edward Everett Horton, and Eric Blore.

Was Walter Brennan really gay when he played those grizzled old sidekicks to such macho stars as Humphrey Bogart, Gary Cooper, and John Wayne? Maybe he fell in love with these boys when they took out their dicks to piss together in the desert.

Also discussed are two additional suspects from the 1930s, "roomies" Randolph Scott and Cary Grant.

Simon

(2004)

Conventions Denied & Differences Overcome

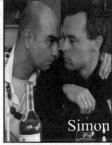

Eddy Terstall directed this 102-minute feature film about an unusual friendship between a shy gay man and a flamboyant womanizer. The straight, Simon Cohen, is played by Cees Geel, the gay, Camiel Vrolijk, by Marcel Hensema, and both do a fine job in etching their screen portraits. There is low-key charm here, even though the social issues portrayed are a bit heavy.

As the film opens, Camiel, a dentist in Amsterdam, accidentally encounters Simon, an old friend with whom he has not bonded in at least a decade and a half. Over the years the friends have become estranged, but via flashback we see how they met under a cloud of trauma, since they originally bonded in an emergency room.

Upon the reunion of these long-lost friends, Camiel is living with his lover, Bram (Dirk Zeelenberg). Camiel's coming together with Simon is fraught with tragedy, as Camiel learns that Simon has a terminal brain tumor. Not only that, but he has adopted two children during a visit to Thailand.

Now for the weighty issues: Voluntary euthanasia emerges, as do gay marriage issues, even parenthood.

WHAT THE CRITICS SAID
"As the film's theme switches abruptly from the joy of hedonism to the terror of death, the transition is smooth and the mood remains remarkably lighthearted. Much of this is due to a strong and eclectic ensemble cast, who respond to Eddy Terstall's relaxed direction (he also wrote the script) with a naturalness that softens the story's sharper edges."
Jeannette Catsoulis, *The New York Times*

Eddy Terstall's mild brand of humor and predictable throat-catching weepiness works strictly along boob-tube illness-of-the-week lines, with plentiful shots of topless women."
Variety

Sin Destino

(2002)

Hustling on the Streets of Mexico City

This is gritty drama by Leopoldo Laborde (its helmer and scripter)—shot on the seedy streets of Mexico City and telling of a 15-year-old bisexual hustler who peddles his meat. In Spanish with English subtitles, it covers a familiar theme on the gay screen that's been better dramatized before.

Sin Destino is a realistic portrait of what it's like hustling on the streets of Mexico City.

When Francisco Rey was 9 years old, he was picked up by Sebastian (Roberto Cobo), a pedophile who wanted to photograph him. The relationship turned sexual.

On the streets as a 15-year-old, the young boy continues to prostitute himself to men for sex and money. As predictable, he's addicted to drugs—cocaine in this case—which is supplied by his dealer David (David Valdez).

Even though Francisco spends most of his nights engaged in gay sex, he's not happy about the situation and wants to have couplings with and lose his virginity to girls closer to his own age.

By chance encounter, Francisco is reunited with Sebastien who wants to rekindle their sexual relationship. At first Francisco rejects Sebastien.

What the boy wants is to have sex with a blonde-haired girl he admires from a distance. But David urges him he must first seduce a whore to gain experience in bed with a woman.

Desperate for money, he calls on Sebastien and offers to be photographed again. Following a struggle, Sebastien knocks the boy out with a walking cane and rapes him.

When Francisco wakes up, he is aware that he's been raped. The boy kills the pedophile and steals his money.

With money for his girlfriend, he takes her to David's place where he forcibly rapes her, causing her death.

The film ends tragically, with body parts in plastic bags being dumped.

A Single Man

(2009)

A Gay Man Grieves Over His Lost Lover

The most enthusiastic viewers of this film called it much more important than *Brokeback Mountain*. Gucci's fashion god, Tom Ford (of all people), both directed and scripted the film based on Christopher Isherwood's 1964 novel.

Because the book is mainly a stream-of-consciousness narrative, there were predictions that it would never make it to the screen. But now it has done so, with Colin Firth in the lead as George and the always-talented Julianne Moore cast as Charlotte.

A homosexual English professor lives in Santa Monica. He's just been told that his lover of 16 years has been killed in a car crash. Regrettably, George can't attend the funeral because his lover's family disapproves of their "sinful" relationship. In the wake of the death, George enters a long period of grief, having lost the only person he ever loved.

Jim, George's lover, is played by Matthew Goode. He is introduced in flashbacks—intimate moments together, how they met.

WHAT THE CRITICS SAID

"Ford evokes the depth of loss that would push a man to suicide through flashbacks, dreams, and image distortions. The opening credits show a naked man floundering underwater, perhaps close to drowning or perhaps living in the water's distorting muffle. The scenes in the present tend to be grainy, muffled, and somewhat colorless as well. The set decoration is precise to period detail, but in a way, this is almost a distraction, as George's story is unmistakably universal and timeless. The one place where period details work beautifully is the night in 1946 when George and Jim met at an overflowing gin joint near George's home. The celebratory post-war atmosphere and Jim looking so handsome in his Navy whites really evoke a time and place that synchs well with this first blush of love."
Marilyn Ferdinand

Small Town Gay Bar

(2006)

Ignorance, Hypocrisy, Oppression

This 81-minute docu was both directed and scripted by Malcolm Ingram, and it won Best Documentary at both the Los Angeles Outfest and the Miami Gay and Lesbian Film Festival.

Ingram's docu trolls the back roads of the Deep South, and comes to a stop at Rumor, a roadside gay bar in Shannon, Mississippi, with a population of 1,657. On the outside, it looks like any weather-beaten shanty. Inside it's a different story, as the gay community holds sway, giving gay nightlife a toehold in the Bible Belt.

Of course, Ingram brings in the requisite interviews with local fag-bashers, none more loathsome than Fred Phelps, who runs his "God Hates Fags" empire out of a nearby town. This demented fool even makes the late Jerry Falwell look like a homophile.

The biggest threat facing Rumors is a slow Thursday night, a sign that former customers have decamped to the bright lights of Memphis, even Mobile. *Small Town Gay Bar* is a valentine—perhaps a black valentine—to rural life, a reminder that not all good things are to be found in a big city.

WHAT THE CRITICS SAID
"We have it good in the city. Sure, we can complain about the cost of living, but we don't generally worry about our license plate numbers being recorded by anti-gay groups as we enter the parking lot of our neighborhood gay bars. That is exactly what happens in small towns in northeastern Mississippi."
Newfest

"Since queer culture went primetime in the U.S., it might be tempting to assume that the community support and political infrastructures accessible to gay men and women in major capitals are available nationwide. Dropping in on the Mississippi Bible Belt, *Small Town Gay Bar* shows that, off the beaten track, the struggle for visibility and dignity is in its infancy."
David Rooney, *Variety*

A Soap

(*En Soap, AKA En såpa*; 2006)

Danish Trannie Addicted to American Soap Operas

In Danish with English subtitles, Pernille Fischer Christensen's debut feature is not for everyone, but is a worthwhile diversion, especially for women.

Newly single Charlotte (Trine Dyrholm), in her 30s, moves into a decaying neighborhood in an unnamed Danish city. She has grown unfulfilled in her relationship with her boyfriend Kristian (Frank Thiel). It's goodbye b.f. and hello Veronica (David Dencik), her neighbor.

Veronica is an introverted transsexual dominatrix who prefers to keep the real world at a distance. "She" takes female hormones and is waiting gender-reassignment surgery. "Johns" pay for Veronica's skills in punishing them for being bad boys.

From this unlikely scenario, a relationship develops between Charlotte and Veronica. Before meeting Veronica, Charlotte engages in one-night stands and shows no interest in post-coital small talk. This suggests she has little interest in men, except for Veronica downstairs who was born Ulrik.

Kristian comes over one night and turns violent toward Charlotte, but Veronica rescues her. Could this be the beginning of a new friendship, even an intimate one? Incidentally, Veronica is addicted to American-style soap operas—hence, the title of this flick.

Chapters within the movie are introduced by an announcer who asks, "Why is it so hard for her to find happiness?"

WHAT THE CRITICS SAID
"At critical moments in their desperately lonely lives, Charlotte and Veronica rescue each other from harm, and their mutual acts of generosity seal a friendship deepened by their shared loneliness. But could such a friendship really flower into passion? Not likely."
Stephen Holden, *The New York Times*

Soldier's Girl

(2003)

Forbidden Love in the U.S. Army

Although little known, this 2003 dramatic film is one of the best ever made in depicting how gay love between two men takes unusual pathways. It also explores—and does so most effectively—how homophobia can lead to brutal murder.

Based on a true story, the film starred the handsome, talented Troy Garity, Jane Fonda's son, as Barry, a private with the 101st Airborne Division of the U.S. Army stationed in Kentucky. In a surprise move, he falls for a showgirl working at a transgendered show. The object of his affection, Calpernia (Lee Pace) is en route to sexual reassignment. The love scenes between Barry and Calpernia are explored with great sensuality and sensitivity.

Soldier's Girl, of course, draws the inevitable comparisons to *Boys Don't Cry* and *The Crying Game*. After seeing *Soldier's Girl*, many viewers, both gay and straight, left with indignation over the military's "Don't Ask, Don't Tell" policy and were horrified at the inadequacy of mental health screening for soldiers trained to feed their aggression.

WHAT THE CRITICS SAID
"For at least half the running time of *Soldier's Girl*, director Frank Pierson and screenwriter Ron Nyswaner's account of the killing at a Kentucky military base in 1999 of a G.I. emotionally involved with a transgendered night club performer is as pedestrian as telemovies come. But pic recovers in later reels, boosted by superior performances and a powerful final act. Both Garith and newcomer Pace give complex, controlled performances, full-bodied and richly empathetic, making the union between this unlikely couple seem entirely plausible and natural."
David Rooney, *Variety*

"Directed with intelligence and sensitivity by the Oscar-winning screenwriter Frank Pierson (*Dog Day Afternoon*), *Soldier's Girl* is one of the most unusual love stories you'll ever see."
DVD Review

Some of My Best Friends Are...

(1971)

"We Believe in Fairies"

This curiosity with an all "star" cast, made before the decadent gay 70s were fully launched, takes place on Christmas Eve in a New York bar, the Blue Jay, a disguised version of Gotham's Zodiac Bar.

The film is derivative of the hit *The Boys in the Band*, made the previous year, but lacks that film's devastating wit. *Best Friends* is more morose. Director Mervyn Nelson, who also wrote the screenplay, has assembled a lonely group of misfits, even Cal Culver who as Casey Donovan starred in that gay porno hit, *The Boys in the Sand*. You don't expect Fannie Flagg or Rue McClanahan (from *The Golden Girls*) to turn up, but they do.

Flagg was cast as the wistful hatcheck girl. She would later write the lesbian-themed novel *Fried Green Tomatoes* in 1991. This time around McClanahan plays a bitchy fag hag.

The love-starved waiter, Nick De Noia, cast as Paul, is cheered up by patrons who chant "We Believe in Fairies." Sylvia Syms appears as the club hostess Sadie, claiming her boys make her feel like a queen.

In another surprise appearance, Candy Darling, the famous Andy Warhol star, is cast as a shy spinster, Karen. Actually, her name is Harry and she's a trannie.

Cast as the aging "Miss Untouchable," Carleton Carpenter lives in his private dream world. His image is forever embedded in a moviegoer's mind when he sang "Aba Daba Honeymoon" with Debbie Reynolds in the 1950 *Two Weeks With Love*.

As the night advances, most of the patrons experience the inevitable crisis. For example, Terry is played by Gary Campbell. His witch-from-hell mother (Peg Murray) arrives in the bar to tell her son that because he's gay he can't go home again. Thanks, Mom, for an old-fashioned Christmas.

But all is not lost. Terry pursues his affair with Scott (Gil Gerard), an airline pilot.

Something for Everyone

(1970)

A Man Shared By Everyone In the Family

One critic called this film "a kind of vengeance on the heterosexual world," suggesting that straight sex is portrayed as "hasty and sordid." At least that's the homophobic point of view. *Something for Everyone* is often linked with *Teorema*, the Pier Paolo Pasolini film that starred Terrence Stamp on full frontal display, as well as Joe Orton's *Entertaining Mr. Sloane*.

Each of these films involves an irresistible hunk, a perfect stranger, who arrives at a home and then charms and seduces everybody in it.

In *Something for Everyone*, directed by Harold Prince from a screenplay by Hugh Wheeler, Michael York as Konrad Ludwig, is a handsome and opportunistic country boy in post-war Austria. He charms his way into a butler position at the castle of the widowed Countess Herthe von Ornstein (Angela Lansbury), who has lost her fortune. As one viewer claimed, "Compared to the von Ornstein family, the MacBeths were just plain folks and the Borgias were a nice Italian family."

Before long, York is launched into an affair with the countess's son (Anthony Higgins) playing Helmuth von Ornstein, and another with the daughter of a rich businessman. There's a wonderful appearance by the Greek actress Despo Diamentidou, Ms. Lansbury's lesbian friend.

WHAT THE CRITICS SAID
"Angela Lansbury is magnificent as a fading countess with a castle in need of repairs, and Michael York is all beautiful, silky, deadly charm and lean, hungry ambition as a young Machiavelli who seduces each member of her family to social-climb. The film is saturated with the howling humor of early Billy Wilder, bathed in the rich, intelligent décor of Ernst Lubitsch, and a monument to artistry and taste."
Rex Reed

"Disguised homosexuality at its distorting worst. For the first time in a major studio release male homosexuals kiss, however stagily and awkwardly. Miss Lansbury looks like an aging female impersonator gone sloppy."
John Simon

Sordid Lives

(2001)

A Menagerie of Southern Grotesques

If George H.W. Bush reviewed Del Shores' comedy, set in a small Texas town, he'd no doubt say, "This family is in deep doo-doo," using the former president's favorite expression.

The small town South, with its stupidity, intolerance, and ignorance, truly deserves this send-up. But the film is not for everyone, unless you enjoy visiting a loony-bin. As one viewer put it, "You have a Tammy Wynette-obsessed tranny, trash-talking trailer queens, a sex-crazed grandma who swings both ways, and Olivia Newton-John as a lesbian country singer."

We meet the family as they are preparing for the funeral of their mother. Newton-John plays Bitsy Mae Harling who provides the chorus back-up for this sordid family tragedy.

The movie opens not long after a woman named Peggy dies after she trips over a pair of wooden legs on the way to the bathroom. She's just had sex with the owner of those legs, G.W. (Beau Bridges), a younger married man with whom she was having an affair.

His wife is Delta Burke cast as Noleta Nethercott, whose best gal pal is LaVonda Dupree (Ann Walker). Don't you love these fried-chicken-eating names? How about Sissy Hickey (Beth Grant), the best named character of all, or "Brother Boy" Ingram (Leslie Jordan)? He has been "put away" for 25 years for being a "homersexual." He's also the one who's convinced that he's Tammy Wynette.

As critic Scott Tobias put it, "This gum-smacking, chain-smoking bunch of rednecks suggest John Waters by way of Jeff Foxworthy, the Deep South as a carnival of Jerry Springer-ready grotesques."

Spartacus

(1960)

Eating Oysters, Eating Snails

In a nutshell, this was the story of the slave Spartacus (played by Kirk Douglas at his peak), who leads a violent revolt against the decadent Roman Empire. It had a grand cast, which included Jean Simmons, Charles Laughton, and Peter Ustinov (who won an Oscar). The movie was inspired by the bestseller by Howard Fast and adapted to the screen by the blacklisted writer Dalton Trumbo. The director was a 31-year-old Stanley Kubrick.

The scene in the film that censors cut back in those pre-Stonewall days of 1960 took place between Laurence Olivier as Marcus and his boy slave Antoninus (Tony Curtis at his most beautiful). The scene occurs in a Roman bath. Both men are wearing bathing trunks, alas.

Here is the dialogue that caused such notoriety:

MARCUS: Do you eat oysters?
ANTONINUS: When I have them, master.
MARCUS: Do you eat snails?
ANTONINUS: No, master.
MARCUS: Do you consider the eating of oysters to be moral and the eating of snails immoral?
ANTONINUS: No, master.
MARCUS: Of course not. It is all a matter of taste.
ANTONINUS: Yes, master.
MARCUS: And taste is not the same as appetite and, therefore, not a question of morals is it?
ANTONINUS: It could be argued so, master.
MARCUS: My noble Antoninus, my taste includes both snails and oysters.

Have you, a movie-goer, ever heard such shocking dialogue on the screen?

A Special Day

(*Una giornata particolare*; 1977)

Marcello Mastroianni Goes Gay—and Likes It

This film—set in Rome during the 1930s—takes place on the day of the first meeting between the two Fascist dictators, Hitler and Mussolini. Alone in her tenement apartment, a bored housewife, Antonietta (Sophia Loren), has been left by her tiresome Fascist husband. She strikes up a friendship with her homosexual neighbor, Gabriele (Marcello Mastroianni).

Their coming together will radically alter both of their outlooks on life. This was a film that made director Ettore Scola famous. *A Special Day* is well made and moving, a love story about two unhappy souls finding comfort in each other.

Oscar nominated as Best Actor for this film with Loren, Mastroianni issued the following statement:

"I have played perverted men in the past, but that has nothing to do with homosexuality. Perversion is kinky sex--some of the lovers I played could only climax during danger, in a strange location, or due to some fetish. The man I played in *A Special Day* was a normal man, only he was homosexual. He did not commit any crime; the law was the crime. In Italy at the time, the Fascist Forties under Mussolini, homosexuals had to be deported. It was a stupid law, and if the Romans or the Renaissance Italians had had it, Italy would not have made half of its great contributions to the world."

"I would like to play more homosexuals, but only if they aren't clowns. I have good homosexual friends, since in Italy and Europe, many, many actors are. But I have to admit it was Sophia Loren who convinced me I had to play this role. I think it was the best of my career."

"I am not a sex addict," Mastroianni told the press after Federico Fellini cast him in *La Dolce Vita*. "I got the job because I have a terribly ordinary face."

In spite of his comment, film audiences continued to think of him as a Latin Lover, a reputation fueled in part by his real life affair with Catherine Deneuve.

Spider Lily
(AKA Spider Lilies)

(2007)

You Know You Want Me

In this film from Taiwan, two young women rekindle a dormant love for each other. Taiwanese docu-maker and director Zero Chou, named her film *Spider Lily* after the flower that is said to line the pathway to hell. The flower contains poison and is said to cause a person to lose memory.

Memory is the key word here. The characters involved question whether their memories are faulty.

Jade (Rainie Yang) plays an Internet web-cam sex worker, who earns her bread peddling smut to horny men seeking guilty pleasure from an on-line peek-a-boo service. Since she was 9 years old, she's been in love with Takeko (Isabella Leong), a tattooist.

Years ago Takeko had a spider lily tattoo engraved on her left arm, and Jade wants one for herself.

Zero Chou told the press, "There was a sense that true love is heavy and sad, and there is love that exists which is deep, and it is in the depths of love that sometimes you experience extreme sadness. However, there are also feelings of happiness. In love, both happiness and sadness co-exist, and life is about change and bitterness and sadness are part and parcel of change. In this film, the power of love and courage are explored."

WHAT THE CRITICS SAID
"Two young women re-awaken a dormant love for each other in *Spider Lilies*. Alas, Chou's scripting abilities and her weakness for dreamy whimsy show only a marginal concomitant upgrade, making this one strictly for the faithful. Mixing innocence and sexuality, countryside flashbacks are pic's best parts; rest is largely Jade teasing her webcam, Takeko struggling with sundry guilt, and an amateurish subplot about a shy Internet cop (Kris Shie)."
Derek Elley, *Variety*

Stage Beauty

(2004)

"Most Beautiful Woman" is Really a Man

Scripter Jeffrey Hatcher based this movie on his play *Compleat Female Stage Beauty* centered around Edward "Ned" Kynaston, a star in London during the Restoration.

Little is known about this actor aside from references in the diaries of Samuel Pepys, who called him "the most beautiful woman on the London stage." Kynaston may have been the lover of the Duke of Buckingham. He was known to have suffered a brutal beating from the hired thugs of Sir Charles Sedley, the protector of Margaret Hughes, believed to be the first actress on the English stage, celebrated for appearing as Desdemona in *Othello*. Up to then, Kynaston was known for his interpretation of that role.

Actor Billy Crudup gives a *tour de force* performance as Kynaston, with Ben Chaplin playing George Villars, the Duke of Buckingham. The role of Sir Charles Sedley was performed by Richard Griffiths, with Zoe Tapper playing the king's mistress, Nell Gwynn. The flawless direction is from Richard Eyre.

Up until the reign (1660-1685) of Charles II, female roles on stage were portrayed by male actors. Marie (Claire Danes) is Kynaston's dresser. She has a great love for the theater, but stage roles are denied her because of her sex. She goes instead to a seedy company putting on plays in a pub and emerges as the actress Margaret Hughes.

Rupert Everett, playing Charles II, is hilarious. His best scene is in drag opposite his mistress, Nell Gwynn.

King Charles II in time changes the rule of the stage, dictating that in the future all female roles will be played by women. Maria in her new incarnation becomes a star. Poor Kynaston is out of work.

WHAT THE CRITICS SAID
"Ned is most comfortable playing a woman both onstage and off. But is he gay? The question doesn't precisely occur in that form."
Roger Ebert

Stagestruck: Gay Theatre in the 20th Century

(2000)

Wilde, Coward, Williams, Orton, Kushner, et al.

For those of us who nod in adoring agreement when Blanche DuBois declares, "I don't want realism, I want magic," this is the film to see.

Gay men, of course, have always been attracted to the theater where, or so it is said, entire worlds as well as the "private self" can be invented and reinvented.

That is exactly what happens in this three-part docu by David Jeffcock. The film shows how playwrights from Oscar Wilde to Noël Coward skewered society's mores, dressing up true stories of gay life in straight clothing. These two stately homos might be credited with inventing the language of camp.

The film goes on to describe how, as time went by and the theater became more straighforward in its depiction of homosexuality, a whole new generation of playwrights emerged. They included William Inge and Tennessee Williams, whose immediate vogue was replaced by that of Edward Albee and Joe Orton, whose work eventually gave way to Tony Kushner's and Larry Kramer's. Kramer and Kushner, in fact, appear in this docu as themselves.

There are also interviews with Albee and Martin Sherman, as well as scenes from *Private Lives, Who's Afraid of Virginia Woolf?* and *Torch Song Trilogy.*

Although it's madly in love with the theater, *Stagestruck* is not just for drama queens.

WHAT THE CRITICS SAID
"The mid-twentieth century would see enormous success for gay playwrights like Terrence Rattigan and Tennessee Williams, but also a proliferation of work that portrayed homosexuality as corrupt and corrupting, with most gay characters either dead before the curtain rose or about to die before it fell. With Edward Albee, Joe Orton, and countless others, the modern, liberated gay stage illuminates the complexities of gay life, including the AIDS epidemic."
Mark Taylor

Stealth

(*Comme des voleurs-à l'Est;* 2007)

Reshaping One's Identity...or Trying To

Switzerland is not a country known for turning out gay cinema, but we had to pay attention to helmer/scripter Lionel Baier's *Stealth (Comme des voleurs)*, his follow-up to the more popular *Garçon Stupide.*

It's a complicated story, but in a nutshell it's the tale of a gay man who, much to the dismay of his BF, Serge (Stephane Rentznik), ends up marrying a Polish woman, Ewa (Alicja Bachleda-Curus), as a means of getting her working papers. Shot in French with English subtitles, *Stealth* stars Baier who has cast himself in the lead, narcissistically calling his character "Lionel."

He learns that his paternal grandfather came from Poland, which becomes an obsession for him. He studies Polish, reads books on Poland, and even cheers the Polish soccer team, which he knows nothing about.

For Lionel's co-adventurer, Natacha Koutchoumov was cast as his older sister Lucie. Together the two of them set off for Warsaw to settle the question of their ancestry once and for all. *Stealth* becomes a sort of road trip picture called by one critic "a reverse-Borat jaunt." The film goes *noirish* when Lionel and his vehicle are stranded in Auschwitz.

He's rescued by Stan (Michael Rudnicki) and ends up in his cabin and his bed. Stan, a gay film student, reorients Lionel's sexual urges in the right direction.

WHAT THE CRITICS SAID
"In what is almost a parody of a personal film, Baier's narcissism is so out there and so closely rhymed to the tonal shift of the narrative it can prove disarming."
Ronnie Scheib, *Variety*

"Being gay or straight isn't the matter here, the idea is just to witness how simple information can turn your way of thinking upside down. Overall, part romantic, part touching, part funny."
Wendy Testaburger

Stoned

(2005)

The Wild and Wicked World of Brian Jones

This movie extends the legend of Brian Jones, the guitarist for the Rolling Stones. When historians record those glorious days of the 1960s, surely they will anoint him as the Pied Piper of 1960s Hedonism.

Officially, Jones' death in 1969 was defined as an "accidental drowning under the influence of drugs and alcohol." His body was found in the swimming pool at his country cottage.

Rumors of foul play persist to this day, spawning three books and now this docu-drama, running for 102 minutes. Brian's building contractor reportedly confessed to the murder before he died in 1993.

Lee Gregory plays the flamboyant Jones, and Paddy Considine is cast as Frank Thorogood, his assistant and possible murderer. The movie does not adequately explore the bisexual undertones of this relationship between the working class (and married) bloke and the dissipated, foppish rock star. There is a lot of tension between these two principals that seems to remain unresolved. Gay viewers would probably have appreciated more diss on the homosexuality of Jones.

Jones' legacy is vague and blurred, especially in this docu. Historically, he is credited with founding the Rolling Stones in 1962, but was kicked out in 1969.

That Jones had talent is undisputed. That he was fucked up in the head is also undisputed. Woolley spent nearly 10 years investigating the death of the dead Stone, and thinks he's come up with the answer—that is, murder. With this docu, Stephen Woolley is making his directorial debut.

Appearing only as shadowy figures are Keith Richards (Ben Whishaw) and Mick Jagger (Luke De Woolfson).

Just for fun, the film includes full frontal male and female nudity and frequent graphic sex.

Stonewall

(1996)

The Fight for the Right to Love

This film takes us back to the late 60s before the Stonewall riots when homosexuals had only meager civil rights and were looked upon as social and medical freaks by a sizable portion of mainstream America.

Let's not get into the debate that all those rights have yet to be realized, that homosexuals are still treated as second-class citizens, but, on the brighter side, we've come a long way, baby, from when the action in this film by director Nigel Finch takes place. Rikki Beadle Blaire adapted it for the screen from a novel by Martin Duberman.

The soup starts to simmer when a hunky young man with a Beatle coif, Matty Dean (Fred Weller), arrives in New York hoping for a better life. He evokes "John Boy" Walton. His arrival is timed only weeks before the famous Stonewall uprising that officially ushered in the era of gay liberation.

In a routine raid on the Stonewall Inn (not the big one), streetwise drag queen LaMiranda (Guillermo Diaz) is roughed up by the police. She repeatedly had her face dunked in a dish pan full of dirty water.

Matty to the rescue. He tries to defend her but a policeman punches him in the nose. At first she's not receptive to Matty, telling him, "I don't do love; there's no percentage in pain." But one night with this hayseed, who presumably delivers some good ol' boy country loving, LaMiranda changes her tune.

The subplots take a back seat to a rather weak re-creation of the 1969 Stonewall riots. Film clips announce the death of Judy Garland, an occasion that may have precipitated the riots, or so some gays believe.

There's some window smashing, some head-banging, and lots of shouts of "Gay Power!" But the real riots were far more dangerous and far more serious than anything depicted in this film.

An impromptu chorus line of drag queens end the night singing to the tune of the "Howdy Doody" theme.

Story of a Cloistered Nun

(Storia di una monaca di clausura; 1973)*

Nunsploitation: Sex Behind the Veil

This Italian nunsploitation film was made before other such films in the genre, including Joe D'Amato's *Images in a Convent*; Sergio Grieco's exploitative *The Sinful Nuns of St. Valentine*, or Jesus Franco's *Letters from a Portuguese Nun*. Domenico Paolella, who also co-scripted the drama with Tonino Cervi, created the best of the Nunsploitationers, with ample nudity but mild violence.

Carmela (Eleonora Giorgi) refuses to marry the man her father has selected for her since she is in love with a peasant named Julian. When she refuses to renounce him, she is sent to a nunnery by her outraged parents. Once inside the convent, she must first undergo degradation to acclimatize her to life in the nunnery, which includes rampant lesbianism by the repressed sisters.

Carmela befriends Sister Elizabeth (Catherine Spaak), who helps her sneak out of the convent for a rendezvous with her lover Julian. The encounter leads to her pregnancy.

Elizabeth has an ulterior motive in aiding Carmela and makes her lesbian intentions known. Carmela turns her down. The scorned woman then takes away the one thing Carmela loves most, Julian.

WHAT THE CRITICS SAID

"Story may be the only film of its type which is actually life-affirming, and the movie ends on a surprisingly positive note (a bloody massacre being the traditional closer in such movies). Story has the fairly unique distinction in its genre of not being entirely corrosive of the institution and faith in general. As such, it inhabits an odd middle ground between the out-and-out sleaze fests that would follow, and the more staid and innocent dramas of the past. Some scenes would not even be out of place in a Hollywood production."
David Austin

"Films in this genre often erupt into lusty lesbian orgies, but not here. Most of the women actually are in the convent to be nuns, not because they yearn for the touch of other women."
Shawn McLoughlin

Straight-Jacket

(2004)

The Life of Rock Hudson Inspired This Flick

No, this is not a re-release of Joan Crawford's 1964 *Strait-Jacket*. This comedy/drama is called "Straight-Jacket," and in it the memory of gay actor Rock Hudson and the "glory" days of 1950s Hollywood live again. Richard Day was both the writer and director.

Actor Matt Letscher is cast as Guy Stone, "America's Most Eligible Bachelor." His career is threatened when he's photographed leaving a gay bar. Tabloid headlines scream: HOMO STAR ARRESTED IN PERV PALACE.

In the film, Guy's rapacious agent is acted brilliantly by Veronica Cartwright playing Jerry. She urges Guy into a loveless marriage with a ditzy secretary, who has the hots for Guy, not knowing he is homosexual.

Something of this nature actually happened to Rock Hudson, except his agent was Henry Willson, who virtually invented the casting couch. Rock Hudson was his chief money maker. Fearing exposure in *Confidential* magazine, Willson urged Rock to marry a secretary in his office.

After the marriage, Guy, in the film, complains that his wife is a "total bottom." In this new twist on the plot, Hudson—that is, Guy Stone—wants to keep his sexual preference a secret, of course, since it would destroy his career as a romantic leading man and prevent him from appearing in a remake of *Ben-Hur*. Another gay actor, Ramon Novarro, had filmed the silent screen version. He was later murdered by hustlers. In real life, the homophobic Charlton Heston got the lead role in the remake of *Ben-Hur*--not Rock Hudson.

The comedy heats up as the secretary, played by Carrie Preston, doesn't seem to realize what's going on. Guy falls for a handsome, Hollywood-hating writer named Rick Foster, as played by Adam Greer.

Richard Day, the writer and director, tosses in a subplot with a McCarthy styled probe of alleged "Commies"—in this case, our hunks, Guy and Rick.

Streamers

(1983)

Homophobia in an Army Barracks

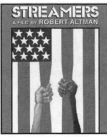

Set within the claustrophobic atmosphere of an Army barracks in 1965, *Streamers* explores homosexuality and homophobia. But not even bare asses and a (blurred) full frontal could tempt gay men to see it. For the director, Robert Altman, this film was no M*A*S*H. *Streamers,* a story of "all-American boys" about to ship out to Vietnam, was too morbid for general audiences. *Streamer's* jocks don't laugh very much.

Altman based his film on a play by David Rabe which won the New York Drama Critics Best Play of the Year award in 1976. The title comes from "streamers"—that is, men whose chutes don't open when they jump from a plane.

Mitchell Lichtenstein (who, incidentally, is the son of the late pop painter Roy Lichtenstein) was cast as the fey Richie, a preening young gay man. In front of his fellow soldiers, Richie is given to saying "outrageous" things.

Billy (Matthew Modine) is a thoughtful but restless recruit who may himself be a closeted homosexual. Richie is paid persistent court by the bisexual outsider Carlyle (Michael Wright), an African-American.

Roger (David Alan Grier) plays a black homophobic straight guy. After Richie accepts Carlyle's crude advances, Roger goes into his faggot denunciations. There is violence here, as when Carlyle stabs Billy with a switchblade. When a drunken sergeant, Guy Boyd, comes into the barracks, he is also murdered.

WHAT THE CRITICS SAID
"On stage, *Streamers* generated an edgy energy and menace. Altman's *Streamers* is curiously disappointedly flat. Although as an ensemble the actors are very good, *Streamers* is visually lethargic as Altman's camera autocratically forbids the eye to roam from talking heads."
Alex Keneas, *Newsday*

"The non-star cast is tremendous, especially Wright as the soldier who triggers a civil war within this troubled Army of a troubled society."
Jack Kroll, *Newsweek*

Suddenly, Last Summer

(1959)

Katharine Hepburn, Homosexuality, and Cannibalism

Suddenly, Last Summer might be the only anti-gay film Tennessee Williams ever wrote. Directed by Joseph Manciewicz, with screenplay by Gore Vidal, it incited the Catholic Church's Legion of Decency to demand that certain cuts be made. Later, they changed their mind. Their reason? "Since the film illustrates the horrors of such a [gay] lifestyle, it can be considered moral in theme even though it deals with sexual perversion."

Williams' most shocking play was deballed a bit, and the cannibalism was muted, but gays got the message, even if general audiences of the time did not.

Hepburn, in what she defined as her "most perverted" role, plays a wealthy widow maneuvering to have her niece Catherine (Elizabeth Taylor) lobotomized by Dr. Kukrowicz (Montgomery Clift) as a means of concealing the awful truth about what happened the previous summer in Spain. Violet claims that Catherine has been "babbling obscenities."

The dreaded secret is that Miss Violet's son, Sebastian, was cannibalized by ravenous youths after a series of presumed sexual adventures. To attract these boys, he was using Catherine as bait, in the same way he had, years before, used his mother.

Some critics defined the film as a product of a "diseased mind." Both Hepburn and Taylor were nominated for Best Actress Oscars, but lost to Simone Signoret for *Room at the Top.*

WHAT THE CRITICS SAID
"Mankiewicz, particularly in his telling of the flashback to last summer, with Miss Taylor's face superimposed over the dread events, has given a vivid, cinematic life to the facets of Williams' play."
Alton Cook, *New York World-Telegram*

"I know films about insane Southern women may not be high up on your list of must-sees, but I urge you to take a gander at this classic tale. Rarely do you see films of this caliber with acting by two of the cinema's best performers ever. It's pretty clear where this film is headed, but the road will keep you strapped to your seat."
Brina Koller

Sugar

(2004)

Gay Teenager Falls in Love With a Street Hustler

This film, in its way, emerges as a tribute to the talent of the late actor André Noble, who in this movie plays Cliff, a puppyish suburban Toronto teen celebrating his 18th birthday. In this stunning, emotional, and homoerotic adaptation of "bad boy" Bruce LaBruce's "JD stories," Cliff, who looks like he's only 14, falls for a gorgeous, crack-addicted street hustler, Butch (Brendan Fehr).

Regrettably Noble died an untimely death, obliterating what might have been a successful acting career. He plays his role with cutting-edge passion. As his fan John Segar said, "Beautiful eyes, gorgeous hair, and a smile that would break a million hearts. His death leaves the film industry without his raw talent and that is a shame."

Butch challenges Cliff's sheltered upbringing by exposing him to street smarts and a very different lifestyle.

Madge (Marnie McPhail) plays Cliff's open-minded yet perennially stressed mother. Haylee Wanstall was cast as the boy's sister Cookie, age 10.

A veteran of the stage, John Palmer directed this film. It was his second venture, having made *Me,* but that was 30 years ago.

WHAT THE CRITICS SAID
"*Sugar* sports the expected *outré* elements—sex, drugs, reckless self-destruction—but also has steaks of tenderness, pathos, and directorial skill. The tale of tortured love between a gay youth and a street hustler juggles a complex load of emotional and tonal colors within an admirably lean runtime."
Dennis Harvey, *Variety*

The Sum of Us

(1994)

Russell Crowe Searching for Mr. Right

Based on a play by David Stevens (he also penned the screenplay), *The Sum of Us* stars two powerful actors, Jack Thompson and Russell Crowe, in this Aussie flick. Thompson plays a widowed father, Harry Mitchell, who is searching for Ms. Right, while his self-effacing son, Jeff Mitchell (Crowe), is searching for Mr. Right.

Unlike most father-son gay dramas that showcase alienation, Harry supports his offspring. Instead of denouncing him as a "poof," the father wants to see his son settle down with a good man who won't break his heart. Crowe is young but not green in the film, and he plays it gay without resorting to any swish mannerisms.

In fact, Harry seems to approve of his son too much. At one point he pokes his head into his son's bedroom while his kid is having sex to ask how everyone would like his tea. When Jeff brings home a new lover Greg (John Polson), the newcomer simply can't handle Harry's acceptance. Unlike Jeff's situation, Greg's father is a sexist brute, who denounced him when he saw him in a gay pride parade. Even so, Greg can't deal with Harry's utter lack of homophobia and bails out.

WHAT THE CRITICS SAID
"In this household Harry is so nosy, benevolent, curious, and obtrusive that Jeff is hardly allowed to have a life, let alone a sex life. Jeff feels some anger and frustration at his father, but not enough, I feel, and as the movie slips into its melodramatic third act, it avoids the issues that are bubbling right beneath the surface of the story in order to get sidetracked with soap opera."
Roger Ebert

"The father-and-son story is a true rarity: a gay-themed film that doesn't compromise for a straight audience, and yet is every bit as accessible to moms and dads because the drama is rooted in family values—not those of the fictional family imagined by the far right, but of the untraditional, loving combinations in which we now live."
Barry Walters, *San Francisco Examiner*

A Summer Day

(*Un jour d'été*; 2006)

Beautiful Boys, Unfulfilled Desires

Made in France, this in its way is another one of those coming-of-age movies. Franck Guérin is making his feature debut (he also co-scripted the drama), and he also knows how to capture the glow of late-summer light or even the naked torso of the film's star, Baptiste Bertin playing Sébastien.

Our hero lives and works with dear old dad (Philippe Fretun), but his heart belongs to his best friend, Mickaël (Théo Frilet). No wonder. As one reviewer put it, Frilet looks like an "erotically charged Botticelli angel."

The bliss is interrupted by the sudden death of the divine Mickaël in a freak soccer accident. In his grief, Sébastien is drawn to Mickaël's mother (Catherine Mouchet). In him, she finds a substitute for her dead son, and he interprets the mother as the figure of his dreams.

We were left wishing that some of those sexual uncertainties had become more certain in this flick, especially after Frilet floored us with his sexual come-hither face.

Director Guérin, when asked what was the meaning of this film, said, "That's open to interpretation." and so it is.

A Summer Day ends without answering any questions and leaves the plot open for speculation. However, this is typical of many French films. Most American films couldn't get away this, although many have tried.

WHAT THE CRITICS SAID
"The sun is high and the hormones raging in a well-to-do provincial town in western France, where Sébastien lives and works with his father in the local garage. Guérin's take on unmanifested gay desire still feels backward for France in 2006. Glances are everything in the film: eyes that avoid and ones that beckon. But the love story is never allowed to emerge. The camera certainly adores the leads."
Jay Weissberg, *Variety*

Summer Storm

(*Sommersturm*; 2004)

Bittersweet Road to Self-Discovery

In this 98-minute comedy/drama shot in German with English subtitles, Tobi (played by Robert Stadlober) and Achim (Kostja Ullmann) are the best of friends and the pride of their local crew club. They do what young boys do together: wrestle, talk about girls, and masturbate with each other. It soon becomes apparent that when masturbating, Tobi is thinking not so much about girls but about Achim.

Stadlober as Tobi clearly steals the film from that dummkopf Achim. He spends quality time with his girlfriend, Sandra (Miriam Morgenstern), who is on the girls' team. Tobi views the relationship of Achim and Sandra with some skepticism.

To complicate matters, Anke (Alicja Bachleda-Curus), a pretty girl, falls for Tobi. To make the plot stew thicker, a gay team arrives from Berlin. In the midst of all this, Toby is "confused."

With the arrival of the athletic, cliché-busting young gay men from Berlin, Tobi needs to come to terms with his fears and hidden longings. The evening before the races begin, the storm that breaks out is more than meteorological.

WHAT THE CRITICS SAID
"An old-fashioned gay romance all the way, courtesy of director Marco Kreuzpaintner, with most of the genre's most beloved conventions—locker room rowdiness, thwarted schoolgirls, swimming scene—and the requisite harmless youth comedy cuteness."
Kelly Vance

"*Summer Storm* is director/co-writer Marco Kreuzpaintner's sharp entry into the 'I'm not gay but my boyfriend is' genre."
James Wegg, *Film Threat*

"Routine in some aspects, but compensates with psychologically sharp writing and performances."
Dennis Harvey, *Variety*

"One of the film's major assets is Stadlober's winningly natural performance—his moody charisma is irresistible."
Elliott Stein, *The Village Voice*

Sunday, Bloody Sunday

(1971)

Being Happy With the Love You Get

This 1951 British film, helmed by gay director John Schlesinger was a breakthrough in its matter-of-fact treatment of bisexuality. Based on a screenplay by Penelope Gilliatt, the story involves two men and a woman in a love triangle.

Peter Finch plays Jewish doctor Daniel Hirsch, who is in love with Bob Elkin (Murray Head), an artist. There are complications: Alex Greville (Glenda Jackson) is also in love with Elkin, and both Hirsch and Greville are aware of each other, since Elkin doesn't believe in keeping secrets. After several famous actresses turned down the role because the film was too risqué, Peggy Ashcroft agreed to play Mrs. Greville, the mother of Alex.

Casting the role of the bisexual young man also proved difficult. Because a hot male-on-male kiss was involved, the original actor, Ian Banne, found the scene so traumatic he turned down this juicy role.

The movie created shock waves when it was released in the early 70s. But today the shock is gone. You can settle back and see a first-rate production, with a talented cast. In fact, *Sunday Bloody Sunday* has become a classic, asking the eternal question, "Is it better to share a lover than to have no lover at all?"

In his role as a gay doctor, Finch is relatively well adjusted. He doesn't seem particularly upset—certainly not suicidal—that he's a gay man.

The film was nominated for four Oscars.

WHAT THE CRITICS SAID
"The glory of *Sunday Bloody Sunday* is supposed to be in the intelligent, sophisticated—civilized!—way in which these two people gracefully accept the loss of a love they had shared. Well, they are graceful as hell about it, and there is a positive glut of being philosophical about the inevitable. But that didn't make me feel better for them, or about them, the way it was supposed to; I felt pity for them. I insist that they would not have been so bloody civilized if either one had felt really deeply about the boy."
Roger Ebert

Swoon

(1992)

A Homoerotic Redefinition of Leopold & Loeb

In May of 1924, the murder of 14-year-old Bobby Frank in Chicago at the hands of Nathan Leopold and Richard Loeb was one of the most shocking tabloid stories of the 1920s. In director Tom Kalin's recitation of their tale, the "thrill killers" appear in archival footage.

Their story has been told on screen before, but in contrast to earlier, squeaky-clean versions, Kalin's includes flashes of homoerotic imagery.

Kalin doesn't flinch from the sexual orientation of these very rich, genius-level kids who killed basically as a mental exercise, deluding themselves that they could outwit the dumb police with their superior intellects.

Conceived to some degree out of boredom, their crime was not one of passion. As relayed by Kalin, it was in some ways like their love affair— a device to relieve boredom more than sexual tension. Daniel Schlachet as Loeb and Craig Chester as Leopold brilliantly bring this arrogant and remorseless duo to life again.

Loeb and Leopold escaped the death penalty because of an impassioned defense at their trial by Clarence Darrow, the best and most famous lawyer of his day. Using their homosexuality to back up his premise, he argued that they were insane.

Expressed in its most horrific terms, the murder of Bobby Frank, as defined by the filmmaker, was an act of sadomasochistic chic.

WHAT THE CRITICS SAID
"Tom Kalin, in his first feature, has taken a different tack from either Alfred Hitchcock's *Rope* or Richard Fleischer's *Compulsion*, one specifically informed by gay politics, essentially equating gayness with outlaw status in a hostile society."
Variety

"The movie may not explain evil, but it certainly gets the feel of it."
Hal Hinson, *The Washington Post*

Taking Woodstock

(2009)

Sex & Drugs & Rock 'n' Roll

After the huge international success of *Brokeback Mountain*, director Ang Lee has once again crafted a film with a gay man as the lead character. Based on the memoirs of Elliot Tiber, it stars Demetri Martin as Elliot. He became neck-deep in "Warhol's 15 Minutes of Fame" when he inadvertently played a role in shaping the direction of 1969's Woodstock Music and Arts Festival.

Tiber was a semi-closeted designer in New York at the time of the Stonewall Riots in 1969. On weekends he ran his parents' failing motel in the Catskills. Lee's most documentary film tells how Tiber used his position as head of the White Lake Chamber of Commerce to bring the festival from Wallkill to Woodstock.

At one point in the film, Tiber contacts Woodstock producer Michael Lang (Jonathan Groft) at Woodstock Ventures to offer his family motel to the promoters and generate some much-needed business. Tiber also introduces Lang to his neighbor, the legendary Max Yasgur (Eugene Levy), who operates a 600-acre dairy farm down the road. At first the farmer wanted $5,000 but when he read in the paper that tickets were being sold, he asked for $75,000. That farm, of course, went down in the annals of music history.

As we know, some half a million people headed for Yasgur's farm for "3 Days of Peace and Music in White Lake."

A minor but compelling character features Lieu Schrieber as "Vilma," the ex-Marine who became a dominatrix drag queen.

Tiber's mother is the villain of the piece, the fiercest and most ferocious of any Jewish mother depicted on the screen up to now. Cast as the overbearing mother is Imela Staunton, who steals every scene she's in. She even takes a broom to chase the nude actresses off the makeshift stage.

It takes a while before we learn that Tiber is actually gay. But when a handsome young man kisses him, and he seems to like it enough to kiss him back, we get the point. There's also a scene showing them nude in bed together.

Tan Lines

(2006)

Surfing Through an Aussie Coming Out Film

Not another coming-of-age story! Fortunately, this one is a bit different, shot on the sun-drenched beaches of Australia with a lot of sexy surfers on display. Ed Aldridge, helmer and scripter, cast real-life surfers with no acting experience in this romance/drama.

Jack Baxter, a cute, likable boy, plays Midget Hollows, a 16-year-old just coming to terms with his sexuality. He lives in a small coastal town on the outskirts of Sydney, sharing a bed with his mother. She seems to have substance abuse problems. His father is unknown. Was dear ol' mum once a hooker?

Midget occupies his time hanging out and surfing with his best mate Dan (Curtis Dickson).

The homecoming of Dan's older brother Cass (Daniel O'Leary) complicates Midget's life for all time. Floppy haired and buff, Cass fled the town four years earlier in the wake of a scandalous affair with his still smitten schoolteacher (Christian Willis).

Almost from the beginning there is a sexual tension between Cass and Midget. Cass helps Midget down the road to becoming queer.

Expect animated erections and talking saints in this film.

WHAT THE CRITICS SAID

"Midget is employed doing part-time 'gardening' for Miss Havisham-like spinster McQuillan (Theresa Kompara) and her boy-crazy niece Alice (Lucy Minter). But in truth, he's expected to mow a lawn of a more pornographic nature under Miss Q's perversely etiquette-minded direction. *Tan Lines* has other oddball, borderline surrealist notions, including the primitive animation of Catholic icons in Cass's bedroom that scold Midget in subtitled Italian."

Dennis Harvey, *Variety*

Taxi to the Toilet

(*Taxi Zum Klo;* 1980)

An Obsessive Hunt for Quick Pickups

Controversial, even revolutionary in its day, this German film displays gay sex very graphically. In the United States, it was rated X, no doubt because of the erect penises and unsimulated fellatio. In one scene, a young man drinks urine direct from the source, the penis of Frank Ripploh, who also wrote and directed this German film.

Ripploh plays "Frank" as a bearded, shaggy-haired schoolteacher with an interest in filmmaking. When not in the classroom, he has one of the most active sex lives in Germany, or so it would seem. The Berlin schoolteacher pursues sex in public toilets, among other venues. The protagonist is depicted as immature and irresponsible.

Frank is seen at times correcting school papers in a public toilet as he awaits his next sexual conquest.

One evening he meets "Bernd" (actor Bernd Broaderup) who becomes his live-in lover. Frank doesn't remain faithful to Berndt very long, and soon he is cruising public places again. His polyamorous lifestyle resumes, and Berndt is aware of what he is doing. How long can their relationship last?

So far, Frank has kept his sexual preferences out of the classroom. However, at the annual Queen's Ball in Berlin, he shows up for class in full drag. His secret is out of the bag.

Even when he is hospitalized for infectious hepatitis, he calls a taxi and escapes to a public toilet for more sex.

As one viewer put it, "Knowingly exposing others to communicable diseases crosses into impeding the lives of others, and is not in the least bit charming."

This movie, not for everyone, is very kinky, very kitchen sink.

Tchaikovsky: The Creation of Genius

(2007)

A Fragile Russian Romantic

This BBC film tells the story of the Russian classical composer Pyotr Ilyich Tchaikovsky (1840-1893) with a mix of live instrumentation, documentary, and dramatic re-creations. Both his disastrously short marriage and his passionate gay love affair are depicted.

Directed and co-written by Matthew Whiteman, *Tchaikovsky* examines the life ("a messy bowl of musical soup") and music of the 19th-century Russian in two parts, each hosted by conductor Charles Hazlewood.

The fragile boy genius never recovered from the loss of his mother when he was very young. In his adult life, he was a tortured homosexual living in fear that public exposure would derail his career. In his public life, in the face of massive skepticism, he struggled to win approval for his daring musical ideas.

This first section is called "The Creation of Greatness."

In Part II, "Fortune and Tragedy," his disastrous marriage of convenience to a young female admirer, Antonina Milyukova, is explored.

Ed Stoppard (*The Pianist*) plays the Russian composer in the re-enactment scenes. The feature is also a concert film, presenting performances of the composer's most well-known and respected musical works, including *Romeo and Juliet*, an erotically charged work composed during an early love affair with Edward Zak, a music academy student.

Presented also are some of Tchaikovsky's ballets, including *Swan Lake* and *Sleeping Beauty*. The climatic performance is saved for his "Pathétique," (Symphony #6) one of the most moving musical compositions ever written.

Intriguing is an episode called "Who Killed Tchaikovsky?" It questions the reported death of the composer at the age of 53. It followed his drinking of a glass of unboiled water during the height of a cholera epidemic. Could it have been suicide? Murder?

Tea and Sympathy

(1956)

"When you speak about this, *and you will*, be kind"

Gay director Vincente Minnelli, who married Judy and fathered Liza, tamed down the homosexuality implicit in the Robert Anderson Broadway play, but the point was nonetheless made.

In this film, Deborah Kerr as Laura Reynolds, John Kerr (no relation) as Tom Robinson Lee, and Leif Erickson as Bill Reynolds re-created their roles on Broadway.

The film is outdated—after all, this was the 50s—but it remains well written and brilliantly acted by the three leads.

Tom is called "sister boy" by his classmates, though he is defended by his roommate, Al (Darryl Hickman). Tom doesn't fit in with the other boys. He doesn't do "manly" things like go out for sports and chase girls.

Headmaster Bill Reynolds' wife, Laura, sees Tom suffering at the hands of his schoolmates (and her husband) and tries to help him "find himself."

In one of the most frightening portrayals, Edward Andress appears as Tom's creepy father. Daddy would rather his son get involved in a scandal with the town tart so it would erase his sister-boy reputation.

Tom endures a disastrous experience at an "arranged" event, when he is thrown together with everyone's party girl, Ellie Martin (Norma Crane).

As the wife of the school's coach, Laura is supposed to supply only "tea and sympathy" to the boys. In Tom's case, she generously offers more.

WHAT THE CRITICS SAID
"The housemaster part, played with muscle-flexing exhibitionism by Leif Erickson, loses some of its meaning in the tone-down. On the stage his efforts at being 'manly' carried the suggestion that he was trying to compensate a fear of a homo trend in his own makeup. The suggestion was diluted to absence in the picture."
Variety

Tell Me That You Love Me, Junie Moon

(1970)

Demented Triplets

Helmer Otto Preminger, turned down directorship of the movie, M*A*S*H, to make this disaster. He based it on a novel and screenplay by Marjorie Kellogg.

When the picture was finished, Liza Minnelli, who plays Junie Moon, announced that she would never again "work with that tyrant," meaning Preminger. During its shooting, her mother, Judy Garland, died.

Her supporting team included Ken Howard and Robert Moore. Liza has been scarred on the face by acid from her kinky boyfriend; Howard suffers strange psychosomatic seizures, and Moore is a homosexual paraplegic.

As the film evolves, we learn that Warren (Moore) was brought up by a gay man (Leonard Frey) and partially paralyzed during a hunting trip by a friend at whom he'd made a pass. Arthur (Ken Howard) had shuttled in and out of various homes for the retarded. Liza emerges as the heart and spunk of the trio; Howard the apparent breadwinner, and Moore the brains.

WHAT THE CRITICS SAID
"*Tell Me That You Love Me, Junie Moon* is one of the most demented movies ever. It concerns a *ménage à trois* between an epileptic, a crippled homosexual with a yen for black bellhops, and a girl whose face has been burned by acid. Instead of making it believable or at least palatable in the sensitive direction of, say, a Carson McCullers tale of survival among the misfits, Preminger accents all the bizarre aspects of Kellogg's novel and none of the poetic ones. The result is that *Junie Moon* is just plain repulsive."
Rex Reed

"This is one of the better Preminger films. It succeeds, among other things, in making human entertainment out of a rather unlikely story. He seduces us into accepting the situation by treating it as entertainment, not soul-searching, tear-jerking *True Confessions*. If Preminger had played on our sympathy, everything would have fallen apart."
Roger Ebert

Teorema

(1968)

Terence Stamp: Is He Jesus or Just a Sexy Hunk?

Over the years many viewers have walked out of any screening of *Teorema*; others have been mesmerized by it, scenes in the film remembered for decades to come.

Pier Paolo Pasolini, who was murdered, was an acknowledged Marxist and atheist. Yet he may have made a religious film of sorts. Is the handsome hunk of a man, Terence Stamp, then at his most beautiful, really Jesus in Second Coming, or at least God?

Pasolini's intent is never clear.

This stranger moves into an upper bourgeois household in Milan. Soon the entire family experiences his "heavenly divining rod," which the well-hung Stamp reveals in a full monty.

He seduces the teenaged daughter Odette (Anne Wiazemsky); the gay son Pietro (Jose Cruz), the mother Lucia (Silvana Mangano), the father Paolo (Massimo Girotti), and even the maid Emilia (Laura Betti). The seduction is a transcendental experience for each of them. When Stamp departs, he leaves each member of the household to collapse in his or her own way.

Upon its release, *Teorema* won the International Catholic Jury Grand Award at the Venice Film Festival. The Vatican, however, reacted in horror, attacking the award in an official statement. Obscenity charges were pressed against Pasolini in the Italian courts, but he won his case.

In spite of what critics said, *Teorema* is the most watchable of Pasolini's films.

WHAT THE CRITICS SAID
"*Teorema* is an allegory in two acts which merges eros and religion in an up-to-date context. Pasolini, ever sensitive to religion, eroticism, homosexuality, and social forces, employs all these elements to detail his premise that a sudden revelation of possible human self-fulfillment can permanently mar the upper strata of society and exalt its sub-strata."
Variety

Testosterone

(2003)

Antonio Sabato Jr. Flashes the Full Monty

Let's face it: the reason many gay men (though far too few, according to box office receipts) went to see this film was because of the publicity about *über*-hunk and former Calvin Klein underwear model/actor, Antonio Sabato Jr., showing the full monty. Thanks to this film,

we at last know what he was keeping under wraps in those celebrated underwear ads on giant billboards in Times Square in New York and other cities.

Of course, Antonio—and certainly not his penis—is not the star of *Testosterone*. That honor goes to a less handsome, Canadian-born actor, David Sutcliffe, who plays Antonio's lover in the film. Antonio is cast as Pablo, David as Dean. David has the ongoing role of Rory's dad in the WB series, *The Gilmore Girls*. He's also starred in his own series, *I'm With Her*, for ABC.

Testosterone has plenty of hormones, and the guy-to-guy action is some of the hottest in any feature film. Dean plays a brilliant graphic novelist living with Pablo in a California beach house. Pablo goes out for a cigarette run and doesn't return. Ever the romantic, Dean blows his deadline and heads for Argentina, the place where Pablo has retreated. The source of that information comes from Pablo's domineering mother (Sonia Braga), who detests her son's choice of lovers.

Arriving in Buenos Aires, one of the world's most decadent and photographable cities, Dean encounters one disaster after another in his search for "closure" with Pablo. In this intriguing locale, more evocative than Bogie's *Casablanca*, Dean soon learns that Pablo is the scion of a powerful local family. Sonia wants Dean out of town and will go to considerable lengths to accomplish her mission, sending scary cops and dangerous thugs after him.

In this obsessive love story, director David Moreton has discovered a more intriguing voice than he did in his 1999 queen teen tract, *Edge of Seventeen*.

226

That Man: Peter Berlin

(2005)

Model, Artist, Porn Star, Legend

Peter Berlin, as every gay man of a certain age already knows, was a gay icon and porn star of the 1970s. With his trademark Dutchboy haircut, he was the poster boy for the hedonistic and sexually liberated 1970s. He wore the tightest pants of any porn star before or since.

Younger viewers not familiar with Berlin's work can treat themselves to his classic film, *That Boy,* now available in a special edition DVD. At least viewers can learn just how "big" a star Berlin actually was. The already mentioned *That Boy* (1974) was preceded by another famous film, *Nights in Black Leather,* released the previous year.

Berlin was the great nephew of the famous fashion photographer, George Hoyningen-Huene. During his early 20s, Berlin worked as a photographer, but his real passion was photographing himself in erotic poses and making skin-tight clothes to wear. He was known for cruising the parks and train stations of Berlin.

His many friends offer their reflections on Berlin and his era. These include campy director, John Waters, author Armistead Maupin, adult film legend, Jack Wrangler, and filmmaker Wakefield Poole.

Peter was also the subject of several Robert Mapplethorpe photographs and six drawings by Tom of Finland. Although he more or less disappeared from the limelight in the 1980s, he still makes videos of himself and walks the streets of San Francisco, where fans of his early porno still recognize him.

WHAT THE CRITICS SAID
"Peter Berlin may have refined narcissism to a fine art, but this captivating and sometimes rambling documentary's stream of photos and verité porn moments presents a man whose beauty is so potent that self-adoration is inescapable."
Dan Buskirk, *Philadelphia Weekly*

"An extraordinarily beautiful documentary....A strange, irresistible picture."
Miami News Times

This Film Is Not Yet Rated

(2006)

An Exposé of the American Movie Ratings Board

Most filmmakers detest the Motion Picture Association of America (MPAA), which, based on their standards of decency, assigns commerically vital ratings to most films shown in the US? Would it surprise you that their prevailing standards are heavily influenced by a motley collection of straight "concerned parents," with opinions often provided by Catholic priests?

In their classification of movies, almost any form of violence is acceptable, but gay sex is often deemed as "aberrational behavior." Except for *Brokeback Mountain,* nearly all indie films that feature some male/male action get an NC-17 rating, thereby limiting their release and advertising. In this film, helmer Kirby Dick makes U.S. censors look like the asses they are.

Some things are just too wild for the censors. They include threesomes (*The Dreamers, American Psycho*), oral sex (*Boys Don't Cry*) and such "gay stuff" as *Where the Truth Lies* and *Mysterious Skin.*

Using archival footage, Dick has assembled an all-star cast of in-the-know sources who comment, sometimes scathingly, on the MPAA's "ratings game." They include, among others, Pierce Brosnan, Richard Burton, Tom Cruise (that very heterosexual actor), Robert De Niro, Michael Douglas, Jane Fonda, William Holden, Jeremy Irons, Jessica Lange, William H. Macy, Kevin Spacey, Hilary Swank, Sharon Stone, Elizabeth Taylor, Jon Voight--even John Wayne

WHAT THE CRITICS SAID
"Kirby Dick obviously has a soft spot in his heart for queer filmmakers, beginning his film with the travails Kimberly Peirce faced in releasing her Academy Award-winning *Boys Don't Cry.* The MPAA, which emerges in Dick's film as a creature of the Hollywood studios, wraps itself in a cloak of morality. But like so much in the United States, what the MPAA presents as protecting children is much more about protecting profits. And it's clear that gay visibility on the silver screen suffers from Hollywood's greed."
Patrick Moore, *The Advocate*

This Filthy World

(2006)

John Waters' Torch Song: Trash as Art

"The first time I met Richard Simmons, I felt homophobic," John Waters confesses in this 90-minute documentary in which helmer John Garlin brings us the fabulous world of this outrageous director. It was filmed over a two-night period at the Harry De Jur Playhouse on the Lower East Side of New York. And how lucky we are it was.

Even if you know Waters only through his Tony-winning musical, *Hairspray*, based on his 1988 film, you'll want to catch him in this, "live." After you do, we predict you'll go out and rent such notorious Waters "staples" as *Pink Flamingos* (1972) and *Polyester* (1981). After all, Waters directed Tab Hunter in his comeback, and even introduced us to dog shit-eating Divine, the divine cross-dresser who re-defined the word slut.

Who but Waters could bring together a cast that included Ricki Lake, Maggie Gyllenhaal, Melanie Griffith, and even Patricia Hearst for Cecil B. Demented.

Waters has a wonderful self-mocking style. He name-drops but in an amazingly kind way. He has a brilliant talent for delivering small, droll stories, and even lets us know that a fellow Baltimorean called him an "asshole."

"When I was a teenager, I wanted to be Visconti," he said. "But now I realize that my career is becoming similar to Paul Lynde's."

WHAT THE CRITICS SAID
"Those who think of the director, John Waters, only as a sicko, a wacko, a pervert, a psycho, a multi-fetishist, a deviant, a menace and/or a nut job will be surprised to discover, through *This Filthy World*, that he would also make an excellent dinner party guest. True, the other guests would need to have a tolerance for stories about singing rectums, but still, the guy is a raconteur of the first order."
Neil Genzlinger, *The New York Times*

Three Dancing Slaves

(*Le clan*, 2006)

A Band of Orphaned Brothers

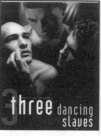

This 90-minute French drama is by openly gay director writer-actor Gaël Morel, who helmed *Full Speed* and acted in *Wild Reeds*. His latest film is filled with hope amidst a violent and unpredictable world. It tells of the emotional lives of three orphaned brothers, providing a glimpse into the complicated world of men and their deepest emotions.

Told in three chapters, the film follows the lives of three handsome siblings. Lonely Marc, 22, idolizes his brother Christophe, who has just been released from prison. Christophe's desire to lead a quiet new life is disrupted when he must become Marc's protector from a band of sadistic toughs who relish taunting the sensitive, younger sibling.

The third brother, Oliver, 17, forms a strong bond with Hicham (Salim Kechiouche), his best friend and "surrogate" brother.

Lovers of French beefcake who like their handsome actors full frontal will find much to admire in this film. One of the most memorable scenes in this homoerotic flick is when Dad discovers his three sons sleeping together naked with their limbs intertwined. He merely observes this, rolls his eyes, and walks away.

WHAT THE CRITICS SAID
"Like so many films that target a gay audience, *Three Dancing Slaves* transpires in an abstract parallel universe where half the population has mysteriously disappeared and the other half works out a lot and often goes unclothed. The only female presence to speak of is the dead mother of the fraternal trio. Even when one of the most macho of the brothers has sex, it's with a bewigged pre-op transsexual whose biological status is of course full-frontally corroborated."
Dennis Lim, *Village Voice*

"The last segment, Olivier, concerns the erotic adventures of the youngest son (Thomas Dumerchez) as he falls in love with another man (Salim Kechiouche) and practices *capoeira*, the dance-like Brazilian martial arts that is the source of the film's English title."
Dana Stevens

Three of Hearts

(2007)

A Hip, Postmodern Family

This docu directed by Susan Kaplin will hold interest for polyamorous people, and maybe some others, too, especially those interested in "trinogamy." Forget same-sex marriage: In this movie, three is not a crowd, but a happy family of open-minded New Yorkers.

Sam and Steven meet in college where they become lovers. Deep into their years-long relationship, they each appear to have bisexual leanings. In their younger years, both of them dated women. The two men decide they need a woman "to share in their happiness."

In their search for a third partner, they don't hit it the first time around. Then they meet attractive, bright, and young Samantha, who seems intrigued with the idea of sharing a bed with two hot men.

Amazingly, this relationship of the three Ss seems to work out. A child is produced. She too takes an S name, in this case Siena. Of course, in a case like this, Samantha doesn't know who the father is, since she's consistently fucked both Sam and Steven.

Of course, there are the inevitable problems, but not as many as you think. Eventually, even the parents of each of the three participants learn about the unusual relationship.

One of the high points of the film is when Sam brings both of his mates to his 20-year high school reunion. An old girlfriend howls, "*That's so cooooool!*"

WHAT THE CRITICS SAID
"This well-told docu follows nine years in the lives of a gay couple and the woman they invited to share their relationship. When we meet this happy threesome, they're trying to get pregnant. In winning interviews, these assertively bourgeois strivers chat about their setup, their decision to marry, their spa business, their mix-and-match sex (There's never a feeling of being left out!)."
Laura Sinagra

Tides of War

(2005)

A Formulaic Submarine Movie with a Gay Twist

This movie first aired in 2005 on Here! TV, the gay pay-per-view satellite channel. It represents a growing phenomenon in films to target gay and lesbian audiences by recycling straight films, changing the plot by throwing in gay scenes. These are called "dual purpose" movies.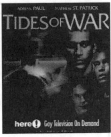

In this gay version, the commander's hunky male assistant is changed from best friend to lover. Most such films, such as *Tides of War*, shoot an extra week, subbing gay content scenes although leaving the plot of the film pretty much as it was.

For example, *Tides of War* starts out with an obligatory gay scene that has little else to do with the remainder of the film. Even with its gay theme, the movie is a rather standard submarine thriller. The drama spins around the cold, dark waters off North Korea, where a U.S. Navy fast attack submarine meets with a mysterious disaster. It's attacked and nearly sunk by an ominous stealth submarine. We won't give away the plot such as it is. But you just know the forces of good (U.S. Navy) will prevail over the phantom ship of the last remaining Stalinist police state (North Korea).

Tides' screenwriter Mark Sanderson was instructed to add at least five scenes that could be altered to a gay theme.

TV stations in many countries were given a choice of gay or straight, with Canada and Britain going mainly with the queer version. Japan opted to go straight, but Argentina went gay. Macho Brazil chose the straight version of *Tides*. It was a mixed call in America.

Outfest executive director Stephen Gutwillig said: "Gays and lesbians grow up transposing themselves into the heads and hearts of straight characters in romantic movies, so it's not much of a leap to say that we deserve and will flock to gay versions of those kinds of films—let alone gay versions of all sorts of other genre films. It represents a maturing of queer storytelling and a broadening of what's possible in commercial release."

Time to Leave

(*Le temps qui reste;* 2005)

Life Is Over Too Soon, and It's Never Complete

The talented French filmmaker, François Ozon, returns with this haunting examination of bereavement and grief. In some respects, *Under the Sand* was a cinematic precursor to Joan Didion's *Year of Magical Thinking.*

As the film opens, Romain (Melvil Pouopaud) is a good-looking man, 31, living in Paris and working as a fashion photographer. Seemingly, he enjoys the good life, aided in no small part by his delicate, slim, and almost child-like boyfriend, Sasha (Christian Sengewald), who is an obvious bottom.

Then Romain is given a diagnosis of brain cancer. There is no hope for him. Death awaits.

He reacts strangely—first, by chasing away his good-looking little bottom who has served him so admirably. Sasha suffers, since Romain is one of the great beauties of the screen. Incidentally, Romain played Naomi Watts's straying husband in *Le Divorce.*

He rejects treatment and decides to face death from his tumor on his own terms. He lashes out at his pregnant sister, but does not tell her of his illness. He is also uncommunicative to his loving and supporting parents.

However, he does confide in his grandmother, played by that national French treasure, Jeanne Moreau. When she asks him why he is confiding in her, he tells her. "Because you're like me, you'll be dying soon." Without his lover, he wanders aimlessly. The leather bar in this movie seems left over from the set of that notorious flick, *Cruising.*

The film takes a detour when Romain has a chance encounter with a roadside waitress played by Valeria Bruni-Tedeschi. Although in love with her husband, she can't have a child with him. With her husband's consent—in fact, he joins them in bed—Romain impregnates the woman. It's his chance to bring one life into the world as he is leaving it. It's a rather tender portrait of a *ménage à trois.*

The Times of Harvey Milk

(1984)

The Gay Politico & the Psycho Fireman

Not to be confused with the Sean Penn film, *Milk, The Times of Harvey Milk* was a docu helmed by Rob Epstein, who was also the co-scripter. In the Epstein film Milk appears as himself in archival footage. The narrator is none other than Harvey Fierstein.

Also in archival footage, you see everybody from Anne Kroneberg to Jerry Brown, and Jimmy Carter to Dianne Feinstein, even the "villain" of the piece, Dan White.

The film was made six years after Dan White assassinated Milk, a member of the San Francisco Board of Supervisors, and Mayor George Moscone. The date was November 27, 1978.

Underlying the assassination were White's social conservatism and Milk's open gayness. He was the first openly gay, elected official in the United States (yes, we know about Abraham Lincoln but he wasn't officially "out").

A highlight of the film is an angry night of rioting that erupted after White received a lenient sentence. "If Dan White had only killed Moscone, he would have gone up for life," one person says in the film. "But he killed a gay, so they let him off easy." Not mentioned in the film, White later committed suicide.

WHAT THE CRITICS SAID
"Epstein is treating his film as he would a piece of fiction. Milk never becomes simply the subject but a living, breathing figure; in effect, we get to know the person before the politics. The positioning of Milk and White within a clear protagonist-antagonist framework furthers this sense of straightforward narrative momentum—the Jewish homosexual versus the clean-cut ex-fireman with smalltown values."
Anthony Nield

Tipping the Velvet

(2002)

Erotic Lesbian Romp through Victorian England

In case you want your lingo to go retro, know that "Tipping the Velvet" was a Victorian euphemism for cunnilingus. Set in the 1890s in England, this lesbian love affair is the story of a male impersonator, music hall star Kitty Butler (Keeley Hawes) and Nan Astley (Rachael Stirling). Both stars admitted that they got drunk before shooting the love scenes, but also said that "kissing a woman was not much different from kissing a man."

Running in 3 parts for 177 minutes, this English film was dramatized from Sarah Waters' acclaimed debut novel, *Tipping the Velvet,* and first shown on BBC TV.

It tells the story of young Nan, who works as a cook and "oyster girl" in her father's seaside restaurant. Her life undergoes profound changes when she witnesses the extraordinary performance of a male impersonator, Kitty. Cross-dresser Kitty, as played by Keeley Hawes (*The Avengers*), beguiles the ladies in the audience the way that Marlene Dietrich did in *Morocco.*

One of the songs in the film, "Following in Father's Footsteps," was originally performed by famous male impersonator Vesta Tilley in the London halls of Victorian England during the late 19th century when *Tipping the Velvet* is set.

A life transformation begins for Nan as she is flung into her love affair. Nan experiences both euphoria and deep disillusion as she embarks on a seven-year journey of self-discovery, finally realizing that a life of sensation just isn't enough.

After her affair with Kitty, Nan becomes a streetwalker, dressing up as a boy picking up older men. The poor wretch eventually is turned into a virtual slave of a wealthy aristocratic dominatrix named Diana Lethaby (as played by Anna Chancellor of *Four Weddings and a Funeral).*

Tipping the Velvet has too much sex and S&M to qualify for a traditional Masterpiece Theater material, but it's getting there.

It was adapted for television by Andrew Davies and directed by Geoffrey Sax.

Tongues Untied

(1990)

Black Men Loving Black Men

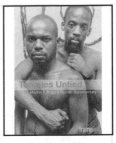

Director Martin Riggs suggests in this docu that black men loving black men is a revolutionary act. As the docu clearly reveals, being homosexual and black is especially difficult because of the rampant homophobia in the African-American community.

In a sense, Riggs' film is a celebration of black-on-black love, as evidenced by footage of black men marching in a gay pride parade.

Riggs gets help from other gay black men, especially the poet Essex Hemphill. *Tongues Untied* is told through poetry, music, and tales from the subjects themselves. There is joy and hope here, but also sadness, particularly when the docu closes with obits of victims of AIDS.

The men have their various comic riffs, but also indulge in social (not just sexual) intercourse with each other, including dancing together and taking lessons in how to snap their fingers, including "the diva snap."

Black homophobia is linked to anti-gay violence. In a montage sequence, church leaders decry homosexual relationships as an "abomination." Some African-American political activists see black + gay as a conflict between loyalties. Fag humor is practically an industry—take Spike Lee and Eddie Murphy as examples.

Regrettably Riggs' "tongue" was tied, so to speak, when he was overcome by AIDS, his life fading away. He was an amazing artist and no doubt had many other documentaries in him that will never be filmed. He died in 1994, age 37.

WHAT THE CRITICS SAID
"*Tongues* weaves poetry, performance, popular culture, and personal testimony and history in a complex pattern that emerges as an essential personal statement. It presents the situation, politics, and culture of black gay men using an intense mixture of styles ranging from social documentary to experimental montage, personal narrative and lyric poetry."
Alex Castro

Torch Song Trilogy

(1988)

The Flamboyant, Unsinkable Arnold Beckoff

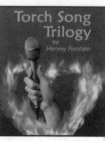

Torch Song Trilogy opens with female impersonator Harvey Fierstein playing Arnold Beckoff and looking more like Marjorie Main than Joan Crawford. The Tony Award-winning actor and playwright, Fierstein, recreates his role as the unsinkable Arnold. The original Broadway production opened at the Little Theater on June 10, 1982 and ran for 1,222 performances.

The film, like the play, is staged in three acts, with Arnold, in the words of one critic, appearing as "nervous, mannered, gravely voiced, overly sensitive, campy, and with a taste for eye-rolling rivaled only by Groucho Marx in modern showbiz annals."

In the first part, Arnold falls in love with Ed (Brian Kerwin), a good-looking, straight-seeming guy who openly announces his bisexuality. Arnold, in spite of the warning, falls for this Middle American hunk. Of course, as was inevitable, Arnold loses Ed to a young woman Laurel (Karen Young).

Along comes Matthew Broderick as Alan Simon, adorably handsome and a fashion model. He started out in life as a hustler. As unprobable as it seems, Alan falls for Arnold. "If anyone asks, I'm the pretty one," Arnold proclaims. But Alan is killed by gay-bashers.

In the third and final part, Arnold, who calls himself a "gay Aunt Jemina," adopts a teenage son and tries to sort out his strained relations with his mother. Ma Beckoff (Anne Bancroft), playing the role rather stridently.

In his new role as a "mother," Arnold talks to the kid like his own mother lectured him. Arnold finally wins his respect from dear ol' mum. He tells her, "there are two things I demand from the people in my life: Love and respect."

WHAT THE CRITICS SAID
"*Torch Song Trilogy* is basically a movie about a man who slowly becomes more comfortable with himself...Homosexuality is not his problem—it is the arena for his problems."
Roger Ebert

Touch of Pink

(2004)

Cary Grant as an Imaginary Friend

The most obvious theme of *Touch of Pink* revolves around a "coming out" conflict, but the larger theme pushes much further. Not only has the hero hidden his sexual identity from his mother; he's virtually divorced himself from his family's South Asian culture as well. Within the depiction of a subculture (gay identities becoming identified and defined) within another subculture (a community of Ismaelian Muslims living in Toronto), the film emphasizes the need for people to live comfortably with who they most naturally are.

The movie contains some of the elements of an old-fashioned screwball comedy, with quaint references to the spirit of a reincarnated Cary Grant. Cheerful and chipper, with a kind of retro charm that's re-created by *Sex in the City*'s Kyle MacLaughlin, he lives within the hero, unbeknownst even to the hero's lover, Giles, as the kind of secret and imaginary friend that lonely children adopt for company.

As the film deepens, *Touch of Pink* explores the way its characters come out of their sexual and cultural closets, learning to love who they are and where they came from, culturally. In the words of one of its co-producers, "it deals with characters that are ultimately required to be true to themselves even though they are slightly out of step with the rest of the world around them."

As played by Jimi Mistry, Alim is a young, sexy, South Asian Canadian who's living in London, working as a still photographer in the movie business, and trying, with the help of his imaginary reincarnation of Cary Grant, to live up to the glamorous standards of old Hollywood. Playing Alim's partner, Giles, actor Kristen Holden-Reid is a handsome English economist who's charming, intelligent, and comfortable with who he is. Nuru (Alim's mother), acted by Sue Mathew, arrives in London for a visit from her home in Toronto, hoping to pull Alim into the orbit of the Ismaelian community, where, she hopes, he'll find a Muslim bride, raise a family, and "do his duty."

Transamerica

(2005)

A Pre-Op Transsexual Copes With Her Son

Let's play that again, Sam. *Desperate Housewives* star Felicity Huffman in *Transamerica* appears as a pre-operative male-to-female transsexual. One reviewer felt that the star of the film "looked like Felicity Huffman's male twin," only to discover that it was Felicity Huffman herself in a surprise role.

Like all films there were many disappointed viewers. One critic claimed that film is too busy "badly treading *Tootsie* turf, where Dustin Hoffman's only mental issues were obstinacy and chauvinism."

Huffman plays "Bree," who had learned that she has a son just one week before her scheduled surgery. Apparently, when she was more fully a man, she fathered a son somewhere along the way in a one-night quickie. Her son, called "Toby" in the film and played by Kevin Zegers, is a teenage runaway hustling "johns" on the streets of New York and selling drugs.

As the director and writer of the film, Duncan Tucker, has it, Bree's shrink will not sign the final paperwork for her transformation operation until she deals with her newly discovered, errant boy.

Bree crosses the country to rescue her street hustler son from a juvie detention center.

For reasons of her own, Bree decides not to reveal her true identity to the boy but poses instead as a church missionary do-gooder. Bree persuades Toby to drive with her from New York back to Los Angeles. At least that justifies the title of *Transamerica.*

But it was Andy—safely tucked away under her skirt—that saved the day. Purchased in a Manhattan sex shop, Andy was a prosthetic male organ, made of rubber, that was surprisingly realistic. In the film, Huffman's son discovers her taking a piss with her decent sized dick, learning for the first time that his traveling companion is actually a man impersonating a woman. He doesn't know at this point that Huffman is his actual father in the film.

Transfixed

(*Mauvais genres;* 2001)

The Sexual Underworld of Brussels

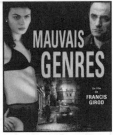

In this French/Belgium thriller, Bo is a transexual prostitute working the mean streets of Brussels after running away from home. Bo's personal style as an *artiste*, as interpreted by Robinson Stévenin, was defined by one critic as "more Doris Day than Rita Hayworth," and by another as "Jeanne Moreau meets Audrey Hepburn."

The director, Francis Girod, co-scripted the film with Philippe Cougrand, who based it on the novel *Transfixions* by Brigitte Aubert. As a beautiful drag artist with a Europeanized style and a fetching kind of feminine/macho swagger, Bo finds himself at the center of two police investigations.

Bo's father, a famous physician (Marcel Dossogne), has been arrested for fondling a child in his clinic. Even though Bo went to the authorities as a pre-teen complaining of child molestation, he was ignored at the time and is now reluctant to testify against dear old dad. Strong points are made about sexual hypocrisy among the bourgeoisie, and the viewer is left with the disturbing realization that it isn't particularly safe to be an out-and-proud drag queen on the sexual edge.

Detective Huysmans (Richard Bohringer) urges Bo to testify against his father.

There are other complications, and serious ones. A serial killer is rampant, attacking transvestite and transsexual entertainers on the back streets of Brussels. Huysmans begins to suspect Bo. Another plot involves Bo's sexual obsession with the handsome Johnny (Stéphane Metzger), a sleazy gigolo associate of Alex (Frédéric Pellegeay).

These men make their living by luring rich American widows into their web, followed by blackmail of their victims. Unknown to Bo, Johnny is actually impotent. Alex uses him as bait to attract the women with his good looks. In one scene Johnny stands naked while Alex seduces a woman.

Johnny regularly insults Bo and humiliates him in public, but the abuse only seems to feed Bo's passion. In order to clear himself, Bo must turn detective.

Trick

(1999)

A Romantic Gay Date Movie

Trick can tell *Billy's Hollywood Screen Kiss* to eat my celluloid dust. Director Jim Fall never seeks the approval of straight audiences. As such, the film is so gay it could be painted lavender.

Gabriel (Christian Campbell) is an aspiring writer of Broadway musicals. On a disconsolate night, he enters a gay bar where he gets a hard-on (we presume), watching go-go boy Mark (John Paul Pitoc) whose nickname is "Beer Can." Later, on the subway, they make eye contact and the fun begins. Their problem involves where to find a place to have sex. The film details the misadventures of a hot-to-trot pair during one long frustrating night.

Insensitive Katherine (Tori Spelling) is in Gabriel's apartment, neurotically printing 500 copies of her résumé. Also, roommate Rich (Brad Beyer) refuses to leave the nest, as he's screwing ditzy but not dumb Judy (Lorri Bagley).

Gabriel and Mark drift through the night looking for a secure bed to get off in, going into drag clubs and diners. Instead of concealing the identity of his new trick, Gabriel brags to people that Mark is a go-go boy, acting, in the words of one critic, "like a conventioneer on a date with a Rockette."

WHAT THE CRITICS SAID
"This delightfully charming film belongs to a new cycle of gay movies that are not about AIDS or social issues but 'simply' deal with situations, such as dating and first love, regardless of sexual orientation. *Trick's* spell depends on the magnetism of its two protagonists and the strong chemistry between the characters who embody them, both perfectly cast."
Emanuel Levy *Variety*

"The message, I suppose, would be that gays should have romantic comedies just as dim and dumb as the straight versions, although I cannot offhand remember many recent straight films this witless. The movie imposes a Doris Day storyline on material that wants to be more sexual; it's about a character whose quasi-virginity is preserved through an improbable series of mishaps and coincidences."
Roger Ebert

Tropical Malady

(*Sud pralad;* 2004)

A Thai Parable About Love and Sacrifice

This Thai film, directed and written by Apichatpong Weerasethakul, is in the drama/fantasy/romance genre. It's the tale of a gay-themed romance between a soldier, Keng (Banlop Lomnoi), and a country boy, Tong (Sakda Kaewbuadee). It's a bit hard to follow but all this drama takes place wrapped around a Thai folk legend involving a shaman with shape-shifting abilities.

With English subtitles, the film shifts into the supernatural at the point Tong retreats from Keng's advances.

In a nutshell, *Tropical Malady* is a love story that evolves into a parable about the sacrifices true love demands. Keng faces a daunting challenge if his desire is to be with Tong. He must rescue him from a dark force or sacrifice oneself in order to be reunited.

WHAT THE CRITICS SAID
"The film has such a dreamy, gentle, floating quality that even at its darker, most dangerous moments it never seems malevolent—and that is perhaps because it is so romantic, at first tethered playfully in the real world and then freed to soar in the realm of the supernatural. Counterpointing the film's tantalizing images is an inspired use of both man-made and natural sounds. *Tropical Malady* is the work of a visionary fabulist."
Kevin Thomas, *Los Angeles Times*

"Instructively titled, *Malady* is a split down the middle between lovesick daydream and malarial delirium. An idyllic first half, which recounts in fleeting fragments an intensifying attraction between handsome soldier Keng and bashful farm boy Tong, gives way to a nocturnal folk tale that likewise traces an anatomy of desire, but this time with the soldier amid an unearthly menagerie of tiger spirits, phantom cattle, and an aphorism-dispensing baboon."
Dennis Lim

Tru Loved

(2008)

Coming Out, Post-Millennium Teen Style

Stewart Wade, who brought us *Coffee Date*, strikes again with this endearing tale of a teenager with two lesbian moms fighting homophobia in her bigoted high school. Wade both directed and wrote this heart-warming tale.

Growing up in gay-friendly San Francisco, Tru (Najarra Townsend) is painfully uprooted from her environment and plunged into a right-wing town in Southern California. Her two lesbian moms are played by Alexandra Paul and Cynda Williams. Tru says goodbye to her friends and even to her two gay fathers.

In school, because of her home situation, Tru feels different from the other kids. However, Lodell (Matthew Thompson), the African-American star quarterback, takes an interest in her. Schoolmates assume they are involved in a hot romance but Tru learns that the football hero is in the closet. He reveals that he's gay, but they agree to keep up their amorous charade for the sake of appearances.

Even so, she decides to face the school's homophobia straight on and forms a Gay-Straight Alliance. She also forms a friendship with hipster Trevor (Jake Abel). This causes some jealousy on Lodell's part. Tru is faced with a dilemma, torn between her friendship with a closet case or following her heart into a new and more meaningful relationship. Trevor is straight and is being brought up by his gay uncle.

Rounding out the cast is the always marvelous Bruce Vilanch, plus Jane Lynch (*The L Word* and *The 40-Year-Old Virgin*), Jasmine Guy (*A Different World*), Alec Mapa (*Ugly Betty*), and Nichelle Nichols (*Star Trek*).

WHAT THE CRITICS SAID
"*Tru Loved* dramatizes a struggle between bigotry and humanity that is too common for lesbian and gay individuals, families, and especially youth in America today...we believe that when this film is shared with a wide audience, it will open people's eyes to the price we all pay for prejudice."
Jody M. Huckaby, Executive Director, PFLAG

The Twenty Fourth Day

(2004)

Power Play Between Captor & Captive

This film is a thriller. Actor Scott Speedman is cast as Tom, who as a married man has lived his whole life straight except for a one-night stand with a man five years ago. After getting diagnosed with HIV, he tracks down Dan, as played by James Marsden, the man he

slept with. The question is this: Was Dan responsible for infecting him?

Tom lures Dan back to his apartment where he ties him up and draws blood for an HIV test. If Dan tests positive, Tom claims he'll kill him. Thus, the stage is set for this battle of brain and brawn between two men locked in a studio apartment, perhaps both ultimately facing their deaths.

First launched as a play in Los Angeles, the script was considerably revamped for the screen. When *The 24th Day* reached the screen, reviews were mixed: Some critics said it was a homophobic piece; others argue that it was just the opposite. That you must decide for yourself.

Even though this independent film, written and directed by Tony Piccirillo, has undergone many changes since it was inaugurated on the stage, there is still the lingering aura of a play about it. It follows the dark, conspiratorial genre of more successful, mainstream films, especially *Death-trap* and *Sleuth*.

Tom has reason to be seriously agitated. He thinks that he infected his wife with the virus, a factor that contributed to her suicide after her discovery that she was ill.

If Dan is the guilty one, Tom reasons, "He must pay." Most of the drama centers around Dan's struggle to get the upper hand and to escape.

At some point, the conclusion becomes predictable, but interest in what's going to happen between the two men rarely lags. The faint-of-heart are warned about the strong language and what is called adult situations between two men. Perhaps the best things about *The 24th Day* are the two leading men, Scott Speedman from *Underworld* and James Marsden from *X-Men*. Both actors handle their roles with skill and panache.

Twist

(2003)

A Hustler's Version of Oliver Twist

Young Jacob Tierney, helmer and scripter, has taken Charles Dickens' classic novel, *Oliver Twist*, and set it on the seedy side of modern-day Toronto. Another Dickens novel, *Great Expectations*, was given a modern setting as well in a 1998 film that starred Robert De Niro and Gwyneth Paltrow.

Tierney has envisioned what Fagin and his renegade gang of Victorian pickpockets would be like if they lived in the 21st century. In the director's contemporary version, Fagin would have a heroin habit and send his young charges out to hustle johns on the streets. Fagin (Gary Farmer) takes his orders from the big boss named Bill. He is never seen on screen, however.

The film doesn't focus on Oliver (Joshua Close) but on Dodge (Nick Stahl), who is the "Artful Dodger." This talented actor clearly steals the picture, even from pretty boy Oliver. He's like a lost soul wandering the cold streets in freezing temperatures hoping to turn a trick.

In addition to selling his meat, Dodge is ordered by Fagin to lure more homeless boys into his den, where he will recruit them as child prostitutes.

The plot swells when Dodge's older brother arrives in Toronto, ostensibly to rescue him. Stahl is very convincing as a shambling, hollowed-out junkie. He seems to personify a twist on Dickens. There are no happy endings for the Oliver Twists of today. They live and die on the cold streets, most often as homeless, broken down junkie whores.

WHAT THE CRITICS SAID

"If a director is going to update *Oliver Twist* to the world of gay hustling, isn't it fair to expect him to display at least some knowledge of the scene? Updating the classics is always fair game, but if a filmmaker has no fresh insights to offer, why bother?"
Lions Gate

"As Oliver's innocence dissolves, both young men [Oliver and Dodge] confront inner and outer demons and, strangely, it is Dodge who finds he cannot escape this past."
Sijit R. Varma

Two Drifters

(Odete, 2005)

Looking for Love, Lost in Dreaming

In Portuguese with English subtitles, this 101-minute film has sex, nudity, violence, and profanity. Otherwise, you wouldn't want to bother with it. Its helmer and co-scripter was João Pedro Rodrigues, the Portuguese filmmaker who made a debut in 2002 with his highly acclaimed feature, *O Fantasma*. That hardcore tale of a libidinal garbage man enthralled certain audiences.

In many ways, *Two Drifters* is less dirty but even more perverse. Its plot, including transmigration of the souls, is easy to parody.

The plot? Here goes. Pedro (João Carreira) and Rui (Nuno Gil) kiss after a first anniversary dinner. The two men exchange rings inscribed with the words, "Two Drifters," the lyric from "Moon River."

Pedro drives home but dies en route in a crash.

The story switches to another pair of very different lovers—Odete (Ana Cristina de Oliveira) and Alberto (Carloto Cotta). They split over her desire to have a child.

Back to Pedro's funeral. Odete lives in the building of the deceased, and she attends the wake, stealing a ring from the dead man, a last gift from Rui. At the gravesite, she behaves hysterically. Later, with Pedro's ring on her finger, she insists she's carrying the dead man's child. In one scene, Odete returns to the cemetery on a rainy night. On Pedro's grave, she cries out to the dead body: "Fuck me! Fuck me!"

Rui, deep in grief, drinks too much and sees Pedro's apparition. While wondering who this crazy chick (Odete) is, Rui cruises for anonymous sex.

Odete begins to push around an empty baby carriage. Rui gets simplistic and rather silly advice from a friend: "Pedro is dead, but you're very much alive."

Can any of this end happily?

Two Moms

(2004)

Two Exceptional Women & Their Unique Family

Helmed by Luiz DeBarros and newcomer Andile Genge, *Two Moms* is an intimate profile of two exceptional South African women and their unique family, It's a riveting docu that's sure to challenge long-standing misconceptions and stereotypes.

The docu profiles lesbian couple Suzanne du Toit and Anna-Marié de Vos, their two adopted children, their six dogs, and four cats. It charts their daily life, as well as their historic struggle to legally adopt children and receive equal treatment under the law.

Two Moms takes a human look at this family, exploring the people behind the headlines. It makes a case for highlighting the similarities between all of us as opposed to emphasizing our differences.

"Our aim involved focusing on the human stories we found within the family, and not on the issues themselves, although these invariably came to the fore in a natural way," said DeBarros.

Genge agreed, adding that, "the Dos Vos Du Toit family gave us extraordinary access into their daily lives, in Pretoria and on their farm."

WHAT THE CRITICS SAID
"In 2001 the women challenged South African child adoption laws and demanded the right to adopt as equal partners. They won the case, changed the law, made international headlines, and assured the rights of gay and lesbian co-adoptive parents in South Africa."
Behind the Mask

Tying the Knot

(2004)

The Union That's Dividing America

Jim de Sève gets nearly all the credit for this docu about same-sex marriages. He directed it, produced it, and edited it.

Extremely relevant, highly entertaining, and utterly humanist, the critically acclaimed film festival favorite poignantly explores one of today's hottest political issues. Along with abortion, right-wing America is enraged about gay marriage. This film is about gay people who want to marry and those who are hell-bent on stopping them.

The movie asks the question, "If you lost the one you love, how would it feel to have your love placed on trial?" It cites the case of a bank robber's bullet ending the life of cop Lois Marrero. Her wife of 13 years, Mickie, discovers a police department willing to accept the lesbian relationship of the two women, but unwilling to release Lois' pension. An Oklahoma rancher, Sam, loses his husband of 25 years. But cousins of the deceased challenge the dead man's will and move to evict Sam from his home.

As Mickie and Sam take up battle stations to defend their lives, *Tying the Knot* digs deep into the past and present to discover the meaning of marriage today, focusing on such key issues as rights, privilege, and love.

There are the usual suspects, including right-wing politicos and interviews with gay activists. Some of the best archival footage features gay hippies storming the Manhattan marriage bureau in 1971.

WHAT THE CRITICS SAID
"Wrenching and skillful."
Stephen Holden, *The New York Times*

"Packs a wallop!"
Max Goldberg, *San Francisco Bay Guardian*

"Brilliant. A potent call to arms."
Gerald Peary, *The Boston Phoenix*

The Underminer

(2005)

"Friend" as an Urban Predator of the Psyche

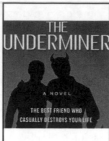

Based on a book by Mike Albo and Virginia Hefferman, Todd Downing's film reveals the insidious tactics of the quintessential New York "underminer," a master of passive aggression who throws his victim into a spiral of self-doubt and hopelessness every time he sees him. Albo plays both the role of the Underminer and Undermined, leaving one to wonder just how much of *The Underminer* comes from within.

When *The Underminer* was published in 2005, its author received critical acclaim. *The New York Times* called Albo "the ultimate satirist of the downtown New York social landscape, and Ron Rosenbaum (see below) proclaimed *The Underminer* as "Raid for the roaches of the soul."

Helmer Downing makes films that appeal to both gay and straight audiences. His short films, ranging from *Dirty Baby Does Fire Island* to *Jeffrey's Hollywood Screen Test*, have been profiled in publications which include everything from *Film Comment* to porno mags. He was recently named one of the "Six Best Directors You've Never Heard Of" by SHOUT! magazine.

WHAT THE CRITICS SAID
"*The Underminer* is a compressed comic classic of New York, a kind of anti-E.B. White fable that focuses on the one unavoidable character everyone in New York runs into, a "friend" bred out of an unstable fusion of ambition and envy, of *Schadenfreude* and *Gluckschmerz*. (You know the former: "A sense of joy based on the failure of others." The latter may be less familiar: "Sadness based on the success of others.") Add a strain of something very American: Oblivious self-congratulation. Fold in an arsenal of barbed compliments, faux flattery, and paranoia-inducing praise, and you've got *The Underminer*, a defining figure of our age, alas."
Ron Rosenbaum

Unveiled

(*Fremde Haut;* 2004)

Female Refugee Becomes a Male Factory Worker

The lesbian filmmaker, Angelina Maccarone, of Germany, faces a daunting challenge in her latest film, *Unveiled*. In a nutshell, it imagines its heroine living in a homophobic and repressive country such as Iran. She flees to Germany to seek asylum. Once in the West, she discovers that Germany has tightened its immigration policies and won't take her in. Her solution? She assumes the identity of a dead man.

The lead role of Fariba Tabrizi is brilliantly played by Jasmin Tabatabai, a riveting Iranian-German who is both an actor and musician. She is convincing as the film's male protagonist.

A child of immigration herself, Maccarone said: "We (meaning herself and co-author Judith Kaufmann) wanted to tell a story about someone who loses basically everything that makes a person a person: her work, where she lives, who her friends are, her family, her language, and her sexual identity." Maccarone's previous film, *Everything Will Be Fine*, was the winner of the 1998 Outfest Audience Award.

In the plot, Fariba falls for a local woman, Anne, as played by Anneke Kim Sarnau.

Both women are day laborers in a sauerkraut factory near Stuttgart. Anne's discovery of her friend's gender, and the subsequent complications, seems a bit far fetched.

WHAT THE CRITICS SAID
"Several large leaps of faith take some of the dramatic steam out of *Unveiled*, an otherwise well-acted and accessible lesbian drama that also flirts with issues like loss of identity and anti-Muslim tensions. As well as being, frankly, unbelievable, this development is further weakened by Fariba's sudden talent for performing a convincing drag act, complete with a 5 o'clock shadow, at a moment's notice. Later scenes show her secretly taking showers in the middle of the night, but at no time is her character allowed any unease or ineptness (comic or otherwise) in assuming the look and gait of a man."
Derek Elley, *Variety*

Urbania

(2000)

An Odyssey of Grief Through NYC Streets

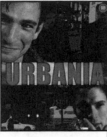

A darkly intriguing thriller-drama, *Urbania* explores the nature of love and the lasting effects of loss. Directed by Jon Shear from a play and screenplay by Daniel Retiz, it is at times painful to watch. It's the story of Charlie (Dan Futterman) who takes a journey of grief during a fall weekend in New York City. The film depicts the inhabitants of Gotham, often at their most unattractive.

Futterman as Charlie delivers a sensitive and complex performance.

Several of the major characters, including Charlie himself, are gay, but *Urbania* doesn't really qualify as a "gay" movie. Gay and straight are blurred in the intricately plotted narrative of Shear's film.

At the beginning of the film, Charlie is traumatized by the loss of his lover, Chris (Matt Keeslar), in a violent incident.

He begins to meet strangers, including his upstairs neighbors (Bill Sage and Megan Dodds), who do little to conceal the sound of their endless lovemaking. An actual encounter with the couple ends violently.

The characters grow more bizarre, including a mysterious, tattooed stranger (Samuel Ball). One of the most significant encounters is with Breet (Alan Cumming), who develops a crush on Charlie. There's also a homeless man (Lothaire Bluteau).

WHAT THE CRITICS SAID

"The drama's more philosophical dimensions, which take center stage in the film's last reel—and its most disturbing chapter—depict Charlie's efforts to regain power and executive justice through revenge against those responsible for his misery. Incidents of gay-bashing and gay counterattacks have appeared in several recent films, but never have these issues been so well integrated into the narrative and so crucial to the characters' transformation."
Emanuel Levy, *Variety*

Vacationland

(2006)

The Seedy Side of Bangor, Maine

For his micro-budgeted *Vacationland*, helmer Todd Verow drew upon his own experiences of growing up gay in Bangor, Maine. *Vacationland* casts Brad Hallowell as Joe (presumably a stand-in for the director himself).

The young man lives with his single mom, Cathy (Jennifer Mallett), and his older sister, Theresa (Hilary Mann), in the notorious Capehart slum projects in Bangor. At the Capehart projects, where young boys grow up fast, there is always something happening such as a woman smothering her baby because she believes he's the anti-Christ. Along with another boy, Joe was molested when he was ten years old but never told anyone about it.

As they work together at a rundown mall next to the projects, Joe and Theresa bond in their joint dream. He wants to go to college, and she wants to sample the glorious life of Los Angeles. They have no money and must scheme to get some to achieve their dreams.

Joe falls for super-hottie, Andrew, his best friend, as engagingly played by Gregory J. Lucas.

The downside of Andrew is that he is a compulsive shoplifter even though he is the school football star. After a drunken night, Joe and Andrew get it on, but their love is complicated by Andrew's manipulative girlfriend, Mandy (Jennifer Stackpole).

When not pursuing Andrew, Joe likes to hang out in toilets in search of such adventures as letting strange men play with his leg hair. He also fools around with his French teacher, Nathan Johnson, blackmailing the man into assisting him with his application to the Rhode Island School of Design. Joe also answers a personal ad, taking a job as a "houseboy-model" to an unattractive old man.

Even though intriguing in part, this sexual burlesque ends on a sour note with a muddled, violent conclusion.

Valentino: The Last Emperor

(2008)

"I Love Beauty--It's Not My Fault"

Couturiers are a dying breed.

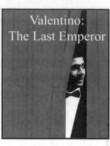
Valentino: The Last Emperor

In this documentary, an exposé of the fashion business, Karl Lagerfeld whispers into Valentino's ear: "You and I are the last two. Everyone else makes rags!" This is more or less the truth.

Director Matt Tymauer traces the life of the legendary fashion designer Valentino in the years 2006 and 2007, leading up to his retirement when he sold his company for $300 million.

It is also a love story of two young men, Valentino Garavani and Giancarlo Giammetti, who met in the heyday of the 1950s *La Dolce Vita* along the Via Veneto and formed a "marriage" and a business partnership that exists to this day.

Giammetti seems perfectly suited to handling Valentino's artistic temperament. Together, they comprised one of the most celebrated—and successful—gay couples in the world.

Valentino shot to international fame when he designed Jackie Kennedy's wedding dress for her marriage to Aristotle Onassis. From sketch to runway, the docu presents a year of him at work, presenting shows, making decisions, hosting glam parties in his French chateau, or tending to his staff, friends, and menagerie of pugs, who seem to steal the picture. Everything is part of the pursuit of beauty, especially when it's presented in "Valentino red."

We were left with a touch of sympathy for the divine and even-tempered Giammetti, who has lived so relentlessly for so many years in the shadow of his lover. He estimates that he hasn't been apart from Valentino for more than 2 months in 45 years.

Overall, the pic provides a fascinating insight into the *haute* world of European fashion and glamour, with a keen eye for the sweat, labor, and human idiosyncrasies that go into its compilation.

Velvet Goldmine

(1998)

Is This Really a Bi Overview of David Bowie?

A trio of Hollywood hotties—Ewan McGregor, Jonathan Rhys Meyers, and Christian Bale—head the cast of this film where much of the dialogue came from the writings of Oscar Wilde. Todd Hayes directed this look at 70s glam rock and was the co-scripter.

Hayes played a trick on his stars. As Bale and McGregor were filming their sex scene, the director cut without letting them know. The two studs continued to simulate the sex act until they realized a trick had been played on them.

The movie was originally supposed to feature some of David Bowie's music—hence the title. The singer learned that much of the script was based on unauthorized biographies of him, including *Stardust: The David Bowie Story*. He threatened a suit, forcing the producers to rewrite the script to avoid too much resemblance between Bowie and the Bowie-like character of Brian Slade (Rhys Meyers).

As a young rock star, Slade inspires numerous teenage boys to paint their nails and explore their own sexuality. When he can no longer stand the role he created for himself, Slade plots his own murder. Later fans discover that the murder is a hoax. His star fades as his fans desert him. All this happened in 1971.

Fast forward to 1984 when Arthur (Bale) a journalist, is assigned to investigate the story of the fake murder of Brian Slade.

The film proceeds like a Citizen Kane-like investigation into the life and career of the vanished superstar.

Slade has an affair with Curt Wild, an outlandish rising rock star (played by Ewan McGregor and perhaps modeled on Kurt Cobain). Wild's act includes flashing his dick, posturing, and diving through flames into the audience---an ejaculatory performance.

A Very Natural Thing

(1974)

Gay Relationships, Gay Liberation

The New York Post claimed this film was an argument for the gay lifestyle—not an entertainment. Critic Judith Crist also had little praise for it. "If the gay lib movement wants its own mediocre movie preachment—here it is." Even A. H. Weiler of *The New York Times* claimed that although the film was sensitive and realistic in its approach, it "is not especially moving."

For its director, Christopher Larkin (who also co-penned the screenplay), it was an act of love. An ex-monk himself, Larkin crafted a story of an ex-monk David (Robert Joel). In his 20s, he meets Mark (Curt Gareth), with whom he falls in love and wants to live with.

No longer a monk, Davis is a young local high school teacher. His new love is a handsome but restless executive type. Clouds gather on the horizon of their relationship.

David breaks up with Mark but enters into another relationship with Jason (Bo White), the new light in his life. Jason has an estranged wife and a little daughter.

"Being gay is a very natural thing," a young lesbian says within the film. But, as noted by one viewer, "The succession of ecstasies, tiffs, quarrels, and searchings for meaning are, despite the essential honesty, the stuff of standard, not unusual, drama."

The film is also a gay travelogue, moving from a Gay Pride rally in New York's Washington Square Park to the gay fleshpots of Fire Island, and to the steam baths where a disillusioned David moves from monogamy to promiscuity.

WHAT THE CRITICS SAID
"Unlike the strictly pornographic exercises on view, *A Very Natural Thing* is sensitive and realistic in its approach, even though the homosexual bars, the local and Fire Island beach soirées, and artistic couplings are not in short supply. And its Manhattan, Fire Island, and Cape Cod vignettes have been captured in pastel colors that are strikingly lovely and lend a documentary effect."
A.H. Weiler, *The New York Times*

A Very Serious Person

(2006)

Drag Legend Charles Busch's Directing Debut

The queen of all drag queens, Charles Busch, both directed and stars in this drama. He even co-wrote it with Charles Andress. The film also marks a return to the screen of Polly Bergen. Busch plays Jan, an itinerant male nurse from Denmark who takes a new job with Mrs. A (Bergen), a terminally ill Manhattan woman raising her parentless, 13-year-old grandson, Gil (P.J. Verhoest).

In this coming-of-age tale, P.J. plays a proto-gay teen. Busch's cloistered caregiver banishes cherry balloons with a disapproving stare, but it's only a matter of time before his star-spangled inner self starts to shine, unlocking his young tagalong's burgeoning sexuality in the bargain. As would be expected, Busch plays the nurse in an effeminate way, as he befriends this sensitive teenager during a summer at the Jersey shore.

As a director, Busch (*Die, Mommie, Die!*) seems a bit out of his element. Maybe he'd better stick to wearing a wig, which he does almost better than any other performer. He makes a directorial thud in this bland drama.

WHAT THE CRITICS SAID
"Charles Busch, celebrated auteur and cross-dressing diva extraordinaire of stage and screen, steps behind the camera and out of drag--mostly--in front of it to helm and star in this autobiographical change-of-pacer, a sweet but never cloying account of a 13-years-old's last summer with his dying grandmother. Aficionados of Busch's bravura femme perfs may initially be put off by his relatively staid depiction of a pony tailed male."
Ronnie Scheib, *Variety*

"Everything is destined to end wistfully, with sighs and shrugs as opposed to *sturms und drang*. It's unusual for Busch to be so subdued and unfortunate that the whole exercise doesn't have a bit more zing to it."
Don Willmott

Victim

(1961)

"The Blackmailer's Charter"

Blackmail was the subject of this pioneering film, written by Janet Green and John McCormick, who'd also penned *Sapphire* in 1959, a thriller about racism. In England during the late 1950s, male homosexuality was illegal, although not lesbianism because Queen Victoria did not think girl/girl sex was possible. It was estimated that 90 percent of all blackmail victims in Britain were gay men.

Although uncut in its current DVD release, *Victim* was a daring, courageous film for its time. Many actors, including Laurence Olivier, turned down the lead, but Dirk Bogarde, a gay actor himself, accepted the challenging role. He did admit that after his portrayal, the 4,000 "fanatical" letters he received every week from lovesick female fans stopped abruptly.

In the role of Melville Farr, Bogarde appeared on the screen as a married barrister (wed to Sylvia Syms). He had had a gay past. Risking his career, Farr goes after a blackmailer threatening homosexual men in London.

The movie was intelligently written and filmed, and is still interesting to watch after all these decades have gone by.

The blackmailer has photos of Farr and a young man who is being blackmailed. He later commits suicide. In the wake of that, Farr tracks down other homosexuals who are being blackmailed by the same man.

Detective Inspector Harris (John Barrie) considers the anti-sodomy law on British books nothing more than an aid to blackmailers. He assists Farr in calling the blackmailer's bluff.

After the public exposure Farr faces at the blackmailer's trial, Farr and his wife Laura come to terms with his homosexuality.

Victim was originally banned from American screens because it dared use the dreaded word "homosexual."

Homosexuality—at long last!—was finally legalized in Britain in 1967.

Victor/Victoria

(1982)

Julie Andrews a Man?

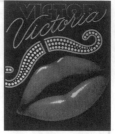

Writer and director Blake Edwards cast his wife, Julie Andrews, in this gender-bending farce that still enjoys a wide gay audience. Edwards denied strong rumors that Tom Selleck was under consideration to play King Marchand, a Chicago night club owner who is shocked finding himself falling for a Polish "gentleman," Victor (Andrews), who passes himself off as a female impersonator.

If you've seen *The Sound of Music* or *Mary Poppins* (who hasn't?), be warned that *Victor/Victoria* is not your typical Julie Andrews movie.

Looking jowly and showing his age, Robert Preston, formerly a handsome leading man, plays the old queen Toddy. One critic found that Preston played the role in the spirit of Ethel Mertz on *I Love Lucy*. Toddy suggests to his friend, Victoria, a poverty-stricken soprano trying to find work in 1930s Paris, that she become a female impersonator, as such acts are in demand. The charade works, and "Victor" is employed in a club.

In the audience, King Marchand (James Garner) finds himself sexually attracted to the impersonator. He finds this hard to believe that he, with strong hetero credentials, could actually be falling for another man. He starts to investigate.

His bodyguard "Squash" Bernstein (Alex Karas), not in the loop, thinks his boss is gay like himself, and he comes roaring out of the closet.

Comic relief is provided by the brilliant Lesley Ann Warren who is Garner's girlfriend. She is fiercely jealous of this new competition. As the gun moll, she seeks revenge using the Chicago mob.

Andrews is cast in one of her finest roles playing a woman playing a man playing a woman.

WHAT THE CRITICS SAID
"*Victor/Victoria* is a sparkling, ultra-sophisticated entertainment from Blake Edwards. Based on a 1933 German film comedy, which was a big hit in its day, pic sees Edwards working in the Lubitsch-Wilder vein of wit and delightful sexual innuendos."
Variety

Walk in the Light

(2005)

Tales from a Black and Gay Church in L.A.

A grassroots church movement was founded in 1982 by the Rev. Carl Bean. Openly accepting of homosexuality, the Unity Fellowship Church set out to show that "Gay Christian" is not an oxymoron.

Walk in the Light explores the lives of people who yearn for a relationship with God but are turned away from traditional churches. Revealing the impact of intolerance and demonstrating the power of self-love, the film explores the lives of three individuals who attend Unity Fellowship Church. The mother church, which later established a branch in San Diego, lies in a gritty section of South Central Los Angeles. Intimate footage and lively gospel music provide the backdrop to a film about struggling to accept others and one's self.

The present pastor of the church, Rev. Charles Lanier, once said, "I began to realize that I was gay as a little boy, but I always loved church. I wanted to be a good little Christian, and so in listening to the teachings, the one subject that they always talk about is homosexuality, and those are the worst sinners, and God does not love them. Subsequently, I started drinking and using marijuana at about 13: anything to escape the self-hatred that had begun to grow inside of me for not being able to accept my feelings." Eventually he discovered Unity Fellowship Church and his real healing began.

Worshippers depicted in the film include Cookie, a transgender female. "At Unity, I feel like I'm fighting for something," she said. An ex-marine and the biological father of two, Cookie always felt her identity was not that of a man. After years of self-denial, Cookie decided to continue her life as a woman.

On the other hand, Claire is more troubled. She wants to be with her partner, Bridget, but her conviction that she will go to hell for being a lesbian haunts the relationship. Together, Bridget and Claire attend Unity Fellowship Church for the first time.

A Walk on the Wild Side

(1982)

Stanwyck as the Dyke Madam of a Bordello

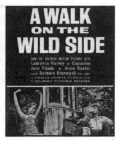

In the early 1980s, taking advantage of new production rules allowing homosexuals on the screen, real-life lesbian Barbara Stanwyck became the first A-list American actress to play a lesbian character in a feature film.

In this film directed by Edward Dmytryk and based on a racy novel by Nelson Algren, Stanwyck plays Jo Courtney, director of the Doll House, a 1930s bordello in New Orleans. Hallie (played by the French actress Capucine, who was sometimes defined as 100% beautiful and 100% talent-free) is the bordello's main attraction, both for male clients and for Jo.

The screenplay suffered through multiple rewrites, including drafts from both Clifford Odets and Ben Hecht. Even so, it goes terribly awry, emerging as evocative of an ill-advised Tennessee Williams' indulgence. *Walk on the Wild Side*, viewed today, is an outdated curiosity.

Algren set the tone for his seedy story. "The book asks why lost people sometimes develop into greater human beings than those who have never been lost in their whole lives."

The male lead is played by gay actor Laurence Harvey. During the filming, Capucine objected to kissing scenes with him, claiming "he's not manly enough." Harvey told her, "Perhaps if you were more of a woman, I would be more of a man. Honey, kissing you is like kissing the side of a beer bottle."

Jane Fonda plays Kitty Twist, an amoral, mentally deficient thief and prostitute. Anne Baxter (yes, Eve Harrington herself) was strangely cast as a love-starved Mexican woman who offers her *chicharrones* to complete strangers. The role called for Rita Moreno or Chita Rivera.

Despite its all-star cast, *Walk on the Wild Side* was not well received by critics. Bosley Crowther of *The New York Times* called it "lurid, tawdry, and sleazy melodrama." He also found Stanwyck "like something out of moth balls as the madame," and the film "naughty as a cornsilk cigarette."

The Walker

(2007)

Woody Harrelson Plays it Courtly and Gay

Woody Harrelson is certainly versatile, playing everybody from the dumb Woody in the 1980s sitcom *Cheers* to the smut peddler in *The People vs. Larry Flynt*. In Paul Schrader's *The Walker*, he plays a southern gentleman—and a gay one at that—the son of a late, great southern senator. "I'm not naïve," he drawls in his role of Carter Page III. "I'm superficial." So is the movie.

Schrader considered *The Walker* the completion of his "lonely man" trilogy, which included *American Gigolo* (1980) and *Light Sleeper* (1992). However, *The Walker* doesn't have their bite. Its gentle, languid pacing matches Carter's drawl.

Schrader drew inspiration for his gay character from Jerry Zipkin, who once escorted Nancy Reagan, Pat Buckley, and Betsy Bloomingdale to various social affairs.

When not dabbling in real estate, Carter "walks" various society ladies to various functions. Chief among them is Lauren Bacall at her most stately. The killer lines are reserved for her, and she delivers them with her usual panache. "Memory is a very unreliable organ," she tells Carter. After a beat, she adds, "It's right up there with the penis."

Schrader takes delight in portraying the vipers of Washington, including Lily Tomlin, one of Carter's ladies. Trouble comes in the form of a senator's wife the stylishly evasive Lynn Lockner (Kristin Scott Thomas). She trusts Carter enough to ask him to drive her to a rendezvous for a tryst she's having with a lobbyist. Once there, she encounters a corpse. To save her husband's career, she asks Carter to cover up for her to protect her politically ambitious husband (Willem Dafoe). Carter cleans up the crime scene, which later makes him the prime suspect.

Carter must solve the murder himself to escape jail. In his investigation, he is aided by his neglected boyfriend Emek Yoglu (Moritz Bleibtreu), a young Turk paparazzo who helps him track down the killer.

The movie is not so much about a murder as it is about the dark side of the human soul.

Wanted

(*Nachbarinnen*; 2006)

Women Who Want to Love and Be Loved

Director Franziska Meletzky's debut is a tragic comedy in the style of the New Berlin School. Starring Dagmar Manzel, Grazyna Szapolowska, Jörg Schüttauf, this is a discreetly lesbian, East German "crimi" drama.

Dora, played by Manzel, lives alone and delivers packages. Her reclusive life takes place in narrow apartment building in Leipzig, Germany. She makes it through the day thanks partly to her dry sense of humor. Her quiet, orderly life is thrown out of balance when she has to hide her mysteriously fascinating neighbor, Jola (Szapolowska). Jola is convinced that she has killed someone. Reluctantly, Dora takes the woman into her home where she becomes attracted to this open and impulsive stranger.

Dora begins to trust her because she asks exactly those questions that no one else dares to ask.

She soon learns that the charges against Jola have been dropped. Instead of telling Jola the truth, Dora invents a fictitious police investigation as a means of keeping Jola in her apartment.

In an interview Meletzky said, "I believe in love and its possibilities but what do they look like? If I'm fascinated by someone, maybe even in love, I want to keep this person. But how do I do that? If I say 'stay!' I lose him or her. If I say 'go!' I lose as well. Saying nothing is probably the worst choice. This is the question and how to deal with it, sometimes tragically and sometimes amusingly, that *Wanted* tackles. In my movie, it's essential that actors reveal themselves. As Billy Wilder once said, 'the director must not get in the way.' I have to give my partners their space. Like an imaginative mother, perhaps; lovingly reliable, with hardly any needs of her own, pushing them on, with discipline, responsibility, fair with reason. My focus is on the actors, just like my passion."

Water Flowing Together

(2007)

Spotlight on Ballet Dancer Jock Soto

Jock Soto

Gwendolen Cates has directed and written a feature-length docu that chronicles the life of the retired ballet dancer Jock Soto, a Navajo/Puerto Rican who was the principal male dancer at the New York City Ballet. The film explores his connection to his mixed heritage and follows him through the last two years of his career up to his retirement on June 19, 2005. It also documents his coming out as a gay man.

Today Soto is still dancing and teaching and running a catering business with his lover and partner, Luis Fuentes, whom he met in a bar.

After 25 years in the ballet, Soto retired at the age of 40. "I wanted to show people how, after dance, you don't just die. You continue on. And I obviously was not embarrassed at all of being gay."

Soto was one of the last dancers selected by Balanchine to perform before the master's death in 1983. But Soto's guiding light was really Peter Martins, who appears in the docu as himself. "He was like my father figure," Soto said. "He sort of guided me through life."

WHAT THE CRITICS SAID
"Soto's formidable talent, charm, and drive are apparent throughout the film, and there is no doubt that he will remain a vital presence in the arts world. *Water Flowing Together* addresses ballet more seriously and more insightfully than most comparable documentaries; it's engrossing as an encapsulation of Mr. Soto's artistry and as an exploration of cultural interface and cultural commonality."
Joel Lobenthal, *The New York Sun*

Water Lilies

(*Naissance des pieuvres;* 2007)

Girls Off the Deep End

If this French film had been made in English several years back, it was suggested that its stars would be Scarlett Johansson, America Ferrera, and Ellen Page.

Instead we get a tomboy brunette, Pauline Acquart, as the late-blooming Marie; a gorgeous blonde swimming star Floriane (Adele Haenel), and Marie's rather unattractive friend Anne (Louise Blachère).

Its original French title translates as "Birth of Octopuses," and that still can be a good description of the complicated relationships in this coming-of-age story, an impressive debut of helmer and scripter Céline Sciamma.

The action takes place in a suburb of Paris where the three girls meet at the local swimming pool. Love and desire make an unexpected, dramatic appearance. It is clearly a picture about teen angst and nascent sexuality.

Boys appear only in relation to the female trio and the backdrop of synchronized swimming.

The girls have some major problems in this flick—sexual desire, puberty, and the pressure of virginity. Another problem involves sorting out the differences between friendship and sexual attraction.

WHAT THE CRITICS SAID
"*Water Lilies* isn't a teen satire or a suburban docudrama or a standard-issue lesbian coming-of-age film. And it isn't porn, either. The sex scene is intense and troubling but not at all graphic. If *Water Lilies* feels like a remarkably realistic rendering of teen culture, that's because teen life is always mythic in scale, at least when you're inside it, and the unrequited, inexpressible and painful desires of Anne, Marie, and Floriane are inside us all."
Nick Pinkerton

Watercolors

(2010)

Creating Art from a Lost Love

The good acting of Tye Olson as Danny and Kyle Clare as Carter bring helmer David Oliveras' drama to life. Danny is a gifted young artist. As the film opens, we see him at his first big New York show, the walls covered with erotic paintings of swimmers. The scene triggers memories of his first love (Carter), a troubled athlete whose depression and self-denial led to suicide.

The New York exhibition takes place 15 years after the Carter affair. Danny faces the possibility of losing Allan (Edward Finlay), his current lover, if he doesn't set aside his still-flaming torch for the long-dead Carter.

Although they are opposites, Danny and Carter are attracted to each other. But their blossoming love affair is made more difficult by homophobic harassment from the other members of the swim team, especially from Coach Brown (Greg Louganis).

Although his father seems rather indifferent to his son, Danny gets moral support from his mother, actress Casey Kramer. When he confides in her that he's been beaten up by the school bullies, he also outs himself to her. In spite of her shock, she offers moral support.

Danny is also aided by his friends, Mrs. Martin (Karen Black), a free-spirited art teacher, and his best friend Andy (Ellie Araiza), a young girl with a severe physical impairment.

WHAT THE CRITICS SAID
"Boil it down: The debut feature from writer/director David Oliveras is an honest, engaging coming-out and coming-of-age movie despite its flaws. What the script does right is take its time in developing Carter and Danny as friends, and then as lovers. They're a mismatched pair from the beginning in every way, helping make their inevitable coming together all the more remarkable. They have a sweetness when they're together, a sense they can both let their guard down without being assaulted for who they are. The obligatory sex scene is beautifully shot and written."
TMR: The Movie Rambler

The Wedding Banquet

(1993)

The Film that Put Ang Lee on the Map

Long before director Ang Lee gave us *Brokeback Mountain*, there was *The Wedding Banquet*. It's a hysterically smart comedy about a gay couple whose relationship is thrown into a tizzy by a green card wedding and the impending arrival of traditional Chinese parents traveling 8,000 miles to attend a sham wedding.

Simon (Mitchell Lichtenstein), an American, and Wai-Tung (Winston Chao), a Taiwanese expatriate, are a happy gay couple living in a Greenwich Village townhouse. Simon is an affable doctor and Wai-Tung is a budding real estate wheeler-dealer.

The Chinaman's parents (Ah Lei Gua and Sihung Lung) are constantly harassing him with long distance calls, urging him to get married and produce a grandson for them.

Wai-Tung is the owner of some slum buildings. Simon suggests that his boyfriend marry Wei-Wei (May Chin), another expat who lives in an apartment in one of Wai-Tung's buildings. She is in the States illegally and desperately needs a green card to stay on.

To silence his parents, Wai-Tung agrees. But there are problems—after all, this is a movie.

Wei-Wei has a crush on her husband-to-be and actually wants it to be a real marriage. All hell breaks loose when Wai-Tung's parents show up for the wedding. The gay couple hurries about their house getting rid of all the male nudes.

The fun has just begun.

WHAT THE CRITICS SAID
"*The Wedding Banquet* is not a particularly slick film; the plot construction feels contrived, and the acting of the two younger men is somewhat self-conscious, although the parents are magnificent. What makes the film work is the underlying validity of the story, the way the filmmakers don't simply go for melodrama and laughs, but pay these characters their due. At the end of the film I was a little surprised how much I cared for them."
Roger Ebert

Wedding Wars

(2006)

Gay People Across the U.S. Go on Strike

The very talented John Stamos goes gay in this film which asks the question, "What would happen if every gay person in America suddenly went on strike?"

"Oh, my God," shouted one viewer. "Uncle Jessie is kissing another man and with passion!" The reference was to Stamos, usually with the top buttons of his shirt unfastened, who became world famous playing his role on *Full House*, the TV sitcom in which three men raise a family in San Francisco. "I love John like he's the sister I never had," said *Full House* co-star Bob Saget.

Not only with *Wedding Wars*, but on the stage, Stamos is taking chances. He appeared barechested (at long last) in the stage version of *Cabaret*, playing the pansexual role of the emcee. With nipples sparkling and in full lipstick with a bow-tie between his naked breasts, "Uncle Jesse" both wowed and shocked audiences in the role Joel Grey made famous and won the Best Supporting Actor Oscar for his characterization in the 1972 film that starred Liza Minnelli.

Stamos said his character in *Cabaret* "would have sex with a squirrel if he had a chance—and he probably did." He learned to "push the boundaries" in *Cabaret* and was prepared to play gay in *Wedding Wars*, where he was cast as a likable gay rights activist.

In the role, he tackles the delicate issue of same-sex marriage but with light humor. Stamos as Shel Grandy takes up the issue of gay marriage after his brother—played by *Grey's Anatomy* Eric Dane (as Ben)—becomes engaged to the daughter of a conservative governor, Conrad Welling (James Brolin), whom we never call Mr. Barbra Streisand.

The film was directed by Jim Fall, who married his own boyfriend on the set in Halifax, Canada.

An argument between the two brothers inadvertently triggers the strike, and it's up to the siblings to solve their differences before the entire country is shut down.

Were the World Mine

(2008)

A Queer Take on *A Midsummer Night's Dream*

This is a rarity. A gay musical on film, a queer-centric take on Shakespeare's *A Midsummer Night's Dream*. This project was conceived by Tom Gustafson, who also co-wrote the screenplay.

For a sensitive gay teen Timothy (Tanner Cohen), all the world's a stage. Of course, Cohen at 6 foot 4 may be a bit big to play a fairy. Nonetheless, he gets cast as Puck in a high school musical version of *Midsummer.*

Timothy is the gay outcast in an all-boys academy. He lives in a world of sweetly sexy fantasies staged as song-and-dance numbers.

He's got a crush on handsome head jock Jonathon (Nathaniel David Becker).

In a bit of a stretch, Timothy creates a love potion to turn Jonathon—and everybody else in town—queer.

Ensnaring family, friends, and enemies in this chaos, Timothy forces them to walk a mile in his musical shoes.

The love potion proves that true love never runs smoothly and is, in fact, a bumpy ride.

Timothy also has to deal with his struggling mother (Judy McLane) and his friends, Max (Rocky Goldman) and Frankie (Zelda Williams, daughter of Robin).

WHAT THE CRITICS SAID
"When the film narrows its focus from big questions addressed through overly broad strokes and instead zooms in on one-on-one interactions and the emotional power of a well-made musical sequence, it taps into a winning sweetness and poignancy."
Ernest Haryd

"As the action unfolds, with dazzling color and crisp choreography, the homophobic boys get the lessons of their lives."
Reyhan Harmanci, *San Francisco Chronicle*

When Boys Fly

(2002)

The World of Gay Circuit Parties

This docu by helmers Stewart Halpern-Fingerhut and Lenind Rolov traces the saga of four men as they find their place on the social ladder of Palm Springs' Circuit Parties. Expect male nudity, gay sex, drug abuse, and disconcerting insights into gay lives lived dangerously.

In case you didn't know, A circuit party is a professionally produced dance event, extending through a night and into the following day. Sometimes perceived as a celebration of gay life and gay sexuality, Circuit parties are sometimes satirized for their superficiality and condemned by health officials for the promiscuous sex and drug use associated with the events.

Tone is a 21-year-old biology student who devotes much of his free time to circuit parties, boozing it up and doing drugs. He's aware that he needs to find some direction in his life, but doesn't seem to get around to traveling that road.

Brandon, age 23, is more conservative and a college student. A virgin on the circuit party scene, he heads to Miami for the next big blast. He wants to find out about the gay world and how he fits into it.

Todd, 35, and Jon, 19, are a couple, Todd came out late in life and has been trying to make up for lost time. He's cheated on all his BFs, including Jon. Todd says that he knows the difference between love and sex. Jon, on the other hand, thinks that's bullshit.

WHAT THE CRITICS SAID
"Audiences have the luxury in 'Circuit' of being able to sit back and tell themselves that the story unfolding in front of them was made up, only that's not the case here. It makes *When Boys Fly* all the more painful to watch. Fortunately, it's extremely mesmerizing, and the people featured in the film are so diverse and different from each other that one cannot help but want to see how they interact and finally how it all turns out. There's grief, sorrow, joy, fulfillment, discovery, and betrayal to be found in these 60 minutes."
DVD Review

When I'm 64

(2004)

A Gay Version of *On Golden Pond?*

This telepic is a BBC production with an unusual subject matter. Alun Armstrong is cast as Jim, a retiring boys' school Latin teacher, with Paul Freeman playing Ray, a widower cabbie. They strike up a "December shadows" friendship that blossoms into a romance. And we thought love was only for the young.

Director Jon Jones and writer Tony Grounds succeed in bringing to life this offbeat drama about friendship at the age of retirement. The two lonely men make for compelling characters. We found ourselves rooting for them and their potential happiness. Both men play their roles with utter realism and sound no false notes.

Ray drives a cab to bring in extra money, having given up his lifetime passion for soccer hooliganry. He laments the loss of his late wife and faces condescension from his grown children, as played by Tamzin Outhwaite and Jason Flemying.

As might have been predicted, he picks up a passenger, Jim, one fine day and his life changes forever. Of course, all is not sunny in this autumnal romance. Ray's nosey kids are mortified at the burgeoning relationship.

We especially like the way the film depicts homosexual longings that have been suppressed for decades. Both actors avoid camp parody, so common when many straights try to play on-screen gay.

The Beatles sang their famous song about reaching the age of 64 to a youth-obsessed culture that viewed such an age as the end of life. But as Ray and Jim discover, it may merely be the beginning of something new.

WHAT THE CRITICS SAID
"The kind of telepic that makes you wish big screen features could manage such intimate yet crowd-pleasing character drama more often. Expertly written, directed and acted tale is a keeper that merits fest books (not just gay ones) as well as offshore niche DVD pickups."
Dennis Harvey, *Variety*

White Shadows

(2005)

Survival and Transformation

This 72-minute docu is based on the life of Dalee Henderson, a celebrity hair stylist and gay African-American man who was reared in the rural, segregated South of the 1950s. Dalee escaped to the West Coast to live life openly and proudly, arriving in Los Angeles in the late 70s.

There he achieved great personal and professional success, amassing a wealth of admirers by virtue of his gregarious nature. His life changed when he learned of his HIV status. But in spite of a deteriorating body, he lived to continue what was called "a triumphant lifestyle."

In October of 2005 Henderson passed away at his home in his sleep. This film is a love letter to him.

In his heyday, Henderson was a stylist of such luminaries as Diana Ross, Stevie Wonder, and Denzel Washington.

"Dalee truly believed that every day was a gift," said director Mialyn Hanna. "This is a story about a man who transcends his disease and chooses to focus on his life. He truly served as an inspiration for many, and I wanted to celebrate his life and the gifts he brought to so many people of all walks of life."

"Dying from AIDS is not an option for me," Henderson said. "I live my life in divine wellness. I claim wellness in my spirit and life with the energy I surrounded myself with, as well as the people that I surround myself with."

White Shadows won several awards, including the best of NewFest at the Brooklyn Academy of Music in New York and the Spirit Award 2006 at Rebelfest International film Festival in Toronto.

WHAT THE CRITICS SAID
"With a deft and gentle hand, with a clear and unsentimental eye, director Mialyn Hanna guides us through the astonishingly joyful end of the life of a man we've never known, but now will never forget."
Hal Ackerman

Whole New Thing

(2005)

Schoolboy Crush on an English Teacher

After years of being home-schooled by his hippie parents, Emerson (Aaron Webber), a precocious 13-year-old, is enrolled at his local public high school.

The intelligent, androgynous youth confounds his classmates but captures the attention of his attractive English teacher, Don Grant (Daniel MacIvor). Mr. Grant has his own problems, struggling with a proclivity for sexual encounters in public toilets. He worries that he made the wrong decision in leaving the big city—and his lover—for this remote outpost. The teacher-student relationship leads to problems where everyone gets involved, including the boy's parents.

The film evolves into a fresh, sweet, and smart coming-of-age story about family, love, lust, and missed connections.

The gay theme is subordinate to the stories of the individuals involved. The boy, who is probably virginal, perhaps bisexual, pursues his crush on his teacher without any regard for its impropriety. His teacher could be fired from the school—or even jailed--for sexually molesting the boy.

The parents, Kaya (Rebecca Jenkins) and Rog (Robert Joy), are concerned that Emerson's social skills have evolved into levels far more advanced than those of his Nova Scotia contemporaries. A few bloody noses ensue.

The film is helmed by Amnon Buchbinder, who also co-wrote the script with Daniel MacIvor, who plays the schoolteacher Grant.

WHAT THE CRITICS SAID
"Coming-of-age teen dramas are a dime a dozen, but when they're executed with a little care and compassion, there are few genres that are more skilled at drilling straight to the heart. *Whole New Thing* heads to some very interesting emotional places, and through fine direction, captures a feeling of a wintry place and heated frustrations that is enormously compelling. It's a film of small intentions, yet the dramatic rewards are mighty."
Brian Orndorf

<table>
<tr><td>

The Whore's Son

(Hurensohn; 2006)

And What Does Your Mama Do for a Living?

</td><td>

Wild Side

(2004)

A *Ménage à Trois* of Misfits

</td></tr>
</table>

This Austrian film in German with English subtitles was the creation of co-scripter and director Michael Sturminger, who is vaguely Fassbinder-ish. In fact, the movie was photographed by the late director's former collaborator, Jurgen Jurges. Its running time of 85 minutes  treats us to a parade of sex, violence, and profanity, all that good old stuff. The results, however, are not always successful.

Sturminger dusts off another coming-of-age plot. Opening with a flashback, the teenager star of the movie, Ozren (Stanislav Lisnic), has just confessed that he's killed his beautiful mother, Silvija (Chulpan Khamatova). When their native Yugoslavia descended into civil wars in the 1980s, mother and son had fled to Vienna.

Orzen at age 3 is played by Gabriel Usein; at age 8 by Emanuel Usein. In spite of the parade of "johns" in her life, Silvija tells the older Orzen (Stanislav) that she is a waitress.

As the film progresses, Silvija moves out of their modest digs, getting her son a job in the brothel being run by a madam downstairs. The teenager's curiosity leads to tragedy.

WHAT THE CRITICS SAID
"Austrian director Michael Sturminger's debut feature creates a visually evocative environment in which to explore some significant themes, from religious repression to Freudian guilt. But our teen protagonist never develops a personality beyond his reactions to Mom's profession, and the movie might have made a greater impact if it focused less upon the whore, and more on the son."
New York Daily News

A French film with English subtitles, and running for 94 minutes, *Wild Side* is Sébastien Lifshitz's second feature. It is a cross between  Patrice Chereaux's *Those Who Love Me Can Take the Train* and *Son Frère*. In this new film, Lifshitz explores the relationship between a transgendered prostitute (Stéphanie Michelini), her lover, a Russian immigrant (Edouard Niktine), and an Arab hustler (Yasmine Belmadi). All three leave Paris to attend the dying mother of the character played by Michelini.

The performers here are rather cold and detached, and it's hard to find anything to like about them. Since Stéphanie can't decide which of the two men she wants long-term, it makes it so much easier that they are attracted to each other.

WHAT THE CRITICS SAID
"Sex frequently disguises itself as friendship and love in *Wild Side*, a morbid and self-important homosexual *Jules & Jim* for the new millennium. Mistaking silence for significance, Gallic helmer Sébastien Lifshitz lets long periods roll by without dialogue, but his intention to shock is unmistakable, with one genital close-up, one anal penetration, and two acts of fellatio in the first few minutes."
Russell Edwards, *Variety*

"Sébastien Lifshitz's gender-blurring mosaic of bruised lives is an alternative family endorsement with a premise that sounds like a barroom joke: Ever hear the one about the bisexual Russian army deserter, the Algerian rent boy, and the pre-op transsexual French hooker? There's nothing lewd about the punchline, though, which proposes a nurturing polyamorous threesome as a sustainable design for living."
Dennis Lim

"The film explains why Stéphanie and her bisexual boyfriends need each other, but doesn't depict why they are drawn to each other, making the *ménage à trois* mechanical, largely due to Stéphanie Michelini's understated and sullen debut performance. The audience will feel just as disconnected as Stéphanie."
Kent Turner

Wild Tigers I Have Known

(2006)

A Lyrical Depiction of Sexual Anguish

Cam Archer both directed and scripted this feature film, with Gus Van Sant serving as one of the executive directors. It's a coming-of-age story, with Malcolm Stumpf playing the misfit kid, Logan.

He pines for the hunky loner, Rodeo (Patrick White), in the co-starring role. The gay 13-year-old Stumpf decides to act on his attraction to the older boy by disguising himself as a girl. In the film he learns to cope with his newfound sexuality and his unrequited love for the cool kid in school.

The film fails in many ways, but is momentarily intriguing if you've got nothing better to do one night. The cast, however, is admirable, including Fairuza Balk as Logan's mom. Max Paradise appears as Joey, Tom Gilroy playing the school principal.

There is something to admire in Archer's attempt to turn a yearning for rough trade into something lyrical and feminine.

WHAT THE CRITICS SAID
"Two high school wrestlers grapple on a fuzzed-out TV screen. A pubescent boy in sunglasses masturbates in a luridly red room. That same lad, wearing lipstick and blond wig, stares into a cracked mirror. Cam Archer's feature debut offers a stunning opening triptych that's a virtual porno-homo filmography, skipping from the pixilated New Queer Cinema of Sadie Benning to Kenneth Anger's colorful cryptography and Andy Warhol's narcissistic *Drag City* in two cuts."
David Fear, *Time Out New York*

"Encouraged by the older boy's attentions, Logan develops a female alter ego he calls Leah, one bold enough to call Rodeo in the middle of the night and come on to him in a way Logan himself could hardly muster."
Kyle Buchanan, *The Advocate*

Without Conscience

(*Verso Nord;* 2004)

The Attraction of Opposites

Gay men in Italy flocked to see this movie because of the appearance of Valerio Foglia Manzillo playing Rollo. For devotees of Italian hunks, the beautiful and charismatic Manzillo is the greatest thing to come along since spaghetti. If directors don't cast him in a raft of future movies, preferably wearing as few clothes as possible, they are fools.

If you can divert your eyes from this Adonis, you might try to follow along with the plot of this Italian drama with English subtitles.

Mauro (Maurizio Mattioli) is a 50-year-old nurse who lives a reclusive life in Rome. To make brownie points with his boss at the hospital, he agrees to escort a young orphan to the Swiss border so he can link up with his adoptive parents. Along the way, Mauro hooks up with Rollo (as played by the divine Manzillo). The two men soon discover they have a lot in common. Both men develop an affection for their young charge, Eddi, as played by Mohamed Ismail Bayed.

With a plot line that's propelled forward by the arrival of a prostitute, Elena (Ana Papadopulu), *Verso Nord* soon takes on the aura of a chase film to the Swiss border.

The unlikely pairing of Mauro and Rollo marks the beginning of a beautiful friendship, to quote from the closing reel of Bogie's *Casablanca*.

Director/writer Stefano Reali handles the drama with great sensitivity.

WHAT THE CRITICS SAID
"Maurizio Mattioli creates a gay character impossible not to love while the inordinately handsome and charismatic Valerio Foglia Manzilo brings a presence to the screen that promises an exciting career! The pacing is breathtaking, the cinematography is magnificent, and the message is timely and universal!"
Grady Harp, *Amazon.com*

Women in Love

(2005)

Lesbian Sex Revolution in San Francisco

Filmmaker Karen Everett's docu is a compelling collective bio of a den of sex radical dykes in the Bay area. It's a portrait captured on film of a generation of creative lesbians, documenting their experiments in love, commitment, and butch/femme erotic dynamics. It also illuminates how they handle child rearing, breaking up, having sex with men, and sustaining a network of comrades over the long haul.

Everett's previous films include *I Shall Not Be Removed* and *The Life of Malron Riggs.*

In her latest film, she aims her camera at her love life and her community of like-minded souls in San Francisco. The docu explores one woman's journey through 15 years of friendship and love through home videos, candid interviews, and video diaries. Everett poses universal questions about the nature of relationships through monogamy and polyamory.

Everett and her friends, now in midlife, were part of the seminal generation of thousands of young lesbians who moved to San Francisco during the 1980s. At the peak of the AIDS epidemic, these queer women refined sexuality in their own style, creating lesbian pornography, strip clubs, sex toy stores, and alternative ways of loving. The film features Jackie Strano and Shar Rednour, leading directors of lesbian pornography, and Phyllis Christopher, one of America's leading photographers of dyke erotica.

WHAT THE CRITICS SAID
"An intelligent, introspective, occasionally very funny look at what happens when timeless desires collide with changing mores. Highly recommended for anyone looking for new kinds of love and new ways of relating."
Catherine A. Liszt, Co-author, *The Ethical Slut*

"This video memoir (59 min) doesn't amount to much more than a self-absorbed intellectual evaluating her commitment problems, but Everett's friends and their ever-shifting relationships are lively and interesting enough to keep this from collapsing into narcissism."
Reece Pendleton

Word Is Out

(1977)

Stories of Some of Our Lives

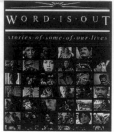

Many viewers across America were stunned when this landmark film appeared in movie theaters and on TV. It was the first feature-length docu about gay and lesbian identity and the first made by gay filmmakers, six people known as the "Mariposa Film Group." It had a huge impact when it was first released and became an icon of the emerging gay rights movement of the 1970s.

In 2010, Milestone Films released a restored DVD version, running 133 minutes. It is a re-mastered digital print of the original docu. The DVD also has special features, including updates on the cast and the filmmakers, including an homage to Peter Adair, who produced the film. He died of AIDS in 1996.

Word Is Out interviewed a very diverse group from the gay and lesbian community, ranging in age from 18 to 77. Locales included venues across the nation, including Boston and San Francisco. Even a sultry drag queen was "interrogated."

WHAT THE CRITICS SAID
"This film provides a window into the evolution of gay cinema, both in the shadow of liberation politics and far beyond it. *Word Is Out* weaves the stories of 26 gay men and lesbians who speak openly about coming out, finding love, and fighting prejudice. When *Word Is Out* was released in theaters and broadcast, more than eight years after the Stonewall Riots, media depictions were still largely confined to unflattering stereotypes, and gay audiences had yet to see their experiences reflected on screen. Reviewing the film in *The Advocate,* Vito Russo declared, 'The silence of gay people on the screen has been broken.'"
Dennis Lim, *The New York Times*

Words & Music
by Jerry Herman

(2007)

The Last Great Showtune Composer

Gay men who "adore" Broadway musicals will be attracted to this docu of Jerry Herman, who in certain circles is a living legend known for such works as *Hello, Dolly!* which, of course, was Carol Channing's greatest hit. Channing appears in this  docu as herself; it was written and directed by Amber Edwards.

Rising from a childhood in Jersey City, Herman was a youthful prodigy. By his early teens, he was writing songs, and in 1955 produced *Sketchbook* at the University of Miami. After college, he moved to New York where his revue *Parade* ran off Broadway for two years. He became known as "the youngest composer-lyricist on Broadway."

But it was *Hello, Dolly!* in 1964 that nailed down his fame. Even Lyndon Johnson was singing it in the White House, having adopted it as his campaign's theme song.

Channing still has great praise for Herman, as does Angela Lansbury, who starred in his post-*Dolly* triumph, *Mame*.

The docu makes note that the Hollywood versions of *Dolly!* with Barbra Streisand and *Mame* with Lucille Ball were disappointing when compared to their Broadway triumphs.

The docu is filled with rare flashback segments, including Pearl Bailey headlining an all-black *Dolly!* with Louis Armstrong singing the hit song.

Various former collaborators also have Herman stories to tell, including Charles Nelson Reilly and cabaret star Michael Feinstein, who admiringly deconstructs several Herman songs at the piano.

Okay, the shows that followed were less successful—*Milk and Honey, Dear World*, and *Mack and Mabel*. But we flocked to them nonetheless. The docu presents Leslie Uggams rehearsing a "Mack and Mabel" number with her ravishing voice.

Herman had another Broadway hit in 1983, *La Cage aux Folles*, at the height of the AIDS crisis.

Herman appears in the film as himself.

The World Unseen

(2007)

Lesbian Longing, Racial Oppression

Shamin Sarif wrote both the novel and screenplay and directed this drama centered on two women who, during the 1950s, get involved in a dangerous love affair during the pressure cooker of South Africa's apartheid era.

Both of the women, we learn as the film begins, were born in India but have been living in South Africa for at least seven years.

Miriam (Lisa Ray) is a traditional Indian mother, hard working and self-effacing. She is trapped in a loveless marriage to Omar (Parvin Dabas), her domineering husband, who's having an affair with another woman. Miriam becomes fascinated by Amina (Sheetal Sheth) who defies society by driving a taxi, and running a café with a local black man named Jacob (David Dennis). At their cafe, racially mixed dining is encouraged. The friendship of the two women flourishes in the face of outraged disapproval. But can they risk acting out their sexual attraction for each other?

To her dismay, when the film's director sent a DVD of her work to the admissions board of a film festival in Dubai, it was returned with a note that stated, "the subject matter does not exist."

WHAT THE CRITICS SAID
"This tale of forbidden love suffers from heavy-handed direction and stodgy exposition, but it is made tolerable by its two central performances. While you may groan at the corny two-shots and the overripe score, you have to acknowledge the aching sincerity of its message-mongering."
Anthony Quinn

"An extremely rare case of a pic version both written and directed by the book's original author, *The World Unseen* reps a strong argument for leaving screen adaptations to other, more capable hands."
Derek Elley, *Variety*

Wrestling With Angels: Playwright Tony Kushner

(2006)

The Devil Behind Angels in America

The scripter and helmer Freida Lee Mock is known mainly for the Oscar-winning *Maya Lin*. Taking on the playwright, Tony Kushner, proved too daunting a challenge.

By now every gay man in America, even straights, know who Kushner is. He's the left-leaning gay political activist who won a Pulitzer Prize for the sweeping stage epic, *Angels in America*, his play about AIDS in the Reagan era.

To appreciate Mock's 98-minute docu on Kushner, it's best to have seen the Mike Nichols-directed HBO movie of this visionary work. This docu highlights not only Nichols but Diane Sawyer, Meryl Streep, and Emma Thompson (the latter in archival footage).

The film is divided into three parts, like a three-act play. Act I, "As a Citizen of the World," focuses on Kushner as activist. He discusses his play, *Homebody/Kabul*, about a middle-class, middle-aged English woman's obsession with Afghanistan. Like a prophet, Kushner wrote this play before 9/11.

Act II, "Mama, I'm a Homosexual," is obviously his coming-out story, but also takes in his involvement in the gay rights movement. At the age of 6, Kushner, who was born in Lake Charles, Louisiana, knew he was gay.

Filmed at Lake Charles on his 80th birthday, Kushner's father talks about his son's homosexuality. William Kushner admits that he would have been "ashamed to have had Tchaikovsky as a son." But time has mellowed him, and now he seems to be content to have a thoroughly out-of-the-closet Tchaikovsky as a son.

Act III, "Collective Action to Overcome Injustice," delves into Kushner's Jewish heritage, including scenes from his play on Jewish immigration, "Why Should It Be Easy When It Can Be Hard."

WTC View

(2005)

The Gay Vista 12 Blocks from Ground Zero

Brian Sloan both wrote and directed this feature film drama, running for 102 minutes. In a nutshell, it tells the story of a young man in SoHo who places an ad in *The Village Voice* for a new roommate on September 11, 2001, "A date that will live in infamy," to borrow words from FDR.

Surprisingly, several candidates show up during that confused period in New York's history. Not only does the young man need to find a roommate, he needs to keep his emotional balance in the wake of 9/11.

Originating as a play, the film made the rounds of gay fests in 2005. The young man, Eric, is played by Michael Urie, more or less well.

Prospective roomies include Jeremy Beazlie, a hotelier from England; a livewire native, Lucas Papaelias; a gay Alex (Nick Potenzieri) with whom Eric shares his bed that night.

Eric even meets a student (Jay Gillespie), whose teacher has urged him to stay in the Big Apple "because the city needs him." There's another potential roomie, a nice straight guy and liberal politician as played by Michael Linstroth.

Urie plays a photographer. The pictures hanging on the wall of his apartment were taken by director Brian Sloan. There are also pictures, including semi-nude males, taken by Craig Hamrick, a New York photographer.

WHAT THE CRITICS SAID
"Urie creates a performance that functions like a pressure cooker, and it only loses credibility when the emotions explode."
Robert Koehler, *Variety*

XXY

(2007)

Boys Who Like Girls Who Are Boys

Not that there's a lot of competition, but *XXY* is probably the best drama ever made about a hermaphrodite—aka known as an intersexual. Director Lucia Puenzo both directed and wrote the screenplay based on Sergio Bizzio's short story *Cinismo*.

Alex (Inés Efron), a 15-year-old intersex person, lives with her parents in a coastal town in Uruguay to escape the mockery she experienced in her native Argentina. Alex lives her life as a woman, which she is from the waist up, although she's a man down below.

Alex was born to a marine biologist named Kraken (Ricardo Darín) and his wife Suli (Valeria Bertuccelli).

Alex's parents decided not to operate on her at birth so that she could choose her own gender when she matured. However, she takes corticoids and is reared as a girl.

One day Suli invites friends to visit for the weekend, a plastic surgeon Ramiro (German Palacios) and his wife Erika (Carolina Peleritti), along with their 15-year-old son Alvaro (Martin Piroyansky). The surgeon is a brute, even suggesting that he suspects his son may be "a fag."

At first the kooky girl annoys Alvaro, but he becomes charmed by her and even falls in love. In what may be the first sexual experience for both kids, he discovers that she's a he! Or maybe something in between.

In one of the most disconcerting scenes in the film, Alex's papa accidentally sights his daughter reaming her new "bend-over" BF. Maybe Alvaro is gay after all. In another disturbing scene, three local teenagers on the beach chase Alex, pinning her down and stripping her to settle the mystery of her physiology.

As critic Aaron Coleman suggested, *XXY* is "heartbreaking, disturbing, and rewarding, shedding hope that every human, no matter their suffering, can find a healing circle of love."

A Year Without Love

(*Un Año Sin Amor*; 2006)

A Writer Dying of AIDS Searches for Meaning

This Argentine film, directed and co-scripted by Anahi Berneri, is the story of a writer dying of AIDS, who searches for a cure and human interaction in the hospitals and sex clubs of Buenos Aires. Set in 1996, Juan Minujin plays Pablo Pérez who is a writer and a French tutor living with his aunt (Mimi Ardú).

Confronted with eroding health because of his HIV-positive status and a lousy love life, he decides to keep a diary. Pérez is a real person and collaborated with Berneri on the script.

Faced with a potential death sentence, Pérez tries to liberate himself from his illness and loneliness. He makes frequent visits to a clinic, but is reluctant to take the medication offered.

Even though the disease is taking its toll, he still looks for someone to give meaning to his life, a life addicted to pornography and casual sex.

He becomes involved deeply in the gay S&M scene in Argentina. He meets a man at an S&M leather party, and enters a relationship based on master-and-slave roles.

The sexual experimentation of Pérez in the film is supposed to be life-affirming, but seems random. Nudity is depicted, along with explicit sex scenes. But just where is all of this headed? To death?

Eventually Pérez meets a kindly older man Báez (Osmar Núñez), which results in sexual fulfillment of an unexpected nature.

As one critic put it, "The strength of the film is in showing, through Pablo, how people are capable of adapting when placed under situations of extreme duress."

WHAT THE CRITICS SAID
"There's nothing gratuitous about *A Year Without Love*, which doesn't try to tug at your heart or needlessly break it. There are some unforgettable images in the film—lingering shots of Pablo walking down the street—even though the story doesn't go much of anywhere."
Peter Hartlaub

Yossi & Jagger	You Are Not Alone
(2002)	*(Du er ikke elene;* 1978)
Macho Israeli Soldiers Make Love, Not War	**Two Boys, Ages 12 & 15, Fall in Love**

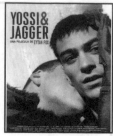

Director Eytan Fox's tender drama is about two hunky Israeli soldiers who fall in love while serving in a remote military outpost near Israel's troubled border with Lebanon. One of the most emotionally moving gay films of 2002, it is in Hebrew with English subtitles. It was a big hit in Israel.

The two young men are well cast, Ohad Knoller playing Yossi and Yehuda Leví cast as Lior Amichal, nicknamed "Jagger" because of his resemblance to the rock star.

Both of these young men try to keep their love affair under their khakis. Jagger is more playful. His company commander is Yossi, beefier and more macho. At one point Jagger asks Yossi, "Is this rape, sir?"

The pressures and privations of military life are brilliantly portrayed in this group of bored soldiers stationed at a cramped outpost. The area they're patrolling is a rutted, snow-covered no-man's land. The lovers' fellow soldiers quickly perceive that they share a lot in common, but they view that as a close bond between men, nothing more than a special friendship.

When the lovers need time along to make love to each other, they steal away on a bogus lookout mission. They make love in the snow (how do they get it up under such cold conditions?).

Jagger is a shameless coquette, pressuring Yossi to leave the army and come live with him in a love nest.

Sexual tension arrives in the form of two female soldiers, Goldie (Hani Furstenberg) and Yaeli (Aya Koren), who disrupt life on the base.

WHAT THE CRITICS SAID
"What the movie lacks in ambition, originality, and grit, it makes up for in pure feeling."
Wesley Morris, *Boston Globe*

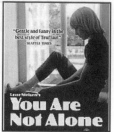

This Danish film takes place in a boarding school, focusing on the love between two boys, 15-year-old Bo (Anders Agens) and 12-year-old Kim (Peter Bjerg). Much of the conflict in the film centers on the boys vs. their stern, old-fashioned headmaster (Ove Sprogøe). To complicate matters, Kim is the son of the headmaster.

The relationship of these two boys is not portrayed in an overtly sexual way, but in an innocent manner. There is no struggle about sexual identities. Their love, as brought to the screen by Ernst Johanse and Lasse Nielsen, is portrayed as something natural.

The boys hug, they shower together, they romp in their skivvies, and they go for romantic idylls in the Danish woods. There is conversation about masturbation, even a debate on whether sex is better with boys or with girls.

Kim, with his innocent face and silky blond hair, appears as only 9 years old, which makes this film a hit with pedophiles.

Tension erupts when one boy, Ole (Ole Meyer), is expelled for exhibiting pornography. The students go on strike, forcing the headmaster to let Ole stay in school.

Kim and Bo decide to come out to the school, their classmates, and their parents. They make a film of their love which concludes with a long and passionate kissing scene.

You Belong to Me

(2007)

Invading *Rosemary's Baby* Territory

This is a nifty little suspense thriller bordering on horror in the creepy apartment building genre as evoked by Roman Polanski's *Rosemary's Baby* or his *The Tenant*. Of course, to make the comparison apt, you'd have to remove the supernatural elements in *You Belong to Me*.

Sam Zalutsky, its helmer and co-writer, traces the story of Jeffrey (Daniel Saull), a young New York architect, who moves into the wrong apartment building.

In the beginning, you think you're seeing a gay rehash of *Fatal Attraction*, that Michael Douglas film.

Jeffrey shacks up with hunky René (Julien Lucas). The architect likes it so much he wants the affair to continue night after night. But René shrugs off further romance. "You're a sweetheart. I am not a sweetheart."

The wandering René returns to the bed of his possessive GF Nicki (Heather Alicia Simms).

When he spots René entering his apartment building, Jeffrey decides to move in himself to be near the object of his affection.

As part of Zalutsky's quirky character development, we meet a landlady from hell, Gladys (Patti D'Arbanville). René is none too pleased when he learns that his one night trick is a fellow apartment dweller. Neither is the jealous Nicki.

The film suddenly shifts from *Fatal Attraction* to horror when Jeffrey hears faint cries of help coming from beneath some floorboards where Gladys lives one floor down.

Some viewers have suggested that you should not watch this film alone.

WHAT THE CRITICS SAID
"Zalutsky's first feature puts a gay spin on creepy-apartment-building-entrapment scenarios. Well-crafted tale of a guy who moves into the wrong flat and finds himself dealing with crazies. It is smart and offbeat."
Dennis Harvey, *Variety*

You I Love

(*Ya lyublyu tebya*; 2004)

Going Gay in Modern Russia

This is a comedy/love story about the lives of young Muscovites today.

Vera, a beautiful TV newsreader, meets and falls in love with Tim, an advertising man. Luckily, he falls in love with her also.

They have much in common: they are underpaid, overworked and severely stressed.

Tim and Vera's relationship seems to have some healing power for them as their love grows stronger, but on the day of their first anniversary dinner, Vera comes home to find Tim in bed with Uloomji, a young Kalmyk male from a distant Russian province. And then the events begin to spin well out of the control for our heroes. The whirlwind pace of modern-day Moscow never allows them a moment to pause and think.

The style is slick, youthful, and ultra-cool. The story urges forward with sudden twists and unpredictable turns of events.

This film demonstrates that for the new generation of Russians, love carries the same crazy feelings it did before, except that now, everyone can be more open about it...or can they?

The film is an attempt to satirize Russia's post-communist economic landscape. But, we are not sure that homophobia in modern-day Russia can be treated in a way that's as jaunty as this film suggests. Gay backlash may not be as severe today in Russia as it is in Red State America, but, even so, it is hardly a laughing matter.

The performances are adequate but without screams for the Academy Awards to recant their choices. There are evocative touches, including that of a Kalmyk day worker who cleans cages at the Moscow Zoo, while secretly harboring a dream of being a circus acrobat.

This unorthodox film may be a harbinger of what is to come for Russian filmmakers who will inhabit a landscape that's radically different from what most of them were born into.

You'll Get Over It

(*Tu verras, ca te passera, AKA Á cause d'un garçon; 2002*)

A Dangerous Passage Called Youth

In this French coming-of-age drama, popular 16-year-old high school student Vincent (Julien Baumgartner) stars on the swim team and dates a pretty girl named Noémie (Julia Maraval). His family, his teachers, his coach all love and admire him, but in one respect, he's misleading them all.

This becomes all too apparent when Benjamin (Jérémie Elkaïm) moves to town, and, seeing through Vincent's façade, pursues him. Vincent's classmates see the two of them together, rumors abound, and somebody completes the "outing" process by spray painting "Vincent is a fag" on one of the schoolyard walls. The swim team ostracizes Vincent, his closest friends are angry about the deceptions, and his parents don't know what to say. Perhaps it's too much for a 16-year-old kid to sort out himself.

Jérémie Elkaïm starred previously in the very successful gay romance *Come Undone* as a troubled young man coping with his sexuality. In *You'll Get Over It*, he takes a role on the other side of the coming-out equation, that of openly gay Benjamin. Elkaïm's previous films include Stephane Kanzadjian's *Sexy Boys*, a French take on *American Pie*, and Catherine Corsini's *The Very Merry Widows* starring Jane Birkin.

Another star of *Sexy Boys*, Julien Baumgartner, teams up again with Jérémie Elkaïm for *You'll Get Over It*. Appearing regularly on French television, his work includes *Un Beau Jour*, *Un Coiffeur*, and *La Tranchée des Espoirs*.

You'll Get Over It was helmed by acclaimed TV and film director Fabrice Cazeneuve. His recent works include the films *Un Fils De Notre Temps* and *La Dette*. He also won the Silver Leopard Award at the Locarno International Film Festival for his film *The King of China*.

The actors portray their characters with sensitivity and depth, turning in nuanced performances. Of course, this coming-of-age theme has been worked a lot in both film and books, but it appears new again in this retelling.

The Young, the Gay, & the Restless

(2006)

A Gay Spoof of Soapy TV Dramas

Spoofs are difficult to pull off, especially when you're satirizing daytime soaps on television. These programs are almost spoofs of themselves. Nonetheless, Joe Castro, who wrote and directed this picture, sticks his toes into waters that have turned scalding for so many other helmers/scripters.

The action, such as it is, spins around the household of Victoria Gaylord, who looks like a drag queen on a bad hair day. She throws a party at which she is stricken with a heart attack but refuses to go to the hospital.

There are various greedy children hovering in the distance, eager to grab her millions. But a handsome doctor and a mysterious black nurse appear.

The doctor, it seems, though flirting with a gay man, has played stud duty to Victoria, who has named him as the executor of her will. The black girl may be Victoria's daughter, though they have no resemblance to each other.

There's a lackluster husband, Mr. Gaylord, hovering about. He has given blow-jobs to all the boys—his sons or otherwise—when they were teenagers. It seems his secret hobby involves sucking young dick.

There's the buffed stud married to one of Victoria's daughters. She accuses him of homophobia because he's always complaining about being hit upon by other guys. He spends most of his time staring at his image in the mirror. He's later accused of standing nude in front of the full-length mirror while he masturbates. We just know that he's pretending to be straight, and that secretively he wants to plug boy-ass.

As the film progresses, three men, plus one Asian girl, are after one hottie, and there's a possible four-way relationship emerging on the horizon.

Yours Emotionally!

(2006)

Gay Love in Homophobic India

Two gay Brit friends, Ravi (Premjit), a British Indian, and Paul (Jack Lamport), set out for a holiday in India. In the early part of the movie, although India is a homophobic country, we're almost led to believe that it's a gay man's paradise.

Sridhar Rangayan, the helmer and co-scripter, comes up with a choppy, unevenly acted film that is nonetheless diverting.

In India, Paul and Ravi get invited to an orgiastic gay party at an ostensible religious center. Once here, Ravi encounters a good-looking boy, Mani (Prateek Gandhi). The two young men go off for a night of erotic and romantic pleasure.

But Mani is no easy catch to haul back to London. Ravi and Paul become guests at a hotel owned by an older homosexual duo (Ajay Rohilla and Akhlaq Khan). Ravi finds that his story parallels that of the older gay couple, who may help him keep his new-found love.

As could be predicted, Mani is bethrothed to be married. In India, young men from virtually every family are always being pressured into marriage. You might ask why, since the country is horribly overpopulated and millions are starving to death.

Mani seems unwilling to fly back to the UK with Ravi. Soon, tension erupts within the long-standing friendship between Ravi and Paul because of the sexually charged Mani.

Tune in to the DVD.

WHAT THE CRITICS SAID
"Prospects of sexual friskiness around every corner goes down easier than the awkward storytelling in director-scenarist Sridhar Rangayan's second feature. More seriously problematic are pic's pointless reality/illusion japes and arbitrary stylistic ones (freeze-frames, occasional B&W), not to mention a weak ending."
Dennis Harvey, *Variety*

Zero Patience

(1993)

A Musical About AIDS

Juggling MTV-style images. a sense of politics derived from the AIDS crisis, and lots of high-octane sexuality, Canadian director John Greyson created an unlikely musical whose concept is more memorable than its delivery. The plot pivots around the controversial "Patient Zero" theory whose premise first appeared in *And the Band Played On* by Randy Shilts, published in 1987. The premise involved a sexually promiscuous French-Canadian airline steward, the "host" who first brought AIDS to North America. The real-life flight attendant was named Gaetan Dugas.

In the Greyson feature, Dugas is reincarnated as "Patient Zero" (Normand Fauteux), who returns to earth to clear his name.

Talk about odd couples: He is matched up with the repressed homosexual Richard Burton (John Robinson), an explorer known for his translations of the *Kama Sutra* and *Arabian Nights*.

The flight attendant appears as a gay ghost in a Jacuzzi, where he sees old friends succumbing to the disease and fighting back against governmental indifference.

Burton has lived an extra century to become chief taxidermist and dioramacist at the Toronto Museum of Natural History. The former explorer is plotting a Patient Zero exhibit in the Hall of Contagion, where he hopes to affirm homo/AIDS phobia designed to "perpetuate bigotry and fetishize blame."

After Burton and Zero become unlikely lovers, Patient Zero becomes in this revisionist view a "heroic slut who inspired safe sex."

The film is filled with musical numbers, including Michael Callen's cameo as a Barbra Streisand-inspired "Miss HIV."

Glenn Schellenberg's well-sung rock score, "Tell Me the Story of My Life," is catchy and visualized with an underwater ballet *à la* Esther Williams.

Campy and quirky, *Zero Patience* is unlike any film you've ever seen.

Zerophilia

(2005)

Being a Woman Doesn't Make You Less of a Man

This 90-minute film, written and directed by Martin Curland, has a strange premise. Its star, Luke (Taylor Handley), can transform from male to female as circumstances dictate.

As a male, he's a real hottie with his Titian curls and lickable tits. Luke has a rare chromosomal disorder, allowing him to switch back and forth between genders before eventually choosing which sex he wants to be. Although he's doing well as a man, the plot gets complicated when he develops a crush on a beautiful man.

This screwy romantic comedy and sexual fantasy raises a question. What if a man, who turns into a woman when he's aroused, meets a woman who turns into a man when she's aroused. That is a hell of a lot to ponder. Call this the oddest romantic comedy of the year.

His girl friend, Luca (Marieh Delfino), is adept in her role. The plot thickens when Luke/Luca meets the dazzling Michelle (Rebecca Mozo), and Luca meets Michelle's hunky brother, Max (Kyle Schmid). Talk about gender confusion. The funniest scene is when Luke sprouts breasts on a romantic dinner date with Michelle.

Cast as Luke's best friends, Dustin Seavey, as Keenan, and Alison Folland, as Janine, deliver keen, upbeat performances.

WHAT THE CRITICS SAID:
"The movie is fresh, suspenseful and lovely to look at, thanks to a fine cast of young hotties. And its final twist will leave you cheering."
Beth Greenfield, *Time Out New York*

"Unrated pic features enough nudity to entice the frat-house set, while putting it out of the reach of slumber party auds. Amid deliberately campy situations and sophomoric jokes, *Zerophilia* offers a disarmingly sweet lesson about learning to identify with the opposite gender."
Peter Debruge, *Variety*

Zoo

(2007)

The Love That Dare Not Speak Its Name

In high school vocabulary we learned the words "Francophile," and "pedophile," but "zoophile" was strangely missing. This beautifully photographed semi-docu, set in the Northwest, aims to remedy our ignorance . . . and does so exceedingly well.

Helmed and co-scripted by Robinson Devor, it tells the strange story of a Seattle man who died as a result of an "unusual encounter" with an Arabian stallion. The death of the Boeing executive made headlines across America. He died from a perforated colon after having sex with a horse.

Zoophiles found an unwitting ally in right-wing talking head, Rush Limbaugh. He suggested in an audio clip, "How in the world can this happen without consent?"

A hit at the Sundance Film Festival, this is a semi-docu in that it is a re-enactment of the true-to-life tale in 2005. It's a sort of blurring of the line between narrative and documentary storytelling. Abandoned by fellow zoophiles at an emergency room in rural Washington, the victim eventually died from internal injuries. The investigation into his death uncovered a nearby horse farm that hid a dark sexual secret. Tapes, including one entitled BIG DICK, were discovered at the farm. The zoophiles communicated with each other over the Internet, arranging various gatherings at this remote farm.

The film, in spite of its subject matter, is not lurid. In fact, it rather gently exposes this hidden subculture in America by presenting both a compassionate portrait and one that is subdued to the point of being almost poetic.

As David Ansen of *Newsweek* so accurately put it, "*Zoo* is transfixing and eerily beautiful, creating a dreamlike, elliptical reverie that neither condemns nor condones what it explores."

Never has bestiality been shown in such an elegant, eerily lyrical way. It sure beats all those big-dog-fucking-putas in Tijuana bestiality films.

Part Two

For Connoisseurs of Queer Cinema

160 Worthy But Less Publicized Queer Films

None of these films was ever considered for an Oscar
BUT SO WHAT?
Neither were thousands of other, less worthy films.

They're intriguing, thought-provoking,
occasionally tacky, and/or a lot of fun,
and that's why we've opted to include them in this guidebook.

"It was supposed to be about homosexuals, and you don't even see the boys kiss each other. What's that?"
Jean Renoir critiquing
Alfred Hitchcock's *Rope* (1948)

"The movies didn't always get history straight. But at least they told the dream."
Charlton Heston (1978)

"I've just gone gay--all of a sudden!"
Cary Grant to May Robson in
Bringing Up Baby (1938)

"It was the first film in which a man said, 'I love you' to another man. I wrote that scene in. I said, 'There's no point in half-measures. We either make a film about queers or we don't."
Dirk Bogarde, discussing
Victim (1961)

BLOOD MOON
Productions, Ltd.

Quotable Hollywood

"Oh, it's sad, believe me, Missy
When you're born to be a sissy
without the vim and voive."

Bert Lahr as
The Cowardly Lion
in *The Wizard of Oz* (1939)

"I did a movie with John Wayne
and was very surprised to find
out he had small feet and wore
lifts and a corset. Hollywood is
seldom what it seems."

Rock Hudson

"The only thing that dikey bitch and I ever had in common
was Billie Burke (a.k.a. Glinda, the Good Witch of the
North), who supported both of us in our first pictures."

Margaret Sullavan, circa 1938,
referring to **Katharine Hepburn**

Alpha Dog

(2006)

Homophobic Morons Smoking Weed and Shitting

Within a film chock-full of *Sturm und Drang*, we get to see Justin Timberlake take off his shirt, revealing that he was heavily tattooed for the role of Frankie, a drug dealer. Although we've seen far greater chests and even better-looking boys, we admit that no one would turn down Timberlake if he came up to them in a gay bar. Although this film about rich boys gone wild received massive condemnation, Timberlake was unscathed—in fact, in review after review, he won praise, proving that he can do more than assist Janet Jackson in her wardrobe malfunction.

Time Out New York pronounced Nick Cassavetes' "cruddy" *Alpha Dog* the worst movie of the year. The magazine had a point, at least for gay men. *Alpha Dog* contains pathetic dialogue such as this: "I fuck bitches. You're a homo." How many guys have said that to us over the years? Countless ones, no doubt. Don't be surprised at such dialogue, though. The sybaritic, monosyllabic, adolescent Angelenos in *Alpha Dog* are scripted as homophobic morons.

The film is based on a true crime story from 2000. Jesse James Hollywood (that was his real name) was a 20-year-old marijuana kingpin in Los Angeles, a teeny Tony Montana. He ordered the kidnapping and later the murder of Nicholas Markowitz because his half brother owed him $1,200 for a dope debt and refused to pay. Young Markowitz was kidnapped while walking near his San Fernando Valley home. Although the kid partied with his captors at first, Hollywood eventually realized the severity of his crime and ordered his henchmen to get rid of the evidence. The victim was shot multiple times and left to rot in a national forest with sweeping views over the Pacific.

After the murder, Hollywood fled to Brazil where he was apprehended in 2004. Since then, four others have been arrested, tried, and sentenced for the death of the Valley teenager.

The cold-blooded execution of the 15-year-old victim was called "a prank gone wrong." To sum up, *Alpha Dog* is a depressing film about some very sick and rabid puppies.

Arisan!

(2003)

Indonesia's First Gay-Themed Movie

An *arisan,* as defined by Kalyana Shira Films, "is a unique Indonesian social practice," when a circle of friends gather each month. The event is hosted by one of the *arisan* members, each of whom must create an escrow account with a predetermined amount of money. A lottery determines who wins all that money. By default, the winner becomes the next *arisan* host.

Director Nia Di Nata, who co-wrote the script with Joko Anwar, has produced Indonesia's first gay-themed cinema. The comedy is so broad, the scenes so delicately etched, that *Arisan!* did not cause homophobic riots in Jakarta.

The movie spotlights three well-off friends pushing or beyond age 30. Cut Mini Theo plays Meimei, a beautiful interior designer who wants to get pregnant by a husband (played by Nico Siahaan) who couldn't care less. He's flirtatious with a roving eye.

Her best friend is Sakti (Tora Sudiro) playing an architect in the same firm that hires Meimei as an interior designer. Gay men will quickly identify him as one of their own, although he's still in the Indonesian version of the closet. His well-groomed good looks and "simply fab" wardrobe suggest he's a Chelsea boy waiting to escape from Jakarta.

As the plot thickens, Meimei agrees to go to an *arisan,* hosted by Andien (played by Aida Nurmala) and attended by rich Jakarta ladies-who-lunch. If you've caught *The Women* on the late show, with Norma Shearer and Joan Crawford, you've been indoctrinated into their catty remarks. When Sakti comes to retrieve Meimei from the catfest, he finds himself chosen to host next month's *arisan.*

At home, Sakti still lives with dear old mom, who is eager to get him married.

We won't give away the plot to tell you how all this is resolved. We will tell you, however, that it has an upbeat conclusion which some viewers found "more flimsy than feel-good."

B. Monkey

(1998)

Lovers: Rupert Everett & Jonathan Rhys Meyers

This little romantic thriller is a showcase for the controversial Italian goddess, Asia Argento, but she's backed up by such hotties as Rupert Everett and Jonathan Rhys Meyers, with Jared Harris also cast in a lackluster role.

The solidly crafted melodrama is directed by Michael Radford, who is not afraid of sexuality, violence, and a drug content.

In this danger-filled love story, Argento plays Beatrice or "B. Monkey" as she is known on the street. The cat burglar and jewel thief claims, "I can get into anything."

She is totally decadent, sharing a glamorous apartment with Everett as Paul and Meyers as Bruno. Meyers emerges as the male beauty of the film. Drug-addled Everett, consuming an ass-load of pot, looks dissolute in his role as a bisexual London criminal.

You get plenty of Eurochic trappings and lots of nudity, mostly from Argento. One reviewer called it a "sort of *Pretty Woman* for the underground."

Harris gets the less exotic role as a schlumpy schoolteacher who falls for the cat burglar. He wants to lure her into a settled lifestyle in the rural bliss of Yorkshire. But Bruno and Paul track her down for a final reckoning.

Variety claimed, "As the hard-assed, cross-tracks lover dogged by a past she can't escape, the husky-voiced Argento, with a monkey tattooed on her shoulder and an angel above her crotch, is suitably exotic casting that benefits the pic by further removing it from any kind of reality."

Basic Instinct 2

(2006)

Stone as an Older *Femme* Is as *Fatale* as Ever

We appreciate the gay-friendly Sharon Stone and were rooting for her success in this sequel to the 1992 hit, *Basic Instinct*, in which she starred with Michael Douglas. Many of her admirers had warned her that *Basic Instinct 2*, in which she reprises the role of the murderous

Catherine Tramell, wasn't a good idea. And significantly, when he was offered the co-starring part in the sequel opposite Ms. Stone, Michael Douglas himself fled to the border.

We knew that things were going wrong after the first 15 minutes: The audience howled in the wrong places. The writers, the husband-and-wife team of Leora Barish and Henry Bean, will absolutely never rival Shakespeare with the quality of their writing. Sample dialogue: "Not even Oedipus saw his mother coming." "Would you like me to come in your mouth?" These screenwriters evoke Jacqueline Susann with a little help from Jeffrey Dahmer.

Yet another non-winning line is delivered when David Thewlis, playing a police detective, says: "Even the truth is a lie with her!" Although their scripted dialogue was weak, the writing team seemed to like their cinematic sex kinky, and accessorized the onscreen activities with garrotes, handcuffs, and chains.

Whereas the original 1992 hit was directed by Paul Verhoeven, the less successful sequel was helmed by Michael Canton-Jones, who captured none of the original sleek wit or craziness. In the sequel, Sharon once again assumes the role of Catherine Tramwell, a mass market crime novelist whose prose style seems inspired by the heat of her sexual energy.

In the sequel, Sharon had a tough act to follow—namely herself when she made the original at the voluptuous age of 34.

In marked contrast to the original version, the sequel subdues any sense of Sharon's bisexuality, except for some Sapphic voodoo that she unleashes upon her co-star, Charlotte Rampling, one of our all-time favorite actresses.

Bazaar Bizarre

(2004)

Hungry for the Taste of Human Flesh

The year was 1988. The place was Kansas City. A screaming young man, Chris Bryson, was seen running down the street. His battered body was naked except for a dog collar and a leash.

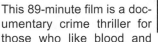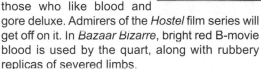

This 89-minute film is a documentary crime thriller for those who like blood and gore deluxe. Admirers of the *Hostel* film series will get off on it. In *Bazaar Bizarre*, bright red B-movie blood is used by the quart, along with rubbery replicas of severed limbs.

This documentary eerily evokes the saga of yet another serial killer, Jeffrey Dahmer, a psycho who liked to torture, rape, and murder young men. He used some of the same techniques as local merchant Robert A. (Bob) Berdella, who's depicted in the photo above. Director Benjamin Meade (*Das Bus*) and writer James Ellroy (*L.A. Confidential*) bring to life the horrid story of this vile piece of shit and methodical killer.

Berdella, however, went Dahmer one better: After finishing with his torture and rape, Berdella cut up the bodies of his victims with an electric chain saw and a bone knife. He then placed the body parts in empty dog food bags, putting them in his trash can for garbage pickup on Monday morning.

For certain organs, such as the liver, he packed them in ice and took them to his food shop, where he mixed them with meat from cows or pigs and served them to his customers.

Berdella also appears on film because an interview he gave was on video. He attacks the press for making him appear a monster and blames the local police for not getting to him sooner.

File this under "believe it or not." There are actual musical numbers in this film, including recordings by the Demon Dogs, a band created by Bill Gladden, the movie's composer.

One critic claimed the docu "walks the line between campy splatter horror and goose bump-inducing true crime."

Beautiful Daughters

(2006)

"The Vagina Monologues" as Performed by Trannies

Just when you thought the world had run out of ideas for docus, along comes *Beautiful Daughters*, either the most misnamed film of the year or the most sensitively subtle. Directed by Josh Aronson and Ariel Orr Jordan, the hour-long film explores the collaborative venture behind a transgendered version of *The Vagina Monologues*.

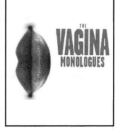

In the film we experience Eve Ensler, author of *Vagina Monologues*, conducting meetings with a selectively varied group of male-to-female trannies. Her goal is to cast her specially rewritten play. First aired on the Logo Channel, the docu reveals the alchemy by which the transgendered women's stories are transformed into dramatic theater, in much the same way that Michael Bennett got those chorus boys and girls to reveal their private behind-the-scenes life for his *A Chorus Line* in the 1970s.

The credited cast lists Calpernia Addams, Lynn Conway, Verba Deo, Andrea James, Valerie Spencer, Leslie Townsend, and Asia Vitale. Of the cast, Calpernia Addams is clearly the drama queen. Her own real-life drama formed the basis for the 2003 *Soldier's Girl*, a marvelous film that was one of the great trannie stories, one that should have had a wider audience.

Calpernia starred in that film with the very handsome Troy Garity, who is the son of Jane Fonda and Tom Hayden. Garity's parents gave him the name of his paternal grandmother for the sake of anonymity. In 1998 *People* magazine named him as one of its "50 Most Beautiful People."

WHAT THE CRITICS SAID:
"The cast represents a wide spectrum from a professor emeritus of computer science, to a pioneer in 'transitioning,' to a stunning ex-stripper/escort-turned-real-estate-agent who has hidden her male past and sees opening night as her coming-out party. As they rehearse, the play's original transcript and performers' unique experiences begin to be an affirmation of reconstitute femininity."
Ronnie Scheib, *Variety*

Bedrooms and Hallways

(1998)

Blurring the Lines Between Gay and Straight

The American director Rose Troche achieved acclaim for her debut feature *Go Fish*. This follow-up film, set in London, finds disconsolately single Leo (Kevin McKidd) love starved and 30 years old. His campy flatmate Darren (Tom Hollander) urges  him to join an ostensibly straight men's therapy group run by New Age guru Keith (Simon Callow).

Once in the group, Leo finds himself attracted to a presumably straight Irishman, Brendan (James Purefoy). Thanks to his dark good looks and mellifluous voice, he's a guy to get hot over.

During a group therapy session, Leo is handed an "honesty stone," and told that its powers ensure that each member of the clan will tell the truth. Leo not only comes clean about his sexual preference, but reveals his attraction to Brendan. Instead of beating him up, Brendan seems flattered by the attention. In the wake of a "wild man" weekend with the group, Leo and Brendan link up sexually.

Goosing up the plot, Robert Farrar then introduces Sally (Jennifer Ehle), Leo's high school sweetheart.

As one reviewer put it, "The film, which aspires toward the playful sophistication of a Noël Coward romp, imagines a brave new world in which the distinctions between gay and straight have begun to dissolve. The characters seem free to experiment sexually, even in homosexuality, without declaring that as their final preference.

WHAT THE CRITICS SAID
"But having begun to explore the ins and outs of bisexuality, *Bedrooms and Hallways* loses its nerve and turns into a shallow sitcom in which everyone is abruptly and mechanically paired off. The potentially incendiary conflicts that the movie had begun to explore are inexplicably dropped. The letdown is so steep it is almost as though the film ran out of time and money before it could be completed."
Stephen Holden, *The New York Times*

Between Love & Goodbye

(2008)

Love Doesn't Have To Be Forever

Laden with an excess of melodrama, this boy-meets-boy story is the tragedy of two young lovers. It's love at first sight when Kyle (Simon Miller) locks eyes with a handsome Frenchman (Justin Tensen). Casper Andreas, known for *Slutty Summer*, both directed and wrote  this well-made, cautionary tale.

Kyle and Marcel move in with each other, but you know trouble is on the way. (Otherwise, there would be no movie.) Marcel is so in love with Kyle that he marries his lesbian girlfriend, Sarah (Jane Elliott).

The arrival of Kyle's sister, April (Rob Harmon), signals the doom of the two lovers. The bitch has some serious gender problems: She's a woman changed from a man and changed back to a woman and then a man again.

If you like your boys naked, you'll enjoy Kyle and Marcel romping around in bed, showing off their beautiful bodies. It's soft core but titillating for devotees of cute tricks.

Tensions mount between Marcel and April, who couch crashes for weeks at a time. Marcel is suspicious, and rightly so, that she's trying to destroy his love affair with her brother. *The New York Times* critic called April "a petulant, mean-spirited home wrecker." She's also an ex-whore and homeless.

Personally we would have liked the movie better if Kyle had kicked out April and kept Marcel between the bed sheets instead. A man is a fool to let a love machine like that slip out the door.

The Los Angeles Times found the film "wrenching, uncompromising, and unpredictable." *New York Post* called it a "dreary gay soap opera," finding the movie a "snooze."

As a film, it is momentarily diverting, worth a look on DVD with three or four beers. We did want love to triumph in the end. We won't tell you what happened, but you won't like it.

Between the Lines: India's Third Gender

(2005)

Why Some Men Prefer Castrated Males

Almost every subject associated with homosexuality, from getting fucked by a horse to boy-molesting priests, has been explored in a film, often a docu. Along comes this 95-minute movie, a surprise package, taking us into the world of the *hijras,* or transsexuals, of India.

Never has the camera focused so vividly on the Indian eunuch, some of whom were voluntarily castrated, others who were forcibly tied up and butchered. Thomas Wartmann, who also co-wrote the screenplay with Dorothea Rieker, reveals this world of men who are often considered pariahs, but in some quarters are viewed as conduits of the supernatural.

Camerawoman Anita Khemka, playing herself, uses a trio of men as guides to this bizarre world. Laxmi, Rhamba, and Asha play themselves in this German-financed film.

A dance instructor, Laxmi prostitutes herself to earn extra money. Technically, Laxmi is a "he," as he has not gone through the complete castration ceremony.

In contrast, Asha used to work as a prostitute servicing men, but now is a street beggar and alcoholic. When someone doesn't give Asha money, she threatens to reveal her disfigured genitals. Her entire life has been painful, and she faces an uncertain future, drowning her sorrows in alcohol.

Rhamba, in contrast to these two lives, is a *hijra* in a temple, performing exorcisms. She seems the most pleased with her life, and in her next incarnation wants to return to the world as a *hijra.* Of the trio, Rhamba is the one most likely to pass for female.

A castration ceremony is lensed. At the moment the knife cuts off the penis, a passing train drowns out the scream.

The film was shot in Mumbai (Bombay), but travels to the religious transsexual festivals in Koovagam.

Beverly Kills

(2005)

Same Sex Love Story with Mass Murder Subplot

This 80-minute feature is the follow-up to writer-helmer Damion Dietz's campy delight *Fag Hag* (2000). This is a rambunctious tale of an aging drag queen, Beverly Jackson (played by Gary Kelley), who vows revenge on Hollywood when she's not cast in a youthful revue, *Balls Out!* To get her revenge, Jackson launches a cult of deadly celebrity impersonators, including a flaky broad whose audition song is "I'm Gonna Fuck My Way to the Top." There's also a dancer who speaks no English but is named Strip after the John Travolta character in his most disastrous picture, *Moment by Moment.*

The plot spirals out of control and inadvertently escalates into the realm of terrorism. The cast of young and talented newcomers is gorgeous, and the film takes an iconoclastic stab at Tinseltown's "cult of celebrity."

Dietz's *Fag Hag*, that underground classic, is now available on DVD with all its trashy behavior and savage fun.

WHAT THE CRITICS SAID
"*Beverly Kills* answers the burning question: 'Do muscular, naked young men performing delectably silly musical numbers belong in such a movie?' with a resounding 'Gosh, you bet!'"
Lisa Nesselson, *Variety*

"Bright and energetic. Director Damion Dietz tells the entire world that it's okay to be who you are."
Film Threat

"This uproariously funny gay-themed film expertly blends boy-meets-boy love story with a screwball revenge plot by a spurned drag queen. The result is a sexy comedy that anyone will enjoy, as long as the film is approached for what it is: a cheesy, silly farce that should not be taken too seriously. Director Damion Dietz concocts a tale that recalls the insane campiness of a John Waters production mixed with charmingly earnest naïveté of *Legally Blonde* but with lots of naked guys."
Raymond So

Beyond Conception

(2004)

Men Having Babies

Johnny Symons' docu is about baby fever—in this case two male lovers who, of course, can't have children biologically and who opt for technology instead. They are obviously fed up with the adoption process, which, in fact, is illegal in such states  as Florida, thanks in no small part to former orange juice warbler, Anita Bryant.

Based in San Francisco, Bruce Gilpin and Paul Moreno turn to a lesbian couple to be their surrogates. Jennifer and Jenna Franet (same last name) also based in San Francisco, already have two children of their own from Jennifer's former hetero marriage.

A 65-minute edition of the film was aired in the summer of 2006 on the Discovery Health Channel, but for those interested in the subject, it's better to see Symons' longer version.

The movie explores the doubts that the male couple have about their choice of the Franets as "birth partners." Apparently, after the eventual birth of the child, the two couples went their separate ways and today lead disconnected lives.

The actual eggs were donated by a young woman known as "Jade." The future male parents even express some doubt about the eggs donated for insemination into the uterus of Jennifer. Although bright and physically alluring, Jade has a medically troubled family history of breast cancer. As seen through the intimate lens of Symons, the plot gets even more complicated. Jenna is trying for her own conception to add to their already existing family. "A child of our own," so to speak.

WHAT THE CRITICS SAID
"Oh brave new rainbow-colored world! Just when you thought you knew everything there was to know about getting in the family way, here's another twist. Gay men on a mission, feisty lesbians with opinions, lots of money, donated eggs, sperm, uteri (or is it uteruses?), surrogate contracts. And let's not forget romance. Just make sure they're separate from the actual act of conception."
15th Annual Florida Film Festival

Beyond Hatred

(*Au delà de la haine*; 2007)

Forgiving French Skinheads for a Murder

Au delà de la haine (its French title) is a documentary written and directed by Olivier Meyrou. For 86 minutes, he follows the travails of a family of a 29-year-old gay Frenchman murdered by skinheads. The family travels down the road to forgiveness as they attempt to  discover the origins of the hatred of their son's killers.

On a September night back in 2002, three psychotic hatemongers, feeling France is being taken over by illegal Arab immigrants, set out on a dark mission to bash an Arab at random.

The setting was Reims, 98 miles northeast of Paris. Instead of an Arab, they encounter a 29-year-old gay male, François Chenu. They beat him unconscious and tossed him into a pond to drown.

In a surprise cinematic move, Meyrou never shows us the face of the victim. Not even the faces of the skinheads.

Against a backdrop of the film's maudlin score, the family of the victim, "730 days" after the murder, set out to understand the factors that influenced the skinheads in their execution of such a violent, senseless act. As Aaron Hillis of *The Village Voice* noted, "The film shows the family members intellectualizing their grief to one another, often talking themselves into a loop while smoking too many cigarettes." Their agenda does not involve a crusade against homophobia, but the pursuit of a path toward closure.

Meyrou asks the question: Will the family forgive "the poor dears" who murdered their family member? Each of the skinheads came from culturally deprived backgrounds awash with brutish violence. Of course, any viewer can guess that these killer creeps had despicable parents.

The film is elliptical, and at times far too slow moving, but it will have appeal for viewers who have been the victims of homophobic violence themselves.

270

Bilitis

(1977)

A Lesbian Romp for Male Fantasies

In a nutshell, this is a French-made coming-of-age story centering on the exploits of a young girl Bilitis (Patti D'Arbanville) during summer vacation. The teenage beauty comes to live with a couple whose marriage is ending. Gilles Kohler plays Pierre, the husband,  Mona Kristensen his wife, Melissa. Bilitis develops a crush on Melissa, but also pursues a local teenage boy Lucas (Bernard Giraudeau).

Men who enjoy watching lesbian movies will delight in nude young women swimming in a pond or taking showers in a gym. There are female on female kisses intertwined with limbs locked in passion. But for their serious relationships, the women in Bilitis seem to turn to men.

Directors David Hamilton and Robert Towne certainly know how to photograph women, often in soft focus with very erotic movements.

Bilitis' guardian, Pierre, is a stern, even brutal guardian, and she sees him rape Melissa. Such behavior sets her up for a lesbian romp. Bilitis moves in to seduce Melissa, who seems to like the experience, but doesn't commit to repeating it.

For reasons known only to herself, Bilitis sets out on a mission to find a more suitable lover than Pierre. She begins to photograph good-looking men, carrying the images back to Melissa. Mikias (Mathieu Carrière) is a suitable candidate.

Mikias doesn't work out as a suitor, but Bilitis turns Melissa over to the rather handsome Lucas. The couple bond, dancing away into the moonlight. Bilitis is left alone.

We know at the end that Bilitis will get over her crush on Melissa and discover another girlfriend, or else settle down with a man. It's unclear at this point. Is her summer love and passion for a woman only a momentary diversion before she pursues heterosexual love for the rest of her life?

Before they part, Lucas, the suitor that never was, suggests to Bilitis that "natural" love must be between a man and woman.

Billy's Hollywood Screen Kiss

(1998)

Will He or Won't He?

This is a totally superficial picture, but totally fun. Billy Collier, the lead, is played by Sean Hayes of *Will & Grace* fame. A gay fine arts photographer, he falls in love with a supposedly straight, blond waiter, Gabriel, who is gorgeous, looking like a square-jawed post-adolescent Leonardo DiCaprio.

Tommy O'Haver is the writer/director and a better director than writer. He labels his debut feature "a trifle," and we don't disagree with the guy.

Billy spends the entire film trying to figure out if Gabriel is straight or gay, or else hoping to get him in bed to find out. The movie also revolves around relationships—and how difficult they are to launch and maintain—regardless of one's sexual preference.

Hoping to entrap Gabriel, Billy wants him to model for his latest project, a series of remakes of famous Hollywood screen kisses, notably Burt Lancaster and Deborah Kerr in *From Here to Eternity*. The difference is that Billy's project will feature exclusively male couples.

Warhol superstar Holly Woodlawn makes a guest appearance. She not only plays herself, but Deborah Kerr. Drag queens appear to enliven the proceedings with music.

A cool, laid-back personality, Billy rooms platonically with Georgiana (Meredith Scott Lynn).

O'Haver satirizes Los Angeles lifestyles, as Billy introduces Gabriel at various parties and gallery openings. Ever the opportunist, Gabriel auditions for top modeling assignments under the patronage of fashion lenser Rex Webster (Paul Bartell), who has lascivious designs.

In his pursuit of Gabriel, Billy finally gets him to his apartment and in his bed, after time lodged on his sofa. We won't give it away by telling you what happened.

Bollywood and Vine

(2004)

An East Indian Version of Norma Desmond in Drag

This is a comedy/crime/romance picture all in one. Edward Jordan co-directed it (along with Donald Farmer) and also wrote it. Shot on a shoestring budget without any stars, it features Jamey Schrick playing Bhuvan Bannerji, an Indian bus driver who takes his sightseers to visit the homes of the stars.

He is particularly intrigued with a "has-been scream queen," Delilah Leigh, as played by Skye Aubrey. She lives in faded *Sunset Blvd.* trappings with her transvestite son, Devin Leigh, as played by J.R. Jones. J.R. Jones is an actor who has impressive acting ability in his female impersonator scenes. As one viewer put it, "the film leans more toward farce than gay activity *per se*—nothing more than *The Birdcage*—but there is a gay kiss or two in the mix." Aubrey, who hasn't made a movie in some two decades, evokes Gloria Swanson as Norma Desmond.

Every day, Bhuvan stops his bus in front of Delilah's home to enthrall his viewers with her former screen career. Her gay son begins to impersonate his mother by appearing in drag in front of the tour bus. Bhuvan wants to take his screen favorite to Bollywood and stage her comeback.

Mother and son, along with Bhuvan, collaborate on a comeback script as the Indian tour guide begins to figure things out. When that happens, Delilah rips a page from the script of *What Ever Happened to Baby Jane* and locks the two boys in the attic together "to work out their differences." In the meantime, the neighbors experience mass hostage-taking, blackmail, and accidental deaths. Police investigations and news reports follow.

WHAT THE CRITICS SAID
"Experienced actress Skye Aubrey (the daughter of James Aubrey, MGM's axeman and joykiller of the early 70s) is excellent as the has-been star of Z-horror films and scenery-chewers featuring demented dames holding people prisoners in attics or basements. Aubrey hits an appropriate tone of 'Tallulah Bankhead in suburbia.'"
Glenn Erickson

The Book of Daniel

(2006)

A Depressed, Pill-Popping Priest with Family Issues

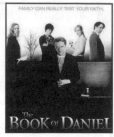

It seemed NBC in this series wanted to add some spice to their nightly line-up and provoke the ire of the religious right as a means of attracting more viewers. The ill-fated series starred the handsome Aidan Quinn as a Vicodin-addicted Episcopal priest who talks to Jesus and has a gay Republican son (Christian Campbell). That's not all. His sister-in-law is bisexual.

The anti-gay American Family Association denounced the dramedy, but its creator, Jack Kenny, seemed none too alarmed. The association in particular objected to the "unconventional" white-robed and bearded Jesus who spoke to Daniel. Kenny responded, "Isn't that the most conventional Jesus there is—white robed and bearded?"

In an interview with *The Advocate*, Kenny was asked: "The Episcopal Church is facing a schism over homosexuality. Will the show address that?"

He responded, "I'm hoping down the line that Peter (Daniel's gay son) will want to get married and have his father perform the ceremony."

Daniel has troubles more pressing than the mere inconvenience of a gay son. His wife, Judith (Susanna Thompson), loves her early-day martinis. Their 16-year-old daughter Grace (Alison Pill) sells pot. They also have an adopted son, Adam (Ivan Shaw), who is Chinese, opening the door for all manner of ethnic jokes. This Chinese son is busted for banging a rich patron's daughter.

There's a subplot as well—a brother-in-law stole the rich patron's money before being murdered by his lesbian girlfriend who is seducing the murdered man's wife.

Garrett Dillahunt plays Jesus Christ as a slow, dull "buddy parent," who has no insights, no healing abilities, and, in the words of one critic, "just passively nags Daniel to quit" his bad habits.

Ellen Burstyn delivers as Bishop Congreve, but she isn't above sampling from Daniel's pill chest.

The helmer links the Catholic church to the Mafia.

Boom!

(1969)

The Angel of Death Visits Liz Taylor

It failed on Broadway twice, the final version with Tallulah Bankhead and Tab Hunter (yes, Tab). Looking gorgeous, he was practically devoured on stage by Tallulah, as queens in the audience screamed their approval.

Those who missed that notorious moment on Broadway can feast on Elizabeth Taylor and Richard Burton in *Boom!*, the movie adaptation of the play, *The Milk Train Doesn't Stop Here Anymore.* Both the play and the film's script were written by Tennessee Williams on a bad hair day. Taylor is too young for the role, Burton too old. Actually the ages and looks of Tab & Tallulah were just about right.

A celebrated beauty and gold digger, Sissy Goforth is the world's richest woman, living out her dying days in an island fortress off the coast of Sardinia. She is visited by a mendicant poet, Chris Flanders (Burton), known along the coast as "the Angel of Death."

When not crying for injections of morphine, Sissy is dictating her memoirs to her long-suffering "Girl Friday," Miss Black, as played by Joanne Shimkus.

The film is rococo lunacy, the script overripe. Of course, you get to hear Taylor say, "Shit on your mother." John Waters proclaimed *Boom!* as his favorite movie, calling it perfect because it is "failed art."

Highlight of the movie is the arrival from the mainland of "the Witch of Capri" (Noël Coward himself) to dine with Sissy on boiled sea monster. Tennessee wrote this part for a woman, but Coward handles it smoothly--so much that you'll think it's autobiographical.

Director Joseph Losey has seen better days. Maybe he wasn't himself. After all, Burton, Taylor, and Losey were said to have launched their mornings with pitchers of Bloody Marys.

This film has long been a favorite of gay men because of its camp, not because of any overtly homosexual activity. Okay, so it's a bad movie. But movies can be so wretchedly bad they become almost masterpieces of cinematic art.

Bowser Makes A Movie

(2005)

Porn for Geniuses, Loan Sharks, and Bandit Nuns

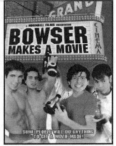

Much to the chagrin of his straight-laced parents, Bowser (Nick Louis) pursues his dream of making his own adult movie.

After Bowser's father proudly proclaims that the mortgage on the family home is totally paid, Bowser disguises himself as his father and re-mortgages in order to finance his film.

That's not all. He overhears a conversation of the top brass of the company, "For Geniuses Corporation," where the president, Mr. Belami (Mathew Goldman), is voicing his discontent regarding slow sales of their books. With tons of chutzpah, Bowser storms into the meeting, hyping his book, *Porn for Geniuses*, which he claims will make a fortune. But that's just a book, right? Where's the movie?

Helmut Schwantz Sauger (Peter Marinelli), the watchdog the president has assigned to Bowser's new task, has his own sleazy agenda. He invests in the X-rated DVD to be produced concurrently as Bowser is writing the book.

Cash in hand, Bowser first loses the money to a nun riding on the famed Chicago El train. Hoping to save the day, his buddy, Adam (Kevin Viol), borrows money from dangerous mob loan sharks. When the loan isn't repaid, the mob pursues Bowser's parents, who have no idea their son has mortgaged their home.

With trouble brewing on all fronts, Bowser wonders if his cinematic dream will ever come true.

Albert Williams for the Chicago Reader called the Bowser film "amateurish," noting that Toby Ross cluttered the story "with contrived complications rather than making his characters believable and therefore funny."

WHAT THE CRITICS SAID
"A fun movie with a lighthearted cast makes this entertaining. A clever story with good writing. The characters are both sincere and quirky. Fun to watch with friends over pizza."
Brian Andrews

Boy Culture

(2006)

Confessions from a Male Escort

The book, *Boy Culture*, by Matthew Rettenmund, went over well with a largely gay male audience. Robert Rodi, author of *Fag Hag*, found it, "An unapologetic, take-no-prisoners comic novel." Lars Eighner, author of *Travels with Lizbeth*, praised it as  "Erotic, insightful, and deliciously funny." Now *Boy Culture* comes to the screen. It's directed by Q. Allan Brocka, who co-authored the screenplay with Philip Pierce.

It's been called a contemporary date movie. Shot in Seattle, the film tells the story of a successful male escort's tangled romantic relationships with his two roommates and an older, enigmatic male client. Hot and sexy, the story deals with such issues as monogamy, fidelity, and the nature of love between interracial and multigenerational gay couples.

The film stars Derek Magyar, Darryl Stephens, Jonathan Trent, and Patrick Bauchau.

Director Brocka was named "one of five gay and lesbian directors to watch" by *Variety*, and his life was an open book—literally—on AMC reality series, gay Hollywood, which followed five openly gay men as they tried to build careers in the entertainment industry.

WHAT THE CRITICS SAID
"A strong cast, formal visual style, and cynical voiceover that propels the action help elevate this Seattle-set gay romp from the ranks of the stereotypical. Brocka's sophomore feature wryly recounts a tragicomic dance of displaced desire as three roommates circle each other warily, uncovering layers of denial, defensiveness, and role-playing. But it's too devoid of angst and too enmeshed in the ironies of gayness to cross over to a wide aud."
Ronnie Scheib, *Variety*

"All told, this is a harmless, well-packaged bit of overly familiar fluff."
Ernest Hardy.

Boy I Am

(2006)

No Room for Transphobia

Running only 60 minutes, this docu, produced and directed by Samantha Feder (sometimes billed as "Sam Feder) and Julie Hollar, is one of the first to seriously tackle the subject of transgender surgery. *Boy I Am* was voted the Best Documentary Feature at the Seat-  tle Gay & Lesbian Film Festival in 2006. The film features FTMs in various stages of "transition." Lesbians also appear, questioning whether transitioning from female-to-male is congruent with feminist principles.

This is not your usual tranny movie. It follows a trio of female-to-male trans as they undergo surgery and hormone therapy. Norrie, Keegan, and Nicco are all in their 20s, facing a completely new and altogether frightening transgender chapter of their lives. Norrie, an African-American, is especially concerned about the pressures of turning into a man.

WHAT THE CRITICS SAID
"*Boy I Am* juxtaposes powerful portraits with a number of articulate women who raise questions and voice doubts that many are thinking about but don't say aloud. The interviews with Judith ("Jack") Halberstam talking about gender are worth the ticket price alone."
Erica Marcus, *San Francisco Bay Times*

"The filmmakers effectively use their tiny DV cameras to make their subjects feel comfortable opening up, and directly address the problems lesbians have with women determined to become men."
Robert Koehler, *Variety*

"At birth we are given a body, and, from that point on, we are constructing our identity."
Blade

Boy's Choir

(Dokuritsu shonen gasshoudan; 2000)

The Quicksilver Passions of Adolescence

This Japanese film garnered many awards at various film festivals in 2000. Although it may be hard to obtain, the work of its director merits attention. At the Berlin International Film Festival, Akira Ogata won a prestigious prize, the Alfred Bauer Award for Best First Feature.

Ogata handles the story of two boys who bond at a boarding school back in the early 70s. They journey, in the words of one critic, "the path from revolutionary ardor to bitter disillusionment traveled by many of the era's student radicals."

Amid a talented cast, actor Teruyuki Kagawa, playing Seino, is clearly the leader of the pack. A leftist radical in his younger days, Seino has become a devout Catholic, a scene-stealer in his depiction of the school's choir director.

The two young boys are Michio (Atsushi Ito) and Yasuo (Sora Tôma), known for his crystalline soprano voice. His dream involves becoming a member of the Vienna Boys' Choir.

Michio, who stutters and is taunted by his classmates, is attracted but intimidated by Yasuo's girlish beauty. Yasuo sides with him and becomes his friend, and something more.

The plot thickens when Satomo (Ryoko Takizawa) demands help from her former comrade, Seino. She's fleeing the police, who are asking questions about a bombing in Tokyo. Seino provides her with a hideaway.

Filled with youthful idealism, the two boys adopt their own form of revolution. Expect a shattering conclusion.

WHAT THE CRITICS SAID
"Boy's Choir is fashionably minimalist in style, with long cuts, a delicate pace, and an emotional palette more subtle than bold. No one is ever going to accuse it of being mall-ready entertainment. Moviegoers may find the film's finely nuanced introspection a hard sit—until the boys lift up their voices in passionate song and deliver the film's final message. The real revolution is not in books nor bombs, but in the heart."
Mark Schilling

The Broken Hearts Club: A Romantic Comedy

(2009)

Best Friends Pushing 30 (Horror)

In the palm-shaded oasis of gay West Hollywood, we meet Dennis (Timothy Olyphant), a promising photographer as he prepares to celebrate his 28th birthday. He ponders his dilemma. "I can't decide if my friends are the best or worst thing that ever happened to me."

"I'm 28 years old and all I'm good at is being gay," complains one of those friends, Marshall (Justin Theroux). Other friends include Howie (Matt McGrath), a psychology grad who is letting life pass him by, and Taylor (Billy Porter), the resident drama queen.

Cole (Dean Cain) is a charismatic actor who makes off with everybody's hunk. Benji (Zach Braff) has a lust for buff gym bodies.

Patrick (Ben Weber) faces self-image problems and must decide if he wants to donate sperm to his lesbian sister and her lover. He's a narcissist, treating men as mere playthings until he hooks up with movie star Kip Rogers.

The broken hearts gather at Jack's Broken Hearts restaurant and lounge. Acting as their father figure, Jack (John Mahoney) is the coach of their softball team and head cheerleader.

Somehow the director and writer Greg Berlanti manages to pull all these queens together in this comedy/drama/romance that suggests that the shortest distance between friends is not always a straight line.

As one critic noted, the writer-director, Berlanti, one of the creators of *Dawson's Creek*, knows "just when to introduce the false crisis, the false dawn, the real crisis, and the real dawn."

WHAT THE CRITICS SAID
"The new movie acts like a progress report from *Boys in the Band* (1970). Instead of angst, Freudian analysis, despair, and self-hate, the new generation sounds like the cast of a sitcom."
Roger Ebert

Broken Sky

(El Cielo Dividido; 2006)

An Artsy Mexican Film About Alienation

Helmer Julian Hernández proceeds at a very slow pace indeed in this tediously long aesthetic exercise. But he had the good taste to cast a trio of handsome young actors in this love triangle played out almost in a pantomime which is virtually dialogue free.

The sensitive one, Gerardo (Miguel Angel Hoppe) is in love with Jonas (Fernando Arroyo), and they seem a happy duo for the moment at their university. But Jonas is dazzled by a fleeting encounter with a stranger in a dance club (Ignacio Pereda). This breaks the heart of Gerardo who turns to Sergio (Alejandro Rojo) for love in hopes that he can mend a broken heart.

In this boring, long, and pretentious film, there are some tender moments, but not enough. Much of the so-called action is repetitious.

Some of the gay press looked far more kindly upon this epic queer romance, Gary Kramer of *Gay City* calling it "a highly stylized masterpiece and one of the sexiest films of the year."

But as one viewer so accurately put it, this is a "dance of love, rejection, pain, new love, guilt, return to old love."

That about says it.

WHAT THE CRITICS SAID
"Auteur Julian Hernández tortures viewers as thoroughly as he does narrative and genre conventions in this punishingly long, overabstracted first-romance tale. Not even Alejandro Cantu's rapturous camerawork can make up for the whimsy-deprived pretentiousness or overall tedium."
Mark Holcomb, *Time Out New York*

"That's the movie—desperate grasps, huffy affronts, gulping kisses, and one juicy (if silent) sex scene, early in the film, before our senses have been deadened by boredom. Without dialogue, we don't know who the characters are, so we can't care about what they do."
Melissa Levine, *Village Voice*

Brüno

(2009)

An Absurdly Flamboyant Austrian *Fashionista*

Like his hit movie *Borat*, Sacha Baron Cohen blends candid camera moments and scripted sketches in *Brüno*. Some fall flat like last night's hard-on.

Cohen is still obsessed with body parts; he still has insane sight gags, and even more filthy jokes than *Borat*.

In the words of one critic, Cohen "can no longer fool the average moron" with his material. Expect a trio of dildos, an anal bleaching, and one gyrating, talking penis.

Regrettably, this gay spoof is an ultimate turn-off in spite of director Larry Charles' guidance. Yet you wouldn't want to be the only gay man who hasn't seen it.

Brüno arrives in Hollywood, wanting to become "the biggest Austrian superstar since Hitler."

One of the funniest scenes is when Ron Paul, the presidential aspirant, is played for a sap. On Brüno's interview show, guest Paula Abdul is asked to sit on the "furniture"—that is, down-on-all-fours *mexicanos*.

WHAT THE CRITICS SAID
"There are numerous jaw-dropping sequences; Brüno's deliberately incendiary interviews with Israelis and radical Palestinians (real? Who knows?); his Madonna- and Angelina-inspired adoption of a black African baby named O.J. and subsequent taunting appearance before an all-black TV studio audience; his attempt to undergo a 'gay cure' through counseling and then via macho martial arts training; a pretty amazing visit to a blue collar swingers' party; and, finally, his goading a mangy, beer-swilling Arkansas crowd into an anti-gay frenzy at a cage-wrestling extravaganza. Real? Once again, who knows?"
Todd McCarthy, *Variety*

Bulldog
in the White House

(2006)

Unconditional Access to the President's Bed

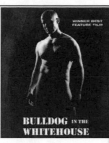

Was this underground film secretly screened at the White House? It depicts George W. Bush as "doe-eyed and dopey" and his Laura as a faghag version of Lady Macbeth. Rumors have it that Karl Rove once arranged such a screening. The Bushes were allegedly enraged, but didn't sue.

This avant-garde adaptation of *Dangerous Liaisons*, Choderlos de Laclos's tale of power and deceit within France's *ancien régime,* depicts the Bush administration's "horny, plotting, and evil" White House. At the Chicago Underground Film Festival in 2006, *Bulldog* won as Best Feature.

Experimental filmmaker Todd Verow directed this film and cast himself as the tenacious Bulldog, a seldom-clothed, hustling power broker going from bed to bed, hoping to acquire a "hard pass" that would grant him access to the bed of our "gay president." Yes, in this daring spoof, the administrators of the White House are all queer—and, in the words of one festival viewer, "ensnared in incestuous webs of diabolical seductions and random hook-ups."

There is a left-wing political point of view here. But, so as not to get too preachy, Verow throws in some gay porno action, perhaps hoping to emulate the decadence associated with the aristocrats of France in the 1700s.

Karl Rove is the grande dame Marquise, who dallies with the hustler, Bulldog (the transposed Valmont) throw up road blocks to thwart an alliance between Bush and a neo-Nazi religious leader, as performed by Michael Burke.

WHAT THE CRITICS SAID

"Cheerfully obscene . . . the semi-coherent narrative tracks as a burlesque revue of Bush II scandals."
The Village Voice

"You can expect cocks, spit and ass to be swapped willy-nilly, all to the detriment of democracy and ultimately for the entertainment of a gurgling Jabba-the-Rove."
New York Underground Film Festival

Can't Stop the Music

(1980)

A Faux Bio of The Village People

This was a gay movie in denial. Of course, there's that quick scene of a group of guys taking a shower, and one even slaps a towel on another's butt. There are also loving, slow-motion scans over buff and oiled jocks, and an all-male synchronized swimming team scene.

But the normally talented Nancy Walker, aided by writers Alan Carr and Bronte Woodward, wants her cake and wants to eat it too. She tries to balance family-friendly with gay-friendly and doesn't succeed at either, although this incredibly bizarre musical has moments of whimsy and charm.

Athlete Bruce Jenner turned down the titular role in *Superman* (1978) to appear in this film. Big mistake. The ex-Olympic decathlon champion doesn't make it in the acting stakes. If he'd stripped down and showed the full monty, he would have been more intriguing. At least we get to view him taking off his pants.

Actor Steve Gutenberg plays Jack Morell, a thinly disguised role of the founder of The Village People, Jacques Morali. He plays a struggling composer desperate to gain fame with his songs. His problem? He needs a group to sing them—hence, the birth of The Village People. His roommate, Samantha Simpson (Valerine Perrine), playing an ex-model with a heart of gold, comes to his rescue.

After the success of *Grease*, the flamboyant producer Alan Carr was hoping to hit paydirt again. But his shovel came up empty with this one, except for those scantily clad young men.

David Hodo plays the Construction Worker; Glenn Hughes the Leatherman; Randy Jones the Cowboy; Felipe Rose the Indian, and Ray Simpson the Police Officer.

Guys old enough to attend movies in the 50s will recognize old-time stars such as Tammy Grimes, June Havoc (sister of Gypsy Rose Lee), and Barbara Rush who got to marry that divinely handsome Jeffrey Hunter when he wasn't fucking other guys.

Cannibal

(*Melancholie der Engel;* 2006)

Aficionados of Human Flesh and Flopping Weiners

Loaded with male nudity and imbued with homoeroticism, this controversial film is based on the true story of the cannibal in Germany who advertised on the Internet, looking for someone to eat.

Director Marian Dora has taken on a daunting challenge in this provocative movie, which was banned in Germany and released as a "Not Rated" DVD in the United States.

Cannibal focuses on the day of the killing and the hours leading up to the actual slaughter. Carsten Frank plays Armin Meiwes, the Rothenburg Cannibal, and Victor Brandi is cast as Bernd Jürgen Brandes, the Flesh. They had a passionate sexual affair prior to the killing. Brandes is longing for a lover, a desire that will literally consume him. Meiwes is smacking his lips and indulging his sexual fetish to consume human flesh.

Dialogue is scarce—"I'm your flesh"—and there is full frontal male nudity and a lot of it. *Cannibal* depicts the slaughter, the freezing, and the preparation of meat for Meiwes' first meal.

In real life, Meiwes was sentenced to life in prison. Until the final sentencing, he maintained that he still had fantasies about consuming human flesh. He even launched gay chatboxes in his search for fresh meat.

Police found the remains of Brandes in the garden of Meiwes' home. They also confiscated a videotape from the night Brandes was killed. In his defense, Meiwes claimed that he did not actually commit murder, but was carrying out Brandes' clearly articulated death wish.

WHAT THE CRITICS SAID
"One of the sickest and freakiest movies ever to come from a nation well known for its freaky and sick movies (Germany). *Cannibal* is shocking, outrageous, sickening . . . and just a little bit interesting because it's based on actual events. One of the men loves to eat human flesh, and the other guy wants to be, well, eaten. It's all very gross, trust me. Once Dora gets down to the slicing and the chomping, the movie's as grisly and off-putting as any horror flick you've ever seen."
Scott Weinberg

Chicken Tikka Masala

(2005)

A Spicy Mix of East and West

Preston, England, not necessarily a locale for filmmakers, is the setting for this British attempt at rib-tickling Anglo-Asian film fare. It continues the array of British films dealing with Asian-based comedy-dramas, except this one has a gay twist.

The plot is familiar. Jimi (Chris Bisson), a young Asian man, is scheduled to wed a family friend's daughter, Simran (Jinder Mahal). There's a problem. Jimi is gay and has a boyfriend, Jack (Peter Ash). The predictable complications arise to keep the plot spinning. Trying to avoid the marriage, Jimi feigns a love child and love itself, with Jack's sister, Vanessa (Sally Bankes).

We don't need to tell you the ending. You know from the start that it'll all work out in the end. After all, this is a comedy—not drama. One weakness of the film is its failure to explore the relationship between the two male lovers, one Indian, Jimi himself, and the other British, Jack. As one critic noted, "They rarely look at each other and have virtually no physical contact."

The film was produced by Sanjay Tandon, co-produced by Rony Ghosh, and directed by Harmage Singh Kalirai.

WHAT THE CRITICS SAID
"Make that *Turkey Tikka Masala*. This is sloppily written, edited with a bread knife, and the musical score is bashed out on what sounds like a Casio synth somebody's bought at a jumble sale. Supposedly, this film is about a gay Asian man getting railroaded into an arranged marriage. The farcical plot is managed utterly without charm or wit, and the ending's a cop-out."
Peter Bradshaw, *The Guardian*

"*Chicken Tikka Masala* is an inept attempt to conflate Ang Lee's *Wedding Banquet* and Stephen Frear's *My Beautiful Laundrette* through the tale of a gay Indian lad with an English lover being forced into an arranged marriage with a Gujarati girl."
Philip French, The Observer

Chuck & Buck

(2000)

Man-Child Stalks Childhood Boyfriend

Mark White pulls out a *tour de force* by writing this drama and also starring in it as Buck O'Brien. He's not the director—that's the job of Miguel Arteta—but White dominates this story of a man-child who tries to reconnect with his childhood friend, Chuck (Chris Weitz), in the wake of the death of Buck's mother.

Chuck grew up and put aside his childhood sexual games and went to Los Angeles, where he became a rising music industry executive. Chuck is also preparing for his upcoming wedding--to a girl, that is.

At his mother's funeral, Buck fondles Chuck's groin during a brotherly hug. The latter flees in haste, too shaken to tell his girlfriend, Carlyn (Beth Colt).

Following him back to Los Angeles, Buck seems to have developed an obsession with Chuck and begins stalking him. The relationship worsens to the point where Chuck and his fiancée stop returning Buck's never-ending calls. Buck wants to reconstruct the relationship they once enjoyed as kids. When he visits Chuck's house, he said, "I noticed there aren't any pictures of me around."

Chuck is deeply embarrassed by Buck's emotional immaturity, and he wants to break the childhood link, a move that shatters love-sick Buck.

When not stalking Chuck, Buck writes an autobiographical play, *Frank & Hank*. We know who that is based on. He even persuades a stage manager (Lupe Ontiveros) to direct it, at least for one night in exchange for $25 an hour for her services.

WHAT THE CRITICS SAID
"What is the movie about? It seems to be about buried sexuality or arrested development, but it's also a fascinating study of behavior that violates the rules."
Roger Ebert

Chutney Popcorn

(1999)

East Indian Immigrants & Urban Dykes

Nisha Ganatra stars in the lead role of Reena in this comedy/drama, and this talented woman also directed the film and co-authored the script. She's part of a New York-based East Indian-American family, consisting of a mother, Meenu (Madhur Jaffrey), and two daughters, including Sarita (Sakina Jaffrey).

Her sister is happily married but is infertile. Reena volunteers to be a surrogate mother for her sister's baby. She hopes that will restore her in the grace of her mother, who disapproves of Reena's lesbianism.

This also brings complications to Reena's Caucasian girlfriend, Lisa (Jill Hennessy). The plot thickens when Sarita finds out that her husband Mitch (Nick Chinlund) is taking an extra special interest in Reena.

WHAT THE CRITICS SAID
"Part portrait of merging cultures, part investigation of the parameters of family loyalty, *Chutney Popcorn* is many things, the most important of which is a very good comedy. With co-writer Susan Carnival, Ganatra draws unexpected parallels between Indian and lesbian communities. Juxtaposing scenes of Indian prayer rituals with those of lesbian bonding, Ganatra illustrates that while the two subcultures could not be more disparate, each has traditions and codes that unite its respective members."
Lael Lowwenstein, *Variety*

"Because *Chutney Popcorn* knows its characters deeply enough to let them determine events, it rises above formula. It is also unusually well acted. Ms. Ganatra's Reena exudes a warm, pillowy sensuality that is complemented by Ms. Hennessy's frisky, high-strung hauteur. But the deepest and most complex performance is Ms. Jaffrey's Meenu. Ms. Jaffrey conveys the pained ambivalence of a devoted parent struggling with her ingrained prejudices and sense of shame."
The New York Times

Ciao

(2008)

Every Ending Has a New Beginning

This film by Malaysian director Yen Tan (who also co-authored the script) certainly had a mixed reaction from the public. "The best gay movie of the year," shouted a fan. "This movie is laughably bad," lamented another. The truth lies somewhere in between.

Its biggest minus is that it is exceedingly slow, with a lot of jabber and more jabber. Jeff (Adam Neal Smith) goes through the e-mails of his friend Mark, who was killed in a car accident. Mark, it seems, has been carrying on an online flirtation with a man named Andrea (Alessendro Calza). In an impetuous moment, Jeff invites Andrea to visit him in Dallas (no, not West Hollywood).

Andrea accepts the invitation, showing up at Jeff's door. The duo spends a long weekend talking mostly about Mark. At one point, they are joined by Ellen, Jeff's stepsister.

It's obvious the two hotties are attracted to each other, although Mark's death still looms over their heads. The tension and chemistry between the two stars makes it somewhat inevitable that they will fall in bed together.

WHAT THE CRITICS SAID
"*Ciao* borders on the brink of soap opera but is saved by an emotional truthfulness and winning performances of the two lead parts. There's not much more to the story. But Smith and Calza inject their characters with feeling."
Ruthe Stein

"*Ciao* is so stylishly lensed (lots of close-ups) and earnestly acted, it's a shame that the film drags under the weight of all that chatter."
V.A. Musetto, *New York Post*

"Shot in muddy video, *Ciao* weds a story that sounds (and often plays) like a pornographic quickie with a torturously ambitious visual style."
Manohla Dargis, *The New York Times*

The Closet

(*Le Placard*; 2001)

Just Pretending to Be Gay

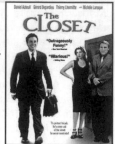

This French film is director/writer Francis Veber's long awaited follow-up to his hit comedy, *The Dinner Game*. The character once again is named François Pignon, acted by Daniel Auteuil, who totally immerses himself in the role of the office nerd. Pignon plays a kindly accountant in a condom factory who is still in love with his ex-wife and also wants some respect from his teenage son.

He soon learns that he's slated to be fired after 20 years of service. His next door neighbor, Berlone (Micxhel Aumont), has a radical solution to prevent that firing. He suggests to François that he should pretend to be gay.

That way, if the company fires him, its executives can be accused of discrimination. Also, no condom factory would want to offend their clients, a majority of which are homosexual.

The Closet, a box office hit in France, turns the tables on *La Cage Aux Folles*, in which a gay man tries to look straight. This is about a straight man trying to appear gay. Word quickly spreads through the office, and Pignon's fellow workers develop a new-found respect for their accountant, finding him more mysterious now as a gay.

Gerald Depardieu, the most macho of all living French actors, plays Santini. He's a homophobe who indulges in gay bashing. Santini is warned by his bosses that he must treat Pignon well or run the risk. Santini's bumbling attempts at positive contact with Pignon provides much of the humor in the movie.

WHAT THE CRITICS SAID
"The movie passes the time pleasantly and has a few good laughs (the loudest is when Pignon rides in a gay pride parade wearing a crown that looks like a jolly giant condom). But the screen relies too much on the first level of its premise and doesn't push into unexpected places. Once we get the setup, we can more or less anticipate the sitcom payoff."
Roger Ebert

Coffee Date

(2006)

Comic Caffeine for Sexual Confusion

Indie gay cinema takes a mincing step forward in this film about the nature of friendship, love, sexual orientation, and sociological subdivisions. Writer/director Stewart Wade took it from a 17-minute short, originally released in 2001, to a 94-minute feature film. As it gets rolling, a blind date unfolds, awkwardly, as a practical joke between a supposedly straight guy Todd (Jonathan Bray) and a gay man, Kelly (Wilson Cruz).

The perpetrator of this *brouhaha* is Todd's endlessly gauche brother, Barry, as played by Jonathan Silverman.

As a result of this encounter, Todd's life begins to spin out of control as an unexpected friendship develops between Todd and Kelly. In the aftermath, Todd's family and co-workers assume, incorrectly, that Todd is gay.

Todd and Kelly decide to take revenge on Barry by reversing the joke. After their "date," the pair saunters past Barry holding hands. Freaking out and convinced that Todd is gay, Barry calls their mother, Mrs. Muller (Oscar nominee Sally Kirkland), to break the news. She's on the next plane.

Todd denies that he's gay to his mother, who has her own opinion. After all, Todd didn't show an interest in sports when growing up, but gravitated to movies.

In a marvelous performance, Kirkland is determined to prove to her son that she loves him regardless of his sexual orientation. After an attempt to prove he's straight with a sexy young woman, Todd starts to wonder. Could his feelings for Kelly be more than he'd ever suspected? Is he, in fact, gay?

Expect camp comedy, beefcake, and a cameo performance by Deborah Gibson who immortalized herself as the 80s pop star, "Debbie" Gibson. This is the kind of film Hollywood used to turn out back in the days of Katharine Hepburn and Cary Grant, or later with Doris Day and Rock Hudson.

Confetti

(2006)

Gay Planners Organize a Nude Wedding

Shot entirely in London as a "fictional docu," *Confetti* is a tale of three couples who compete to win a magazine contest. They vie for the title of "Most Original Wedding of the Year."

Matt and Sam (Martin Freeman and Jessica Stevenson) envision their wedding as a musical ceremony *à la* Busby Berkeley. In their dream, leggy maids-of-honor will gyrate on a three-tier wedding cake.

Josef and his Canadian fiancée, Isabella (Stephen Mangan and Meredith MacNeill) are superb athletes and plan a Wimbledon-inspired "tennis wedding," complete with dancing ball-boys, a preacher dressed as a referee, even a sudden rainstorm.

Michael and Joanna (Robert Webb and Olivia Colman) are nudists who want to express their "I Dos" in the buff, despite the mag's objection to running pictures of "naturists."

The heroes of *Confetti* are the dowdy, hyper-emotional gay wedding planners, played by Vincent Franklin and Jason Watkins. These fussbudgets provide marital counseling to the straight couples, and tell off overbearing mothers-in-laws. They even procure has-been English pop star Cliff Richard to make a surprise appearance.

The film stars some of the brightest lights in British comedy, including Freeman (*The Office*), Jessica Stevenson (*Bob and Rose*), and Olivia Colman (*Look Around You*).

Cast as the magazine's publisher, comic Jimmy Carr is hilarious. "I'm a bride's best friend," he proclaims, then adds with resignation—"and I'm not gay!"

Those tantalized by full frontal male or female nudity will get some here, but it's decidedly unsexy.

With all this hetero love on display, the most fully functional pair are the gay wedding planners themselves.

Debbie Isitt (*Nasty Neighbors*) has created an amiable mock-docu with funny moments, but scenes sometimes fall flat.

Conspiracy of Silence

(2003)

Two Hail Marys and One Father Flanigan

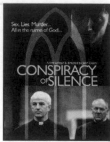

This controversial film addresses the Catholic Church and its policies on gay priests and celibacy. Made in Britain, and running for 90 minutes, it was both directed and written by John Deery.

Ripped from today's headlines, the film asks the question: how far will the Catholic Church go to cover up its own corruption? Set in modern-day Ireland, *Conspiracy of Silence* begins with two seemingly unrelated events—the unexpected suicide of the well-respected (gay and closeted) Father Frank Sweeny, and the expulsion of an idealistic, young seminary student, Daniel McLaughlin.

Local investigative reporter David Foley aggressively pursues the two stories and begins to uncover a deadly secret that links both incidents and leads to the highest ranks of the church.

His suspicions are confirmed when he receives anonymous threats and is chased by shadowy figures. As he digs deeper, he unwillingly puts his and his young family's lives in grave danger.

Meanwhile, Daniel is forced to make a decision that could haunt him forever. Will he return to the church and help cover up its lies and deceit, or will he surrender all dreams of becoming a priest and return to the beautiful girl he left behind?

WHAT THE CRITICS SAID
"An unquestionably sincere call for a change in the Catholic Church, *Conspiracy of Silence* unfortunately presents its cause with desperate earnestness. Arguing for the elimination of priestly vows of chastity, Deery lays out a story devoid of subtlety, in which characters are too easily pigeonholed and issues exist only in absolutes. Set amid such movies as *The Magdalene Sisters* and *The Boys of St. Vincent*, plus regular headlines about pedophile priests, there's doubtless an audience for another tale of church's ailments, even if it's as heavy-handed as this one."
Jay Weissberg, *Variety*

"A well-intentioned but ultimately incompetent Irish dud."
Nathan Rabin, *The Onion* (A.V. Club)

Cover

(2007)

A Black Version of *Brokeback Mountain*

This was the most homophobic movie of 2007. What is Patti LaBelle doing in a film like this?

Director Bill Duke tells this story of two male (and black) lovers from the viewpoint of the initially clueless spouse. The director tries to be making a Tyler Perry type of movie, combining the saintly with the taboo. But his approach is leaden.

Valerie Maas (Aunjanue Ellis) is accused of murder after she finds her middle-class Philly hubby in the shower with another man.

"I'm a Christian, not a murderer," she tells detective Louis Gossett Jr. Valerie wins support from her fanatical church support group for wives whose husbands are on the "down low" with other gay or bisexual men. This none-too-bright group informs Valerie that HIV is a "white man's disease," so the audience can see what an unenlightened coven this really is.

Valerie's strong character and her Christian faith keep her moving as she learns of her husband's betrayals that threaten to destroy her life.

Flashbacks reveal that she and her errant husband Dutch (Razaaq Adoti) have become immersed in the tawdry lives of his boss (Roger Guenveur Smith) and a rap star known as "Leon."

This movie bombs in spite of its intentions, but is such a bizarre, off-the-wall drama that it held a certain fascination for us. At some point, though, you may be rolling your eyes in disbelief.

WHAT THE CRITICS SAID
"This wackily uneven drama is a weirdly schizophrenic movie, one that's light on the murder mystery and heavy on the sermonizing, particularly when Valerie's church-basement women's group starts wailing about the devilish temptations luring African-American men from God and family."
Church Wilson

Cowboy Junction

(2006)

Is That a Pistol in Your Jeans?

The best reason to see this movie is to gaze upon the beautiful body of James Michael Bobby who plays a young cowboy in the film. Fortunately, he's not clothed for most of the running time, though there's nothing frontal.

The work is really the statement of Gregory Christian, who not only co-stars as "The Husband," but also directed and scripted the film. He was the executive producer as well. Talk about wearing many hats.

Christian picks up Bobby in the desert and has hot sex in a car with him before bringing him home to his wife, Elyse Mirto, cast in the always thankless role of a woman married to a gay man.

Ostensibly, Bobby is hired as a caretaker of the property and lives in a cottage out back. When hubby goes off to work, wifey appears scantily clad in the garden, trying to turn the cowboy onto her charms. But he tells her that he's more into cowboys than cowgirls.

Nonetheless, alone in her bed she fantasizes that cowboy is seducing her. Fantasies are about all she has left, since husband has stopped fucking her now that cowboy has moved out back.

When cowboy tries to fuck husband, he protests that he can't take it but later turns out to be a natural bottom. There's a subplot of a hit-and-run accident, and the cowboy suffers nightmares at the loss of his friend who was killed by a car. It doesn't take an Einstein to figure out who was the driver of the car who killed cowboy's friend.

WHAT THE CRITICS SAID
"Before you think this is a rip-off of *Brokeback Mountain*, think again. Christian stars as an unhappily married man who takes a trip to Cowboy Junction, a place where male hustlers hang out with the hope of making a few extra bucks. For those who travel to the desolate desert, life may never be the same again."
Eric Tuchelske

Creatures from the Pink Lagoon

(2006)

A Gay Version of *Night of the Living Dead*

Homophobes need not apply. This is a wacky film for gay men only, preferably those already stoned.

Director Chris Diani (also the co-scripter) is sending up 50s horror flicks. Imagine *Boys in the Band* meeting *The Night of the Living Zombies*. In a nod to Ed Wood, who made the worst movies of all time, there are giant monster mosquitoes and everything here from Judy Garland to sex toys.

In a small town in America in 1967, Philip (Nick Garrison) is planning to celebrate his birthday at a beach cottage. All of his friends are expected to be there, even Randall (Philip D. Clarke), a bitter, chain-smoking queen.

Hang on to your bra. Here's the plot. Gay men infected by schlock-inspired mosquitoes are turned into dildo-licking zombies.

Back at the party, Stan has an unfaithful but buff boyfriend Billy (Vincent Kovar), who will let anybody go down on him.

Billy breaks free from the party for some hot gay sex with Gary (John Kaufmann). On seeing a severed arm on the beach, Gary lets out a screeching scream. Another party is about to begin. You even get to see zombies dance. Could this have been inspired by Michael Jackson's "Thriller" album?

WHAT THE CRITICS SAID
"Get ready to play some water sports with the boys, enjoy the constant gay banter, admire the low-budget charm, gay dancing to show tunes, pink filtered point of view, shots of flaming zombies, and a shitload of gigantic dildos. Watch gays cheat on each other, form new relationships, gossip and team together to take out zombies that play for the pink team!"
Russ Rutter

"*Creatures from the Pink Lagoon* is a theatrically minded romp that makes fun of *Night of the Living Dead's* low-tech insanity."
DVD Verdict Review

Cycles of Porn: Sex/Life in LA, Part 2

(2005)

When Sex, Art, and Business Collide

Jochen Hick's follow-up to his gritty 1998 documentary, *Sex/Life in L.A.*, presents another revealing glimpse into a world where sex, art, and business collide in the City of Angels. Despite it's name, this is not a film to jerk off to.

Jochen Hick issued an excellent statement about the changing porn industry as depicted in this film: "Driven by a sense of adventure or their own narcissism, young men today are still keen to put their own stamp on porn cinema. But the days of a purely non-commercial fulfillment of one's sexual desires has long gone, and the interests of consumers, models and producers no longer coincide. Gay life—like the entire industry—has become something of a profession and is now thoroughly commercialized. Young models begin their sexual careers in internet containers; they enter the business fully aware of their self-exploitation and yet, at the same time, they are somehow unconscious of how they are being exploited. Meanwhile, bareback video producers scout the country in their motor homes on the lookout for new protagonists. But can there be winners in this game? Is there anything left of sex itself? And is there a life after porn?"

It is Los Angeles in the year 2005 as nineteen-year-old boys move through an apartment that has been equipped with web cams and looks like some sort of "futuristic internet doll's house."

All the stars in the cast appear as themselves, although we assume that their names were devised just for the screen. Johnny Law appears as himself, as do Will West, Kevin Kramer, Cole Tucker, Damian Ford, and several others. Of course, the fabulous Chi Chi La Rue appears uncredited but we know it's as "herself."

This is a docu about sordid aspects of lives of actors in the gay porn business. *Sex/Life in L.A. 2* shatters the few remaining illusions that consumers may retain about the porn industry. Instead of portraying the stars as glam models, it reveals widespread exploitation, suffering, and the messed-up lives of many porn stars.

The D Word

(2005)

A Parody of "That Other" Sapphic Series

Same Sex. Same City. This comedy, directed by Noelle Brower and Maggie Burkle, follows a group of young queer friends and family as they stumble through work and sex lives with tongue placed firmly in cheek and other bodily orifices. It runs for only 61 minutes.

The plot, such as it is, spins around Dot Parker (played by Marga Gómez), the director of a downtown theater, and her partner of seven years, Dina Cunnard (Jessica Horstman), described as a "crunchy granola dyke." They're seeking a sperm donor.

The sub-characters are all christened with Ds. There's Daynisha Dykmann (Rose Sias), a closeted WNBA player. Comedian Julie Goldman shines as Drea McClay, more butch than even the Shane character on *The L Word*.

Other D characters include Dixie Lipshitz (Victoria Soyer), a bisexual journalist into S&M, and Dex Parker (Geo Wyeth), Dot's young musician sibling. Daria (Melyss'ah Mavour) plays the owner of the Drunken Pussycat, a bar where the Ds gather to gossip and kvetch their way through this Big Apple dyke drama.

The main creator of this parody is Dasha Snyder, who shares writing credits with Cherien Dabis. One reviewer predicted that Snyder was destined to become the lesbian Mel Brooks.

WHAT THE CRITICS SAID
"When it's funny, this perceptive parody of Showtime's ensemble lesbian dramedy, *The L Word*, is hilarious. But it's also knowingly amateurish and, at about an hour, the lampooning goes on long enough for the sketches to start embracing the cheesiness they mock."
Boston Globe

"Originally filmed as five 10-minute episodes for Dyke TV, this daft lampoon of *The L Word* is satire at its ugliest...tired storyline...irritatingly spoofish...deplorable. There is only one word to describe *The D Word*: Dreadful."
Ashlea Halpern

D.E.B.S.

(2004)

Crime-Fighting Hotties with Killer Bodies

In this lesbian parody of *Charlie's Angels,* plaid-skirted schoolgirls are groomed by a secret government agency as the newest members of the elite national-defense group. D.E.B.S. (Discipline, Energy, Beauty, and Strength).

Written and directed by Angela Robinson, the racy 91-minute film, in which the women are depicted in revealing uniforms, turns out to be a tale of lesbian love.

Keeping their lipstick intact while lying, cheating, and fighting for the U.S. government are such characters as Amy (Sara Foster), Max (Meagan Good), Janet (Jill Ritchie), and Dominique (Devon Aoki). Their mission is to capture the hot vixen, Lucy Diamond (Jordana Brewster), the deadliest criminal the world has ever known. When Amy falls for Lucy, chaos erupts and the D.E.B.S. loyalty is put to the test.

WHAT THE CRITICS SAID
"This girl-on-girl romance barely raises a chuckle, a hormone, or an audience eyebrow. Cardboard-thin and terribly shot, D.E.B.S. is a low-budget even by indie standards, and that's a major disadvantage when you're taking off on a genre that would scarcely exist apart from its turbo cheesecake style. The movie has no wit, no charm, no cleverness, no traction. Simply put, it is no fun."
Owen Gleiberman, *Entertainment Weekly*

"The forced spoof seems to be targeted at lesbian couples and hetero men with severe schoolgirl fetishes; that may be a legitimate market, but I'd hate to be sitting between them."
J.R. Jones, *Chicago Reader*

"The film has no idea of how to develop its one-joke premise. The tepid love scenes are as erotically charged as a home movie of a little girl hugging her Barbie doll, and the satire is as cutting as the blunt edge of a plastic butter knife."
Stephen Holden, *The New York Times*

"D.E.B.S. is a H.O.O.T."
Duane Byrge, *The Hollywood Reporter*

Dante's Cove

(2005)

Possessed and Undressed

Do you really want to know the tangled plot of this TV series? One reviewer suggested that you watch *Dante's Cove* only to see the hot, sexy "alternative people" and that you should turn off the sound and skip all those trivial scenes—"you know, the ones about the plot. Just stick to all that naked passion." Frankly, we think this is good advice.

The series is gay soft-core porn, with some real hotties appearing shirtless (or with even less) in sexy sweat. It's a campy soap. Helmer San Irvin put the boys through their romantic and very hot sex scenes.

Oh, yes, that plot: In the 19th century, Ambrosius Vallin (William Gregory Lee) is out for revenge against a coven of witches known as the " Tresum." He woos one of the bitches, Grace (Tracy Scoggins), hoping to marry her and learn the secret of the coven's power.

But she catches her groom *en flagrante* with her butler. Naturally, the butler has got to die. But she has other plans for Vallin. He's imprisoned in the dungeon beneath her home where he'll be trapped in the body of an old man. He won't be free until a Prince Charming comes along to kiss him.

Switch to the present where we find lovers Kevin (Gregory Michael) and Toby (Charlie David) having problems in their relationship. Even so, Kevin, after trouble with his family, travels to Dante's Cove where Toby is a bartender.

Complications spew forth as Kevin and Toby find themselves being used as pawns in a deadly game of revenge between Ambrosius and Grace (yes, the witch is still around, looking fabulous, after all these years). Now that Ambrosius has been kissed by Kevin, he's developed the hots for his liberator.

We won't go on and on with this plot, which suggests that "some loves will haunt you forever."

WHAT THE CRITICS SAID
"As Baphomet is my witness, the series' mystical underpinnings are of an exclusively Tantric variety."
Keith J. Olexa

Daughters of Darkness

(Les lèvres rouges; 1971)

Looking for Virginal Female Flesh

This French film is an erotic nightmare of vampire lust. It may be the all-time camp classic of the lesbian vampire thrillers so popular in the 1970s.

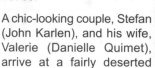

A chic-looking couple, Stefan (John Karlen), and his wife, Valerie (Danielle Quimet), arrive at a fairly deserted seaside hotel after eloping. He is an Englishman with a streak of sadism, and she is a bright Swedish woman.

Two new guests also arrive and they are stunning: the Hungarian countess, Elizabeth Bathory (as played by Delphine Seyrig), and her voluptuous protégée, Ilona (Andrea Rau). The star of the picture is clearly the countess.

Her arrival comes as a surprise to the hotel porter. He gulps, remembering her visit 40 years ago when he was a bellboy. "And you haven't changed—not in all those years." What the porter doesn't know is that the countess has stayed eternally young by bathing regularly in the blood of virgins. Of course, virgins are getting harder and harder to come by.

That couple in the room next door are a bit weird too. When Valerie finally gets Stefan to call his mother to tell her of their marriage, it turns out that dear ol' Mum is actually a man who eats purple orchids for lunch.

Bodies drained of blood are discovered in a nearby town, and a wary detective suspects the countess.

The countess has her eye on Stefan, and eventually reveals to him the delight of vampiric feasts and sadistic orgies. When he beats his wife, she falls into the clutches of the countess as well. In the meantime, Ilona is seducing Stefan.

There's trouble in the land, lots of trouble, lots of blood.

In time, director Harry Kümel's art house lesbian vampire flick became a cult classic.

Deliver Us from Evil

(2006)

Child Sex Abuse Within the Catholic Church

Father Oliver O'Grady, now living in quiet retirement in Ireland, was an equal opportunity seducer. He went for both little boys and little girls, including within his roster of conquests a nine-month-old female infant. The Rev. O'Grady is pretty creepy. He

was defrocked and later imprisoned before he was deported to his native Ireland after serving seven years in jail. In his 60s, he now roams free.

In this docu, director Amy Berg paints a portrait of a preying—and betraying—man. O'Grady himself appears in the film, his face showing no signs of shame even as he admits to the awful acts he perpetrated.

O'Grady is a twinkly eyed Irish priest straight out of Central Casting. But during his reign of terror, the priest raped and sodomized hundreds of boys and girls across California.

At one point it is revealed that he seduced an older mother in order to get to her teenage son for sex. It is also revealed—not surprisingly—that O'Grady himself was also abused by a priest when he was a boy.

"People gotta understand," moans Bob Jyono, a parent of one of the abuse victims, "he's not a pedophile, he's a rapist!"

Indicted is the Catholic Church which shunted the pedophile priest from one central California parish to another, ignoring oft-repeated accusations against him. In each of his new parishes, he continued to abuse children until forced to move on again. The docu includes interviews with the defrocked priest and also with some of his grown and deeply bitter victims.

One of the most shocking elements of the docu is watching court testimony of some of O'Grady's superiors in the Catholic Church. One such official has the temerity to make a distinction between abusing little girls and little boys. The first act, or so it was said, was one of "curiosity," the second act—that is, raping young boys—"was far worse in that it may constitute homosexuality."

Die, Mommie Die!

(2003)

It's a Dirty Town, But Someone Has to Do It

Since an aging Bette Davis or an over-the-hill Joan Crawford weren't around to make this drag send-up of a 1950s genre film, why not Charles Busch himself, cast as ex-pop singer, Angela Arden? For years, Busch reigned as America's leading drag queen; he might refer to himself as a female impersonator.

A lampoon of cherished straight conventions, *Die, Mommie Die!* was helmed by Mark Rucker, who lets Busch be his most outrageous self. Cast as Angela's young lover is the handsome Jason Priestley as hustler Tony Parker. According to legend, Priestley is "the biggest star in Hollywood," at least in one department.

Actually, Angela has a husband. He's a failing Hollywood producer Sol Sussman (Philip Baker Hall). She wants to divorce him, but he nixes the idea. "We're a famous couple, Angela, and we're going to stay together."

Completing the household is a gay pothead son Lance (Stark Sands). That is not a misprint. Who knows what his real name is? We thought agent Henry Willson was dead. He created all those names like "Rock," "Tab," or "Troy." The slutty daughter Edith (Natasha Lyonne) also fills out the bill.

Sol is suffering from constipation, and his suppository is poisoned. Hence, the plot thickens. All fingers point to Angela as the killer, but was she (he) really the one?

WHAT THE CRITICS SAID
"Some of the dialogue and many of the gags are in fact funny. But the movie's reason for being is Busch's drag performance, and I didn't find anything funny because he was a man in drag. What was funny worked despite that fact. A woman in the role might have been funnier, because then we wouldn't have had to be thinking about two things at once. The gag, and the drag."
Roger Ebert

A Different Story

(1978)

A Gay Man & A Lesbian in Love

It's a relic now, but a breakthrough movie of its day, running 108 minutes. Paul Aaron's *A Different Story* follows an illegal alien, Albert (a very handsome Perry King), who is the toy boy of an obnoxious classical conductor (Peter Donat), with a roving eye for good-looking guys on the hoof. When the conductor meets younger meat, Albert is fired as the chauffeur and replaced as a lover by the younger man.

Enter gorgeous Stella (Meg Foster), a real estate agent with several hot women under her belt. She discovers Albert living in an empty house and befriends him. At home as a majordomo, he takes over her house—she's a slob. In the course of their burgeoning friendship, she reveals she's a lesbian, with a neurotic, suicidal, ex-girlfriend (Valerine Curtin) still hovering about.

Immigration catches up with Albert and plans to deport him to Belgium, until Stella saves the day by marrying him. After one boozy night, the platonic pair heads to bed, an encounter that leaves Stella pregnant. Albert must be some stud. Seemingly, overnight he converts her from the lesbian life to the hetero. She turns him from gay man hanging out in the baths to a faithful husband raising a kid. Henry Olek's offbeat, somewhat erotic comedy/drama wanes toward the end, devolving into an updated TV sitcom with superficial marital problems. That's not a man Stella catches Albert with in the shower, but a shapely female model, although at first the viewer thinks it's going to be the naked ass of a man.

The film has been controversial since its release. Janet Maslin of *The New York Times* claimed, "This movie's use of homosexuality is indeed exploitative, insensitive, and offensive." Sylvester Stallone advised Perry King, "Don't play no fags."

Sadly, this now classic film reinforced the Born Again theory that gays can "go straight," and that the straight-and-narrow path is the trail to take.

WHAT THE CRITICS SAID
"Admirable work except for the flawed script."
Variety

Dirty Laundry

(2003)

Black Southern Matriarch Copes with Gay Son

Written and directed by Maurice Jamal, this is the story of a prodigal son. A magazine writer, Sheldon (Rockmond Dunbar) is living an ideal life until one day there is a knock on his door. Opening it, he discovers his traditional southern family on the other side, whose members he hasn't seen in a decade or so.

Once Loretta Devine as Evelyn barges in, the picture is hers, as she delivers a brilliant interpretation of a Georgia mom coming to terms with her disaffected gay son. Evelyn shocks him with the news that he has a 10-year-old boy named Gabriel (Aaron Grady Shaw). His family knows their offspring as Sheldon, but he insists that he be called "Patrick."

The picture flashes back to reveal Sheldon's life in the big city. We learn he has a boyfriend, Ryan (Joey Costello). Later Sheldon is fired from the magazine. When mama, back in the south, asks him to come home, he agrees to it but lies to his b.f., claiming he's visiting relatives in France.

WHAT THE CRITICS SAID
"Jamal (who also plays Sheldon's bitter, blue-collar brother) does all he can to milk social comedy out of the clash between opposites inside African American culture, but his efforts tend to produce broad stereotypes rather than deeply felt comic creations. As Evelyn's floridly self-centered sister, Lettuce, Jenifer Lewis plays every moment like she's working the back row of seats."
Robert Koehler, *Variety*

"If the beans ain't cooking, there's something wrong with the crockpot!" exclaims Loretta Devine's fat, sassy matriarch in what is surely the best line of *Dirty Laundry* (there isn't much competition). She's referring to her daughter-in-law's uterus here (yeah, ew), but she might as well be talking about the own cheesy crockpot of a film she's starring in. Anyway, with gay, elitist Sheldon back among his wacky, loud, fried-chicken-chomping family, hijinx ensue."
Julia Wallace

Dorian Blues

(2004)

Another Coming Out Story

Exhibited at virtually every film festival between Cleveland and Copenhagen, the 88-minute film represents Tennyson Bardwell's writing and directing debut. It documents a coming out story—in this case, that of a suburban teen, Dorian Lagatos, as portrayed by Michael McMillian.

Naturally, this sensitive lad has a star athlete brother, Nicky Lagatos (Lea Coco); a homophobic father (Charles Fletcher), and a Stepford Wife mother (Mo Quigley).

The jock brother tries to cure his younger sibling of his gayness. That endeavor involves both therapy and religious counseling, even the hiring of a female stripper. Fortunately, a boyfriend for Dorian is waiting in the wings.

WHAT THE CRITICS SAID
"While Bardwell's screenplay wobbles somewhat in tone, it displays enough wit and charm to compensate for its lack of polish. Helping matters appreciably is McMillian, who brings a refreshing edge to his performance that helps reduce the proceedings of their more cloying and clichéd aspects."
Frank Scheck, *The Hollywood Reporter*

"With rueful humor and keen insight, Bardwell charts Dorian's ordeal, his escape to NYU, the joy and pain of fleeting first love, and the realization that he's got to overcome a personality that in its flip, critical anger is too much like his father's. With its moments of comic relief overly exaggerated and at odds with its realistic tone, *Dorian Blues* is at its best at its most serious. The linchpin relationship is the underlying deep bond between the two brothers, and the scenes between McMillian and Coco are well written and equally well played."
Kevin Thomas, *Los Angeles Times*

"The movie is slyly comical, with a lot of big laughs. The director aims for big slapstick in Dorian's pickup in an S&M bar, but it was so ludicrous that it took away from the offbeat, realistic tone of the rest of the movie. It was pure cartoon."
Alan Jacobs

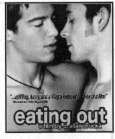

The Village Voice got it right: "The best straight-plays-gay, straight-goes-gay flick since *Harry Potter and the Chamber of Secrets.*

Take a deep breath and try to follow the plot of Allan Brocka's slight sex comedy that in some ways seems better suited for the stage. According to the plot, Scott Lunsford, playing Caleb Peterson, can't get a girl in spite of the fact he's strikingly handsome. Frankly, he'd be grabbed up in a minute by whatever sexual preference he so desired.

He has the hots for Gwen (Emily Stiles). But she's got this thing for gay guys. Caleb's gay roommate, Kyle (Jim Verraros) suggests that Caleb come on to Gwen's gay roommate, Marc (Ryan Carnes). In Kyle's way of thinking, that will make Gwen attracted to Caleb. Remember, she likes gay guys. Kyle thinks this gay impostor routine will eventually lead to Caleb and Gwen getting together. That way, Kyle will be free to pursue Marc himself. Is anyone still with us at this point?

The best sex scene in many a gay film in many a year is when Caleb, still pretending to be gay, has phone sex with Gwen while allowing himself to be serviced by Marc.

WHAT THE CRITICS SAID
"Most of the gay characters here—and even a few of the straight ones—talk anything but normally, batting such a barrage of zingers, *bon mots*, and pop culture references back and forth that each of them winds up sounding like a cross between Bruce Vilanch, Carson Kressley, Steven Cojocaru, and a reincarnated Oscar Wilde."
Michael O. Sullivan, *Washington Post*

"Mass-produced plastic toys might be more distinguishable from one another than the cast members of *Eating Out*, a generic assortment of smooth-skinned gym bunnies who sit around dishing shrill *double-entendres* and strained banter. The one surprise in the cast is Mr. Verraros, a former contestant on *American Idol.*"
Dana Stevens, *The New York Times*

Directed and co-scripted by Philip J. Bartell, this film is a bit funnier and faster paced than the original version from 2004—but not much. In the original, Kyle (Jim Verraros) convinced his straight roommate to pretend to be gay to get the girl. In the sequel, Kyle pretends to be straight as a means of landing Troy (Marco Dapper), the new kid on the block who also just happens to be a nude model in an art class. Dapper's a hottie who would be welcome to drop trou for most gay men.

Troy supposedly is hetero, but Kyle and fag hags Gwen (Emily Brooke Hands) and slutty Tiffani (Rebekah Kochan) aren't convinced. To scope out Troy, Kyle escorts him to a "go straight" session that makes for some satirical targets.

Kyle's ex-boyfriend, Marc (Brett Chukerman), is horrified at Kyle pretending to be straight to nab Troy. He decides to pursue the sexually confused Troy with his own tactic—being his own out gay self. Who will win Troy in the final reel? In this boy-eat-boy rat race, the stakes get raised as sexual boundaries are obliterated. The answer is surprising.

John Waters' longtime cohort, Mink Stole, provides sass as Verraros' earthy mother.

WHAT THE CRITICS SAID
"The horny gay and straight young folks from *Eating Out* continue to crack wise and snuff out partners in *Eating Out 2: Sloppy Seconds*—and the filmmaking continues to be just as sloppy. Sequel is no more than a cheapo campy goof, but this edition does contain a higher quota of laugh lines and an unsubtle message that efforts to make gay youth 'go straight' are destined to fail."
Robert Koehler, *Variety*

"As before, the fun is somewhat capped by the absurdly stilted acting and daytime-soap-quality DVD, but the nonstop sub-Araki glibbage is plenty peppy and so is Rebekah Kochan's ding-a-ling Tiffani."
Rob Nelson, *Village Voice*

Eighteen

(2004)

A Complex Emotional Vortex

This 101-minute Canadian film takes us into the life of Pip Anders (Paul Anthony), a depressed and cynical young man who is living on the streets of Vancouver. He has fled from his dysfunctional upper middle-class family.

When he turns 18, he receives a cassette tape and player from his recently deceased grandfather. In a sort of memoir, the older man relates his time serving with the British army in France, and his attempt to help his mortally wounded comrade avoid capture by the Nazis.

On the tape we recognize the voice of England's stately homo, Ian McKellen. The scenes the grandfather relates are pictured in flashbacks. These flashbacks alternate with scenes in Pip's present life as a street kid.

We are also exposed to "the dark secret" of why Pip fled his home.

Richard Bell (*Two Brothers*) brought this ambitious project to the screen, having the gay and straight roles treated equally in their relationships with each other.

On the lam, Pip encounters Clark (Clarence Sponagle), a gay street hustler on the make. He also meets Jenny (Carly Pope), a social worker who tempts Nip with feelings of love and domesticity. Pip also forms a relationship with a local priest, Father Chris (Alan Cumming). He tells the priest his deepest secret, not only about the death of his brother, but the heinous act his father committed against him.

WHAT THE CRITICS SAID
"*Eighteen* packs far too much plot inside 1 hour, 45 minutes. The World War II flashbacks are a stretch but tie in to the modern story, and the film seems at odds with itself to make the two timelines mesh seamlessly. Some scenes are quite powerful and work, while others seem to fall either melodramatically over the top or flat."
Brett Cullum

Eleven Men Out

(2005)

Star Football Player Reveals He's Gay

This rare Icelandic film, with English subtitles, concerns the star player of the country's top soccer team who admits he's gay to his teammates.

The handsome star player is Ottar Thor (Björn Hlynur Haraldsson), who doesn't consider the implications when he speaks to a reporter in the locker room after a game, confiding in him that he's gay. News of his homosexuality seems to freak out the Right Wing owners of the team, his fellow teammates and everybody else it seems. The star athlete is banned from play.

Ottar is the divorced husband of a former Miss Iceland (Lilja Nótt) playing Gugga, who has become an alcoholic. With Ottar, she shares custody of their adolescent son, Magnus (Arnmundur Ernst Björnsson).

Writer/director Róbert I. Douglas steers this rocky Viking ship along its way. Our hero calls it quits and joins a small amateur team, composed of other gay guys along with more tolerant teammates. Soon more gays turn up to join the team. This new squad skyrockets to a winning streak, mainly because rival teams refuse to play against "queers."

Faced with a backlash from the public, Ottar's former team wants him back.

Ottar tries domestic bliss with one of his fellow teammates, but it doesn't work out. His new lover is just as shallow as he is.

WHAT THE CRITICS SAID
"Róbert Douglas' film follows an Icelandic soccer star who is ousted from his club. The movie's tone is disastrously off, particularly in a putatively comic scene where Ottar fools around with his new boy-toy while his teenage son watches in disbelief. Apart from the chance to hear 'Walk Away Renee' in Icelandic, it's hard to recommend a soccer movie where we never see anyone kick a ball."
Dennis Harvey, *Variety*

Ethan Mao

(2004)

A Gay Hustler Holds His Family Hostage

Quentin Lee's melodrama is a would-be thriller. Ostracized from his right-wing household, Ethan Mao (played by Jun Hee Lee) is a gay Los Angeles teenager suddenly cut loose on the streets by an unforgiving family. He's soon taken in by a hustler, Remigio (Jerry Hernandez). At first they appear to be only friends, but we suspect that romance is in the air.

Lee, one of the best known of gay directors, delivers an intensive and provocative drama to us, telling how the young gay man is forced to hold his own family hostage. Before this family tragedy occurs, Ethan has discovered he's the perfect type for older guys wanting to taste some Asian chicken—they're called "rice queens."

Ethan and Remigio invade Ethan's former abode after Ethan tells them that the family will be away for Thanksgiving. As might have been predicted in the plot, the family returns unexpectedly. The director takes us off into a day filled with suspense, as the family is held hostage over a necklace.

WHAT THE CRITICS SAID
"In the following increasingly desperate hours, the family and Remigio are forced to confront their unresolved conflicts between each other. As the tension between Ethan and his family escalates, their inner demons and secrets unravel in this suspenseful and touching drama."
Scott Cranin

"This is Quentin Lee's third and least accomplished film. *Ethan Mao*, like its anti-hero, never quite knows which way to go once things get started. Film shares ingrained senses of lament and suspense with Lee's *Shopping for Fangs* and *Drift*, but messy admixtures of drama and mockery crucially undermine pic's serious message."
Robert Koehler, *Variety*

"Jun Hee Lee appears in almost every scene, but he's not convincing as an anguished son wronged by his authoritarian dad (Raymond May) or as a drug-addicted hustler."
Andrea Gronvall, *Chicago Reader*

Everyone

(2004)

A Black Comedy About a Gay Marriage

This 89-minute Canadian comedy/drama introduces us to Ryan and Grant, who are getting married and whose keywords are family life, gay male, marriage, parenting, and of course, romance. One viewer said that the film should be "a wake-up call for those who believe that real life should be like an episode in a 1950s sitcom."

With a cast led by Michael Chase and Matt Fentiman, *Everyone* marks the writing-directing debut of Bill Marchant, who is also an actor himself. He tackles all the foibles and traumas in modern-day relationships in this intimate movie.

Besides extramarital affairs, a decoration-crazed mother, and an angry alcoholic brother, there is also a mysterious guest (Brendan Fletcher), who has his eyes on one of the grooms, as Ryan and Grant plot their wedding in their backyard. *Everyone* was named Best Canadian Film at the Montréal Film Festival.

Five couples, siblings and spouses of the bound-for-the-altar boys, all prepare for the day's celebration with one thing on their minds: the state of their own relationships. Reflection and a few shattered conversations reveal that true love travels on a gravel road, as we follow these lovers through booze, babies, bulimia, and a host of other trappings.

Ryan starts the day with cold feet, but that might just be because he's meditating nude in the garden. Grant has other plans, donning a tuxedo to add a bit of traditional flair to the proceedings and maybe to mask his own possible misgivings about matrimony and lifetime commitment.

The clash of styles starts the day off on the wrong foot—opening up a debate between the pair as to whether gay couples should even get married at all. The ensuing fireworks end in a kiss-and-tumble match in the kitchen, but all is not settled.

WHAT THE CRITICS SAID
"Pic feels like a stapled-together contrivance of contempo 'issues' and forced dramatic crises rather than an organic exploration of character and situation."
Dennis Harvey, *Variety*

Family Hero

(*Le Héros de la famille*; 2006)

Feather Boas at the Blue Parrot

This French drama was directed by Thierry Klifa and written by Christopher Thompson. *La Cage aux Folles* it isn't, although in some ways it resembles it.

The plot begins to percolate when the septuagenarian, cross-dressing owner of the Blue Parrot nightclub in Nice, Gabriel Stern (Claude Brasseur), expires. Only the night before he'd asked his surrogate son Nicky Guazzini (played brilliantly by Gérard Lanvin) to lock up. All seemed well until the next morning when Gabriel was discovered dead.

But instead of giving the cabaret to his Nicky, his heir apparent, Gabriel specifies in his will that Le perroquet bleu should be deeded to his godchildren, Nino Bensalem (Michaël Cohen) and Marianne Bensalem (Géraldine Pailhas). The news of this postmortem betrayal reaches Nino in Paris, where he works as an accountant and lives with a much younger boyfriend, Fabrice (Pierrick Lilliu). Nino immediately catches a flight to Nice, where he joins forces with his half-sister and co-heir, Marianne. Both the heirs are in their 30s, Marianne a hotshot Judith Regan-type editor of a popular women's magazine.

Into all this mess walks the co-star of the film, the still-beautiful Catherine Deneuve playing the role of Alice Mirmont, Nino's mother. The great Deneuve is quite humorous in this film, becoming less cold as she ages. In a self-mocking role, she enters the family pow-wow, in the words of one reviewer, "to the sound of thunderclaps as the electricity flickers; couples (gay and straight) embrace as fireworks explode over the Nice waterfront. Deneuve as the mother is the free spirit in this dour, grief-stricken crowd. Nino at one point examines her face, asking, "You've had some work done, haven't you?"

Other cast members include the pulpy Emmanuelle Béart (Léa O'Connor), who delivers comic lines while being poured into seductive gowns. On stage she'll deliver warbling torch songs in English.

Fantasya (AKA Pantasya): Gay Illusion on Men-in-Uniform

(2007)

How ya doin', Sailor!

International gay men viewed this film from the Philippines differently, one viewer finding that its director, Brilante Mendoza, orchestrated the vignettes "with a deft hand and a throbbing hard-on," noting that the steamy sex scenes were

shot with fearless intimacy, "as the boys' hungry mouths devour one another's lithe bodies."

In contrast, Andreis Visockis from Latvia claimed, "The plot summary for this film is actually misleading. It isn't about men in uniforms at all. It was probably the film's international distributors who insisted on a more 'sell-able' title in English. *Fantasya* is about loneliness, a desire to belong, and the daydreaming that comes as a result."

This digital feature is divided into five episodes dealing with gay fantasies. "Biyahe" concerns a jilted taxi driver and his jealous passenger who find comfort in each other's lovesick arms. This is followed by "Linya," about a man whose phone goes dead. Two good-looking repairmen arrive to fix it, and a *ménage à trois* develops.

"Laro" is about four basketball players showering in the locker room after a game. A shy guy is a peeping tom, checking out the equipment and later joining in for fun and games.

"Bilis" concerns a pizza delivery boy who arrives at the office of a bored yuppie. There is an instant attraction. Finally, Episode No. 5, "Bantay," is about a horny security guard working the graveyard shift. He overhears two lovers fighting. One lover, Rhyme, dumps his BF Jon, who then finds satisfaction with that guard.

Even though the young Filipino protagonists long for love and happiness, only in their fantasies can they feel truly fulfilled.

FAQs

(2005)

"Straight-Bash-Fest"

This indie film, the oeuvre of helmer/scripter Everett Lewis, seems to be delivering a message that straight people and cops are evil. Let's face it: some of them are. But not all, of course. Even though the world is filled with gay bashers, let's not get carried away here with that premise,

India (Joe Lia) is rescued from the tough streets of Los Angeles. This Colorado boy is the victim of a pair of suburban gay bashers (Adam Larson and Josh Paul). His avenging angel is named Destiny (Allan Louis), a pistol-packing drag queen.

Destiny takes India home where he meets a troubled lesbian, Lester (Minerva Vier). This strange trio form a bizarre family unit.

Joining the family is Spencer (Lance Lee Davis), a troubled young man obsessed with killing his abusive parents with a homemade bomb.

India has a theory that Guy and Quentin, her abusers, are actually gay themselves. In the meantime, Destiny falls for a local police detective, Vic Damone (Vince Parenti).

WHAT THE CRITICS SAID
"India joins Destiny in keeping the lost and lonely off the streets, and the film becomes more about their mutual desire to resist succumbing to the temptation of violence that rules the straight world. The one-bedroom apartment becomes increasingly crowded as India begins to collect cute boys like so many stray cats. The campier aspects of the film are not enough to make up for its lapses into melodrama and just plain silliness. Though Destiny's vigilante diva is a striking mix of Grace Jones and Catwoman, there are far too many scenes of angry adolescents declaiming death unto the heterosexual world and waxing poetic about the power of love."
Kevin Crust, *Los Angeles Times*

Filthy Gorgeous, The Trannyshack Story

(2005)

Glammy Drag Queens of San Francisco

If you don't live in San Francisco and don't attend the famous drag show every Tuesday at Trannyshack, you might not completely enjoy this 90-minute docu. The helmer, Sean Mullens, makes his feature film debut in this bizarre piece of entertainment.

Spotlighted are such queens as Peaches Christ, Glamamore, Rusty Hips, Princess Kennedy, and Precious Moments. As one of these ladies—we forgot which one—told us one night at Trannyshack, "I'm God damn gorgeous and you'd better write that or I'll rip off your left ball!"

There are also audience shots of the likes of David Bowie or Papa Roach spliced with plainsclothes interviews with the queens themselves. Without their flamboyant drag, they come off as completely different characters.

WHAT THE CRITICS SAID
"You know you're at a gay and lesbian film festival when a glammy queen pulls an American flag out of her ass while lip-syncing 'The Star Spangled Banner' and not a single person boos. Sean Mullens' debut doc about San Francisco's infamous Tuesday night cabaret is all lip-liner, hairspray and bags of cocaine—the foundations upon which their country was built. Self-congratulatory and skin-deep, *Filthy Gorgeous* has earned its seat in the pantheon of glittery drag documentaries, despite its inability to wipe away the eyelash glue."
Ashlea Halpern

"The cutting—sometimes even stage blood-drawing—edge of drag performance is displayed in *Trannyshack*, Sean Mullens' survey of the notorious weekly San Francisco club's first decade. A far cry from the 'old-school drag' acts of glamorous female impersonation and show tunes, *Trannyshack* has drawn loyal, mixed audiences to witness sometimes X-rated rock 'n' roll wig out by self-proclaimed freaks hell-bent on provocation and outrage."
Dennis Harvey, *Variety*

Finn's Girl

(2007)

Angst, Death Threats, Abortion, & Love

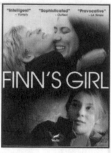

Longtime documentary collaborators Dominique Cardona and Laurie Colbert have turned out a smart, sexy, and suspenseful tale of the lives of Dr. Finn Jeffries (Brooke Johnson) and her daughter, Zelly (Maya Ritter). Finn's life would be busy even without a child. She's a doctor running an abortion clinic and a single lesbian re-entering the dating scene.

The breast cancer death of her former partner has left her alone to rear the latter's stubborn 11-year-old daughter Zelly. The kid's sperm-donor father Paul (Richard Clarkin) spends much of his screen time trivializing Finn's parenting skills.

In her professional life, Finn faces protests from pro-lifers at her abortion clinic.

Fearing that Finn will be killed, the police assign a pair of mismatched officers, Diana (Yanna McIntosh) and Xavier (Gilles Lemaire) to protect her.

They are a lesbian/ladies-man odd couple. But, as one viewer claimed, "The end is a crock that solves everything even though it solves nothing."

WHAT THE CRITICS SAID
"*Finn's Girl* reps an intelligent juggling of disparate elements including pubescent unrest, single parenting, lesbian widowhood, and anti-abortionist violence. While the agenda grows a bit overloaded, solid perfs and polished execution on a low budget help the writing-directing duo pargely pull it off."
Dennis Harvey, *Variety*

"Actually filmed in parts of Toronto's Morgentaler Clinic, *Finn's Girl* is a plain steamroller of a drama that bulldozes its way to a dubious *Deus ex machina* surprise ending. The title character (Brooke Johnson), a crusty, leather-wearing, biker-chick, fertility specialist, spends her days dodging bullets from the screaming pro-lifers who are planted permanently outside her clinic and who even track her down to her home."
Jim Slotek

Fixing Frank

(2002)

A Svengali Who Turns Gay Men Straight

This controversial film directed by Michael Selditch was based n the Ken Hanes play. It deals with "reverse therapy," a scientifically unproven—and much revived—method of directing homosexual sexual behavior down a more straight-and-narrow path.

A gay psychotherapist, Dr. Jonathan Baldwin (Paul Provenza), is outraged at the damage caused to gay men by Dr. Arthur Apsey (Dan Butler). To expose him, Dr. Baldwin enlists his lover of six years, Frank Johnson (Andrew Elvis Miller), who is a freelance journalist. His job? To go undercover and reveal Dr. Apsey to be a dangerous fraud.

Dr. Apsey proves a difficult subject to crack. A man of personality and intellect, he is no Born Again Christian goon like Pat Robertson. The man who would "cure" homosexuality seems not to be practicing either Christian or aversion therapy, but "mind over the matter of sexual orientation." Not really prepared to be an investigative journalist in such a complicated matter. Johnson seems to be the hapless pawn in the struggle between the two warring psychologists.

This movie may raise more questions than it answers. As one viewer put it: "Can gay people really be made straight? If they are born that way, what if they are very unhappy? Can or should they be allowed to change their sexual orientation? How much of this is because of the gay political climate? Is there really pressure to remain gay if someone wants to be stressed?"

WHAT THE CRITICS SAID
"In *Fixing Frank*, Baldwin seems foolish, not to mention unethical, in what he asks of Johnson, who has only written features on subjects like antique shows and fall colors and it would seem that Baldwin, in his understandable frustration in trying to nail Apsey, has been blinded to his lover's lack of suitability for the undertaking. Still, *Fixing Frank* is 'good theater.'"
Kevin Thomas, *Los Angeles Times*

Flirting with Anthony

(2005)

"Gay Porn Bondage and Road Trip Freakout"

There's not much flirting going on in this misnamed movie. The attractive actors just get down and do it, often showing the full monty. A dizzying crosscut of graphic violence and gay sex, *Flirting* seems to be the fantasy of its helmer/scripter Christian Calson. The only thing Christian about this artist is his name, not his plot.

Flirting opens with 15 minutes of intense violence and sexual perversion. Of course, there's nothing wrong with that if it's going to lead somewhere.

The film's title character, Anthony (Daniel Cartier), is kidnapped and beaten. He's hauled off to a garage where he's tied up in bondage for a kinky torture session conducted by some tough guys. Perhaps they are also going to kill him. To the rescue comes Jack (an actor billed only as "Linus"). He rescues Anthony, becoming bruised and bloody as part of the process.

Time goes by. Anthony is living in trashy circumstances with his low-rent girlfriend Donna (Lowe Taylor). After the death of her father, she heads for the funeral as part of a road trip with Anthony.

Their love-making has grown stale, so in a trashy motel they rent a pink-haired gay hooker for a *ménage à trois*. Is Anthony gay? Bisexual? Or just sexual?

The following night Anthony and Donna each hire hookers for a tour-way—called "fourgy" in slang.

At a roadside gas station, who should appear but Jack, Anthony's hero. He's fit and fine now, and we see Jack and Anthony indulge in hot homo sex in the dirty bathroom. Donna waits impatiently outside for these two young men to exchange body fluids. When the two of them come out of the dirty room zipping up, Donna has cause to pause.

WHAT THE CRITICS SAID
"What's really going on here is Calson projecting his own sexual fantasies (bondage, jockstraps, seedy motel rooms) onto the screen."
Dom Willmott

Formula 17

(2004)

"Rice Queen Delight" from Taiwan

No film has ever gone this far and with such delight in depicting Taiwanese gay teen life. It's a frothy boy-meets-boy romantic comedy.

As the song goes, it's the same old story, a fight for love and glory. In this case, boy finds boy, boy loses boy, and boy gets boy back.

A virginal 17, Tien (Tony Yang) is the new boy in town arriving with a red suitcase and looking for love. He wants to lose his virginity, but he's got a requirement: he wants to have sex with someone he loves.

At a gay bar, Tien spots a vision with flowing hair and a Gucci wardrobe. He's the playboy of Taiwan, the dashing Tai Tieh-nan (Duncan Lai), who is known as "Never Beds Twice." Playing the hot, studly young architect Bai, Duncan is a Hong Kong model.

The 93-minute film is in Mandarin and Cantonese, with English subtitles.

In case it matters one damn bit to you, the uptight, ass-plugged censors of Singapore banned *Formula 17*.

WHAT THE CRITICS SAID
"It can seem unfair to call any movie a 'gay movie.' After all, we don't usually talk about 'straight movies.' But it must be said that *Formula 17* is a really gay movie, at least in the sense that every character who appears on the screen is gay. Straight people simply never show up in this depiction of bustling Taipei."
Don Willmott, *Filmcritic.com*

"While the broadly played, goofy comedy and stereotypical queeniness of Tien's friends get tiresome, the relatively sanitized central romance is disarmingly played within an entirely insular gay-male world, in which not one heterosexual character appears. Sharply packaged on a modest budget, this first feature from femme director DJ Chen makes up in exuberance for what it lacks in complexity."
David Rooney, *Variety*

Freshman Orientation

(2005)

A Billy Wilder-esque Bait of Pretending

Originally called *Home of Phobia* when it premiered at the Sundance Film Festival, the title was changed to *Freshman Orientation* to attract wider audiences (read that straight). It's a bit of a potboiler, but has some serious moments.

A typical Midwestern 18-year-old freshman at a large state university is eager to delve into college party life. Instead he discovers that school is not the beer-driven, sexual fantasy of his imagination.

Determined to do anything to obtain the girl of his dreams, he decides to adopt a gay identity as a means of insinuating himself into her life.

This casual charade quickly lands him in a morass of campus activism, gender warfare, fraternity hazes, sorority torture, "coming out" narratives, political martyrdom, and, ultimately, a university-wide meltdown.

As the freshman Clay (Sam Huntington), he asks a gay bartender Rodney (John Goodman) to coach him in how to become a gay stereotype. This leads to Clay's gay roommate Matt (Mike Erwin) bristling at the cultural appropriation.

As the plot takes off, helmer/scripter Ryan Shiraki gets a lot of mileage out of the idea of a college as a dressing room where labels can be tried on or shrugged off like a discarded garment.

Clay's interest is in sorority girl Amanda (Kaitlin Doubleday). Urged on by megabitch Serena (Jud Taylor), Amanda is sent on a mission to woo and then dump various "loser" guys. Her target candidate is supposed to be gay, and she zeros in on hapless Clay, who plays along with the game, hoping to bed her.

Some viewers found the movie homophobic. One disgruntled member of the audience claimed, "I found myself groaning at every scene as gay stereotypes are reinforced and the entire depiction of life in college and gay rights activists is warped so severely that it becomes unrecognizable except as a caricature to be used like a punching bag for the movie's comedy."

Gasoline

(*Benzina;* 2001)

Moribund Hybrid of Thelma and Louise

In Italian with English subtitles, this first-time feature by director Monica Stambrini is a lesbian-themed thriller that needed a little more gas in its sex drive.

It stars Regina Orioli as Lenni, a timid woman working at a grubby Italian petrol station where this runaway lives with her grease monkey lover Stella (Maya Sansa). Lenni receives an unwanted visit from her disapproving mother (Mariella Valenti) who is a fussy floozy.

La Madre is determined to break up her daughter's lesbian affair with Stella. The mother attacks Lenni but Stella comes to her aid, throwing a right hook to the woman's face. She is knocked over, hitting her head on a cabinet. She dies instantly.

With a corpse on their hands, the young women realize they must flee to stay together. Stella conceives of an idea to dump the body and drive off.

Three wild, psychotic teenagers appear out of nowhere and, for reasons not fully explained, began to chase and torment Stella and Lenni.

These crazies pop up occasionally to keep the plot pot boiling. They don't seem to be hassling Stella because she's a lesbian, so they're not necessary homophobes but just doped-up garden-variety idiots.

WHAT THE CRITICS SAID
"This is a low-octane item. Pic slows down considerably, as duo drops body in a dump, plays cat-and-mouse with pursuers, recovers mom, and returns to station and participates in the combustible climax. A sluggish ride would improve considerably if helmer Stambrini would get the lead out."
Eddie Cockrell, *Variety*

Gay Hollywood

(2003)

Even in Hollywood, Being Gay Can Be a Drag

One actor in this 88-minute docu proclaims that Los Angeles is the gayest city in the world. So, thank God, we can skip all that anti-gay bigotry stuff that would have arisen had it been shot in a homophobic redneck hellhole like Crawford, Texas, or Washington, Georgia. LA may be gay, and two men can indeed walk hand in hand, at least in West Hollywood, but being out in Tinseltown isn't a guarantee of success. That's why at least ten A-list male movie stars still live in the closet, two at least famously so in spite of South Park urging them to come out of that closet.

In other words, if you can still get someone of the opposite gender to parade themselves as your Significant Other, it's a savvy career move to make extroverted displays of affection for that person—at least when you're on Oprah or on Candid Camera.

Jeremy Simmons both produced and directed this docu with a quintet of performers playing themselves, taking bit parts while waiting for the right doors to open

Gay Hollywood gets moving when Dustin Lance Black voices objection to the docu, claiming that the helmer is "stacking the deck with stereotypically flamboyant gay men." His complaint against stereotypes doesn't seem completely justified except in the case of Micah McCain who steals the flick. Who can compete with him in his silly drag queen persona as "Bridgett of Madison County?"

A bit duller is Benjamin Morgan, who is a struggling writer trying to peddle scripts to bored TV execs who don't give him much encouragement, but deliver stinging critiques like those delivered by Simon Cowell on *American Idol*.

Robert Laughlin is the film's best example of a struggling, out-of-work actor who needs to pay the rent while waiting beside a phone that never rings. Occasionally a job will emerge, perhaps as an extra in a cheapie soft-core porn video shoot.

Q. Allan Brocka has a famous uncle, the Filipino filmmaker, Lino Brocka, although this is not part of the docu. Instead we see the unknown young Brocka taking on such projects as directing a cheesy video.

Ghosted

(2009)

Cross-Cultural Lesbian Love Triangle

In this romantic, lush mystery, filmmaker Monika Treut (*The Virgin Machine*), who also co-scripted the project, develops a lesbian love story that's partly set in Taipei, which is beautifully depicted.

The unsolved murder of her young Taiwanese lover Ai-Ling (Huan-Ru Ke) leaves Hamburg artist Sophie Schmitt (Inga Busch) completely disoriented. Sophie makes a video commemorating her lover's life and death and travels to Taipei to exhibit and dedicate it to her slain friend.

Once there, she encounters a seductive journalist Mei-Li (Ting Ting Hu). Sophie, still in love with the memory of her dead friend, rejects Mei-Li's advances and returns to her native Hamburg.

Unannounced and uninvited, Mei-Li turns up on Sophie's doorstep in Hamburg. Sophie takes her in and eventually succumbs to her sexual charms. Bursts of memory explode in Sophie's head. In time she learns that there is no Mei-Li working for a Taiwanese newspaper, and that no one by that name ever entered Germany. Just who is this mysterious stranger?

There are problems with *Ghosted*. The script is uneven, the dialogue rather stilted, and the ghost story is distracting, rather gimmicky.

WHAT THE CRITICS SAID
"Sophie isn't much of an artist—her works consist of obsessive, bland portraiture—but she makes for a striking protagonist. Bearing the most imposing bone structure this side of Sarah Bernhardt, and an irresistible air of butch, German mystery, she is a serious lady-killer, though not, as we discover through a series of flashbacks, the person responsible for Ai-Ling's death."
Nathan Lee, *The New York Times*

<table>
<tr>
<td>

The Girl

(2003)

A Lesbian-Themed *Of Human Bondage*

</td>
<td>

Go West

(2005)

Wartime Drama

</td>
</tr>
</table>

This is an Anglo/French art movie, shot in England. Upon its release, it attracted fans of lesbian writer Monique Wittig, who also wrote the screenplay, which was directed by Sande Zeig in a debut feature.

It's the story of "The Painter" (Agathe de la Boulaye) who links up with a glamorous nightclub chanteuse "The Girl" (Claire Keim). A one-night stand turns serious. "The sheets are soaked vivid with our perfume," says The Painter in a voice-over.

The Girl is not exactly a free agent. The Man (Cyril Lecomte) shows up. Even though he doesn't have a mustache to twirl, he is the villain, sending his henchman to break up this new love affair. Despite the arrival of goons, the two female lovers have plenty of time in the sack, about a dozen such scenes. One shot is in such close-up you can't tell an elbow from a vagina.

WHAT THE CRITICS SAID

"Numbingly dull and repetitive, *The Girl* is at least pretty to look at for a time. Actresses Keim and de la Boulaye make a lovely pair, and the movie portrays an intimate, enticing Paris of cobblestone streets, artists' lofts and smoky nightclubs. De la Boulaye plays the narrator, referred to only as The Painter—because she apparently aspires to do more than just smoke incessantly. All the characters have generic names, a conceit that's either minimalist or just stupid."
Carla Meyer

You probably haven't seen too many movies from Bosnia-Herzegovina. Here's one that's daring but awkward, the tale of unlikely lovers, a Muslim and a Serbian. Perhaps a master like Ernst Lubitsch could have pulled it off. But for helmer Ahmed Imamovic, the challenge was daunting.

A classical musician, Kenan (Mario Drmac), is a Muslim living with his lover, a Bosnian Serb, Milan (played by Tarik Filipovic). They live together quietly, fearing retribution from their homophobic neighbors.

When war comes in 1992, their home town of Sarajevo is under siege. Together they flee but are forced off a train by Serbian militiamen. Kenan fears he will be shot to death. To save him, Milan comes up with the improbable idea of disguising Kenan as his girlfriend. Amazingly, he manages to pass in this disguise.

Eventually the lovers reach Milan's village in Eastern Bosnia, and the protection of his father, Ljubo (played by veteran actor Rade Serbedzija). Here this "man and wife" plan to wait until they can escape to Holland. Regrettably, Milan is drafted into the army, and the situation becomes almost intolerable for Kenan.

His one companion is Ranka, a waitress in a local café who possesses dark secrets. Ranka (Mirjana Karanovic) is a sex-starved woman who discovers that Kenan is a man. She seduces him several times, and, out of jealousy, then sets out to destroy his love affair with Milan.

Ultimately, Ljubo will come to Kenan's rescue and send him off to the West.

The great Jeanne Moreau, an associate producer of the film, offers a strange final cameo, playing a French TV interviewer.

WHAT THE CRITICS SAID

"This clumsy back-and-forth between historical tragedy and grotesque comedy just stops working after a while. Motivation is also iffy."
Deborah Young, *Variety*

Guys and Balls

(Männer wie wir; 2004)

Classic Sports Underdog Movie Writ Gay

This German film is a comedy/romance of sorts. Although predictable, it's rather entertaining. The star is Maximilian Brückner who is a decent goalie for his city-league soccer team. Right after giving up the winning goal in the big game, he is discovered drunkenly kissing another teammate after the game. The nasty homophobic footballers kick Eric off the team.

He vows to beat them with an all-queer team in just two months. To do that, he sets about to assemble a ragtag group of soccer wannabees. Of course, they are terrible players in the beginning, and you get no points for guessing who emerges as the winner of this grudge match. The tender moment comes when Eric overcomes his awkwardness with a first boyfriend.

The film does score some laughs, as when Eric recruits a *ménage à trois* of leathermen. His other recruits also include gay fathers, transvestites, and immigrant drama queens. There aren't a lot of surprises in store for you. Every sports cliché seems to have been dug up from the films of yesterday. But with grave reservations, critic Ryan Godfrey found the gay angle "fresh and often funny—a breezy, likable winner the net result."

The movie is mainly for straights wanting to laugh at gay stereotypes. Even gay sex is treated as being of lesser value than the hetero kind.

WHAT THE CRITICS SAID
"A by-the-numbers ensemble dramedy that hits every underdog and gay-fish-out-of-the-water cliché on the nose, German *Guys and Balls* is so derivative it might as well be called *Bend Over, Beckham*. Though helmer Sherry Hormann pushes the right crowd-pleasing buttons in slickly handled item, TV-bred Benedikt Gollhardt's first big-screen script may pander too blatantly for pic to get the good reviews needed to lure auds offshore."
Dennis Harvey, *Variety*

"I've seen spookier reruns of Paul Lynde as center square."
Paul Morales

Gypsy 83

(2001)

A Tale of Two Young Misfits

This is a tale of two young misfits, who decide to flee Ohio and pursue their dreams in New York. Sara Rue, who brilliantly portrayed Gypsy, deserves to be cast in other films. She plays an aspiring singer and songwriter working at a temp job in a drive-through photo shop. As one reviewer accurately noted, Rue plays Gypsy with "just the right combination of sweetness, sexuality, and sass." Her best friend, who shares many of her musical ambitions, is Clive. Actor Kett Turton played this gay teenager.

Together they drive to New York to participate in something called "The Night of 1,000 Stevies," a Stevie Nicks look-alike competition, and both of the teenagers worship Stevie Nicks.

En route to their dreams, clouds get in their way. Surely this film has one of the most colorful casts of supporting players in many a year, including Polly Pearl (Stephanie McVay), White Trash Mommy (Nancy Arons), and Chi Chi Valenti (Vera Beren). Even Karen Black gets in on the action as Bambi LeBleau (don't you love that name?), playing an over-the-hill roadhouse chanteuse and karaoke hostess.

Oh, and lest we forget, the entire film is presented by director/writer Todd Stephens in the bizarre clothing of a Goth cult. And, surely, no woman in America wears her large Goth clothing with more style and daring than the Junoesque Sara Rue. If there's somebody still living in the boonies who doesn't know what Goth dress is, it's worn by young people who dress up like embalmers at a Victorian funeral parlor and who paint their faces with heavy amounts of black mascara.

Peter Debruges of Premier said, "Films like this have a way of finding their own devoted fan base, and *Gypsy 83* deserves to be discovered not only by Goth and gay crowds, but by anyone who runs screaming from all things average. Such rebel spirits should enjoy following Clive and Gypsy's road trip as they encounter a wayward Amish hunk, a washed-up lounge singer, and a corruptible frat boy en route to New York."

Hard Pill

(2005)

A Pill Designed to Turn Gay Man Straight

This provocative drama, both directed and written by John Baumgartner, is the tale of a despondent gay man who throws both his life and his relationships into turmoil when he volunteers for a controversial pharmaceutical study for a drug designed to turn gay men straight.

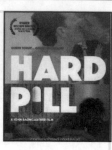

As a gay man, Tim (Jonathan Slavin) is morose. In desperate need of love, he's just not making it with other gay guys. His straight friend Don (Mike Begovich) will submit to that occasional blow-job, but that's about it. Don is already married . . . to a woman.

Instead of Don, the man of Tim's dreams is really the new guy in his office, Matt (Jason Bushman). To complicate matters, Tim's co-worker, Sally (Susan Slome), has the hots for Tim. Only problem is, she's a girl. Joey (Scotch Ellis Loring) tries to get Tim laid, proclaiming that there is "a sea of fags at his disposal and he stays home with a straight man."

To change his life around, Tim agrees to swallow the pill. His world changes at once. He jumps into bed with Sally, but he backs away from her since the treatment includes avoiding emotional involvement with any one woman right away. His new straight "genes" drives him into the arms of Tanya (Jennifer Elise Cox), who is unaware of his gay past.

On a curious note, Baumgartner underlines the human gradation of sexuality by introducing each character with a graphic, including name and tendencies rated on a straight-to-gay scale.

In addition to the drama unfolding, Baumgartner also has brief interludes of TV newsman-on-the-street interviews about the new "gay cure." On an alarming note, the pro-cure people interviewed are presented as average people, not right-wing lunatics from hell as they are most often depicted in such dramas. Because they are so average, they come off as even more frightening.

Hardcore

(2004)

Teenage Hookers Fall in Love

Ignore the title. This is not a porno flick. A Greek film, it runs for 96 minutes and tells the story of two teenage girls who meet and fall in love. By trade, both are hookers. Its footage evokes the films of Quentin Tarantino.

Writer-director Dennis Iliadis brings this urban fairytale of love and betrayal to life.

The performances by the leads are compulsively watchable. The two young (16 and 17 years old) Greek prostitutes are called Martha and Nadia and played by actresses Katerina Tsavalou and Danai Skiadi.

They ply their trade in a seedy whorehouse run by Manos (Andreas Marianos). His brothel is staffed by teenage runaways—both male and female—who respond to his ads. He breaks in his new girls in a private room with a mammoth rubber dildo. Nice guy, this Manos.

Nadia and Martha fall in love even though they're dating two of the rent boys (hustlers) they work with.

Soon the girls are renting an apartment of their own. One day, studly Argyris (Ioannis Papazisis), Nadia's boyfriend, arrives at the apartment with a gun that one of his johns has presented to him. That sets the stage for Nadia to enlist the support of both Argyris and Martha to go with her back to the whorehouse to seek revenge on their employer who owes them money. Their pimp ends up dead, and two prostitutes are also killed.

Nadia shifts the blame onto Argyris, and she and Martha flee. Nadia seems to enjoy her newly found notoriety. To an increasing degree, she becomes adored by the public as she weaves a lurid story of how she suffered abuse from the whorehouse master and his clients. All this leads to an estrangement from Martha.

WHAT THE CRITICS SAID
"It unfolds very much like a traditional Greek tragedy, just with more hot pants, lesbianism, beat heavy dance music, orgy scenes, and coke snorting than usual."
Ian Jane

Hearts Cracked Open

(2004)

Improving Lesbian Sex with Tantra

This 57-minute docu deals with the ancient practice of Tantra long enjoyed by straight couples. In this film, women who love women tune in to walk this spiritual/sexual path.

As depicted in the film, California (but, of course) is leading the way in the so-called Tantric revolution. *Hearts Cracked Open* strives to bring a daily allegiance to Tantric sexual techniques to the lesbian community worldwide.

What's the promise of Tantra? Intimacy. Ecstasy. Bliss. Lesbian sex is linked to a spiritual connection.

In the film, Tantra teacher and Shaman leader, Marcia Singer, introduces pupils to Tantra 101: The sacred touch, the eye-to-eye gazing, deep and rhythmic breathing. Sex expert Pamela Madison, who runs a tantra clinic in Santa Barbara, demonstrates the "fire-breath orgasm." This peak fulfillment can be reached while a partner is fully clothed. It's a question of breathing, movement, and sound. Madison's techniques also involve the G-spot massage and usage of sex toys.

Evalena Rose's advanced six-month, women-only Tantra group gives the viewer an inside look at the exercises and ritual practices of a puja (worshipful circle), with its dancing, sensual feasting, and techniques to awaken the sexual energy in the body.

Annie Sprinkle, renowned sex goddess pundit, shares her own personal Tantric path which has been culled from fellow teachers around the world.

The title of the film comes from the claim made from Tantra, that it "cracks open the heart" to a wider range of emotions and deeply felt sensations. Everyone from frustrated housewives with lesbian leanings to motorcycle mama dykes is said to benefit from Tantric sexuality.

Or as Sprinkle puts it, "a Tantric lesbian is a happy lesbian."

Hellbent

(2004)

Gay Slasher Movie

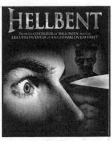

The tagline for this thriller is, "When the night belongs to the Devil, the party goes to hell." Director/writer Paul Etheredge-Ouzts, a former set designer, is the helmer who brought this not always successful film to the screen. There's talent behind the production, however. One of its executive producers, Joseph Wolf, performed similar duties on *A Nightmare on Elm Street*.

The film gets off to a murky start when the serial killer puts a gory end to a gay tryst in a parked car in West Hollywood.

The New York Times compared the buff masked killer to a "cross between Batman and the Grim Peeper." He slices his victims' heads cleanly off and keeps them as souvenirs.

Much of the film takes place at the West Hollywood Halloween Carnival. A group of four gay friends have to fight for their lives to make it through the night. Expect flamboyant costumes and beautiful people.

The main characters include Eddie (Dylan Fergus), a young police officer with a past. He spots hunky stranger Jake (Bryan Kirkwood), who has been praised for turning in the film's best performance as a Marlon Brando-style *Wild One* motorcycle heartthrob. The boyish, inexperienced Joey is played by Hank Harris, and Tobey is interpreted by Matt Phillpps playing "a sensitive underwear model," who is also a pushy drag queen. A brash bisexual, Chaz (Andrew Levitas) appears as a cowboy.

WHAT THE CRITICS SAID

"Despite colorful, campy costumes, even an Amish viewer would predict the killing order of the victims. The villain is an unspeaking, scythe-wielding muscleman who wears a metallic devil's cowl and little else. Why he's running around with a bad attitude is anybody's guess. The pity is that buried under the genre familiarity, the interactions between the principals and the Eddie-Jake relationship comes close to displaying dimension and pathos."

Luke Sader, *The Hollywood Reporter*

Holding Trevor

(2007)

20-Somethings Drifting in La-La Land

Holding Trevor was called a vanity project for Brent Gorski, who both wrote and stars in the film as Trevor. Our "hero" is dissatisfied with his life (who isn't?) but seems stuck in a stalemate with his bitchy friends.

He's involved in an unhealthy love affair with Darrell (Christopher Wylie), a heroin addict. Trevor's fag hag roomie Andie (Melissa Searing) doesn't add much support, nor does his best friend (Jake), a singer.

When Darrell inevitably overdoses, he's taken to a hospital. Here Trevor meets a medical intern Ephram (Eli Kranski) who seems a much better candidate as a BF. He's certainly handsome enough.

The question is then posed: Is Ephram, with his cuddly warmth and security, man enough to take Trevor away from the hapless Darrell? Trevor's celebration of a negative HIV test explodes into horror when an uninvited Darrell shows up. Ephram is having second thoughts about Trevor. Is he mature enough for a man-on-man relationship?

Gorski's script places the vapid party scene in L.A. on boring display.

WHAT THE CRITICS SAID
"There's nothing to fill up the 88 minutes of the film except for the idle bitchery spewed by nearly every character. Are there really people out there who are so irredeemably nasty to their friends and lovers, while actually managing to keep them as friends and lovers?"
Julia Wallace

"With friends like Trevor's, and a rudderless job at an answering service (they still exist?), you might think Trevor should grab adoring Ephram, get the hell outta Dodge, and leave his buddies behind to sort out their own crap. *Ergo,* the pic's noble sacrifice conclusion rings false: these people seem too self-absorbed."
Dennis Harvey, *Variety*

The Hole

(2003)

Lots of Beefcake, Erotica With a Plot

Wash West gave us *The Fluffer*, that hot, hottie of a film. He's back with another steamy soft-core pic. Unlike Chi Chi LaRue, West pays as much attention to the script as to the sex scenes.

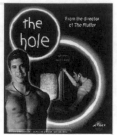

For this pumped-up beefcake epic, he's assembled a cast of some of the hottest male stars today, including Jason Adonis (Daddy, buy me that for Christmas). Other hot men include Tag Eriksson, Josh Hammer, Kip Bravo, and the aptly named Rex Everthing.

This porno pastiche opens with Josh Hammer and Derec Lang recounting the story of a videotape that, when viewed, will turn one gay within seven days. Inspired by a recent viewing of that tape, the two buffed young men get it on in a vivid sex romp.

The hotel room where Hammer and Lang swapped body fluids is later rented to a reporter, Swedish hunk Tag Eriksson. He finds the mysterious tape and watches it. He also picks up the receiver to hear a mysterious voice warning him, "In seven days you'll be gay."

Eriksson encounters Jason Adonis who informs him that he, along with Sam Tyson, also watched the tape and were no longer the straight jocks they were before viewing. We learn that these former "pussyhounds" (Tyson and Adonis) now find that fucking male ass "like, totally rocks, dude!"

There's more fun on the way, including a major circle jerk and a soft-core orgy. Some deep-kissing scenes lead to spectacular depictions of male/male love-making.

WHAT THE CRITICS SAID
"The dicks are hard, the sex seemingly endless and the boys breathtaking. Remember this is soft-core, no cum-shots, no penetration—but Wash takes us as far and as deep as we can go into *The Hole*."
TLAvideo.com

<table>
<tr>
<td>

Hollywood Dreams

(2006)

To Live & Die (& Cry) in Los Angeles

</td>
<td>

The House of Adam

(2006)

Some Secrets Can No Longer Remain Silent

</td>
</tr>
</table>

London-born helmer and scripter, Henry Jaglom, invades the City of Angels with this offbeat comedy/drama about people who pursue crazy dreams in LA. From this director came *Sitting Ducks* in 1980 and *Someone to Love* in 1987, the latter flick featuring Orson Welles.

To his repertoire, he adds his latest, *Hollywood Dreams*, featuring a red-haired newcomer, Tanna Frederick, playing Margie Chizek, a hayseed who drops off the potato wagon from Iowa, landing incongruously in La-La Land.

What a strange choice for a leading role. At times Frederick evokes Ronald Reagan Jr. in drag; at other times, she could be Chelsea Clinton's ugly sister.

Naturally, she's desperate to make it as an actress in Hollywood. Who isn't? She loves old movies of Hollywood's golden age as well as men in lingerie. Her favorite actor Is Robert Williams, who died after his one big role in the 1931 *Platinum Blonde,* with sexy Jean Harlow.

In this film, Jaglom is musing over the burdens of fame and the awful price one pays for success in Hollywood. Of course, that tale has been done so many times, although Jaglom, as in all his 14 other films, provides his own improvisational style.

Margie is rescued from sleeping in her car by a kindly producer, Kaz (Zack Norman). He takes her, along with her tumbling Titian curls, to live in a lavish home with his lover, Caesar (David Proval). About to be married in a same-sex wedding, they are not the most macho of boyfriends.

In this home she meets a young actor, the rather handsome Justin Kirk, playing Robin. Unlike the usual, Robin is straight but pretending to be gay to get ahead in Hollywood. In Hollywood, isn't it the other way around?—particularly for some high profile stars devoted to Scientology.

"I know six A-list actors who are gay and pretend to be straight," Robin tells Margie. "I'm the only one who pretends to be gay."

Jorge Ameer wrote and directed this crime drama/mystery/romance. He also directed *The Singing Forest.* The plot spins around Adam (Jared Cadwell), a recluse in a small town. A trio of religious fanatics murder him.

A closeted police detective (John Shaw as Anthony Ross) must find the remains of his former lover and come to terms with his own loss.

In a bit of irony, he becomes the victim of his own double-sided values, and the results, as they spin along, are both tragic and traumatic for him.

Ameer delves into the supernatural here, as Adam's spirit, which lingers between the living and the dead, remains within the cozy but isolated cabin where he lived. Only a proper burial can give closure to Adam's spirit as it haunts the cabin. The little nest is sold to innocent newlyweds who later become terrified.

HX Magazine called the film "perfect after a long day at the beach."

WHAT THE CRITICS SAID
"The filmmaker should continue with this style of filmmaking. I like it. He deals with some very heavy subject matter here but handles it in a way (dark comedic tongue in cheek) that you can't help to laugh at the absurdity of the situations some people put themselves into in real life. I applaud the filmmaker for that and look forward to seeing more of his work."
Jason McKensey

"Had Jorge Ameer aimed for high-flying camp instead of low-rent earnestness, his movie might have stood a fighting chance. As it is, this mopey tale of love that dare not speak its name is no more than an inept wallow in closeted torment. From risible horror (a newlywed is fellated by Adam's severed head) to amateurish action (punches land several inches from their targets), *The House of Adam* is an unmitigated bore. I'd pay to see the further adventures of the severed head, though."
Jeannette Catsoulis, *The New York Times*

Living in Seattle is a conventional husband Ben (Mark Duplass), who is in a baby-making mode with his wife Anna (Alycia Delmore). Suddenly, his best buddy from college, Andrew (Joshua Leonard) shows up, a sort of warmed-over Jack Kerouac figure. Andrew was always the wilder of the pair, and he naturally has a beard, even tattoos.

Written and directed by Lynn Shelton, the film explores straight male bonding rituals, but goes a bit far.

Andrew invites Ben to a wild party hosted by a bi woman Monica (Lynn Shelton). Ben learns that several of Monica's guests are involved in an experimental homemade porno film festival.

Under influence from the weed, Andrew and Ben need to show they are unflappably cool. These two hipsters announce that they will make a gay porno film clip starring each other. Each man naturally assumes he'll be the one to "do" the other one.

WHAT THE CRITICS SAID
"The static story (nothing much ever happens), stock characters, and blathery talk reinforce the unpleasantness of eyeball-scalding lighting, a sound design that makes each conversation seem like a hubcap rattling on a concrete floor, and my-cameraman-has-epilepsy photography."
Kyle Smith, *New York Post*

"The camera's view of the characters, although intimate, is almost antiseptic. The film sees Ben and Andrew the way they see each other: as blobs of flesh with hairy parts but without the tiniest suggestion of latent heat. Neither Ben nor Andrew is especially good looking (in a beauty contest, Andrew would probably win), but neither is ugly. A question the movie doesn't address is how Ben and Andrew imagine they can complete the project without any sexual attraction between them."
Stephen Holden, *The New York Times*

What an oddity. In this vampire film, David Bowie is the leading man to Catherine Deneuve and Susan Sarandon. Deneuve plays a bisexual Egyptian vampire, Lady Miriam, who subsists upon the blood of her lovers.

In return for their blood-letting, her guys or girls don't age. Well, in most cases they don't age.

Let's face it: What put this movie over at the time were rumors of the seduction scene between the age-old vampire, Deneuve, and her latest victim, Sarandon. A-list actresses usually don't play lesbian sex scenes. The two women use lips and tongues on each other's breasts.

The controversial scene, the focus of incredible rumors at the time of its making, is rather dreamily erotic more than raunchy or too explicit.

After years of service to the vampire queen, Bowie has that disease where you age suddenly as in *Lost Horizons*. He needs transfusions of fresh blood to keep going, which leads him to appeal to Sarandon, a medical researcher, incidentally, for help.

He's beginning to look like Methuselah. Sarandon visits the town house where Deneuve and Bowie practice blood sucking. A glass of sherry leads to her bloody seduction. And when it comes to bloodthirsty lesbian love scenes, no one delivers like Deneuve and Sarandon.

WHAT THE CRITICS SAID
"In his feature debut, Tony Scott (brother of Ridley), exhibits the same penchant for elaborate art direction, minimal, humorless dialogue, and shooting in smoking rooms. *The Hunger*—from the novel by Whitley Strieber—is all visual and aural flash, although this modern vampire story looks so great, as do its three principal performers, and is so bizarre that it possesses a certain perverse appeal."
Variety

Hustler White

(1996)

Madonna's Former Lover Plays Male Hustler

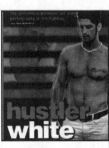

If you get off on L.A. hustlers hawking their wares along Santa Monica Boulevard, this oddball film is your cuppa. It's even got a few real-life gay porn stars thrown in for good measure. A lot of actual hustlers also appear in shorty short shorts.

At the time of its release, most of the interest focused on Tony Ward, who once had underground fame as Madonna's toyboy. Gay men got to see a lot of what turned Madonna on. Ward isn't as handsome as Andy Warhol's Joe Dallesandro, but no one would turn him down in a gay bar. For about $200, Ward will do anything with any guy.

Filled with kinky adventures, *Hustler White* follows the trail of Jurgen Anger (Bruce LaBruce), a writer and "sexual tourist," who has winged into L.A. to research a book about male prostitutes. Ward as a young male hooker is employed as his tour guide. LaBruce and Rick Castro both helmed and scripted this soft core adventure. LaBruce later gets to suck face with a male ho.

Some of the scenes are not for the faint of heart, as when a group of black men take turns pounding a blond muscle boy. It becomes a titillating freak show when a tattooed mortician changes into dominatrix drag and mummifies a young hooker in duct tape, or when another john with an amputee fetish is depicted, evoking a short story by Tennessee Williams.

With all its flaws, this is a fairly accurate portrait of hustlers, their hangouts, and the outrageous demands of their johns. In one scene, a john is strung up from the ceiling and delicately slashed across his chest and back with razor blades. In a British accent, he demands, "Cut me, dear boy!"

WHAT THE CRITICS SAID
"LaBruce fancies himself a 90s answer to Andy Warhol. *Hustler White* is a direct descendant of Warhol's *Flesh*, right down to its allusion to *Sunset Blvd*. The opening scene finds Monti (Tony Ward) floating face down in a Jacuzzi and narrating the story of how he got there."
Stephen Holden, *The New York Times*

I Can't Think Straight

(2008)

Soft-Focus Passion & Hard-Line Prejudice

Tala (Lisa Ray) is from Jordan. She's planning to get married until she meets Shee Leyla (Sheetal Sheth) in London. Leyla also has a BF, but the two women create sparks when they collide.

Rather predictably, the two women have mothers who have other plans for them. To complicate matters, Leyla is dating Tala's best friend Ali (Rez Kempton). From these complications, a plot ensues.

This is the debut film of Shamin Sarif, and is based on her own novel. She takes the viewer from the spires of Oxford to the sun-splashed hills of Jordan. The world the helmer depicts is without doubt a fictional one. Everybody seems well off. As one viewer said, "It's a window into make-believe, where the endings we dream of sometimes do come true."

WHAT THE CRITICS SAID
"Before all the burning questions in this film can be answered, the plot must plod through a confetti storm of obstacles—religion, ethnicity, overbearing mothers—all of which are overcome in dewy, unsmudged close-up. This isn't a movie, it's an alternative lifestyles campaign for Maybelline."
Jeannette Catsoulis, *The New York Times*

"Stacked decks and straw men are the order of the day In this simplistic lesbian romance about the forbidden affair between a Palestinian bride-to-be and a British-Indian free spirit. Clunky direction doesn't help, though a likable cast does what it can."
Miranda Siegel, *New York Magazine*

"Sarif wraps a story of same-sex attraction into a narrative that explores other issues of identity and politics. The questions of Jews and Israel is never far from the lips of Tala's mother, Reema (Antonia Frering), who calls her daughter 'an Arab hater' because she said Israel is the closest thing to a democracy we have in the Middle East. In *I Can't Think Straight*, it's the older generation of women—not men—who come off as more closed-minded to the changing world around them."
Jonathan Curiel, *San Francisco Chronicle*

I Dreamt Under Water

(J'ai rêvé sous l'eau; 2007)

A Sexually Frank (Whoa!) French Drama

This savagely engaging French film (with English subtitles) is filled with heart, lust, and emotion. It's a bi-sexual man's private odyssey through the dark Parisian night, which opens his mind to a myriad of sexual adventures and possibilities.

As reviewer Jason P. Vargo put it, "The trailer runs just over 6 ½ minutes in total and is perhaps the most sexually graphic film advertisement for a non-porn production in history. If you cut together a trailer involving the genitalia of both genders, a transsexual, a close-up of a freshly deflowered anus, and other such images, doesn't it stand to reason that these body parts should play a major role in the film? What kind of story is going to be wrapped around all of this?"

Antonin (Hubert Benhamdine) is in emotional and psychological torment. Playing in a band, he meets singer Alex (Franck Victor) and is entranced with him. When tragedy intervenes, Antonin is plunged into despair, becoming a hustler more to lose himself than to make money.

He meets Juliette and love is professed. But not all is as it seems. Her past will emerge to haunt our hero.

Co-writer and director, "Hormoz," often bites off more than he can chew with a complicated plot.

WHAT THE CRITICS SAID
"The verbal explanation of Antonin's feelings for Alex never add up to his actions. He doesn't attend the funeral. He does little more than sulk for his dead friend. If this person is an unrequited love, every fiber of his being should be shaken. It's not, as far as we can tell. Maybe it's enough for some audience to take Antonin's word for it, that he really is distraught and teetering on the edge."
DVD Review

In Her Line of Fire

(2006)

A Dyke Defends the Vice President

Mariel Hemingway has played a Secret Service agent twice and a lesbian three times. Here she is again playing a lesbian Rambo type whose job as a Secret Service agent is to defend the vice president when his plane goes down on a remote South American island. He is kidnapped by rebel forces and held for ransom. It's up to her and a press secretary to infiltrate the guerilla camp and save him.

The Mariel who hangs in there is tougher than Stallone, although both she and the original Rambo are a bit past their prime. Her love interest, attractive and brave, is Jill Bennett (Sharon Serrano). The preoccupation of this film is action, action, and more action. Sergeant Major Lynn Delaney (Mariel) and Jill don't have time to pick the flowers in the jungle, much less take a nude swim together.

Playing Vice President Walker is David Keith, who'd get our vote over Dick Cheney. He offers the greatest advice a straight man can give to a heavily armed lesbian. "You're a marine. Act like one. Go for it!"

The guerilla force holding the veep is portrayed by the cliché-prone mercenary David Millbern.

Made at an estimated cool million, the film took in $232 over a weekend when it opened in the States on two screens.

The fledgling script could depict the heroine having her breasts enlarged for a movie role, and how she had to have the implants removed after one ruptured.

Why will Mariel live on in movie history? She was the first famous-name actress to ever appear nude on screen. The film was T*ales from the Crypt* (1989). Lesbians remember Mariel with the greatest fondness because of her 1982 role as Chris Cahill in *Personal Best*, which caused her to be inserted as a clip in The Celluloid Closet in 1995.

At least Mariel changed the cliché of having lesbians always portrayed as vampires from Sodom.

Irma Vap—She's Back

(Irma Vap—O Retorno; 2006)

A Grotesque Parody of "Baby Jane"

In Brazil, Charles Ludham's Theater of the Ridiculous smash hit, *The Mystery of Irma Vep*, set a Guinness world record for the longest running play with the same cast. But that doesn't mean it's going to lend itself to a good film. Shot in Brazil, this 80-minute movie is in Portuguese with English subtitles.

The storyline of the film, however, deviates greatly from that of the play. A Brazilian actress, Carla Camurati, directed the film. Marco Nanini and Ney Latorraca star in the film version, as they did in the play. But on stage they assumed all the roles. By far, Nanini is the scene stealer here, especially with the parody of *What Ever Happened to Baby Jane*? This actor delivers a tour de force performance, combining feminine fluttering with masculine klutziness.

You'll laugh and be delighted as Nanini as Cleide grotesquely reprises her "Sunbathing by Moonlight" kid star hit tune. Treat yourself, as the young lead, Thiago Fragoso, does, to a "zaftig middle-aged Cleide in gossamer hoops and pigtails coyly sliding down a column," in the words of one viewer.

The movie met with very mixed reviews in Brazil, most of them bad. One critic called it "the worst movie I have ever seen."

WHAT THE CRITICS SAID
"Its impact depends on the spectacle of two actors playing all the parts in the show via lightning-quick cross-dressing changes, which is irrelevant on film. Therefore, Brazilian actress-turned-director Carla Camurati opts instead for an absurdist movie about a revival of Irma Vap encompassing off-stage shenanigans supposedly nuttier than those on stage. The result is a mixed bag."
Ronnie Scheib, *Variety*

Karl Rove, I Love You

(2007)

Falling for George W. Bush's Turd Blossom

The film asks the question, "What if the role of a lifetime became the love of your life?"

Out actor Dan Butler, starring in the film, is also its co-director and co-scripter.

It is election year 2004. A docu takes a surprising turn when Butler ("Bulldog" from the TV series *Frasier*) becomes smitten with the idea of playing Karl Rove, whom the ex-President fondly referred to as "turd blossom."

Rove, of course, was Bush's notorious senior advisor, and may have tipped the 2004 election by his Republican-directed campaign against gay marriage. Butler's initial intent was bringing Rove down, but as he gets deeper and deeper into his character, he actually falls in love with the little creep.

As critic Ed Gonzalez accurately claimed, "Shrill tone chokes this sitcom-ish affair, but Butler and co-director Phil Leirness still manage to lob a cherry bomb at the insularity of Hollywood liberals."

The Independent Critic came down hard on the film. "The idea of loving Karl Rove strikes us as obscene."

WHAT THE CRITICS SAID
"Initially ignorant of who Rove is, Butler excitedly realizes the reptilian Bush intimate is his equivalent, the ultimate "supporting player." With Leirness' camera documenting, the developmental process stalls until an acting coach tells Butler, 'You have to see the world through his eyes.' Thesp takes that advice to extremes that eventually prompt an intervention by worried friends, then vault into conspiracy-theory terrain. Complete with convincing Rove impersonator, credibly quasi-verité pic drolly mocks liberal Hollywood insularity at least as much as it mocks right-wing D.C."
Dennis Harvey, *Variety*

Keillers Park

(2006)

A Story of Sexual Awakening

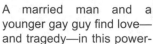

This moody film noir from Sweden, in its ads, raised some questions: "You've got everything. You meet the love of your life. How much are you ready to sacrifice?"

A married man and a younger gay guy find love—and tragedy—in this powerful bittersweet love story inspired by a real-life 1997 hate crime in Gothenburg. This striking love story/thriller has a strong visual sense, hot sex scenes, suspense, and the requisite male nudity.

Directed by Susanna Edwards, from a script by Pia Gradvall, *Keillers Park* captures the joy and fear of a sexual coming out in an inventive way. Sensitive use of flashbacks reveal how all this came about for Peter (Mårten Klingberg), who is the rich son of an engineer. Attractive and in his early 30s, he's involved with a beautiful artist Maria (Karin Bergquist).

By chance Peter encounters Nassim (Pjotr Giro), a handsome Algerian. Just a glance is exchanged between them, but it's enough to awaken long dormant homosexuality in Peter.

Peter and Nassim meet in Keillers Park to begin their secret love affair. Their first sexual encounter is erotically captured on film.

Peter's involvement with the Algerian leads to a personal disaster in his own life. Not only does Maria desert him, but his father disowns him. He is left unemployed and alone.

After Nassim is found beaten to death in the park, Peter is roused by the police and accused of the murder. At the police station, the story of his affair with Nassim is revealed in flashbacks.

WHAT THE CRITICS SAID
"Striking to look at, but lacking the passion to make the central story convince, *Keillers Park* is a fact-based story of a gay hate crime in Gothenburg. Feature debut by docu-maker Susanna Edwards shows an assured hand on the technical side but lacks the same skills with her actors."
Gunnar Rehlin, *Variety*

Key West: City of Colors

(2004)

The Inventor of the Rainbow Flag

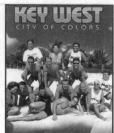

Talmadge Heyward created this 64-minute docu on the favorite resort of many gay men and lesbians. The southernmost city of the United States was for decades a gay mecca, especially in the heyday of the Navy presence during the Eisenhower era and beyond. As a gay resort, it reached its pinnacle in the 1970s—it once even had a gay mayor.

Today it attracts cruise ships and a high percentage of mainstream visitors, but the gay presence is nonetheless felt more here than in any other city south of P-Town.

With a cast that includes Gilbert Baker playing himself, the film might be of interest to members of the G&L community who have never visited. It's a fine little docu that focuses on the unraveling of a 1¼ mile long Rainbow Flag along the length of Duval Street, linking the Atlantic with the Gulf of Mexico. This film was shot in 2003, marking the 25th anniversary of the creation of the flag by Baker. (Call him Betsy Ross).

The docu is mainly a celebration of the little island and the people who live there. It was done with a kind, somewhat sentimental view—not a hard-nosed approach.

Despite the implications of this documentary, Key West is not universally permeated with love and understanding. There is bigotry, prejudice, and stupidity here, like anywhere else. But its level of tolerance is greater than anywhere else in Florida, with the possible exception of South Beach and the Lauderdale area.

WHAT THE CRITICS SAID
"The most important part of this documentary was seeing Gilbert Baker, the inventor of the rainbow flag. Like a reptile who lays an egg and moves on, I had only known that a veteran made the rainbow flag one day. I didn't know he was queeny and very invested in gay rights. It is great to see a middle-aged San Francisco denizen alive when so many of his peers have passed away due to the epidemic."
Jeffrey Mingo

The Libertine

(2004)

Depp and Debauchery in 17th Century England

It was perfect casting for Laurence Dunmore to put Johnny Depp in the role of John Wilmot (1647-80), the second Earl of Rochester who self-destructed with terrifying velocity. He was also one of England's most notorious bisexuals, although  Dunmore shies away from portraying the homosexual side of the dissipated rake. He died at the age of 33 (same as Jesus) from the ravages of syphilis (the sores vividly seen on Depp's face) and from chronic drunkenness.

There were reports of a passionate kiss between Depp as the debauched poet and the character's male lover, but, alas, this lip-lock didn't make the final cut—and the film is much less than what it could have been.

Gay men, being among the most sophisticated and tolerant of all movie-goers, would have preferred the original version of the naughty Miramax movie. The MPAA was so scandalized by "the graphic sexuality and nudity" in the original version that its ratings board hit it with an NC-17, which meant that many newspapers wouldn't carry ads for the randy film. Sitting on a shelf for almost a year, it was "sanitized" to earn itself an R-rating. Even so, a poster shows Depp—known in Hollywood as "Donkey Dong"—being pleasured by actress Samantha Morton.

This is a dark and dreary film—yes, Dunmore insists on showing the mudholes in which the booted feet of the 17th century landed. Even the rats are filmed. Dialogue is often mumbled and very hard to understand, even for those to whom English is a first language.

Depp, as the rake, continues a film tradition launched with Philip Kaufman's *2000 Quills* (the story of the Marquis de Sade), in depicting history's most debauched literary figures.

The grainy images of the film appear to have been shot in candlelight, but perhaps this is appropriate to the 17th century. Instead of an arresting biographical drama, this film emerges somewhat as a Gothic horror movie.

Love Sick

(*Legaturi Bolnaviciose*; 2006)

Lesbians from Transylvania

This film from Transylvania does not feature Count Dracula, but two romantic Romanian college students who embark on a sapphic affair. In case you care, the  drama was entitled *Legaturi Bolnaviciose* in Romania when it was released there by director Tudor Giurgiu.

To the world, Alex (Ioana Barbu) and Kiki (Maria Popistasu) are just good friends. They met on their first day at college and immediately fell for each other.

There's an incest theme here too, although it is handled rather matter-of-factly. Kiki and Sandu (Tudor Chirila) are sister and brother—and nighttime lovers as well. The relationship with the older brother is never completely spelled out, but he acts like a jealous boyfriend with Alex—and because of the attraction of the two women for each other, he has reason enough to be jealous.

WHAT THE CRITICS SAID

"The two girls are polar opposites. Alex, from the countryside, is quiet and studious, eager to make her parents proud; Kiki, from Bucharest itself, is always ready to put fun (including smooching) above books. But there's a perceptible attraction between the two that comes across with very little sex shown onscreen."
Derek Elley, *Variety*

"The tag line for *Love Sick* is, 'It may look sick, but it's deep and it hurts.' So my big dilemma is: are they equating incest with homosexuality? Is there an underlying subtext that Kiki's relationships with Alex and Sandu are equally 'sick'?"
www.moviepie.com

Loving Annabelle

(2006)

One Student, One Teacher, One Secret

This film was inspired by the once-notorious *Maedchen in Uniform*, a German classic released in 1931 and dealing with student-teacher love. This remake of that classic is a soft-core lesbian sexual fantasy, the work of scripter-director Katherine Brooks. It relates the story of a Catholic boarding school teacher, Simone Bradley (Diane Gaidry), who has an affair with a female student, Annabelle (Erin Kelly).

The pushy 17-year-old Annabelle pursues her teacher (a 30-something-year-old) with the result being that the teacher falls for her. But after they acquiesce to their lusts, the lesbian relationship is revealed—and Simone is arrested.

WHAT THE CRITICS SAID
"Climatic bliss is interrupted by tragic intervention of gossips, prudes and police. Gauzy lensing, nubiles lounging in lingerie, and some high-drama moments verging on unintentional camp keep slick but silly item well removed from any semblance of real life."
Dennis Harvey, *Variety*

"The result is a disappointing, choppy, dimly lit and entirely by-the-numbers hybrid of a bad soap opera, a cheesy lesbian romance novel and any number of movies set in that clichéd hot-bed of same-sex action: The all-girls' high school."
www.moviepie.com

"*Loving Anabelle* vacillates between rosy-tinted fantasy romance, soft-core titillation, and serious drama, and it never finds a home in any of those places."
Johnny Web (Uncle Scoopy)

Make the Yuletide Gay

(2009)

Now We Don Our Gay Apparel

Rob Williams, the scripter and helmer, has emerged with a PG-rated gay holiday flick. The jokes are corny, and the plot formulaic, but it's mildly amusing as you cuddle on the sofa by the Christmas tree with your year-round Santa.

Gustav (Gunn) Gunderseon (Keith Jordan) is an out college student, but not to his Midwestern parents (Derek Long and Kelly Keaton). He has to shed his gay apparel and crawl back into his old duds, and into the closet, as he sets out for Christmas with Mom and Pa, who plan to set him up with his high school sweetheart, Abby (Hallee Hirsh).

Gunn has to kiss his boyfriend Nathan (Adamo Ruggiero) goodbye and head home. When Nathan goes to visit his own parents, he finds they have gone on a cruise through the Holy Land. Nathan then decides to surprise Gunn by showing up on his doorstep as a treat from Santa. In Wisconsin, he learns that Gunn's parents think their son is straight—not a ho ho homo.

Obviously the plot will spin out of control at this point, especially when Nathan gets bored with sleeping alone in his bunk bed.

At one point Nathan tells Gunn, "You're 22 years old." One BF thinks the other BF should come out to his parents.

WHAT THE CRITICS SAID
"Other than a short cameo by Alison Arngrim (the great Nelie Oleson) as a bitchy neighbor, little of interest happens until the inevitable revelation. While Ruggiero is relaxed and excellent in his role, everyone else comes across as an inauthentic caricature, and that prevents any authentic emotion from coming through. In this, his fourth feature, Rob Williams once again keeps things relatively low key, at least in comparison to other movies in the same genre. That's sort of admirable but also sort of risky. A story needs some drama, even when it's as light and easy-going as this one."
Dom Willmott

A dynamic duo, Michael D. Akers, the helmer and co-scripter, and Sandon Berg (writer and co-star), released this spoof on gay marriage and reality TV, not that the latter needs any spoofing. The couple also produced *Gone, But Not Forgotten.*

Call this one a "mockumentary." Straight guy Malcolm Caulfield (Rick Federman, a recurring actor on *Passions*) is about to be cut off by his rich parents.

As an aspiring actor, he figures his best option is to go on a reality show where he could make a million dollars. The catch is he has to pretend to be gay and has to marry another man.

His "husband" shows up, Spencer Finch (Sandon Berg), a backwoods rube whose family eats possum. The most hilarious moments come when the parents of the two grooms come together. At least the rednecks are used to inter-family marriages, but not gay ones. The question the film asks is, "Can a 'gay for pay' groom handle the pressures of gay marriage?"

Expect a lot of punch lines about fags and backwoods hicks.

WHAT THE CRITICS SAID
"The world is full of gay stereotypes, and I didn't buy the ones offered here. *Matrimonium* proves that real life is stranger than fiction, and movies can be a sad substitute for reality. When art stoops to the lows of broadcast television and broad stereotypes, it hacks at its own medium. Some people may find a laugh or two here, but I felt the movie was lacking any soul. But here's to hoping the filmmakers get it right next time. At least they had a good idea, and they're trying. I give them an 'E' for effort."
Anonymous

This film, shot in South Africa, will introduce you to one of the most outrageous characters you'll ever meet—the notorious Granny Lee, who was also known as Granny Con, Queen Cobra, and the White Queen of Africa. The film begins with her death at the age of 81 in a car crash and then flashes back.

Granny was actually a South African black man (Du Plooy) who lived most of his adult life as a white woman. Although such a deception would be controversial in any society, under the repressive Apartheid of South Africa at the time, his "deception" took on larger, in some cases, legal implications than they'd have had in, say, the U.S. or Canada. Using one of the techniques later made famous by Michael Jackson, he got away with his charade because his skin had been lightened by vitiligo, a chronic disorder that causes depigmentation in patches of skin.

In this 52-minute docu, Granny Lee lives again in re-creations of her life in which actress Ruth Barter plays the disco diva. Granny lived life on the edge, and attracted a number of young male admirers, and she also openly defied the repressive Apartheid regime of the time.

Luiz DeBarros both helmed and scripted the outrageous camp of this unusual docu that includes a gruesome reconstruction of the fatal accident and even a creepy audio message Granny Lee recorded for his/her own funeral.

WHAT THE CRITICS SAID
"Sometimes moving and always outrageous, Granny Lee's life was obviously much more colorful than this slightly timid film."
Rich Cline

Middle Sexes

(2005)

Gore Vidal's Take on Hermaphrodites

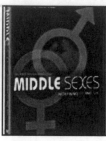

First, let's get one thing "straight": We know that the word, hermaphrodites, is yesterday's news. The newly emerged term, and the only politically correct one, is "intersexuals," which is a lot easier to pronounce and to spell.

We don't have a clue as to why America's leading gay author, Mr. Vidal, looking more and more like "the oldest man in the U.S. Senate," a position he never—much to our regret—obtained, should lend his distinguished voice to narrating this sensationalist docu by Antony Thomas. But, for whatever reason, Vidal lends his voice to a world tour of intersexuals, transvestites, and transsexuals, among other categories.

The film, which had its premiere on HBO in December of 2005, was written by vet docu helmer, Antony Thomas, a native of South Africa, who has created such shows as the 1999 *A Question of Miracles.*

The premiere showing of *Middle Sexes* came at the same time that two movies about fictional transgendered people, opened across America: *Breakfast on Pluto* and *Transamerica.* These films followed such dramatic flicks—based on true stories—as *Boys Don't Cry* and Showtime's Emmy-nominated *Soldier's Girl.*

The cast of characters includes an eight-year-old boy, Noah, who is shown dancing and raving about acting and fashion. Does he possess "the soul of a girl?" The decision of his parents is to love him unconditionally despite the negative scrutiny. In India, a man undergoes a sex change to become a *hijra* (we used to call them eunuchs). These people are traditionally accepted in society as a "third sex," having special magical and intuitive powers.

In Thailand, beautiful "lady-boys" are popular as models and cabaret performers. They are both transsexual and transvestite. Many men—often handsome, virile, young ones—seek out these lady-boys for sexual pleasure, as many of them are said to be very skilled in fellatio and as bottoms.

The Mostly Unfabulous Social Life of Ethan Green

(2005)

Cheerful but Stereotypical Sitcom

Ethan (Daniel Letterle) is presented as a self-absorbed twerp in this comedy/romance directed by George Bamber and based on a screenplay by David Vernon.

Ethan is in love with Kyle (Diego Serrano), a former big league ballplayer who has emerged from the closet. To complicate matters, a former boyfriend, Leo Worth (David Monahan), is attempting to sell the house in which Ethan resides.

If he doesn't want to be homeless, Ethan has to sabotage the house sale. To do that, he enlists the help of Sunny Deal (a real estate agent from hell) and Punch (Dean Shelton), a teenage sex machine.

A lot of supporting players give the "stars" competition, especially Meredith Baxter as Harper Green, Ethan's mother, a planner of gay weddings.

The film is bright at times, even a bit cheerful, and always predictable.

WHAT THE CRITICS SAID
"*The Mostly Unfabulous Social Life of Ethan Green* is a frothy lark with a decided sense of the outrageous, sincere affection for its characters and their romantic plights. Based on the comic strip by Eric Orner, pic may be so aggressively gay as to limit its appeal even among intended auds."
John Anderson, *Variety*

"A gay romantic comedy that's as shallow as its hetero Hollywood templates, *The Mostly Unfabulous Social Life of Ethan Green* is an adaptation of a long-running comic strip. But *Sin City* this ain't: there's zero artistry here, just a bunch of sketchy stereotypes being put through their sitcom-level paces by an apparently indifferent director."
Adam Nayman

Mr. Leather

(2004)

Orphans, You May Find Daddy Yet

This 95-minute docu revolves around modern-day Leathermen and leather competitions, following nine contestants in a Mr. L.A. Leather Contest. It delves beneath the hide of the leather scene, revealing its manly yet (surprisingly) sweet-natured devotees—that is, in many cases.

Helmer Jason Garrett's debut feature is a journey into the leather subculture, exposing the dreams, hopes, and conceits of guys in leather, including their kinks, sense of sexual freedom, and brotherly bonding.

With all the whips, chains, chaps, harnesses, and jock straps, the contest isn't the Miss America pageant. Some S&M contestants talk of their fondness for flagellation.

WHAT THE CRITICS SAID
"Basically, the film seems to exist to validate a marginalized minority—which is exactly what the Mr. Leather contests are doing. What's a bit peculiar is how seriously all these guys take the competition. There is no sense of irony at all here, despite an edge of campy excess that surrounds the entire event. Yes, leather is a legitimate fetish that adds to the diversity of society. But it's also just a bit of racy fun for those who find it a turn-on. So, laugh about it. Because for the rest of us it seems rather comical, really."
Rich Cline

"Thanks to the human-interest information provided by the filmmakers, I understood why the judges in this contest arrived at their final conclusions. What came through was the degree to which this "marginalized community" (the filmmaker's words) were committed to selecting pageant winners who would most articulately and most authentically represent the values of the leather community to America at large. Now if only I'd been invited to the filmmakers' after-party......"
Jacques Pepin

Naked Boys Singing

(2007)

Nude Dudes with Vocal Training

This is the filmed version of the "full monty" stage musical that has run for so many years off Broadway it's a virtual institution. Featured are 10 buff guys who show it all—no opera glasses needed here as in the theatrical performance.

From its opening number "Gratuitous Nudity," the viewer knows what awaits him. We go on a whirlwind tour exploring such themes as masturbation, circumcision, and even "the locker room experience." "Fight the urge" takes the viewer into the high school locker room where an unwanted erection could spell an Outing.

Only one song, an ode to actor Robert Mitchum, is clothed. The numbers are by various composers and lyricists, the score evoking the sound of the 70s and 80s.

There's also a cute fugue composed solely of different words for the male member, as well as Kevin Stea's saucy "Naked Maid."

For the DVD viewer, it's like inviting a bevy of ten gorgeous, talented, and intelligent men into your living room for fun and games. No show on or off Broadway has a more accurate title than this chunk of male burlesque. Call it a film about nude dudes.

This musical celebration of the male physique was directed by Troy Christian and Robert Schrock, and was shot on video before a live audience.

Naked Boys Singing is bawdy, outrageous entertainment, poking fun at the stuffy conventions of the Broadway musical theater.

WHAT THE CRITICS SAID
"It's important to note that most of the songs are performed completely in the buff, and that's no small accomplishment. Even if one rejects the music on a purely personal taste level, there has to be a hefty amount of respect paid to the actors for their skills executing elaborate dance choreography while their bits and pieces sway two moves behind."
Brian Orndorf

Naked Fame

(2004)

The Hard Road from Porn to Pop

Former Colt model and porn star, Colton Ford, made it big (a play on words, of course) in skin flicks. At the opening of this documentary/biography, as he's working nude at his home computer, he turns around for a full monty shot. And if you haven't already caught one of Colton's gay male porn flicks, you'll soon grasp one of the reasons for his success in porn. Directed by Christopher Long, this 82-minute film might have been entitled: *A Star Isn't Born*.

Approaching the big Four-O, Colton faces a career dilemma: His pecs and glutes are still firm but that goatee has turned salt and pepper. His dick's still as formidable as ever, but the muscle-bound star of 11 hard-core flicks must inevitably face a career change. He wants to go back to his original dream of becoming a singer.

ChiChi LaRue (playing himself—or is it herself?—in the film) very accurately suggests how difficult the road will be for Colton.

As one viewer commented, "As a trained vocalist with a sizable range, Mr. Ford wants fans to love him for his larynx and leave the rest of him alone."

Those pecs, glutes, and a big dick got him into porn. But Colton soon discovers that you just can't fly from Los Angeles to New York and come back with a big record contract.

In film all he had to do was walk into a gym or a gay bar and get someone within minutes to go down on his dick. Not so in the music world. His father in the film and in life suggests that Colton might advance himself much quicker in the music world if he allowed his dick to be sucked by the right promoters.

To complicate matters, Colton has a live-in lover. He's another porn star, Blake Harper, who also plays himself. Devotees of Blake have seen him hard, ready, and pumping in some 60 skin flicks. Also aging, Blake is fed up with the seedy skin industry. At their "love and raw hotel," their every sexual indulgence is recorded by ceiling-mounted cameras for the viewing pleasure of online voyeurs.

Nina's Heavenly Delights

(2006)

Part Foodie Fest, Part Lesbian Romance

If you like lesbian love combined with chicken shakuti, this is your simmering pot of curry, the creation of helmer Pratibha Parmar, who co-authored the script with Andrea Gibb. It's a refreshing comedy about complex identities.

In a nutshell, it tells of a lesbian daughter of a Scottish-Indian family, who returns home to Glasgow to help put the family restaurant back on its feet. While on Scottish soil, she romances an old schoolmate and practices her Bollywood moves.

The director manages to incorporate a trio of cross-cultural romances—gay, lesbian, and straight—everything headed to a televised curry competition. As was noted by viewers, the food is hotter than the implied sex.

Indo-Scottish Nina Shah (Shelley Conn) dumped her GF Sanjay (Raji James) when she left Glasgow three years previously. But the gas burner might light up again.

Her departed father's curry palace may be lost to rivals unless Nina wins the "Best of the West" cooking finale. Nina and her fellow chef Lisa (Laura Fraser), in the words of *Variety*, "are soon using their tongues on more than recipes."

The movie is enlivened by silly musical numbers, compliments of Bobbi (Ronny Jhutti), Nina's flamboyant Bollywood-obsessed drag queen friend.

Nina gets inspiration from the ghost of her dead father (we kid you not). He offers "follow-your-heart" chestnuts.

Each member of Nina's family has a secret—her brother (Atta Yaqub); her mother (Veena Sood), and even her younger sister (Zoe Henretty). The inevitable complications follow.

But, as one viewer pointed out, "This harmless celebration of multi-culturalism is not exactly *My Beautiful Laundrette*."

Nine Lives

(2004)

A Totally Gay *La Ronde*

The writer/actor Michael Kearns was not content to have immortalized himself in that watershed gay porn film, *L.A. Tool and Die*. He also wrote a play, *Complications*, which helmer Dean Howell turned into a screenplay with a large cast, starring eight guys and one woman in this film of erotic candor where men are stripped emotionally and physically for the camera's eye.

Kearns himself appears in the star part of Ronnie. Sex is the glue that binds nine monologues in which stories of the gay lifestyle are revealed, as well as issues associated with infidelity, drug use, sex addiction, aging, and the state of being HIV+.

In the role of Ronnie, Kearns is middle aged and living in West Hollywood, having lost one lover on the rice paddies of Vietnam and two more to AIDS. Tired of burying his husbands, he wants to party.

By chance, he encounters a hunky Latino pool cleaner, Carlos (Eric Dean). Revelatory words coming from Carlos include "Fuck me, daddy!"

Carlos also meets and sleeps with (on an individual basis) a gay couple, Corey (Steve Callahan) and Daniel (Nick Salamone). Is their relationship dysfunctional? We'd say so. Of the two, Corey is the nice guy, Daniel the shithead.

A closeted TV writer and racist on the side, Daniel rents Bo (John Ganun), a hustler with a six pack of abs.

Carrying on with these microcosms of gay life, the plot thickens as Bo himself picks up Mikey (Dennis Christopher) for hot fuck sessions. Mikey, it turns out, is a drug dealer, who makes a delivery to James (Dean Howell) who begs him for sex.

After having Mikey, James is seen in a steamy bathhouse where he encounters Ralph (William Christian), who is married to Lisa (Debra Wilson). She's the one woman we referred to. Ralph obviously is leading a secret life.

This film delivers a lot of hot sex, while sending messages about shame, self-love, and the dangers of barebacking.

November Son

(2008)

Gay Gore & a Lot More

The helmer and scripter of *November Son*, Jason Paul Collum, had an original dream film which was released as *October Moon* in 2004. It was the tale of a closet case who fell real big for his sexy male boss. *November Son*, more or less, could be called a sequel.

The plot, as stated by B+B Productions, gets a bit murky. See if you can follow along.

It's been nearly two years since an obsessive love destroyed not only the lives of three young men, but also those they left behind. Emily Hamilton (Judith O'Dea) tries to cope with not only the loss of her son Elliot (Jerold Howard), but also the guilt of possibly driving him down his obsessive, murderous path.

Nancy (Brinke Stevens) is desperate to find the love, friendship and support of a man similar to Corin (Sean Michael Lambrecht). Maggie (Darcey Vanderhoef) desires the companionship of a best friend, someone to be her confidante in the same vein as Jake (Jeff Dylan Graham). And Marti (Tina Ona Paukstelis) has deteriorated into a shell of a human being, harboring a secret so deeply connected to those in Elliot's life that she has had no choice but to run from it for the last two years.

Enter Eli (Sacha Sacket) and George (Lloyd Pedersen), two men who have become a part of these women's lives, and who hold the keys to saving them from their misery . . . or perhaps creating it. The men have a shared secret about their own pasts which will force the women to confront their own fears and guilt over the events which have already destroyed them. When the truth comes out, the terror once again begins as each of the women and both men are tossed into scenario after scenario of bloodshed, torture and the ultimate hell of death, mutilation and destruction. Who is the *November Son*, and what secrets does his own past hold that will either leave these women saved . . . or buried six feet under?

One to Another

(*Chacun sa nuit;* 2006)

Nudity In the First Degree

Both the female lead and the young men in this French drama are the epitome of Gallic beauty. And they don't mind showing you the full monty. Filmmakers Pascal Arnold and Jean-Marc Barr insist their actors bare it all.

Pierre (Arthur Dupont) and Lucie (Lizzie Brocheré) are brother and sister engaged in an incestuous relationship. They lie around naked, with matching strawberry birthmarks prominently displayed on their cheek-to-cheek posteriors.

Pierre doesn't just have sex with his sister. He seems to live for sex—and sometimes gets paid for it. He also has sex with other boys, or with older men.

The siblings hang out with three other male beauties—Nicolas Nollet, Guillaume Baché, and Pierre Perrier. None of these young men seems to have reservations about stripping down or bed-hopping.

Then one sad day, Pierre (the Dupont character) is found murdered in a field. Lucie, becoming a kind of Nancy Drew, sets out to find his killer, even if it means bedding a man if it will help her solve the mystery of her brother's death.

WHAT THE CRITICS SAID
"Only the French would make a movie like this. You'll enjoy it if you turn off your brain and concentrate on the eye candy."
V.A. Musetto, *New York Post*

"Pascal Arnold and Jean-Marc Barr's expedition into the outer limits of narcissistic sexuality, *One to Another*, loosely wraps itself around a true crime story so it can weave suspense through its tableaux of naked adolescents frolicking under the sun. But uneven thesping, assorted inanities, and a narrow focus turn the potentially fascinating tale into a bland, perverse round-robin of teen angst."
Ronnie Scheib, *Variety*

Partners

(1982)

Two Cops: One Gay, One Straight

"Watch it and wince!" asserted one viewer. Ryan O'Neal (Sergeant Benson) plays a straight detective who teams up with an effeminate, in-the-closet desk cop, John Hurt (Kerwin). They go undercover as gay lovers to investigate a serial killer. Some gays considered *Partners* the most offensive gay movie ever made. Others loved it. You decide.

O'Neal is a macho, womanizing cop who can barely tolerate his fey partner, Hurt, who plays it blandly asexual, not posing any potential threat for the removal of the shorty short shorts O'Neal wears in the film.

As undercover agents, the two men have to be flamboyant enough to attract the attention of the serial killer. O'Neal's character finds this rather disturbing. The question the movie asks, "Can an uptight straight and a mousey gay form a meaningful relationship?" The film isn't as anti-gay as some have claimed. In the end, the two men not only nab the killer but end up with newfound respect for each other.

As part of their gay disguise, the two cops have a lavender Volkswagen, a lavender jogging outfit for Hurt, and tight-fitting jeans and tank tops for O'Neal. They also live in an apartment house populated almost exclusively by homosexuals.

WHAT THE CRITICS SAID
"Mr. Hurt (*The Elephant Man*) has an especially unhappy time, being required to behave so ineffectually that he confirms all of the most blatant stereotypes about limp-wristedness. The only way this fellow could have gotten on the Los Angeles police force is if his mom had been the commissioner. Mr. O'Neal, a good, robust comedian, makes Benson's discomfort often amusing, but the spirit of the film is mangy and foolish. If it had the courage of its clichés, it would end—like all similar heterosexual comedies—with the two mismatched leads falling in love and living happily ever after."
Vincent Canby, *The New York Times*

The Pervert's Guide to Cinema

(2006)

But Who's the Pervert?

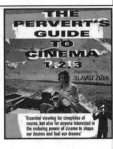

First, let's dispense with the title. This is not a film review of movies dealing with sexual perversion. As director Sophie Fiennes (sister of Ralph and Joseph) explained it, "The title is something of a McGuffin, just a way to get you into this network."

So be it. All serious cinephiles will want to take this one in, whether they are straight, gay, bi, lesbian, or anything in transition.

The director takes us on an exhilarating ride through some of the greatest movies ever made, as we explore the works of Hitchcock, Lynch, Tarkovsky, and others.

The star of the film is the bearded, rather unkempt looking Slovenian philosopher, Slavoj Zizek. Fiennes gives Zizek ample time to expound on his more extravagant theories.

To make the docu visually intriguing, Zizek turns up appearing to actually be on the sets of the movies he's discussing. We see him in a rowboat on Bodega Bay watching the invasion of Hitchcock's *The Birds*; again tiptoeing in and around rooms #771 and #773 of the former Jack Tar Hotel in San Francisco deconstructing the toilet scene in Francis Ford Coppola's *The Conversation*; in the Bates basement in *Psycho*; and perched on the corner of Dorothy's couch in David Lynch's *Blue Velvet*. Zizek applies a Freudian theory to his view of films, and you may not always buy his philosophy. Do you think, for example, that the moral of *Vertigo* is "the only good woman is a dead woman?"

WHAT THE CRITICS SAID
"A virtuoso marriage of image and thought, *The Pervert's Guide to Cinema* is a propulsive, stream-of-consciousness sprint through the movie-projector mind of Slovenian philosopher and psychoanalyst Slavoj Zizek, who uses clean and properly framed clips from some 43 mostly high-profile films to illustrate his ideas on sexuality, subjectivity and that old standby, fantasy vs. reality."
Eddie Cockrell, *Variety*

Poison

(1991)

Wake Up and Smell Jean Genet's Latrine

Director Todd Hayes based his script on the writings of the gay French author, Jean Genet (1910-1986). To get inside the messy, at times psychotic brain of Genet was a daunting challenge, which Haynes may not always have met.

The film, originally named *H*; contains three separate sub-sections: *The Hero, The Horror*, and *The Homo*. It's a clever work of art, but hardly everyone's must-see movie.

The stories predictably concern sex and violence—after all, it was based on Genet.

In *Hero*, Richie, age 7, kills his father and ascends into the heavens. *The Horror* is about a researcher who isolates the essence of the human sex drive. After accidentally drinking the potion, he becomes a festering, contagious murderer. A woman who loves him tries to help him, but at her peril. Finally, *Homo* is the story of a prisoner who develops a perverse fascination with another inmate.

Poison received a small portion of its funding from the National Endowment of the Arts. This caused that Right Wing psycho, Senator Jesse Helms of North Carolina, to shit his pants. He falsely referred to *Poison* as "gay pornography."

The current DVD release includes two scenes cut from the original—one which included views of a penis and another not particularly explicit gay sex scene. Both of these, of course, were from the "Homo" episode.

WHAT THE CRITICS SAID
"Todd Haynes's *Poison* is a vision of unrelenting, febrile darkness. Its effect is like that of an especially vile infection that moves diabolically through your system, spreading fever and nausea as it goes. For Genet, his entry into the gutter realms was an attempt to achieve redemption. The universe he created was lurid, sadistic, and unabashedly homoerotic, but there was always a promise of transcendence in his descents. Haynes captures the cruel, unflinching spirit of Genet without really realizing the writer's objectives."
Hal Hinson, *Washington Post*

Poltergay

(2006)

Gay Ghosts in the Cellar

This French film is flawed but has a few laughs. It can be viewed by both straight and gay audiences. A married couple Marc (Clovis Cornillac) and Emma (Julie Depardieu) move into a spooky old mansion which they bought for a fire sale price.

Marc sets out to make the dump livable. But he begins to hear sounds, such as loud music coming from the basement in the early hours of the morning. To his surprise, he finds five homosexuals occupying his cellar.

Trouble is, he's the only one who can see these guys. These visions cause ripples in his marriage. He's suspected of being gay himself. Perhaps he's just fantasizing about five hot men in his cellar.

Other strange events begin to occur. Drawings of cocks pop up on his walls, and he finds his blue jeans neatly pressed.

All this drives Mark to a psychiatrist, who tells him that he's a closeted homosexual. In a bit of a stretch, Marc is forced to turn to his gay quintet to help him win Emma back.

Director Eric Lavaine, working from a script by Hector Cabello Reyes, certainly had his job cut out for him in this comedy/fantasy/gay thriller.

WHAT THE CRITICS SAID
"Things look clearer once a parapsychologist (Michael Duchaussoy) is called in and he, too, sees the mincing apparitions. Turns out the nocturnal revelers, killed in a freak explosion when the cellar was a gay disco, are trapped by four magic stones embedded in the house by the Templars. Cornillac and Depardieu disport themselves with tongue-in-cheek relish, but the gags aren't clever enough and most of the camp material dates from way before the Village People."
Jay Weissberg, *Variety*

Prom Queen: The Marc Hall Story

(2004)

A High School Graduation that Rocked Canada

There may come a day when a boy friend will routinely invite his BF, or a girl friend will routinely invite her GF to the senior prom. Of course, even today that happens, but it still is a hot button issue evoking almost as much right-wing rage as same-sex marriage.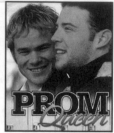

This Canadian film, helmed by John L'Ecuyer, is based on an actual incident that occurred in Ontario in 2002. The film version is set in the fictional blue collar town of Inniston.

The plot centers on Marc Hall (Aarom Ashmore), who is a popular student even though most of his classmates seem to know he is gay. Somehow he manages to avoid the inevitable harassment most gay kids face in a small town.

Trouble emerges when he invites his boyfriend Jason (Mac Fyfe) to his senior prom. Almost overnight, Marc finds himself involved in a media-covered scandal and becomes known across Canada for "stepping over the line." No longer is he struggling for his right to date, but he becomes an icon in the advancement of gay rights. Eventually, he endures a face-off with Catholic authorities.

The principal of the school Mike Shields (David Ferry) is from hell, but Marc's parents are supportive. Marie Tifjo and Paul Zabriskie shine in their roles.

WHAT THE CRITICS SAID
"Based on an actual *cause célèbre*, pic is flatter-than-flat made for tube throwback to the after-school special tradition, with its teenybopper comedy nods and socially progressive messages. Messages and staging couldn't be more elementary, as if teens couldn't grasp a more nuanced approach."
Robert Koehler, *Variety*

R.U. Invited

(2006)

Five Guys and a Sex Party

In this film, helmed and written by Israel Luna, five guys are invited to an underground sex party. Well, not really invited. There's a catch. First, to qualify for an invitation, each invitee must submit revealing, full frontal photos and go through a screening process.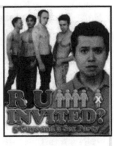

Devotees of skin will delight as the all-male quintet strip down to pose in front of the camera.

John de los Santos playing Ben wants to qualify. He's the boy-toy of Anderson (Phil Harrington), his rich sugar daddy, who doesn't seem to have many objections to his boy joining in the sex romp, where, as promised, "anything goes."

Jason (David Matherly) is no great actor, but when he strips down, all is forgiven. Jason agrees to pose for Ben's digital lens. Mondo (Gabriel Praddo), his BF (they have a relationship of six months) looks on. When both Ben and Mondo notice that Jason's dick has done a major retreat, Mondo suggests that Ben make the pecker look more impressive with a fluffing.

Charlie (Christopher Jones) is an old hand at flashing his naked jewels before the camera, but doesn't mind flapping the hang once more. This ho-hunk is "married" to a makeup artist Helen Beedd (Chase Wade), a drag queen. When she gets wind of the sex romp, she goes after her philandering stud and she gives him a thrashing.

Oscar Contreras appears as Gordy, the overweight one among the buff boys. You can't have all of them looking body perfect. He boldly bares all.

WHAT THE CRITICS SAID
"As the lads wait for the results of their nude screening pics, there's ample opportunity to chat about drugs (the jury is split as to whether poppers are an illegal substance), communication strategies (the horny quintet imagines being 'done' by numerous partners at the sex-fest as their own friends and lovers look on), and, of course, position preference...There's a hilarious scene of 'my first enema.'"
S. James Wegg

The Raspberry Reich

(2003)

Homo Love as the Highest Form of Class Struggle

Written and directed by Bruce La Bruce, *The Raspberry Reich* is a film about "radical chic," specifically the penchant of the modern Radical Left in Germany today adopting the postures and vocabulary of extreme left-wing movements of the 1970s, particularly the Red  Army Faction, also known as the Baader-Meinhoff Gang.

The movie starts off with the abduction of the film's protagonist, Patrick, by a gang of bumbling, would-be terrorists. Patrick is the son of one of the wealthiest bankers in Germany. Chaos and slapstick humor ensues when Clyde, one of the aspiring terrorists—or activists, as they prefer to call themselves—accidentally handcuffs himself to the kidnapping victim and is forced to join him in the trunk of their stolen BMW.

Unbeknownst to the rest of the gang, Clyde, whose job it is to follow Patrick and report his whereabouts to his cohorts, has already enjoyed a sexual liaison with Patrick. Even in advance of the abduction, Clyde is already planning Patrick's escape.

The gang does not know that Patrick's father disowned and disinherited him when Patrick came out as being gay, and therefore he has no value as a hostage. Nothing seems to go right for this idealistic but ineffectual gang of aspiring terrorists.

In the meantime, the leader of the Raspberry Reich, Gudrun, a charismatic young woman who has patterned herself after Gudren Ensslin, one of the main players within the Baader-Meinhoff Gang, has indoctrinated the other gang members to her cause. Gudrun, a strict devotee of Wilhelm Reich and Herbert Marcuse, believes that heterosexual monogamy is a bourgeois conceit that must be smashed in order to achieve True Revolution. To that end, she forces her straight male followers to have sex with each other to prove their mettle as authentic revolutionaries. When Holger, one of her followers, protests that he is her boyfriend, Gudrun tells him not to be ridiculous, that The Revolution is her boyfriend.

The Ritz

(1976)

A Straight Guy in a Gay NYC Bathhouse

This farce was adapted from gay playwright Terrence McNally's Broadway hit, a riotous farce that stars Jack Weston, playing Gaetano Proclo, a straight Cleveland garbage collector hiding from the Mafia in a gay New York City bathhouse. Here, he en-  counters an active steam room and a bevy of towel-clad studs. Since the onslaught of AIDS, no one shows this movie very much anymore.

On his deathbed, the father of Carmine Vespucci (Jerry Stiller) tells his son to "get Proclo." Hearing of this, Gaetano tries to flee to where the mob can't find him. A taxi delivers him to a gay bathhouse, The Ritz.

Once his main character is in the bathhouse, director Richard Lester goes wild. One of the funniest moments is when Gaetano finds himself the victim of a chubby-chaser played by Paul B. Price. He plies Weston with candy bars, pounces on him from behind potted plants, and stalks him down corridors.

Coogie Gomez (Rita Moreno) thinks Gaetano is a big-time Broadway producer, who will discover her. Moreno has some of the funniest moments in the film, playing the singer in the baths, no doubt a role modeled on Bette Midler at the Continental.

Gaetano seems rather slow catching on to what the men are doing when they disappear into those cubicles. Trouble is on the way. Is there any safe place to hide from the mob?

Weston doesn't figure on the gangland family's diversified business interests, or on the ingenuity of Weston's wife, as played by Kaye Ballard. The handsome hunk, Treat Williams, has a nice turn as Michael Brick, a half-naked detective.

WHAT THE CRITICS SAID
"To have a tolerance, or even acceptance of homosexuality doesn't rule out having an underlying physical distaste for it. Inevitably, perhaps, the camera emphasizes the physical element far more than it was emphasized on the stage. To put it bluntly, it shoves up too close—for most of us, I think—too much pale flesh."
Richard Elder, *The New York Times*

Robin's Hood

(2003)

Gay Versions of Bonnie & Clyde

Sara Millman, along with her co-scripter Khahtee V. Turner, raised the money for this low-budget pic through garage sales and the solicitation of donations on the street.

Robin (the writer, Turner herself) is a bisexual African-American woman living in a tough East Oakland ghetto. Her desire is to try to "give back and change" things in her job as a social worker. Her bosses accuse her of getting too close to her charity-based clients, mostly welfare recipients struggling with parole violations or drug addiction.

In the course of her struggles, Robin falls for Brooklyn (Clody Cates), a white French woman who's a thief with dreams of running a motorcycle repair shop.

Mesmerized by Brooklyn, Robin agrees to participate in a series of Bonnie & Clyde robberies so that she can fund much-needed community projects. In essence, Robin lives up to her namesake, Robin Hood, stealing from the rich to give to the poor.

Disaster seems inevitable as Robin plans "one last job" that predictably goes awry.

WHAT THE CRITICS SAID
"Robin is a well-rounded character; sexy, butch, French-speaking outlaw-type Brooklyn remains rather more of a romantic conceit. Thus despite decent lead perfs and chemistry, premise never quite convinces."
Dennis Harvey, *Variety*

Say Uncle

(2005)

When Is a Pedophile Not a Pedophile?

Most of us know actor Peter Paige from his portrayal of the witty, fashion-evolved Emmett on *Queer as Folk*. But whatever was he thinking when he made this inauspicious debut as a writer/director?

After his godson's parents wisely move to Japan, he develops an unhealthy obsession with children. After he loses his job as a telemarketer, he starts to hang out at playgrounds, even inviting young kids to his apartment.

He even advertises his services as a "nanny," although there are no takers. Small wonder. The Xeroxed babysitting flyers sport terrifying images of his pasty visage.

A homophobic mother (Kathy Najimy) organizes a lynch mob in Portland (Oregon) to deal with this suspicious character.

Frankly, we like Paige as the unapologetically queeny Emmett on *Queer as Folk* much better. But as David Ehrenstein asked in *The Advocate*: "How do you top *Queer as Folk*? With something even queerer, that's how."

WHAT THE CRITICS SAID
"Laughless, pointless, and downright creepy, *Say Uncle* is a would-be-black comedy about a young gay man who is wrongly suspected of being a pedophile. *Say Uncle* argues unconvincingly that Paul—an artist who rebuffs romantic approaches by a co-worker—is emotionally stunted and misunderstood because of childhood trauma. Stay away."
Lou Lumenick, *New York Post*

"You'll be begging for mercy well before the end of this self-righteous, thoroughly unsavory 'farce' about a lonely gay man who—gosh darn it—can't seem to stop getting mistaken for a pedophile. Hmmm. Do you think it could have something to do with his odd habit of playing with strangers' children in public parks?"
Scott Foundas, *Village Voice*

Serbis (Service)

(2008)

A *Ship of Fools* With Blowjobs

Award-winning director Brillante Mendoza is not the first to set his movie in a theater. *Goodbye, Dragon Inn* also focused on a dilapidated single-screen theater on its last legs.

Service is set in a shabby Filipino porno movie house. The family owners show straight porno to gay hustlers and their johns, with "service" provided in the seats. It is a film about a "labyrinth of lost and wandering lives," as one critic put it.

If you're looking for extended sex scenes, you won't find them here. Sexual encounters are hurried, and it's a buyer's market.

One of the most disgusting scenes of the movie focuses on the butt of the projectionist, who has a horrible boil on his ass. We get to see his explosive self-treatment for this affliction.

When not roaming the corridors of this porno house, the movie focuses on members of the Pineda family, who run it.

The film opens with Nayda (Jaclyn Jose), wandering the bowels of the theater looking for her mother Flora (Gina Pareno), the matriarch of the family. She has a court appearance that day, a bigamy case against her estranged husband. One of her family members is Roxanne Jewel (Roxanne Jordan), who is first seen naked in an extended sequence

WHAT THE CRITICS SAID
"Presumably Mendoza is looking to use one family's economic struggle and indifference to the sordidness around them as a metaphor for Filipino society as a whole, though his slice-of-life realism often feels more exploitative than enlightening, unlike his super Foster Child."
Jay Weissberg, *Variety*

"This is not a film most people will enjoy. Its qualities are apparent only if one appreciates cinematic style for itself. I enjoyed it because I got into Mendoza's visual use of corridors and staircases and their life rhythms. Most people will find that annoying."
Roger Ebert

Sex, Politics, & Cocktails

(2002)

Queer Eye for the Bi Guy

This is a film about the pursuit of finding someone to permanently "spoon" with. In the film, 30-year-old Sebastien Cortez (as played by both the director and writer, Julien Hernandez) is unable to tie the knot with his Prozac-loving girlfriend, 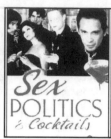 played by Gina Vetro. He turns in desperation to a friend and fag hag, Daria (Marisa Petroro), who introduces him to her mixed medley of gays. Sebastien is sexy but unsophisticated as he wanders like a deer into the headlights in this complicated morass of dubious morals and sexual politics.

Sebastien, an aspiring filmmaker, manages to get a gig filming a trio of documentaries about gay relationships. Much of the film is devoted to Sebastien recognizing the gay man staring back at him in the mirror.

The movie sends up the toxic world of the gay dating scene as uniquely lived in West Hollywood.

Along the way Sebastien meets Michael, a style snob (Seth Marcari); an anorexic piece of Eurotrash (Jonathan Zenz), and under-endowed Paulie (Alex Douglas-hopefully not typecast). These gay belles are known for two things: making margaritas that would have pleased Papa Hemingway and hitting on any hot man Daria introduces them to.

We're treated—if that's the right word—to Sebastien having anonymous gay bathroom sex. One scene, which might have been deleted, is a sexual encounter with a banana that only leads to a hospital emergency room.

WHAT THE CRITICS SAID
"Novice-writer-director Julian Hernandez plays Sebastien, a 'straight' director hired to chronicle L.A.'s gay-dating scene. By the time he finishes documenting all the fun other guys are having, of course, he's desperate to join in. Enthusiastic performances help, but without a logical script or confident direction, the fizz very quickly goes flat."
Elizabeth Weitzman

She's the Man

(2006)

A Bizarre Spin on *Twelfth Night*

When she learns that her high school is dropping its girls' soccer program, she-jock Viola Hastings (Amanda Bynes) decides to join the boys' team. And how does she do that? She disguises herself as her "twin" brother, Sebastian (James Kirk).  She's aided by her stylist sidekick, Paul (Jonathan Sadowski, a dead ringer for Jude Law), who helps her butch it up. The film's original working title was *Walk Like a Man, Talk Like a Man.*

Her befuddled teammate is Duke (Channing Tatum), who's a real hunk. He wants Olivia (Laura Ramsey), a fellow schoolmate. But Olivia seems attracted to Sebastian/Viola, who develops a crush on Duke because he speaks with such sensitivity about women.

Stated another way, Duke wants Olivia who likes Sebastian who is really Viola whose brother is dating Monique (Alexandra Breckenridge), so she hates Olivia who's with Duke to make Sebastian jealous who is really Viola who's crushing on Duke who thinks she's a guy.

If this complicated plot sounds vaguely familiar, it's loosely based on Shakespeare's gender-bending *Twelfth Night*.

Bynes, of course, is the TV star of *What I Like About You.* Elizabeth Weitzman of the *New York Daily News* got it right when she wrote: "As the Bard himself observed, 'some are born great, some achieve greatness and some have greatness thrust upon 'em.' Others should probably head back to TV, where greatness is optional." Or, put another way, he's a she and no great shakes."

WHAT THE CRITICS SAID
"Fickman mostly soft-pedals the play's homosexual panic, generating a comedy that lacks the verbal sophistication of its source and the sexual sophistication of its target audiences."
J.R. Jones, *Chicago Reader*

Show Me

(2004)

Squeegee Kids as Kidnappers

On our Gaydar, this Canadian film would rank two out of a possible ten. Directed and written by Cassandra Nicolaou, it stars two squeegee kids, Kenna (Katharine Isabelle of *Ginger Snaps*) and Jack (Kett Turton). They barge into the luxury car of yuppie Sarah (Michelle Nolden), taking her hostage and forcing her to drive to an isolated cottage where mind games, violence, and sexual tension flow.

In the end, Sarah is forced to make a choice—between being rescued or taking a chance on rescuing Jenna and Jackson herself.

WHAT THE CRITICS SAID

"You'd think a movie about a babelicious yuppie (Michelle Nolden) forced at knife point to take two squeegee kids (Kett Turton and Katharine Isabelle, now way past her disaffected teen prime) to her cottage would be sleazy-creepy mindless fun. You're wrong. *Show Me* takes itself seriously in that inimitably dull, Canadian-cinema way. All three characters are grimly unlikable, and novice filmmaker Nicolaou doesn't know what to do with them at the cottage except explore their dark, irrelevant secrets. It's one thing to exploit the revelation of a character's homosexuality as a plot point; it's another to pull back from a promised threesome. If a movie's going to be offensive, it should at least be that way on purpose."
Kim Linekin

"The lesbian angle gives *Show Me* (awful title) an interesting spin, but for the most part this is a rehash of similar films like *Knife in the Water* and its indie remake, *Kaaterskill Falls*, though the stakes feel lower and the tension rarely ratchets up. Too much of *Show Me* revolves around some extremely unlikely sexual shenanigans, and though these characters are fun to watch over the course of their escapade, it's hard to believe any of this would ever really go down this way in the real world."
Christopher Null

Sideline Secrets

(2004)

Romance, Suspense, & Secrets

This is far from the innocent film it first appears to be. As it unfolds, there is a bevy of "goodies" awaiting us—child molestation, murder, street hustling, kidnapped boys, lesbianism. There is also a lot of frontal nudity among boys who look barely legal, but it's strangely not erotic, incapable of producing a hard-on even in somebody called "Ever Ready."

Stephen Vasquez both directed and co-scripted this feature film with help from another writer, James Townsend, who also plays the lead as a blond high schooler in the flick, Devon Tyler. As the film begins, Devon seemingly has the perfect life. A girlfriend, middle-class parents, including a stepfather who is a psychologist. Devon is about to graduate at the top of his class, but something is wrong. Perhaps it's the far and distant longing reflected in his eyes.

As he becomes more and more aware of his sexual identity, his girlfriend grows more overbearing. The viewer already knows that they were meant to be "sisters," not male/female lovers.

His mother seems to have genuine love for her son, and perhaps his stepfather does too, but not of the socially acceptable kind. Could there possibly be a hidden camera in Devon's bedroom, photographing his frequent masturbation?

A new boy, Brian (Alex Wilson), enters the picture. He's even handsomer than the rather bland Devon and has far more charm and personal magnetism. Devon's life begins to unravel, as an affair develops between the two young men.

For a psychologist, the stepfather doesn't have much cool and kicks Devon out of the house when he learns of his homosexuality. What a hypocrite. As the viewer begins to suspect, the psychologist is not adverse to a little white boy ass from time to time.

The melodrama, especially the violent conclusion, unfolds without conviction.

Ski Trip

(2004)

Black & Latino Gays Invade the Catskills

It's no doubt true that Maurice Jamal, its helmer and scripter, will never produce his own version of *Citizen Kane*, to judge by this so-called romance film.

Our hero, Corey Brown (Jamal himself), has reached the big 3-0. He's also been dumped by his boyfriend. Time to get out of Dodge, which in this case is actually Gotham.

To escape his problems, including a comic book career and finances taking a nose-dive, he joins friends for a ski trip without skis.

The crew of friends is both motley and riddled with gay stereotypes. There's the mincing drag queen (Daren Fleming); a so-called best friend pining for Corey (John Rankin), and, of course, an acerbic lesbian (Cassandra Cruz). Throw in a bitchy hottie (Nathan Hale), and the lesbian's pickup girlfriend, who is deaf, and you've got a gay road trip.

It's party time in the Catskills. The film drew some strong attacks from its viewers, including one that was almost rabid. Wrote one non-fan: "Channel surfing and caught this on LOGO. It was one of those have to watch this because it's so horribly bad moments, like *Roadhouse* without the joy. The writing is atrocious; completely inane, and the acting is throw-up-in-your-mouth bad."

WHAT THE CRITICS SAID
"Deliberately over-the-top laffer gathers a gaggle of dressed-for-the-art black and Latino gay stereotypes, parades them around Gotham, then hustles them to a cabin in the Catskills for a game of truth. Pic's characters are all play-acting to cover their insecurities, and humor in Jamal's debut outing never feels reductive. Unfortunately, it's not especially funny either—aside from Jamal himself, few of the thesps have the wherewithal to suggest much substance beneath the madcap posturing."
Ronnie Scheib, *Variety*

Slutty Summer

(2004)

The Horny, Hunk-Infested Waters of NYC

This is a movie about a bevy of humpy men craving for sex. A drama/comedy, *Slutty Summer* (it's not all that slutty) tells the story of Markus (played by Casper Andreas) who returns home to find his boyfriend of four years naked with another man. Breaking off the relationship, Markus descends on New York's Chelsea district, where he takes a job as a waiter at a swinging hotspot.

Here Markus meets a cast of colorful characters, including lascivious Luke (Jesse Archer), who believes that sleeping around is the best cure for heartbreak. Marilyn (Virginia Bryan) wows Markus with her "dating commandments," and Peter (Jeffrey Christopher Todd), who claims he is holding out for the real deal. Predictably, Markus falls for a guy who turns out to be gorgeous model Tyler (Jamie Hsatchett), who doesn't "do relationships." There is brief nudity, explicit language, and sexual situations.

WHAT THE CRITICS SAID
"Tries to be a gay version of *Sex and the City*, which was pretty gay to begin with."
Lou Lumenick, *New York Post*

"First-time Casper Andreas approaches the subject with the subtlety of a wrecking ball."
Matt Singer, *Village Voice*

"The film is a labor of love for Casper Andreas, who wrote, directed, and starred in this first feature. For the actors he has chosen, it's a labor of lust, with copious necking and grappling required. For the audience, it's just labor."
Ned Martel, *The New York Times*

"While the filmmaker raises some interesting issues and captures his chosen milieu with an entertaining degree of verisimilitude, the film lacks the wit necessary to compensate for its stereotypical characterizations and predictable plot elements. Although some of the dialogue, which concentrates all too heavily on sexual themes, is amusing in a ribald way, you can feel the strain of both cast and screenplay trying too hard to be outrageous and titillating."
Frank Scheck, *Hollywood Reporter*

Staircase

(1969)

Rex Harrison and Richard Burton Play It Gay

When *Staircase* was released, some movie critics said it was a heterosexual revenge for Edward Albee's *Who's Afraid of Virginia Woolf?*

We may never know why director Stanley Donen (*Singin' in the Rain*) was attracted to this weak script by Charles Dyer, based on Dyer's own play. That he got two of the leading stars of British theater, Rex Harrison as Charles Dyer and Richard Burton as Harry Leeds, to play gay is yet another puzzle.

Unlike Harrison, Burton in real life was not a homophobe. He once told *People* magazine: "Perhaps most actors are latent homosexuals, and we cover it with drink. I was once a homosexual, but it didn't work."

Charles and Harry have been living together for nearly 20 years. Both earn a living as hairdressers in the West End of London, but they don't really like each other. Both men, however, care deeply for their mothers.

One of Harrison's character's big concerns involves his recent arrest for soliciting in drag.

WHAT THE CRITICS SAID
"We're not asked to watch a movie about homosexuals, but a movie about Harrison and Burton playing homosexuals. They play them with embarrassing clumsiness. I wonder if that was deliberate. Harrison minces about in a parody of homosexual mannerisms—not that many (or perhaps any) homosexuals ever acted as he portrays them. Maybe he's trying to tell us he's so straight he can't even play a homosexual. But he doesn't even play a character. Neither he nor Burton is believable for more than seconds."
Roger Ebert

"Harrison is the flighty dagger-tongued roommate of fellow hair stylist Burton, offering a portrait of a bitter, disenchanted man living in terror of being alone. Burton, almost stoic, commands respect and, at the same time, sympathy. Harrison and Burton have dared risky roles and have triumphed."
Variety

Starrbooty

(2007)

RuPaul as a Secret Agent and Hooker

The one and only RuPaul stars in this sex-filled, jaw-droppingly crude, down-'n-dirty send-up of secret agent "blaxploitation" flicks.

Gays will be particularly intrigued that some big name porn stars appear in cock cameos—Michael Lucas and Owen Hawk, for example. RuPaul admitted to the press that she got turned on by Hawk after watching him fingering himself while screwing a guy in a Chi Chi LaRue film. "Porn stars are like heroes in this world because we're such a sexually repressed culture that here are these young men who let it all hang out. They should be put on a pedestal."

In this politically incorrect film, a raunchy romp, RuPaul plays a tough agent who goes undercover as a hooker who's described as "a no shitting taking sex worker." The drag queen said she "loved movies where bitches kiss ass."

Critic Dom Willmott claimed that *Starrbooty*, Ru's self-produced do-it-yourself vehicle was "her *Mahogany*, a big candy-colored misfire that will have you alternately groaning and averting your eyes."

Ru's assignment as a secret agent is to find her niece, who has been abducted by Ru's nemesis Annaka Manners (Candis Cayne, a trannie). Assisting Ru is her best friend Page Turner (Lahoma Van Zandt), who's also very familiar with whoring.

WHAT THE CRITICS SAID
"The plot just tumbles along from one outrageous hooker costume change to the next. RuPaul populates her film with an A-list of gay porn stars, most of whom are more than happy to whip it out when the screenplay dictates. Also popping up is gay singer Ari Gold, who plays the part of a gay Hasidic pimp who favors silver leather assless chaps. When Starrbooty gives him a serious beat down, it's a cinematic moment to remember. Somebody actually wrote this!"
Dom Willmott

Suddenly

(Tan de Repente; 2002)

Charged Human Particles in a Collision Chamber

This sleeper film out of the "new" Argentina is chiefly the work of Diego Lerman, both helmer and co-scripter. You might call it a lesbian road movie about punks and a fat woman, but that would be demeaning both to the actors and to this comedy-drama.

Rejected by her boyfriend after a two-year involvement, Marcia (Tatiana Saphir) has put on the pounds, and she's in a dead-end job selling lingerie to a diminishing number of customers.

She is kidnapped at knife point by two sullen lesbian punks, the oddly named Mao and Lenin. Carla Crespo is Mao, Veronica Hassan is Lenin. Both women haul her away, telling her how much they want to have sex with her.

Marcia is hauled to the town of Rosario, a seabordering place outside Buenos Aires. Lenin's seventy-year-old Aunt Blanca (Beatriz Thibaudin) is the most charming person to appear on screen. She has two tenants, a painter, Delia (Maria Merlino), and the shy Felipe (Marcos Ferrante), a biology student.

After having her way with Marcia, Mao, seemingly without motivation, focuses her attention on Felipe.

Confusion reigns, as relationships form or break up, deepen or else shift into various configurations. The characters bounce off each other like pinballs.

"Where is all this going?", you'll ask.

Critic Dennis Lim came up with a subhead: "How to Turn a Lesbian Straight, and Vice Versa, Without Assistance from Ben Affleck."

Sun Kissed

(2006)

Sexy But Surreal & Oh Mama, That Garden Hose

When we stopped over in the Castro area of San Francisco in the summer of 2006, the most watched film among gay men was *Sun Kissed*, a drama/romance scripted and helmed by Patrick McGuinn. After sitting through this movie with its hallucinogenic plotline, the question might be asked—why?

The boys are beautiful, and the director doesn't believe in providing them with shirts. That's the good news. The bad news is this flick is hard to follow.

Teddy (John Ort) is a young writer who ventures to an isolated desert house owned by his professor in southeastern California. There he plans to write a novel.

Instead of undertaking that ambitious project, he becomes enthralled with a handsome, possibly bisexual caretaker, Leo (Gregory Marcel). Leo just might also be murderous. Teddy seduces the mysterious caretaker. Layers of memory and hallucinations unfold that intertwine the two studs who aren't ashamed to show off their physical assets.

The two hotties like to battle each other with a garden hose.

You can file this bit of information under "Who cares?" Director McGuinn is the son of Roger of *The Byrds*. As a reviewer pointed out, someone must care about this biographical tidbit because the press material mentioned it repeatedly.

WHAT THE CRITICS SAID
"When a movie aspires to be gay pornography, but can't even manage that, well, you know you've got a bad movie. The film, about five minutes' worth of plot stretched to more than an hour and a half, tells its thin tale with clumsy dialogue, clumsy editing and clumsy cinematography. At least it's consistent."
Neil Genzlinger, *The New York Times*

The Time We Killed

(2004)

After 9/11, a Time for Reflection

Not everyone's cuppa, this is an evocative but ultimately shapeless meditation on the depression and loneliness of a bisexual, agoraphobic writer Robyn (Lisa Jarnot), who holes up in her Brooklyn apartment in the wake of the tragic events of September 11, 2001.

Drinking cocktails and watching TV coverage of the attack on America and the subsequent anthrax scare, Robyn sinks deeper and deeper into solitude. The film becomes an evocation of lost lovers, memories of childhood, and even her own failed suicide attempt.

WHAT THE CRITICS SAID
"Scenes shot outside the apartment are filmed in high-contrast 16-millimeter, while the interior shots of Robyn's life appear in crisp digital video. Both formats provide black-and-white imagery of surpassing beauty (light reflecting off the East River, raindrops trembling on the ladder of a fire escape.) But the free associate voice-over, written by Jennifer Todd Reeves and Lisa Jarnot and delivered by the latter in an uninflected monotone, soon begins to grate. *The Time We Killed* has the raw intimacy of a filmed diary, but as with reading a stranger's journal, it eventually gets dull."
Dana Stevens, *The New York Times*

"Best known as an accomplished abstract filmmaker, first-time feature director Jennifer Reeves wrings bitter truth, confused paranoia, and impotent rage from an all-too-recent period, infusing them into the story of an agoraphobic poet, Robyn (real-life poet Lisa Jarnot). Robyn's verbal and visual stream of consciousness provides an internal narrative in more ways than one, as her observations blend into a lyrical swirl of sunny reverie, muted trauma, and inescapable reality. 'Every day is an echo of some shit time I already had,' she says."
Ed Halter, *The Village Voice*

Times Have Been Better

(*Le ciel sur la tête;* 2006)

Coming Out to a Liberal French Family

Made for TV, this French film is available on DVD. It's about opening the closet door, with all its perils and rewards.

Directed by Régis Musset in broad, conventional strokes, the film is based on a story and screenplay by Nicolas Mercier. This is a sophisticated comedy about what happens within a liberal French family when they learn their son is gay.

Jérémy (Arnauld Binard) is a successful business executive in Paris. He pays a surprise visit to his parents, Rosine (Charlotte de Turckheim) and Guy (Bernard le Coq). For years he's had a good relationship with his younger brother Robin (Olivier Guéritée), who has known that his brother is gay for some time.

His mother, in a brilliant performance by Turckheim, has suspected that her older son might be gay. But Guy has not. He has some issues. One of his biggest concerns is that his son might be "the girl."

The son is already 30 years old, so his coming out is rather belated. After meeting his son's lover, Marc (Pierre Deny), Guy realizes that the gay man is closer to his own age than his son's. For such a supposedly liberal father, he takes this rather badly. As one critic dramatically put it, "He bitterly lashes out at his wife, wishes his offspring dead, and generally alienates everyone in sight, his reactions decreasingly funny and increasingly pathological."

In contrast, the mother races about taking a course in Homosexuality 101. She copes by gauchely trying to bond with her condescending gay co-worker. Rosine even journeys to Paris to see her son's home, bond with his lover, and meet his new friends. After confronting some of her own suppressed needs, she returns to her nest an altered person.

Times Have Been Better is an affirming coming-out film for confident kids and their uneasy parents.

Too Outrageous!

(1987)

Too Little, Too Late

There was no need for female impersonator Craig Russell to follow his cult hit, *Outrageous!*, a decade later with a sequel. What had been clever and fresh in the 70s seemed sad and frayed in the 80s, as AIDS swept across the gay world. In fact,  both Russell and his writer-director Dick Benner would die of the disease in 1990.

In *Too Outrageous!*, Russell's act has grown tired. In one sequence, he was overshadowed by cast member Jimmy James doing a brilliant impersonation of Marilyn Monroe.

To break from the tired routine of impersonating Mae West and other divas, Russell tried to bring freshness into his act by donning blackface, and doing Tina Turner and Eartha Kitt, but he never hit the kind of stride he had with older divas such as Peggy Lee or Carol Channing.

In *Too Outrageous!* Benner reteamed Russell with his original co-stars, Hollis McLaren and David McIlwraith. Cast again as Russell's roommate, Liza Connors, McLaren seems to have controlled her schizophrenia in the sequel, mainly through drugs.

In this version, Craig as Robin Turner finds a hunky lover, a singer, Tony Sparks (Paul Eves).

WHAT THE CRITICS SAID
"Too maudlin! Ten years later, Robin Turner (Russell) picks up the frayed hem of his life. Still an undiscovered diva of gay dives, he lives with Liza (Hollis McLauren), his dresser and functioning schizophrenic who writes to purge her head of 'voices.' He's discovered by a big-time New York agent (Lynne Cormack) and sent back to Toronto to polish his act in preparation for a one-man/woman show on Broadway. The purpose of all this is to teach Robin 'the prices of success,' which he discovers is too high. On top of everything else, female impersonation is an art form that only tourists can tolerate in 105-minute doses."
Helen Knode, *Los Angeles Weekly*

The Trip

(2002)

"I Just Love Dick" (Nixon, That Is...)

Helmer and scripter Miles Swain has a contemporary gay romance, the tale of Tommy (Steve Braun) and Alan (Larry Sullivan), who are political opposites. Tommy, 19 years old, is a gay rights activist, Alan a 24-year-old Republican. They  first met in 1973, and in spite of their differences, formed a long-term relationship.

The Trip

In 1977, during the campaign in Dade County of Anita Bryant, the so-called singer and OJ queen, an anti-gay book Alan wrote is published. He'd written it years before, and it was published without his consent. The book intrudes on Tommy's life, destroying his credibility as a gay activist.

Because of the incident, Tommy and Alan break up, but reunite seven years later. Alan is given a second chance to set things right between them, since they are obviously attracted to each other.

A host of actors—defined by one critic as "a motley array of supporting loons"—surrounds the two men. Most of them are clichés, such as Sirena Irwin as a ditzy blonde or Alexis Arquette as a perpetually horny opportunist. The surprise in the cast is the appearance of Jill St. John as Alan's supportive but flaky kleptomaniac mother. One critic suggested that St. John was just looking for a little exposure in the role, perhaps hoping that *The Trip* would become a camp classic.

The setting for much of the film is Falcon's Lair, the former abode of Rudolph Valentino and later Doris Duke and Gloria Swanson.

Stated succinctly, *The Trip* is a trip.

V for Vendetta

(2005)

Graphic Novel Lost in Translation

The year is 2020 and a totalitarian government is ruling England, its symbol a modified crucifix. Its slogan is "Strength Through Unity, Unity Through Faith." The action takes place after a series of devastating terrorist attacks.

The avenger (Hugo Weaving) is known only as V. Like a lurking Phantom of the Opera in a Guy Fawkes mask, he conducts guerilla warfare against the government. When he rescues a normal young woman, Evey (Natalie Portman), these two citizens unite, wanting to put an end to this fascist state.

V wins Evey's confidence because he rescues her from a life-and-death situation. V not only does that, but he ignites a revolution when he detonates two London landmarks and takes over the government-controlled airwaves, urging his fellow citizens to rise up against tyranny and oppression.

V is out to restore individuality and reclaim freedom for the people, even at the expense of their happiness. The movie suggests that a future totalitarian state might repress not just homosexuality, but Islam, too.

Millions of movie fans identified with V, who can be defined either as a terrorist or a freedom fighter, depending on your point of view. Many fans who flocked to the movie were enthralled by the graphic novel of the same name by Alan Moore. Moore disassociated himself from the movie and had his name removed from the credits.

WHAT THE CRITICS SAID
"Helmed by James Mcteigue, pic suffers from many of same problems as last two installations of producers Andy and Larry Wachowski's *Matrix* franchise: Indigestible dialogue, pacing difficulties, and too much pseudo-philosophical info."
Leslie Felperin, *Variety*

Whispering Moon

(*Das flustern des mondes*; 2006)

Something Strange This Way Comes

If you like a movie about hoaxes, exposés, young love, poisonous tree frogs, and a lot more, wander into the mind of writer/director Michael Satzinger who helmed this Austrian entry. Dominik Hartl, Julian Stampfer, and Liane Wagner star in this film which tries to push the borders of conventional movie photography.

Playful, subversive, and scintillating, *Whispering Moon* is visually stunning, like nothing you've probably seen before. It blends media, narratives, and skin to tell "a story about storytelling."

Jannis and his mute lover, Patrick, are a pair of young techno rebels living in the not-too-distant future, a world of conspiracy and paranoia. These two boys set up surveillance cameras at a circus that may—or may not—be raising poisonous frogs to kill politicians.

Might the frog conspiracy also involve Mo, a young woman who lives with the circus and suffers from *Xeroderma pigmentosa*, a malady of the skin which forces her to live by night and avoid all ultraviolet light? Such people are often called "Children of the Moon."

The movie blends traditional film, digital video, computer graphics, and animation, allowing the main character to stop the action and make changes to the story at will.

The movie is in German, with English subtitles.

WHAT THE CRITICS SAID:
"Using a variety of cinematic techniques, this movie takes the viewer on a journey through the complexity of young love and devotion. It is certainly not a film for those who want a narrative that starts, builds, and finishes, but it does challenge the viewer and at times even disturbs. The two young men at the heart of the movie are complex characters—not two dimensional cut-outs."
Peter Schultz

Wonderland
(The Fruit Machine)

(1998)

A Rent Boy, Dolphins, & A Killer

Released in the U.S. as *Wonderland,* and in the UK as *The Fruit Machine*, director Philip Saville's movie tells of the bonding between two 17-year-old boys in Liverpool. Each comes from working-class families, and both of them are gay, but their differences are enormous.

Michael (Tony Forsyth) is a punk kid who is quite beautiful. After having escaped from a youth detention center, he is picked up by older men who want him for sex.

On the other hand, the somewhat effeminate Eddie (Emile Charles) lives with his mother and spends his days watching old movies.

When Tony meets Michael, they spend time at both the video arcade and at The Fruit Machine, which is a trannie club. It's run by a very obese man, Annabelle (Robbie Coltrance). He dresses in what one critic called "castoffs from Little Orphan Auntie."

While hanging out late at the club, the boys witness an altercation between Annabelle and Echo (Bruce Payne), who plays a hit man. It seems that Annabelle hasn't been making his protection payments.

Annabelle is killed by the hit man, and, because they're witnesses, Eddie and Michael flee to Brighton. There they find refuge in the home of an opera singer, Vincent (Robert Stephens) and his manager, Eva (Clare Higgins). To pay for his room and board, Michael allows himself to be seduced.

Eddie, on the other hand, is a dolphin lover and checks out the animals at a nearby aquatic park called "Wonderland." He feels that these beautiful animals are trapped and mistreated, and he wants to set them free.

Toward the end, the movie doesn't make a lot of sense. When Eddie is stabbed by the hit man who has followed the boys to Brighton, Michael doesn't rush him to the hospital in an ambulance. Instead he heads to Wonderland to free the dolphins.

PART THREE

50 YEARS OF QUEER CINEMA
GOES BEHIND THE SCENES

THIS SECTION IS DEVOTED TO LORE,
INSIDER-ISH GOSSIP, CASTING DRAMAS,
AND HOW VARIOUS DIVAS ACTED AND REACTED
UNDER PRESSURE FROM THE SLINGS AND ARROWS
OF HOLLYWOOD OUTRAGE.

The Father of New Queer Cinema
Derek Jarman
Gay, Punk, a Genius, and Ever the Provocateur

"heterosexuality isn't normal it's just common."
—derek jarman

New Queer Cinema is the name given to contemporary indies that deal openly, even aggressively, with queer culture and politics. The phrase dates from 1992, just two years before the death of British director **Derek Jarman** (photo above left), who is now hailed as the father of the new art form.

The term originated with B. Ruby Rich in an article in *The Village Voice,* who noted that many films were beginning to represent sexualities which were "unashamedly neither fixed nor conventional," and that certainly included the gay lifestyle. Jarman's films challenged the "heteronormative status quo."

DEREK JARMAN
DEFINING PROMISCUOUS SEX IN PUBLIC PLACES AS "REVENGE" AGAINST BRITAIN'S THATCHERITE MAJORITY

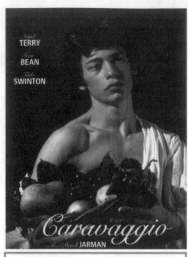

Not as well known as he should be to a lot of young gay filmmakers, the British movie director, stage designer, artist, and writer, Derek Jarman (1942-1994), is hailed as the founding father of New Queer Cinema. Other New Queer filmmakers, following in the master's footsteps, include Todd Haynes (*Poison*) and Tom Kalin (*Swoon*).

Jarman's fame derived from his controversial films whose themes move quickly from erotic to bitter to elegiac; from his outspoken openness about his homosexuality; his never-ending public fight for gay rights; and his personal struggle with AIDS, which finally took his life. His legend also derives from a poignant sense of ambiguity about symbolism: Gardens, for example, can evoke either Eden or Gethsemane, and the costuming of his "period dramas" can be inspired, within the same film, by anything from the English Renaissance to the Jazz Age, depending on the taste, preferences, and texture of the character who "inhabits" them. In his films, even Christ might be recast as a pair of persecuted Queer lovers.

On December 22, 1986, Jarman was diagnosed as HIV-positive. Many gay men at the time kept news of their HIV status deep in the closet. Not so Jarman. He even appeared on the British "telly" to discuss his medical condition in front of millions.

As a result of recent DVD re-releases of some of his landmark films, notably *Sebastiane* (1976), or *Caravaggio* (1986), Jarman's films are being discovered anew by an entire generation of gay men. (See this guidebook's separate reviews of *Caravaggio* and *Sebastiane*.)

Working from a script by Tilda Swinton, directors Isaac Julien and Bernard Roser have produced a documentary, *Derek* (2008) about the enduring importance of Jarman to the film world, especially its gay subdivisions. The film combines clips from Jarman's films, excerpts from a 1990 interview, and a ruminative voice-over by actress/scripter Swinton.

Art historians don't know a lot about the Italian Renaissance painter, **Caravaggio**, so Jarman had to use his fertile imagination during the shooting of this film released in 1986.

Critic Paul Attanasio of *The Washington Post* referred to the cinematic interpretation of this bisexual voluptuary as "an act of vandalism." Another critic viewed the film as an assassination of Caravaggio himself.

Gay men loved it, in part because of the humanization of an otherwise obscure historical figure, and in part because of the lusty sexual themes, especially of the homo variety, as well as the film's profanity, graphic violence, and macho swagger.

Jarman's 1979 adaptation of Shakespeare's **The Tempest** was praised by some of the Bard's chroniclers, but viciously attacked by others as a mere "homosexual metaphor."

American audiences seemed more accepting of it than British viewers.

Swinton's first appearance in a Jarman film was in the 1986 *Caravaggio*, which relates how the Renaisance Italian painter, beginning as a homeless teenager, was taken under the patronage of other artists and rose to fame, using street urchins and prostitutes as models, flaunting his bisexuality, and fashioning homoerotic paintings when he wasn't brawling or getting into knife fights and an involvement in at least one incidence, in 1606, of murder. In *Caravaggio,* Jarman and Swinton were credited with fighting against "the dead hand of good taste" in a Britain then ruled by the conservative Tory hand of the "Iron Lady," Margaret Thatcher.

Jarman's *Sebastiane* remains—arguably—his most controversial film. Shot on a shoestring budget and released in 1976, it's performed in low-end Latin, as might have been spoken by a low-ranking Roman soldier, with English-language subtitles. Examining the relation of sex and power, it's the story, of course, of the martyrdom of St. Sebastian, a saint whose arrow-pierced depictions in medieval and Renaissance painting have often been associated with subliminal homoeroticism. The film became infamous for its overt depiction of queer desire onscreen, and, as such, is now cited as a major example of a British film featuring positive images of gay sexuality. It became even better known for being the first major mainstream film release that exposed a man's fully out and proud erection.

The occasionally chaotic British studio in which Jarman and Swinton operated has been likened to Andy Warhol's The Factory in Manhattan.

The docu, *Derek,* depicts Jarman's final, AIDS-ravaged days in which he opted to live in a cozy, shingle-covered cottage built of tarred timber and incongruously positioned amid a bleak industrial landscape a few steps from the monolithic hulk of the antiquated, ecologically disastrous Dungeness (southeastern England) Nuclear Power Station. He likened the surreal nature of his home to that of the Kansas farmhouse in which the character of Dorothy (Judy Garland) lived in *The Wizard of Oz.*

Dennis Lim, writing in *The New York Times,* claimed that Jarman "drew heavily on the example of previous generations. His poetic sensibility owes a debt to the outlaw lyricism of Jean Cocteau and Jean Genet. His taste for the baroque calls to mind British filmmakers like Michael Powell and Ken Russell, who hired Jarman to work as a set designer on his film *The Devils* (1970).

"Heterosexuals have so colonized and fucked the screen that there's hardly room for us to kiss," Jarman once said.

He described having public sex as "revenge" against

In the film, Caravaggio discovers the object of his desire, Ranuccio, in a bare-knuckles boxing match, and in the aftermath, quickly invites him to his bed.

Jarman cast actor **Sean Bean** (above) in the role.

Visually striking, as the scene above clearly indicates, **Sebastiane** delivered a blatantly homoerotic version of the martyrdom of a figure later embraced by the Catholic church as a martyred saint. A classical scholar took special pains to translate all of its dialogue into a low dialect of working-class Latin akin to what Roman soldiers in the barracks would have used, rather than the oratorical speech of the Caesars.

Jarman, it was rumored, took "director's privilege" and set up private auditions, Roman-style, with some of the actors.

years of repression by England's sense of propriety and decorum, as then defined by the country's Thatcherite majority.

Jarman was fascinated with the plays of Shakespeare, especially *The Tempest,* a screen version of which he crafted and filmed in 1979. "*The Tempest* is really about uncovering a secret world. Secrets are a canker which destroys. Destroying secrets is what I like to do."

Within his version of *The Tempest,* Jarman was very liberal with the Bard's text, adjusting the dialogue whenever it was convenient, and using Shakespeare's original theatrical vision as a springboard for his own ideas and interpretations. It included abundant nudity, mostly male, and instead of an island setting, *à la* Shakespeare, Jarman set his dreamy film within a decaying mansion, and systematically dissected the Shakespearian texts, infusing those that remained with visions of the occult. As was inevitable, traditionalists denounced both Jarman and his film.

In Jarman's words, "I cut away the dead wood (particularly the comedy) so that the original play's great speeches were concertinaed. Then the play was rearranged and opened up: the theatrical magic had to be replaced...*The Tempest* obsesses me. I would like to make it again, would be happy to make it three times."

Examples of his other idiosyncratic, homoerotic visions include his films *Jubilee* (1977) and *Edward II* (1991). Incidentally "straight" storytelling, so to speak, was never Jarman's strongest suit. Nor was it even a principal goal of his cinema.

In *Edward II* Jarman succeeds at evoking a modern-day resonance within the 17th-century Marlowe texts; queer activists appear in crowd scenes to protest homophobia because, as Jarman said, "the play's whole central relationship...is mirrored by today's institutionalized homophobia. There's also a sense in which the making of the film is about reclaiming history, because there's been a long tradition of denying the homosexual side of the relationship between Edward and Gaveston."

Critics attacked Jarman for his 1985 release of *The Angelic Conversation,* one irate writer defining it as an hour or so of "pretentious gay artsiness," another as "indulgent schmaltz," but many fans of Jarman loved it.

The film's only spoken dialogue involved an unseen woman reciting some of Shakespeare's love sonnets--14 in all--as a man wordlessly seeks his heart's desire, as in the scene depicted above.

The woman's voice, incidentally, emanated from the very talented Dame Judi Dench

Zeitgeist Films, which introduced Jarman to American audiences, has released a DVD set called *Glitterbox,* a boxed set which contains a cross-section of three of Jarman's films. They include the neo-Brechtian *Caravaggio* (1986), and *Wittgenstein* (1993). It also contains the homoerotic reverie *The Angelic Conversation* (1985), a "Super 8 experiment"in which (Dame) Judi Dench reads twelve of Shakespeare's sonnets, the film's only dialogue, as background for visual images that illuminate the emotional and sexual bond between two young men (Phillip Williamson and Paul Reynolds). The tableaux are those glimpsed from the windows of an Elizabethan House as the lovers find and eventually lose each other.

Wittgenstein is a dramatization, in modern theatrical style, of the life and thoughts of the Viennese-born, Cambridge-edu-

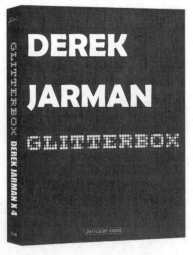

DEREK JARMAN
GLITTERBOX

cated philosopher Ludwig Wittgenstein (1889-1951) whose principal interest was the nature and limits of language.

A homosexual, Wittgenstein, an associate of Bertrand Russell and John Maynard Keyes, was hailed as a "perfectionistic thinker generally regarded as a genius." *Variety* called *Wittgenstein* "an immaculately lensed, intellectual joke that's more of a divertissement than a substantial addition to Jarman's quirky *oeuvre*."

Running parallel with the intellectual stuff is an exploration of Wittgenstein's repressed homosexuality.

Jarman's final film, *Blue* (1993), made when he was terminally ill and going blind, asked audiences to stare at a blue screen and listen to evocative monologues that would conjure images within the blank field of color. *Blue,* which was defined as Jarman's "monochrome valediction," is as mysterious, enigmatic, and emotional as any epitaph an artist ever composed for himself.

Desson Howe of *The Washington Post* wrote: "Blue it is after 10 minutes. Blue it is after 30 minutes. Blue after an hour. Blue, blue, blue for 76 minutes."

Frankly, the trio of Jarman films incorporated within *Glitterbox* was packaged for fans who are already familiar with Jarman's work. If you wander unaware among its presuppositions, you might think you've come to the wrong address. But therein lies the challenge and potential satisfaction of discovering the legacy of an avant-garde filmmaker.

Once, when asked what it means to be queer, Jarman answered, "Queer means to fuck with gender. Our sexuality is unique. It's not about whether you fuck with boys or girls...QUEER IS NOT ABOUT GAY OR LESBIAN--IT'S ABOUT SEX."

As one film student, Philip Sooley, told us, "In my way of thinking, Jarman's greatest contribution to cinema will be in bringing the erect dick to the screen. I'm tired of looking at all those limp dicks. Gotta love Jarman."

During the final years of his life, before he died of AIDS, **Jarman** spent a lot of time nurturing his famous garden, growing healthy plants in gravel, even though it was adjacent to an industrial site, a decaying nuclear power station in southeastern England. In the background is his simple, wood-sided, century-old fisherman's cottage.

TILDA SWINTON

"THERE IS ONLY ONE YOU. ONLY ONE."

Tilda Swinton is a British actress who was born in London in 1960. She became famous not only as the muse for Derek Jarman, but as a world-class, A-list actress who also made arthouse flicks.

She won an Academy Award for Best Supporting Actress for her brilliant work opposite George Clooney in *Michael Clayton* (2008). Swinton also appeared in *The Curious Case of Benjamin Button* alongside Brad Pitt.

Swinton's *au naturel* appearance has surprised some movie-goers. But as stylist Jerry Stafford said, "This is skin born of the Scottish Highlands, so why hide it? Why the hell put foundation on it and all this garish lipstick?"

Swinton understood the artistic impact of Derek Jarman better than anyone else on the planet. In an interview with Holly Willis, Swinton said, "Derek lived and worked outside of any industrial model as a filmmaker. That, in itself, is a powerful thing to look at at any time, but now, when filmmakers are constantly being told that we cannot do what we want to, according to some kind of rule book set by the market, it is a vital reminder of a possibility we may have forgotten.

Derek was an artist first and foremost, the idea of making work within any kind of map laid down by anybody's cultural men, or by anyone's allegiance to financial viability or profit motives was an anathema to him. He simply didn't care about any of that.

He collected his friends, and anyone who looked right for the images he was intersted in playing with. He turned on the camera and we played. Sometimes, there were words written down in scenes, but more often than not, we were in silent home movies, shot from the hip, resulting in hypnotic reveries made up of fire and wind and light, wild at heart and passionately amateur in spirit."

Photos, above, left, **Tilda Swinton**, *au naturel*, and above right, modeling a dress by Yves St-Laurent.

IN MEMORY OF DEREK JARMAN
(R.I.P.)
SEX AS AN ACT OF REVENGE

We've inserted the photo, left, in deference to Derek Jarman's definition of promiscuous sex in public places as a form of "revenge" against Britain's Thatcherite majority, and by extension, as a potential form of protest against bourgeois, repressive morals everywhere.

The Cinematic Legacy of
Tennessee Williams
Going Naked On Stage

Born into a genteel Southern family wallowing in hypocrisy, gay playwright **Tennessee Williams** would become America's most fabled (read that "notorious") author at the midpoint of the 20th century. From the 1944 premiere of his play *The Glass Menagerie* until 1961, he produced an astonishing body of work, including *A Streetcar Named Desire* and *Cat on a Hot Tin Roof.* Each of those plays earned him separate Pulitzer Prizes.

Yet his self-destructive impulses consumed him in the 60s, as he retreated into alcohol, pills, drugs, and wildly promiscuous sex as he wandered the globe, searching, but never finding, what he needed for self-fulfillment.

"I understand the lost," he told author Darwin Porter. "I write about these wretched souls. I sail on the same ship as they do. We are heading into dark waters. I'm thinking of entitling my next play *Forlorn Destinies.*"

"FLEE, FLEE THIS SAD HOTEL"
(THE ORIGINAL TITLE OF TENNESSEE WILLIAMS' MEMOIRS)

Playwright Tennessee Williams brought echoes of homosexuality to the stage, and later to films, in an era when the word could not even be mentioned.

Never before in history had a playwright brought such subjects as rape, castration, and even cannibalism to the Broadway stage.

His increasing openness about promiscuous homosexuality became the scandal of the theater. When asked on nationwide TV about rumors of his homosexuality, he snickered and said, "I've walked the waterfront."

Although he denied ever promoting an actor after a session on the casting couch, he did seduce both Paul Newman and Marlon Brando, among others. There were also rumors about Williams and Warren Beatty, who got cast in *The Roman Spring of Mrs. Stone.*

Williams one night, during pillow talk, confessed to his lover, Frank Merlo, that he'd seduced Brando long before the role of Stanley Kowalski was even conceived.

"Tenn got his man," Merlo claimed. "It happened in the early 40s in Provincetown. As Tenn put it, a slightly drunken Marlon offered his sexual favors as the 'tide lapped under the wharf and the hungry seagulls screeched overhead.'"

"I managed to extract two offerings from that magnificent tool before I would remove the treasure from my mouth," Williams allegedly told Merlo. "By the time Marlon's cannon shot for the last time, the early streaks of dawn were in the sky. Although Marlon that summer temporarily turned his splendid body over to me, it was a vessel I was to possess only briefly. He was destined to share his magnificence with others. *So many others.*"

In many ways, Williams' own life was a nonstop performance. He peopled his plays with outcasts, misfits, and fugitives, the way he saw himself. He often used frustrated women as his alter egos, as he did with the character of Flora Goforth in *The Milk Train Doesn't Stop Here Anymore.*

A lonely wanderer, traveling aimlessly around the globe, Williams succumbed to drugs, alcohol, and an endless parade of hustlers, each evoking Chance Wayne in *Sweet Bird of Youth.*

His critics claimed that "the talent that Williams once had failed him in the last two decades of his life. Much that he writes, in spite of the occasional poetry, is the result of a brain long pickled. Where is Stanley Kowalski? Where is Amanda Wingfield? Where is Blanche? They would never come from his typewriter again."

A friend, Dotson Rader, described the playwright's condition in his memoir, *Tennessee: Cry of the Heart.* "I first met Tennessee Williams shortly after he got out of what he called Barnacle Hospital (actually Barnes Hospital) in St. Louis, where he had been confined by his brother, Dakin, in 1969. Tennessee had flipped out on copious amounts of Doriden, Mellaril, Seconal, Ritalin, Demerol, amphetamines, and too much sorrow in Key West. He thought his house was surrounded by assassins, rifles pointed at him through the thick foliage, terrorists lurking inside the walls."

Born in 1911, with roots in the Deep South, Williams led a life that was as disturbing and dramatic as any of the memorable characters he created. His friend, Darwin Porter, once asked

Williams, "Who was the inspiration for the character of Blanche DuBois in *A Streetcar Named Desire?*"

Williams responded, "I am Blanche, right down to her moth-eaten finery."

The career of the playwright embraced such classics as *The Glass Menagerie*, *A Streetcar Named Desire*, and *Cat On a Hot Tin Roof*, among other memorable works such as *The Night of the Iguana*; *The Rose Tattoo*; *Sweet Bird of Youth*; *Suddenly, Last Summer*; and *Summer and Smoke*.

Beginning with *The Glass Menagerie*, the plays he produced between 1944 when he was thirty-four years old through 1961 were astonishing both in volume and distinction. That distinction earned him two Pulitzer Prizes and made him rich, an international celebrity.

He wined and dined with some of the most celebrated people on the planet, ranging from Elizabeth Taylor and Bette Davis to Vivien Leigh and Lord Laurence Olivier, even John F. Kennedy and Jacqueline. He told Gore Vidal that JFK "has a nice ass."

He would continue to write until his death in 1983, but never again would he enjoy his early success. His finest works were each crafted prior to 1962. He once confided to Gore Vidal, "I slept through the 1960s."

Vidal assured him, "Tenn, you didn't miss a thing."

His greatest love was Frank (aka Frankie) Merlo, a New Jersey-born Navy veteran, a second generation Sicilian. He was short, muscular, and strikingly handsome. Tennessee often referred to him as "Horse." Merlo moved in with Tennessee, thereby catalyzing the playwright's longest and deepest experience with intimacy.

But shortly before Merlo's early death, Williams called it quits and asked him to leave. For a while the discarded lover stayed with author Darwin Porter in his Manhattan penthouse apartment until his violent coughing forced him into a hospital.

Before he did, and because he needed the money, he dictated to Porter his memories of his life with Williams, which illuminated one of the most memorable sagas of any playwright in history. He never lived to complete the project.

A heavy smoker throughout his life, Merlo was diagnosed with inoperable lung cancer. He died in 1963. In some ways, Williams never recovered from the loss, even though he had kicked Merlo out of his life only months before.

In summing up his life, Williams said, "I have had a remarkably fortunate life which has contained a great many moments of joy, both pure and impure."

One night near the end of his life, Williams told writers Porter and James Leo Herlihy, "There have been so many young men in my life. With an exception or two, like Frankie and a few others, I remember only their first names. But tonight even those names elude me, the experiences growing dimmer and dimmer."

Whenever Tennessee was away from his Key West cottage, his longtime love, **Frankie Merlo** (seated in the chair at the far right of photo above) would play with his comrade-in-arms and the reigning queen of Key West, Danny Stirrup (far left).

Together, they'd entertain visiting sailors. An orgy would usually follow.

Williams loved the raffish charm of Key West, and its steady supply of sailors, both foreign and domestic. The playwright's beloved bulldog looks on, indulgently, at this gay debauchery.

CELEBRATING
THE TENNESSEE WILLIAMS'
FILM COLLECTION
(2006)
Southern Repressive and Gothic,
But With an All-Star Hollywood Cast

At long last in one DVD collection, you can see the film versions of six of Tennessee's plays, including an uncensored, two-disc director's cut of *A Streetcar Named Desire*, starring Vivien Leigh as Blanche DuBois and Marlon Brando as Stanley Kowalski. Also part of the collection is *Cat on a Hot Tin Roof*, with Elizabeth Taylor as Maggie the Cat and Paul Newman as Britt, her sexually confused husband.

Also part of the collection, making their DVD debuts, are *Sweet Bird of Youth*, *The Night of the Iguana*, *Baby Doll*, and *The Roman Spring of Mrs. Stone*. The latter starred Warren Beatty and Vivien Leigh and was the only film of his works that Williams actually liked.

> In almost every case, playwright Tennessee Williams intensely disliked how Hollywood adapted his plays for the screen. But even though the film versions of his plays suffered from the censorship standards of the time, they still captured some of the playwright's qualities of compassion, black humor, and his sense that human souls were constantly tortured with internal and external conflicts.
>
> According to Tennessee (or was it according to his fictitious creation, Blanche DuBois?) "The enemies of the delicate always tried to destroy the sensitive soul of the artist, but I defied them."

This collection also includes the little-known *Tennessee Williams' South*, an offbeat documentary that had its TV premiere in 1973.

The films in the collection offer remarkable performances, sharp direction, and the lusty poetry of the Southern playwright. Many viewers will discover many of these movies for the first time. *Baby Doll*, directed by Elia Kazan, was defined by one reviewer as "at least 20 years ahead of its time."

Not included in the collection, yet available from other studios, are such other Williams plays-as-films, including *Suddenly, Last Summer,* starring Katharine Hepburn and Elizabeth Taylor, and *The Rose Tattoo*, starring Anna Magnani and Burt Lancaster.

WHAT THE CRITICS SAID

"The collection's only drawback is its dearth of commentaries. Tracks for *Street* and *Cat on a Hot Tin Roof* are ripping good fun, with Karl Malden shining on the former as a generous, warm-hearted storyteller. It would have been nice to hear similar anecdotes about, say, Warren Beatty's turn in *The Roman Spring of Mrs. Stone*. But this box still captures the potency of a legendary American writer and the cinematic era he helped create."
Mark Blankenship, *Variety*

[Note: *A Streetcar Named Desire*, *Cat on a Hot Tin Roof*, and *Suddenly, Last Summer*—which is not included within this film collection—are reviewed elsewhere within this book.]

BABY DOLL
(1956)
Race to the Teenage Virgin

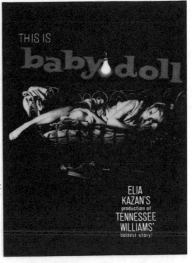

***

BABY DOLL: Excuse me, Mr. Vacarro, but I wouldn't dream of eatin' a nut that a man had cracked in his mouth.

SILVA VACARRO: You've got many refinements.

***

Such is the dialogue that permeates this notorious movie that outraged the Legion of Decency back in the Eisenhower 50s. Director Elia Kazan based the film on a screenplay by Tennessee Williams.

It's a steamy tale of two Southern rivals and a sensuous 19-year-old virgin. Williams himself based the work on two of his one-act plays, *Twenty-seven Wagons Full of Cotton* and *The Unsatisfactory Supper*.

In spite of its notoriety, the film brought Oscar nominations for Carroll Baker in the leading role of Baby Doll Meighan. Mildred Dunnock was nominated for Best Supporting Actress, and Williams himself received a nod for Best Screenplay.

Karl Malden played Archie Lee Meighan, with Eli Wallach cast as Silva Vacarro.

Archie Lee, the middle-aged owner of a cotton gin, can hardly wait for the 20th birthday of his child-like bride Baby Doll, to deflower her. She still sleeps in a crib and sucks her thumb.

Earlier, Archie Lee had promised Baby Doll's dying father that he would not touch his daughter until she was "ready for marriage."

Archie Lee's arch enemy is a flashy Sicilian business rival (Wallach), who has forced Archie's decrepit cotton gin out of business. One night, in desperation, Archie Lee burns down his rival's new cotton gin. You don't do that to a Sicilian without expecting a vendetta.

The plot simmers and boils over.

Williams resisted Kazan's efforts to bring this material to the screen, but eventually gave in. He even agreed to travel to Benoit, Mississippi, where the film was to be shot. Soon after, he left Benoit, telling Kazan that he didn't like the way people looked at him in the street. Previously, he'd left Mississippi when he was only 17, at the time (he thought) for ever. "Those people chased me out of here. I left the South because of their attitude toward me. They don't approve of homosexuals, and I don't want to be insulted."

THE ROMAN SPRING OF MRS. STONE
(1961)
Scarlett O'Hara Amongst Those Roman Gigolos

Based on a novel by Tennessee Williams, this film cast Vivien Leigh as the fading actress Karen Stone.

She escapes to Rome after the death of her husband where she falls into the clutches of a scheming Contessa (brilliantly played by Lotte Lenya) and a handsome young gigolo (Paoli di Leo). As Williams conceived the character, Paoli hustles both men and women, although this is not made entirely clear in the movie version of the novel.

Once again, Leigh brought her luminous talent to a Williams' character. Of course, no one, not even the critics, felt she would equal her performance as Blanche DuBois in *A Streetcar Named Desire*.

In his memoirs, Williams explained his fascination with the Italian gigolo. "Prostitution is really the world's oldest profession in all Mediterranean countries, with the possible exception of Spain. It is due largely to their physical beauty and to their warmth of blood, their natural eroticism. In Rome, you rarely see a young man on the street who does not have a slight erection. Often they walk along the Veneto with hand in pocket, caressing their genitals quite unconsciously, and this regardless of whether or not they are hustling or cruising. They are raised without any of our particular reserves about sex."

The playwright's long-time friend, Donald Windham, realized that Karen Stone was Williams' "first fictionalized self-portrait after his success—and it displays a hair-raising degree of self-knowledge."

The most evocative moment of the film comes at the end, when Mrs. Stone throws her keys down from her balcony to the young gigolo who has been stalking her. Her motion was compared by one writer to "a grotesque Juliet or a decadent Rapunzel."

As Williams himself described the plight of Mrs. Stone: "The opposite force had been time, time the imponderable, not moving amicably with her but treacherously against her, and finally meeting her and arresting her in mid-flight with a shattering crash."

As an Italian gigolo (read that "hustler") in Rome, **Warren Beatty** tries to bleed what money he can out of Mrs. Stone (**Vivien Leigh**), an aging actress who fled from Broadway for the decadent life in Rome, where she's "drifting" and a prey for rich, handsome young men willing to sell their bodies in exchange for the loosening of her purse strings.

Beatty's gal pal, Joan Collins, recalled at the time: "His hair had been darkened for the part. He had a deep tan, which, although it was out of a bottle, looked as if it came straight from Portofino. He wore a beautifully cut beige silk suit from Brioni, a cream-colored crepe de chine shirt from Battaglia, and a brown-and-beige St-Laurent tie. The Warren Beatty-as-sex-symbol was beginning to emerge."

SWEET BIRD OF YOUTH

(1962)
Castrating Tennessee Williams

Sweet Bird of Youth was a hit on Broadway when it starred Paul Newman as the hustler, Chance Wayne, and Geraldine Page as the fading celluloid diva, Alexandra Del Lago. Chance returns to a small Southern town, dominated by a leering political boss, with the dissipated movie queen. After a previous visit to the same town, he'd left the despot's daughter, Heavenly Finley, with a venereal disease.

In many ways, the character of Alexandra Del Lago mirrored Williams' own concerns—drug abuse, paying for sex, a career in chaos.

In the Broadway version, Williams claimed that he wrote one line specifically for its star, Newman. As part of the playwright's instructions to the play's leading male character, Williams wrote: "Your body is designed for satin sheets."

The playwright had long lusted after Newman, whom he considered remarkably handsome. Once, when asked about his relationship with Newman, Williams claimed, "I have never auditioned actors on the casting couch. Besides, Paul Newman is too big a star to lie on the casting couch."

At the time, however, Williams was clearly aware of Newman's career-advancing moves during the early 50s, when he lay on that lavender couch for both William Inge and Joshua Logan, playwright and director, respectively, of the stage vehicle (*Picnic*) which launched Newman's career as an actor.

Before the stage opening of *Sweet Bird*, Newman didn't have to accept Williams' invitation to join him at El Convento Hotel in San Juan. But he did. He flew there to be with the playwright, whom he liked and admired.

"Let's just call it *The Lost Weekend*," Newman told director Elia Kazan upon his return. The star was referring to a film Ray Milland made in 1945, where Milland had won an Oscar for playing an alcoholic whose amnesiac binge lasted a full three days.

Williams maintained a promiscuously open relationship with his lover Frank Merlo. Upon his return to Key West, Williams reported to Merlo what Newman had told him before flying out of San Juan. "Now, God damn it, the next time you have a great part, you come to me, not Marlon Brando. Who's the man, baby?"

The curtain line for Chance Wayne became one of the most memorable ever uttered in the theater. "I don't ask for your pity, but just for your understanding—not even that, no. Just for your recognition of me in you, and the enemy, Time, in us all."

In the play's film version, Geraldine Page and Paul Newman repeated the roles they'd developed on Broadway, as did Rip Torn and Madeline Sherwood. Ed Begley contracted to play Boss Finley in the film version, and Shirley Knight signed on as Heavenly, Chance's former girlfriend. The very talented actress, Mildred Dunnock, was assigned the role of Heavenly's Aunt

Nonny, who is sympathetic to Chance.

Because of studio pressure, director Richard Brooks was forced to water down the play script. Instead of the castration Chance endures at the end of the play, he suffers a beating at the hand of Boss Finley's goons. And instead of having been infected with a venereal disease, film-goers are informed that Heavenly, impregnated by her earlier adventure with Chance, has suffered through an abortion.

The biggest change, however, and one that particularly infuriated Williams, involved the happy ending Brooks crafted for the film. Heavenly and Chance run away, presumably toward a happy future, although that hardly seems likely after what has already gone down.

Page lost the Best Actress Oscar that year to Anne Bancroft as she appeared in *The Miracle Worker*.

In 1989, Elizabeth Taylor would re-create the role of Alexandra Del Lago on television, with Mark Harmon cast in the hustler role.

Geraldine Page (left) immortalized herself as the fading actress, Alexandra Del Lago, in Tennessee's evocative *Sweet Bird of Youth*. Many actresses were auditioned for the part--Ava Gardner, Lana Turner, Rita Hayworth--but Page was allowed to re-create the role she'd developed for the stage onscreen, and she did so magnificently.

Shirtless for part of the movie, **Paul Newman** was cast as the hustler, Chance Wayne. Elvis Presley wanted to play the role of the male whore, but his dictatorial manager, Col. Tom Parker, refused to allow it, forcing Elvis into safer, forgettable roles instead.

THE NIGHT OF THE IGUANA
(1964)
Illicit Liaisons Both On & Off the Screen

When director John Huston flew his crew to Puerto Vallarta to film Tennessee Williams' play, it put the then-seedy Mexican backwater on the map. Before that, it didn't even have scheduled air service. Now it's a top Mexican resort destination with hundreds of hotel rooms. Cruise ships regularly call.

Of course, it could be argued that it was Elizabeth Taylor who really put the town on the map. She flew here to join the star, Richard Burton. Their scandalous affair became tabloid fodder.

The Broadway version of *The Night of the Iguana* had starred Bette Davis in a red fright wig. On stage, the play was epigrammatic and full of Williams' faux poetry. But Huston brought it into sharper focus, rewriting some key lines and casting Richard Burton as the defrocked priest, Dr. T. Lawrence Shannon, who leads a bus load of middle-aged Baptist women on a tour of the Mexican coast.

They land at a seedy hotel run by Ava Gardner as Maxine Faulk, who has this thing for muscled beach boys. She plays it like an Ava Gardner gone to seed.

Deborah Kerr is rigorously ladylike, as in most of her films, and Sue Lyon plays an aging Lolita. It was Grayson Hall, cast as an uptight and very tense lesbian, who received an Oscar nomination for Best Supporting Actress.

Throughout the filming, both Taylor and Burton were drinking heavily on the set. She was fussing over him, worrying about his hair and makeup. The Richard Burton cocktail was invented in Puerto Vallarta. It goes like this: "First take 21 tequilas..."

Burton began drinking beer every morning at 7am. By noon he'd finished off a case and switched to tequila. The nights were long.

There were many more illicit romances going on offset than in front of the cameras. Gardner, in ways equivalent to the character she was playing, developed a passion for Mexican beach boys and enjoyed the charms of quite a few. Williams arrived with some young man he'd picked up in a bar in New York. Fresh from her key role in Stanley Kubrick's *Lolita*, Sue Lyon arrived with "a tall, pale youth ravaged by love who haunted the surrounding flora," according to Lawrence Grobel, Huston's biographer.

It seemed that Deborah Kerr was the only one in the cast who wasn't shacking up with someone, although both Burton and Huston made plays for her. "They were drunk at the time, and I didn't take them seriously," she later recalled.

Gardner and Burton gave off sparks, but Taylor intervened. Gardner backed off. The two *femme fatales* had known each other since their early days at MGM and didn't want a mere man to become between them. On many previous occasions, each of them had seduced the same men,

349

not only Frank Sinatra, but Peter Lawford, et al.

On November 22, 1963, Huston told his assembled stars: "I have bad news. President Kennedy has been assassinated in Dallas."

Huston later confided to friends in Hollywood that both "Elizabeth and Ava wept. Speaking with each of them separately later that night, I learned that each of these pussies had fucked JFK. God, did that guy get around."

Later, Eddie Fisher revealed that during the filming in Puerto Vallarta, Burton managed to slip away from Taylor and have a brief fling with Lyon. Fisher, according to reports, claimed that he learned that when he himself had an affair with Lyon. "She wanted to compare my sexual prowess with Burton's."

Scenes from *The Night of the Iguana*, wherein **Ava Gardner** and **Richard Burton** were defined as its stars, **Sue Lyon**, lower right, seemed to be reprising her recent role as Lolita as she pays a call on the wicked, recently defrocked reverend, as portrayed by Burton. Burton, with Elizabeth Taylor, then at the height of their tabloid notoriety, arrived in Puerto Vallarta (Mexico) for the filming.

Jealous Elizabeth, kept a watchful eye on Burton's delectable female co-stars--Gardner, Deborah Kerr, and "Lolita" Lyon. "I didn't want him falling into the wrong honeypot at night," she said.

Even so, "illicit" romances flourished and prevailed across the set. Tennessee arrived with a very young boyfriend; Sue Lyon, a ripe 17 at the time, appeared with "a tall pale youth ravaged by love," according to biographer Lawrence Grobel.

Whenever they weren't getting "pickled on tequila," Burton and Taylor could be heard screaming out their passion during lovemaking. Deborah Kerr joked that "I was the only one not getting plugged. Ava told me she took on as many as five *mexicanos* one drunken night, and invited me to share them with her, but I politely refused."

TENNESSEE WILLIAMS' SOUTH
(1973)
"I Always Had a Feeling I Was Black"

In this sensitive, poetic documentary made for Canadian TV, helmer/writer Harry Rasky captures the essence of the great playwright, Tennessee Williams, as no one ever has before. Now available on DVD, either separately or as part of the collection, Williams' look at his peculiar South is told in his own words, and set in key points that include both New Orleans and Key West.

In addition to filmclips of brilliant scenes from Grade A actors, Williams reads some of his best poetry. As filmmaker, Rasky illustrates Tennessee's poetry with scenes from nature.

The harmonious Southern accent of the playwright is often mesmerizing. Williams hesitates in his choice of words at times, carefully searching for the right one to describe the emotion he wants to convey.

He points out that he grew up in the segregated South, where whites and blacks didn't often mix. But he claims he identifies with the black culture, and credits African Americans with contributions to the idiomatic speech patterns of many Southerners. For example, he said that he borrowed the title for one of his most popular plays, *Cat on a Hot Tin Roof*, from the idiomatic speech patterns of the American South.

Between bouts of poetry from Williams, scenes from some of his works, both memorable and lesser known, are performed by some of the leading lights of the theater. None is more notable than Miss Jessica Tandy, re-creating a famous monologue from her role as the original Blanche DuBois on Broadway in the late 40s.

She laments her own role in the death of her young husband, who was a homosexual. The night she told him he "disgusted" her was the night he killed himself. This stage scene was considered too controversial for movie audiences at the time.

Tandy's Blanche DuBois is very different from the same role played by Vivien Leigh in the movie version with Marlon Brando. Williams conceived Blanche as a moth—"a tiger moth, perhaps"—but a moth nonetheless, a woman frightened by "the enemies of the delicate everywhere."

In her Oscar-winning portrayal, Leigh evoked that moth-like quality. Tandy's Blanche is a much stronger woman—nothing moth-like about her at all.

As the "gentleman caller," the miscast Michael York performs a scene from *The Glass Menagerie*, with Maureen Stapleton playing the mother, Amanda Wingfield, and Carol Williard cast as the emotionally delicate daughter, Laura.

Perhaps the grandest performance is by "Big Daddy" himself, Burl Ives, playing a shoe salesman, Charlie Colton, lamenting the passing of the Old South.

John Colicos captures the essence of the Rev. Dr. T. Lawrence, the defrocked priest in the stage version of *The Night of the Iguana*. Richard Burton played the reverend on the screen opposite Ava Gardner. In the docu, Colleen Dewhurst delivers a sensitive performance as Hannah

Jelkes.

Some of the scenes acted out in the docu never actually appeared in Williams' plays but were the playwright's extenuations of his character's thoughts and emotions.

Many viewers found the docu disappointing and not very insightful. We disagree, of course, although admitting the film is for aficionados.

WHAT THE CRITICS SAID

"'It seems to be that I'm the head of my own country,' Williams says. The movie adaptations of his plays are fine—a couple are first-rate—but Williams' 'my own country' and its troubled population always existed first on the stage, where his unfiltered scripts grab us by the collar better than in any other medium. *Tennessee Williams' South* is an entry-level and stylistically dated look at Williams, but we recommend it for newbie enthusiasts, American Lit or drama students, and film buffs wondering where all these poetic dreamers, misfits, and good ol' boys came from."
DVD Journal

Getting Violent with "The Enemies of the Delicate"

"Oh Laura, Laura, I tried to leave you behind me, but I am more faithful than I intended to be! I reach for a cigarette, I cross the street, I run into the movies or a bar, I buy a drink, I speak to the nearest stranger—anything that can blow your candles out! For nowadays the world is lit by lightning! Blow out your candles, Laura—and so good-bye."

from Tennessee Williams' *The Glass Menagerie*

Literary Gossip from the Past: How to Win a Pulitzer Prize

In 1955, Joseph Pulitzer, Jr. had a hard time convincing his fellow jurors to award one of America's most coveted literary prizes to *Cat On a Hot Tin Roof.* Of the five nominees under consideration, the play by Williams was viewed as the weakest, with many strikes against it because of its homosexual undercurrents. One juror referred to the work as "amateurishly constructed," another labeled it "annoyingly pretentious." Until they were persuaded otherwise, most jurors wanted to award the prize to the now-obscure *The Flowering Peach* by Clifford Odets, or else to *The Bad Seed,* a play by Maxwell Anderson based on a novel by William March.

Another gay playwright, Edward Albee, faced the same prejudice in 1963 when his brilliant *Who's Afraid of Virginia Woolf?* was passed over by the Pulitzer committee because of its sexual themes and use of profanity.

Sunset Blvd.

"There's nothing else...Just us, and the cameras,
and all those wonderful people out there in the dark." (Norma Desmond)

Gloria Swanson's performance as the fading silent screen actress Norma Desmond in *Sunset Blvd.* represented one of the great comebacks in cinematic history. Her striking, stylized performance as a demented former screen goddess made her almost a shoo-in for the Oscar. Alas, defining Swanson as an Oscar winner wasn't meant to be, in spite of her getting the sentimental vote from the Academy.

With five unsuccessful marriages behind her, Swanson admitted on the set that, "I looked pretty good for fifty-two."

Even before filming began, she was painfully aware that the public had largely forgotten her sweeping successes as an actress on the Silent Screen back in the 20s. In a rare moment of self-analysis (and this from an actress who wasn't noted either for her humor or her ability to self-satirize), she said, "In order to spring back to them in a single leap, I had to have a bigger-than-life part. Perhaps I played the part too well. On very rare artistic occasions the actor actually becomes the part—Barrymore *is* Hamlet, Garbo *is* Camille, and Swanson *is* Norma Desmond."

BOULEVARD OF
BROKEN DREAMS

For thousands upon thousands of gay males, at least those over 50, *Sunset Blvd.,* released in 1950 and directed by Billy Wilder, remains their all-time fave. And the film isn't even gay.

In her greatest role as a has-been vamp of the silent screen, Gloria Swanson, as *über*-diva Norma Desmond, appealed to the exaggerated sense of camp that secretly (or not so secretly) lives within the heart of most gay men.

Lines from the film have become imbedded in the gay psyche. Many gays have memorized and in some cases adopted the film's most famous line, uttered with a sense of unreality as Norma descends a palatial staircase on the way to her doom: "I'm ready for my closeup, Mr. DeMille."

Who can forget screenwriter Joe Gillis interacting with the fallen star.

JOE: You're Norma Desmond. You used to be in silent pictures. You used to be big!
NORMA: I AM big! It's the pictures that got small.

Let's not forget William Holden playing the down-and-out screen hack, Joe Gillis himself. It was fun watching Holden, then at his sexiest, play a scriptwriter/male whore to the aging star.

As fine as his performance was, Montgomery Clift probably could have delivered greater magic with the role. But he turned it down. At the time of the offer, the homosexual actor's career was on fire. He could have had almost any role in Hollywood he wanted. He was also considered the most beautiful male face in Tinseltown.

At first, Clift jumped at the role. But weeks later he changed his mind, asserting: "I can't be convincing making love to a woman twice my age."

That wasn't the real reason. His *inamorata* and mentor since 1942, the scandal-soaked Jazz Age singer Libby Holman had urged him to reject the role.

[Holman had been infamously associated with the widely publicized society murder or was it suicide of her young bisexual husband, Zachary Smith Reynolds, on July 6, 1932 in Winston-Salem, North Carolina. Always the target of sometimes justified gossip, Holman was afraid that critics would draw unflattering parallels to her relationship with the pretty young actor, 15 years her junior.]

Like the character of Norma Desmond, Holman was also a has-been, a celebrity fossil from another era. In the movie, Norma shoots Joe Gillis when he tries to leave her. The smell of gunsmoke also lingered around the aroma of Holman.

Taming the Shrews

A Director's Perilous Task:
Convincing an Actress That She'd be Fabulous in the Role of a Hollywood Has-Been

Mae West was Billy Wilder's first choice for the role of Norma Desmond. Maurice Zolotow, Wilder's biographer, said that West represented "a platonic idea of the whore whose mystery Wilder was forever trying to unravel. There was about her a certain vulgarity and fleshiness which reminded him of Viennese and *Berliner* prostitutes."

But when Wilder asked West, then aged 55, if she'd accept the role of the almost-forgotten star, West reacted in horror. "I'm no faded flower, and I'm no has-been. I'm the Venus's Flytrap that is still snaring men in her trap. Besides, I could never be convincing playing any woman older than twenty-six."

After Mae West rejected the role of Norma Desmond, **Mary Pickford** (left), once celebrated as "America's Little Sweetheart" and by some estimates one of the dozen most famous persons in the world, was offered the part. In the early version of the script she was shown, the role of Joe Gillis was the dominating part. Although she was intrigued with the script, she told director Billy Wilder that he had to expand her part, thereby making her the star of the movie. "Only then can I make a triumphant comeback," she said.

Wilder later commented, "She was a star. She would always be a star. Nothing had changed since the days of the silent pictures for Mary Pickford. She was what the movie was about--the persistence of a sense of the past to the degree that the present is but a pale shadow against those memories."

As a screen vamp of the silent screen, Poland-born **Pola Negri**, falsely credited with being the long-time lover of Rudolf Valentino, was the often bitter rival of Gloria Swanson. Had she controlled herself better, it would have been Negri herself taking over the role of Norma Desmond. But her initial meeting with Wilder didn't go well. Famous for her volatile temperament, she denounced him. "How dare you suggest that I'm a has-been. I'm still a reigning star. Still getting thousands of fan letters every day." She was exaggerating, of course.

Wilder tried to cajole and placate her, pretending that he wanted her because of her superb acting skills. "She was shrewd enough to see that he was capitalizing on her decline," said Maurice Zolotow. "She did not want to be food for the vultures."

Charles Brackett, producer of *Sunset Blvd.*, incorporated broad associations with Holman's late husband—whom he re-named *Smith* Wetherby—in his novel *Entirely Surrounded*, and years later, Holman was still fuming at that thinly disguised portrait.

Gloria Swanson was not Wilder's first choice either. File this under *believe it or not* but he first offered the role of Norma to Mae West. She rejected the idea, loudly asserting, "None of my fans would believe me as a has-been."

In the movie, Norma hires Gillis, a scriptwriter, to help her with her screenplay *Salome* for what she preferred to call "a return to pictures...not a comeback."

(In a real-life parallel, when Mae West returned to pictures in 1970, starring in Gore Vidal's *Myra Breckinridge*, her first movie in 27 years, she said, "I'm not making a comeback. I never went away.")

As part of yet another early casting attempt, both Brackett and Wilder called on Mary Pickford, a genuine has-been who, decades previously, during the Silent Screen era, had been known throughout the world as "America's Little Sweetheart." Wilder later claimed that during their dialogues, she was too drunk to even make sense of the project.

Her biographer, Scott Eyman, disagreed, claiming Pickford was interested and would have considered the script but she wanted the role of Norma Desmond expanded so that she, Pickford, not Holden, would be the true star of the picture.

Pola Negri, the rival of Swanson as screen vamp goddess of the silent screen, was also considered. By 1949 (when *Sunset* was filmed), Negri had also evolved into a true has-been. She'd made her last picture in 1943. She'd make an attempt at yet another comeback in 1964 in *The Moon-Spinners* with Hayley Mills.

But nothing worked out for her. Thanks to the sponsorship of a wealthy lesbian lover, she eventually settled in San Antonio, Texas, where she lived in Norma Desmond seclusion until her death in 1987.

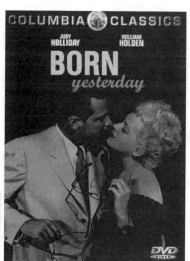

Finally, someone suggested to Wilder that the part of Norma Desmond called for "A bad actress...a Gloria Swanson type." Wilder agreed, but added, "Instead of a Gloria Swanson type, let's get Gloria Swanson herself."

Swanson later lamented that her fans, especially the gay ones, for ever after believed that she was actually Norma

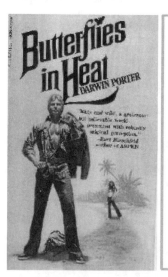

In the late 1970s, Gloria Swanson was offered yet another film role, "an *après-comeback comeback*," starring as the aging fashion mogul in the film adaptation of Darwin Porter's bestselling potboiler about love, loneliness, and sex in Key West, ***Butterflies in Heat***. Regrettably, she was ill-advised, and even more irritable and temperamental than she'd been during her temperamental heyday. It was true that, indeed, the filmscript included a scene of her climbing into bed with a studly young man, but she'd already played an equivalent scene with William Holden in *Sunset Blvd.*

She later admitted that, "I was misled. I wouldn't have had to take off my clothes. I'd have worn an elegant silk robe that I could have designed myself."

It (1950) was **William Holden**'s golden year. He starred opposite Gloria Swanson in *Sunset Blvd.*, as well as opposite **Judy Holliday** in *Born Yesterday* (a scene from which is depicted above) The Oscar that year went to Holliday for her memorable comedic role as the "kinda smart but kinda dumb" heroine.

Swanson was bitter that her portrayal of Norma Desmond had lost the Oscar until the day she died.

Desmond, and that she was merely playing herself on the screen.

In her memoirs, she revealed that after the release of *Sunset Blvd.,* most of the scripts she was offered dealt with imperious, aging, and eccentric actresses.

"It was Hollywood's old trick: Repeat a successful formula until it dies. The problem for me was that if I had played the part of a spry fifty-one year old, I could obviously go on playing it for many variations to come, until at least I became some sort of creepy parody of myself, or rather, of Norma Desmond—a shadow of a shadow."

It was for that reason that she turned down the role of an aging dress designer, Leonora de la Mer, in the screen adaptation of Darwin Porter's bestselling novel, *Butterflies in Heat.* The role called for her to play an aging dress designer living in a decaying mansion, not on Sunset Blvd., but in Key West. Here, she becomes involved with a young man on the make, a blond hustler demigod named Numie Chase.

She was ready to do the role until the news broke in Hollywood that Gloria Swanson would soon appear in "a porno remake of *Sunset Blvd.*" The charge, of course, was ridiculous, completely untrue, but she was so humiliated by these false tabloid reports that she took out an ad in *Variety,* stating "to whom it may concern" that she was dropping out of the picture.

The role went instead to stage actress Barbara Baxley, one of Tennessee Williams' favorites. Later, Swanson requested a private screening of the film, which was released as *Tropic of Desire.* She called author Darwin Porter and said, "I made a terrible mistake. The part was written with my name on it. There was nothing pornographic about it. I would have insisted that the producer Jerry Wheeler enlarge my part. The role of Leonora could have brought me my first Oscar, the one that was denied me by those lesbians."

"You mean, Judy Holliday?"

Holliday won Best Actress that year (1950) for *Born Yesterday.*

"Yes, I mean her, but I also mean Bette Davis. Davis, whom I always loathed, and I were both playing aging actresses. I think we cancelled each other out. Defeated by another lesbian."

"I've heard stories but you don't really believe that Miss Davis is a lesbian, do you?"

"Of course, I believe she's a lesbian. The poor dear just hasn't figured it out yet."

***

Sunset Blvd. remains the best drama ever made about the movies. And although the film sees through the industry's illusions, Norma does not.

"Poor devil," Joe Gillis (William Holden) says, "still waving proudly to a parade which had long since passed her by."

Alas for Norma, who hisses psychotic and self-delusional commentary as she's led off either to jail or an asylum, "There's nothing else. Just us, and the cameras, and those wonderful people out there in the dark."

ERICH OSWALD STROHEIM

(aka Count Erich Oswald Hans Carl Maria von Stroheim und Nordenwall)

(1885-1957)

Before we sign off on *Sunset Blvd.*, it would be a crime not to mention the film's third lead, Erich von Stroheim, famously known for playing villainous German roles, during one of which the character he was playing threw a baby out an open window. Film critics at the time referred to him as "The Man You Love to Hate." Born in Vienna in 1885, von Stroheim was a rigorous and imperial "fantasist" who shamelessly embroidered misinformation about his (dubious) aristocratic past. One of the great film directors of the silent screen era, von Stroheim had immortalized himself for the direction of his masterpiece, *Greed,* which the studio later edited and censored to the point where it was virtually unrecognizable.

In 1929, he directed Swanson in the ill-fated *Queen Kelly,* a horrendously over-budget film financed by her lover at the time, Joseph Kennedy, Sr., father of the future U.S. president. Although it was never completed, partly because of ongoing conflicts with Kennedy and Swanson herself, scenes from that (fiscally disastrous) picture were featured within the context of *Sunset Blvd.*

In *Sunset Blvd.,* the autocratic and humorless von Stroheim was cast into "the lousy butler part" (his words). The character he played, as explained near the end of the movie, had been one of Norma's former husbands. In his capacity as her ex-husband and presently, her butler, his self-defined duties included the crafting of fan letters which deluded her into thinking that they'd came from passionately enthusiastic audiences who had never forgotten her.

Despite the fact that von Stroheim delivered one of the most brilliant and poignant performances of his long career, he never liked his role in the Wilder film.

In the words of his biographer, Thomas Quinn Curtiss, "Von Stroheim felt that the role capitalized on his own downfall, and indeed the whole film was a mockery of the old-time Hollywood in which he had accomplished his best work."

PITHY WISDOM FROM VON STROHEIM

"Lubitsch shows you first the king on the throne, then as he is in the bedroom. I show you the king in the bedroom so you'll know just what he is when you see him on his throne."

"If you live in France, for instance, and you have written one good book, or painted one good picture, or directed one outstanding film fifty years ago and nothing else since, you are still re'ognized and honored accordingly. People take their hats off to you and call you '*maître.*' They do not forget. In Hollywood —in Hollywood, you're as good as your last picture. If you didn't have one in production within the last three months, you're forgotten, no matter what you have achieved before this."

Between 1928 and 1929, **Erich von Stroheim** (two photos, above), one of the greatest of all film directors, directed Gloria Swanson in the notorious *Queen Kelly*, a silent film financed by her lover, Joseph Kennedy, Sr., and never completed. The director and his then-leading-lady met decades later on the set of *Sunset Blvd.* "Once I was your director—the greatest of them all—and now I'm cast as your butler," he told her. "Such are the vagaries of fate."

For budgetary reasons, Von Stroheim's cinematic masterpiece, *Greed,* released in 1924, was cut to one-fourth of its intended length by hack film editors, and the footage destroyed. Film historians have mourned its loss ever since.

The notorious cabaret singer and actress **Libby Holman** (photo top right) is seen here in a publicity still promoting her 1931 Cole Porter hit, "Love for Sale," which was also a theme song--more or less--for Gloria Swanson. It was because of Holman that Montgomery Clift, the original choice for the role of Joe Gillis, turned down the role of the screenwriter/male whore. "Too close to home," Wilder later said. "Clift thought *Sunset Blvd.* would be interpreted as a thinly disguised film version of what had happened between Libby Holman and himself."

Although Clift had claimed that he could never realistically portray a young man in love with an old woman, he was in the grip of a romantic obsession with Holman, who was thirty years older than he was, give or take, mostly give."

In *Sunset Blvd.,* Norma Desmond shoots and kills Joe Gillis. Decades before, in real life, Holman had shot and killed her young gay husband, R.J. Reynolds, heir to a tobacco fortune, in Winston-Salem, North Carolina. Years later, Holman, always good at histrionics, threatened to kill herself if Clift played Gillis.

An author of this guidebook, Darwin Porter, was once in a Manhattan elevator with film icon **Tallulah Bankhead** (photo lower right). Into the elevator came a wizened version of the towering seductress that used to be Libby Holman. The dialogue that ensued went like this:

> **HOLMAN**: Tallulah...Time does march on, I can see.
> **BANKHEAD**: Libby, dahling....Taking a break between murders?

How to Lose an Oscar, Diva-Style

Arguably, the person who cost Gloria Swanson her well-deserved Oscar for Best Actress in 1950 was the formidable **Bette Davis** (top photo, left) in her defining role as Margo Channing in *All About Eve.* Both Swanson and Davis were cast as aging actresses, Swanson a Hollywood diva, Davis an over-the-hill Broadway baby.

To make the race even more complicated, **Anne Baxter** (left-hand figure in lower photo) who had played Eve Harrington opposite Davis in *All About Eve,* added to the tension by insisting that her entry into the Oscar sweepstakes be as Best Actress, not Best Supporting Actress. Suddenly, the judges found themselves confronted with three A-list contenders (Swanson, Davis, and Baxter), each portraying ambitious actresses, thereby splitting the panel's votes even further.

This was the dynamic that paved the way for the designation of "fourth ringer" Judy Holliday, the romantic lead in *Born Yesterday,* that year as Best Actress. Screams of protest were heard throughout America, but the judges' decision was final.

Dishing the Divas / More Casting Drama

Bette Davis is remembered today for her portrayal of one of the most autocratically flamboyant characters in film history, the "fasten your seat belts, it's gonna be a bumpy night" Margo Channing. But even though in hindsight, she was the obvious choice for the role, she was not the studio's first choice.

Darryl F. Zanuck wanted Marlene Dietrich, but when the film's director, Joseph L. Mankiewicz, strenuously objected, Claudette Colbert was offered the part. When Colbert seriously injured her back and had to bow out, Zanuck offered the role to Ingrid Bergman, even though everyone was aware that she was a bit young for a diva who'd gone way over the hill.

Finally, in desperation, Bette Davis got the part. At the time (1949), her Hollywood career was considered "all but dead," a fact that because the character she was playing faced the same dilemma, seemed oddly appropriate.

Marilyn Monroe (bottom photo, between **Bette** and **George Sanders**, said, "I should have been Eve."

Brokeback Mountain

Liberation and Love Are Forces of Nature

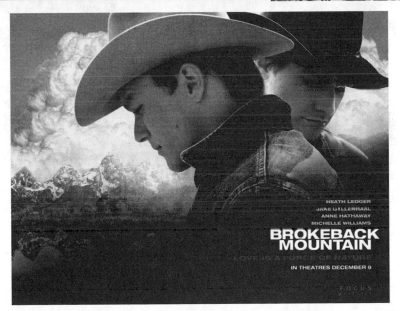

Director Ang Lee said, "Westerns usually contain a lot of homo subtext. A cowboy has always been homoerotic for the gay community, like the Chinese martial arts heroes in the East."

Producer James Schamus more or less suggested that the film's characters could ride 'em, cowboy, and let the yokels be damned. "The aim of the film was not to make a political point about intolerance toward gays," said Schamus. "We are using the codes and convention of romance that have always applied to straight people very un-apologetically. We don't care if anyone is going to be upset about it. There's not a conscious political program one way or another."

BROKEBACK MOUNTAIN
HOMO ON THE RANGE

John Wayne may be rolling over in his grave, but director Ang Lee made the epic American western, a history-making "gay cowboy movie" that will probably continue to be screened a half-century from now. It's the story of two cowboys, as portrayed by Jake Gyllenhaal and Heath Ledger, who fall in love almost by accident, beginning a furtive, frustrated romance that spans two decades.

Ledger delivers an Oscar-winning performance as the tight-lipped Ennis Del Mar, who at first doesn't seem to know what's happening to him. Gyllenhaal as Jack Twist became the new poster boy of the gay world. Such former heartthrobs as Brad Pitt and the very heterosexual Tom Cruise should start shopping for middle-aged daddy roles.

Set in Wyoming, the film was actually shot in Alberta. It all begins one night when Ledger's campfire dies, and he's shivering in the biting cold. The spark is lit when he enters Jack's tent. That spark turns into an undying flame that would last beyond the grave.

In the shadows of the cramped tent, Jack makes overtures to Ennis who at first resents him. Then, in a sudden outburst of long-suppressed desires, he takes to gay sex as if he were born for it. Jack quickly becomes his everloving bottom, as this handsome cowboy discovers an ecstasy he never dreamed possible. Once inside Jack, he wants to stay there forever.

Of course, there is the inevitable morning after and the usual denials.

ENNIS: I'm no queer.
JACK: Me neither.

We sensed what a powerful movie this would make when we first read Annie Proulx's short story in *The New Yorker* in 1997. Larry McMurtry and Diana Ossana also recognized the possibilities and adapted it for the screen.

Sam Mendes, who directed **Jake Gyllenhaal** in *Jarhead*, said, "I don't think I had realized until I saw him onstage how masculine he is. He's a big guy, and he has a combination of soulfulness and a 'man of action' aura that I was looking for. Also, he's very accessible. His face is accessible. His soul is accessible."

Brokeback Mountain contains a nude scene in which Heath Ledger and Jake Gyllenhall jump into a cold lake. Ang Lee intended to edit out any actual frontal nudity. But a paparazzo caught photos of Ledger with a digital camera, and these shots appeared soon after on the Internet.

For the film's official version of that "go jump in the lake" nude scene, body doubles were enlisted. That's not because Gyllenhaal has anything to be ashamed of. In *Jarhead*, in a shower scene, he does the full Monty, but only for a glimpse and in shadows. It's a tantalizing glimpse.

But their screenplay went begging for eight years. McMurtry knows about the loneliness and despair of Western America. His novel, *The Last Picture Show*, was made into a movie 34 years ago by Peter Bogdanovich. No major studio would touch *Brokeback Mountain* until Ang Lee came along. The rest is cinematic history.

Lee was brilliant in his magnificent film, *Crouching Tiger, Hidden Dragon*. Regrettably, he followed it with the execrable *Hulk*. With the release of *Brokeback Mountain*, the director lived up to his promise as never before.

In 1963, when the story begins, the word "gay" had not even made it into the vocabulary of the people of Wyoming. When Jean Bullis, the real-life editor of a small-town newspaper, first learned that men make love to each other, her first response was, "that's impossible. For a man to make love, he's got to have a hole to stick it into. Women have holes. Men don't have holes."

Surely the world has grown a bit more sophisticated than when this yokel made such an utterance.

Various writers and artists have called attention to the homoerotic strain in American culture way before *Brokeback Mountain* was ever heard of. Critic Leslie Fiedler nailed it in his controversial *Partisan Review* essay published back in 1948. "Come Back to the Raft Ag'in, Huck Honey." The writer characterized the bond between Jim (the run-away slave) and Huckleberry Finn as the unconscious romantic attachment shared by two men—one black, the other white.

There are other examples: The Lone Ranger and Tonto; and that buddy movie, *Red River*, with John Wayne and gay actor Montgomery Clift. And back in the 70s, openly gay author James Leo Herlihy once admitted to us that *Midnight Cowboy* was at its core a love story between two men.

The beat goes on, notably with Paul Newman and Robert Redford, both looking gorgeous in *Butch Cassidy and the Sundance Kid*. Of course, all this male bonding did not explore the phenomenon's shadow side. Ang Lee had the balls to do that in *Brokeback Mountain*.

Randy Quaid delivers a brilliant short performance as Joe Aguirre, the hard-boiled rancher and homophobe who hires these two down-and-out sheepherders to work the flock and keep them safe from coyotes in Wyoming high country. Once isolated, the boozy friendship of the two men begins. It's fueled by whiskey and testosterone, and nourished by the canned beans on which they subsist.

Both men come from tragic backgrounds, Ennis raised by a brother and sister after his par-

Frank Rich, arguably the most culturally hip columnist in America, wrote in *The New York Times:* "Although *Brokeback Mountain* is not a western, it's been directed by **Ang Lee** (photo above) with the austerity and langourous gait of a John Ford epic. These aesthetics couldn't be more country miles removed from *The Bird Cage* or *Will & Grace*. The audience is forced to recognize that gay people were fixtures in the Red State of Wyoming (and every other corner of the country, too) long before Matthew Shepard and Mary Cheney were born.

"This laconic film dramatizes homosexuality as an inherent and immutable identity, rather than some aberrant and 'elective agenda' concocted by conspiratorial 'elites' in Chelsea, the Castro, and South Beach, as anti-gay proselytizers would have it. Ennis and Jack long for a life together, not for what gay baiters pejoratively label as a 'lifestyle.'"

ents died in a car crash. Brought up in the rodeo, Jack is more talkative than the taciturn and bottled-up Ennis. His father, a bull rider, was the last kind of Wyoming father a gay man needs to bring him up. Jack's father, when he's finally introduced at the end of the film, is a stunning portrait of Gothic America with all its horrors. He's more frightening than Freddy Kruger in *A Nightmare on Elm Street* (1984).

At the end of their summer of isolated bliss on Brokeback Mountain, Ennis and Jack go their separate ways. Instead of a hug and a kiss, Ennis delivers a tight-lipped farewell: "See you around."

At that point, not even conceiving that it was possible to pursue a gay lifestyle as a spiritually married couple, the two handsome men drift into straight relationships. Ennis marries his girlfriend. Alma (Michelle Williams) delivers a stunning performance as his wife that will push those of borderline preferences quickly to the gay side of the fence. Less brilliant, but also effective in a lesser role, is Lureen (played by Anne Hathaway), a self-centered Texas rodeo queen, who falls for Jack. Ultimately he joins her redneck father's farm equipment business. Naturally, the narrow-minded Daddy hates Jack and humiliates him whenever possible.

If there are any gay men still out there contemplating a traditional marriage to a woman, they need to see *Brokeback Mountain*. Both Jack and Ennis enter crumbling marriages orchestrated in Hell. Although fully aware that her husband, Ennis, is gay, she keeps the news and its pain bottled up inside. Her bile doesn't rise to the surface until

In this scene from *Brokeback Mountain,* **Jake Gyllenhaal** might have been dancing with his make-believe darling--in this case, **Anne Hathaway**--but we know that in his heart, he's eager to return to the panoramas and blue skies of the West, where Heath Ledger is waiting for him.

In his private life, Gyllenhaal has gracefully confronted gay rumors. "You know, it's flattering when there's a rumor that I'm bisexual. I'm open to whatever people want to call me. I've never really been attracted to men sexually, but I don't think I would be afraid if it happened."

Both **Michelle Williams** and **Heath Ledger** signed on for key roles in doomed love stories (both celluloid and real-life) when she took him into her bed for the first time. Their romance blossomed in 2004 in Calgary, Alberta, when they were shooting *Brokeback Mountain*.

At first, it was idyllic. After she injured her knee on set, Ledger told Ang Lee, "I feel I have to look after her. We just fell very deeply into each other's arms. Our bodies definitely made the decision for us."

The result was a beautiful daughter they named Matilda.

after she divorces her husband. Although the audience won't like her, Williams, as Alma, gives a performance worthy of a best supporting actress Oscar.

Jack deals with his unsatisfactory marriage to Lureen by entering a robotic shell. To answer the desperate sexual and emotional needs not fulfilled by Ennis, he has clandestine encounters with other men, picking one up on a "gay alley" in a sleazy Mexican town.

Four long and painful years pass before Jack and Ennis link up again. From his home in Texas, Jack sends a postcard to Ennis marked general delivery. He's planning to return to Wyoming on a visit. Held intact all these years, Ennis's passion for Jack explodes when they reunite in a spontaneous clinch. Tongue down the throat. Hot, throbbing cock pressed against hot, throbbing cock. This kissing scene is so powerful that Ledger nearly broke Gyllenhaal's nose while filming it. Unfortunately for her, Alma witnesses it all. She is heartbroken, as her husband rushes off to check into a bleak motel with his newly rediscovered lover.

Jack, the more "out" of the two, wants to forge a romantic bond with Ennis, setting up a shared life on their own ranch together. Ennis is the reluctant groom. He still remembers an incident from his childhood when his father took him to see the mutilated body of a rancher. He was tortured and beaten to death for living with another man, his cock ripped from his body.

It should be painfully noted that the murder of Matthew Shepard took place in "Brokeback Country." Inspired by the then-sitting president of the United States, the homophobes of Wyoming, and elsewhere, are just as ignorant, dangerous, and stupid today as they always were.

Even though four years have passed, Jack remembers the bond he had created with Ennis that previous summer on *Brokeback*. In the words of Ms. Proulx, he fondly recalled when "Ennis had come up behind him and pulled him close, the silent embrace satisfying some shared and sexless hunger."

Because of the refusal of Ennis to enter into a clearly defined permanent relationship, Jack must confine his visits to his lover to so-called fishing trips once or twice a year. No fish is ever caught on these trips.

In the film, the love between Jack and Ennis may be pure, but the secrecy of the relationship is a poison that visits itself on the two men and their families.

Heath Ledger and **Michelle Williams** participated in an on-screen marriage ceremony in *Brokeback Mountain*. In real life, such a wedding never occurred. Whereas they lived together and produced a daughter, marriage was never an issue.

As actors within the film, at least, they gave the appearance of being a stereotypical Wyoming couple of that era, each evoking a touch of local yokel in the characters they were playing.

Although the film is about two gay cowboys, it's not really a gay film of the genre that came to prominence in the 70s. It's too honest, too real for that type of exploitation.

The characters as played by Ledger and Gyllenhaal become so real that even a homophobe might come to view them as two human beings in love—not two cowboys fucking each other. But perhaps that would give homophobes too much credit.

The film came as a disappointment to many gay fans who had hoped that after that night in the tent the two handsome actors, Heath and Jake, would make it permanent and set up housekeeping.

Alas, we can dream, can't we?

Even before the film opened, the Drudge Report managed to dredge up a playwright from Wyoming, who claimed that she had never met a homosexual cowboy. She accused Ang Lee of ruining the state's image. Isn't that moron adorable?

Brokeback Mountain is not about sex. It's about love. Love discovered. Love frustrated by society. Love held forever in the sorrowful heart of Ennis who missed out on his own chance to find happiness and meaning in life and ends up alone in a bleak trailer to live out his days with the memory of loving Jack dooming him to sorrow, with longing in his heart for what is gone forever.

The life-long bond formed by the two men is by turns ecstatic, bitter, and conflicted. The complications, joys, and tragedies of the relationship provide a testament to the endurance and power of love.

WHAT THE CRITICS SAID

"Our hearts go out to these lovers and the yearning that binds them together over the long and lonely years. It is a crime that passion like this continues to be denigrated, hated, and fought as if it were the vilest thing that a human being could ever do."
Frederic and Mary Ann Brussat

"Unmissable and unforgettable! Hits you like a shot in the heart! The classic in making ranks high on the list of the year's best movies. It's a landmark film and a triumph for Heath Ledger and Jake Gyllenhaal. Heath Ledger's performance is an acting miracle. Anne Hathaway excels. Michelle Williams is a revelation."
Peter Travers, *Rolling Stone*

"This is one of the best serious films about homosexuality ever made, but though it's sad and sobering, it's still only a rough draft of a great movie. The sex scene that follows is fairly graphic, and director Ang Lee must know that he could have tripled his audience by trimming 60 seconds. But the scene is there, and if it will make some viewers uncomfortable it also plants us firmly in reality. *Brokeback Mountain* will be rightly praised for honestly assessing the emotional wreckage done to men and women by the closeting of homosexuality. That idea is so powerful and so little explored on screen that it's bound to be revisited in a more complete film in the future."
Kyle Smith, *New York Post*

"A big, sweeping, and rapturous Hollywood love story! It could turn out to be the most revolutionary movie of the year. A film in which love feels almost as if it were being in-

vented. It is also a rare crowd-pleaser with the potential to change hearts and minds."
Owen Gleiberman, *Entertainment Weekly*

"Focus, which finally financed the film, must be hoping that some higher powered culture warriors will attack their movie as a manifestation of the Antichrist—or, at least, the anti-Mel Gibson. The sex scenes may be hot but it's difficult to believe that Madonna found them 'shocking.' All is tasteful, and far more convincing than the movie's representation of passion is its evocation of a punishing social order. The closet has never seemed more cruelly constricting than in comparison to the wide open spaces of what Americans are pleased to call God's country."
J. Hoberman, *Village Voice*

"Ang Lee twists each genre with the film he enters into it, and now with *Brokeback Mountain*, he aims to wring the western genre with a beautiful and honest love story. It'll be met with controversy, especially in today's political climate where homophobia reigns along with stiff, intolerant religious values even in the highest of political positions. But it's a story that doesn't aim to preach a message of acceptance and tolerance. Its only objective is to tell its story, as any great film aims to do, and do so with as much honesty and affection as possible."
Sam Osborn

"A quick sex scene in which Ennis flips his wife over on her stomach tells us all we need to know about his true preference. With critical support, Focus Features should have little trouble stirring interest among older, sophisticated viewers in urban markets, but trying to cross this risky venture over into wider release reps a marketing challenge for

Never looking this sexy before, **Michelle Williams** lured Heath Ledger into a romance, but it turned sour when she couldn't keep him away from drugs and alchohol. Ironically, their tormented romance paralleled the one that had been portrayed onscreen between Ennis del Mar and Jack Twist.

For three years, Williams was an eyewitness to Heath's self-destruction, watching him ingest lots of cocaine, heroin, and an assortment of pills.

For a time, the troubled duo even wore rings, although they never confirmed either an engagement or a marriage.

THE LINE-UP (LEFT TO RIGHT):

Anne Hathaway, Ang Lee, Heath Ledger, and **Jake Gyllenhaal**. During the shoot, the theory arose that had *Brokeback Mountain* been filmed during the *I Love Lucy* homophobic 1950s, the director would have cast Paul Newman as Ennis and Montgomery Clift as Jack Twist.

Lee was pleased, post-millennium, with his final choices. Stephen Holder in *The New York Times* agreed: "Both Mr. Ledger and Mr. Gyllenhaal make this anguished love story physically palpable. Mr. Ledger magically and mysteriously disappears beneath the skin of his lean, sinewy character. It's a great screen performance that's as good as the best of Marlon Brando or Sean Penn. The pain and disappointment felt by Jack, who is softer, more self-aware, and more self-accepting, continually registers in Mr. Gyllenhaal's sad, expectant, silver-dollar eyes."

the ages; paradoxically, young women may well constitute the group that will like the film best."
Todd McCarthy, *Variety*

"The film could easily have become exploitative, pigeonholing its leads as two drama queens in cowboy boots, but Lee portrays them both as virile men who know the pain and suffering of forbidden love and despite their virility are not able to enjoy their romantic moments together. It has elements of a cowboy film but it is not a cowboy film. It has elements of a forbidden love drama but neither is it simply that; *Brokeback Mountain* dives headlong into the two characters of Ennis and Jack; two men who suffer because of love and each other."
Boyd van Hoeij

"Never mind that the dusty duo is still whining about their tragic fate into the late 1970s. They are, after all, in the west. But for me, this dramatic excuse that seems to want to excuse the lack of choice made by these two very strong, very focused men, is a complete cop-out. If these men want to be together so badly, why not risk it? My God, even after getting a divorce, one of the characters can't move forward into his life. The last 15 minutes or some of the film does, in a quiet way, suppose to bring the perspective of the other characters into play . . . finally! But too little, too late. If you are willing to put blinders on to how thin the movie is and if you are into mushy romance, you will probably love it."
David Poland

"It's always what we always knew to be true: beneath the tight jeans, sweaty chaps, and weathered countenance, the American cowboy is an ass-pounder waiting to be born. Ang Lee's *Brokeback Mountain* shocked the hell out of me. It's a gracious, tender film of such depth and dignity that were this nation not packed to the gills with homophobic creeps, it would go down as the year's most powerful love story. As Woody Allen has said, 'the heart wants what the heart wants,' and what better case could be made for letting love take its course. One of the year's best."
ruthlessreviews.com

"*Brokeback* feels like a landmark film. No American film before has portrayed love between two men as something this pure and sacred. As such, it has the potential to change the national conversation and to challenge people's ideas about the value and validity of same-sex relationships. In the meantime, it's already upended decades of Hollywood conventional wisdom."
Newsweek

"As adapted by Larry McMurtry and writing partner Diana Ossana, the result is something like *Lonesome Dove* refashioned as *Doctor Zhivago*, with a serial grandeur attained largely by adhering closely to the 30-page source material, populated by characters with-

out the emotional vocabulary to cope with the profound changes wrought in them."
Paul Cullum

"I don't normally feel bad for movie stars, but seeing Brokeback leads Jake Gyllenhaal and Heath Ledger bombarded with queries along the lines of 'Ah-hur-hur, what was it like to kiss another guy, ah-hur-hur?' is a little dispiriting. I'm almost surprised nobody's asked, 'Did you two touch each others' pee-pees?' But maybe I just haven't seen that particular *Entertainment Tonight* episode yet."
Premiere

"The cast relies on very little makeup to suggest the passage of two decades, time passing instead through clothes, music, and hair (particularly Hathaway's). But it is these outer cues that are the most poignant, because eventually the 1960s give way to the '70s and '80s. In another part of the United States, Stonewall was taking place, gay men were establishing a beachhead in San Francisco's Castro district, and the closet was starting to fly open. But, for Ennis and Jack, all of that may as well be happening on Mars. While Jack complains that their relationship is limited to 'a couple of high-altitude fucks' and would happily start over somewhere else, Ennis is more circumspect. 'We could end up dead,' he cautions Jack, terrified at what might happen if anyone finds out about the true nature of their friendship. It never occurs to him that his reticence by itself constitutes a tragedy."
Paul Grady

"*An Affair to Remember* meets *Boys in Buckskin*. If anybody can make a gay cowboy movie that appeals to the mainstream U.S. audience, it's Ang Lee. Homophobia is the shadowy villain stalking this romance, and homophobia is the only thing that can keep it from enjoying a roaring success. Ang Lee's adaptation of Annie Proulx's short story about a closeted love affair between two gay ranch hands in the 1960s Wyoming may be too much for Red-State audiences, but it gives the liberal-leaning academy a great chance to stick its thumb in conservatives' eyes."
Jack Mathews, *New York Daily News*

"Forbidden love is forbidden love; no recent American movie feels as solidly traditional and satisfying in its dark romantic swoon. 'It's because of you that I'm like this,' Ennis bawls to Jack. It's the film's most staggering revelation. It's possible that such exchanges would trigger squirms even in a hetero context; *Brokeback Mountain* is nothing if not a full-on weepie, and a conservative one at that. It literally ends in a closet. Such may be the essence of its appeal, paradoxically, to mall crawlers soon confronted with matinee man-love. But the film is also a fine tragedy, fiercely alive with sympathy for people in a culturally dark place and time. Sadly, that hasn't changed much; here's to a film with the balls to depict such shortcomings where we least suspect them, a rocky terrain where the men are, most bravely and tenderly, men."
Joshua Rothkopf, *Time Out New York*

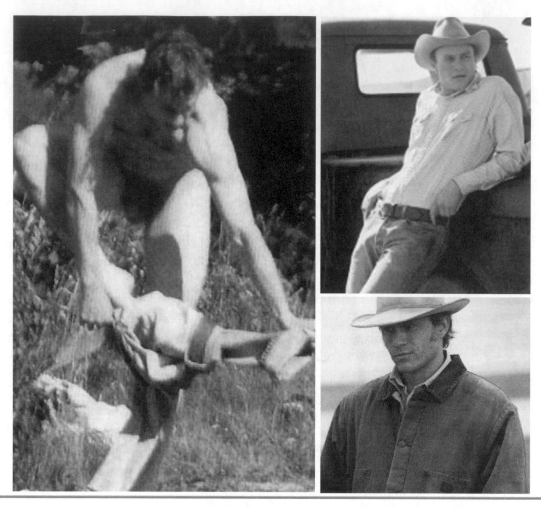

So LONG, PARTNER

Heath Ledger's early death left fans around the world fretting that his life had been unfulfilled, and that there were many more movies he could have made. We can at least be grateful that he gave us the performance of a lifetime in his Oscar-nominated role as Ennis Del Mar in *Brokeback Mountain*.

When it came to dropping trou, he was no sissy, showing us the full monty in the candid snapshot above. Ledger's take on the brooding sexual tension between two men has rarely been equaled on screen.

As Kyle Buchanan wrote: "For a population who grew up on a filmic diet of doomed gays and lesbians, Ledger's real-life death adds an extra layer of tragedy to his character in *Brokeback Mountain*. The life Ennis had carved out was not a happy one, but he was, at least, a survivor. With a minimum of makeup, Ledger has taken the character into his 30s and 40s, ages the actor will now never see. The compromised triumph of Ennis Del Mar——the idea of a happy life gone unlived——grows more bittersweet when coupled with thoughts of what Ledger himself might have gone on to accomplish."

HEATH LEDGER
TRAGIC HEARTTHROB
FROM DOWN UNDER

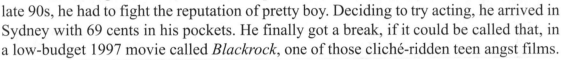

Born in 1979 in Perth in Western Australia, Heath Ledger faced a busy year in 2005: *Candy*, *Lords of Dogtown*, *The Brothers Grimm*, *Casanova*, and, of course, the history-making *Brokeback Mountain*, which is likely to be remembered when all those other films are forgotten.

First, coming to the attention of the public in the late 90s, he had to fight the reputation of pretty boy. Deciding to try acting, he arrived in Sydney with 69 cents in his pockets. He finally got a break, if it could be called that, in a low-budget 1997 movie called *Blackrock*, one of those cliché-ridden teen angst films.

Coming to America, he was named one of *People Magazine*'s Most Beautiful People in 2001. Originally, he was slated to star in Oliver Stone's 2004 *Alexander*, but the role went to big-dicked Colin Farrell with the dyed blond job.

Directors Gus Van Sant and Joel Schumacher rejected both *Brokeback Mountain* itself and the idea of Heath Ledger playing a gay cowboy, but not Ang Lee, who took chances on both the offbeat script and on the Australian actor for the leading role.

The critical acclaim from Venice to Toronto was immediate. The buzz was out: the picture to see when it opened in December of 2005 was *Brokeback Mountain*. Some producers in Hollywood predicted that it would destroy Heath Ledger's career. Actually, the role of Ennis brought the actor his most critical acclaim. He's brilliant in the part, his performance heralded as a "revelation" by critics.

"Ennis Del Mar is probably the most masculine character I've played to date," Ledger told reporters. "This is a somewhat homophobic guy who's in love with another man. That's his story, and that's what I was attracted to about the role—his choices, or his lack of choice. It's why the violence is so important, because he doesn't accept it himself. He needs someone else to kick the shit out of him."

Heath was no longer a decorative element as he was in such earlier light-headed Hollywood fare as *10 Things I Hate About You* (1999), *A Knight's Tale* (2001), and *The Four Feathers* (2002). He tried to rough up his image with a role in *Monster's Ball* in 2001.

Of Heath's performance in Brokeback, director Lee says, "I think it's always Ennis's movie, not in terms of the love story, but when you think about carrying the Western mood, that nonverbal, brooding elegiac mood. The sort of hidden agenda, which is fear and violence, that was all pretty much carried by Ennis."

In endless press interviews, Ledger was constantly pressed on the gay issue. At one point, he said, "With society today, anybody who still has an issue with it [homosexuality] is a little bit immature." We'd second that, but we'd rewrite the comment to read. "It's a hell of a lot immature, not a little bit."

Later, Ledger added, "It baffles me that we have to voice our opinions or disgust about the way people choose to love each other. Shouldn't we be doing that about the way people express anger?"

There were rumors that Ledger got "turned on" during the love scenes with Gyllenhaal. He did admit to the press that he found his co-star "awfully cute."

On the set, Heath fell for actress Michelle Williams, who played his wife in the film. On October 28, 2005, they gave birth to a baby, Matilda.

Ledger was found dead on January 22, 2008 inside his New York City apartment. An autopsy failed to reveal exactly how the actor died, although it appeared to be a drug overdose. At least five different bottles of prescription drugs were found around his apartment.

In the wake of his death, American media destroyed his reputation as a clean living guy. Magazines dug up data about his previous drug past which was cited as the reason for his breakup with the actress Michelle Williams.

A spokesperson for the New York Police Department, Paul Browne, told the press, "There was no obvious indication of suicide."

Ledger's death sparked interest in the latest of the Batman pictures, *The Dark Knight*, in which he delivered a performance of The Joker that was radically different from that of Jack Nicholson. Nicholson played The Joker in the first Batman movie released in 1989.

At the time of his untimely death, Ledger was filming *The Imaginarium of Doctor Parnassus*. The 28-year-old star's last movie was rescued by a trio of friends playing his role—Johnny Depp, Jude Law, and Colin Farrell.

His friend Christopher Plummer told the press, "I like to think of Heath as not having disappeared. Because the one thing that the screen does, that the theater does not, is to make you immortal. He was a joy and he'll go on being a joy. Heath will be with us forever."

Henderson   McKinney

A tragic portrait (left photo) of two psychotic, gay-bashing killers, **Russell Arthur Henderson** and **Aaron James McKinney**. They are each serving life sentences at the Wyoming State Penitentiary South Facility in Rawlins, Wyoming, for the October 1998 torture and slaying of gay University of Wyoming student **Matthew Shepard** (right photo).

Young Matthew's brutal death revealed that gay men are killed in the state of Wyoming for being gay. *Brokeback Mountain*'s premise was not mere fiction.

COMPARISONS OF *BROKEBACK* TO ROCK HUDSON AND JAMES DEAN IN *GIANT*

Brokeback Mountain evoked memories of James Dean in *Giant* for many critics, including Manohla Dargis of *The New York Times*. In Brokeback, when Ennis pushes his Stetson down to obscure his face, his gesture recalls James Dean pushing down his Stetson in the 1956 film, *Giant*. Based on a story by Edna Ferber about a Texas ranching dynasty and the changes it faces when oil is discovered on their property, it co-starred gay actor Rock Hudson and the world's most gay-friendly A-list actress, Elizabeth Taylor. James Dean was killed in a car accident just before the release of this film.

As *Brokeback* progresses, to indicate the passage of time, Jake Gyllenhaal sprouts a mustache to show that he's reached middle age. Even so, he still looks like a schoolboy to us. The "aging" of Heath Ledger and Gyllenhaal evokes the so-called aging of James Dean and Rock Hudson in *Giant*. Silver hair and painted-on wrinkles didn't really age Dean and Hudson either.

Like the characters in *Brokeback Mountain*, actors Hudson and Dean were forced to live in the closet of the 1950s. Dean was still in the closet when he died. Even today, so-called "close friends" deny that he was gay, in spite of hundreds of witnesses who relate up-close and personal encounters to prove the opposite. Hudson was only forced out of the closet by his battle with AIDS.

Dargis indulges in some fascinating speculation. "James Dean was about the same age as Mr. Gyllenhaal when he made *Giant*. It would be nice to think that if Dean and Hudson were alive today they would be out of their respective closets and would be enjoying the kind of marquee muscle that could get a project like *Brokeback Mountain* off the ground and into the theaters."

IT'S
GIANT!

Three movie icons beloved by the gay community are pictured in these movie stills from *Giant*. Showcased in the upper row of photos (left to right) are **James Dean, Elizabeth Taylor,** and **Rock Hudson,** who never looked handsomer and more macho.

In the bottom left-hand photo, **Taylor** looks like she's begging to give gun-toting **Dean** a blow-job. In the photo on the lower right, gay **Hudson** is pretending to make love to **Taylor**, perhaps not very convincingly.

Originally, Taylor objected to her West Texas wardrobe--brogue shoes, a long, somewhat frumpy skirt, and a man's slouch hat. "I look like a lesbian in drag," she complained.

Hudson and Dean began the filming of *Giant* as real-life sex buddies, but later turned against each other. Taylor befriended both of them.

Although for years she refused to discuss the sexuality of her male co-stars, she later claimed that she helped "Jimmy and Rock get out of the closet."

Pop Guru
Andy Warhol

"Without Moi, There Would Be No Queer Cinema!"

"Warhol was the most hated person of his time. Hated as a cold fish--cold-blooded, calculating, power-hungry."
Ronnie Tavel

***

Of the thousands of cultural icons of the 20th century, **Andy Warhol** (1928-1987) most clearly represented the celebration of celebrity itself. Of course, he had his detractors, but legions of devotees celebrated virtually everything he said and did. No one, however, ever awarded him any nice guy plaques. At times, he became more of an "after dark phenomenon" than an artist, per se, although some of his iconic pop art made its way into major-league museums. At the time of his death and beyond, much of his personality remained a deliberately enigmatic mystery.

He was a man of few words. Sometimes hours would pass wherein he'd utter only the phrase, "Gee, that's great."

Warhol had an instinct for knowing where the action would be on any given Manhattan night, and as such was photographed with a frequently surreal medley of glitterati from all spectrums of society. Popping up frequently within his orbit were the likes of Mick Jagger, Fellini, Calvin Klein, John Lennon, Elizabeth Taylor, Cher, Madonna, Jackie Onassis, Truman Capote, Presidents Reagan, Ford, and Carter, and spectacularly eccentric members of his inner circle, known collectively as "The Factory."

THE PSYCHIC PRICE OF FREAKDOM

A homosexual young man, not surprisingly, became the centerpiece of that visual movement known as Pop Art. Warhol enjoyed a lot more than "15 minutes of fame." Warhol's biographer, Victor Bockris, called him "the single most important artist of the 20th century."

He also became a lot richer after his death than he was during his lifetime. In 2009, his 1963 canvas, *Eight Elvises* fetched $100 million, the highest price ever paid for a Warhol. At the height of the art market boom, in 2007, auction sales of his work totaled $428 million. Since 1994, the Andy Warhol Museum in his native Pittsburgh, a collabortive extension of the Carnegie Institute, has honored his life and legacy.

His startling genius began to be appreciated in the 60s with his iconic paintings of American cultural mainstays that included cans of Campbell's soup and Coca-Cola. His paintings of celebrities also earned him fame—Marilyn Monroe, Elvis Presley, Elizabeth Taylor. He even painted Troy Donahue.

One of the most famous events in Warhol's life occurred on June 3, 1968 when a deranged member of his inner sanctum, Valerie Solanas, shot Warhol in his studio, "The Factory." T h e founder of S.C.U.M. (Society for Cutting Up Men), and an advocate of "male gendercide," Solanas had appeared in Warhol's 1968 film, *I, A Man*. Solanas escaped with a light sentence—three years in prison. Warhol nearly died from his wound and was saved by doctors, who opened his chest and massaged his heart to stimulate movement once again. Intimates report that he lived in pain from the wounds till the day he died.

By the 1980s, Warhol had started to lose favor with the public, who denounced both him and his work as "too commercial." His exhibits were judged as "superficial and facile, without depth." After his death, however, he was reappraised by critics, some of whom referred to him as "the most brilliant mirror of our times." Warhol had, in fact, in the words of one appraiser, "captured something irresistible about the *Zeitgeist* of American culture in the 70s."

Although thought of as asexual, Warhol did have an active sex life, seducing some of the icons of his day and taking on an occasional lover. He produced many drawings and shot erotic photographs of male nudes. Some of his films, such as *My Hustler*, held their previews in gay porn houses.

At 6:32am, on February 22, 1987, death came suddenly to Warhol. He'd entered New York Hospital for routine gallbladder surgery. All his life he'd never trusted doctors or hospitals.

He was buried resting under his platinum wig, wearing sunglasses.

***

What was the most bizarre story we ever learned about how Warhol created some of his art?

His oxidation paintings were canvases that were prepared with copper paint that needed to be oxidized—in this case, with urine. He called them "my piss paintings."

Warhol himself may have been the first to piss on his own paintings. He would often invite handsome young men to his studio and give them lots of wine before asking them to "piss on my paintings." He was never turned down. Superstar Candy Darling once said, "Andy just loved to watch young men piss on his paintings."

Left photo above: On the set of *Querelle,* German director **Rainer Werner Maria Fassbinder** (left) with film star **Brad** (*Midnight Express, see separate review*) **Dexter** and **Warhol** (right). Warhol to Dexter: "I want to draw your dick."

Center photo above: Warhol captured this candid shot of his idol, the pixie-like, pill-addicted **Truman Capote**, in the summer of 1978 near Truman's apartment at Manhattan's U.N. Plaza.

Right photo above: Warhol created this likeness of **Lennon** for the cover the 1986 album *Menlove Ave.,"* released posthumous to Lennon's death by Yoko. At least five of the songs on it were produced by the notorious Phil Spector.

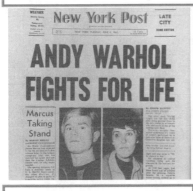

"I SHOT ANDY WARHOL. HE HAD TOO MUCH CONTROL OF MY LIFE."

So said the infamous Valerie Solanas. At The Factory on June 3, 1968, she shot at Warhol three times, hitting him once. As she aimed the gun, in a sequence that seemed oddly inspired by the pop art that had become the artist's trademark, Warhol, in vain, screamed, "No! No! Valerie, don't do it!"

A psychiatrist who evaluated her shortly afterwards concluded that she was "a Schizophrenic Reaction, paranoid type with marked depression and potential for acting out." Many of her detractors derided her as a "crazed lesbian." For reasons never fully explained, Andy refused to testify against her.

ALL YOU NEED IS LOVE

In February of 1978, Warhol was caught kissing John Lennon. "Next time, use your tongue," Lennon told him.

CROTCH GRABBING AMONGST THE RICH AND TERRIBLY FAMOUS:

Yoko Ono (left), Warhol (center), and Lennon (right). Warhol to Lennon: "I just love your uncut cock!"

Warhol confessed this to fellow artist Keith Haring, who told everybody at Studio 54.

ANDY WARHOL:
A DOCUMENTARY FILM
(2006)

A Voyeur With a Voracious Appetite for Fame

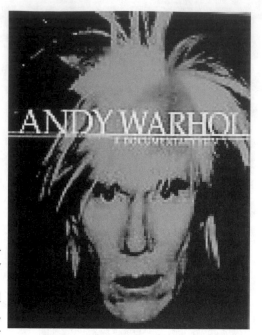

First, the bad news for anyone suffering from Attention Deficit Disorder. This portrait of the artist, Andy Warhol, is 4 hours long—so be duly warned.

Is there anyone alive who doesn't know who Warhol (1928-1987) was? Artist, filmmaker, photographer, writer, publisher, interviewer, model, actor, businessman, fashion consultant, set designer, TV show host, rock choreographer, record producer, gourmet, jet-setter, trendsetter, dog lover, and modern dancer. Dare we add homosexual? Warhol, of course, became the leading exponent of Pop Art, the artist who gave us those silk-screen portraits of Marilyn Monroe, Elizabeth Taylor, and Elvis Presley that still hang in our bathrooms, sometimes directly imprinted on our shower curtains.

The film assures us that Warhol was the greatest artist of the second half of the 20th century, the first part of that century going to Pablo Picasso, of course.

Ric Burns was both the director and co-author (along with James Sanders). The helmer told the press that it was a hard sell raising money for his documentary. Previously he'd done docus on Eugene O'Neill, the playwright, and on Ansel Adams, the photographer. "People hate Andy and they love him," Burns said in an interview with *The New York Times*.

"Warhol is the American dream, but in the minds of corporations it could be the American nightmare," said Donald Rosenfeld, who produced the film with Daniel Wolf. "He's peculiar looking—not of this world." Wolf added a footnote: "Warhol was branded as this gay, weird, party-going genius—and not the great artist he should have been known as."

Burns blended interviews with archival footage. Narration by Laurie Anderson is a bit too reverent when a more dispassionate tone might have been called for.

Paul Morrissey, who wrote and directed such Warhol-produced films as *Trash, Heat*, and *Flesh*, is barely mentioned in the movie. Yet in some respects those films, starring superstud Joe Dallesandro, form one of Warhol's most enduring legacies.

The docu traces Warhol from his origins on the seedy side of Pittsburgh, where he was poor, physically frail, and very effeminate. He was forced to share a bed with his two brothers. When he finally reached New York, he met Truman Capote, sensing a kindred spirit.

Ever since he'd seen the notoriously fey portrait of Capote on the book jacket of his first novel, *Other Voices, Other Rooms*, Warhol had been obsessed with the writer and even stalked him. Capote rejected Warhol's overtures of friendship. When not stalking Capote, Warhol delivered completed versions of his early commercial artwork in brown paper bags, his colleagues mocking him as "Raggedy Andy."

To record his drama, the filmmakers rounded up all the usual suspects, including Warhol's best biographer, Wayne Koestenbaum. They even tracked down Warhol's brother, John Warhola. Warhola was Andy's original name. A typesetter at a magazine where the artist was working accidentally dropped the final "A."

Warhol liked his revised name and stuck with it for the rest of his life.

Like a one-man Collyer Brothers, Warhol left a vast trail of documentation, even dinner invitations and fan mail. If we have any criticism at all, it's that the praise in the film is a bit too effusive. How many times do we need to hear that Warhol was a genius?

After exploring Warhol's early attempts at commercial art in the Big Apple, the second half of the docu turns to The Factory, both its 47th Street and Union Square locations. Peopled with hustlers, drug addicts, wannabees, "superstars," and drag queens, The Factory's opening party in 1964—or so it was said—was "the night the 60s were born."

In the drugged out bliss of The Factory, films were made, and art, music, and even dance were presented. It was here that Warhol created such alleged masterpieces as *The Chelsea Girls*. It was also here that that man-hating crackpot, Valerie Solanas, shot Warhol. She'd convinced herself that the artist had conspired with her publisher to steal her ideas. As Warhol recovered, his business was generating a cool million a year for him before he died of medical malfeasance in 1987. He was an unripe 58.

Although Warhol with his blotched skin, bulbous nose, and early hair loss concealed by bad wigs gained international fame, he never achieved his childhood dream of becoming Shirley Temple. He didn't achieve his adult dream of becoming Marilyn Monroe either.

WHAT THE CRITICS SAID

"Andy Warhol had a reputation for shallowness and superficiality; his assembly-line paintings and artless movies were initially received as elaborate put-ons. But in *Andy Warhol*, director Ric Burns parades a legion of critics, biographers, and former acolytes who attribute unexpectedly profound meanings to his deceptive *oeuvre*. A four-hour running time may seem unduly long, but Andy Warhol, like its enigmatic subject, is never boring."
Tom Beer, *Time Out New York*

"Before Madonna and Paris Hilton, there was Warhol. But to assume, as some still do, that Warhol's vision was nihilistic and steeped in irony is to look only at the chilly industrialized surfaces of art that sprang from a passionate, quasi-religious workshop of pop culture and its icons."
Stephen Holden, *The New York Times*

"One misses the voices of Lou Reed and John Cale, Rauschenberg or the critics who pegged the soup cans a vulgar joke. There's little sense of what Warhol had to overcome in the art establishment—or how he helped create a new art establishment—or the state of mind of individuals who rode a Warhol wave through the 60s."
Variety

"Even with 240 minutes at his disposal, director Ric Burns can't quite decode the enigma that was Andy Warhol. Nevertheless, his epic examination of the artist is consistently compelling and required viewing for anyone remotely interested in pop culture. We need all four hours, and even more, to understand the man who so prophetically divided the world into 15-minute increments."
The New York Daily News

FILM REVIEW
ABSOLUTE WARHOLA
(2001)

Wherein Viewers Learn That Andy is Descended From Country Yokels

The gay pop artist Andy Warhol was actually born in Pittsburgh. His parents were working-class immigrants from Miková in northeastern Slovakia, then under the rule of the Austro-Hungarian Empire.

Andy's father, Ondrej Warhola (Andy dropped the a), immigrated to the United States in 1914, the year World War I broke out. He found work in a coal mine in Pennsylvania. The mother, Ulja, immigrated in 1921.

Often bedridden as a child, suffering from chorea (a disease of the nervous system), Andy drew pictures in bed, listened to the radio, and collected pictures of handsome movie stars like Clark Gable, Errol Flynn, Tyrone Power, and Robert Taylor.

Helmer/scripter Stanislaw Mucha journeyed to Miková to discover the Warhola family still living, their lives under the shadow of Chernobyl, a memory erased with the consumption of a lot of vodka—hence, the title.

For a documentary, the 80-minute film rambles, and tells you absolutely nothing about the artist's work—nor anything about his private life. These Eastern European yokels, who never knew Warhol, are adamant about only one aspect of his life: Each man or woman interviewed emphatically denied that their relative was a homosexual. Of course, homophobia is deeply ingrained in Eastern Europe, less so in the break-away Czech Republic where Prague is a center of Europe's gay porno industry. Dozens of handsome young Czech men have migrated to Germany to sell their meat to that country's vast array of homosexuals.

The film is less about Warhol than the Slovak region of Ruthenia, ancestral birthplace of the Warholas. The film crew also visited Medzilaborce, home of the Andy Warhol Museum. The museum displays a permanent collection of many of Warhol's works, but the roof is constantly leaking. Local gypsies complain that they are banned from the museum. As noted by Warhol's cousin, Janko Zavacky, the relatives didn't know they had a famous member of the family until 1978. "Before democracy," Zavacky claimed, "Andy was forbidden."

When Warhol shipped his family a package of drawings and paintings, they didn't like or understand the art. Family members rolled some of the drawings up to use as paper cones. Others were destroyed when a home was flooded. Later the Warhola family learned they had tossed out millions of dollars worth of art.

The docu is quirky but touching.

WHAT THE CRITICS SAID

"Stanislaw Mucha's docu is an agreeably loose and free record of a visit to the east Slovakian villages that claim Andy Warhol as their own, but with an undercurrent of sadness that makes this the film equivalent of a pleasant white wine with a kicker to it. Mucha has mastered the art of flying by the seat of his pants and keeping his eyes open to anything that happens within view of his camera. Pic gains further grace by not making profound points but simply observing."
Robert Koehler, *Variety*

Andy's first "painting." 1937

When Warhol shipped one of his famous **Campbell's soup cans** (top left photo) back to the Old Country and his East Slovakian relatives, they didn't know what to do with it. At first, they thought it would provide tomato soup for the village. "But it was empty," one of his relatives said. Although the pop art object could have been sold for thousands of dollars, these relatives used it to catch rain water.

The top right-hand photo above shows some of Warhol's country-bumpkin **relatives**. Even though these hicks had never been outside their village and had never met their famous American relative, they adamantly swore on camera that he was not a homosexual.

Below, **Andy Warhol** in 1937, recently arrived in Pittsburgh, looked like an innocent cherub posing with his garishly colored interpretation of *Madonna with Child*. He was already plotting his future. "It would be just high school for me. College is nothing." Thin and pale, he was a bit effeminate, and was known for developing crushes on his school's macho jocks.

PSST! HAVE YOU HEARD?
THE WARHOL / MORRISSEY UNDERGROUND FILMS
(WE'RE TALKING ABOUT EVERYBODY'S CULT FAVES)
FLESH, TRASH, AND HEAT
ARE NOW AVAILABLE ON DVD!

As defined by his repeated appearances in underground films, Warhol's superstar, **Joe Dallesandro,** born in 1948, was one of the 20th century's most famous male sex symbols. In the gay subculture, he was a king, praised by John Waters as "a wonderful actor who forever changed male sexuality on the screen." Even Warhol himself later claimed, "In my movies, everyone's in love with Joe Dallesandro."

"My introduction to the gay world did two things," Dallesandro was quoted as saying. "One, it saved me from life in prison for murder, which is probably where I would have wound up. How? Because the gay world showed me that you didn't have to beat up every man you saw or hurt people to make a point. Two it taught me never to be homophobic."

When Tennessee Williams first met Joe at a party, he was so overcome with his beauty that he fainted in his arms.

JOE DALLESANDRO
Warhol's Underground Sex Symbol

Paul Morrissey, who first ventured into the Warhol Factory in 1965, functioned as Andy's manager for nearly 10 years and was the creative force behind his best films—the so-called *Flesh* trilogy. These included *Flesh* in 1968, *Trash* in 1970, and *Heat* in 1971.

On the scantiest of budgets provided by Warhol (virtually his only contribution), the talented Morrissey, who had already directed a number of shorts, wrote, photographed, and edited these now classic underground films.

Thanks to Image Entertainment, Warhol's famous trilogy—*Flesh, Trash*, and *Heat*—are available once again. The controversial DVDs are packed in one box: *The Warhol Paul Morrissey Boxed Set*.

Joe Dallesandro plays the lead in all three films. He's sexy in *Flesh*, sleazy in *Trash*, and scandalous in *Heat*. Each film is a wonder of wanton, perverted pleasures as lensed through the pop vision of Warhol and Morrissey.

Morrissey's camera was clearly enamored of Dallesandro. Never before, except in porno, had the naked male been more closely observed with such naturalness in major release American films.

In each movie within the trilogy, Dallesandro is a mostly immobile, solid block of masculinity. His main acting assignment is the maintenance of his cool. Unlike the enigmatic star, the women in the Morrissey films talk nonstop.

In 1962, at the age of 15, Dallesandro was a professional car thief. During a heist, he was shot—obviously not fatally—by the police and sent to prison, where he must have given a lot of sexually repressed

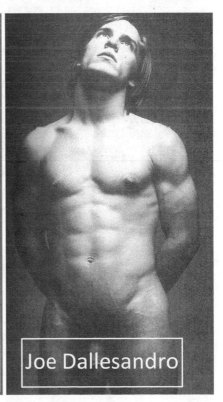

Joe Dallesandro

LITTLE JOE?

In a 2005 appraisal of **Joe Dallesandro**, Michael Ferguson wrote: "Ambivalent about his fame as a Warhol superstar, he cannot escape the power of his allure in those films, nor the power his image has wielded over each succeeding generation to discover him during the last 40 years. As the first openly eroticized male sex symbol of the movies to walk naked across the the screen, he not only transcended the convention of being an actor, but he spoke to our fantasies and liberated the male nude as an object of beauty in cinema. He liked to tell interviewers that all he ever had to do in a Warhol/Morrissey film was to show up. He was right. He's a natural."

At Studio 54, back during Dallesandro's cinematic heyday, John Lennon once told Warhol and the ever-gossipy Truman Capote: "My ultimate dream in life is to spend an afternoon sucking the world's most magnificent penis, which is found between the legs of Joe Dallesandro. I want to put it in my mouth and not remove it for five hours, even if Joe has to take a piss during that time."

After his many battles with drug addiction and liquor, "Little Joe" is still hangin' today, still an erotic fantasy to thousands of gay men who view DVD redigitalizations of his old movies. Dallesandro is alive and well today, at last report running a small hotel in Hollywood and granting the rare interview.

men big-time hard-ons. It was in prison that he acquired his famous "Little Joe tattoo."

Upon his release from jail, he worked as a nude model for *Physique Pictorial*. Quite by accident, he met Warhol and Morrissey in 1965. Both men were "taken" by his stunning male beauty. He was subsequently cast in *Flesh, Trash*, and *Heat*.

Both horny women and hot-to-trot gay men were attracted to Joe, with his stunning face, his humpy body, and a dick that he never seemed to mind showing off. Joe, in fact, became the eroticized male sex symbol of the early 1970s, ending up on the cover of The Rolling Stones' *Sticky Fingers* album.

As his career evolved, he moved to Europe where he worked with film directors Louis Malle and Jacques Rivette, and French singer/songwriter Serge Gainsbourg. Upon his return to the U.S., he was directed by Francis Ford Coppola, John Waters, and Steven Soderbergh. He found his true calling when he modeled for underwear commercials with Kate Moss. In 2004, *The New York Times* reported that the "Joe Hustler haircut" was back in style.

Flesh, Trash, and *Heat* are somber, seedy examples of pop, late 60s and early 70s cinematic experimentation. They are a decidedly mixed bag of goodies, with *Heat* (set in Los Angeles) being a cobbled together finale to this so-called trilogy, which at best are only randomly sequential or interrelated.

So although they can be a hell of a lot of fun, the DVD trio is a tainted triptych, representing a vanished era—the epitome of then-popular indie chic.

Andy Warhol posed **Joe Dallesandro** in a pair of clinging blue jeans, leaving clear instructions for him not to wear his famous white jockey shorts beneath them. As if in anticipation of a future Calvin Klein ad campaign, Warhol said, "I don't want anything to come between your skin and those jeans." The photograph, which depicted Joe's inordinately large crotch bulge, eventually graced the famous front cover of the Rolling Stones' album *Sticky Fingers*.

The 1980s British band, "The Smiths," would also use a photograph of "Little Joe" from the notorious film *Flesh* as part of the cover of their debut album.

What was Dallesandro's reaction to the notoriety catalyzed by these album covers? His response was enigmatic: "If you have to ask, we'll be glad to tell you."

Tell Us That It Isn't True:
Has Paul Morrissey Become a Right-Wing Conservative?
And What If He's Correct?

The scriptwriter and director of *Flesh, Trash*, and *Heat* is starting to sound like a right-wing reactionary. Catholic Republican writer Maurice Yacowar quotes Morrissey: "All the sensible values of a solid education and a moral foundation have been flushed down the liberal toilet in order to sell sex, drugs, and rock and roll."

Filmmaker Paul Morrissey

384

FILM REVIEW
FLESH
(1968)

Humpy Joe Reveals All!

Originally released in 1968, this once-shocking film is more Paul Morrissey than Andy Warhol. Andy lent his name as in "Andy Warhol Presents," but the film is clearly the achievement of Morrissey.

Flesh examines—rather painfully—the hippy-druggy sub-culture of New York in the late 1960s. Viewers see a day in the life of Joe Dallesandro playing a male prostitute who works the streets of New York to support his life. His character is simply titled, "Joe, the Hustler."

Geraldine Smith plays Geri, Joe's wife. They have a child, but also need to raise money to pay for an abortion for Geri's lover, Patti D'Arbanville, who plays a character also called "Patti" in the film.

Before the day expires, Joe will pose for an aging artist, Maurice Braddell, cast as "the Artist," and will spend some time with gym bunny "David, the Gymnast" (Louis Waldon). He'll also spend quality time with two drag queens, the once infamous Candy Darling and the lesser known Jackie Curtis. Because Joe is so beautiful, everyone in the film wants him naked. The movie is about body worship. Morrissey's camera absolutely loved Dallesandro, especially when he doesn't have any clothes on.

The film broke ground in the way it framed the body and face of humpy Dallesandro. Before Little Joe came along, only women were photographed so lovingly by the camera. Remember Rita Hayworth in *Gilda*?

Flesh attacked "the code" in a frontal assault. It became the first non-pornographic film ever to display an erect penis.

Flesh has a two-minute tender moment, and it became celebrated. Before going out to hustle his dick, Joe takes time to play with his baby daughter on the floor and to feed her a cupcake.

WHAT THE CRITICS SAID ABOUT FLESH

"Though it tends to track in vignettes instead of a single sound narrative, and can't quite make up its mind what it wants to say in the end, it is still a remarkable time capsule to an era where free love was no longer a luxury, and getting paid for being laid was a reasonable attempt at carving a niche out of the numbness of metropolitan malaise. Peppered with sequences both sad and scandalous, Morrissey and his actors turn New York into one big smoldering smut pit, a place where the person and the prurient no longer matter."
DVD Verdict

"The bracingly relaxed tone of the film feels far head of its time, as does the rough editing style (the film feels like it was cut with a butter knife and spliced with duct tape). Some of it feels a bit repetitive and indulgent, but there's always a point to it; none of the conversation is irrelevant, even though several scenes drag on and feel rather dull. But the way Morrissey keeps things natural and real is both bracing and important. And compelling."
Rich Cline

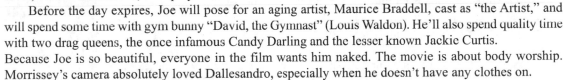

FILM REVIEW
TRASH
(1970)
Recycle It!

In the wake of the success of *Flesh* in 1968, *Trash* was conceived two years later as a reference to the expression, "Sex, drugs, and rock 'n' roll."

The film is a send-up of scenes shanghaied from Hollywood's golden age in the 1930s. Yes, the tinny movie music is taken from Josef von Sternberg's *The Blue Angel*, starring his one-and-only creation, Fraulein Marlene Dietrich.

In *Trash*, poor "Little Joe" (Joe Dallesandro) has evolved from a street hustler into a heroin addict. He wants to keep selling his meat to pay for his drug of choice. But he's got a real problem.

After Morrissey opens the movie with a shot that focuses on Joe's pimply butt, we learn he's impotent. What a waste of a good cock. But Joe can't even get it up. The question *Trash* asks is, "How is Joe going to get it up to score?"

This is the dilemma facing our hero in this second installment of the three Little Joe films directed by Paul Morrissey but produced by Andy Warhol, who may have contributed no more than the use of his name.

Morrissey's cameras, in a very nonjudgmental way, introduce us to a world of "junkies, cross-dressers, and street johns."

Stealing the picture from Joe is the "super star" drag queen, Holly Woodlawn herself. Of course, it's not hard to steal this picture, considering that Joe is comatose throughout most of it. There is no reference made to Holly being a transvestite. But in case you didn't grow up in the 70s, we thought we'd clue you in.

Holly supports herself by stealing trash from the streets, often to sell as furniture. Before he developed erectile dysfunction problems, Holly had a good sex life with studly Joe.

In addition to facing the dilemma of Joe's flaccid dick, Holly needs to go on welfare as a means of supporting her sister's kid. Sis is about to birth a baby at any minute.

Will Joe kick his drug habit and get his dick up and running again? Will Holly achieve her dream about going on welfare? The plot churns.

In one memorable scene, when Holly fails to arouse Joe, she desperately masturbates with a beer bottle, grasping his hand as she climaxes, begging him to kick the habit so that they can really make out again like they used to.

In the film, there are many people who'd like to get it on with Junkie Joe if only he could raise a boner. Other than his wife, Holly Woodlawn, there's his stripper friend, Geri Miller, playing Geri the go-go dancer who'd like to get porked by Joe. Who wouldn't, as a matter of fact?

A rich girl, Andrea Feldman, also tries to get Joe interested and aroused. When Feldman is on the screen, she steals the show, even from Woodlawn's drag dementia. One reviewer claimed that Feldman combined elements of the British, "nasal New York-ese, a sprinkling of Sparkle Farkle, and the call of a castrated collie dog—Andrea proves there is nothing more fabulously funny than a ditzy dunderhead spewing random thoughts off the top of her head in crazed cartoon-like convulsions."

Jane Forth appears as Jane, a middle-class bimbo, who bickers mindlessly with her new husband, Bruce Pecher (playing "Bruce") as Joe ODs on their floor.

Meanwhile Holly has problems of her own, as she concocts scams involving her homeless pregnant sister, Diane Podel, and a naïve teen (John Putnam) in search of drugs. But it's a welfare investigator, Michael Sklar, as "Mr. Michaels," who crosses the line. In one of the more outrageous scenes, he thinks Holly's silver shoes would make a great lamp.

WHAT THE CRITICS SAID ABOUT TRASH

"All feelings, all values are turned upside down and played for laughs, with the result that it's difficult for me to take *Trash* more seriously than it takes itself. At heart, the film is a kind of exuberant exhibition of total apathy. Mr. Morrissey is, I think, a talented moviemaker, even though much of the effect of *Trash* depends on outrageous shock or on rather curious plays on pathos. Holly Woodlawn, especially, is something to behold, a comic book Mother Courage who fancies herself as Marlene Dietrich but sounds more often like Phil Silvers. *Trash* is alive, but like the people in it, it continually parodies itself, and thus represents a kind of dead end in filmmaking."
Vincent Canby, **The New York Times**

"Andy Warhol's *Trash*, written and directed by Paul Morrissey, is an exception to the rule. It seems to have some bedrock understanding of how ridiculous semi-pornographic exploitation films really are. *Trash* goes for laughs, not eroticism, and I was relieved to find the audience laughing with it (and at it). *Trash* is the first semi-hard core movie to approach the naïve charm, the Rabelaisian healthiness of *Vixen*, or the Isabel Sarli epics from Argentina."
Roger Ebert

"In hypnotizingly minimal, almost home-movie-ish *Trash*—the warmest and funniest of the three— Dallesandro is an East Village junkie with crab lice and a potency problem. He's quite poignant in the role, but the extraordinary transvestite Holly Woodlawn (the erstwhile Harold Danhaki) steals the film as Joe's compulsive, trash-collecting lover. The director doesn't use Woodlawn as a drag queen—on screen she's a woman whose dreams of family and normalcy are constantly frustrated, played by an actress giving a superb performance often marked by zany, self-deprecating humor. *Trash* takes a deglamorizing line on hard drugs, but wisely stops short of moralizing. In its heart of hearts, it's the cleanest dirty movie ever made."
Elliott Stein, *The Village Voice*

"Much of the film is blackly hysterical. And for a film about life on the sleazy edge of society, the film looks gorgeous, crabs and all."
Rich Cline

Happily, this pre-Viagra, classic Andy Warhol production is returning to the screen after shaking up America three decades ago, and it hasn't dated an iota. The still shocking film that brought the underground and Little Joe's privates uptown, cleared the path for Almodóvar, Van Sant, and Araki. It is as hilarious and poignant as ever."
PopcornQ Movies

HOLLY WOODLAWN

?

Gender-bending pioneer Holly Woodlawn shot to fame in *Trash*. There was even Oscar talk for her (him?). But as some wag noted, would you have given Holly Best Supporting Actress or Best Supporting Actor Oscars?

Arriving in New York with eleven dollars to her name, Holly shaved her legs and plucked her eyebrows. The rest is film history. She met Morrissey, who cast her as the costar of *Trash*. The year was 1969.

When *Trash* held its world premiere in New York, Holly couldn't attend. She was in the slammer. She'd been arrested while impersonating the wife of a French diplomat, trying to withdraw $2,000 from the socialite's bank account.

Hauled off to the women's detention center, she was forced to hike up her dress. Surprise!

Unable to pay her $1,000 bail, she sat in jail. She tried to call Warhol but he wouldn't speak to her. Eventually artist Larry Rivers came along to bail her out. Headlines in *Daily Variety* revealed "*Trash* Star Found in Trash Can."

Her fame rooted solidly back in the 1970s, Holly lives today in a modest apartment in West Hollywood (where else?). Perhaps her fame will be revived with the re-release of *Trash*, as a newer generation discovers her drag queen charms.

Holly did not benefit from the millions that *Trash* earned and the money that it may earn again on DVD. She signed away everything. Morrissey gave her $125, all that she ever got of the millions *Trash* earned.

Holly wrote an autobiography, *A Lowlife in High Heels*. There was even talk of a movie project for it, with Madonna playing Holly.

But the Hollywood Hills are filled with stars of yesterday, many with dreams equivalent.

Thankfully, Holly's performances are available again, this time via DVD.

FILM REVIEW
HEAT
(1972)

A Faggot Rehash of Sunset Blvd.?

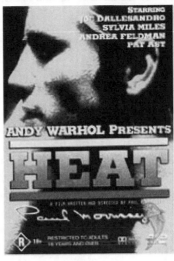

Written and directed by Paul Morrissey, and first released in 1972, *Heat* is a comedy/drama that adds a final chapter to the *Flesh* and *Trash* trilogy. Once again it stars that bare-assed hunk of studliness, Joe Dallesandro, playing an unemployed ex-child actor.

This time he is cast against the formidable Sylvia Miles as Sally Todd and Pat Ast as the hideous Lydia. *Trash* is actually a parody of that 1950 Billy Wilder film, *Sunset Blvd.*, that starred Gloria Swanson as Norma Desmond.

Expect funny one-liners, some brilliant acting, and lots of flesh. The film is better plotted than either *Flesh* or *Trash*

Set in seedy parts of Los Angeles, Joe Dallesandro plays a former child star whose 15 minutes of fame came when he was a child star in a fictitious TV series called *The Big Ranch*. As a means of paying the rent on his battered room in a backwater motel, he offers his sexual favors to his tarty landlady, Ast.

Then he meets his slutty neighbor, Andrea Feldman, who turns out to be the lesbian daughter of one of his former costars, Sylvia Miles playing Sally Todd. Miles is living in Hollywood Hills luxury. The granting of additional sexual favors are on the way for the overworked Joe who has a lot of holes to plug.

No one can play a slutty B-movie character better than Miles, who gave a performance matched only by her Oscar-nominated turn as an aging hooker in James Leo Herlihy's *Midnight Cowboy*.

Pat Ast, as the trashy, slobbering sex machine, was called "the mother of all rednecks."

Sally tries to help Joey, until he realizes that she just isn't well connected enough to be of any service to reactivate a stalled career. The affair is complicated by Sally's psychotic, lesbian daughter, Jessica (Andrea Feldman), who tries to muscle in on her mother's relationship with Joe.

The film's tortured plot feels like something akin to a porn movie.

WHAT THE CRITICS SAID ABOUT HEAT

"Morrissey maintains a sunny, silly tone. The characters' overt selfish ambition shines bright in every scene, and the jagged improvised dialog is simply brilliant. With a much bigger budget, slicker editing, glorious photography, and even a strong John Cale score, this is a more polished, dialog-based film than the previous two; and it's also much more aware of the film censor. But as it takes a swipe at everything from sexuality to showbiz, it stays consistently entertaining and very telling."
Rich Cline

"The movie is absorbing mostly because Morrissey has assembled an outrageous cast, given them an impossible situation and then all but dared them to act their way out of it. Incredibly Sylvia Miles does. She handles this material in the only possible way, by taking it perfectly seriously. If she's a semi-retired actress, having an affair with an androgynous robot, so be it. The robot has never met anyone like HER before."
Roger Ebert

FIFTEEN MINUTES OF FAME

ANDY WARHOL SCREEN TESTS
THE FILMS OF ANDY WARHOL CATALOGUE RAISONNÉ   CALLIE ANGELL

We seem to be in the midst of an Andy Warhol renaissance. Of course, Warhol has never gone out of style. Nor has he ever become forgotten.

Andy Warhol Screen Tests: *The Films of Andy Warhol, Catalogue Raisonné, Volume One,* from art publishers Harry Abrams, is priced at $60 per copy. In her review of this book, Grace Hendris in the *New York Post*, suggested that these screen tests "might just be Warhol's greatest work of art," although encased in a book with an academic title that "sounds about as interesting as paste."

Warhol began filming his living portraits in 1963, asking each of his subjects, from Dennis Hopper to Susan Sontag, to sit still for three minutes in front of the camera. Over a period of two years, he filmed 472 of these living portraits.

Even Bob Dylan and Salvador Dalí agreed to a sitting. Of course, these are famous subjects. Some of the names in the tests have been assigned to the dustbin of history, including Warhol's friend, Willard Maas, whose troubled marriage reportedly was the inspiration for Edward Albee's *Who's Afraid of Virginia Woolf?*

Although not as revealing as the actual film clips, the catalogue provides a series of still photographs of Warhol's subjects, who range from drag queens to socialites. There is the occasional famous face but mostly the artist's subjects were unknown. Biographical blurbs provide information about who they were. Sometimes a bio is quite tantalizing, as in the case of Freddy Herko who "danced out the window" of John Dodd's fifth-floor apartment."

If nothing else, this book reveals that Warhol thought nothing was more fascinating than the human face, and in the case of poet Allen Ginsberg, a close friend of Warhol's, that might be true.

**Famous Faces Among Warhol's
"Greatest Work of Art"**

Top to Bottom:
Young **Edie Sedgwick** and
queer, Beat Generation poet/writers
Allen Ginsberg and
William Burroughs

FACTORY GIRL
(2006)

Holly Golightly
on the Road to Hell

Sex, nudity, foul language, and drugs, it's all that you would expect in this semi-fictionalized account of the rise and fall of Andy Warhol's ill-fated 60s muse, Edie Sedgwick.

As if you didn't know, Edie Sedgwick (1943-71) was that leggy 60s heiress who became a *Vogue* "youth-quaker" and fleeting superstar for Andy Warhol. She led a tragic, supernova life that ended in California when her husband, Michael Post, woke up on the morning of November 16, 1971, to find Edie lying dead next to him.

Ever since 1966, her star had gone into eclipse, never to shine again. At moments of desperation in the late 60s, she stole art and antiques from her grandmother's apartment to fund her drug habit, which eventually led to her death.

The film traces her odyssey from Radcliffe to the streets of New York where she wanted to become the next Holly Golightly. Although she appears rather innocent at the beginning of this film, she was actually a fag hag in Boston before meeting fame slut Andy Warhol in New York.

Since the pop artist was gay, there was no romance between them, but for months they appeared everywhere together, perhaps becoming one of New York's most famous couples of the 60s. Edie became the Queen of Underground Art and Fashion. If F. Scott Fitzgerald had lived, he might have romantically included her among his "The Beautiful and the Damned."

As director of this unforgiving movie, George Hickenlooper tells the same old story that movies have told since the beginning of the 20th century. Innocent girl—pretty, of course—hits town and slips into a decadent lifestyle, only to pay for the wages of her "sins." In Edie's case, those sins carried a very high price tag.

The helmer relies heavily on the performance of Sienna Miller as Edie and English actor Guy Pearce as Warhol to pull off this movie. They can't save the film but it is not for lack of trying. Pearce brilliantly portrays Warhol as physically repulsive—"an almost soulless puppet master clueless in his cruelties," as one columnist put it. The Cambridge-born actor is the best Warhol to date. Yes, better than David Bowie, Cripsin Glover, Jared Harris, and Sean Gregory Sullivan.

Pearce is one busy actor. Many gay men saw him for the first time in *The Adventures of Priscilla, Queen of the Desert* (1994). His latest starring role is *Death Defying Acts*, based on the life of Harry Houdini.

Warhol in real life was like one of those creatures that can mate with itself—in other words, the ideal narcissist. Pearce cuts into this character with a sharpened knife and the skill of a brain surgeon. When he's "used up" someone—in this case the vulnerable Edie—he tosses the person aside like a box of stale pizza—the kind that might have been delivered to The Factory several days before.

A writer with the improbable name of "Captain Mauzner" penned this problematic biopic, just as he did another problem film, *Wonderland*, centered around the life of porn star John C. Holmes (13 ½").

Edie's would-be rescuer appears as "The Musician," played stiffly by the good-looking but bland Hayden Christensen. We know that this folk singer is a representation of the real-life Bob Dylan, but that Dylan is never specifically named because of the folk singer's threatened lawsuit. Dylan's lawyers claimed that their client never had an affair with Edie. In real life, the exact nature of the Sedgwick/Dylan involvement (or lack thereof) may never be known. The answer is blowin' in the wind.

Like Eve Harrington replacing Margo Channing, Edie sees "the new girl" at The Factory. She's Ingrid Superstar, who burst onto the scene in 1966 as *Hedy, the Shoplifter*, obviously inspired by the late Hedy Lamarr. Her fate wasn't any better than Edie's. On December 7, 1986, she disappeared and is presumed dead, although her body has never been found.

Like Edie herself, actress Sienna Miller is no stranger to scandal. Her on-and-off relationship with dashing Jude Law made her an overnight celebrity. Following reports that he had a fling with the nanny of his three children, Sienna broke off their engagement. She learned Law's secret. But we know a secret about her. She dips her French fries into chocolate milkshakes.

After the Law scandal, Miller was reinstated into the role of Edie. She'd originally been given the part but the producers decided she was not famous enough. But after the headlines that trumpeted the subject of Jude Law's infidelity, Miller was deemed a big enough name to carry the role. In other words, she'd become A-list famous. "If you're in the papers for virtually any reason, you've made the grade and American producers want you," said one commentator.

Sienna made her own headlines after the release of *Factory Girl*. She revealed that she takes drugs because "they're fun." But she upset the good people of that sweet city, Pittsburgh, when she called it "Shitsburgh." The remark was doubly insulting because of Warhol's links to Pittsburgh.

She later claimed that her rants were the result of suffering from a form of Tourette's syndrome, which, of course, is a neurological disorder associated with the exclamation of derogatory or obscene remarks. What's Mel Gibson's excuse?

One-time Warhol acolyte and rock god Lou Reed told the press his opinion of *Factory Girl* even before filming ended. "They're all a bunch of whores," referring to helmer Hickenlooper and his cast. Reed claimed that he read the script. "It's one of the most disgusting, foul things I've seen by any illiterate retard in a long time. There's no limit to how low some people will go to write something to make money." Allegedly, Reed at one point was asked to be part of the project but the rocker gave the film a fuck-you.

WHAT THE CRITICS SAID

"*Factory Girl* burns brightly and then snuffs herself out. It's a peculiar movie, frantic and useless, with a hyperactive camera that gives us no more than fleeting impressions of Edie ecstatic at parties, Edie strung out on drugs, Edie lying mostly naked on a bed, with her skin blotchy from injections. Whatever shrewdness or charm Sedgwick possessed that caused people to believe that she was a revolutionary figure in New York night life, it doesn't come through in this movie."
The New Yorker

"Perhaps any biopic on as inimitable a figure as Edie Sedgwick would have been doomed to fail. There's a particular disconnect when Hollywood tries to 'do' the Warhol scene, going all the way back to 1969s *Midnight Cowboy*."
Melissa Anderson, *New York Magazine*

"*Factory Girl* is the sort of compulsively enjoyable bad movie that Andy himself would have loved. And he might even have perversely enjoyed being portrayed therein as an ultra-unattractive creep, a shallow villain with a talent only for exploitation."
Liz Smith

"Sienna Miller is unnervingly vulnerable as Edie Sedgwick, the classic actress/model/whatever and idle heiress ('My grandfather invented the elevator') who in 1965 New York decided to make a career out of being famous."
Kyle Smith, *New York Post*

"The world through which Sedgwick blazed and burned out was one that lived and died by the camera. It existed to be seen and drooled over. But God help you if you actually lived it. In the movie's hostile portrayal of Warhol, the pop art giant comes across as an emotional vampire who loathed his own appearance and used Sedgwick as a vicarious mirror, then turned his back when she became troublesome. In this simplistic tug-of-war, Mr. Dylan is the God of authenticity and inner truth and Warhol the Devil of superficiality and glitter, but you wouldn't know it from the ludicrous mumbo-jumbo muttered by the Dylan character."
Stephen Holden, *The New York Times*

Siena Miller playing Edie Sedgewick

astride Guy Pearce playing Andy Warhol

Sienna Miller

Edie Sedgwick

Guy Pearce

Andy Warhol

Hayden Christensen

Bob Dylan

Warhol's Factory Girl: Edie Sedgwick

A WALK INTO THE SEA
(2007)

A Designated Whipping Boy
for Warhol's Sadism

If you got off on *Factory Girl*, a semi-fictionalized feature on the ill-fated Edie Sedgwick, you might be up for seeing the story of another ill-fated Andy Warhol favorite, Danny Williams. "Who in hell was Danny Williams?" you might legitimately ask.

Among his other credentials, Danny was Warhol's lover. He was not a very sexy guy, standing about five feet ten. He was nice looking rather than beautiful--a bit chunky, but not unpleasantly so.

In 1965, soon after he and Warhol met, Danny moved into Warhol's home on Lexington Avenue. As Warhol biographer, Victor Bockris, relates, "Soon Danny was wearing the same boat-neck striped shirts Andy and Edie were wearing and regularly accompanying Warhol on their social rounds. However, after two months, the relationship broke down."

At one point in a restaurant on Christopher Street in Greenwich Village, Danny jumped up from the table and pulled off Warhol's wig. Friends at the table got a rare chance to see Warhol bald before he grabbed the wig from Danny and plopped it back onto his head.

Danny moved into Warhol's Factory after he got kicked out of Warhol's home. He slept there throughout most of 1966, having set up a workshop for himself. He knew how to work the lights and record sound.

Like Edie, Danny transformed himself from a Harvard preppie into an addict, his hair becoming matted and stringy, his skin looking ghostly. According to Bockris, Danny became The Factory's whipping boy, and Warhol constantly screamed at him.

An observer at the time, Henry Geldzahler, summed up the Danny/Warhol relationship this way: "Andy was a voyeur-sadist and he needed exhibitionist-masochists in order to fulfill both halves of his destiny. And it's obvious that an exhibitionist-masochist is not going to last very long."

Such was the case with Danny. In July of 1966 Danny showed up at the house of his grandmother, Nadia Williams, who appears as herself in the docu. He borrowed her auto for a drive to the ocean "to get some fresh air." He never came back. His disappearance remains a mystery to this day.

Like Norman Maine in *A Star is Born* (played by James Mason) opposite Judy Garland, Danny did drive to the ocean. Once there, he stripped off his clothing, leaving the apparel in a neat pile by the vehicle. He apparently jumped into the sea and drowned. Presumably, he was washed out to sea where he might have become a shark's dinner.

When Warhol was informed of Danny's death, he said, "Oh, I don't care. What a pain in the ass Danny was. He was just an amphetamine addict!" He spent no time mourning his former lover.

The docu was directed by Esther B. Robinson, who was the niece of Danny. If you look quickly, you can see Edie Sedgwick herself in a clip from one of Danny's movies.

Robinson has assembled an impressive list of interviewees to tell Danny's story, including director Paul Morrissey. Many of the subjects appear in archive footage. The famous filmmaker, Albert Maysles, tells how the 21-year-old Danny worked on his early films, including *Showman* in 1963 and *What's Happening! The Beatles In the U.S.A.* in 1964.

The 16mm black-and-white short, *Factory*, is shown in its entirely in this docu. In addition to Edie and Warhol, Danny captures Billy Name on film as well, as well as Velvet Underground member John Cale.

Over the years, virtually everyone connected with Warhol's Factory has come up with wildly different accounts of what actually happened there.

Even though it's a docu on his life, at the end of the film, Danny Williams remains an enigmatic figure. Except for some film work he left behind, there only remains this docu, a few photos, and some distant memories.

WHAT THE CRITICS SAID

"Even allowing for the fact that *A Walk Into the Sea* is a sober-sided docu, and *Factory Girl* a sensationalist, semi-fictionalized feature, both depict The Factory's milieu as a vicious circle, where creativity was indeed fostered but rivalries could turn poisonous, presided over by the fickle Warhol himself. Both films illustrate how Warhol made a habit of elevating favorites such as Danny Williams, and then tossing them aside."
Leslie Felperin, *Variety*

"Danny had no second act," said the designer, Halston, who once took **Danny Williams** (photo, right) to bed. "The young man had talent and could have made it on his own, but he was suckered into that 15 minutes of fame shit because of his two-month gig in Warhol's bed. He was a great cocksucker but a sad case. I used to see him sitting alone at The Factory just staring at the strobe lights. Any time Andy was frustrated, he would rip into that boy. I don't know how Danny took it."

In the Good Old Days, When New York's Meatpacking District Was Still Skanky, William Friedkin made

Cruising

And Gay People Rushed to Condemn It. Why? We Wondered

Nearly three decades after the release of **Cruising**, gay leaders are still divided over the film's merits—or lact thereof. It was made after the Stonewall riots, when the gay-rights movement was coming into bloom and making steady political gains.

William Friedkin, who had previously directed the controversial *The Boys in the Band,* claimed that "*Cruising* was inspired by actual crimes against gays, but, I must admit, it is a far from perfect movie."

Pacino was conspicuously absent from the documentaries and commentary associated with the re-release of the film as a DVD.

The Godfather Gets Kinky
or
Jack the Ripper Among The Fegalah

Some three decades after its initial release in 1980, *Cruising*, starring Al Pacino, remains the most controversial film ever shot on New York streets. In its new DVD release, as before, Pacino plays a cop who goes undercover in New York's gay S&M haunts and leather bars to catch a serial killer.

William Friedkin's notorious thriller attracted thousands of gay protesters during filming in Greenwich Village in the summer of 1979. And well it should. *The Village Voice*'s Arthur Bell called it "the most oppressive, ugly, bigoted look at homosexuality ever presented on the screen."

The decades have gone by and times have changed. Michael Musto, who replaced Bell on the *Village Voice*, claimed, "with a multitude of gay images all over the place, the movie can be seen more objectively—and it's not bad at all!"

Helmer Friedkin, incidentally, also directed the pioneering *The Boys in the Band*.

Damone Romine of the Gay & Lesbian Alliance Against Defamation, recalled seeing *Cuising* upon its initial release. "Without any other examples of gay men in the media to balance it out, *Cruising* sent a very dangerous message and scared me to death," he said.

Upon the film's release, it took a drubbing from critics for its lurid depiction of gruesome stabbings and leather bars patronized by sex-obsessed, half-naked men. Friedkin later admitted that *Cruising* "is far from the perfect movie."

At the time of the film's release, *Time* magazine, before it became more enlightened, reported that "homosexual homicides are frequent—and often gruesome; dismembered corpses and mutilated genitals are common."

New York's closeted gay mayor at the time, Ed Koch, said, "Whether it is a group that seeks to make the gay life exciting or to make it negative, it's not our job to look into that."

Upon its re-release, gay leaders are still divided over *Cruising*, although it was warmly received for the most part at the Cannes Film Festival.

Time Out New York put down the gauntlet. "See if Friedkin's dark tale, set in the then-skanky Meatpacking District and starring a fresh-faced Pacino, gets you as riled up as it got those old school gays."

Mick LaSalle of the *San Francisco Chronicle* suggested that *Cruising* can be seen "as a glimpse of pre-AIDS subculture. Or as an opportunity to see Pacino looking uncomfortable in skin-tight leather pants and a tank top."

The killer is played by Richard Cox, who is tall and thin. He wears the regulation sunglasses, chains, biker jacket, and hat. He doesn't have sex in mind, as this is a slasher movie.

He picks up gay guys, ties them up, and hacks them to death. Amazingly [and this is a

398

spoiler], viewers learn before the end of the movie that he is a graduate student preparing his thesis on the roots of the American musical theater.

To sum up, Friedkin's downbeat, soulless, dark, ambivalent, and "flamboyantly pervy fag noir" was a critical and box office disappointment. But for some viewers, the leather life it depicted, with all its drawbacks and AIDS-related tragedies, was indeed fun while it lasted.

A "Slashing" Look at the Heyday of Barebacking

These scenes in a leather bar set off massive protests in Greenwich Village during filming because of its tawdry depiction of gay life.

As part of the plot, in the immediate wake of the film's depiction of one of the murders, the visuals cut to a scene in the morgue, where a naked man lies ass up on a slab as the coroner delivers a lecture on semen and anal penetration.

Friedkin later said he opted for a knife as the killer's weapon because it penetrates the flesh. Andrew Holleran, author of the best-selling gay novel *Dancer from the Dance,* asserted, "that's what makes *Cruising* still so hard to watch: It's really about the fear of being *schtupped.*"

WHAT THE CRITICS SAID

"*Cruising* mixes gay sex and Grand Guignol without any psychological insight or sense of reality. The truth is, the men in those leather bars in the 1970s (as Friedkin concedes) were largely psychiatrists and lawyers, curators, and composers. It was theater run along lines as strict as anything in Emily Post—and in the end, primarily a refuge for people in search of masculinity."
Andrew Holleran

"The movie plays like a recruiting poster for an Anita Bryant parade. It is like taking a Hamburg brothel as the site for an examination of heterosexuality."
Charles Champlin, *Los Angeles Times*

"The movie insinuates obliquely that the undercover cop (Pacino) realizes he's a latent homosexual when he poses as one. The movie can even be interpreted as implying that the shock of recognition may have transformed the cop into the same kind of killer as the one he was hunting."
Joseph Gelmis, *Newsday*

"William Friedkin's Performing Homosexuals acted like small grateful puppies at the master's table. The master didn't say 'Bark,' he said, 'Cruise.' The master didn't say 'Roll Over,' he said 'Fistfuck.' The master didn't say 'Fetch,' he said 'Fellatio.' Sometimes the master didn't say anything at all. The puppies knew what to do."
Charles Ortleb, *Christopher Street*

"*Cruising* is a mediocre thriller but an amazing time capsule—a heady, horny, flashback to the last gasp of full-blown sexual abandon, and easily the most graphic depiction of gay sex ever seen in a mainstream movie. *Cruising* is a lurid fever dream of popper fumes, color-coded hankies, hardcore disco footage, and Crisco-coated forearms. Nowadays, when the naughtiest thing you can do in a New York gay club is light a cigarette, it's bracing—and, let's admit, pretty fucking hot—to travel back to a moment when getting your ass plowed in public was as blasé as ordering a Red Bull. Friedkin imagines the entire West Side of Manhattan as an expanse of sticky asphalt swarming with tumescent Honcho sluts. Grotesquerie abounds—leering sex fiends, freaky bondage weirdos, fugly trannies—but so does a palpable sense of fun. The atmosphere of uninhibited sexual camaraderie—invisible to the protesters and long since vanished from the scene—overpowers the trite homophobic conceits. *Cruising*'s lasting legacy isn't political but archival. One year after the film was released, the first symptoms of AIDS were detected in New York City."
Nathan Lee

With most of its plot unfolding within a dark, sweaty, high-testosterone leather bar, the kind that used to be much more common in New York City, **Cruising** should probably have been renamed *The Scent of a Man*. Within it, **Al Pacino**'s odyssey as an actor associates him with the gay underground.

One of the film's most evocative scenes occurs when Pacino abruptly pulls his pants down as if he's going to take a shit. "Hips or lips?" is the phrase he utters as a means of confronting the man he thinks is the serial killer.

Few films have been re-released as DVDs with as much historical baggage as *Cruising*. A reviewer for London's *Gay Times* said, "More surprising is just how hot and horny [*Cruising*] often is; or is that just nostalgia for a time before both AIDS and Rudy Giuliani put twin pincers on New York's delirious, thrill-seeking sexual scene?"

BUT HE LOOKS LIKE SUCH A NICE BOY

This is a picture of *Crusing's* murderous, perverted, leather-clad villain. Or was the perceived villain the leather scene he was pursuing at the time?

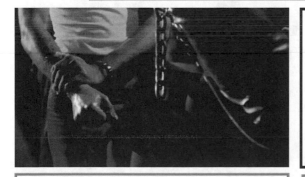

NO
SEXUAL
ACTIVITY
ALLOWED

You will be arrested

MEMORIES....

Is that a sling and someone's willing leather-clad butt we see depicted in this scene from *Cruising*?

BUT MAYBE SEX ISN'T SQUEAKY-CLEAN IN CYBERSPACE THESE DAYS, EITHER

Here's a leaflet that was routinely distributed at NYC's raunchy The Cock recently, showcasing the difference between then and now.

This Page is Dedicated to the Earthy Camaraderie of
THE LEATHER COMMUNITY—LONG MAY IT PROSPER—
Gay, Straight, and Transgendered

In Memory of
Jack Wrangler

In the Pre-Condom 1970s,
He Was the Gay World's Most Popular Porn Star

Although at first he seems like an unlikely choice, gay porn star **Jack Wrangler** (1946-2009) became an icon of the gay liberation movement.

Outcyclopedia, a gay-oriented online reference, wrote: "Many gay men in the early 70s and 80s cited Jack as an integral part of their coming-out process, as his against-the-stereotypes on-screen persona helped show them that a man can be gay and still be a man."

"I created the Wrangler persona," he claimed, "to help me get over my insecurity and timidness."

JACK WRANGLER

During the 1970s, before Jeff Stryker and Michael Lucas, Wrangler was the number one name in gay porn. His notable hits included *Kansas City Trucking Co.* in 1976; *Sex Machine* and *Heavy Equipment*, both in 1977; and the box office champion, *A Night at the Adonis* in 1978.

Once, as a long-term house guest of this guidebook's author, Darwin Porter, Wrangler frankly admitted, "I wouldn't make it in gay porno today. There are so many other guys out there who are better at it than I was. They have bigger dicks too. I'm no John C. Holmes. My dick looks big because I have a small frame. My body is buff but I'm no Hercules. Actually, I'm sort of a little guy. My super macho image was just a play act."

His self-appraisal was accurate. Both on screen and in the flesh, Wrangler could, at times, be effeminate, evoking some of the same girlish mannerisms as fellow porn star Cal Culver, who, as Casey Donovan, scored such a bit hit in *Boys in the Sand*, a landmark gay porn feature.

Wrangler was born John Robert Stillman in Beverly Hills. His father was the famous Robert Stillman, Hollywood film and TV producer who had directed such hits as *Champion* and *Home of the Brave*, both of them released in 1949. Stillman became even better known when he pro-

A star-struck seven-year-old in Hollywood, **Jack Stillman** (later, **Wrangler**) adopted a white bunny (left-hand photo, above) as a pet. These early pictures gave no clue about the stunning young porno star he'd become in later years. Ironically, in his autobiography, he claimed that even at that early age, "the permannet uglies had already set in."

For a Valentine's party at his parents' home, and only for a day, Jack wanted to grow up to be a cowboy star like Roy Rogers. By the time he posed for the picture on the right, that dream had vanished, replaced with a dream of becoming a song-and-dance man on Broadway.

On the variety/talent showcase, *Vaudebeat*, hosted by the homophobic Buddy Ebsen, Jack performed what he later referred to as "my famous triple-tap and goldfish imitation."

duced the long running hit television series *Bonanza*. Wrangler's mother was Ruth Clark Stillman, a former dancer in Busby Berkeley musicals. Rumors—many of them deliberately amplified by the porn star himself— that Jack's mother was actress Dolores Hart— are false. (Trivia Note: Dolores Hart, born in 1963, was one of the few Hollywood actresses who withdrew from the entertainment industry and became a nun. Prior to her retreat, she'd enjoyed roles in, among others, *King Creole* in 1958 and *Where the Boys Are* in 1960. She entered the strictly cloistered Regina Laudis Benedictine Monastery, in Bethlehem, Connecticut, where, at presstime for this film guide, she remains today, functioning as the prioress.)

At the age of nine, Wrangler was employed in the religion-based TV series, *The Faith of Our Children* (1953-1955), which starred Eleanor Powell of tap-dancing fame (former wife of Glenn Ford). At the age of 10, Wrangler became aware of his homosexuality.

He struggled for a time in the summer stock and dinner theater circuit, trying to "pull the pieces" of Betty Hutton together and more or less succeeding at the resurrection of Ruth Roman. He coped with the egos of Hermione Gingold and Andy Devine (of all people), and soothed the tempers of everybody from big-busted Jane Russell to Mamie Van Doren, Yvonne De Carlo, and Ann Sothern.

In 1970, after several failed attempts on the stage as a dancer and actor, he changed his name to Jack Wrangler. He took his last name from the label inside his work shirt and stuck with it ever after. That was the year he made his debut appearance in a male strip show.

He launched himself into gay porno with an appearance in *Eyes of a Stranger* (1970), one of the first hard-core gay adult films to be released commercially (in this case by Magnum Stu-

As a starry-eyed (and somewhat effeminate) adolescent, Jack dreamed of a career in show biz--one where he'd keep his pants on and not show his dick. The left-hand photo shows him as host of a radio program, *The Jack Stillman Show,* broadcast by Chicago's WNUR. In that capacity, the young man hosted famous guests who included Hugh O'Brian, the lover of his future wife, Margaret Whiting. Otto Preminger also appeared on the show, even Van Johnson, with whom Jack enjoyed a brief fling.

Enrolled at Chicago's Northwestern University, Jack (left-hand figure in center photo) claimed that he was the "top celebrity" on campus, a position he maintained to some degree by exaggerating his theatrical credentials. They landed him a leading role in a musical variety act called *The Little Ones' ABCs*.

Fortunately for fans of gay male porn, within a few years he would no longer be performing for children.

dios) in the United States. It wasn't entirely clear at the time whether gay porn was technically legal. This was the launch pad. During the course of his career, he made nearly 85 films, the majority of them gay.

One of Wrangler's most popular gay porn series was marketed as the "Roger-Wrangler Trilogy." In these movies, he co-starred with a well-endowed stud known simply as "Roger."

During the production of these films, Wrangler learned that Roger's manager worked overtime scheduling many dozens of off-the-record "appointments" for his star. For a brief time, Roger became the most expensive and the most sought-after hustler in New York City. Roger's manager, according to Wrangler, would allow a client exactly 30 minutes with Roger. That manager strictly timed these seductions "standing outside a hotel room with a stopwatch," according to Wrangler.

These experiences and many more are revealed in his 1984 autobiography *The Jack Wrangler Story or What's a Nice Boy Like You Doing?* (written with Carl Johnes).

The memoir is highly censored, omitting details about his dozens of romances with young men in New York and Hollywood.

Despite his naked appeal onscreen, there's no evidence that Wrangler made it a point to sell his meat for pay. He never evolved into the "fuck or get fucked on demand" playmate that Cal Culver became. Cal was an out and proud rent boy, enthusiastically for hire to anybody willing and able to pay the charges.

Wrangler was, however, frequently star-struck, perhaps a by-product of his Hollywood childhood. So whenever the likes of Roddy McDowall or Rock Hudson called, he donned his Wrangler jeans and ventured forth into the night to answer the summons.

Ironically but not surprisingly, despite his success in male porn, Wrangler really wanted to become a legitimate mainstream actor. One of his biggest disappointment came when he was denied the role of the "blond god" male prostitute, Numie Chase, in the film adaptation of Darwin Porter's bestselling novel, *Butterflies in Heat*.

Instead, the role went to the supermodel and super beauty, Matt Collins, the highest paid male model of the 70s. The novel's film adaptation, which became a cult classic, was released under the title of *Tropic of Desire*.

In 1978, Jack was offered a fee that justified his switch to straight porno, making his debut in *China Sisters*, which included his first cinematically recorded sexual encounter with a woman. Up to that point, he was, sexually speaking, a cinematic virgin, at least insofar as women were concerned.

The plot of *China Sisters* seemed close to home. In the film, two Chinese sisters recall their sexual adventures. He is supposed to be gay but by fucking him they make him straight. As Wrangler later recalled, "Talk about the perfect crossover film! The picture was me."

Gay actor James Coco liked **Jack's autobiography**, referring to it as "a startling, often hilarious account of a world few people know. It's hot, it's cool, it zips."

In the book Jack tells of how he went from enrollment in socially correct schools to a directing career in summer stock, struggling with the "burning egos" of such divas as Andy Devine, Hermione Gingold, Jane Russell, Mamie Van Doren, Yvonne De Carlo, and the emotionally troubled Betty Hutton.

It also reveals how one day he discovered that he was, "the hottest star in the gay porn industry."

Several other XXX films for straight adults followed, including *Jack and Jill* (1979), *Roommates* (1981), and *The Devil in Miss Jones 2*.

His favorite director was the openly gay Chuck Vincent. Instead of concentrating on traditional pornographic views of the female body, he focused on Wrangler's body and directed the viewer's eye to the male sexual experience instead. Perhaps for that reason, many gays also flocked to see (or purchased, for private viewings) these nominally "straight" films as well.

The strangest pairing in a somewhat bizarre life was yet to come. In 1976 Wrangler met the famous singer, Margaret Whiting, who was known for such hits as "Springtime in Vermont," and who had first made her reputation as a singer in the 1940s and 50s. She was 22 years Wrangler's senior.

Whiting is the daughter of the songwriter Richard Whiting, who composed such hits as "Hooray for Hollywood" and "Too Marvelous for Words."

The chanteuse also wrote a

Best Wishes

Love,
Jack 'n Jill

When offers came in for roles as a mainstream (i.e., "hetero") porn star, **Jack** would reinvent himself as a "crossover" performer. Here he's seen with **Samantha Fox** in *Jack 'n Jill*.

In *Two China Sisters*, he was cast as a gay man who became straight after the sisters jointly seduced him. *[Psst!-- gossip from the fluffers: Maybe having a dildo pushed up Jack's ass helped him perform.]*

He also posed for the cover of *Ultra*, a rip-off publication that tried to imitate *Playgirl*. The cover that's illustrated above was the last edition of this ill-fated magazine ever published.

memoir, calling it *It Might As Well Be Spring*. Long before Wrangler, she had enjoyed affairs with A-list studs who had included both John Garfield and Hugh O'Brian of *Wyatt Earp* fame.

Their romance got off to a slow start, but eventually blossomed. Some of Wrangler's fans berated him for betraying his inner (gay) core. Other less charitable critics claimed, "Wrangler's in it just for the money."

Wrangler himself was somewhat enigmatic claiming, "I'm not bisexual and I'm not straight. I'm gay, but I could never live a gay lifestyle, because I'm much too competitive."

Whiting, aware of Wrangler's history as a gay porn star and alert to his fleeting romances with young men, once told the author and art director Stanley Mills Haggart, "Sometimes he comes on like gangbusters."

Their emotional links were strong, however, and their friendship endured. Wrangler married Whiting in 1994. Once, she informed a reporter that she knew that her husband was gay, "but only around the edges, dear."

In New York City in 1998, when Whiting broke her hip by tripping over a loose pavement, she and Wrangler sued the city for $3 million. The suit, which catalyzed a river of gay witticisms, demanded not only settlement for her injuries, but $1 million in compensation "for loss of conjugal relations."

On April 7, 2009, still relatively young and still looking good, but based on years of smoking cigarettes, Wrangler died at the age of 62 from complications related to emphysema.

His films, however, especially the gay porn, still rack up handsome sales figures.

Backstage, **Jack Wrangler** (rarely photographed in glasses) and **Margaret Whiting** embrace **Charles Pierce** (center), one of America's greatest female impersonators, who's rarely photographed without his wig. (Many of them appear on the shelf behind him.)

Wrangler and Whiting finally married in 1994 after living together for years. Soon after becoming involved with Whiting, Wrangler retired from porn and devoted his time to his first love, musical theater. At the time this picture was taken, Wranger and Whiting were familiar faces on the Broadway scene, and were active in their support and promotion of AIDS charities.

MANDATE
THE NATIONAL MAGAZINE of ENTERTAINMENT & EROS

YESTERDAY'S BEAUTY YESTERDAY'S ICON

Jack Wrangler, born John Robert Stillman in Beverly Hills in 1946, still lives on in gay porn collections today.

Taking his name from the label on a pair of blue jeans, he first appeared in the mid-70s as "Jack Wrangler." A career in gay porn soon followed, as he starred in such films as *Boots and Saddles, Gemini, Heavy Equipment, Junior Cadets, Kansas City Trucking Co.,* and *Navy Blue.* One of his most memorable films was *A Night at the Adonis.*

As a straight porn star, he appeared most notably in *Devil in Miss Jones II* and the phenomenally profitable *Debbie Does Dallas.* His first sexual encounter with a woman was actually on screen in front of a camera.

In the lower right, a gray-haired Wrangler is shown shortly before his death in 2009 from emphysema.

FILM REVIEW
WRANGLER: ANATOMY OF AN ICON
(2008)

Out, Proud, and Pornographic

With his rugged good looks, blond hair, steely blue eyes, and macho-posturing, Jack Wrangler, the 1970s' most visible and highest-grossing gay male porn star, appeared in at least 30 gay sex films. Within their steamy contexts, he both topped and bottomed.

This docu by Jeffrey Schwarz traces the odyssey of Wrangler's bizarre life and career

In his own words, Wrangler said, "I did porn because I felt unattractive. I wanted to be lusted after."

And so he was by thousands of young gay men coming out in the 1970s, the heyday of this ruggedly handsome but rather small (5'10" tall, 140 lbs.) actor who photographed "big" on the screen.

After his porn heyday, he "graduated" to a brief career in pornographic hetero films. Or should we say was downgraded to hetero.

> At first, **Jack Wrangler** was reluctant to cooperate with the producers of this documentary about his incredible life, but finally, he was seduced. The film includes archival materials from Jack's life and interviews. There are glimpses of full-frontal Jack in stills, but the porn clips aren't particularly graphic. Sigh.

Born Jack Stillman in Beverly Hills, the son of a big-time Hollywood producer, Wrangler (as he came to call himself) wanted to be independent. After a try in legit theater, he developed a core of fans as a partially undressed go-go dancer. Later, he appeared nude in a racy San Francisco gay play.

That led to magazine layouts and 8mm porn loops before he moved into gay films, some of them directed by porn master Jack Deveau.

Thanks partly to his unbridled posturing, and an aggressive pursuit of an intensely sexual persona, Wrangler was on his way. He became a household word, albeit only in gay households.

In one of the strangest emotional bonds of his career, the gay actor came to live with songbird Margaret Whiting, a jazz and pop icon from the late 40s and 50s. Whiting was the original cougar. Perhaps she evoked the witchcraft of her big hit "That Old Black Magic," and worked her spell on Wrangler.

The couple married in 1994, and Wrangler eventually began to write and direct cabaret shows, some with Whiting performing. He helped conceive the 1997 Broadway revue *Dream*, which starred Whiting in a tribute to her friend, the South Carolina songwriter Johnny Mercer.

Whiting appears as herself in Schwarz's documentary. Other persons appearing as themselves include Bruce Vilanch, Michael Musto, Chi Chi LaRue, Jamie Gillis, pornographer Al Goldstein, founder of *Screw* Magazine, poet Rod McKuen, and Debbi Whiting (Margaret's daughter).

When asked in later years about his career as a porn performer, Wrangler said, "I'm proud of it, and there's nothing I can do about it."

Homage to

Miss Bette Davis

*Uncompromising, Intractable, Tactless, Disagreeable, Unforgiving,
Impossibly Temperamental, and LARGER THAN LIFE*

:"*Bette Davis, who died Friday in Paris at the age of 81, always made the world aware of her presence. And she often made Hollywood quake in that presence. She also changed the course of women in film.*"
Robert Osborne (1989)

Bette Davis, her name synonymous with movie legend, had a career that spanned six decades. She also survived four disastrous marriages, including one to her *All About Eve* co-star, Gary Merrill, who ridiculed her in a "Wifey Dearest" tome, as did her ungrateful daughter, B.D. Hyman, who orchestrated a "Mommie Dearest" attack on her in a book of her own.

Long after her critics are dead, buried, and forgotten, the name of **Bette Davis** is likely to live as long as her films are shown. *The Little Foxes, Jezebel, All About Eve, What Ever Happened to Baby Jane?,* and *Now, Voyager* are only a few of her cinematic triumphs.

Davis even survived Joan Crawford, her arch rival. Director Vincent Sherman, who bedded both actresses, said, "Joan called Bette 'a bitch,' and Bette shot back that Joan was 'a whore,' and then Bette went on to say that while Joan was at MGM, 'she fucked everybody except Lassie.'"

MISS BETTE DAVIS

Bette Davis appeared second on a list compiled in 1999 by the American Film Institute of the greatest female movie stars of all time. Yet even though she went over the top in many of her performances, many gay men consider her the greatest female star Hollywood ever produced. Arguably, she should have beaten the also vastly talented Katharine Hepburn for the number one spot.

Her enduring legacy was the subject of two recent documentaries, each of them reviewed on the pages which immediately follow.

"A pitfall for the high-powered woman is a tendency to choose weak men. The successful Hollywood actress often is attracted to rather neutral characters from outside her profession."
Bette Davis, 1955

"I've always liked men much better than women. From high school onward, all my friends were boys. I like the male mind better. Men aren't as pretty as women, but they're more interesting. I miss their company."
Bette Davis, 1983

QUEER ICON:
THE CULT OF BETTE DAVIS
(2010)

We should send roses to the brother/sister team of Mike Black and Carole Summer for putting together this docu. Incorporating film clips of the diva's iconic moments, it interviews gay men about why they worship Bette. Collectively, at least 20 self-professed gay men tackle an intriguing subject: Why did the sometimes disagreeable actress evolve into such a *Queer Icon*? And do gay men within today's more liberated society still need role models akin to Bette Davis?

She was an odd choice for gay men to select as their standard-bearer. Perhaps the more obviously gay-friendly Joan Crawford might have been a better candidate. But gay men voted with their hearts, and have done so for decades. They adore Bette—and that is that.

"Peaches Christ," one of the men interviewed in the documentary, delivered the money quote: "There's a collective understanding that Bette is God."

The documentary includes campy burlesques of Bette by impersonators who include Charles Pierce, Matthew Martin, and Arthur Blake. Blake, of course, is the *grand dame* of all Davis impersonators. During her shooting of *Deception* (released in 1946), Bette actually saw his impersonation of her at the Trocadero Night Club in Los Angeles. The next day she entertained *Deception's* cast and crew by doing an impersonation of Blake impersonating her.

Although some of Blake's routines pissed her off, she later admitted that he was the most brilliant of her many impersonators. "Unless you consider Tallulah Bankhead," Davis added sarcastically. It was Tallulah who insisted that Bette had impersonated her in her portrayal of Margo Channing in *All About Eve*.

Rumors of Bette's own lesbian past, some of them associated with Barbara Stanwyck and Bette during the filming of *So Big* in 1932, have never been verified. A smoking gun, however, may emerge in future biographies, as more details become known. In the meanwhile, however, we have to take Bette at her word: She often proclaimed, loudly, that she could not understand how anyone, male or female, could be sexually attracted to someone of their own gender.

Throughout her life she never lent her support to gay rights, and sometimes in private she would make homophobic remarks. "It completely baffles me," she often said in reference to all things light and gay.

Yet, in contrast, as the years went by, she softened her position. In her declining years, she became especially impressed with the realization that her biggest fans and supporters were gay.

"A more appreciative, artistic group of people for the arts does not exist," she said. "Conceited as it may sound, a great deal of it has to do with their approval of my work. They are knowing and loving of the arts. They make the average male look stupid."

A drawback to *Queer Icon* involves the fact that the only interviewee (and this is an educated guess), who has seen every movie Bette ever made is Darwin Porter, the biographer of celebrities who is, incidentally, co-author of this guidebook to Queer Films. "When I was a kid," Porter said, "old movies weren't so readily available. There were few revival houses and no DVDs. Luckily, when I was a young teenager in Miami, a decaying movie house on Flagler Street sponsored a revival that screened all of Bette's films. At the time, Bette was a role model to my mother, who made it an ongoing point to dress and make herself up to look like Bette. Perhaps my darling mama was the first real Bette Davis impersonator."

"She took me to every one of Bette's movies, including the really obscure ones like *Bad Sister* (1931) and *The Golden Arrow* (1936). Since that faraway time in Miami, her movies have entered the mainstream, each being more readily available and better known. But I also remember *The Working Man* (1933); *Fog Over Frisco* (1934); *The Menace* (1932), and *Jimmy the Gent* (1934)—all of them. How many impersonators can mimic Bette in *Dark House* (1932)? In that political comedy, starring Warren William (remember him?), Bette played Kay Russell, a secretary whose idea of a woman's place in politics was under her boss's bedsheets."

WHAT THE CRITICS SAID

"That been-around the block moxie; that sultry sophistication; and, of course, those eyes. There are many reasons why Bette Davis was one of the greatest actresses ever to grace the silver screen, but her X-factor has long held—indeed, continues to hold—particular sway over gay men."
Matt Sussman

"*Queer Icon* is a bona fide treat. Rates three boxes of popcorn."
Buzzin' Lee Hartgrave

"*Queer Icon* brings the career and *oeuvre* of the divine Bette Davis into focus. Whether you prefer her as a ruthless and amoral southern belle (Regina Giddens in *The Little Foxes)*; as a mousey but soulful heiress (Charlotte Vale in *Now, Voyager)*; as a volcanic and temperamental diva (Margo Channing in *All About Eve*); or as a vulgar, aging psychopath (Jane Hudson in *What Ever Happened to Baby Jane?),* in *Queer Icon*, the legacy of Miss Davis lives again. Of special interest is the docu's ongoing discussion of why she's always been so passionately imitated by drag queens. "
Danforth Prince

STARDUST: THE BETTE DAVIS STORY

(2006)

Mother Goddamn's Bumpy Ride to Stardom

Fasten your seat belts, as you're in for a bumpy ride in this made-for-TV bio which was first aired on Turner Classic Movies with narration by Susan Sarandon. Emmy-winning helmer Peter Jones, along with Mark A. Catalena, pulled together this cigarette-twirling, ball-breaking homage to the great film diva, with Jones also crafting the script.

They had unprecedented access to Davis's personal archives and were granted many original interviews, although it's hard to come up with a lot of new stuff about a woman whose life has already been so heavily investigated by other biographers.

Stardust emerges as an excellent docu about one of the greatest stars of the so-called golden era. Davis herself would have rewritten that line as "I was *the* greatest star—not *one* of the greatest."

In archival footage appear such characters as Bette's own Mommie Dearest, Ruthie Davis. We also get "memories" from B.D. Hyman, who wrote a tell-all book in 1985 entitled *My Mother's Keeper*. B.D.'s book was published seven years after Christina Crawford libeled her mother Joan in her own notorious portrait, *Mommie Dearest*.

Davis' relatively loving and charitable son, Michael Merrill, son of Davis' fourth husband, Gary Merrill, is also interviewed, admitting that Davis did take a drink or two on occasion.

The late Vincent Sherman, Davis's director and lover, also weighs in, along with Ellen Burstyn and Jane Fonda. In archival footage, George Arliss appears (he made *The Man Who Played God* with Bette in 1932). We're also treated to archival footage of Bette's boss, the dreaded Jack L. Warner.

The most stunning revelations—relayed with obvious venom—come from Marion Richards, Davis's maid, who married her boss's ex-husband, William Grant Sherry. She leaves the distinct

impression that Davis was implicated in the death of her second husband, Arthur Farnsworth, in 1943. The poor man died of head injuries, but from whom?

Davis's greatest triumphs are carefully documented, including her participation in William Wyler's *Jezebel* and in *Dark Victory*, a role Garbo turned down. We also see Davis in *Now, Voyager* (the two cigarette moon-and-stars thing), and in *The Little Foxes*, which Tallulah Bankhead had used previously as a vehicle for success on Broadway.

The directors could hardly leave out Bette Davis's crowning achievement, the role of Margo Channing in the 1950 *All About Eve*. Fox called Davis in at the last minute to take over the role of Margo. Originally, the studio had cast Claudette Colbert, who had to drop out because of a back injury. That year, Davis and Gloria Swanson, playing Norma Desmond in *Sunset Blvd.*, lost the Oscar to lesbian actress Judy Holliday in *Born Yesterday*. A shame, really, We only wish the Oscars could have been a tie that year between Ms. Channing and Ms. Desmond. Neither Swanson nor Davis had ever played such spectacular roles before, and, alas, never would again.

And, of course, we get *What Ever Happened to Baby Jane?*, co-starring her nemesis, Lady Crawford. *Stardust* reveals what we already know—that Joan Crawford hated Bette Davis. Yet they came together for a shooting schedule of only 21 days in *Baby Jane*, Joan's first picture in four years. Both were smart enough to know that they had to get along, and both of these fading stars needed a hit.

On learning of Joan's death, Bette said, "You should never say bad things about the dead. You should only say good. Joan Crawford is dead, good."

Aside from *All About Eve* or *Baby Jane*, what gay man can resist Bette's campy portrait of Rosa Moline in *Beyond the Forest* (1949). It provided dozens Davis's drag impersonators with the immortal line, "What a dump!"

Actually Davis was as big as the movies themselves and often bigger than many of her lesser efforts. Her life was stormy both on and off the screen. The docu attempts to deal with some myths, including the one that Davis was "never considered as a candidate in anybody's mind"—but her own—to play Scarlett O'Hara in *Gone With the Wind*.

Bette Davis died in France at the age of 81 in 1989 when the man she called "little Ronnie Reagan" was presiding over the Free World.

She did not live to see a certain biographer suggest she had a lesbian past.

WHAT THE CRITICS SAID

"The gay sensibility is brought home by author James McCourt, Charles Busch, and a gem of a clip of Charles Pierce doing his famous impersonation. Trivia: Davis's tombstone reads, 'She did it the hard way.' This portrait of her tumultuous life certainly reflects that."
Christopher Harrity, *The Advocate*

"When *Stardust* isn't demonstrating what made Davis great, it is allowing her to speak for herself in television interviews with Dick Cavett, Jack Paar, Phil Donahue, and others. 'I never cared how I looked, as long as I looked like the character,' she said in one exchange."
Anita Gates, *The New York Times*

COMPARING BREASTS

When he was only 19, Douglas Fairbanks Jr. was famously married, albeit for only a short, high-profile period (1929-1933) to Joan Crawford. Bette Davis met the dashing young actor, son of a famous father, during her first two years in Hollywood.

In 1933, Davis and Fairbanks, Jr. were cast together in that dud, *Parachute Jumper*. Robert Aldrich would mock the film some three decades later when he featured a clip of it in *What Ever Happened to Baby Jane?*, presumably to demonstrate one of the actress's cinematic failures.

Tipsy, Fairbanks walked up to Bette at a Hollywood party, encountering her in a low-cut gown. Drink in hand, he told her, "You're not particularly pretty. In fact, you're rather plain." He reached into her gown and exposed her left breast. He fondled it for a few seconds. "Joan Crawford has better breasts than you do." Then he walked away, leaving a shocked Bette standing there with one breast exposed.

Characteristically, Bette had a lot to say about that episode, and about Fairbanks, Jr., in later years. Famously included with those remarks was her oft-repeated observation, "We live in a tit culture."

Douglas Fairbanks, Jr., and **Joan Crawford**, shortly after their marriage of 1929. He liked her looks and her tits better than he did those of Bette Davis.

In a discussion about *Parachute Jumper* (1933), an unmemorable film he made with Davis which she remembered as one of her worst, he recalled, "I didn't appreciate my new young leading lady, fresh from the stage. She was not particularly pretty, in fact, I thought her rather plain, but one didn't easily forget her unique personality. She was always conscientious and serious, and seemed devoid of humor of any kind."

THE QUEER QUOTIENT: BETTE'S MOST FAMOUS LINES

"I'd like to kiss you, but I just washed my hair."
Madge Norwood in *The Cabin in the Cotton* (1932)

"I want you to have a party and be gay. Very, very gay!"
Judith Traherne in *Dark Victory* (1939)

"With all my heart, I still love the man I killed."
Leslie Crosbie in *The Letter* (1940)

"Oh, Jerry don't let's ask for the moon. We have the stars."
Charlotte Vale in *Now, Voyager* (1942)

"What a dump!"
Rosa Moline in *Beyond the Forest* (1949)

"Fasten your seatbelts, it's going to be a bumpy night."
Margo Channing in *All About Eve* (1950)

Famously Bitchy Bette

(and we all know how much gay men love famously bitchy divas)

Catalyzed Some Famously Bitchy Commentary

HERE'S MERELY THE TIP OF THE ICEBERG:

"Bette Davis is a no-good, sexless son of a bitch!"
Hungary-born film director **Michael Curtiz,** for whom English
was a second language.
In 1939, he directed Bette in *Elizabeth and Essex*

"I hear she screws like a mink!"
Jack Carson

"Bette Davis is an egotistical little bitch."
Barbara Stanwyck

---

*"Bette Davis was like a greedy little girl at a party table who just has to sample
other women's cupcakes."*
Miriam Hopkins

---

*"That dame is too uptight. What she needs is a good screw from a man who
knows how to do it."*
Humphrey Bogart

---

*"I admit I may have seen better days, but I'm still not to be had for the price
of a cocktail!"*
Bette Davis as **Margo Channing** in *All About Eve*

The Making of
Ben-Hur

How The Homoeroticism of Ancient Rome
Was Camouflaged, Oh-So-Delicately, in the Age of Sputnik

The pressure was on. **Charlton Heston** (photo above) not only had to win that famous chariot race, but he had to save MGM too. If *Ben-Hur* failed at the box office, the nearly bankrupt Metro-Goldwyn-Mayer, once the most famous studio in the world, would have closed its doors.

Although the studio was losing $5 million a year, in a nail-biting gamble, it agreed to bankroll *Ben-Hur* at a then-staggering cost of $10 million.

William Wyler turned down the role of director six times before finally accepting. He'd worked as an assistant on the original production of *Ben-Hur* in 1926. His first recommendation involved hiring Charlton Heston to play the villain, Messala.

"But who, then, will play *Ben-Hur?*" asked producer Sam Zimbalist.

"There's only one man who can pull it off," Wyler said. "Rock Hudson. He's got a great body, and Ben-Hur is going to be naked throughout most of the film. Hudson's a fag, but he's good at butching it up in front of the camera."

WHO CENSORED THE CENTURIONS?
How MGM Camouflaged the Ancient World's Lust With Delicate Subliminal Codes

It was altogether appropriate that director William Wyler either auditioned or interviewed a wide spectrum actors for the title role of *Ben-Hur*, Wyler's 1959 remake of the 1925 silent film that had starred gay actor Ramon Novarro, the lover of Rudolph Valentino. Much more than just a sword-and-sandal epic, it was the big-budget third film interpretation of Lew Wallace's fictional 1880 novel, *Ben-Hur: A Tale of the Christ.*

For the male lead of Ben-Hur, Metro-Goldwyn-Mayer's producer Sam Zimbalist had originally wanted Paul Newman. His preference was revealed during a well-documented script conference with gay author and the film's scriptwriter, Gore Vidal, Newman's best friend at the time. Vidal promptly informed Zimbalist that Newman would never accept such a role.

"Why not?" Zimbalist asked. "It's the most coveted role in town."

"After his disastrous debut in *The Silver Chalice*, Paul swore he'd never appear again on screen in a cocktail dress," Vidal said. "Besides, he always claims his legs are too skinny."

In the wake of that meeting, Zimbalist conferred with Wyler, then jointly decided that Rock Hudson would be ideal as Ben-Hur. "He's certainly got the physique for it," Zimbalist said. But when he called Universal to pop the question, studio executives there refused to release Hudson from his pre-existing contract.

Next on the list was Marlon Brando. He'd hated himself on the screen in *Julius Caesar* and wasn't anxious to return to Rome for the filming of another "swords and sandals" epic ever again.

Then Burt Lancaster, another actor with a great physique, was pitched the script as the studio's choice for Ben-Hur. Lancaster, to his regret, had already contracted for another picture, and couldn't resolve their conflicting schedules.

Charlton Heston (left), **Stephen Boyd** (center) and director **William Wyler** (right) were all smiles and cooperation during the early weeks of film production on *Ben-Hur,* although the inevitable tensions arose as production dragged on.

At first, Heston had applauded Wyler's choice of the Irish actor, Boyd. Soon he was calling him "Steve."

"I'm glad you cast a manly man like myself in the role—not one of those homosexual boys you were considering," Heston told Wyler. "Between us, Steve and I can produce enough testosterone to give birth to *Ben-Hur.* The 'baby' that Stevie boy and I can produce will grow into a giant at the box office. MGM will be rescued—take my word for it."

By coincidence, in one of the great gay ironies associated with casting issues in Hollywood, each of the actors noted above were either homosexual or bisexual.

Finally, however, Charlton Heston was offered and accepted the role. He signed his contract despite the stated objections of Gore Vidal, who remarked at the time, "He has all the charm of a wooden Indian."

Casting the role of Messala, the film's Roman officer, was almost as convoluted. Victor Mature, who'd scored a big hit in *Samson and Delilah*, was the first choice. Soon-after, that proposed deal collapsed, as did a similar pitch to Steve Cochran. (Voyeuristic note to size-queens: Cochran and Mature were known at the time for swinging the two biggest clubs in Hollywood.)

In the end, Stephen Boyd (1928-1977), the ruggedly handsome Northern Irish Protestant actor, accepted the choice role of Messala. In yet another (parallel) coincidence, Mature, Cochran, and Boyd were each also bisexuals.

By now, on-set wags had noted how appropriate it was that a film script about repressed homosexuality was being cast with mostly repressed homosexual actors—a literal gay houseparty whose offscreen permissiveness might have vaguely reflected the sexual mores of ancient Rome at the time.

Regrettably, Sam Zimbalist died in 1958 and never got to see "my dream film" or any of the various awards it generated.

During his compilation of the filmscript, Vidal faced many perplexing challenges. Ben-Hur and Messala had been intimate childhood friends. Years later, they meet as strong-willed, testosterone-permeated adults whose personalities and political allegiances have by now been clearly defined: Heston is a land-owning, fervently patriotic Zionist Jew, Messala is an aristocratic Roman officer [i.e., a ruthless and hostile foreign conquerer.]

Initially, their reunion is affectionate, but soon, Ben-Hur and Messala quarrel bitterly over sovereignty and the politics of the day.

A mutual loathing follows, with rivalry that leads to Messala's death in that famous chariot race.

Early in the filming, as scriptwriter, Vidal protested to Wyler that there was "no motivation for all this fury," but subsequently he came up with

Charlton Heston (left, in photo above) and **Stephen Boyd** take time out for a sightseeing tour of Rome, in a style inspired, perhaps, by what Gregory Peck and Audrey Hepburn had done in *Roman Holiday* (1953), six years before.

When Boyd saw this candid shot of themselves on a motorcycle, he told Wyler, "My legs are more shapely than Chuck's. Mine look like they were sculpted by Michelangelo. Chuck's look a little too toothpickey. And before this shoot is over, I plan to find out if, under the tunic, he's as much of a man as he says he is."

In one of the most controversial scenes in *Ben-Hur*, **Boyd** (left) and **Heston** (right) share a communal bond in memory of their boyhood when they were best friends. "Chuck is trying to look macho throughout our bonding," Boyd later said, "but I was playing Messala like Gore Vidal intended. We had been boyhood lovers, according to Vidal's version, and I'm looking at Chuck with lust in my eyes. Any fool can see that. But Chuck missed the point of the scene."

a motivation.

He reckoned that Ben-Hur and Messala had been boyhood lovers. Meeting again as adults, the more decadent and more permissive of the two, Messala, is still in love with Ben-Hur and wants to resume pounding his ass.

Ben-Hur, as a virtuous Old Testament-thumping Zionist, righteously rebuffs Messala's come-on. As for Messala, hell hath no fury like a horny Roman officer rejected in love, "from a Jew, no less."

A very reluctant Wyler agreed to go along with this homosexually motivated plot device, providing that it was so understated and so subtle that relatively naïve mainstream audiences of 1959 wouldn't get it, but gay men would.

Wyler, Vidal, and their collaborators decided to bring the sexually sophisticated Boyd into the loop. Wyler knew that the Irish homosexual had deflowered a lot of boy-ass in his day. Wyler, however, insisted that Heston should not be informed that the scenes he'd be filming with Boyd contained a homoerotic undercurrent, subliminal or not.

In his literary memoirs, Vidal noted: "Chuck (i.e., Heston) was now imitating Francis X. Bushman in the 1925 silent screen version, tossing his head, chin held high, oblivious of what was going on. Boyd at one point winked at me. *He* was in character."

In countless newspaper and magazine articles, Heston has been made the butt of jokes. "How dumb can an actor be?" Wyler once asked. "How can an actor play a gay love scene and not even know it? When Heston saw the rushes, couldn't he see the gleam in Boyd's eyes?"

As the years went by, Heston gave the impression of having been more enlightened. During his lifetime, at least, his own sexual decadence had never been revealed in any lurid *Confidential* magazine way. Only the underground press ever got a whiff of what was really going with Heston when the cameras weren't rolling.

In a 1977 interview, he got the message. Perhaps he had assessed the gay undercurrent at the time of its filming, yet never reached out to inform Wyler, Boyd or Vidal that he understood.

"The story behind *Ben-Hur* isn't really about Christ," Heston recalled. "It's certainly not a story about Ben-Hur and Esther, either. It's a love story between Ben-Hur and Messala, and the destruction of that love and the world they had known. In the wake of that destruction, there remained only hatred and revenge—it's a vendetta story."

Incidentally, the 1959

Not since D.W. Griffith's *Intolerance* (1916) had such a gigantic filmset ever been constructed. The scene involved the bitter chariot race between the characters of Messala and Judah Ben-Hur. An army of Italian craftsmen had constructed the largest set in the history of cinema as an evocation, sprawling over 18 acres, of the ancient arena at Antioch.

The night before the shoot, a drunken Boyd, in the bar of a hotel on the Via Veneto, had come on strong to **Heston** (charioteer in the photo above), who had scornfully rejected him, thereby ending their friendship in a way that eerily paralleled the scenario of the movie itself.

remake of *Ben-Hur* saved MGM from bankruptcy and won a record 11 Oscars out of a dozen nominations. When it was re-released in 2010 on Warner Home Video, it was viewed by consumers who were infinitely more sophisticated, sexually speaking, than those white-bread-with-vanilla viewers of 1959. Hip modern-day critics immediately noted the "homoerotic relationship" simmering between Ben-Hur and Messala.

Years later, in a bar in Dublin, near the end of his short life, and after too many drinks, the still-very-handsome Boyd swaggeringly but only half-jokingly told his hangers-on: "I never got around to plugging Chuck Heston during the filming of *Ben-Hur*, but I have no doubt he would have bottomed for me."

Whoever said pictures don't lie? This candid snapshot of *Ben-Hur's* (left to right) director **William Wilder**, screenwriter **Christopher Fry**, **Gore Vidal**, and **Charlton Heston** does not reveal the seething rage transpiring behind the scenes among this unholy quartet of egos and frustrations.

Pressured by the studio, Wyler had brought in Christopher Fry, the English poet and playwright, to rework much of the script Vidal had previously written. Wyler had objected to the homosexual dynamics that Vidal was establishing between Ben-Hur and Messala.

Although in the picture, Heston is amicably placing his ringed hand on Vidal's shoulder, he actually despised him. In his memoirs, *In the Arena,* Heston had nothing but praise for Fry, but referred to Vidal as "a tart, embittered man, an odd choice" for the screenplay of *Ben-Hur.*

Vidal, Heston claimed, was sent packing, with Fry taking control of the script. In years to come, Heston repeatedly downplayed Vidal's contribution, although Vidal claimed "I rewrote the script from the first page through the chariot race. Fry wrote the rest."

The debate continues to this day. At any rate, Vidal never got the credit he deserved. In fact, at MGM the false legend persisted for years—at least until many of the participants in the affair died— that Vidal had tried to turn *Ben-Hur* into "a fag picture."

On the night **Susan Hayward** presented **Charlton Heston** with his Best Actor Oscar for his portrayal of Ben-Hur, they posed for cameramen backstage after the show. Here, Hayward looks approvingly at Heston, although she could be quite candid about him in private.

Six years before, she'd co-starred with him in *The President's Lady,* a costume drama about former U.S. president Andrew Jackson. Heston, of course, had been cast as Old Hickory.

"We had a brief fling at the time," Hayward confided to her assistant, Peter Pell, in Fort Lauderdale. "I had a mirrored wall in my dressing room. All during the fuck, Heston kept staring at himself in action and didn't once look into my eyes, even though he was right on top of me. Later, I learned that he much preferred very young women—or young boys, as the Hollywood grapevine had it at the time."

MGM's 1959 release of *Ben-Hur* was not Hollywood's first attempt to get some cinematic mileage out of Lew Wallace's 1880 novel. MGM had produced an earlier, silent version in 1925 with just as many queer subliminal behind-the-scenes dramas. Shamelessly promoted at the time as "The Picture Every Christian Ought to See," it was the most expensive silent film ever made.

In 1997, it was selected for preservation in the United States National Film Registry by the Library of Congress as being "culturally, historically, and aesthetically significant."

We dedicate this page to the version of *Ben-Hur* that "didn't get it quite right," as was generally believed at MGM as they were reprising it during their 1959 push.

We also dedicate this page to the (closeted gay) star of *Ben-Hur*'s 1925 version, Latino heartthrob **Ramon Novarro**.

RAMON NOVARRO (1899-1968)
BEN-HUR'S ORIGINAL CINEMATIC STAR

At the time, Metro claimed that their budding star, **Ramon Sameniagos** (later **Ramon Novarro**; two photos above) was "Michelangelo's David with the face of an El Greco Don." The "too-beautiful" Ramon loved to be topped, especially by his arch-rival, Valentino, and by Latin heartthrob Antonio Moreno.

Before his tragic death in 1968, the result of a psychotic hustler who stuffed Valentino's Art Deco dildo down his throat, Ramon was a sweet, adorable youth and a nude model.

With its S&M implications, *Ben-Hur* was the role of a lifetime for **Ramon** as Ben-Hur (right in photo above) and the cinematic comeback for horse-hung but faded matinee idol **Francis X. Bushman** as Messala (left). Here, they glare at each other, perhaps re-activating the sexual role-playing they'd enjoyed together during their romantic heyday six years before.

"The noblest Roman of them all," **Ramon Novarro** as Judah Ben-Hur was both a romantic lover and a swashbuckling hero. Billed as "a second Valentino," in the photo (left) he plays golf in Rome wearing a stripped-down version of gladiator fetish during a break in the filming.

Ramon as a naked galley slave in a publicity still for MGM's 1925 version of *Ben-Hur*. Even his pubic hair was showing, a first ever for a male film star.

The caption read, "This photograph proves rather conclusively that he has no intention of ever joining a monastery."

EDITOR'S NOTE: For more about what was being swept under the carpets during the bad old days of early Hollywood, refer to Darwin Porter's bawdy info-novel, ***Hollywood's Silent Closet*** (ISBN 978-0-9668030-2-0). Based on eyewitness accounts of the debauched excesses of the Silent Era's closeted and very lavender past, it was reviewed by critics as "The most intimate and realistic account of sex, murder, degradation, and blackmail in early Hollywood ever written...a brilliant primer for *Who Was Queer and Who Was Who*."

Some Like it Hot

Swing, Sex, Slapstick, and Drag

Arguably, *Some Like It Hot* was one of the best movies ever shot. Without **Marilyn Monroe** and her director, Billy Wilder, it might have been another of those forgotten comedies of the late 1950s.

Thanks, indeed, that Wilder abandoned his original plan to cast Danny Kaye and Bob Hope as the drag queens, settling instead on **Jack Lemmon** (photo far right, above) and **Tony Curtis**.

Wilder also wanted to cast Mitzi Gaynor in the part of Sugar. But what did he know? At first, he wanted Mae West to play Norma Desmond in *Sunset Blvd.* When Marilyn agreed to film *Some Like It Hot,* she hadn't made a movie in two years and needed the money.

Some Like It Hot ranks #150 on the list of Top Grossing Films of the 20th Century.

In Billy Wilder's Sexually Ambiguous Film about the Game of Love,
Nobody Was Perfect

In Marilyn Monroe's greatest film, and the best comedy ever turned out by Hollywood, she is a blonde bombshell of thermonuclear dimensions. She seems poured into her clothes like giant bon-bons for boys who are in and out of drag.

As Jack Lemmon tells Tony Curtis, "Look how she moves. Like Jell-O on springs. She must have some sort of built-in motor. I tell you, it's a whole different sex."

The plot is fairly simple: Joe and Jerry (Curtis and Lemmon) are musicians who witness the St. Valentine's Day Massacre in Chicago of 1929. Before fleeing town, they disguise themselves as women and join an all-girl band headed for a musical gig in Palm Beach, Florida.

Curtis becomes "Josephine" and Lemmon assumes the role of "Daphne." In her most comedic role as Sugar, Marilyn plays an untalented singer fully capable of stopping any show. She digs saxophone players. Guess what? Curtis, whether he's dressed as his male persona or as Josephine, is a saxophone player. Shades of lesbianism here.

Sugar wants to marry a millionaire, any millionaire, in Palm Beach, and Curtis, now into his male persona again, impersonates the millionaire of her dreams. He even talks like Cary Grant.

Contrary to expectation, it's Daphne (i.e., Jack Lemmon) who snares him/herself a real millionaire, the sexually aggressive, much-married Osgood Fielding III, who has, we assume at first, mistaken Daphne for a biological woman. Joe E. Brown as Osgood stars in his most triumphant role.

The dialogue was written by I.A.L. Diamond, with help from director Billy Wilder. Some of it, though still comic, has not weathered the changing fashions of time. For example, when Lemmon tells Curtis that he's

As **Tony Curtis** (left figure in photo above) looks on, **Jack Lemmon** as Daphne (second from left figure, above) seems to be telling **Marilyn** that his legs are more shapely than hers. At least he's posed them more seductively than Marilyn, who was rarely caught standing flat-footed (as she is above) when a camera was nearby.

Curtis, despite his protestations, bedded Monroe during the making of the film, but he'd also done that a decade earlier when they were both struggling "starlets."

engaged to Osgood, Curtis protests, "You're not a girl! You're a guy! Why would a guy want to marry a guy?" In this day of same-sex marriage debates, that question would never be asked.

Amazingly, both Monroe and Wilder had wanted Frank Sinatra to play Daphne. Of course, Ol' Blue Eyes turned it down. The idea of Sinatra in drag is comic, but hard to imagine. He'd probably have been more comfortable in the gangster role as played by George Raft, who doubled as a tough, part-time gangster in real life. Throughout the film, of course, Raft & Co. want the eyewitnesses to the Chicago massacre, Curtis and Lemmon, rubbed out.

After Sinatra rejected the crossdressing role, Wilder turned to Danny Kaye and Bob Hope. When they said no, offers went first to Anthony Perkins and then Jerry Lewis. Both of them declined as well.

Monroe was not Wilder's first choice for Daphne—originally he'd wanted Mitzi Gaynor. What a different movie that would have been.

At the time of filming, Monroe was going through one of the most difficult periods of her private life. Pregnant during the filming, she later had a miscarriage. The troubled star would

A DOUBLE DOSE OF UNREQUITED LOVE

Tony Curtis (left figure in left-hand photo, above) claimed that, in spite of their former conjugal link, kissing **Marilyn Monroe** was like kissing Hitler. Later, he retracted that statement. But Marilyn heard about it, and responded publicly, "I don't understand why people aren't a little more generous with each other. I don't like to say this, but I'm afraid there is a lot of envy in this business. For instance, you've read that there's some actor who said that kissing me was like kissing Hitler. Well, I think that's *his* problem."

Love takes many forms. In the movie, the much-married **Joe E. Brown** (left figure in right-hand photo, above) seems mesmerized with **Lemmon playing Daphne**, who's vampishly holding a flower between her teeth.

Wilder said that Joe E. Brown was one "crazy guy--old enough to play Osgood and loony enough, too." He instructed Brown to play Osgood as if he were truly in love with Daphne and planned to marry her/him even though he'd long ago figured out that Daphne's female credentials were suspicious.

As Wilder instructed, "Your character of Osgood has been seducing women for decades. In his declining years, he's decided to try a man for a change. Just don't let the audience in on our little secret."

often refuse to leave her dressing room, and when she did, she couldn't get her lines straight. Once, it took 47 takes for her to say, "It's me, Sugar," correctly.

Wilder had his own impression of Marilyn. "The question is whether Marilyn is a person at all. Perhaps she's one of the greatest DuPont products ever invented. She has breasts like granite. She defies gravity. She has a brain full of holes, like Swiss cheese. She hasn't the vaguest conception of the time of day. She arrives late and tells you she couldn't find the studio when she's been working there for years."

The film's original title was *Not Tonight, Josephine*, and immediately after its release, it ran into trouble: The Catholic Legion of Decency gave it a "C" (meaning "condemned") rating. But *Some Like It Hot*, along with Alfred Hitchcock's *Psycho* (1960), plus other films, led to the collapse of the Production Code in the 60s. Since it did not receive the Production Code approval, United Artists released it without the MPAA logo in the credits or title sequence.

Why is this film, even today, considered so gay, so hip, and such a romp? It's partly because both its male stars, Curtis and Lemmon, even though the plot firmly establishes them as heterosexuals, are in drag throughout most of the film. But more importantly, it was Monroe's greatest film, and hailed by critics as the finest comedy film ever made. "It is the *Citizen Kane* of comedies," wrote one critic.

Wilder deliberately chose not to photograph it in color so it wouldn't look like a "flaming faggot picture." From the reaction of the film's preview audience, Wilder didn't realize he'd created a cinematic landmark. Only one person out of an audience of 800 laughed—it was Steve Allen.

During the shoot, Monroe feuded with Wilder, and virtually everybody ended up hating each other. But as Billy Wilder's biographer, Maurice Zolotow, wrote: "With the passing of time, the bitter words and the memories of bad events were forgotten, because *Some Like It Hot* emerged as a magnificent film, a sensation at the box office the whole world over, a critical triumph for Monroe, a critical triumph for Wilder, an all-around bonanza. Suddenly, Wilder, the dishonorable cad, became Monroe's favorite director again. Suddenly, Monroe, that irresponsible and arrogant bitch, became the most luminous of all film actresses since Garbo."

Wilder was playing a joke on the more naïve 1950s audiences. The joke involved the fact that the Osgood character, as interpreted by Joe E. Brown, and in hot pursuit of "Daphne," knew all along that "she" was a man. Gay men in the 50s got it; straight audiences, or at least most of them, did not.

The final piece of dialogue in the film was never meant to be. Wilder kept it in only because he and his creative team couldn't think of anything better. It became one of the most memorable pieces of dialogue in film history. Jerry protests that he can't marry Osgood and, as if to prove his point, pulls off his wig. With his excessive makeup smudged, his earrings and other jewelry swinging, and with his (false) breasts heaving from exertion, he yells, "You can't marry me because I'm a man!"

Without missing a beat, and in response, Osgood proclaims, "Well, nobody's perfect!"

***

As for famous lines delivered offscreen, Curtis' most bitchy and infamous quip involved Marilyn, with whom he had argued, bitterly and frequently, throughout the shooting. "Kissing Monroe was like kissing Adolf Hitler." Yet after watching the two of them make love aboard Osgood's yacht, a viewer can only conclude that Adolf must have been a hell of a smoocher.

Despite of that remark, which Curtis later denied ever making, Curtis asserted that sometime during the filming, Marilyn invited him to her hotel room. "Making love with her—on the screen or in real life—was a unique, unforgettable experience," he claimed.

In his memoir, *The Making of Some Like It Hot*, Curtis wrote about his final, anti-climactic, and somewhat depressing interaction with Monroe, whom he encountered some time later at a party at Peter's Lawford's beach house.

"Marilyn was there," Curtis wrote. "She looked tired and unhappy. But her eyes lit up when she saw me across the room. I went over to her."

"Where's your green convertible?" she asked me.

"You mean the one with the Dynaflow Drive?"

"I guess so," she smiled, a little vaguely. "Yeah. Uh huh. That one."

"In Buick heaven."

"That's nice."

"I squeezed her hand and excused myself. And that was the last I ever saw of her."

IS <u>EVERYBODY</u> IN DRAG?

PHOTO, ABOVE: Running from the Chicago mob, **Tony Curtis** (left figure in photo, above) impersonates Josephine, a member of an all-girl band in Palm Beach.

His co-star in drag, **Jack Lemmon** (right) gave one of the screen's most brilliant drag performances as Daphne.

PHOTO, ABOVE RIGHT: In this hard-liner lineup of cardinals in their lace petticoats, the figure on the extreme right is outfitted more elaborately than any *grande folle.* (That's French for "an outrageously over-the-top cross-dresser").

He's the **Rt. Rev. John Timothy McNicholas** (1877-1950), Bishop of Duluth and Archbishop of Cincinnati and founder, in 1933, of the National Legion of Decency as a means of countering the influence of "salacious cinema."

The organization, which boasted more than 22 million Catholics as members, boycotted films that were not morally approved by the Catholic Church. The film industry rushed to cooperate with the Legion and edited many films for content to avoid receiving a "C" ("Condemned") rating. McNicholas fought to prevent the word "homosexual" from even being mentioned on-screen.

MEN WE DISLIKE, MEN WE THINK ARE DANGEROUS

In 1933, **Archbishop John McNicholas** (portrait bust, left) composed a membership pledge for the Legion of Decency. Between nine and eleven million Catholics signed it. Here's how it was worded:

I wish to join the Legion of Decency, which condemns vile and unwholesome moving pictures. I unite with all who protest against them as a grave menace to youth, to home life, to country and to religion. I condemn absolutely those salacious motion pictures which, with other degrading agencies, are corrupting public morals and promoting a sex mania in our land. … Considering these evils, I hereby promise to remain away from all motion pictures except those which do not offend decency and Christian morality.

Editorial P.S.: We LOVE the archbishop's neck dress--it reminds us of a wardrobe malfunction from an old Irene Dunne movie!

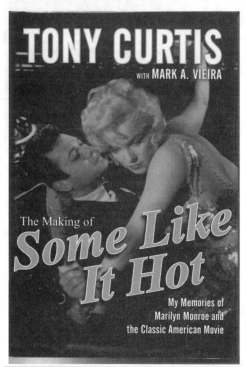

The movie's director and most of its stars are long gone. Only **Tony Curtis** remained to write the history of *Some Like It Hot.* His version appeared as a memoir (see photo above).

In his "behind the scenes saga," he relates his "uncensored" story, but, of course, it's his version. Marilyn might have dictated quite a different tale.

In his book, he discusses the trauma of how "the best looking kid in Hollywood" was forced to dress as a girl.

In the photo above, **Curtis** and **Monroe** share an off-screen joke during a light-hearted moment that did not reveal the tension behind the scenes. Marilyn tried his patience because of her chronic tardiness.

Curtis relates in his memoir that at one point, he almost turned into a prune while waiting in bath water for "the goddess" to show up.

430

GIRLS WILL BE GIRLS **Curtis** (left) walks from the studio's makeup department with **Lemmon** (right), both dressed in high heels as 1920s-era vamps wearing the kind of fashion they probably remember being worn by their mothers.

In Technicolor, their skin tones appeared as unnaturally green, so Wilder decided to shoot the picture in black and white.

During one of his waits for Marilyn to show up, Curtis, in a dress, minus the wig, played poker with movieland gangster George Raft and Wilder.

Curtis claimed that he and Lemmon made a great acting team. "He never played the prima donna. Marilyn all by herself, of course, was enough prima donna for one movie."

Curtis also said that after *Some Like It Hot,* he witnessed Marilyn "becoming spoiled, slovenly, deluded, and addicted. It got to be a very sad spectacle."

When she returned to the screen after a two-year absence, Marilyn looked sumptuous, sexier than ever, even though she was undergoing a difficult period in her life. Her marriage to playwright Arthur Miller was crumbling.

Curtis (far right figure in photo above) surveys Marilyn's ascent to join the gals, including Daphne, in their bunk beds in this celebrated scene in a Pullman-style railway car.

"Getting Marilyn's magic onto the screen was sometimes a challenge," Curtis asserted. "And sometimes a pain. And sometimes maddening. But (director) Billy (Wilder) did it."

"All this talk about me playing Daphne was pure bullshit," **Frank Sinatra** (photo above left) said. "Billy Wilder never approached me about the role. If he did, I would have bloodied his fucking nose. I've been accused of many things in my life, but no one ever said Frank Sinatra was a drag queen either on or off the screen. As for **Mitzi Gaynor** (photo above right) as Sugar, she was perky in a non-threatening way. She was limited as an actress, but she could dance around a bit, and the kid had a certain show biz pizzazz before her act went out of style. But she was no Marilyn."

The famous yacht scene looked so intimate onscreen, but it wasn't. At least 50 members of the film crew were checking out **Monroe**, and scads of locals behaved like Peeping Toms. Impersonating a rich play-boy, **Curtis** sounded like Cary Grant. When Grant saw the movie, he said, "I don't sound anything like that. He must have been impersonating David Niven."

Role models **Cary Grant** (left) and **David Niven** (right)

50 Years of Queer Cinema
Will Now Dish the Divas Who Starred in
Three Camp Classics
of the 1970s

Consider this as a possibility for a gloriously faggy weekend: Invite a party of friends, pop the popcorn, and settle back with a lover for back-to-back screenings of three infamous camp classics from the 1970s: Gore Vidal's *Myra Breckinridge*, Mae West's *Sextette*, and Darwin Porter's *Butterflies in Heat / Tropic of Desire*.

This trio of outrageous films, perhaps because of their stunning flaws, live on whenever and wherever "camp followers" gather.

MYRA BRECKINRIDGE
(1970)
GORE VIDAL'S X-RATED GENDER-BENDER

Based on Gore Vidal's literary send-up of Old Hollywood, *Myra Breckinridge* is one of the most notorious films ever made. At the box office, it was a colossal flop, yet it nonetheless lives on as a camp classic in ways comparable to *Mommie Dearest*. At the time, it's newsworthiness was partly based on the fact that after a 27-year retreat from any active film role, Mae West, the campiest woman alive at the time, made a cinematic comeback, playing a nymphomanical 77-year-old casting agent whose skills were reserved only "for leading men."

In the thankless role of Myra Breckinridge, Raquel Welch was cast as the post-op transsexual after Elizabeth Taylor wisely turned down the role. During a brief interlude, the film's British helmer, Michael Sarne, actually considered casting a real transgendered person into the key role instead.

Then an enthusiastic neophyte, Sarne, quickly realized that he had wandered into a web of egomaniacal spiders and that each of them could and would draw blood.

A then-unknown Farrah Fawcett was also cast, making what has since been called "The Most Embarrassing Movie Debut of All Time." Other well-known actors who signed on to film this travesty included Jim Backus, John Carradine, and the homophobic Andy Devine, cast as Coyote Bill.

Playing Myra's alter ego, the character she'd been before her sex change, was film critic Rex Reed. A rival critic, John Simon, was particularly vicious as regard the choice of Reed for the role: "I had hoped that this campy butterfly and self-styled critic—cast, I am told, so as to make certain things about Myron obvious without the script's having to spell them out—would portray himself on screen so that on the

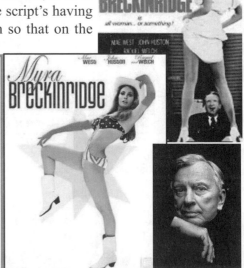

Gay author **Gore Vidal,** (photo, lower right corner) looks on in dismay as **Raquel Welch** struts her stuff or flashes her goodies in her portrayal of the outrageous transsexual, Myra Breckinridge.

Vidal, who wasn't happy with the film treatment of his novel, is surveying one of the most notorious flops ever made. Critiqued or not, Welch delivers the finest performance of her career, for whatever that's worth. Originally X-rated in 1970, *Myra Breckinridge* is Vidal's omnisexual showbiz lampoon. Its musings on the kitschy ridiculousness of Golden Age Hollywood glamor and free love culture are inane, of course, and unfunny, but why, then, did we love it so?

strength of his success, we would be rid of him as a writer. No such luck. His acting is on a par with his writing."

On the set, Sarne not only had to cope with the demands of Miss West (no small feat), but a cast that included veteran actor John Huston as Buck Loner (a character defined by one critic as the Ghengis Khan of psychotically decadent pansexual men).

As director, one of Sarne's most obvious traps involved a volcanic feud that erupted between female stars Mae West and Raquel Welch. Both of the women refused to appear in any scene together. They fought over everything: Billing, screen time, and wardrobe.

Even the clips from vintage movies which Sarne inserted into the context of his modern-day film sometimes got him in trouble with divas from the Golden Age who had appeared in the original clips. When she heard about the association of her likeness with the campy and controversial then-new film, Loretta Young, for example, demanded that her appearance on screen "be excised from this tasteless mess."

Welch and West weren't the only divas engaging in on-the-set feuds. There was also Huston vs. Reed, and Reed vs. Welch. Welch seemed to have catalyzed a feud with everyone, and virtually everyone seemed to be feuding with Sarne as well.

Gore Vidal is a well-respected, major league writer whose literary legacy will survive the ages. And although his original vision for the character of Myra might have been inspired by Daniel Defoe's 1722 classic, *Moll Flanders*, it had nothing to do with the campfest that eventually reached the screen. Vidal's biographer, Fred Kaplan, wrote, "Myra (who had once been Myron) was more victim than victimizer. The sex-change operation embodied his/her capabilities for bisexual roles. But in her tormented expression of sexual and psychological instability, it also disembodied society's self-destructive rules about sex and gender. Deeply anti-Christian, the novel attacked a civilization that had forced many people to be at lifelong

 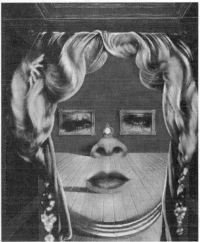

"Every time **Loretta Young** (photo above) 'sins,' she builds a church. That's why there are so many Catholic churches in Hollywood." So said Marlene Dietrich, who loathed Miss Young.

In spite of her saintly image and her religious devotion, Young had a list of lovers that stretches around Forest Lawn—George Brent, Louis Calhern, Douglas Fairbanks, Jr., Richard Greene, Wayne Morris, David Niven, Tyrone Power, Gilbert Roland, Jimmy Stewart. Spencer Tracy, Darryl F. Zanuck, et al.

She had an illegitimate child with Clark Gable when she made *Call of the Wild* with him in 1935. But in spite of her dozens of amorous adventures, she rather prudishly demanded that a film clip of her in the 1930s be removed from *Myra Breckinridge,* which she loudly and publicly denounced as "a tasteless bore."

ICONIC LIPS, ICONIC HIPS, ICONIC MAE WEST. It took the crazed Surrealist artist, Salvador Dalí, to capture the "essence" of Miss West. The mad artist called his concept of West "a persistence of vision," suggesting that West is best experienced as a surrealist illusion. Dalí never met West, but in 1935, he painted his infamous *Mae West's Face Which Can Be Used as a Surrealist Apartment* (photo, above).

In the words of author Simon Louvish, "he portrayed her as a univeral receptacle; her eyes gaze out of framed city landscapes, her lips form a blood-red sofa, her nose is a fireplace topped by an ornamental clock, her blonde hair as drapes drawn back from the lower part of her, which is represented by bare stage boards. The stage is ready for the play, the divan for romance."

war with themselves."

Once the irrepressible Miss West was cast, and began filtering the novel's intentions through her dialogue, Vidal's intent evaporated with her suggestive one-liners.

As for the character played by Welch, she seemed more intent on showing off her new pussy after her sex change operation than she was in conveying Vidal's complex vision of her character

As filming progressed, it became obvious that part of the problem involved the plotline's premises: Among the least logical includes Vidal's premise about how Myron (Rex Reed), manages in the immediate aftermath of a sex-change operation, to emerge like a reincarnation of Venus as the spectacularly attractive, sexually voracious Myra (Welch).

Under the threat of blackmail, Uncle Buck (Huston) offers Myra a bizarre teaching position at his California acting school.

Once aboard, Myra unleashes her crusade to "destroy American manhood," which involves rectally raping the hunky Rusty (Roger Harren). Like an Amazon on the rampage, she administers a dildo treatment to the unwitting and unwilling "last stronghold of masculinity in this Disneyland of perversion."

Miss West demanded $350,000 for her appearance in the movie, and 20th Century Fox reluctantly agreed. She also insisted on writing her own scenes. Perhaps most frivolous of all, she insisted that the spelling of her character's name be changed from Le*ti*cia to Le*tic*ia.

The geriatric star deluded herself with high hopes for the financial success of this film. "I know I've still got a public out there," she told executives at Fox. "On my last birthday, I got more than 90 phone calls from Europe—and at least 350 altogether. Which ain't bad for one day. Yuh know what I mean?"

West seemed especially pleased with the casting of handsome Tom Selleck, who played the role of "Stud." She claimed "I taught him how to drape himself so he wouldn't be too tall for me—like I did Cary Grant."

As stated by film critic Aaron Hillis, "West's comeback film features a female-on-male rape played for yuks—poor thing—but the screen legend still spouts innuendos like a septuagenarian trooper, and sings either the greatest or worst version of Otis Redding's 'Hard to Handle' ever heard."

One of the most notorious casts ever assembled in Hollywood brought (left to right in photo above) **John Huston, Raquel Welch, Mae West,** and **Rex Reed** onto the set of the ill-fated *Myra Breckinridge*. The only person missing from this motley crew was the director, Michael Sarne, himself, who sometimes suffered at the hands of his actors. The acid-tongued Reed told a columnist that Sarne "looked like a wolf with rabies."

The feud between West and Welch rivaled that of Joan Crawford and Bette Davis. Welch and West fought over everything, including costumes and who could or couldn't wear the black and white that stands out in Technicolor .

John Huston managed to remain neutral throughout these storms, claiming, "I managed to put in a day's work without become involved in this crap—like a piano player in a whorehouse. Even so, I got fucked in the end."

"*Myra Breckinridge* is one of the most notorious, commercial, critical, and production debacles in history," Hillis continued. "Though its musings on the kitschy ridiculousness of both Old Hollywood glamour and free love culture are too inane, coarse, and unfunny to register as more than a cult curiosity, one might nonetheless appreciate its latest DVD release."

Myra Breckinridge's DVD release offers two audio commentaries, one from Raquel Welch herself, who is at her bitchiest. At one point she compares her co-star, the late diva, Miss West, "to a dock-worker in drag."

In contrast, and in retrospect, Sarne sees his film as a "daring, visionary masterpiece featuring Welch's all-time best performance."

Nathan Rabin wrote: "In what's easily the least-warranted display of arrogance this side of Joe Eszterhas' autobiography, Sarne insisted that *Myra Breckinridge* is both a voyeuristic gay movie lover's Hollywood fantasia of power and perversity, and an ostensibly heterosexual broad drag comedy about a man who wants to be a woman." Many latter-day appraisals of this infamous film have been issued, none more destructive than the one penned by critic Nathan Reed and aimed at Sarne. According to Reed: "In this film, Sarne dishes out casual homophobia with gross egotism. He insists that transsexuals and gays are essentially pathetic, deluded creatures whose campy facades hide deep reservoirs of shame. He even refers to Vidal and Rex Reed as 'screaming fags' who are pathetically pretending to be straight."

Rex Reed (no relation to the above-mentioned Nathan Reed) was no great promoter of the film he had had a role in. He wrote about it as a fiasco in *Playboy* magazine, and even attacked it on *The Mike Douglas Show* as one of the Ten Worst Films Ever Made.

Ultimately, the widely derided film fails, though it's more compelling to think of it as a cinephile's wet dream than as an unfunny, gratingly over-the-top comedy.

Years later, in his literary memoir, *Palimpsest*, Vidal claimed that the *animus* of Myra's character was actually that of the fabled

Director Michael Sarne claimed that he'd received "divine inspiration" when he had the idea to cast **Mae West**--Paramount's most profitable box-office attraction during the early 30s-- as the sexually rapacious talent agent Leticia Van Allen. Simon Louvish, a biographer of W.C. Fields (whom Mae West hated), referred to her as a "sex goddess, Hollywood star, transgressive playwright, author, blues singer, vaudeville brat, and the 20th century's greatest comedienne."

Problems arose the moment she walked onto the set. She immediately informed Sarne that he'd have to rewrite all her lines, and then pulled her oft-repeated one-liners and quips out of a vaudeville trunk. Typical quotes included, "I don't expect too much from a man-- just what he's got." Another vintage quip she suddenly renewed was, "The wages of sin are sables and a film contract." None of these actually made it into the final cut.

A letter to the editor of *The Los Angeles Times* from "J. Gorrell," published when *Myra* was released, articulated a prevailing attitude among many of Mae's fans or former fans. "Mae has become a tiresome old bore, forever talking about how wonderful she was, and thinks she still is. At almost 80, I can put up with her ego to some extent, for she is a gabby old girl, but at her present age, she is not the Mae West of 40 years ago, and I was a fan of hers then. She belongs to the past, and only in the past. An old lady who thinks of herself as a sex symbol is sad and somewhat revolting."

diarist, Anaïs Nin "in all the flowing megalomania of her diaries." [Jointly, in a series of poisonous counterattacks that involved most of the literary world at the time, Nin and Vidal later launched one of the major literary feuds of the 20th century.]

Gore Vidal's ultimate summation: "*Myra Breckenridge* was not just a bad movie, it was an awful joke."

Mae West's final movie, *Sextette,* tarnished her legend and was an inglorious end to a fabulous career which, during its heyday, had captured the attention of the world. A critic for *Time* Magazine called *Sextette* "one of those movies rarely seen these days, a work so bad, so ferally innocent, that it is good, an instant classic treasured by connoisseurs of the genre everywhere."

In the *Village Voice,* Randy Shilts wasn't kind. "Yes, Mae West is a legend still living—but only barely. Once robust and lovely, the octogenarian now seems petite and fragile, like a grandmother who needs to be escorted from chair to chair. Yes, her face looks ageless—ageless because it is impossible to make out any featuere, even age, under the pounds of pancake make-up which only partially conceal the inevitable erosions of the years."

SEXTETTE

(1978)

DIAMOND LIL MEETS JAMES BOND

Lured out of retirement, the unsinkable Mae West, forgetting she'd appeared eight years before in the disastrous *Myra Breckenridge*, faced the cameras for the final time. It was the worst mistake of her film career.

She should never have made *Sextette*, released two years before her death in 1980. Age 84 at the time of its filming, she was far too old to play Marlo Manners/Lady Barrington, based on a character defined as a sex bombshell in her 20s. Rushing to her defense, her press agent de-livered a statement that was phrased in the campy spirit of the movie itself: "She loves short weddings and long honeymoons."

In the movie's final cut, it was painfully obvious that West had slowed down. Her delivery was stilted and slurred. Indeed, she deliv-ered some of her oft-re-peated world-famous lines: "It's not the men in your life, it's the life in your men." But perhaps as a means of enriching her legacy, she added a few new ones: "You gotta get up early in the morning to catch a fox, but you have to stay up late at night to get a mink."

With an utter lack of both humor and chivalry, film critic Rex Reed ranted, "*Sextette* will probably be shown decades hence as a monument of ghoulish camp. Mae West looks like

The producers of *Sextette* asked viewers to believe that a stunning beauty like **Timothy Dalton** (both photos above) would marry an aging diva (born in 1893) like **Mae West**. In the film, West was cast as "Marlo," who is dictating her sala-cious memoirs. After tons of lovers and many husbands, she has found "true love" with Dalton who, she has just learned, is a top British spy, "Bigger than 007," she proclaims, although later admitting "I never got a chance to take his measurements."

Actually, West frequently told her confidants that she was deadly accurate in guessing the size of a man's penis even when he was fully dressed. In Dalton's case," she said, "I'd give him seven inches, maybe 7 1/2 if he went to bed with me, because I've always inspired men to produce that extra half inch or even and inch and a half."

In the film's convoluted plot, the revelations within Marlo's memoirs force world leaders into a peace pact. In the movie's final scene aboard a yacht with Dalton, he tells her that she's done more for her country than Paul Revere. Her re-sponse? "Well, as he said—the British are *cumming*."

something they found in the basement of a pyramid."

Timothy Dalton, the future James Bond, played her 6th husband, Sir Michael Barrington. This wouldn't be called a May/December romance, more of a highly artificial January/December mating.

Earlier she'd objected to the casting of Louis Jourdan, once one of the handsomest men in the world and still looking good. She predicted that, "I'll make a star out of Dalton like I did that gay boy, Cary Grant."

Tony Curtis was cast as one of her six husbands, but Mae, then an octogenarian herself, considered him too old to play one of her former husbands. Shortly after meeting him, she jabbed, "You're gonna do something to cover up that bald spot, right?"

Famous stars of yesterday, George Raft and Walter Pidgeon, were each engaged for cameos. Raft had appeared in West's first film, *Night After Night*, in 1932. "She was supposed to play a supporting role, but she stole the God damn film from me," Raft said. "Just for that, I'll never fuck her again."

In the plot, Marlo Manners is trying to enjoy her honeymoon with Lord Barrington, husband no. 6, at a posh European hotel. But the honeymoon is frequently interrupted with appearances from various of her ex-husbands on the scene, some of whom are attending a conference at the hotel in an effort to save the world from imminent destruction. As part of the plot, Marlo is taping her scandalous memoirs, which, for legal reasons, her harrassed manager (Dom DeLuise) is desperately trying to destroy.

Director Ken Hughes wondered if mass audiences would accept the premise that six sexy males, one of whom was George Hamilton, would compete with one another to get a woman of her age into bed.

West showed up on the set with a curled blonde shoulder-length wig to hide the hint of a dowager's hump. A microphone was placed within her wig so that her lines could be "broadcast" to her, just prior to her repeating them on camera. Lifts attached at her temples and linked by a

Sextette's director surrounded Mae with icons from the 70s, including **Ringo Starr** (left in photo above). Aiming a gun at his head, Starr seems to be making a statement about how he feels about being perceived as one of West's paramours, cast as he is as Mae's husband #4.

Even rock musician **Alice Cooper** (right-hand photo above) was cast into a small role in the film as a piano-playing waiter. When Mae heart that Cooper had been cast, she asked, "And what role will *she* play? I'm not gonna get into a catfight like I did with Raquel Welch over another dame who thinks she's a sexpot."

rubber band smoothed out any hint of sagging facial muscles. A light patina of pink-and-white pancake enhanced her color.

She was pleased at the casting of Hamilton as one of her husbands. She was told that the casting of Ringo Starr, Keith Moon (drummer for *The Who*), and heavy metal singer/songwriter Alice Cooper would bring in the youth market.

But scripter Herbert Baker was asking a lot for a movie audience to think that the Beatles star, Mr. Ringo himself, could ever have been an ex-husband of Mae West.

The press generated after the film's premiere was disastrous.

Variety blasted, "West is on screen for most of the film, mostly attempting Mae West imitations and lip-synching a series of undistinguished musical numbers. It's an embarrassing attempt at camp from the lady who helped invent the word. Only Dom DeLuise is occasionally amusing as West's agent."

Originally the director had wanted Danny Kaye for the DeLuise role, but West nixed that idea. "I need to be seen with something fresher, perhaps Gene Kelly."

The worst barbs came from *The New York Times*, which noted, "*Sextette* is a disorienting freak show in which Mae West, now 87 years old, does a frail imitation of the personality that wasn't all that interesting 45 years ago. The movie is a poetic, terrifying reminder of how a virtually disembodied ego can survive total physical decay and a loss of common sense. The character we see in this peculiar film looks less like the Mae West one remembers from even *Myra Breckinridge* than like a plump sheep that's been stood on its hind legs, dressed in a drag-queen's

Although it first appeared in 1976, *Butterflies in Heat* continues to sell, with various publishers commissioning different artwork for the covers of its various editions. The raciest of its many covers (far right) was commissioned as part of a collaboration between The Florida and the Georgia Literary Associations, which bought the rights to a photo of a successful Cuban-America masseur and model at the time, **Diego von Bismarck**, who revealed his more-than-ample endowment as a sales incentive for the book. Sales skyrocketed, propelling the novel onto the GLBT bestseller lists many years after the book's original release.

When the book's author, Darwin Porter, sold it to the movies, he recommended that Lauren Bacall be cast into the role of fashion designer Leonora de la Mer, and that Warren Beatty be cast as the male hustler, Numie.

The film's producer, alas, did not heed the author's advice and never sent a copy of the book or the script for its screen adaptation to either Bacall or Beatty. Beatty, however, did end up convincingly portraying a hustler, but in a different film: the screen adaptation of Tennessee Williams' *The Roman Spring of Mrs. Stone*.

idea of chic, bewigged, and then smeared with pink plaster. The creature inside this get-up seems game but arthritic and perplexed. She walks with apparent difficulty. One eye sometimes sags and the voice, despite Hollywood's electronic skills, cracks like the voice of the old lady she really is. Under these circumstances, the sexual innuendos are embarrassing. Granny should have her mouth washed out with soap, along with her teeth."

Not everything is bad. We do get to see Alice Cooper singing a sappy ballad wearing a Barry Manilow wig.

The question remains: Why would any sane person want to see this travesty today?

Self-styled "Mae West fanatic," Aaron Giler, phrased it like this: "Would you at least watch a porno movie where Obama is fucking Tom Cruise? Sure, you would. Camp followers of West, yesterday and today, can't resist her final *adieu*. I think it has to do with the lovely idea that America's movie-going public might like to know that there's still a well-rounded sex life going on among the denizens of Forest Lawn."

  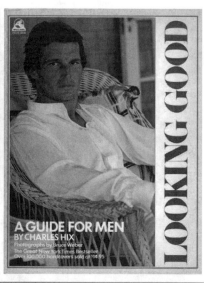

The star who landed the coveted role of Numie Chase in *Tropic of Desire* was **Matt Collins**, the highest-paid male model of the 1970s. Throughout Japan, he was known as the spokesman for Marlboro cigarettes.

When the editors of an instruction manual for good male grooming, *Looking Good,* went in search of "the perfect man," they chose Matt as their poster boy. Later, although he posed for the cover of *Playgirl*, he never completed a nude centerfold for the inside. Too bad. "A lot of horny women and gay guys would have loved it," said Jerry B. Wheeler, the producer who eventually cast Matt as the star of *Tropic of Desire* (originally filmed with the name *The Last Resort.)*

TROPIC OF DESIRE

(1979)

CASTING WORKING HUSTLERS AND REAL-LIFE
TRANSSEXUALS IN SCREEN ADAPTATIONS OF BEST-SELLING NOVELS

In the 1950s, when he was 18 years old, a rookie journalist from Miami wrote a steamy novel, *Butterflies in Heat*, about a staggeringly good-looking but emotionally vulnerable blond hustler named Numie Chase. When it was finished, he decided that the world wasn't ready for such a book and stashed it away in a trunk.

There it remained until the mid-70s, when the journalist met gay literary agent Jay Garon, founder and president of the then-flourishing New York City-based Garon-Brooke Literary Agency.

Garon, who later became famous for discovering and then launching the career of multi-million-copy bestselling suspense author John Grisham, asked the author [Darwin Porter] for a copy of the dusty manuscript. The savvy (some say, ruthless) literary agent immediately saw

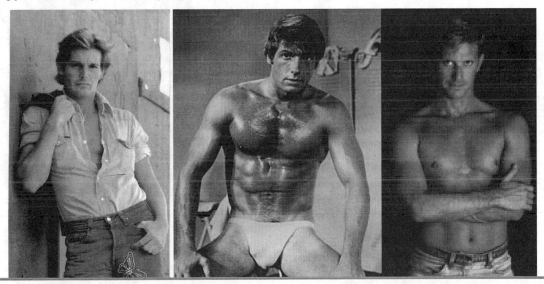

Competing for the role of the male hustler, Numie Chase, in the film adaptation of *Butterflies in Heat* were three charming, handsome, and well-endowed men. They included (left to right) **Matt Collins**, **Jack Wrangler**, and **Cal Culver**. Matt nabbed the role partly because his public image carried less "baggage" than his two competitors. Soon afterward, the wardrobe department sewed a butterfly onto the crotch of his hustler jeans.

In the center, an almost nude **Jack Wranger** was the leading gay porno star of the 1970s. He was born Jack Stillman, the privileged son of a Beverly Hills show-biz family--his father had produced the hit TV series, *Bonanza*.

Cal Culver (right-hand photo) had been billed as Casey Donovan in *Boys in the Sand*. Like Wrangler, he was educated and articulate, and had enjoyed some success as a teacher in a private Manhattan prep school before turning to gay porn. Onscreen, during their porn performances, Culver and Wrangler were "dick-to-dick rivals in seeing which of them could give a viewer the biggest hard-on," in the words of the well-known New York-based literary agent, Jay Garon.

blockbuster sales figures dancing before his eyes, and decided that in the sexy 70s, the world was ripe for such a novel.

He arranged with Manor Books, known for its pulpy, mass-market paperbacks, to publish the book. During its first months in print, thanks partly to aggressive sales promotions in gay meccas which included Fire Island, Palm Springs, and Key West, it sold more than a million copies. One critic referred to it as "a defining piece of gay literature."

Adding to its luster, the novel received praise from Tennessee Williams, James Kirkwood (co-author of *A Chorus Line*), and James Leo Herlihy (author of the novel on which the film *Midnight Cowboy* was eventually based).

Sales materials for the novel included phrases like this:

In the searing heat of a tropical cay [read that as "Key West"] *the strikingly handsome Numie Chase would arouse passions in six flamboyant but vulnerable people whose lives mesh under the blood-red sun.*

Bestsellers wrote,

"We know from the beginning that we're getting into a hotbed that has morbid fascination for potential readers. The novel evolves, in fact, into one massive melee of malevolence, vendetta, and e-v-i-l, stunningly absorbing alone for its sheer and unrelenting exploration of the lower depths."

The outrageous characters introduced as part of the novel's plotline included Leonora de la Mer, an imperious, rapidly aging dress designer, a sort of American Chanel, who lives in the town's grandest mansion which she calls Sacré-Coeur. Her nemesis is a black (male) drag diva named Lola La Mour. Leonora's emotionally bludgeoned assistant is an open-hearted tub of lard, Tangerine, who appreciates moonshine and well-hung men.

Also depicted are an alienated gay man and his long-suffering (heterosexual) wife, both of whom compete for a piece of the emotionally bruised Numie, who is also in search of love himself.

The film's producer, Jerry B. Wheeler, acquired the rights for a film adaptation of the novel, but as the project progressed, he became worried about the gay implications of both the plot and the title. His fears were to some degree justified by the fact that funding for the project derived to some extent from an investment division of family-friendly, well-respected Safeway Supermarket chain.

Against the advice of the novel's author, Wheeler changed the film's title to *The Last Resort*, and aggressively adapted the screenplay into a relatively conventional [i.e., heterosexual and mainstream] tale about love and alienation, marketing it as "a desperate love story at the end of the rainbow."

"A tragic mistake," **Gloria Swanson** said after viewing *The Last Resort,* a film adaptation of *Butterflies in Heat.* Pictured above as the demented Norma Desmond in *Sunset Blvd.,* Swanson said she'd been misled by press reports that *The Last Resort* would be pornographic. "I was made for the role of Leonora de la Mer, and I wish I had read it before making a bad judgment. I could have played it like an American version of Coco Chanel. Unlike Norma, Leonora's character was sane and brutally realistic--it would have been the proper swan song for me."

Filming began in Key West in 1979, but not before some flamboyant issues associated with the film's casting bashed their way into the national press.

For the role of the script's regal and imperious *couturier*, the producers approached Jazz-Age diva Gloria Swanson (remember her?). In terms of the history of her real life, dressmaking had been one of her early professions. Gamely, Swanson had been receptive to accepting the role until a gossipy article within *The New York Post* asserted that she'd be filming a porno re-en-actment of *Sunset Blvd.* That was, of course, spectacularly untrue. Regardless of that statement's inaccuracy, Swanson was so enraged that she took out an ad in *Variety* which asserted that she was not part of the movie, and that she'd never be part of the movie. Later, after she saw the actual film, she regretted her decision.

The role of dragon-lady Leonora de la Mer was ultimately awarded to the distinguished stage actress, Barbara Baxley, a proud recipient of Broadway's 1961 Tony Award as that year's best dramatic actress. Baxley had made her stage debut in 1948, starring with Tallulah Bankhead in Noël Coward's *Private Lives.* The two women lived together for a number of years (there was talk). She even named one of her cats Tulah.

Then there arose the dilemma about whether or not, in allegiance to the novel's original premise, to cast a real-life drag queen into the role of Lola La Mour. In a nod to the financial backing of Safeway, and partly because he was afraid that box-office receipts would suffer if he got too radical, Wheeler diluted the novel's plot to incorporate a real (i.e. biological) woman, and shoehorned Eartha Kitt into the role. Playing an obsessively seductive cabaret *artiste* with a platinum-blonde wig and performing some well-executed musical numbers, Kitt was stunning.

For the dozens of gay men observing the dramas-within-the-drama, the juiciest gossip began when the pre-eminent gay porno stars of the 70s— Jack Wrangler and Cal Culver (aka Casey Donovan)—both looking like gods and both of them blond or *faux-blond*— let it be understood that each of them would do virtually anything for a role in the film as Numie, the film's hustler/protagonist and hero.

In a decision that virtually everyone regretted later, Wheeler refused to cast either of them into the role "because of their porno backgrounds. We aren't making that kind of movie," he told the disappointed young men, both of whom are dead today.

Instead, he cast Matt Collins, the most visible and highest-paid male model of the 1970s. Previously, a *fashionista* magazine had defined Collins as "the most beautiful male animal on earth." Tall and lean, with sandy hair, dark eyes, strong cheekbones, and a past which had included years training

Eartha Kitt, pictured on a Key West alleyway in a blonde wig as Lola La Mour in *The Last Resort,* never bothered to conceal her ego. "When I'm on the screen as Lola, what other actor in the frame has a chance against me? Although I was supposed to be a real woman in the film, I preferred the book's description of my character as that of a transvestite. I didn't care what the director said. I played the fucking role like a gender-reassigned drag queen, and my fans knew exactly what I was doing."

445

horses on ranches in Virginia, he had a somewhat sullen demeanor which, according to the fashion of the time at least, added to his allure.

Prior to his new-found gig as an actor, various modeling agencies, including Wilhelmina Models, had fallen over each other to sign him. Soon, his brooding effigy was promoting beer, business suits, and "every shirt you can imagine." He was designated as Marlboro Cigarette's emissary to the world at large (i.e., "the Marlboro Man"), spearheading with his own image a sales campaign that was particularly successful Asia, especially Japan. "I'm giving cancer to the Japanese," Collins frequently quipped.

As footage from *The Last Resort* abundantly reveals, Matt photographed beautifully. Although he'd been offered other film roles during the course of his long modeling career, the first major film role he accepted was as *The Last Resort's* Numie Chase.

As filming progressed, Matt found himself drawn, psychically and spiritually, into the character of the role he was portraying—that of a breathtakingly good looking, morally ambiguous young man searching for love in all the wrong places.

Directed by Cash Baxter, the film also starred the late character actor Tom Ewell playing a grizzled and impossibly corrupt small-town lawyer. In 1955, he had immortalized himself starring with Marilyn Monroe in *The Seven Year Itch*.

Other featured players included Louisiana-born Pat Carroll, who had, during her long career, played everything from chatterbox wives to wicked stepsisters, and Don Porter, best remembered for his role as Miss Sothern's boss in "The Ann Sothern Show," which had been preceded by his earlier portrayal of her exasperated boss in the 1953 TV series "Private Secretary." Roxanne Gregory got the role of the newly heterosexual Numie's love interest, and Bert Williams played the town's corrupt and psychotic sheriff.

Years later, Jerry B. Wheeler, *Tropic of Desire's* producer, had deep regrets about his misguided adaptation of the novel. "I should have followed the storyline and I should definitely have kept the title *Butterflies in Heat*. I should have shot Darwin's story the way it was written—raw, powerful, uncensored, and cutting edge. I watered it down, and I made a mistake. Unfortunately, in Hollywood you often aren't allowed to make mistakes."

"And right at the beginning, I should have let Gloria Swanson read the actual script before she became a victim of those stupid rumors about how this would be a porno flick," Wheeler said. "How stupid! And when she turned it down, I should have hired the other stars who wanted to be in it. They were Rita Hayworth, who would have been fabulous as Leonora de la Mer, and her former husband, Orson Welles, who would have been brilliant as the Commodore. But when I met with Miss Hayworth, I thought she was drunk, or at least having a bad reaction to her pills. What I didn't realize at the

Kentucky-born **Tom Ewell** was the American actor who's mainly remembered for his appearance (above) with **Marilyn Monroe** in *The Seven Year Itch*. The scene where Ewell slyly admires Monroe as she stands on a subway grate with her skirt billowing upward has become one of her most iconic moments in film. "I adored her," Ewell said. "But I was also envious. I'd love to have bedded one-quarter of the studs she screwed, especially that Joe DiMaggio. Forget about that famous nude picture of him in a locker room. Marilyn told me Joe was a grower—not a show-er."

Although Ewell was twice married, he had a lifelong fondness for well-endowed male hustlers. "I was never pretty," he admitted to Jerry B. Wheeler, producer of *The Last Resort*. "I always had to pay for sex, even when I was a young man."

time was that actually, the fabled star of *Gilda* was already showing signs of the Alzheimer's disease which eventually killed her. And complicating matters was the fact that our insurance agent was afraid of the litigation risks involved with transporting the rotund, impossibly obese Orson Welles down to Key West."

Wheeler continued his litany of regrets. "Ironically, Eartha Kitt would have agreed to play Lola as a drag queen instead of the way I insisted—as a biological woman. I should have let her. And Shelley Winters would have been ideal as Tangerine, but I'd heard she was too temperamental, and she wanted more scenes written in for herself."

"I worked well with most of the cast and crew except for an ongoing problem with Tom Ewell," Wheeler claimed. "He was on his last legs. Even during his glory years, he never really looked good on the screen. But at this point in his life, he was a wreck. In Key West, as part of his compensation, he demanded I hire hustlers for him. As a means of placating him, I sent over two or three of them, but after they each took a look at him, they refused to have sex with him. Poor man. When a gay guy gets rejected by a pay-for-play hustler, you know he's in serious trouble."

Completed in 1979, *The Last Resort* was evaluated, pre-release, by audiences as "highly enjoyable," but not critically well received. Then, when Wheeler died prematurely, the film was tied up in litigation and its release was delayed indefinitely

Years later, after the settlement of his much-contested estate, the film's new promoters retitled it *Tropic of Desire* and, after much delay, released it. Since then, this campy tale of sex, drugs, and male prostitution in Key West has developed a cult following.

It's often been compared to a homoerotic version of James Leo Herlihy's *Midnight Cowboy* or Tennessee Williams' *Sweet Bird of Youth*. But in the words of critic Brook Peters, "the novel has more in common with Henry Fielding's picaresque *Tom Jones*."

In 1997, the Florida Literary Foundation (a subdivision of StarBooks), recognizing the book for the gay classic it was, re-released the novel in a "silver edition," which featured a very well-endowed model (Diego von Bismarck) on the cover. At New York City's now-defunct Oscar Wilde Bookstore, the novel remained a number one bestseller for weeks, as such getting re-introduced to an entire new generation of gay men.

In an industry where working titles change as frequently as cast assignments, the very gay ***Butterflies in Heat*** became the somewhat gay ***The Last Resort***, but was ultimately released on DVD as the somewhat vanilla, mostly heterosexual ***Tropic of Desire***. Depicted on its cover are Matt Collins embracing Roxanne Gregory, further evidence of how the backers of this film made it progressively more mainstream throughout its various manifestations.

Fortunately, there's still the original novel on which the film was based, a study in "perversion" if it could be called that, and mendacity. One reviewer defined its examination of lost souls with love for sale as "Pure E-V-I-L."

447

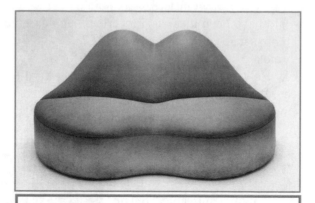

MORE ABOUT MAE

Commissioned by Edward James, a wealthy British patron of the Surrealists in the 1930s, and manufactured from satin and wood, it has been called "the campiest piece of furniture ever designed." Salvador Dalí designed it in 1937 in honor of Mae West's lips.

IS IT AGONY OR MERELY S&M?

Perhaps the artist was alluding to the way gay themes and gay talent have traditionally been handled by the megacorporations of Hollywood.

TELL US THAT IT ISN'T SO:

For an Actor in the Entertainment Industry

Playing it Gay

Is the Kiss of Death. False or True??

Not so, as proven in the photos above and moving clockwise: Al Pacino getting sweaty with his leather buddies on the dance floor in *Cruising;* William Hurt getting glam in *Kiss of the Spider Woman*; Brando crotch-conscious as a gay army officer in *Reflections in a Golden Eye*; Michael Caine playing gay blade and theatrical agent to his onscreen wife (Maggie Smith) in *California Suite;* James Dean puckering up for Sal Mineo in a scene from *Rebel Without a Cause*; and Ledger/Gyllenhaal as a romantic team in *Brokeback Mountain*.

We love them for it...And their careers survived, and in some cases, thrived!

FAMOUS STARS PLAYING GAY
To Be Cast as Queer:
Career Breaker or Career Maker?

Ever since permission was granted for the word *homosexual* to be uttered onscreen, and ever since screenwriters began factoring gay and lesbian characters into their screenplays, a myth persisted that it was career suicide to play homo on the range.

The myth is not true. Many straight actors (and several we'd label as bisexual) have shouldered gay roles and their careers not only survived, but in some cases, prospered. A classic example is Robert Redford, a straight who played Natalie Wood's gay husband in *Inside Daisy Clover* (1965). Redford was warned not to make the movie, but he deliberately ignored the advice. He said, "Some movie-goers thought my character was straight—that they didn't hear right.

LEFT PHOTO, ABOVE: Two of the biggest movie stars in the world, **Marlon Brando** and **Elizabeth Taylor,** couldn't quite rescue Carson McCullers' *Reflections in a Golden Eye.* Macho actors William Holden, Robert Mitchum, and Lee Marvin turned down the gay role, but Brando went for it, especially the $750,000 salary. Brando claimed that Elizabeth flirted with him during the filming, but he rejected her advances "because her ass is just too small.'

CENTER PHOTO, ABOVE: **Robert Redford** went gay with *Inside Daisy Clover,* although his managers expressed fear that it would "taint his image." The line that was cut from many screenings of the film was spoken by Melora (Katharine Bard), who addressed Natalie Wood about the man she married (Wade Lewis played by Redford). "Your husband could never resist a charming boy," Natalie is informed about her new groom.

RIGHT PHOTO, ABOVE: **Al Pacino**'s *Cruising* became his most notorious film (see separate feature). Pacino's career was not harmed by accepting the role, except that he earned the ire of the gay community. Charles Champlin, writing in the *Los Angeles Times,* said: "You don't have to be homosexual to dislike *Cruising,* but the gay community is not wrong to worry that William Friedkin's movie plays like a recruiting poster for an Anita Bryant parade. It is like taking a Hamburg brothel as the site for an examination of heterosexuality."

I guess people see and hear what they want to. But the point is, *Daisy Clover* didn't ruin my career. I'm still here."

Another example of a famous actor who played it gay is Marlon Brando, who starred in *Reflections in a Golden Eye* opposite Elizabeth Taylor. Brando played a married military officer who tries to repress his consuming sexual desire for the handsome private he stalks so relentlessly.

Released in 1967, *Reflections* foreshadowed by a year a similar theme in *The Sergeant*, starring Rod Steiger. In this film, the very macho Rod Steiger has the hots for the very beautiful John Philip Law of *Barbarella* fame. The film relates a story about the sergeant's discovery of his gayness. The story ends in suicide in a way that once was almost mandatory as an ending for gay-themed novels. We hope we won't have any more movies like that.

Richard Burton, who admitted in a 1970 TV interview that he was bisexual, played it campy gay alongside straight actor Rex Harrison in that horrendous film *Staircase* (1969). At first Harrison was reluctant to take the part. He called Burton and asked him what he thought. Burton said that he and Elizabeth loved it, and thought it was hilarious. So Harrison said, sportingly, "I'll do it if you do it."

Another bisexual English actor, Laurence Olivier, lusted after a young, cute Tony Curtis in *Spartacus* (1960). Their notorious scene where Olivier as Marcus asks Curtis as Antoninus if he eats

ROD STEIGER STUNS AS THE SERGEANT

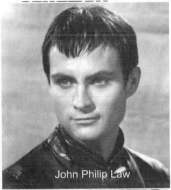

John Philip Law

Rod Steiger (photo at top of this page) later said that his career began to go wrong after he played a homosexual Army sergeant with a fixation on a handsom private (**John Philip Law**). "It wasn't because I played a homosexual," Steiger said. "It was because I appeared in a depressing movie that nobody wanted to see. The most controversial part was the famous kiss scene. I didn't mind doing that," Steiger said. "John Philip Law was prettier than most gals I've kissed." Privately, Law told Steiger, "I like to be kissed by macho men, but let's keep that a secret."

Rex Harrison agreed to play a homosexual barber and the lover of **Richard Burton** in *Staircase*. "The film was a risk," Harrison later told a reporter. "I felt I was old enough and rich enough to take a risk. And I think Richard did too. So we did it. It was a mistake. It was a dreadful mistake. But that's what risks are all about."

Burton later said, "I loved its caustic wit, but I think it was lost on almost everyone who thought it was just a campy story about two poofs played by two actors who are rather notorious for being anything but poofs."

oysters and snails was cut from the movie's original release as too homosexual in content, but it's been restored in DVD. Gay men knew all along that the discussion about oysters vs. snails was really a thinly disguised attempt to determine sexual proclivities.

Back when homosexuality dared not speak its name on the screen, the proclivities of some characters depended on your gaydar. For example, Warren Beatty played it gay in *Bonnie and Clyde* (1967), depending on how you interpreted the film's beginning. Al Pacino was gay in *Cruising* (1980), depending on how you interpreted the ending. Of course, there could be no doubt about Pacino's orientation as the gay bank robber in *Dog Day Afternoon* (1975), for which he received an Oscar nomination.

Some portraits of gay characters in films were far more rounded than those mentioned. In other words, you did not have to guess a character's sexual orientation.

British actor Michael Caine played the stylish and cheerful gay husband of Maggie Smith in the 1978 *California Suite*.

Caine later told a gay magazine: "I wasn't the least bit scared to do it. He was a very decent, typical sort of man, who had worked out an arrangement that suited him. He enjoyed his life, was successful. Not many heterosexuals can boast of that. And as you saw, he was a masculine man. Masculinity has little to do with sexuality. For most of my roles, I try to draw on my feminine side. For example, my sensitivity—I'm an extraordinarily sensitive man, and it makes me a better artist. This man I played is glad he is homosexual; his one unhappiness comes from not being able to please his wife. She can't understand you can't convert a gay, any more than you can convert a straight."

Italian heartthrob Marcello Mastroianni later said that the gay male he played in *A Special Day*, opposite Sophia Loren, was the best role of his career. He told the press, "I have played perverted men in the past, but that has nothing to do with homosexuality. Perversion is kinky sex—some of the lovers I played could only climax during danger, in a strange location, or due to some fetish. The man I played in *A Special Day* was a normal man, only he

Who to believe? The original script for *Bonnie and Clyde* called for a *ménage à trois* between Beatty, Dunaway, and Michael J. Pollard, who had a face that, according to one of his detractors, "looked like it had been shaped from Silly Putty." Beatty allegedly asserted, "I ain't gonna play no fag. They're gonna piss all over my leg."

He was referring to the audience, which might not have accepted him in the role. Beatty, according to some reports, later said he had no problem with the role, and denied reports to the contrary. Finally, it was decided to make Clyde impotent, and not so much a homosexual. "Impotence is fine with me," Beatty allegedly said, "so long as Clyde overcomes it before the final credits roll."

Beatty, one of the great Romeos in the history of Hollywood, played it impotent in the beginning. For him, that was a bit of a stretch.

A Special Day teamed **Sophia Loren** with **Marcello Mastroianni.** Instead of making love to her, as audiences might have expected, he played a homosexual.

Although he was a sex symbol to both gay men and women, he always downplayed his role as a Latin lover. "Well, to tell you the truth, I'm not a great fucker," he told Dick Cavett on TV. [The word "fucker," of course, was blipped.]

"Marcello is a man who thinks like a man, talks like a man--is a man!" said Loren. "He has so much magnetism, he brings out the very soul in a woman."

was homosexual. He did not commit any crime; the *law* was the crime—in Italy at the time, the Fascist Forties under Mussolini, homosexuals had to be deported. It was a stupid law, and if the Romans or the Renaissance Italians had had it, Italy would not have made half of its great contributions to the world."

Leonard Frey broke ground when he starred in *The Boys in the Band* (1970). "When I did *Boys*, it was just about the first gay thing to hit the national consciousness. And some people were shocked at my particular role, since they didn't know there even were Jewish homosexuals. Afterwards, some of the film's cast members immediately played straight parts, to get away from the association, but I did a gay cameo in *The Magic Christian*, a gay vampire. I think no matter what you are or what you think, if you're an actor, you act. That means playing everyone from Christ to De Sade."

Frey later became an Oscar nominee for his role in *Fiddler on the Roof*.

Laurence Luckingbill, who was cast in the part of the bisexual school teacher in *The Boys in the Band*, was warned by his agent not to accept the role. For him that might have been good advice. He immediately lost a cigarette commercial worth $15,000. The casting director told Luckingbill: "No fags smoke our fags." That snide comment, however, did not prevent the actor from accepting two subsequent gay parts.

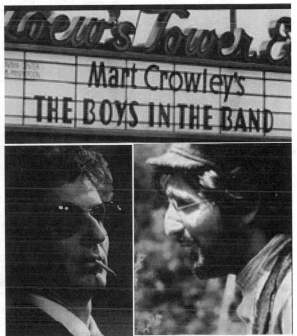

Luckingbill ruefully admitted that after filming *The Boys in the Band,* most of the cast did their best to set audiences "straight"—and to let them know they were, at heart, macho men. "We straight guys spent a lot of time being photographed with cigars in our mouths with our dogs, wives, and children."

Martin Balsam played a campy interior decorator in *The Anderson Tapes*. "It's more fun to be a character actor than a leading man," he later said. "You get in touch with more human experiences. I had only a small role, but I turned out to be the only comic relief in the picture. Even though the guy was outrageous, it's important to point out that he didn't feel guilty. He liked himself, he was liked by the straight characters, and he was a partner in a gang of toughs that included Sean Connery. He got what he wanted in the end. So even if your first inclination was to laugh at him, he was one of the strongest characters in the film, and you laughed *with* him. There's a huge difference."

WHAT, ME WORRY? **Leonard Frey** feared that his role as Howard, a decadent homosexual in *The Boys in the Band,* would typecast him into equivalent roles forever. Ironically, one of his next parts was that of an innocent, untested, and wholesome (heterosexual) suitor several years later in *Fiddler on the Roof.*

Torn between two lovers, Peter Finch and Glenda Jackson in *Sunday, Bloody Sunday*, Murray Head played a bisexual. "I didn't like my part," Head recalled. "My two older lovers—Finch and Jackson—knew what they wanted, but my character was too wishy-washy, stuck in a sexual twilight zone. I do think Finch deserved the Oscar that year, but it was a landmark anyway, because he was the first man ever nominated for a gay role. I heard that some people walked out during the scene where Finch and I kissed, but at the time I thought it was rather tame. We didn't go farther because the Finch part was that of a conservative homosexual. Another landmark is that it may be the first time where the gay part came off as the best—Finch was definitely the brightest of us all, and the best survivor."

After Jack Coleman completed his portrayal of the bisexual Steven Carrington on TV's *Dynasty*, he wondered what would happen to his career. "On network TV," he said, "you're strongly identified with a role. Week in, week out, you come into people's houses. And since they don't pay, it seems less like a performance and more like a slice of life."

A. Scott Berg, the biographer of such notables as Katharine Hepburn and Samuel Goldwyn, conceived the story for *Making Love*, which was filmed in 1982 with Harry Hamlin and Michael Ontkean as the gay lovers.

After six of his personal friends came out after getting married to women, Berg got the idea for the movie. He told the press, "This is the next big social movement—men leaving their wives for other men. What the black movement was in the sixties, and the feminist movement in the seventies, the gay movement will be in the eighties."

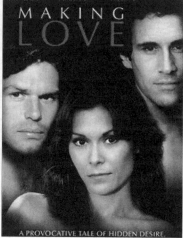

A PROVOCATIVE TALE OF HIDDEN DESIRE.

What Berg didn't know is that the specter of AIDS was looming to darken the lives of thousands of gays.

After the screening of *Making Love*, Hamlin faced casting prejudice. Even though he was living with sultry Ursula Andress at the time, casting directors identified him as gay. His career suffered until it was lifted by TV's *L.A. Law*.

In 1986, he told *The Washington Post*, "A guy can play an ax murderer and still be considered sexy and still get another role as a leading man. But if you play a homosexual, suddenly you're not in contention anymore for an ax murderer."

Drag roles are somehow different—take Harvey Fierstein's *Torch Song Trilogy* or the popular movie and musical versions of *La Cage aux Folles*. Drag roles are outside the range

John Forsythe (left) and actor **Jack Coleman** (right) hit paydirt in the TV series *Dynasty*. Born in 1958, Coleman is still known today for replacing Al Corley in the bisexual role of Steven Carrington in the 1980s prime time soap opera. One of the first gay characters on television, Coleman stayed in the role until 1988.

A sixth generation descendant of Benjamin Franklin, he never really made it big like he'd wanted to. Did playing gay so prominently hurt his career? The jury's still out on that one. Eventually, he ended up portraying Noah Bennet in the science fiction drama series *Heroes*.

Harrison Ford, Michael Douglas, and Richard Gere all turned down the male lead in the gay love story *Making Love*. Each of them cited "the subject matter" as the reason.

The subject matter was homosexuality. **Michael Ontkean** and **Harry Hamlin** had the cojones to accept the roles of the gay lovers. The movie flopped and Hamlin, at least, felt his playing gay might have harmed his career. The movie had a poor script, and ultimately that is what might have harmed the careers of everyone involved, even **Kate Jackson**, who played Ontkean's wife in the flick.

of ordinary experience, and men in drag, cinematic precedents for which date from the early 20th century, have been accepted by straight audiences who seem to want some subdivision within society to mock and ridicule.

For some reason, famous actors who played not only gay but camp seemed to have done fine, delivering *tour de force* performances. No one ever seemed to confuse their real self with their reel self. Take Robert Preston, who played an outrageous queen in *Victor/Victoria*; or Tom Courtenay who was the prissy, mincing backstage assistant in *The Dresser*; even William Hurt, the flamboyant spinner of dreams in *Kiss of the Spider Woman*.

Back in the 1970s and 80s, gay actors, with the possible exception of Roddy McDowall, simply did not accept gay roles. It was safer for the likes of Rock Hudson to play a ladies' man or Tab Hunter to portray a tough marine. That is changing, but actor Rupert Everett once complained to the press that he'd been typecast, and therefore restricted in terms of parts he'd get in Hollywood and was heading back to London.

We could go on and on with our survey—Sal Mineo lusting for James Dean in *Rebel Without a Cause* (1955). A kissing scene between these two hotties was cut from that landmark film's final print.

In their early cinematic outings, lesbians were depicted as monsters. But their image improved after appearances in such films as *The Killing of Sister George* (1968), with Beryl Reid giving her greatest performance, or in *The Fox* (also 1968), based on the D.H. Lawrence story about a romantic liaison between empathetic characters portrayed by Sandy Dennis and Anne Heywood.

Bisexuality was prevalent in 1972 *Cabaret* (1972), as Liza Minnelli and Michael York realize to their horror that the same German baron has made love, and made the same insincere promises, to each of them.

Robert   Morley,

AL PACINO in DOG DAY AFTERNOON

The robbery should have taken ten minutes.
Eight hours later, it was the hottest thing on live TV.

Al Pacino wasn't worried that playing gay in *Dog Day Afternoon* would harm his career at all. In fact, he ended up with an Oscar nomination. "Give me a good script, and a good director" (in this case, Sidney Lumet) "and I'm up for it," he said.

Pacino's credentials as a heterosexual were so firmly established with such stars as Debra Winger, Tuesday Weld, and Diane Keaton that playing gay hardly damaged his standing. One of his female lovers said, "He's the kind of man who takes you to great heights of ecstasy and knows what to do when he gets you there."

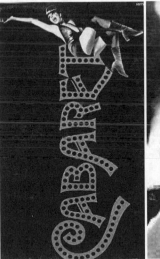

Playing in a gay scenario didn't phase **Liza Minnelli** at all. She and her mother often married gay.

In *Cabaret*, she understood her character. "Sally is a girl who improvises her whole life, and her fantasy of tomorrrow is so strong that she really can't take a good look at *now*."

Michael York's career was hardly damaged by playing it gay in *Cabaret*. As Samuel Goldwyn once said, "If a picture makes millions at the box office, an actor can play anything, even a serial killer, and he'll be applauded."

who portrayed Oscar Wilde in *Oscar Wilde* (1960), said, "It's a wonder that you have any homosexuals in America, because daily, the country's children are bombarded with anti-gay propaganda. I believe that if more people were exposed to homosexuality, in the films and on the telly, everybody would have a better understanding. We certainly have enough films about heterosexual affairs and all their problems with marriage and the kiddies."

Morley's wish, after decades of struggle in the movies, is beginning to come true.

English actor **Rupert Everett** came out of the closet a long time ago, and has been openly gay on the screen, including when he played a homosexual student at an English public school in *Another Country* (1984). In Paris in 1989, Everett came out as gay and also wrote a novel, *Hello, Darling, Are You Working?*

His emergence from the closet was perceived as damaging to his career. He responded with an award-winning performance playing Julia Robert's gay friend in *My Best Friend's Wedding* (1997). He also played Madonna's gay best friend in *The Next Best Thing* (2000).

Kirk Douglas (center top photo) was the star of *Spartacus*. The scene from that movie in the lower photo, above, became infamous, as it depicted **Laurence Olivier** (right) coming on to the slave boy as played by **Tony Curtis** in a scene so provocative that it was cut from the original release.

When the bath scene was re-inserted for the re-release of the film, the soundtrack associated with that clip had been lost. Tony Curtis was still around to deliver his lines for a dubbing. But since Olivier had died in 1989, actor Anthony Hocking was hired to replicate Olivier's voice.

Danny Kaye, the lover of Laurence Olivier, frequently pestered director Billy Wilder to play a musician, in drag, in *Some Like It Hot*. But Wilder never thought his presence would add anything to the plot. Instead, he pitched the idea to **Jack Lemmon**.

Lemmon later claimed that "I would have run like a jackrabbit if any director other than Wilder had asked me to appear in drag." Before Lemmon, Wilder seriously considered using Frank Sinatra in the role, although he couldn't imaging the crooner dressing up as a woman for the duration of the shoot.

In 1968, *The Killing of Sister George*, starring **Beryl Reid** and **Susannah York**, became America's first X-rated A-list film. Beryl Reid's large-as-life portrayal of a lesbian character, June, in the film, has become one of the landmarks in lesbian cinema.

Before it could be released in Britain, however, the British Board of Film Censors demanded that four minutes of a lesbian love scene be removed. The movie flopped upon its release. Its director, Robert Aldrich, claimed that had he made it in 1975 instead of in 1968, *Sister George* would have been a hit. Eventually, the film did break even because of its videocassette sales.

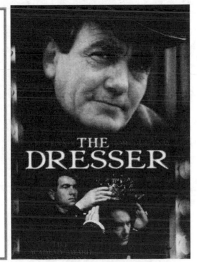

Director/producer Peter Yates released *The Dresser* in 1983, starring **Albert Finney** as the aging actor and **Tom Courtenay** as he dresser. It was the story of a master-servant relationship. The film was so successful that both Finney and Courtenay were Oscar-nominated as Best Actor in 1984.

By the 80s, critics were onto who was playing it gay and who wasn't. *Vanity Fair* recalled Courtenay's performance as "all lavender-tinted prissiness— *The Boys in the Band* style gay-farce." Many gays were offended by the actor's mincing mannerisms.

Director Mark Rydell took D.H. Lawrence's novel, *The Fox* (1922), and turned it into a graphic depiction of lesbians in love. **Sandy Dennis** and **Anne Heywood** were cast as the lesbians, with handsome Keir Dullea as the male intruder on their remote farmstead in Canada.

As a movie, it was far more graphic in depicting Sapphic love than other mainstream films that had preceded it. Released in 1968, *The Fox* came out just as the old Production Code was breaking down. The most shocking scene, at least to audiences of the late 60s, was Heywood's controversial on-camera masturbation scene.

457

When offered the role of a gay man in *Sunday, Bloody Sunday,* **Peter Finch** immediately said, "I'm not a queer." His agent, Olive Harding, responded, "No, dear, but I'd like to see you play one to prove you're an actor."

As it happened, no one ever seriously believed that Finch was queer just because he'd played it gay. He'd had plenty of "dollybirds," as he called his female tricks. They had included Vivien Leigh, the daughter of an African chieftain, a Sabena Airlines stewardess, and many prostitutes.

Later in life, however, he issued this enigmatic statement; "A high libido and a sense of life's absurdities can breed queer bedfellows," he once said, "and in the good old days, I landed up in some pretty queer situations."

Sidney Lumet's 1971 *The Anderson Tapes,* starring Sean Connery, was a big hit--a fast-paced thriller about an ex-con's master holdup plan. In a small but seminal role, **Martin Balsam** (photo, right) played a homosexual interior decorator.

"It certainly didn't harm my career," he said, "and I got generally good reviews. I'm sort of an ugly, stocky guy, and I had no romantic image to protect. My whole career was built on character parts, and a flamboyant gay guy was just fine with me."

Playing gay never hurt the career of **Harvey Fierstein**, (three photos above) seen in left photo above slipping into a 25-pound body suit padded with foam and silicone. Of course, it was for his appearance as a woman in the live version of *Hairspray.* John Travolta would perform the role in the movie. When Harvey draped a dress over the body suit and appeared as Edna at the Neil Simon Theater, he made Broadway history. Fierstein is also known for playing a female impersonator in the Tony-winning play and movie *Torch Song Trilogy.*

As for his role of Edna, Fierstein said, "I'm playing Edna as a woman, not as a drag role. It's a lot of work, especially dressing up for the part. I couldn't resist the chance to make an audience believe that they were seeing a real woman, not a drag queen. The challenge for me is to make Edna a believable person."

McQueen and Newman as Butch and His Sundancer

BUT WITH MCQUEEN AND NEWMAN ON A DOUBLE-BILLING,
Who'd Be the Top?

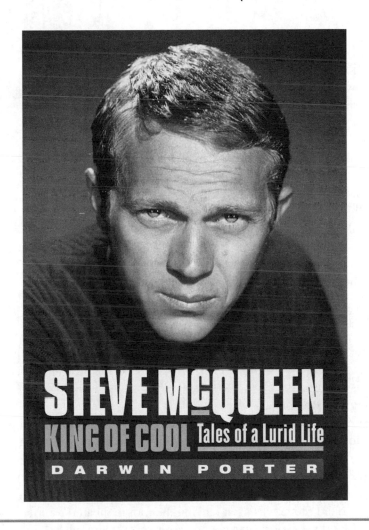

The private life of **Steve McQueen**, screen macho, was exposed for the first time in Darwin Porter's 2009 biography. (See cover above).

As a young boy, McQueen was brutally molested by one of his "stepfathers," who forced him to work as a child prostitute along Santa Monica Boulevard, a situation that led to his gang rape. As a teenager, he worked in bordellos in Havana, Santo Domingo, and Port Arthur, Texas. He earned a living through appearances on camera in porn, and on the stage in an erotic revue, his skit entitled, "The Cream in Her Coffee."

After a tour of duty in the Marine Corps, he landed in Greenwich Village, where he hustled rich homosexuals.

AND THE CASTING DRAMAS THAT ENSUED

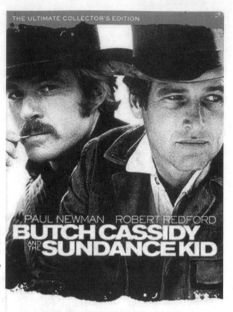

At the peak of his career, when he was reigning as king of the box office, Steve McQueen made a major mistake. He turned down a leading role in *Sundance Kid and Butch Cassidy* (its original title). But he devoted some time to thinking about it first.

Both Steve and Paul Newman had originally been the leading choices to play the cold-blooded killers in the film version of Truman Capote's *In Cold Blood*. Capote himself wanted Steve and Paul, although the producers feared they were too well known. Eventually, the roles went instead to Robert Blake and Scott Wilson.

When both Steve and Paul saw the finished result in 1967 after the film was released, they regretted turning down the roles. They vowed that if a good script came along featuring two equal male parts, they'd go for it.

Over the years Paul had maintained a friendly rivalry with Steve. When Paul was filming *Winning* (1968),

> With the exception of Steve McQueen, many of Hollywood's leading actors were considered for the role of The Sundance Kid, including some of Newman's private, closeted lovers such as John Derek, Sal Mineo, and Brando De Wilde. Even Newman's son, Scott, who later killed himself, wanted the role.
>
> Jack Lemmon, Warren Beatty, and Dustin Hoffman were also in the race, and perhaps Marlon Brando for the role of either Sundance or Butch Cassidy.

Steve, now number one at the box office, called Paul. "Hey, it's lonely at the top, old pal, old buddy," Steve said. "Come for a motorcycle ride with me in the desert. I'll fuck you in the sand until you get cactus up your ass."

"Dream on, faggot" Paul said.

Although they talked "dirty" to each other, each man, although a rival, still maintained a deep and abiding love and respect for each other. Paul liked Steve so much that in the months ahead, he would invite him to join him as an investor in a new film production company.

When Steve went to see Paul's film, *Winning*, his take on a race car driver, Steve was clearly jealous that his rival had beat him to the screen with a picture about his own favorite sport.

As a drunken, stoned Steve was seen leaving the movie theater, a reporter asked him if his interest, and that of Paul's, in sports car racing expressed a death wish.

"Either of us can fuck anybody in the world we want," Steve said. "All we have to do is call 'em on the phone, and they come running. There have been rumors about Paul and me, about most actors. There have even been suggestions that we're not masculine. But out on those race tracks, we show those faggot reporters who's the man, baby."

Marlon Brando was asked to star in *Butch Cassidy and the Sundance Kid*, but bowed out, claiming, "I'm just too tired to make another God damn movie." He called Paul and told him of his decision to withdraw his name from the roster of candidates. "Why don't you get Steve Mc-Queen to play Sundance?" Brando asked.

Richard Zanuck of 20th Century Fox called George Roy Hill, who had signed on as director of the Butch and Sundance film. "Newman and McQueen are two of the world's biggest stars," Zanuck said. "With those guys on the marquee, millions around the world will flock to see them. Of course, there will be the problem of top billing. They're both number one."

Meeting with the "suits" at Fox, Zanuck claimed that "McQueen is a born screen cowboy," citing his role in *The Magnificent Seven*. He contacted Steve directly and sent over a script, by-passing his agent.

Three days later, Steve called Zanuck. "I'm your Sundance. Draw up the contract. I don't work cheap. Remember that."

For years Paul and Steve had discussed appearing in a film together, and the roles of Butch and Sundance now seemed to provide that chance. In dialogues night after night, they became so fired up over the movie's possibilities that Paul proposed that they acquire the rights to the script themselves, each of them investing $200,000 from their own pockets. Steve rejected that idea.

The question of billing kept coming up, Steve demanding top billing but Paul refusing to re-linquish his star status. Fox intervened when they heard of this argument and proposed a stag-gered but equal billing.

After endless debates with himself, and after negotiating an agreement with Paul to appear opposite him, Steve suddenly and impulsively rejected the movie offer. "There's no way in hell that I'm gonna play Newman's bitch," Steve told the stunned executives at Fox. He had finally figured out that *Butch Cassidy and the Sundance Kid* was the story of a love affair between two homosexual outlaws.

Many months later, after it had become obvious that *Butch Cassidy and the Sundance Kid* had been a staggering success, Paul called Steve to chide him. "How does it feel to be dethroned, old buddy, old pal?" Paul asked. "And to think you could have been riding in the saddle with me if you'd signed on as Sundance."

"Wasn't my role Butch?" Steve asked, "With you playing that faggot, Sundance? You might be number one at the box office—at least for 1969—but my dick is bigger than yours, and there's not a God damn thing you can do about that, fucker. Say, kid, since you're now the Queen of the Box Office, let's get together for some beer. I'll let you feel it under the table so you'll know what a real man is like." Having uttered that, he put down the phone.

Its gay wardrobe master claimed that the film, *The Magnificent Seven*, was actually the average measure of the penis sizes for this splendid array of talented manhood.

Left to right: Yul Brynner, Steve McQueen, Horst Buchholz, Charles Bronson, Robert Vaughn, Brad Dexter, and James Coburn. During filming, McQueen and Brynner, both bisexuals, vied for the nighttime services of the gay German actor, Buchholz.

PAUL NEWMAN AND STEVE MCQUEEN WERE LOVERS!

The Globe, based on revelations derived from Darwin Porter's biography of Steve McQueen, broke the news to millions of readers, exposing what thousands from "insider Hollywood" had known for years. During the 1950s, Newman and McQueen were lovers—or at least fuck-buddies.

In an article by Peter Sheridan, *The Globe* reported: "Movie hunk Steve McQueen used his macho good looks to sleep his way to the top of the Hollywood heap, bedding the biggest female and MALE stars—including his screen rival, Paul Newman!"

McQueen was an alley cat who had "no morals--he would have sex with anyone." In the case of heartthrob Newman, "McQueen desperately wanted to cut him down to size." *The Globe* went on to say, "McQueen told friends, 'I thought Newman was arrogant. When I finally got him into bed, I taught him who the man was.'"

Porter said the screen rivals, who later co-starred together in *The Towering Inferno,* never defined themselves as gay, but "simply saw themselves as men enjoying their sexuality."

McQueen also bedded James Dean, the pretty one in *Rebel Without a Cause.* "He was sleeping with both Newman and Dean and neither of them knew that," Porter said.

In 1980, at the age of 50, McQueen died of cancer. He was married three times--to Broadway actress Neile Adams, actress Ali MacGraw, and model Barbara Minty, his widow. But he was never faithful to any of them.

McQueen frequently expressed his contempt for homosexuals, but that didn't stop him from having sex with them. McQueen also bedded some of Hollywood's leading stars, including Monroe, Ava Gardner, and scores of others, even some of the aged A-list *duennas* from yesteryear. As he told Rock Hudson, "From time to time, I like antique pussy." Once, he even asked Rock to set him up with his friend, Miss Mae West. Talk about antique.....

FILM ICONS WHOSE MYSTERIES LAY BEHIND THEIR BABY BLUES
SEX BUDDIES AND FILM RIVALS STEVE MCQUEEN (TOP ROW) AND PAUL NEWMAN

The Front Runner

How the film based on a hot, gay-themed, multi-million copy bestseller
NEVER GOT MADE.

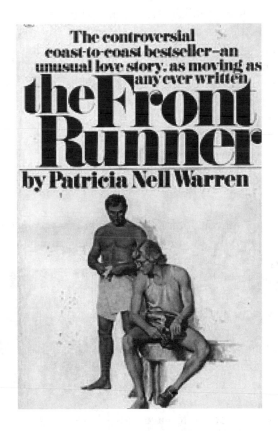

At curbside in front of *A Different Light,* the leading gay bookstore of Los Angeles, a sleek black limosine pulled up. From the front seat, the driver, clad in an elephant gray uniform, jumped out. He opened the limosine's back door. The year was 1974.

Sidewalk gawkers first got a view of one of the shapeliest pair of gams in the world--and the most celebrated. They belonged to Marlene Dietrich, who had come to the store to buy a copy of *The Front Runner,* a novel about two men in love, by Patricia Nell Warren.

Dietrich wasn't alone in her quest for this book. The story of a tough, conservative ex-Marine track coach and his love for an Olympic-bound long distance runner would ultimately sell 10 million copies worldwide, in multiple languages. It would inspire two sequels--*Harlan's Race* and *Billy's Boy.*

THE FRONT RUNNER
AN OLYMPIC LOVE STORY

But a Slow Mover on the Track

In 1974, Patricia Nell Warren published a novel, *The Front Runner,* that sold more than ten million copies, and which is today a classic in gay literature. Shortly after its release, even Marlene Dietrich pulled up in a chauffeur-driven limousine and purchased a copy from *A Different Light* bookstore in Los Angeles.

The novel is the story of a cross-country coach, Harlan Brown, who, at an obscure college in New York State, falls in love with a young Olympic runner named Billy Sive, the affair leading to disaster.

The plot very tenderly and with great sensitivity explores the developing love relation between the track coach (an ex-Marine) and his openly gay athlete. *The Front Runner* became the first contemporary novel about gay love to be listed on *The New York Times* bestseller list. In publishing, it was defined as a cross-over novel, meaning that it appealed to both straight and gay readers.

It was Paul Newman's producer, John Foreman, who first read the novel, buying a copy at an airport and reading it on his flight to London. When he returned to Los Angeles, he sent it to Paul with a note: "Do we dare?" the note asked. As a whimsical postscript, he scribbled, "I know you still look devastatingly young and gorgeous, but I had you in mind for the coach, not the young Front Runner."

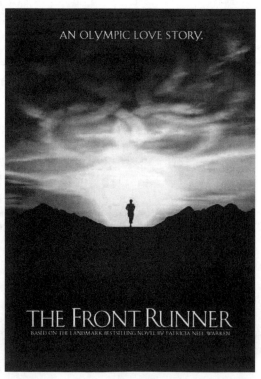

AN OLYMPIC LOVE STORY.

THE FRONT RUNNER

BASED ON THE LANDMARK BESTSELLING NOVEL BY PATRICIA NELL WARREN

Paul read the novel that weekend and was intrigued at the prospect of bringing an openly gay love story to the big screen. He ordered his staff to acquire the film rights to *The Front Runner*.

But within a few weeks, he began to have serious doubts. The director, George Roy Hill, reminded Paul, "No one will believe Paul Newman playing a homosexual." Hill seemed to forget that Paul had already played gay, both on the screen, though heavily masked, in *Cat on a Hot Tin Roof*, and on stage in *Baby Want a Kiss*.

To make the story work, the onscreen chemistry between Paul and the actor playing Billy Sive had to be both idyllic and explosive. Ever since he'd made *Butch Cassidy and the Sundance Kid*, followed by *The Sting*, he and Redford had promised each other that they'd both be on the lookout for the perfect script in which they could co-star again, hopefully as successfully as they did in their previous ventures together.

Reports exist that Paul wanted Robert Redford to play Billy. However, by the mid-1970s Redford had entered middle age—after all, he was born on August 18, 1937—although he didn't look it. Because of Redford's age, some sources claim he was never seriously considered by Paul for the role. Actually, he was.

At that time in Redford's career, and with the right kind of makeup, almost twenty years, or at least fifteen, could be removed from his face.

"One night," Foreman claimed, "perhaps when he'd had too much beer, Paul talked with great enthusiasm about playing love scenes on screen with Redford. Perhaps he knew in his heart that's the only way he could make love to Redford—that is, in front of a camera." Foreman at the time was well aware of Paul's bisexuality.

Paul sent Redford an early draft of the movie script for *The Front Runner*. If the reports about the matter can be believed, Redford read the script and flat-out rejected it. "There's no way I'm going to appear on the screen with you, playing a homosexual."

Redford, or so it was said, had been deeply troubled over his gay-bisexual role in *Inside Daisy Clover* and didn't seem inclined to repeat the experience with a role as an openly gay athlete. Throughout his career, Redford has never been the supporter of gay rights to the extent that Paul was.

"I don't know what Redford's problem is," wrote reporter Barry Devlin after hearing about Redford's rejection of *The Front Runner*. "For those who could see with any sort of open mind, both Redford and Newman had already played homosexual lovers in *Butch Cassidy and the Sundance Kid* and in *The Sting*. With that in mind, look at *The*

"The Sundance Kid" (**Robert Redford**, left) and **Paul Newman** (right) were first gossiped about in the press as potential stars of *The Front Runner*. But middle-aged Redford--his age clearly revealed in this portrait--was far too old to play the young runner, Billy Sive. Reportedly, Redford told Newman he would never consider the role, even if age hadn't been a factor.

(Left photo, above) **Paul Newman** was ideal for the role of coach Harlan Brown. "He was ideal except for one thing," said the novelist James Leo Herlihy (*Midnight Cowboy*). "He didn't have the *cojones* for it. He told me he feared his fans would stay away if he played such an obviously gay character. I told him to go for it and to include at least one love scene with him naked in bed, making love to Billy."

(Right photo, above). **Patricia Nell Warren**, an openly lesbian American author, can, amazingly, write with sensitivity about love between two men. The best-selling author is widely known as "The Mother of Frontrunners," those GLBT running and walking clubs that were launched in Los Angeles and immediately spread to other cities around the world.

Called "Patches" by her fans, Warren often appears as a speaker at the invitation of various gay rights groups. Born in 1936, she is one of the most popular and renowned authors of gay lit in the world. She's come a long way from that cattle ranch where she grew up in Montana.

Sting again and decide for yourself."

Paul may have had his feelings hurt at so abrupt a rejection. Nonetheless, he didn't hold a grudge against Redford. That Christmas he sent him a paperweight containing sparkling blue eyes in porcelain. It was inscribed simply FORGET ME NOT.

Perhaps to counter the sentimentality of Paul's gift, Redford sent Paul a wrecked Porsche. To get back at him, and perhaps embarrassed at the sentimentality of his earlier gift, Paul shipped Redford two boxes of toilet paper with Redford's face illustrating every sheet.

"Paul's wooing of Redford, such as it was, was about as successful as Joan Crawford's attempt to seduce Bette Davis," said Foreman.

With Redford removed from consideration, Paul conjured up his own choice for the character of Bill Sive. "The Front Runner," at least for a few weeks, was Richard Thomas, the young actor who'd played his son in the race car picture, *Winning*.

Then for a brief time, Paul considered Robby Benson, who had starred with him in *Harry and Son,* a serious drama they had made together in 1984. (The tagline for that film? "They were two men with nothing in common. They were father and son.") Foreman reminded Paul that Benson had been nominated for a "Razzie Award" after his dreadful appearance in that film. Foreman also warned Paul that neither Benson nor Thomas were handsome enough for the part. "Billy should be blond, blue eyed, and gorgeous, Robert Redford in 1962, in other words."

"As if to answer a maiden's prayer" [Foreman's words], a picture and resumé arrived from Cal Culver. Foreman rushed it to Paul. It was what Paul had been dreaming of, a photograph of a young, beautiful, and sexy Robert Redford reincarnate. Except, as both Foreman and Paul learned, Cal Culver carried a certain baggage.

Identified by the screen name "Casey Donovan," Cal had appeared in *Boys in the Sand* (1971), a landmark film in the history of gay pornography. Born in 1943, he was five years younger than Redford, but looked much younger than that.

In addition to evoking images of Redford, Cal's glorious physicality also suggested Guy Madison, Troy Donahue, and Tab Hunter at the peak of their beauty.

With Foreman beside him, Paul watched a screening of *Boys in the Sand*. Both men agreed that the handsome young actor was stunning. But a question was raised: Would Cal's previous appearances in porno ruin him for mainstream films? Foreman thought not. "He has a large gay following, maybe millions have seen *Boys in the Sand*, and that would only increase box office

| Donahue | Redford | Hunter | Madison |

Paul Newman's producer, John Foreman, articulated the "look" he wanted for whatever actor would be cast into the role of Billy Sive. At various times, he suggested a "young" **Troy Donahue**, as he appeared in *A Summer Place;* a "young" **Robert Redford**, as he starred in *Barefoot in the Park;* a "young" **Tab Hunter** as he looked in *Island of Desire;* and a *"young"* **Guy Madison** as he was in *Since You Went Away*.

for us. Straight audiences, however, would not have seen *Boys in the Sand*, and could not possibly care."

"Fly him to Hollywood," Paul said. "I'd like to meet this angel."

It can't be ascertained exactly what Paul was expecting when he first met Cal, but perhaps it was not the well-educated actor and model who appeared before him. Cal was charming, charismatic, articulate, and full of grace. "He was a knockout," Paul told Foreman the next day.

In Key West in the late 1970s, Cal told author Darwin Porter that "I seduced Newman the first night we got together. It was the easiest thing I've ever done. I'm a take-charge kind of guy, and I just moved in on him. He put up no resistance at all. To judge by the moans, I gave him great sex. As for me, I've had better. But he *was* Paul Newman, and I was thrilled to submit to the casting couch. Of course, it became a question of just who was casting who on that casting couch."

"I had described myself to Newman as Robert Redford's younger brother," Cal claimed, "and he seemed to agree. For a full month, I was in Hollywood, with Newman paying all my bills. The only off-key note was one night when we were going at it, and he called me 'Robert.' I didn't like that, but I forgave him. After all, it was I who had been promoting the image of my own similarity in looks to Redford's. What could I expect?"

"We had great times together," Cal recalled. "Newman convinced me we were going to make the movie, and that we'd actually appear nude on the screen together—no full frontals, of course. He seemed to be looking forward to it."

"I was bouncing around up there in the clouds," Cal claimed. "In spite of my porno background, I really wanted to go legit. After all, I'd appeared on stage with Ingrid Bergman. This was going to be my big breakthrough role. I even told myself that I might allow myself to fall in love with Newman, although another actor, Tom Tryon, already had his stamp on me."

Tryon had been the star of Otto Preminger's *The Cardinal* (1963).

John Foreman, Paul Newman's producer, was the first to read *The Front Runner,* and thought it would be ideal for the screen, in spite of it being a homosexual love story.

He reportedly told Newman, "It's time we saw two gorgeous men make love to each other on the screen. There's a hell of a lot of that going on in Hollywood already."

History does not record the private demons that led to **Newman** refusing to go ahead with the production of *The Front Runner.* Physically, he was ideal for the part, and it would give him another chance to show off his body, which he seemed to want to do in every film.

"Ultimately, maybe it was just sheer vanity," Shelley Winters told author Darwin Porter. "Paul told me he was worried about showing off his body stacked alongside someone so much younger. I get the feeling myself whenever I see a pretty girl in a nude scene."

Paul Newman--like hundreds of other gay men--became mesmerized by porn actor **Cal Culver** who had billed himself as **Casey Donovan** in *Boys in the Sand.* But Paul reserved judgement until Culver was flown to Hollywood to test for the role of Billy Sive in *The Front Runner.*

At the time, Newman didn't know that the handsome, well-built actor was also a world-class star fucker. Culver's specialty involved opening the door on closeted actors, at least in private. Before the rooster crowed, Culver had Newman in the sack. "It was no trouble at all," he said. But later, Newman fled both from Culver and from the film project too.

"Late one morning," Cal recalled with a definite bitterness, "the sky fell in on me. I came down from the clouds. Newman called shortly before noon. I was still asleep, groggy from the previous night. He told me that he had abandoned plans to film *The Front Runner*, and that our relationship was over. Before hanging up, he also told me that a check was in the mail. He put down the phone and that was it. The end of my big, silly dream."

"I was devastated," Cal said. "Newman's check never arrived, but John Foreman called me. I came by his office where five thousand dollars in one hundred dollar bills were waiting for me. That's a hell of a lot more than either Liberace or Merv Griffin gave me for similar services. I flew to Miami knowing it was all over for me. Eventually even Tom Tryon didn't want me anymore. It was back to hustling and porno. I was, after all, known as the gay Adam."

"Quite by chance I ran into Paul one night in New York," Cal said. "I thought he'd ignore me, but he didn't. He stopped and chatted for a minute or two, apologizing that *The Front Runner* didn't work out for either of us. I suggested that he might like to come back to my apartment for a drink, but he turned me down. He told me that his affairs were over, that he was going back to settle down in New England. 'Everyone who's been a whore has to get out of the profession sooner or later—and that goes for you too, kid.' Those were his last words to me."

On the Sunday of August 10, 1987, Cal died of a lung infection associated with AIDS. Jay McKenna, writing in *The Advocate*, referred to him as "the first widely embraced gay symbol to appear during the post-Stonewall years."

Years later, Paul claimed he regretted not making *The Front Runner*. "I made *Slap Shot* instead, and who cares about that fucker today? Had I made *The Front Runner*, it could have been a landmark—a turning point, really—in the history of cinema. Too bad I didn't have the balls. Cal Culver and I would have become the screen's new romantic lovers." He hesitated. "In the Greek tradition, of course."

Toward the end of 1975, the author, Patricia Nell Warren, read a script of *The Front Runner*, as defined by the movie's official website. "When I read it, my heart sank. It backed away from portraying a love relationship between two gay men. The poignant romance of my book had been reduced to a one-night stand before the Olympic Games. So little remained of the original story that when I met with Newman's business partner, George Englund, to discuss my reaction to the script, I told him: 'Why are you paying me money to call this *The Front Runner*? You can title it something else, and not pay me a nickel. Because this is not what I wrote.'"

With Newman in the closet, Frank Perry, who filmed that notorious and degrading libel of Joan Crawford, *Mommie Dearest* (released in 1981 after the publication in 1978 of a defamatory biography, by Christina Crawford, with the same name) appeared as *The Front Runner's* next suitor. Though he struggled for years, he was not successful in launching a film version.

After many unrelated, and failed, intra-Hollywood struggles, Jerry B. Wheeler, an independent producer, wanted in on *The Front Runner* game. In 1977, he had already produced Darwin Porter's *Tropic of Desire*, starring

Unknown to Paul Newman, who was paying Cal Culver's rent in Los Angeles, the porn star had other "sponsors," notably **Tom Tryon,** the New England-born actor and Yale graduate who became famous when Otto Preminger cast him as the male lead in the 1963 picture, *The Cardinal*.

When Tryon's acting career faded, he turned to novel writing, creating, among other successes, *The Dark Secret of Harvest Home,* which was adapted into a movie with Bette Davis in 1978.

Tryon became Cal's long-time romantic squeeze, but the relationship became too hot for the older actor to handle, and the two men eventually separated.

Matt Collins and Eartha Kitt, based on Porter's bestselling novel, *Butterflies in Heat*.

Jack Wrangler, the leading gay porno star of the 1970s, approached Wheeler to play Billy Sive, but was rejected because of his cinematic history. This time around, the project's fantasy dream cast, as defined by Wheeler, included Robert Redford playing the coach (not Billy), and with Tom Cruise cast as Billy.

In 1988, Wheeler ran an ad in *Variety*, virtually "begging" for a star to play either role. Many actors he approached had already turned down the part. Even Jon Pennell, a talented young actor, refused to sign on as the coach's lover, even though the film could have made his career.

"There was a general feeling that homosexuality is a dangerous subject," said Director Marshall W. Mason, who made his name in the theater with such plays as *Fifth of July*, which had homosexual characters.

Wheeler died in 1990, and seemingly the hope of ever transforming *The Front Runner* into a film went to the grave with him.

After many a battle, often in court, Patricia, the original writer of the novel, eventually reacquired the film rights to *The Front Runner*.

By 2010, it would seem that those earlier barriers against the production of a gay film have collapsed, especially with the release of such films as *Philadelphia* with Tom Hanks or *Brokeback Mountain* with Heath Ledger and Jake Gyllenhaal.

As of this writing, this marvelous novel, despite numerous attempts, has yet to be filmed.

Where is Ang Lee now that we need him?

At one point after the release of *Boys in the Sand,* **Merv Griffin** wanted to produce an entire episode of his daytime-TV talk show on the emergence of gay porn as a legitimate art expression whose freedom had recently been endorsed by the American courts. Merv envisioned a joint interview with both Cal Culver and Wakefield Poole, the director of *Boys in the Sand,* the most acclaimed male porno movie in the history of cinema.

Griffin never had the nerve to actually tape the show, although he enjoyed the private show (and casting couch audition) Culver staged for him in anticipation of a televised event that never came to be. Culver later claimed, "I liberated Merv sexually on the first night I met him."

Although never publicly admitting to homosexuality--in fact, blatantly denying it until the end of his life--**Liberace** was another A-list patron of Cal Culver.

After seeing him emote in *Boys in the Sand,* Liberace sent Culver one-half of a thousand-dollar bill. "To get the other half of this bill, give me a ring," Liberace wrote. "There's more where that came from."

Paul Newman even rejected a young Tom Cruise for a role in *Harry & Son* (1984), endorsing **Robby Benson** (photo above) for the role instead.

John Foreman, the designated producer of *The Front Runner,* opposed the choice of Benson. "Robby is not handsome enough for the part. Billy should be blond, blue eyed, and goregous, in other words, Robert Redford in 1962."

Ironically, in 1983, Benson was cast as the long-distance runner, Billy Mills, in another film, *Running Brave,* a story about an Oglala Sioux who against all odds achieves greatness.

After Robby Benson was deemed unsuitable, Both Newman and Foreman considered **Richard Thomas** for the co-starring role of Billy in *The Front Runner.* Thomas had become a household word because of his long-running portrayal of John-Boy on the hit series *The Waltons.*

For whatever reason, when movie critic Rex Reed heard of this casting and the possibility of a nude scene between Newman and Thomas, he denounced the idea and the entire project too.

Why this bit of on-screen romance should have gotten Reed so hot under the collar remains the subject of lurid speculation.

Cal Culver wasn't the only porn star pursuing the role of Billy Sive in *The Front Runner.* **Jack Wrangler,** the most popular gay porn star of the 1970s, also wanted the part. Ironically, at about the same time, both actors were also competing for the lead role of a male hustler in the film adaptation of Darwin Porter's *Butterflies in Heat,* which was eventually released as a film entitled *Tropic of Desire,* co-starring Eartha Kitt.

Both of the porn stars were denied the leads in both projects. Jerry B. Wheeler, who produced *Tropic of Desire,* also bid aggressively for the status of producer of *The Front Runner.* "But there's no way I'm going to cast a porn star, Cal or Jack, in my movie. I'm not making that kind of picture. I'll go to bed with them, and I did, but they're not getting the part. Of course, I didn't tell them that when I was propositioning them."

Joe Gage

Porn Poet of the Queer Working Class

Joe Gage (aka Tim Kincaid, aka Mac Larson) is famous today for his legendary gay porn trilogy--*Kansas City Trucking Co., El Paso Wrecking Corp.,* and *L.A. Tool and Die.* He is the greatest gay porn director in cinematic history.

Frank Rodriguez, who interviewed Gage for *Butt Magazine,* said, "He was the first artist to suggest that sex between men was more about camaraderie than romance, more about hot action than a lifestyle. While his characters were always working class joes, his 70s epics became blueprints of sexual tension building and were also stylistically innovative."

Latter-day critics have praised his films for their portrayals of male/male sex occurring between masculine-looking men from blue-collar and usually rural backgrounds. Gage's characters consistently related to each other as equal partners, altogether avoiding the sometimes judgmental stereotypes of dominant vs. submissive role playing.

Since Gage, the concept of a gay man's potentiality as a "macho bottom" has never been the same.

471

JOE GAGE

GLORY HOLES AT THE TRUCK STOP

Young gay men who weren't around in the late 70s can now see, on DVD, the restored films of Joe Gage that formed what became known as the "Working Man's Trilogy." Each of these legendary porn features have been restored to their original glory, or glory holes in the case of some of the scenes in these films.

If you happen to believe that gay porn can be an art form, you can test that theory by watching *Kansas City Trucking Co.* (1976), *El Paso Wrecking Corp.* (1977), and, the final entry, *L.A. Tool and Die* (1979). These road movies featured some of the leading porn stars of the genre, replete with lots of raunchy sex.

But, first things first. Joe Gage is really a pseudonym for Tim Kincaid (born 1944), an American film director, script writer, and producer. He was sometimes credited as Mac Larson.

Let's call him Gage. His trilogy of gay porn featured man-on-man sex between rugged machos who came from blue collar, often rural backgrounds. The actors in these films were viewed as equal partners, with no references to macho or fem roles, or labels associated with top vs. bottom.

Sex never occurred in these films in boudoirs with satin sheets. Often the venue was within truck stop toilets. Many of the actors (in both real and reel life) were bisexuals. Many of them were married with kids, but didn't mind homo sex with another man as rugged as they were.

Gage (or at least the persona he evoked) was credited with a "significant impact" on gay

Still a hot seller today, **Gage's porn trilogy** (see above) is hailed by some gay men as the hottest films of that genre ever made. They were road movies with a loose narrative and loads of raunchy sex, including toilet fucks and golden showers, with plenty of group gropes.

Some of the men featured in these flicks became porn legends. They included Jack Wrangler, Fred Halsted, and Richard Locke. All of these flicks were pre-condom, of course.

male culture in the halcyon pre-AIDS days before the plague descended in the early 80s.

He went on to direct films in the early 80s, including *Closed Sets* and *Heatstroke*, working under the pseudonym of Mac Larson, but these low-budget flicks didn't become the staples of his trucker trilogy movies. He did enjoy success with his Men's Room series, most of which included some kind of water sports. His latest film (2010) is tantalizingly entitled *Jock Park*.

Gage tried to cast "average joes" (that is, if they were big dicked) instead of Chelsea-style gym bunnies.

Some of the leading porn stars of the day, including Richard Locke, appeared in these movies. Locke, in fact, appeared in all the trucking trilogy films back when bare-backing was the norm.

Set in bars, desert shacks, or toilets riddled with glory holes, these films were hypermacho. Unlike a lot of today's porn—perhaps flicks released by Falcon where the emphasis is just on sexual acts—Gage's films had storylines, characters, dramatic conflict, and even dramatic resolutions.

Kansas City Trucking Co. starred not only Locke but Jack Wrangler, the "King of Gay Porn" in the 1970s. Locke played Hank, Wrangler a guy named Jack. Steve Boyd played Joe. Joe and Hank masturbate together on the road and later join an all-male orgy at a trucker's bunkhouse in Los Angeles.

The original cut featured a golden shower scene in which Locke and Wrangler were seen urinating on some unknown man. Later Locke and Boyd piss on Wrangler.

El Paso Wrecking Corp. starred not only Locke but Fred Halsted, a famous gay filmmaker in his own right. Women were also featured in this film, including Georgina Spelvin as Mille, roadhouse owner. Clay Russell appeared as a park ranger.

In the final flick of the trilogy, *L.A. Tool and Die*, the movie starred Locke, Will Seagers, and Paul Barresi, whose appearance was limited to a straight sex scene.

In 2009, Joe, then in his early sixties, was instrumental in the compilation of a new film, *Dad Takes a Fishing Trip,* for his *oeuvre* of porn pics. Its tagline, from a seasoned director for whom the age of a performer was always less important than his sex appeal?

"Intergenerational was never so sensational."

When **Joe Gage** (photo, above right) called for "Action!" on the set of one of his porn films, he meant it—and how! The trickle-down effect of his films on the aesthetics of gay male culture as it was developing in the 1970s and 1980s was huge.

In the early 1980s, he shocked his gay fans when he got married—to a biological woman, that is—and left the porn factory. He settled down, fathered two sons, wrote a novel, directed a play, and made some non-porno B-movie flicks.

At presstime for this edition of this guidebook, Joe, we heard, in his early 60s, had returned to gay porn, with a new banger under construction. Will he be performing, we wondered, as he'd done in rare instances in his cinematic past?

As recorded in an interview by Frank Rodriguez for *Butt Matgazine*, "For me it's really simple: performers can do anything they want to sell a movie, or themselves for that matter. Directors, however, should keep it zipped up, unless they're performing as well."

MICHAEL KEARNS

In *L.A. Tool and Die*, the respected mainstream actor **Michael Kearns** graced audiences with a cameo role in an orgy scene, a rare instance of a mainstream "legitimate" actor performing explicit sex acts in a hardcore porn film. Since then, Michael has come a long, way, baby, as an activist and spokesman for out and proud gay causes.

Back in the mid-70s, when coming out of the closet was considered a death wish for a career move in the entertainment industry, Kearns was the first Hollywood actor on record to come out, confronting as a result a shocking amount of homophobia.

In 1989, Kearns' solo performance piece, *Intimacies*, in which he played six wildly divergent characters who are urgently affected by HIV/AIDS, was a landmark theatrical event. As reviewed by *L.A.Weekly*, *"Kearns' carefully observed monologues achieve a balance of sympathy (without manipulating sentiment), humor and quiet heroism that communicates its personal struggles without losing sense of the larger social and political qualifiers."*

He went even further in 1991, making television history by announcing on *Entertainment Tonight* that he was HIV positive. Since then, he's portrayed HIV-positive characters on, among others, episodes of ABC TV's *Life Goes On* in which he played a character who had the virus. He played Cleve Jones in the HBO adaptation of Randy Shilts' *And The Band Played On*; *A Mother's Prayer;* and *It's My Party,* and had a recurring role on *Beverly Hills 90210*... often in a capacity that depicted the human aspects of HIV/AIDS.

Kearns' other television and film credits lend credence to the belief that Hollywood can and will overlook past (porno-related) indiscretions when it comes to getting meaty roles. Mr. Kearns has done a bang-up job on episodes of, among others, *Cheers, Murder She Wrote, The Waltons, Knots Landing, General Hospital,* and *Days of Our Lives,* and in feature films which have included *The Fall Guy, A River Made To Drown In, Kentucky Fried Movie,* and Brian DePalma's *Body Double.*

Actor Vincent De Paul as a Case Study of

The New Hollywood

How to Maneuver Your Way Through a Post-Millennium Acting Career in La-La Land

A highly visible figure among both *fashionistas* and the celluloid colony, **Vincent De Paul** is an actor and model who's equally at home in the pages of fashion magazines and with roles in such blockbusters as *Hairspray (*1988), *Hitch* (2005), or *Poseidon* (2006).

One of his most recent films is *Make a Wish* (2010), directed by David Grotell, who has spearheaded one of the annual Sundance Film Festivals. It pays homage to that dolce vita 1954 classic, *Three Coins in a Fountain* that starred everybody from Louis Jourdan to Jean Peters.

Vincent often appears at charity events such as "Cuties for Canines" in West Los Angeles, or he can be seen at premieres escorting lovely stars such as Jennifer Hudson along red carpets.

Vincent is a true *Metrosexual,* the name of a 2007 film in which he also appeared.

STAYING ALIVE, STAYING CONNECTED, AND
PLAYING WELL WITH OTHERS IN
THE NEW HOLLYWOOD

The pretty boys of the 30s—Robert Taylor, Tyrone Power, and Errol Flynn—are relatively unknown to the modern generation. Some younger gays, when queried, don't even know who Rock Hudson was. For some, Paul Newman is remembered as the face on a can of spaghetti sauce. Even the former "King of Hollywood," Clark Gable, is a fading memory except for his constantly revived role of Rhett Butler in *Gone With the Wind.*

But as the 21ˢᵗ century grows up into its "teens," an emerging crop of new actors has emerged. In many ways one such actor, Vincent De Paul, represents the New Hollywood.

Soft-spoken and extraordinarily handsome, with golden brown eyes and dark wavy hair, he stands 6' 1" tall and has an appealing sense of self-deprecation about his pre-Wilhelmina origins in Baltimore as Vincent Zannino. He plays soccer, badminton, and basketball, and is a master swimmer. He keeps in shape in case he's asked to appear in the buff in some tropical paradise, as he did in the film *Contadora Is for Lovers* (see separate film review).

Should some Hollywood producer ever get around to bringing sloe-eyed Valentino (not the designer) back to the screen, post-millennium, Vincent is our choice to play the role in any re-make of *The Sheik*, a film that thrilled silent screen audiences of the 20s. Vincent would also be brilliant if producers in the future decide to redo the James Bond series as gay. Even Daniel

Dressed or undressed, Vincent De Paul is known as a Hollywood hottie, a young man combining brains, brawn, and talent, all within one attractive package. His underwear photo (see above) promoted Ralph Lauren's POLO line.

"Who needs that old Marky Mark now that we've got Vincent De Paul?" wrote one fan. Smooth, suave, and a civic-minded gentleman, well educated and perfectly chiseled, he can move from roles as a clothes (or underwear) model to a variety of other roles as characters both sane and insane--including playing a psychopath if he has to.

Just 'cause he's pretty doesn't mean he's dumb.
Johns Hopkins, his Alma Mater

476

Craig, the most recent of the "Bond Boys," has suggested the commercial viability of a movie featuring a gay James Bond.

Originally, Vincent did not intend to be an actor. He began his adult life as a medical student at Johns Hopkins University where he studied epidemiology, biomedical ethics, and bio-statistics—heavy stuff, indeed. When he graduated, he went south for a medical internship at the Mount Sinai Medical Center in Miami Beach.

During a jog along South Beach, a chance meeting with Versace led to an abrupt career change. Vincent's dark, good looks got him cast as a model with representation by Wilhelmina. Soonafter, he appeared in *GQ*, *Vogue*, *Men's Health*, and *Cosmopolitan* (no, not as a nude centerfold like Massachusetts Republican Senator Scott Brown).

Later, as he juggled an increasing number of modeling assignments, Vincent nabbed a role opposite Drew Barrymore in *Riding in Cars With Boys*, cast as a hunkily adorable football player—the type all of us secretly wished we'd dated in high school (and some of us did!).

Vincent grew up in Baltimore, like John Waters, one of his cultural heroes. Born as Vincent Zannino, he later adopted the name of "De Paul," perhaps in a nod to the 17th-century Catholic saint, Vincent de Paul (canonized 1737), famous for being sold into slavery in Tunis, converting his master to Christianity, and later, for multiple acts of charity which were later endorsed by the French monarchs. John Waters cast the modern-day Vincent De Paul in *Hairspray*, which any screen aficionado knows was set in Baltimore.

Vincent is the son of a mortuary scientist, and this somewhat macabre background may have prepared him for his role as a character in Season 2 of *Six Feet Under*. In it, he was cast as a Hollywood junkie snorting the ashes of his cremated friend.

For some 20 years, Vincent has been working in film and TV. As a clothes model, he is an easy fit for almost any wardrobe—formal or casual.

He lives mostly in Los Angeles, but also has a residence in Miami Beach. Like Waters himself, he frequently returns to his native Baltimore and his supportive family.

Unlike the majority of wannabes in Hollywood, Vincent is a meticulously organized working actor, appearing frequently on screen in such films as the 2010 *Baby Jane*, a drag parody of *What Ever Happened to Baby Jane?*, the Bette Davis/Joan Crawford box office hit from 1962. The 2010 film, which included multiple location shoots in the Castro district of San Francisco, was directed by Billy Clift, a relative of the late actor Montgomery Clift. In it, Vincent was cast as Detective Bill Kovacks. Matthew Martin was cast as Baby Jane, with J. Conrad Frank as Blanche.

Whether it involves previous roles in *Exploring Love* or buried *Six Feet Under*, Vincent De Paul is that rarity in Hollywood--a working actor.

In addition to other roles, Vincent appears as a college counselor in the 2010 film *Sebastian*, about a woman dying of cancer who is miraculously cured by a handsome young stranger who claims to be the soul of her aborted child. Director Gregori J. Martin cast Daeg Faerc as Sebastian.

Other Vincent films of recent vintage include Brent Bambic's *Exploring Love* (2008), a drama/romance about a single man struggling to find deeper meaning in his materialistic life. The film starred Matthew Pearson as Sean, with Vincent cast as "Mr. Buggati."

Violet Tendencies (2010), directed by Casper Andreas, found Vincent playing Chase, with Mindy Cohn cast as Violet. The comedy is about a woman trying to distance herself from her gay friends so she can land a straight boyfriend. Approaching 40, Violet is known as Manhattan's "most fabulous fruit fly."

Vincent feels that it's easier today for a young actor to break into films than it was back in the days of the tyrannical movie moguls such as Harry Cohn, Louis B. Mayer, and Darryl F. Zanuck.

"It's easier and less costly today to produce a film than it was in the Hollywood of yesterday," Vincent said. "An actor can often get a role in a feature or a short film, which can be a showcase for his talents. That was much more difficult in the 40s when an aspiring actor or actress like Marilyn Monroe had to pursue that elusive studio contract. Often when a star was dropped, there were no other takers at the major studios."

Today the cameras are turning out shorts or features in greater numbers than ever before. Admittedly, most of these films will end up in the dustbin of celluloid history, but future stars will emerge from it all, regardless of how lowly the project that launched them.

Both Sylvester Stallone and Joan Crawford, for example, started at the bottom of the film industry by appearing in porno.

Director Billy Clift

Fans of the famous 1962 flick *What Ever Happened to Baby Jane?* eagerly await the drag parody *Baby Jane?* (2010), in which Vincent De Paul has a role as an occasionally undressed stud. Matthew Martin as Baby Jane and Conrad Frank as Blanche succeeded in the post-millennium version without ever (at least on film) resorting to violence.

The real-life animosity between Miss Davis and Miss Crawford was known as "The Divine Feud." Sandwiched in the photo (center, above) between the two ferocious divas is the film's producer and director, **Billy Clift,** who's related to that late gay icon, Montgomery Clift, formerly known as "the most beautiful man on the planet."

478

TO PLAY IT GAY . . . OR NOT?

When Perry King signed for *A Different Story* (see separate review), Sylvester Stallone called him and said: "Don't play no fag." Denzel Washington phoned Will Smith and begged him not to film a scene that called for him to kiss a man. Heath Ledger was warned not to make *Brokeback Mountain*. His managers claimed, "It will destroy what appears to be one of the most promising careers in Hollywood."

Vincent De Paul thinks that these opinions do not necessarily reflect the direction that both New York and Hollywood are moving today. "An evolution has occurred," he said.

"Agents and actors alike—for the most part, that is—embrace gay or bisexual roles if the script is worthy," Vincent said. "If the screenplay is compelling, regardless of the sexual preference of a character, most of today's actors will take it on."

"When I'm offered a role in a film, I would never turn it down based on the sexual orientation of the character," Vincent said. "I enjoy flexing my muscles as an actor and expanding. I like to play a diversity of roles . . . and have."

A Different Story, in which Perry King played a gay man, was filmed in 1978. Obviously King didn't take Stallone's advice. The two actors had starred together in the 1974 *The Lords of Flatbush*. In that film King played Chico, although originally the role was cast with Richard Gere. Beginning the first day on the set, Stallone and Gere fought constantly, at one point coming to blows (no inference meant). Stallone demanded that Gere be fired, and he was.

Perry King (left photo, above) played a gay character in *A Different Story* (1978--see separate review),. He regretted his decision to play gay, claiming (if reports are to be believed) that it "stunted" his career. Perhaps King wished he'd taken the advice of **Sylvester Stallone** (center photo, above), who counselled against "going queer" in the film, again according to reporters.

John Travolta (right photo above) was a long way from dressing in drag when he appeared on the cover of *Rolling Stone*. Here, he's playing it strictly hetero. But during the summer of 2007, gay men in the millions flocked to see him in a dress in *Hairspray*. Despite the fact that various tabloids have tried to Out the star in "Second Coming" headlines, Travolta still had the balls to dress in drag, donning latex padding and a wig. In *Hairspray,* with great style, he played a role previously inhabited by such gay icons as Divine, Harvey Fierstein, and Bruce Villach.

As a director, Stallone showed far greater sensitivity with fellow actor John Travolta, whom he cast in the 1983 *Staying Alive*. Travolta played Tony Manero, who tries to make it as a professional dancer on Broadway in a sequel (that is, a sort of sequel) to *Saturday Night Fever*.

The role of the dancer required intense physical training, and Stallone also directed Travolta's off-screen physical training, forming a strong male bond with him as part of the process. "That's me up there on the screen," Stallone later said.

Incidentally, *Staying Alive* won the Golden Raspberry Award as being among the "100 Most Enjoyable Bad Movies" ever made.

For the 1994 suspense thriller *The Specialist*, Stallone flew to Florida with his fellow co-stars, Sharon Stone, James Woods, Rod Steiger, and Eric Roberts.

Stallone was not the first choice for the role of Ray Quick, a former government agent who uses his expertise as a bomb specialist to help a woman seek revenge against the Miami underworld.

The original choice for the role, Steve Seagal, demanded $9 million for his appearance and was turned down. The producers called Stallone and pitched the role to him. Amazingly, he was given only a 15-minute deadline to make up his mind. Otherwise, the producers threatened to drop him and go with Warren Beatty instead.

In Miami, Vincent De Paul met Stallone. Vincent said that even though Stallone might have made that remark—"Don't play no fag"—to King, he seemed to have matured since then.

"I sat down with him over drinks, and we were joined by Gianni Versace. Stallone expressed great admiration for the fashion icon and seemed to respect him and his work."

At table were Angie Everhart, an American actress and former fashion model, and Antonio D'Amico, a fashion designer and former model best known as Versace's lover. D'Amico's long-term relationship with Versace lasted 15 years until Versace's assassination by a demented for-

(Left photo above) **Denzel Washington** (born in 1954) has never endeared himself to the gay community, especially when reports leaked out that he allegedly advised Will Smith not to kiss a man in a movie. Washington also didn't earn any gay brownie points when he appeared in *Philadelphia* with Tom Hanks in 1993 (see separate review), playing Joe Miller, the AIDs-ridden Hanks' homophobic lawyer. Was this type casting?

The much younger **Will Smith** (right photo above), is far more talented and diverse than Washington. He doesn't seem to have any hang-ups about playing a wide variety of roles, and is the reigning African-American box office champ of them all.

In *Brokeback Mountain*, **Jake Gyllenhaal** (left figure in photo above) and the late **Heath Ledger** (right) didn't have any reservations about going gay in *Brokeback Mountain*.

The gay cowboy *schtick*s didn't harm their careers at all-- in fact, each of the talented actors delivered their most moving performances. Writing in *The Advocate*, Kyle Buchanan said, "One of the most compelling stories, one likely to grow with time, compares Ledger to James Dean. Beyond its most obvious connection, it's an instructive primer of the homoerotic ingredients that go into creating a masculine icon."

mer model, Andrew Cunanen, in 1997.

To judge from Vincent's recollection, "Rocky" handled himself well within a gathering of sophisticated people and certainly didn't come off as the Neanderthal homophobe his remark to King indicated.

Footnote: In Versace's will, D'Amico was left a "pension" of about $26,000 a month for the rest of his life, and the right to live in any of the designer's homes in the United States or Italy.

But whereas Versace appeared to have sincerely loved D'Amico, relationships were always strained between D'Amico and Versace's sister and heir to the administration of his empire, Donatella. She told the press, "My relationship with Antonio is exactly as it was when Gianni was alive. I respected him as the boyfriend of my brother, but I never liked him as a person. So the relationship has stayed the same."

Back to the subject of gay roles: The late Heath Ledger, after completing *Brokeback Mountain*, was asked if he'd ever play gay again on the screen. "Bring 'em on!" was his answer. Those same words could certainly be echoed by many young actors, gay or straight, in today's Hollywood.

Vincent's attitude increasingly seems to be the norm. As Jake Gyllenhaal has said, "I'll have no problem playing gay in the future, and I'm sure I will many times to come."

HANGING OUT ON SOUTH BEACH

Players in the New Hollywood often appear along the sands of South Beach, Miami. Time was when you might spot model **Angie Everhart** (upper left) or hatted **Vincent De Paul** (lower left). They were seen hanging out with lovers **Antonio D'Amico** and **Gianni Versace** (left and right in upper right photo), and, of all people, the ferocious-looking **Sylvester Stallone** (lower right), who apparently isn't really Rambo offscreen.

D'Amico, a model and fashion designer born near Brindisi in southern Italy, met Versace in 1982 and embarked on a 15-year relationship that lasted until the designer's murder in 1997. Versace also "discovered" Vincent walking along the sands of South Beach, and steered him toward a career as a male model.

SALLY KIRKLAND
QUEEN OF THE INDIES

Vincent De Paul is a young man about town, either in New York, Hollywood, or Miami Beach. He has been seen and photographed escorting such stars as Oscar winner Jennifer Hudson.

But a special place in his heart is reserved for Sally Kirkland, the "Queen of the Indies." This gay-friendly American film and TV actress was the goddaughter of Shelley Winters and was a student of Lee Strasberg at the Actors Studio in New York. For a while she was part of the coterie associated with Andy Warhol.

Her greatest achievement came when she was Oscar nominated for Best Actress in the 1987 *Anna*. For that same film, she also won the Golden Globe for Best Actress in a Drama.

Many of Sally's fans believed that Cher robbed Sally of the deserved Oscar. Cher won for *Moonstruck*.

Today, when not appearing in films, Sally is an ordained minister in the Church of the Movement of Spiritual Inner Awareness. An artist, she also teaches drama, yoga, and meditation, and is a health activist, especially as an advocate for women harmed by breast implants.

Vincent hails Sally as "my teacher, mentor, and inspiration. She has always wanted me to strive and become greater and better."

Vincent and Sally have appeared in films together, including *The Ear of the Beholder* in 2008, a comedy/drama/romance.

The film was helmed by maverick director Francis Xavier—who, like Vincent, bears a name that's evocative of a Renaissance saint, in this case, Francis Xavier (1506-1552), missionary and founder of the Jesuits. Xavier, the modern-day filmmaker, is a sort of Renaissance man of films—writer, cinematographer, composer, actor, film editor, producer, and director.

Sally and Vince also worked together in *Oak Hill* (2007), scripted and directed by Peter LaVilla. This is a drama about three women and their struggle to co-exist within a flophouse in New Jersey. In this film, Sally plays an alcoholic, aging movie star, and Vincent plays a homeless man ("Moose") who's living in a shelter.

Vincent also appeared with Sally in the 2009 *Devil's Land* directed by Val Tasso and Jonathan Kutner, a short horror thriller.

One of Vincent's most recent films with Sally was *Make a Wish* (2010), helmed and scripted by David Grotell and inspired by the 1954 classic about the glamor of Italy during the 1950s, *Three Coins in the Fountain*. Grotell's story charts the journey of three men seeking love in Hollywood with Vincent cast as "Adam."

Assessing Sally both as an artist and as a personal friend, Vincent refers to her as "a national treasure."

Anna was the film that most celebrated the career of **Sally Kirkland**. Her role in it earned her an Oscar nomination for Best Actress in 1987, and a Golden Globe award as one of the five best acting performances by a woman in the 1980s.

FRANCO & TATUM

STARS OF TOMORROW

Vincent was asked to name some actors who are coming along to replace Brad Pitt, Tom Cruise, Tom Hanks, Matt Damon, and Ben Affleck (remember him?).

"I feel there's definitely a new crop waiting in the wings, many trained in the techniques once promulgated by Stella Adler, who taught Brando, and Lee Strasberg, who coached a bevy of actors who later became icons," Vincent said. "Marilyn Monroe frequented Strasberg's Actors Studio, as did a young James Dean and Marlon Brando."

"I find that James Franco is so very good at everything he does," Vincent said. "He's a brooding, organic actor."

Born in Palo Alto, California in 1978, Franco is not just an actor, but a director, screenwriter, producer, and painter. He came to prominence when he played the title role in Mark Rydell's TV biography of *James Dean*. For that interpretation, he earned a Golden Globe for Best Actor in a Miniseries or Television Film.

Franco's real fame came with his portrayal of Harry Osborn in the *Spider Man* Trilogy. He portrayed the son of the villainous Green Goblin (Willem Defoe), the best friend of the title character (Tobey Maquire). Originally Franco was considered for the lead of Spider Man/Peter Parker, although the lead eventually went to Maguire.

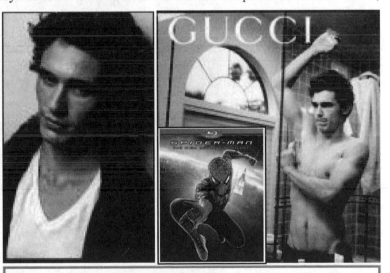

Franco came to the attention of many gays who hadn't seen the *Spider Man* movies when he starred opposite Sean Penn in *Milk* (2008). In that movie, he played Scott Smith, the lover of Harvey Milk (Penn), proving that Franco wasn't afraid to take on a gay role. "Franco is a nice match for Penn as the lover who finally has enough of political life," wrote critic Kenneth Turan of the *Los Angeles Times*. For his performance in *Milk*, Franco won the 2008 Independent Spirit Award for Best Supporting Actor.

One of Franco's most recent films is *Howl*, which had its premier at the Sundance

Just how thin should a rising young actor actually be? In the right-hand photo above, **James Franco**, former star of several teen films and of the Spider-Man trilogy, models his underarms for Gucci, He's lean and beautiful--no wonder the character played by Sean Penn took him as a lover in *Milk*.

In 2008, Franco was named as the new face in Gucci's men's fragrance line. The guy is not only gorgeous, but he's well educated and a talented artist. In fact, he's been a painter longer than he's been an actor. Some people are referring to him as "The New James Dean," perhaps because he appeared as James Dean in a film of the same name in 2001.

Film Festival in 2010. It is based on the life of gay poet Allen Ginsberg, a leading rebel of "The Beat Generation."

Hailed as a sex symbol, Franco in 2008 was designated as the new face of Gucci's men's fragrance line. The following year he was named "Sexiest Man Living" by Salon.com.

Vincent also cited Channing Tatum as a star to watch. At the urging of Vincent, he was a fixture at one of his first fashion shows, walking the runway at South Beach in Florida. According to Vincent, "I spotted talent when I first saw him, and he is living up to my earlier expectations for him."

Born in Alabama in 1980, Tatum was an athlete in school, playing football, track, baseball, as well as practicing martial arts. Reportedly, he once worked for about a year as an "exotic dancer" at a night club under the stage name of "Chan Crawford."

In 2010 he told an Australian newspaper that he'd like to make a movie about his experiences as a male stripper. "I've already got the director picked out," he said. "I'd like Nicolas Refn, who did the movie *Bronson*, to do it because he's insane for it."

Writer, producer, and director Nicolas Winding Refn was born in Copenhagen in 1970. One of his more recent films is *Valhalla Rising* (2009). A native of Denmark, Refn, recipient of numerous film awards, is known in France and the rest of Europe as as *l'Enfant sauvage,* ("The Wild Child").

If Tatum carries through on his wish to play a guy who sheds his skivvies, half the women in America will go to see it, along with every red-blooded gay guy as well. "The film about the stripper needs to be a bit crazy, and, under Refn's direction, it's possible to do a cute, romantic movie," Tatum said.

Tatum broke into show business as a dancer in Ricky Martin's "She Bangs" music video for which he was paid $400. By 2001 Tatum was picked as one of *Tear Sheet* magazine's "50 Most Beautiful Faces."

Launching himself as an actor in 2004, he appeared in the TV series *CSI: Miami*, although his first feature film role came a year later in *Coach Carter*. In this high school drama, he played a basketball player.

Other films have included *Step Up* in 2006, a dance-themed romance in which Tatum played a rebellious hip-hop dancer. That same year he teamed with Robert Downing Jr. and Shia LaBeouf to make *A Guide to Recognizing Your Saints*, a coming-of-

Sexy **Channing Tatum** used to be a male stripper, and he'd like to play one on the screen. In the left-hand photo above, he displays that he's got the lean, mean body as well as the "package" for the part.

His 2009 film was entitled *The Rise of Cobra,* and we can just imagine what that would be like. Gay men can only swoon because, according to Channing, "Girls were my biggest distraction in school." There, with gusto, he played football, went out for track, hit baseballs, and specialized in the martial arts, especially *kung fu.*

age drama about a boy growing up in Astoria, New York, in the 80s, where his friends end up dead, on drugs, or in prison. Tatum received an Independent Spirit Award nomination for "Best Supporting Actor."

While filming *The Eagle of the Ninth* in Scotland, a crew member accidentally poured boiling water down Tatum's wet suit. He was supposed to have diluted the scalding water with cold river water. Tatum attempted to escape from the wet suit, but the boiling water reached his crotch and severely burned his penis.

"The boiling water pretty much burned the skin off the head of my dick," Tatum told the press. "It was the most painful thing I've ever experienced in my life."

After his recovery, Tatum claimed, "Now my penis is fantastic! One hundred percent recovered."

For verification, you can check with his wife, Jenna Dewan. The couple was married on July 11, 2009, in Malibu.

Vincent's prediction about Tatum's stardom is coming true even as we speak. In *Dear John* (2010), a film he shot with Amanda Seyfried, based on a novel by Nicholas Sparks, the movie opened to mild reviews but major box office, shortly after the wildly popular *Avatar* had moved down to second place.

In reviewing *Dear John,* A.O. Scott, of *The New York Times,* said: "Mr. Tatum has shown himself to be an actor of narrow range. But his potential is evident, and his magnetism is undeniable. He is shrewd enough to stay within his comfort zone, and able to make the most of his interactions with more nimble performers."

A STAR ON THE RISE: **Channing Tatum** (left) appears with veteran thespian **Donald Sutherland** (right) in the 2010 release of *The Eagle of the Ninth*. Rosemary Sutcliff's novel, back in 1954, sold more than a million copies worldwide.

The story is set in Roman Britain during the 2nd Century AD, following the construction of Hadrian's Wall. Channing was cast as centurion Marcus Aquila.

channing tatum   amanda seyfried

From Nicholas Sparks, best-selling author of THE NOTEBOOK

DEAR JOHN

What would you do with a letter that changed everything?

Screen Gems presents in association with Relativity Media
a Temple Hill and Relativity Media production a film by Lasse Hallström
Channing Tatum Amanda Seyfried "Dear John" Henry Thomas Scott Porter
and Richard Jenkins Joanna Colbert csa Richard Mento csa
Dana Campbell Happy Walters Season Kent Deborah Lurie
Kristina Boden Kara Lindstrom Terry Stacey asc
Michael Disco Kenneth Halsband Jamie Linden
Jeremiah Samuels Toby Emmerich Michele Weiss Tucker Tooley
Marty Bowen Wyck Godfrey Ryan Kavanaugh Nicholas Sparks
Jamie Linden Lasse Hallström

FEBRUARY

In a previous role, *Dear John,* also released in 2010, Channing plays a modern-day US soldier who falls for a conservative North Carolina college student played by **Amanda Seyfried** when he's home on leave.

Part of the film's attraction for both gay men as well as for hordes of screaming female teenagers involved watching buffed Channing on the South Carolina beachfront.

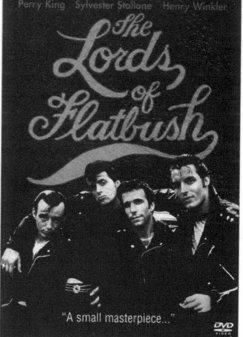

"A small masterpiece..."

Richard Gere, whose star is beginning to flicker, shows off his chest when he appeared in *American Gigolo* in 1980, the Paul Schrader film that focused on some of the unsexiest sex scenes ever filmed. In spite of the dim reviews, gay men flocked to see Gere in one scene where, as a hustler, he flashed the full monty.

Gere dropped out of *The Lords of Flatbush* after disputes with Stallone, the role eventually going to Perry King.

INDEX OF NAMES & TITLES
IN PART THREE

INDEX OF FILMS
REVIEWED IN THIS GUIDEBOOK

BLOOD MOON PRODUCTIONS

Entertainment About How America Interprets Its Celebrities

Blood Moon Productions originated in 1997 as *The Georgia Literary Association*, a vehicle for the promotion of obscure writers from America's Deep South. Today, Blood Moon is based in New York City, and staffed with writers who otherwise devote their energies to *THE FROMMER GUIDES*, a trusted name in travel publishing.

Since 2004, Blood Moon has generated at least nine different literary awards. They've included both silver and bronze medals from the IPPY (Independent Publishers Assn.) Awards; four nominations and two Honorable Mentions for BOOK OF THE YEAR from Foreword Magazine; and two Honorable Mentions from the Hollywood Book Festival.

Our corporate mission involves researching and salvaging the oral histories of America's entertainment industry--those "off the record" events which at the time might have been defined as either indecent or libelous, but which are now pertinent to America's understanding of its origins and cultural roots.

For more about us, and the books we're planning, click on our website, or refer to the pages which immediately follow.

Thanks for your interest, best wishes, and happy reading.

Danforth Prince, President
Blood Moon Productions
www.BloodMoonProductions.com

BLOOD MOON Productions, Ltd.

Salvaging the unrecorded oral histories of the Entertainment Industry's "off the record" past

And its affiliate, the Georgia Literary Assn

THE GEORGIA LITERARY ASSOCIATION
ENTERTAINMENT YOU WOULDN'T NECESSARILY EXPECT FROM THE DEEP SOUTH

by **Darwin Porter** and **Roy Moseley**

DAMN YOU, SCARLETT O'HARA

Here, for the first time, is a biography that raises the curtain on the secret lives of (Lord) **Laurence Oliver**, known for his interpretation of the brooding and tormented Heathcliff of Emily Brontë's *Wuthering Heights,* and **Vivien Leigh**, who immortalized herself with her Oscar-winning portrayals of Scarlett O'Hara in Margaret Mitchell's *Gone With the Wind*, and as Blanche DuBois in Tennessee Williams' *A Streetcar Named Desire.*

Even though the spotlight shone on this famous pair throughout most of their tabloid-fueled careers, much of what went on behind the velvet curtain remained hidden from view until the publication of this ground-breaking biography. The PRIVATE LIVES (to borrow a phrase from their gossipy contemporary, Noël Coward) of this famous couple are exposed with searing insights into their sexual excess and personal anguish.

Dashing and "impossibly handsome," Laurence Oliver was pursued by some of the most dazzling luminaries, both male and female, of the movie and theater worlds. The influential theatrical producer David Lewis asserted, "He would have slept with anyone." That included Richard Burton, who fell madly in love with him, as did Noël Coward. Lord Olivier's promiscuous, emotionally disturbed wife (Viv to her lovers) led a tumultuous off-the-record life whose paramours ranged from the A-list to men she picked up off the street. None of the brilliant roles depicted by Lord and Lady Olivier, on stage or on screen, ever matched the power and drama of personal imbroglios which wavered between Wagnerian opera and Greek tragedy. **Damn You, Scarlett O'Hara** will emerge as the definitive and most revelatory portrait ever published of the most talented and tormented actor and actress of the 20th century.

Darwin Porter is the co-author of this seminal work. Winner of numerous awards for his headline-generating biographies, he has shed new light on Marlon Brando, Steve McQueen, Paul Newman, Humphrey Bogart, Merv Griffin, Michael Jackson, and Howard Hughes.

Roy Moseley, this book's other co-author, was the godson and intimate friend of Lord and Lady Olivier, maintaining a decades-long association with the famous couple, nurturing them through a tumultuous life of artistic triumphs, emotional breakdowns, and streams of suppressed scandal. Moseley even had the painful honor of being present at the deathbed rituals of Lady Olivier. Moseley has written biographies of Queen Elizabeth and Prince Philip, Rex Harrison, Cary Grant, Merle Oberon, Roger Moore, and Moseley's long-time companion during the final years of her life, Miss Bette Davis.

DAMN YOU, SCARLETT O'HARA
THE PRIVATE LIFES OF LAURENCE OLIVIER AND VIVIEN LEIGH
by Darwin Porter and Roy Moseley
ISBN 978-1-936003-15-0   Hardcover, 435 pages, $27.95

Finally--A COOL Biography that was too HOT to be published during the lifetime of its subject. TALES OF A LURID LIFE!

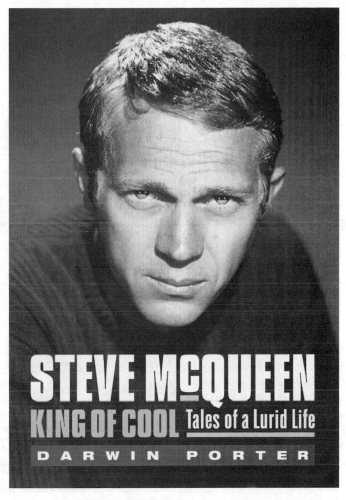

The drama of Steve McQueen's personal life far exceeded any role he ever played on screen. Born to a prostitute, he was brutally molested by some of his mother's "johns," and endured gang rape in reform school. His drift into prostitution began when he was hired as a towel boy in the most notorious bordello in the Dominican Republic, where he starred in a string of cheap porno films. Returning to New York before migrating to Hollywood, he hustled men on Times Square and, as a "gentleman escort" in a borrowed tux, rich older women.

And then, sudden stardom as he became the world's top box office attraction. The abused became the abuser. "I live for myself, and I answer to nobody," he proclaimed. "The last thing I want to do is fall in love with a broad."

Thus began a string of seductions that included hundreds of overnight pickups--both male and female. Topping his A-list conquests were James Dean, Paul Newman, Marilyn Monroe, and Barbra Streisand. Finally, this pioneering biography explores the mysterious death of Steve McQueen. Were those salacious rumors really true?

Steve McQueen   *King of Cool*   *Tales of a Lurid Life*
by Darwin Porter

ISBN 978-1-936003-05-1   Hardcover   **$26.95**

PAUL NEWMAN
THE MAN BEHIND THE BABY BLUES, HIS SECRET LIFE EXPOSED

by Darwin Porter

THE MOST COMPELLING BIOGRAPHY OF THE ICONIC ACTOR EVER PUBLISHED

Drawn from firsthand interviews with insiders who knew Paul Newman intimately, and compiled over a period of nearly a half-century, this is the world's most honest and most revelatory biography about Hollywood's pre-eminent male sex symbol, with dozens of potentially shocking revelations.

Whereas the situations it exposes were widely known within Hollywood's inner circles, they've never before been revealed to the general public.

If you're a fan of Newman (and who do you know who isn't) you really should look at this book. It's a respectful but candid cornucopia of information about the sexual and emotional adventures of a young man on Broadway and in Hollywood.

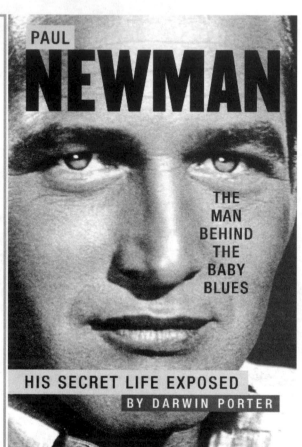

PAUL
NEWMAN
THE
MAN
BEHIND
THE
BABY
BLUES

HIS SECRET LIFE EXPOSED
BY DARWIN PORTER

WINNER OF AN HONORABLE MENTION
AT THE **2009** NEW ENGLAND BOOK FESTIVAL

This is a pioneering and posthumous biography of a charismatic American icon. His rule over the hearts of American moviegoers lasted for more than half a century. Paul Newman was a potent, desirable, and ambiguous sex symbol, a former sailor from Shaker Heights, Ohio, who parlayed his ambisexual charm and extraordinary good looks into one of the most successful careers in Hollywood.

It's all here, as recorded by celebrity chronicler Darwin Porter--the giddy heights and agonizing lows of a great American star, with revelations never before published in any other biography.

Paul Newman, The Man Behind the Baby Blues
His Secret Life Exposed
ISBN 978-0-9786465-1-6 $26.95
Hardcover,   520 pages, with dozens of photos.

"One wonders
how he managed
to avoid public scrutiny
for so long."

BLOOD
MOON
Productions, Ltd.

MERV GRIFFIN
A Life in the Closet

by Darwin Porter

"Darwin Porter told me why he tore the door off Merv's closet.......*Heeeere's Merv! is 560 pages, 100 photos, a truckload of gossip, and a bedful of unauthorized dish.*"

Cindy Adams, The NY Post

"Darwin Porter tears the door off Merv Griffin's closet with gusto in this sizzling, superlatively researched biography...It brims with insider gossip that's about Hollywood legends, writ large, smart, and with great style."

Richard LaBonte, BOOKMARKS

Merv Griffin, A Life in the Closet

Merv Griffin began his career as a Big Band singer, moved on to a failed career as a romantic hero in the movies, and eventually rewrote the rules of everything associated with the broadcasting industry. Along the way, he met and befriended virtually everyone who mattered, made billions operating casinos and developing jingles, contests, and word games. All of this while maintaining a male harem and a secret life as America's most famously closeted homosexual.

In this comprehensive biography--the first published since Merv's death in 2007--celebrity biographer Darwin Porter reveals the amazing details behind the richest, most successful, and in some ways, the most notorious mogul in the history of America's entertainment industry.

Most of his viewers (they numbered 20 million per day) thought that **Merv Griffin**'s life was an ongoing series of chatty segués--amiable, seamless, uncontroversial.
But things were far more complicated than viewers at the time ever thought. Here, from the writer who unzipped **Marlon Brando**, is the first post-mortem, unauthorized overview of the mysterious life of **the richest and most notorious man in television**

HOT, CONTROVERSIAL, & RIGOROUSLY RESEARCHED

HERE'S MERV!
Hardcover, with photos

ISBN 978-0-9786465-0-9 $26.95

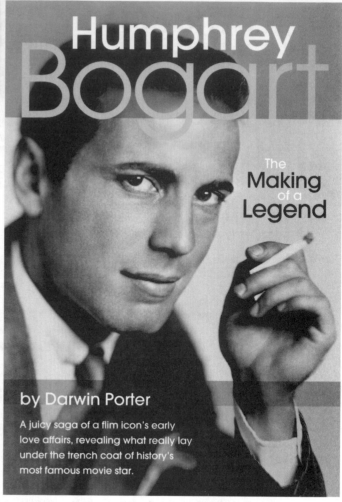

This "entertainingly outrageous" (FRONTIERS MAGAZINE) biography provides a definitive,
blow-by-blow description of the "hot, provocative, and barely under control drama" that was the life
of America's most famous Postwar actor.

Brando Unzipped

by Darwin Porter

"Lurid, raunchy, perceptive, and certainly worth reading...One of the ten best show-biz biographies of 2006." **The Sunday Times (London)**

"<u>Yummy</u>. An irresistably flamboyant romp of a read."
Books to Watch Out For

"Astonishing. An extraordinarily detailed portrait of Brando that's as blunt, uncompromising, and X-rated as the man himself."
Women's Weekly

"This shocking new book is sparking a major reassessment of Brando's legacy as one of Hollywood's most macho lotharios."
Daily Express (London)

"As author Darwin Porter finds, it wasn't just the acting world Marlon Brando conquered. It was the actors, too."
Gay Times (London)

"*Brando Unzipped* is the definitive gossip guide to the late, great actor's life."
The New York Daily News

Hardcover, 625 indexed pages,
with hundreds of photos.

ISBN 978-0-9748118-2-6. $26.95

This is one of our most visible and most frequently reviewed titles. A best-seller, it's now in its fifth printing, with French, Portuguese, and Dutch editions selling briskly in Europe. Shortly after its release, this title was extensively serialized by THE SUNDAY TIMES in the UK, and in other major Sunday supplements in mainland Europe and Australia.

Katharine the Great
(KATHARINE HEPBURN)
A Lifetime of Secrets Revealed

A softcover that fans of old Hollywood find fascinating.

by Darwin Porter
569 pages, with photos $16.95
ISBN   978-0-9748118-0-2

Katharine Hepburn was the world's greatest screen diva--the most famous actress in American history. But until the appearance of this biography, no one had ever published the intimate details of her complicated and ferociously secretive private life. Thanks to the "deferential and obsequious whitewashes" which followed in the wake of her death, readers probably know WHAT KATE REMEMBERED. Here, however, is an unvarnished account of what Katharine Hepburn desperately wanted to forget.

"Behind the scenes of her movies, Katharine Hepburn played the temptress to as many women as she did men, ranted and raved with her co-stars and directors, and broke into her neighbors' homes for fun. And somehow, she managed to keep all of it out of the press. As they say, *Katharine the Great* is hard to put down."
The Dallas Voice

"The door to Hepburn's closet has finally been opened. This is the most honest and least apologetic biography of Hollywood's most ferociously private actress ever written."
Senior Life Magazine, Miami

"In Porter's biography of Katharine Hepburn, details about the inner workings of a movie studio (RKO in the early 30s), are relished."
The Bottom Line, Palm Springs

Katharine
The Great

a lifetime
of secrets...
revealed   by Darwin Porter

"Darwin Porter's biography of Hepburn cannot be lightly dismissed or ignored. Connoisseurs of Hepburn's life would do well to seek it out as a forbidden supplement."
The Sunday Times (London)

Katharine Hepburn was the most obsessively secretive actress in Hollywood. Her androgynous, pan-sexual appeal usually went over big with movie audiences--until those disastrous flops when it didn't. This book tells the how and why of Kate Hepburn's most closely guarded secrets.

Jacko
His Rise and Fall

The Social and Sexual History of Michael Jackson

by celebrity chronicler Darwin Porter.

ISBN 978-0-936003-10-5. Hardcover
600 indexed pages ©2009 $27.95

Rigorously updated in the wake of MJ's death, this is the most thorough, best-researched, and most comprehensive biography of the superstar ever published.

A DEMENTED BILLIONAIRE:

From his reckless pursuit of love as a rich teenager to his final days as a demented fossil, Howard Hughes tasted the best and worst of the century he occupied. Along the way, he changed the worlds of aviation and entertainment forever. This biography reveals inside details about his destructive and usually scandalous associations with other Hollywood players.

Howard Hughes
Hell's Angel by Darwin Porter

Set amid descriptions of the unimaginable changes that affected America between Hughes's birth in 1905 and his death in 1976, this book gives an insider's perspective about what money can buy--and what it can't.

"Darwin Porter's access to film industry insiders and other Hughes confidants supplied him with the resources he needed to create a portrait of Hughes that both corroborates what other Hughes biographies have divulged, and go them one better." **Foreword Magazine**

"Thanks to this bio of Howard Hughes, we'll never be able to look at the old pin-ups in quite the same way again."
The Times (London)

A BIG comprehensive hardcover, Approx 814 pages, with photos, Available in August, 2010
$32.95
ISBN 978-1-936003-13-6

Hughes--A young billionaire looks toward his notorious future.

"The Aviator flew both ways. Porter's biography presents new allegations about Hughes' shady dealings with some of the biggest names of the 20th century"

New York Daily News

Billie Dove-- duenna of the Silent Screen. She gave him syphilis.

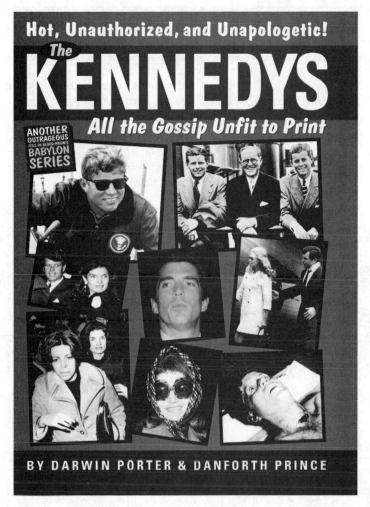

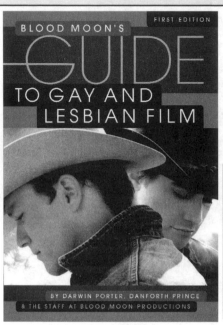

Midnight in Savannah

Sexual Eccentricities in the Deep South
Perversity in Extremis

by Darwin Porter

Trade Paperback   498 pages   **$16.95**
ISBN   978-0-9668030-1-3

After its publication in 2000, Darwin Porter's *Midnight in Savannah* quickly established itself as one of the best-selling gay novels in the history of the Deep South.

Eugene Raymond, a filmmaker in Nashville, writes, "Porter disturbs by showing the world as a *film noir* cul-de-sac.   Corruption has no respect for gender or much of anything else.

"In MIDNIGHT, both Lavender Morgan (at 72, the world's oldest courtesan) and Tipper Zelda (an obese, fading chanteuse taunted as 'the black widow) purchase lust from sexually conflicted young men with drop-dead faces, chiseled bodies, and genetically gifted crotches. These women once relied on their physicality to steal the hearts and fortunes of the world's richest and most powerful men. Now, as they slide closer every day to joining the corpses of their former husbands, these once-beautiful women must depend, in a perverse twist of fate, on sexual outlaws for *le petit mort*. And to survive, the hustlers must idle their personal dreams while struggling to cajole what they need from a sexual liaison they detest. Mendacity reigns. Physical beauty as living hell. CAT ON A HOT TIN ROOF's Big Daddy must be spinning in his grave right now."

"If you're not already a Darwin Porter fan, this novel will make you one!   We've come a long way, baby, since Gore Vidal's The City and the Pillar."
Time Out for Books

"An artfully brutal saga of corruption, greed, sexual tension, and murder, highlighted by the eccentricities of the Deep South. Compulsive Reading."
The Georgia Literary Assn.

"I've just booked the next flight to Savannah! Nothing like a good Georgia boy on a chilly night in Dixie!"
Out!

Wild, orgiastic nights in pre-code Hollywood

Hollywood's Silent Closet

by Darwin Porter

Trade Paper 7" x 10" 746 pages. 60 photos $24.95

ISBN 978-0-9668030-2-0

a novel by
Darwin Porter

"The Little Tramp" **Charlie Chaplin** (above) was one of the most recklessly debauched players in Hollywood.

Disillusioned In her later years, **Mary Pickford** (left) declared herself a recluse and virtually never left her bedroom.

An anthology of star-studded scandal from Tinseltown's very gay and very lavender past, it focuses on Hollywood's secrets from the 1920s, including the controversial backgrounds of the great lovers of the Silent Screen.

Valentino, Ramon Novarro, Charlie Chaplin, Fatty Arbuckle, Pola Negri, Mary Pickford, and many others figure into eyewitness accounts of the debauched excesses that went on behind closed doors. It also documents the often tragic endings of America's first screen idols, some of whom admitted to being more famous than the monarchs of England and Jesus Christ combined.

The first book of its kind, it's the most intimate and most realistic novel about sex, murder, blackmail, and degradation in early Hollywood ever written.

"The *Myra Breckinridge* of the Silent-Screen era. Lush, luscious, and langorously decadent. A brilliant primer of *Who Was Who* in early Hollywood."

Gay Times, London

A banquet of information about the pansexual intrigues of Hollywood between 1919 and 1926 compiled from eyewitness interviews with men and women, all of them insiders, who flourished in its midst. Not for the timid, it names names and doesn't spare the guilty.   If you believe, like Truman Capote, that the literary treatment of gossip will become the literature of the 21st century, then you will love *Hollywood's Silent Closet.*

Millions of fans lusted after **Gary Cooper** (background) and **Rudolph Valentino** (foreground) but until the release of this book, **The Public Never Knew**.

BLOOD MOON
A sexy, horrifying spellbinder

by Darwin Porter

In 2008, this title was designated as one of the ten best horror novels ever published in a survey conducted by **Boiz Who Read**

ISBN 978-0-9668030-4-4

A controversial, compelling, and artfully potboiling paperback $10.99

Blood Moon exposes the murky labyrinths of fanatical Christianity in America today, all within a spunky context of male eroticism. If you never thought that sex, psychosis, right-wing religion, and violence aren't linked, think again.

"In the gay genre, Blood Moon does for the novel what Danielle Steele and John Grisham have been publishing in the straight world for years."
Frank Fenton

Rose Phillips, Blood Moon's charismatic and deviant evangelist, and her shocking but beautiful gay son, Shelley, were surely written in hell. Together, they're a brilliant--and jarring--depiction of a fiercely aggressive Oedipal couple competing for the same male prizes.

*"**Blood Moon** reads like an IMAX spectacle about the power of male beauty, with red-hot icons, a breathless climax, and erotica that's akin to Anaïs Nin on Viagra with a bump of meth."*
Eugene Raymond

519

Rhinestone Country
by Darwin Porter

All that glitter, all that publicity, all that applause, all that pain...

WHAT COUNTRY MUSIC LEGEND INSPIRED THIS NOVEL?

ISBN 978-0-9668030-3-7   Trade Paper   569 pages. $15.99

The *True Grit* of show-biz novels, *Rhinestone Country* is a provocative, realistic, and tender portrayal of the Country-Western music industry, closeted lives south of the Mason-Dixon line, and three of the singers who clawed their way to stardom.

Rhinestone Country reads like a scalding gulp of rotgut whiskey on a snowy night in a bow-jacks honky-tonk.

-Mississippi Pearl

"*Beautifully crafted, Rhinestone Country sweeps with power and tenderness across the racial, social, and sexual landscapes of the Deep South. This is a daring and dazzling work about trauma, deception, and pain, all of it with a Southern accent.*"   **Peter Tompkins**

"*A gay and erotic treatment of the Country-Western music industry? Nashville has come out of the closet at last!*"

The Georgia Literary Assn.

BUTTERFLIES IN HEAT

by Darwin Porter

A compellingly retro softcover expressing some eternal truths about
love, hate, greed, and sex. ISBN 978-0-9668030-9-9 $14.95

Tennessee Williams, who understood a thing or two about loss, love, and drama, had this to say about **Butterflies in Heat:**

"I'd walk the waterfront for Numie any day."

"The most SCORCHING novel of the BIZ-ZARE, the FLAMBOYANT, the CORRUPT since Midnight Cowboy. The strikingly beautiful blond hustler, Numie, has come to the end of the line. Here, in the SEARING HEAT of a tropical cay, he arouses PASSIONS that explode under the BLOOD-RED SUN."
Manor Reviews

"A well-established cult classic. How does Darwin Porter's garden grow? Only in the moonlight, and only at midnight, when man-eating vegetation in any color but green bursts into full bloom to devour the latest offerings."

James Leo Herlihy, author of
MIDNIGHT COWBOY

This title, a cult classic now in its ***16th printing***, has sold steadily to a coterie of Darwin Porter fans since its inauguration in 1976, when it was the thing EVERYBODY in Key West was talking about, and the inspiration for the movie (The Last Resort/ Tropic of Desire) that EVERYBODY wanted to be in.

"Darwin Porter writes with an incredible understanding of the milieu--hot enough to singe the wings off any butterfly."
James Kirkwood, co-author of *A CHORUS LINE*

"We know from the beginning that we're getting into a hotbed that has morbid fascination for potential readers. The novel evolves, in fact, into one massive melée of malevolence, vendetta, and e-v-i-l, stunningly absorbing alone for its sheer and unrelenting exploration of the lower depths."
BESTSELLERS

ABOUT THE AUTHORS

This guidebook represents the latest in dozens of previous collaborations between **Darwin Porter** and **Danforth Prince**, who share emotional and journalistic links through their long-standing co-authorship of many past and present editions of THE FROMMER GUIDES, North America's most respected travel authority. Since 1982, their shared responsibility has included editorial coverage of the travel landscapes of Europe, The Caribbean, and America's Deep South.

Darwin is also the respected author of at least twenty books and biographies, some of them award-winners, about Hollywood. Many of them are described within the end pages of this guidebook. Each of them outlines, often with glaring clarity, the sometimes bizarre sociology of America's entertainment industry and the corrosive effects of fame.

Danforth, a former employee of the Paris bureau of *The New York Times*, is founder and president of The Georgia Literary Association, Blood Moon Productions, The Porter & Prince Corporation, and other media-related firms.